## WORRIED ABOUT THE COMPUTER ON THE COVER GETTING WET?

Have no fear. This cover was computer-generated to combine two separate photos. With a simple click of a mouse, the designer could move the laptop out of the surf, or even up into the palm trees! One objective of this scene, then, is to show you how computer-generated graphic images can be made to look very real indeed. We also selected the cover because it reflects the four themes highlighted in our book: that computers are making the world smaller, making us smarter, making us more creative, and bringing us closer together. More importantly, we hope this cover will help you to view the Information Age as an era in which computers can give us more leisure time to enjoy this beautiful world of ours and, by so doing, improve the quality of our lives.

*To Melanie and Lori*

# COMPUTING
# IN THE INFORMATION AGE

## Nancy Stern

*Hofstra University*

## Robert A. Stern

*Nassau Community College*

**John Wiley & Sons**

New York    Chichester    Brisbane    Toronto    Singapore

COVER   Photograph of Hikkaduwa Beach: David Ball/The Stock Market
        Designed by Ann Marie Renzi

| | |
|---|---|
| ACQUISITIONS EDITOR | Beth Lang Golub |
| DEVELOPMENTAL EDITOR | Johnna Barto |
| MARKETING MANAGER | Carolyn Henderson |
| PRODUCTION SUPERVISOR | Charlotte Hyland |
| DESIGN SUPERVISOR | Ann Marie Renzi |
| MANUFACTURING MANAGER | Andrea Price |
| COPY EDITING SUPERVISOR | Marjorie Shustak |
| PHOTO EDITOR | Jennifer Atkins |
| PHOTO RESEARCH DIRECTOR | Stella Kupferberg |
| ILLUSTRATION | Anna Melhorn |
| TEXT DESIGN | Levavi & Levavi |

This book was set in Palatino by GTS Graphics, Inc. and printed and bound by
Von Hoffmann. The cover was printed by Phoenix Color Corp.

*Library of Congress Cataloging in Publication Data:*

Stern, Nancy B.
  Computing in the information age / Nancy Stern, Robert A. Stern.
      p.     cm.
  Includes indexes.
  ISBN 0-471-55487-1
    1. Business—Data processing.    2. Information technology.
I. Stern, Robert A.   II. Title.
HF5548.2.S7817    1993                                    92-30940
658'.05—dc20                                                  CIP

Printed in the United States of America

10 9 8 7 6 5 4 3 2 1

# PREFACE

We have written *Computing in the Information Age* for introductory students. While the focus is on business applications, the book, which draws on our experience as instructors and textbook authors, is appropriate for a wide range of course offerings. Our main objective is to explain computing today in a clear and meaningful way and to focus on those concepts likely to have the greatest impact as we approach the next century and the next phase of the information revolution.

## ▶ A More Balanced Approach to Concepts and Hands-On Training

We believe that introductory computing courses are moving into a new phase. While teaching students in a laboratory setting how to use software remains important, hands-on learning is but one milestone in the broader quest toward understanding how computers can enrich our lives, how they work, and how computer information systems can help people make decisions and solve problems.

During the past decade, the focus of introductory courses shifted from the lecture hall to the lab. We believe that the emphasis now is toward a more balanced approach, beyond the microcomputer lab and back toward concepts. Instructors are working to give their students more than hands-on experience with application software packages. While the lab remains vital, a useful text for the introductory course must offer more than tutorials with just a smattering of concepts.

Students must learn to look critically at three main elements—hardware, software, and systems—as well as at the techniques used for connecting them. Only then can they appreciate and anticipate the fruits of the Information Age.

We integrate application software concepts with our information processing focus so that students learn *why* major productivity tools and other types of programs are important. Once the student understands the applicability of the software, we present a conceptual explanation of *how* each major type of tool is used. Because instructors tend to have differing ideas about the best package to use, we keep our software discussions generic. Note, however, that we have retained an appendix on DOS as a transition to hands-on software tutorials. A *Getting Started* series on all the major productivity tools and on Structured BASIC Programming is also available (see list on back cover).

## ▶ PassPort — Multimedia Software To Help Customize Your Course and Reinforce the Text

*Computing in the Information Age* approaches computer processing from a user perspective. We begin with the common properties of any computerized information system—hardware, software, connectivity, and people—and move on to the concepts and principles that form the basis of software applications. We use the latest technology to support our text. *PassPort: A Multimedia Tour of the Information Age* extends textbook information in the form of two add-on sets of disks that

1. Introduce productivity tool concepts (*TechTools*)
2. Provide interesting explorations of new products through *TechTours* and new technologies through *TechBytes*

**PassPort** is a collection of multimedia programs that uses text, graphics, photos, animation, and sound (if you have a sound board) to enhance and extend the information provided in the text. These programs can be used either in a lecture hall using a projection system, in a computer lab, or individually by students. They have been designed to allow instructors to customize their courses by using one or all of the programs depending on the course style and content.

### TECHTOOLS

In the lab, instructors can teach the productivity tools they desire for word processing, spreadsheets, or database management. In the classroom, instructors can use TechTools to teach the reasons why productivity tools are so important to today's users. Each TechTool is unique in its generic approach to productivity software, focusing on the *whys* of the tools rather than the *hows* so that students really learn the significance of each tool. Instructors can also choose from a wide array of software available from John Wiley & Sons to supplement the text.

### TECHTOURS AND TECHBYTES

This software emphasizes the value of technology through exploration of how computers are used in different environments. TechTours and TechBytes relate to the four themes of the text:

- **Computers Are Making the World Smaller:** The TechTour for this theme is on the air express industry and how laser guns, satellite technology, and computers allow for fast delivery and tracking of packages enroute to a destination. The TechBytes are on smart cards, laser guns, and pen-based systems.

- **Computers Are Making the World Smarter:** The TechTour for this theme is on the Tron House, a smart house with many new uses for technology including computer-assisted cooking, electronic storage, environmental controls, and automatic gardening. The TechBytes are on smart maps, smart cameras, and robotics.

- **Computers Are Making the World More Creative:** The TechTour for this theme is on multimedia systems. The TechBytes are on CAD systems, virtual reality, expert systems, and computer viruses.

- **Computers Are Bringing the World Closer Together:** The TechTour for this theme is on electronic education and how electronic networks, computers, video, and other technologies are enabling instructors to collaborate with one another to create new course material. The TechBytes are on cellular phones, ISDN, and computing for the disabled.

All PassPort programs contain a Toolbar enabling easy access to a main menu, a glossary of key words, text page references, a Bookmark that allows place marks to be stored on selected screens, a Notebook to store individual comments, a Quiz for testing student understanding of the material presented in the programs, some critical thinking questions, and other navigational tools that make using PassPort easy and useful. PassPort requires an 80386 or 80486 computer, 2MB of RAM, and Windows 3.0 or higher.

## ▶ Other Distinguishing Characteristics of This Text

In addition to providing a more balanced approach and unique multimedia software, *Computing in the Information Age* offers several other features that distinguish it from other texts in the marketplace.

### CONNECTIVITY AND THE HUMAN FACTOR

We go beyond the traditional units of hardware, software, and systems that appear in most books and add two very important perspectives: Connectivity and the Human Factor.

Throughout the text we emphasize connectivity and the human factor and, in addition, we focus on these topics in more detail in Part Four. For example, the networking of computers and other devices such as fax machines and CD-ROM drives has begun to change the focus of computing, and we highlight how these changes have occurred and what the long-term impact is likely to be.

Similarly, social, ethical, and legal issues continue to be important topics in education, as well they should. We integrate these issues throughout the text and give them special emphasis in Part Four.

## CRITICAL THINKING

The text combines a conceptual, management-oriented focus with a "nuts and bolts" approach. To achieve a proper balance, we include our traditional step-by-step, self-teaching pedagogy along with the usual set of teaching aids, but, in addition, we focus on *critical thinking*. The objective is to present issues and brief analytical problems in computing designed to get the student thinking about various topics and to ask pertinent questions relating to them. Critical thinking items appear both in text margins and in the form of brief cases at the end of each chapter. The multimedia PassPort disks also focus on critical thinking.

One main objective of the text is to help students evaluate products and resources. We focus, of course, on the state-of-the-art, but if that is all we did, the book would become obsolete very quickly. We also include techniques used by managers to evaluate software, hardware, networks, and information systems so that readers will be able to understand and assess future developments and their probable impact on society. We feature products and advertisements for students to analyze and evaluate as part of our critical thinking and product analysis focus.

In general, the goal is to examine controversies and current events in computing, to help students really understand them, and to teach students how to ask the right questions—in short, to encourage critical thinking in our readers.

## APPLICATIONS ORIENTATION

Discussions of technology are integrated with discussions of applications in a meaningful way so that students are not overwhelmed by complex concepts or by an overemphasis on terms. We try to make complex concepts understandable as well as factual by presenting introductory material in a clear, well-organized manner that contains an appropriate mix of technology and applications. In this market, we believe that knowing when to stop is at least as important as knowing what to focus on. Books that "touch base" with every conceivable subject are not usually the best books. We hope we have achieved an acceptable level of in-depth discussions as well as an appropriate breadth of coverage.

## FROM MICROS TO MAMMOTHS

Our book begins with the concept that all computers process data in essentially the same way, keeping in mind that the differences among categories of computers are essentially differences of degree. Since many students enter introductory courses having had some exposure to personal computers, we begin with micro concepts and build up to mainframes in Part One. Then all subsequent chapters reinforce the fact that mainframes are simply larger, faster, more expensive, and more powerful than micros. In this way, the distinctions among computers are not cast in stone, and students gradually lose their fear about "big" machines. We attempt to make the point that with proper connectivity, it could be virtually transparent to users whether they are on a mainframe, mini (midrange), or microcomputer.

Although mainframes can be viewed as quantifiably different from micros, we also emphasize the fact that certain tasks are best performed on larger machines. We make the point that a mainframe is to a micro what a mass transportation system is to a personal car. The former is most efficient for handling the needs of the largest number of users, but it requires users to follow more rules and schedules. Many books today emphasize the micro so much that the importance of mainframes is virtually ignored. We attempt to put these types of machines and their relationship to one another back into perspective.

While we emphasize IBM micros and their compatibles when discussing personal computers, we do not ignore the Macintosh. Indeed, we highlight the features that make the Macintosh ideally suited for some applications.

## ▶ Pedagogy

All chapters have a common structure designed to facilitate self-study and retention, beginning with a brief description of an event or issue in computing that pertains to the chapter. The **Preview Questions** that follow relate directly to the chapter's main text sections. Answering these questions is the student's learning objective. A **Chapter Outline** appears as well, for reference.

Another feature of our text is its layered, "building block" approach to topics and themes. That is, topics are introduced in a simplified way, then expanded on at key points throughout the text.

Whenever our themes are discussed in the text itself they are identified with an **icon:**

- Computers Are Making the World Smaller

- Computers Are Making the World Smarter

● Computers Are Making the World More Creative

● Computers Are Bringing the World Closer Together

We include these icons throughout the text as pointers so that students understand that the concept under discussion is actually being developed from chapter to chapter. In this way, themes are reinforced as they apply to specific subjects.

Throughout each chapter, marginal notes called **In a Nutshell** highlight relevant material (e.g., "criteria used to evaluate computers") and include, where appropriate, brief summaries, in outline or list form, of major topics. **Looking Back** boxes provide a historical perspective on major innovations, and **Looking Ahead** boxes project into the future. Along the way, **Critical Thinking** questions challenge readers to integrate what they are learning about computers with what they know about life.

Each main text section is followed by a short **Self-Test,** with solutions, to help reinforce the material just presented. Photographs and line drawings illustrate concepts in a clear and meaningful way. Captions are detailed and clearly tie the art to the chapter.

End-of-chapter material contains a concepts-oriented **Summary** structured around the preview questions. A full **Chapter Self-Test,** with answers, follows. A separate **Key Terms** list follows and provides the text page number where each term is defined.

As a final challenge for the student, we conclude each chapter with **Review Questions** followed by a short **Product Analysis Case** relating to an event or recent innovation in computing, along with relevant critical thinking questions. This end-of-chapter Product Analysis Case summarizes and reinforces the concepts presented in the chapter.

In summary, the objective of this text is student understanding of both the "tools" and the "whys and hows" of computing. We focus on the unique applicability of computers to business and to life, the advantages we gain from knowing how and why to use computers, and the potential of computers to enrich our lives. And while *Computing in the Information Age* is more substantive than a tutorial, it is by no means an encyclopedia. Rather, we have taken great care to provide what we regard as the ideal mix of concepts that belong in the introductory course, along with optional, add-on interactive multimedia software to supplement the text for instructors who want a more customized approach.

## ▶ Supplements

The following supplemental material is available to support the text:

- *Instructor's Resource Guide* includes sample course syllabi, notes to the first-time instructor, teaching tips, discussion topics, points to emphasize, common misconceptions, lecture outlines, chapter objectives, projects and activities, suggested answers to critical thinking questions, suggestions for using PassPort, and answers to end-of-chapter material as well as general guides to public domain software, journals, major products, and term paper topics.

- *Test Bank* includes approximately 150 test items per chapter (multiple-choice, true/false, and essay).

- *Computerized Test Bank (MicroTest)* is available in IBM 5¼-inch and 3½-inch disk versions.

- *Color Transparencies* include more than 75 full-color acetates of key figures from the text.

- *Student Study Guide* includes chapter outlines, key terms, fill-in exercises, sample test questions, games and exercises, and common misconceptions demystified.

- *Video Series* provide audiovisual supplements that relate directly to the text themes as well as to other issues.

- *Prodigy Demonstration Pack* includes a disk on the popular subscriber service, Prodigy, and a discount coupon for new subscribers.

- *Make Your Point Software* is an electronic slide show incorporating text and graphics that summarizes and illustrates key concepts for each chapter. This is truly a unique presentation graphics tool for the instructor.

- *Getting Started Series* is an array of software manuals offered by Wiley to supplement the text. They are listed on the back cover of this text.

## ▶ Acknowledgments

We wish to thank the following reviewers for their invaluable comments, suggestions, and criticisms that helped us to develop *Computing in the Information Age:*

Virginia Anderson
University of North Dakota

Marilyn Meyer
Fresno City College

Gary Baker
Marshalltown Community College

Anne Olsen
Wingate College

Patrick Fenton
West Valley College

Jane Ritter
University of Oregon

Jeff Frates
Los Meandos College

Linda Salchenberger
Loyola University (Chicago)

Randi Goldberg
Marist College

Bruce Sophie
North Harris College

Jan Harris
Lewis & Clark Community College

Allan Spielman
Hofstra University

Charles Inglis
Algonquin College

Susan Traynor
Clarion University

M.B. Kahn
California State University

Lanny Udey
Hofstra University

Habib Kashani
Vancouver Community College
   (Langara)

James R. Walters
Pikes Peak Community College

Frank Whittle
Dutchess Community College

Connie A. Knapp
Pace University

Floyd Winters
Manatee Community College

Mack Lundy
Trident Technical College

Margaret Zinky
Phoenix College

Elias Majdalani
Marshall University

Projects such as this one are dependent on the work of many people. The Wiley team has been dedicated, committed, and enthusiastic about this book from the onset. We are very grateful to them for their support. This book is, in no small measure, a tribute to their efforts. We would specifically like to thank the following people:

Editorial—Beth Golub, Bill Oldsey, Bonnie Lieberman

Development—Johnna Barto, Sean Culhane, Barbara Brooks, Mary Konstant, Fran Minters

Marketing—Carolyn Henderson, Steve Kraham

Production—Charlotte Hyland, Katy Rubin, Ann Berlin

Design and Illustration—Ann Marie Renzi, Maddy Lesure, Anna Melhorn, Ishaya Monokoff

Photo Research—Jennifer Atkins, Stella Kupferberg, Charles Hamilton, Eloise Marion, Monica Suder

New Technology—Randi Goldsmith, Susan Saltrick

Ancillaries—Andrea Bryant

Proofreading—Shelley Flannery

We also thank Dennis Obukowicz at Asymetrix who worked tirelessly on PassPort and Carol Eisen for typing—and retyping—this manuscript.

We welcome your comments, suggestions, and even criticisms. We can be reached through Beth Golub at John Wiley and Sons, 605 Third Avenue, New York, NY 10158, via Bitnet at ACSNNS@HOFSTRA, via Internet at ACSNNS@VAXC.HOFSTRA.EDU, and via CompuServe at 76505,1222.

Nancy Stern
Robert A. Stern

# CONTENTS

PART THREE SOFTWARE AND SYSTEMS DRIVE
THE INFORMATION AGE                                254

**COMPUTERS ARE MAKING THE WORLD MORE CREATIVE**

PART FOUR CONNECTIVITY UNITES
THE INFORMATION AGE                                 422

**COMPUTERS ARE BRINGING THE WORLD CLOSER TOGETHER**

# APPENDIXES                                                          551

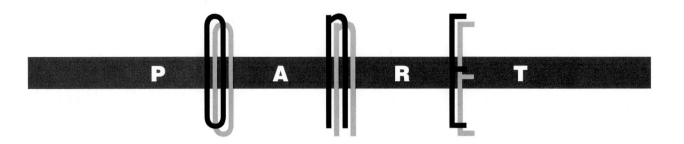

# PART

# COMPUTERS AND
# INFORMATION PROCESSING

 ow often have you heard people say that the world is getting smaller? Of course when people say this, they are not talking about the incredible shrinking planet. Instead, they are reflecting about how technology, from transportation to communications satellites, is shrinking time and distance around the globe, for businesses and for people. Computers and information processing are at the forefront of these changes, and computers themselves are getting smaller and more portable all the time. In Part One, you will learn how computers are making the world smaller.

In the parts that follow you will learn how computers are making the world—and all of us in it—work smarter and more creatively and how information technology is bringing us closer together. You will learn the how and the why. You will learn, too, what living in this Information Age means for you—for your education, your work, your family, and your world.

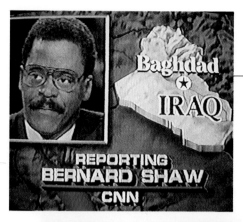

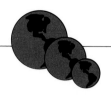

Maybe it first struck you as you watched the Persian Gulf War unfold on television. During the afternoon you watched a live report from Saudi Arabia, but over there it was nighttime. In Japan and Australia, it's already tomorrow. The world is getting smaller all right. Information technology makes time and distance melt away as it gives all of us access to any place on earth at any hour of the day or night.

1

Computers play a big part in the publishing business today. Newspapers, magazines, and books are printed on massive rolls of paper that weave through the presses to be printed and folded into pages in an electronically controlled operation. Computers also are making it possible, on a small scale, for individuals to publish high-quality flyers, newsletters, or books, without rolling the presses.

Many computers today—even the very smallest ones—are pen-based, which means that you can enter data using a stylus or pen. These machines are often used for filling out forms and taking notes.

The power of small computers is constantly increasing while their size decreases. We can use them for all sorts of tasks including accessing databases, desktop publishing, and entertainment. Microcomputers are often used for generating high-quality graphics and for multimedia presentations in which voice, illustrations, video, animated displays, and text are combined.

I f you appreciate how computers are making the world smaller, think for a moment about how people are making computers smaller. The earliest computers filled entire rooms, which had to be specially prepared and kept cool and completely free of dust. Today, you can buy a personal computer with more power than those early machines, and you may be able to take it with you anywhere you go because some of them fit into the palm of your hand.

# THE BASICS OF COMPUTING: HARDWARE, SOFTWARE, CONNECTIVITY, AND PEOPLE

**W**ithin your lifetime, computers and information technology have changed the world more than any machine invented during the entire 200 years of the Industrial Revolution, *including* the automobile. We are moving far beyond the Industrial Revolution into the Information Age, and what an age it is.

To some degree, you probably already are **computer literate:** you are aware of computers and sometimes even use them without knowing it. Every day you interact with devices actually created or enhanced by computing technology—the TV, the telephone, remote controls, cars, even this book. In this sense, you are a computer **user.** The purpose of this book is to increase and refine your computer literacy, especially as it applies to business systems. We will help you understand how computers operate and how they are used in business today. We will take you from computer literacy to computer fluency. This book is also about the future and how you will use computers in your career and throughout your life.

We begin in Chapter 1 to describe computers and their uses, or **application** areas, by answering the following questions:

▶ How do computers process data to produce information?

▶ How do organizations use computers for information processing?

▶ How has information processing been revolutionized by computers?

# 1.1  INTRODUCING COMPUTER SYSTEMS: INPUT-PROCESS-OUTPUT

IN A

**NUT SHELL**

A computer system has the following components.

1. **Input devices** accept data from the user.
2. Main memory stores data so that the **central processing unit (CPU)** can operate on that data to produce useful information.
3. **Output devices** produce information for the user.
4. **Storage devices** hold the program, input data, and output information so that they can be used again.

The main purpose of using computers, regardless of the application area, is **processing** or manipulating data quickly and efficiently so that the information obtained is complete, accurate, timely, economical, and relevant. Computers read incoming data called **input,** process the data, and display outgoing information called **output. Data** itself consists of raw facts; data that is processed or operated on produces structured, meaningful **information. Information processing** is a set of procedures used to operate on data and produce meaningful results. The computer actually consists of numerous devices that input data, process it, and produce output information.

Computers have created a revolution in the production, processing, and transfer of information, primarily because of their ability to handle enormous amounts of data quickly. And the changes continue. In a single decade, business computing has changed dramatically. It was once completely dominated by large computers dedicated to churning out payrolls and financial reports and dependent on technically trained specialists to satisfy all information processing needs. Now, small, powerful **personal computers (PCs)** are widely available to individual workers who can access information from larger systems and increase their own personal productivity. Computer users today often are not computer professionals;

rather, they are people like you who need information to do their jobs effectively. Business users include people who work with computers to process customer orders, prepare budgets, or make decisions about hiring personnel or selecting a marketing strategy.

In this chapter, we look at the various components of *computer systems*—whether they are large, company-wide computers; small, personal computers; or combinations of the two. Think of this chapter as an introduction to computing; we will cover each of its topics in depth in later chapters.

## ▶ The Computer System and How It Processes Data

We use the word *system* in many different ways. There are, for example, telephone systems, nervous systems, grading systems, and betting systems. For our purposes, a **computer system** is a group of machines, or **hardware,** that accept data, process it, and display information. The main reason for using computer systems is to process data quickly and efficiently so that the information obtained is timely, meaningful, and accurate. A computer system performs its information processing operations under the control of sets of instructions called **programs.** As shown in Figure 1.1, a computer system consists of the following components:

*Figure 1.1* A computer system consists of the following hardware components: input devices; main memory and the processor; output devices; and storage devices.

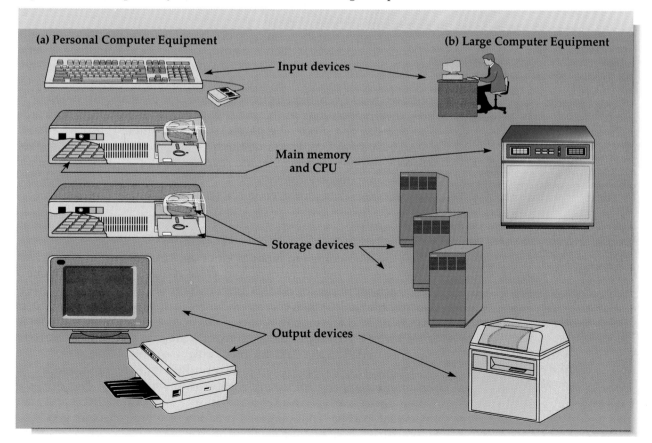

**(a) Personal Computer Equipment**

**(b) Large Computer Equipment**

Input devices

Main memory and CPU

Storage devices

Output devices

Storage units

Processing units

Input and output units

(a)

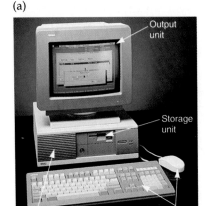

Output unit

Storage unit

Processor

Input units

(b)

*Figure 1.2* Computers of all sizes like (a) a large computer system, and (b) a personal computer have main memory, a CPU, input devices, output devices, and storage devices. Hardware in a computer system differs mainly in terms of size and processing power.

How do computers process data to produce information?

input devices; main memory and the central processing unit; output devices; and storage devices.

When people use the term *computer,* or *computer system,* they are really referring to hardware, which is a group of machines. Computer systems come in various sizes from personal computers to much larger systems. Figure 1.2 compares the major components of a PC to a typical large computer system. Even though these systems are dramatically different in size, they process data in the same way. Their differences are primarily those of size and processing power.

All businesses—and computer users—have individual needs, so they choose computer systems that are specially equipped, or **configured,** to include components or devices that meet their specific needs. Each system processes data, however, in the following way.

## INPUT DEVICES READ INCOMING DATA

There are many different types of input devices: keyboards, disk drives, page scanners, optical readers, and voice recognition units, to name a few. Each input device reads a specific form of data; for example, keyboards transmit typed characters whereas scanners "read" typed or handwritten characters from documents or images from graphs, photos, or drawings. Any input device converts data into electronic pulses that are transmitted to the CPU for processing.

Different businesses are apt to have various types of input devices. An insurance company, for example, may use keyboards and disk drives as input devices; a supermarket may use electronic cash registers and scanners that read bar codes on food products or other consumer goods.

(a)

(b)

*Organizations have different comput-ing needs. (a) Sometimes basic key-board/screen units with disk drives suf-fice, as in many insurance companies. (b) Sometimes applications require dif-ferent types of devices. Supermarket checkout counters use scanners to read codes on consumer goods so that they can be processed by electronic cash registers.*

## MAIN MEMORY AND THE CENTRAL PROCESSING UNIT

Main memory stores programs and data for processing and the central processing unit, or CPU, controls all computer operations. The CPU reads data into main memory from an input device, processes the data according to program instructions, and produces information by activat-ing an output device. The CPU is the "brains" of the computer system.

The unit that houses main memory and the CPU must be linked by cables or by communication channels such as telephone lines to all input and output devices in the computer system. The program, or set of instructions for processing data, is read into main memory by the CPU before data can be entered and processed and information generated.

## OUTPUT DEVICES PRODUCE OUTGOING INFORMATION

Each output device in a computer system accepts information from main memory under the control of the CPU, and converts it to an appropriate output form. A printer, for example, is an output device that prints reports or graphs based on information that the CPU has processed and produced. Similarly, a video monitor is an output device that displays both text and graphics on a screen.

## STORING PROGRAMS AND DATA FOR FUTURE PROCESSING

Once you turn off a computer, the data and instructions operated on by the CPU are lost. For this reason, separate storage devices are needed to keep the data and instructions in electronic form for them to be conve-niently used again and again. **Disks** are common storage media for PCs and for larger computer systems. See Figure 1.2.

**CRITICAL THINKING**

Computer systems are like automo-biles. To use either, you do not need to know, in detail, how each com-ponent works. In what other ways are computers like automobiles? Think about

1. The reasons why people buy new cars.
2. How manufacturers often tout their products as being unique, when basically most devices op-erate in a similar manner.

## ▶ Software Makes It Work

### THE STORED PROGRAM CONCEPT

Before computer hardware can actually read data, process it, and produce information, it needs a set of instructions—a program—that actually controls the CPU's operations. Programs, like data, are read into main memory under the control of the CPU. We say that computers are **stored-program devices** because they require a set of instructions to be stored in the computer's main memory before data can be processed.

Computer professionals called **programmers** write programs for each user need or application area. The total set of programs that enables the computer system to process data is referred to as **software.** Typically, software is available on disk. A computer system for a medium-sized company, for example, may have hundreds of programs for a variety of application areas such as payroll, accounting, inventory control, and sales forecasting. A home computer system may have dozens of programs for typing reports, playing games, or balancing the checkbook. See Figure 1.3.

### TYPES OF SOFTWARE: SYSTEMS SOFTWARE AND APPLICATION SOFTWARE

Computers require two types of software: (1) **systems software** to monitor and supervise the overall operations of the computer system and (2) **application software** to manipulate input data and provide users with meaningful output information.

*Figure 1.3* PCs are currently found in 40 percent of American homes. They help businesspeople work at home, yet stay connected to the office; they help children and adults learn with computer-based training; and they provide access to large databases of information. They improve the quality of life for consumers by helping them perform day-to-day operations like balancing their checkbooks or shopping at home.

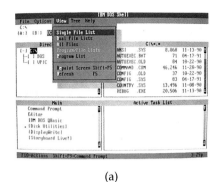

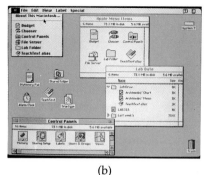

(a)                                           (b)                                           (c)

**Systems Software.**   Computers use a series of control programs, called the **operating system,** that moves data in and out of main memory and monitors the running of application programs. The operating system is the primary component of systems software. Some computers have built-in operating systems, but these cannot be easily changed or updated. Most computer manufacturers either provide their own operating system, usually on disk, or allow users to purchase disks containing the more popular operating systems.

The IBM Personal Computer (IBM PC) and IBM Personal System/2 (PS/2), for example, have their own operating systems—usually **DOS,** which means *d*isk *o*perating *s*ystem, or OS/2 (for the PS/2), which means *O*perating *S*ystem/2. They can, however, use other operating systems as well. Some Apple computers use Apple DOS, while the Apple Macintosh family uses its own operating system. Similarly, large computer systems have various operating systems that control their overall processing.

Operating systems interact with users by means of a **user interface.** Some operating systems, especially those for larger computer systems, are text based and require the user to learn a set of commands. Some operating systems for PCs, like the Macintosh operating system, permit users to select commands from graphic symbols, or **icons,** displayed on a screen. Text-based operating systems, like DOS for IBM and IBM-compatible computers, can work in conjunction with graphical user interfaces like **Windows,** which make them easier to use or more **user-friendly.** See Figure 1.4.

Each operating system has unique ways to process and store data. A disk that is prepared for one operating system may not work on another system, even if the disk fits into the machine. Application programs are written for a particular operating system as well. Programs and data that are designed for different operating systems are often **incompatible;** that is, they cannot be used together. As a result, programs written for one computer are frequently not usable on another computer. Similarly, hardware devices often can be used only with certain computers. Lack of hardware and software compatibility is a common problem for users. We will soon see how the problem of compatibility is being resolved.

**Application Programs.**   Application programs are designed to satisfy user needs by operating on input data to perform a given job, for example, to prepare a report, update a master payroll file, or print customer bills.

*Figure 1.4* (a) *IBM and IBM-compatibles most often use a text-based operating system called DOS, which either requires commands to be typed or uses a shell for selecting commands from a menu. (b) The Macintosh has always had a user-friendly operating system where commands are represented as symbols or icons that are selected by the user. (c) Windows is a user-friendly interface that enables DOS users to select commands represented as icons. DOS with Windows as its interface makes IBM and IBM-compatible computers similar to a Macintosh when selecting commands.*

IN A

**NUT SHELL**

**TYPES OF SOFTWARE**

| | |
|---|---|
| Systems software (includes the operating system) | Supervises and controls the overall operations of a computer system |
| Application programs | Designed to satisfy user needs |
| • Packaged | Inexpensive software often purchased off-the-shelf; designed for a wide range of users; comes with extensive documentation |
| • Custom | Designed to satisfy a specific user's needs; expensive and time consuming to develop |

*Figure 1.5 Packaged software is usually supplied on disk along with boxed manuals that indicate how to set up the software, how to use it, and what to do if an error occurs.*

Typically, application programs are acquired in one of two ways: (1) **packaged programs** purchased off-the-shelf from a software retailer or (2) **custom programs** designed especially for the unique needs of an individual or an organization.

Application packages are sold or leased by computer vendors, self-employed programmers, or software developers, and they are designed for general use in organizations or for personal use. Packaged programs allow limited customization, but they really are intended to be used as is by a broad range of users. Although they may not meet all aspects of every user's needs, application packages are inexpensive compared to custom programs and are supplied with comprehensive user reference manuals called **documentation** (Figure 1.5).

Custom software, on the other hand, is written by programmers within an organization, by outside consultants, or by self-employed programmers. Custom programs are designed to meet the precise needs of users, but they are very time consuming and costly to develop.

Users of large computer systems may more likely be satisfied with custom programs than packaged programs, particularly for major application areas like accounting and inventory; nevertheless, the expense and time required to develop custom programs often are not justified. As a result, organizations frequently buy packaged programs and then either have computer professionals modify the package or sacrifice some of their specific needs.

One category of application programs called **productivity tools** is designed to help PC users perform day-to-day business activities and to assist users in making decisions. Productivity tools help users create written documents, maintain information, develop worksheets for preparing budgets and financial statements, and communicate with one another. As the term implies, productivity tools make users more productive by enabling them to complete business tasks more efficiently, search for information faster, and analyze alternatives more effectively.

## SOFTWARE DRIVES HARDWARE

The rule of thumb when you become a computer user is to decide on the software you need *before* deciding what hardware to buy. In other words, first determine what programmed instructions you need and whether application packages exist that can satisfy your needs. Then find hardware that is compatible with that software. In the computing field, we say that software drives hardware!

Inexperienced purchasers of PCs often buy what they think is "the biggest and the best" only to find that the software they really need cannot run on the PC they own. Experienced computer users know better: they select their software first!

### ▶ SELF-TEST

1. Data that has been processed by a computer so that it is in meaningful form is called _____.
2. Instructions that read input, process it, and produce output are part of a _____.
3. List the major components of a computer system and the purpose of each.
4. The software that controls and monitors the overall operations of the computer is called _____.
5. Programs that are developed to satisfy user needs are called _____.

Solutions
1. information
2. computer program
3. input devices that read incoming data; main memory and the CPU, which process the data; output devices that produce information; storage devices that hold programs and data for future processing
4. systems software or the operating system
5. application programs or software

---

## UNDERSTANDING INFORMATION PROCESSING  `1.2`

### ▶ Computer Systems Automate Information Processing

We have seen that computer systems—the hardware—consist of input units that read incoming data; main memory and a central processing unit that process that incoming data and convert it to meaningful information; storage devices that store data and programs; and output units that produce information in a usable form. We have also seen that computers are stored program devices: software instructs the computer system to read and process data and to store or produce output.

How do organizations use computers for information processing?

*Figure 1.6 Computers are used in business systems to generate output, to help individual managers make decisions, and to provide executives with integrated information on the company as a whole.*

Organizations began using computers to automate business tasks decades ago. Within each business function, tasks from order fulfillment to preparing payroll checks to listing out-of-stock items all require a set of procedures—a system. The integration of tasks and procedures in each business area is a **business system.** See Figure 1.6. The major business systems or functional areas within organizations are:

- Accounting and finance: systems for keeping the books, generating bills and payrolls, and investing money.
- Human resources: systems for managing employee benefit plans and recruiting new employees.
- Marketing: systems for promoting, pricing, distributing, and selling the organization's products and services.
- Production: systems for controlling inventory, scheduling production, manufacturing, and purchasing.

Computerized information processing results in information systems that enable these various business systems to work together and hence contribute to the organization's goal of earning a profit.

In general, computers are used to more efficiently operate on data that would otherwise be processed by hand. Hardware and software enable employees to work more productively, search for information faster, and analyze options better. Note too that it takes more than hardware and software to computerize a business system. The following sections introduce two more basic components of computing: connectivity and people.

## ▶ Connectivity Links Hardware, Software, and People

A wide variety of computer systems and software are available to satisfy a range of user needs. For each application or type of computer, there are also a wide variety of users, in offices, homes, and schools.

In recent years, computing power has been more effectively harnessed with the use of systems that permit resources to be shared, where resources include computing power, software, and input/output units. The concept that enables the sharing of resources is called **connectivity** and is achieved by the use of an integrated computer system referred to as a **network.**

Networks have been widely used for some years now, but only recently have they become prevalent in many organizations. Not only do networks make more efficient use of information resources, they also enable incompatible hardware and software to work together. Thus networks provide an organization with better control and more effective utilization of its overall computing resources.

The types of computers linked together in a network depend on the application areas and the processing capabilities of the networked computers. Operations performed by a large computer system today are apt to be relegated to PCs tomorrow. Similarly, as large-system capabilities

(a)

(b)

*Figure 1.7* (a) *Some networks enable users within an organization to share information and other resources.* (b) *Other networks, like those that are used by stock exchanges, enable brokers throughout the world to access information.*

increase, some tasks performed independently by each PC may be taken over, at a later date, by a single, larger computer system.

Because the capabilities of computer systems change, the tasks they perform also change. Remember: The relationship between personal computers and larger systems is dynamic—it changes frequently as smaller computers become more powerful, enabling larger computers to perform other tasks. Since many users work primarily with PCs, they may think that the era of the big computer is coming to an end. This is a misconception. The tasks performed by large computer systems are apt to change over time, but with the increasing use of networks, larger systems are likely to remain an integral part of an organization's computing facility.

Connectivity makes sharing of resources by compatible computers less expensive. For example, an organization can obtain a software developer's permission to allow all computers for which the software is compatible to access it, at a relatively low cost, whenever desired. Suppose an organization has 300 PCs that all use the same application program. It would be much cheaper and more efficient to have all these computers access one program rather than purchasing 300 separate software packages, one for each computer. Moreover, if hardware is compatible, users can share input and output devices as well as software. A facility with 10 PCs may be able to share as few as four printers with no loss of productivity. See Figure 1.7.

## ▶ The Human Factor: People and Computing

Computer systems operate under the control of software, which provides the necessary instructions for inputting data, for processing the data and converting it into information, and for displaying or printing output. Connectivity enables computer systems to share hardware and software resources for greater productivity.

But information resources must be controlled by people. People determine the needs, implement and control the systems, and supervise the overall computing process. Recall that information processing procedures differ, depending on the application area or business system. **Systems analysts** are the computer professionals within an organization who are responsible for developing business information systems that rely on information processing techniques. Systems analysts work closely with programmers and other computer professionals to develop computerized systems, but they begin the process with the help of computer users and rely on those users to guide them through the development phase.

The first goal in computerizing business systems is understanding user needs. Among the computer users in business who require effective information systems to perform their jobs are

- Managers, who analyze information in order to make decisions. An executive may depend on a profit/loss statement, for example, to decide whether a price increase is warranted.
- Operating staff, who use computers to perform day-to-day tasks, such as billing, answering customer inquiries, and so on.
- Data entry operators, who interact directly with a computer to update the information in a business system. Tellers in banks and cashiers in stores perform data entry operations. See Figure 1.8.

Ideally, systems analysts and computer users at all levels work together exchanging knowledge and ideas. Computer users must communicate what they need from the system. Systems analysts must help users understand what they can reasonably expect from the system. Computerizing business systems is a process that begins and ends with computer users.

*Figure 1.8 Data entry operators, like those who work for the Internal Revenue Service, key data into computers. Some IRS offices process tens of thousands of income tax returns a day.*

## ▶ The Pros of Computing

Organizations spend a great deal of time and money designing, developing, implementing, and maintaining information systems so that they will be effective in providing essential management support. In addition to the costs of hardware, software, and networks are organizational costs such as training users, upgrading systems, support costs, overhead, and so on—hidden costs that sometimes constitute the bulk of the total information processing expenses in an organization! Despite these costs, organizations continue to use computers because of the significant benefits they provide. Here are five reasons for using computers.

### COMPUTERS ARE FAST

Most modern computers process data in speeds measured in fractions of a second. Some computers can process hundreds of thousands of data items and perform millions of calculations in seconds or minutes.

### COMPUTERS ARE ACCURATE

Electronic technology is so precise that when a computer is programmed correctly and when input is entered properly, the accuracy of the output is virtually guaranteed. This is not to say that *output* from a computer is always correct; rather, when inaccuracies occur, most often they are the result of human error—incorrect input or a programming error—and almost never the result of a computer error.

### COMPUTERS OFFER COMPACT STORAGE

Data and information previously stored in a room full of file cabinets can be stored compactly on computer media in a fraction of the space. See Figure 1.9. Moreover, data can be retrieved from storage quickly and in a variety of useful forms.

### COMPUTERS ARE ECONOMICAL

The overall cost of computers for large applications is often far less than the cost for manual systems. In fact, many of today's business and industrial application areas such as oil exploration, genetic research, and airline reservations systems could not even be accomplished manually. The computations required would be too expensive or too time consuming.

### COMPUTERS HAVE INTANGIBLE BENEFITS

The benefits of information processing often exceed the tangible gains of greater speed or lower cost. Intangible benefits are hard to measure but easy to demonstrate. For example, the quality of computer-produced information may improve the decision-making process and speed the flow of information through an organization. Such benefits can enhance

*Figure 1.9 Most organizations use disks of all sizes to store data. A single compact disk can store 650 million characters, the equivalent of 325,000 pages of information.*

(a)

(b)

*Sometimes computers are used to perform tasks that would be nearly impossible to perform manually because the cost would be prohibitive. (a) Control of nuclear facilities, (b) predicting the weather, and (c) genetic research are some application areas that require computers.*

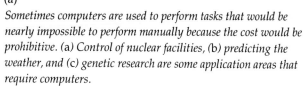

(c)

the company's reputation or improve its service by helping employees respond more quickly to customer requests and questions, provide better quality control, and improve the overall delivery of goods and services.

On another level, computers in the home and the workplace have the potential for improving the overall quality of life in our society. Consider these examples. "Smart" devices with built-in computers can be programmed to maximize energy efficiency and can be controlled by a stan-

## LOOKING BACK

After the Persian Gulf War in 1991, the United States and its allies were judged winners not only in the military war but in the information war. During Operation Desert Storm, the main challenge of the U.S. military and its allies was to create a network between the United States and Saudi Arabia. Connectivity was es-

tablished within hours between the Saudi Arabian Ministry of Defense and the National Military Command Center in Washington, DC. After the first week, voice and data communications between the two countries were in place. Networks had to be rebuilt and altered on a daily basis to keep up with the movement of the

armed forces.

Computers also played a pivotal role in planning bombing missions. It would have been virtually an impossible task to execute the high number of concurrent aerial missions without computers.

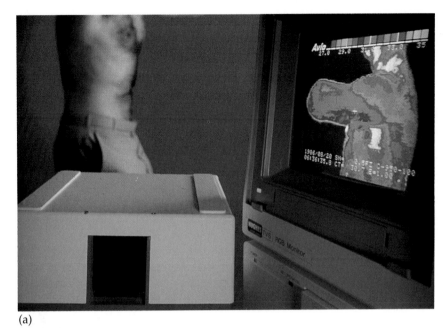

(a)

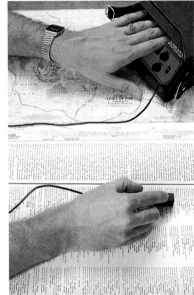

(b)

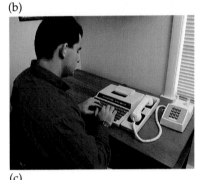

(c)

dard Touch-Tone phone, remote control unit, or a PC. Smart appliances make day-to-day jobs in the home easier as well. Smart cars make driving safer.

The disabled have benefited greatly from computer technology. Computer scanners convert printed text to verbal output or to Braille for the visually impaired; similarly, telephones and other voice recognition equipment convert speech to printed or displayed output for the hearing impaired. Computerized components in pacemakers, artificial limbs, and other medical wonders have not only improved the quality of life for some people but extended their lives as well. See Figure 1.10.

*Figure 1.10* (a) *Large and small computers are used for scanning the body and displaying images used by physicians for making diagnoses.*
(b) *Computers can help the visually impaired to read. This person scans a document with her right hand, and with her left she reads the text which the computer has converted to Braille.*
(c) *This hearing impaired person receives telephone messages that have been converted to screen displays, and then types his message, which is converted to a verbal response.*

### ▶ Avoiding the Cons of Computing

Despite the advantages, computers sometimes prove dissatisfying to users. Hardware and software incompatibility is one reason, although connectivity is helping to alleviate that problem. Another reason is too much or too little information, or information that is simply not useful— such as outdated sales figures, inaccurate billing dates, or a listing of client ZIP codes when you need their phone numbers.

Users and computer professionals can work together to overcome most cons of computing. The secret is communication. Users must understand what they reasonably can expect a software package or an information system to do, and they must be able to convey their computing needs to the professionals who develop or select software and systems. Professionals must understand what matters to users, for example, how often sales need updating, how to catch billing errors before they are processed, and what data the system should be collecting.

Working together, users and professionals can minimize compatibility

To be useful, information must be current, complete, accurate, and meaningful.

## *LOOKING* AHEAD

**HACKERS GO LEGIT**

You may be surprised to learn that only in the past few years have hackers gained notoriety as computer criminals. Most technically proficient computer users (the old definition of *hacker*) are law-abiding folks. But a few find the challenge of breaking into systems and networks irresistible. Some make their living breaking into systems in order to show business executives the weak points in their information systems and then, for a fee, develop techniques for making the systems more secure.

problems and overcome the drawbacks of useless information, poorly developed systems, and even user resistance to computing, by focusing on the six steps that follow.

## MINIMIZE PROGRAMMING AND INPUT ERRORS

Computer systems should be designed to minimize downtime, or breakdowns, and information systems should be designed to minimize errors. Both damage a company's relations with customers and make employees' work more difficult. Mistakes occur as a result of programming errors, input errors, and poor management of the computer system.

Most "computer errors" result from input mistakes. Users and data entry operators need to check the data they enter into the computer to make sure that it is relatively free of errors. Moreover, programmers should include in their programs tests that check input for accuracy. For example, programs can test to ensure that paycheck amounts are within an established range and that birth dates or transaction dates are reasonable.

## PROVIDE ADEQUATE CONTROLS AND PROPER SECURITY

Security is a major issue in designing information systems. Computer software and critical data need protection from natural disasters such as fire, flood, and earthquakes, as well as from people working against the organization's interests. Computers are sometimes used as tools for white-collar crime or even for revenge. Computer **hackers** who are unauthorized users make news when they penetrate huge networked systems with schemes that overwork the system or contaminate data. The resulting errors and computer failures could be avoided if the computer system and its software and data were made more secure.

As the number of computer users continues to grow, the need for proper control and security measures increases dramatically. Networks that provide access to users in far-reaching locales are at great risk. To maintain the integrity of programs and data, users and computer professionals must work together to prevent unauthorized access of their systems.

## GET USERS MORE INVOLVED IN SYSTEMS DEVELOPMENT

One main reason that computers fail to satisfy user needs is poor communication. Either users do not understand an information system's limitations and potential, or systems analysts do not fully understand user needs. Poor communication sometimes results in computer phobia; that is, people fear computers and do not trust the output produced by them. Initially, those fears were coupled with the concern that computers would produce mass unemployment. But the evidence has shown that more jobs are generated by computers than are lost by them, except in certain areas such as automated factories. When computers generate growth in a company, more labor is needed to operate the computer and to develop the information systems.

People who remain leery of computing can benefit from a better understanding of what computers can accomplish and how problems can be minimized. Employees should learn, for example, that some of the tedious tasks they currently perform manually are apt to be tasks easily performed by computing. Here are three ways to get users more involved in what we call **systems development,** which consists of designing and implementing information systems.

**Involve Users in Planning.**  Users are apt to resist a computerized system if they did not work with the systems analysts and programmers in its design. Without the cooperation of users, information systems will almost always fail to meet expectations.

**Be Sure Development Goals Are Realistic.**  In their enthusiasm, computer professionals may underestimate the time and resources needed to build an information system and fail to provide for unanticipated delays and obstacles. Such overoptimism can create difficulties for users working within a fixed budget and a projected schedule for computer use.

**Guarantee Privacy to Workers.**  Many people in organizations resist using computers because they are concerned about invasion of their privacy. A computerized payroll system that contains salary information may be accessible to so many users that many employees fear their privacy is being violated. Medical information for insurance purposes may also be widely available, and an employee's personal health records may be compromised. For employees to cooperate in the design and use of computers, they must feel confident that accepted business procedures are being properly followed and that sensitive information is available only to those with a need to know.

## MINIMIZE INFORMATION OVERLOAD (MORE IS NOT NECESSARILY BETTER)

One result of computerization in many organizations is the proliferation of information and its consequent overload of output, usually in the form of paper. Providing users with a great deal of information may seem a worthwhile goal; but it may, in fact, prove more a burden than a blessing. The objective of computing is to provide meaningful and timely information that users need to perform day-to-day tasks and to help them make decisions. Giving users more than they need can be as ineffective as giving them less than they need.

One of the original objectives of bringing computers into the office was the "paperless office"—to virtually eliminate paper documents or at least to significantly minimize them. That goal has yet to be realized. Indeed, many office workers believe that far more paper is generated now than before. See Figure 1.11. When people have a great deal of information at their fingertips, they are apt to want to capture it on paper.

The objective of reducing paper in the office is still an important one, however. The technology exists to dramatically decrease the amount of paper generated. As users continue to realize the drawbacks of information overload, output in paper form is likely to be reduced.

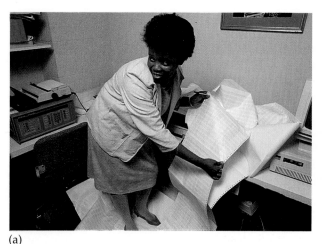
(a)

(b)

*Figure 1.11* (a) *More is not necessarily better when generating printed output.* (b) *Sometimes a picture is worth more than a thousand words. The objective is to provide users with the right amount of information to do their jobs.*

## PROMOTE AND DEVELOP COMPUTING STANDARDS

Because the computing industry changes so rapidly, there are few established standards. As we have seen, computer systems within the same office can be incompatible. Some input/output devices can be used only with specific types of computers. Similarly, some software works only on certain types of computers. Even networked software and hardware are not always usable with all types of systems and with all types of programs. Computer professionals and users must drive the industry by promoting the need for standards in hardware, software, and connectivity.

## INSIST ON COMPLETE AND ACCURATE DOCUMENTATION

Hardware, software, and systems that are properly developed are easier to use, maintain, modify, control, and evaluate. But in the final analysis, the effectiveness of information depends on adequate documentation. User manuals should be clear, complete, and accurate. Information systems are virtually useless if no one knows how the software and hardware work. Custom software developed by programmers for information systems must have proper documentation as well.

## ▶ SELF-TEST

1. (T or F) When business systems are being computerized, it is best to provide users with as much output information as possible in the belief that they will ultimately need all they can get.
2. _____ is a concept that enables different computers to share hardware and software, even if the computers are not compatible.
3. Two basic categories of people who work with computers are _____ and _____.
4. Computer errors are most often caused by _____ and _____.
5. (T or F) Computer professionals can more efficiently and effectively perform their jobs if they work independently to generate an information system and then show users how to work with it.

Solutions
1. F
2. Connectivity
3. computer users; computer professionals (systems analysts and programmers)
4. input errors; program errors
5. F—Users and computer professionals must work closely together.

# COMPUTING   IN   THE   INFORMATION   AGE          **1.3**

Our objective in this book is to help you become more proficient in computing, and that involves both showing you how to use computers and increasing your understanding of the concepts of computing: hardware, software, connectivity, and people. To assist you in thinking critically about how these concepts are related, we focus throughout this book on four major ways in which computing affects our lives now and will continue to affect us in the future.

Computers are making the world smaller, smarter, more creative, and they are also bringing the world closer together. As you will see, we emphasize these aspects of computing because we view them as particularly crucial in the years ahead. We also view them as being interrelated. To be more connected, for example, requires a world that is smaller, smarter, and more creative.

> How has information processing been revolutionized by computers?

## ► Computers Are Making the World Smaller

Initially, computer systems were the size of large rooms. The trend, however, is toward smaller computing devices with greater power. Today, a PC that fits in the palm of your hand has computing power hundreds of times that of the first electronic computers.

The ability of tiny computing devices to control complex operations has transformed the way many tasks are performed, ranging from how scientific research is undertaken to how some consumer products are produced. Tiny "computers on a chip" are used in medical equipment, home appliances, cars, and toys. Workers use handheld computing devices to collect data at a customer site, to generate forms, to control inventory, and to replace a notebook or desktop organizer.

Smaller computers, in fact, are making the world itself smaller. In this book we highlight small computing devices that not only contribute to business but have the potential for improving the overall quality of life. Look for the icon with three world images in decreasing sizes that appears in the text at various places. It means that the topic being discussed focuses on how the world is getting smaller with the use of computers.

**COMPUTERS ARE MAKING THE WORLD SMALLER**

As we consider how computers are making our world smaller, we will emphasize examples such as these.

1. Personal computers that weigh about a pound have the computing power of larger systems.
2. Handheld data collection devices keep inventory systems up to date.
3. Miniature computers perform complex operations for users in business, research, and even at home.

**COMPUTING APPLICATION**

Executives who once measured status by the size of their home or the cost of their automobile have found the ultimate symbol of power and success—the portable computer. For most business people who travel, the smaller and lighter a computer is and the more power it wields, the more impressive it is. Portables began as "luggables" weighing in at 30 pounds with cases that made them look like sewing machines. Businesspeople who transported them looked like salespeople for heavy-duty machinery. Today, executives travel in style with their notebook or palmtop computers carried in their attaché case or breast pocket! These machines are leaner and meaner; they weigh as little as a few pounds or even less, but often are as powerful as the big and bulky desktop versions. Notebook and palmtop computers are not only better because they are smaller, they run longer on their AA batteries, and

many of them have pens that enable users to take handwritten notes that can be saved for future reference.

The applicability of these computers extends beyond the executive level. Salespeople who travel to customers to get information and to

*Even marine biologists need computers; like most professionals on the go, they find that "leaner and meaner" PCs can be taken anywhere.*

make sales may find these compact machines to be invaluable.

## ► Computers Are Making the World Smarter

Not only is computing equipment getting smaller, it is getting more sophisticated. Computers are part of many machines and devices that once required continual human supervision and control. Today, computers in security systems result in safer environments, computers in cars improve energy efficiency, and computers in phones provide features such as call forwarding, call monitoring, and call answering.

These smart machines are designed to take over some of the basic tasks performed by people; by so doing, they make life a little easier and a little more pleasant. In this book we highlight these smart machines. Look for the globe icon with the mortarboard that appears in the margin at various places. It means that the topic being discussed focuses on how computers are making the world smarter.

As we look at how computers make our world smarter, we will emphasize examples such as these:

1. Smart devices like phones and appliances have built-in computers.

**COMPUTING APPLICATION**

A central automation system is the brains behind the smart house. It enables home owners to program functions for all appliances, audio and video systems, heating and cooling equipment, lighting systems, lawn-watering equipment, and security devices. Moreover, the computerized heating and cooling systems are designed to be as efficient as possible.

Approach the TRON house in Tokyo, Japan, and the lights turn on automatically. You can set a timer by phone to draw a bath, turn on the oven, or set the thermostat. If it starts to rain, the windows close automatically. Plants are watered by a timer.

TRON stands for *The Real Time Operating System Nucleus*, and a community of such homes is being planned in Tokyo. The development is sponsored by 18 Japanese companies including Nippon, Mitsubishi Electric, and Sibu Department Stores.

Other smart devices in the smart home include washers that can adjust the wash cycle depending on how dirty the clothes are, microwaves that can adjust temperature and cooking time for proper heating, and vacuum cleaners that adjust to type of dirt and carpet conditions. These devices can also "learn" to adjust to people's preferences. If

*The homeowner can control lighting, security, sprinklers, climate, and various electrical circuits in a smart house by simply selecting entries from a screen.*

you like your food well done, you can teach your oven to cook accordingly.

2. Smart houses and factories have built-in monitoring and control systems.
3. Smart cards store vital information.

## ▶ Computers Are Making the World More Creative

With small computing devices available for performing smart tasks like cooking dinner, programming the VCR, and controlling the flow of information in an organization, people are able to spend more time doing what they often do best—being creative. Computers can help people work more creatively.

In this book we highlight the ways in which computers are making our world more creative. Look for the light bulb icon for topics that focus on how computers can expand your creative power.

As we learn how computers are making our world more creative, we will emphasize examples such as the following:

**COMPUTING APPLICATION**

Expert systems have been developed in a wide variety of areas to help users make decisions. An expert system is software that simulates the "thinking" of an expert. It contains both facts and knowledge along with a set of rules that recommend a course of action for the user. An expert system can be used by a physician who enters a patient's symptoms and obtains as output a possible diagnosis. Another expert system can diagnose the cause of a machine malfunction. A third expert system can evaluate a customer's credit history and determine whether to recommend a loan. Such expert systems make the world more creative by assisting users as they evaluate situations and make decisions.

*This expert system provides diagnostic testing of an automobile.*

1. **Expert systems** simulate the decision-making capability of an expert in science, medicine, law, and other fields.
2. Systems accept spoken data as input and can respond verbally as well.
3. **Multimedia** in computing is the use of sound, animation, video, graphics, text, and images to convey information, to make presentations, and to provide computer-based training.

## ▶ Computers Are Bringing the World Closer Together

Connectivity enables computers and software that might otherwise be incompatible to communicate and to share resources. Now that computers are proliferating in many areas and networks are available for people to access data and communicate with others, personal computers really are *inter*personal PCs. They have the potential to significantly improve the way we relate to each other. With the proper tools, for example, a hospital staff can get a diagnosis from a medical expert hundreds or thousands of miles away. Similarly, the disabled can communicate more effectively with others using computers.

With connectivity, however, comes responsibilities, such as the need to respect others' privacy and to keep data secure. In this book, we highlight connectivity, along with the human factor, as critical concepts in computing that help bring the world closer together. Look for the handshaking icon that appears in the margin throughout the text. It means that the topic being discussed focuses on how computers are making the world more interconnected.

**COMPUTING APPLICATION**

Business researchers estimate that people in approximately 20 million U.S. households use computing technology to earn money at home. These workers may be self-employed, or they may be **telecommuting** employees of an organization. Telecommuters represent a growing segment of the U.S. work force. By using computers at home, employees can be in constant communication with the office and thus perform some or all of their duties without the time, expense, and stress of the everyday commute.

For society, fewer commuters means decreased energy use and less pollution as well as reduced stress and expense for individuals. So telecommuting has the potential to improve our quality of life. As a rule, however, businesses have been slow to accept the virtues of telecommuting. Managers fear the loss of control over employees and projects and are concerned that employees may misrepresent the number of hours worked. Probably most important, managers worry about the effects of decreased face-to-face interaction in the workplace.

What has happened in most cases, however, is that telecommu-ters tend to work additional hours at home using their PCs. Although these workers often find that the greater flexibility they enjoy makes them more productive, they also may find that they are "on call" at all hours. Leisure time becomes less enjoyable. As connectivity continues to link computer users together, telecommuting will likely grow more prevalent. To enjoy its benefits fully, employers and employees must maintain a proper perspective.

*Telecommuting enables people with computers to work at home and still have access to the office. Because there is less tension in their lives, employees are happier, which may improve their productivity. Telecommuting on a large scale has the potential to ease urban problems relating to mass transportation, energy use, and pollution.*

As we analyze how computers are bringing the world closer together, we will emphasize examples such as these.

1. Computer and communication networks link computer users within organizations, between organizations, and all over the world.
2. Networks link users with enormous data banks, both public and private, bringing the knowledge of the world to the computer screen.
3. Private, secure, user-friendly systems provide users with effective, integrated information from many sources that may lead to a better quality of life.

▶ **SELF-TEST**

1. (T or F) Miniature computers are often used in home appliances, cars, and toys.
2. (T or F) Computers are often used in machines to control and supervise tasks.

**CRITICAL THINKING**

Are employers justified in their fears about telecommuting? Does telecommuting have any potential disadvantages for workers in terms of their quality of life?

3. (T or F) A smart machine such as a smart phone is typically one that has a built-in computer.
4. Multimedia incorporates _____ in conveying information.
5. To bring the world closer together, computers must be able to _____.

Solutions
1. T
2. T
3. T
4. graphics, video, animation, and sound
5. share resources or communicate with one another

## ▶ Chapter Summary

When computer systems were first used for information processing, the Information Age began. Anyone who has gone to school or to work in the past decade already is, to some degree, **computer literate** and may also be a computer **user.** Chapter 1 describes computing basics and computer **applications.**

### 1.1 INTRODUCING COMPUTER SYSTEMS: INPUT-PROCESS-OUTPUT

How do computers process data to produce information?

Computers read incoming **data**—raw facts—as **input, process** these raw facts into meaningful **information,** and produce **output. Information processing** techniques vary depending on the application area. Today, small, powerful **personal computers (PCs)** allow any computer user access to information from larger computers.

Computer systems operate under the control of **programs. Input devices** accept data from the user and store it in main memory. The **CPU** transforms input data into information, which is produced for the user via **output devices. Storage devices** hold programs, data, and information on **disk** for later use. The set of computer devices in a system is called the **hardware.** Large or small, specially **configured** or not, all computer systems operate in basically the same way: input-process-output. The real differences among computer systems relate to their relative size and processing power.

Computers are **stored-program devices.** Professional computer **programmers** write sets of programs for any user need. This **software,** available on disk, comes in two forms. **Systems software** controls computer operations through an **operating system,** such as **DOS** for IBM PCs, and communicates with users via a **user interface. User-friendly** graphical interfaces with **icons** are becoming more popular than text-based interfaces. **Windows** is the graphical user interface for DOS.

**Application programs** for specific information processing tasks may be **packaged** for retail sale or **custom** designed for a unique need. **Productivity tools** are application programs used to perform day-to-day business tasks and to assist users in decision making. Packaged programs usually provide users with comprehensive reference manuals called **documentation.**

Software and hardware **incompatibility** is a major issue in the computing industry. Smart computer users select their software before they decide on their hardware.

## 1.2 UNDERSTANDING INFORMATION PROCESSING

In organizations, computer systems automate information processing for major **business systems**—accounting, human resources, production, and marketing. Hardware and software enable employees to work more productively, search for information faster, and analyze results better.

**Connectivity** enables even incompatible software and hardware to share information and resources with the use of a communications **network.**

People control the entire computing process. Computer users at all levels depend on effective information systems to do their jobs. When user needs change, computer professionals—programmers and **systems analysts** among them—modify existing business systems or create new ones in the continuing cycle of **systems development.**

There are many reasons for developing computerized information systems. Computers are fast, accurate, and economical. Computers systems can store vast amounts of information in a compact space, and computing offers intangible benefits, such as improved productivity and better quality control.

To eliminate or minimize the cons of computing, users and computer professionals work to improve communication. To ensure effective systems development, users must understand what to expect from computerized information processing; professionals must understand users' information needs. Other techniques to avoid the cons of computing include correcting errors in programming or incoming data; providing system security against natural disasters or unauthorized use by **hackers** or others; avoiding information overload; promoting computing standards; and insisting on complete, accurate documentation.

*How do organizations use computers for information processing?*

## 1.3 COMPUTING IN THE INFORMATION AGE

To be proficient in computing, you need to develop your skills in using systems and software, and you also need to understand the basic concepts behind hardware, software, and connectivity. This book explains how these components of computing interrelate and why computers are making the world smaller, smarter, more creative, and more interconnected.

In just two generations, computers moved from the laboratory to the dormitory, home, and office. Even smaller and more powerful personal computers can be carried in a briefcase or pocket while larger computers bring the entire world to your fingertips. Computers are making the world smaller.

Smart cars, telephones, and children's toys are just the beginning. One day you will use smart cards as money and come home to a smart house.

*How has information processing been revolutionized by computers?*

Smart computing devices take some of the drudgery out of work and make life a little easier. Computers are making the world smarter.

With smart devices at work, you are free to be more creative with your time. High-powered software and systems expand your creativity, no matter what field interests you, personally or professionally, as the potential of **expert systems** and **multimedia** illustrate. Computers are making the world more creative.

Connectivity links both computing resources and people. As interpersonal machines, PCs have the potential to bring the world to your fingertips. Computer networks on a global scale help businesses and nations meet their needs for information. More personally, networks have the potential for improving the quality of life. **Telecommuting** is one growing network application. Computers are making the world more interconnected.

## ▶ Chapter Self-test

1. Incoming data, or raw facts, is called _____ and information produced by a computer is called _____.
2. The computer device that actually manipulates and operates on input to produce output is called the _____.
3. The set of instructions that specifies what operations a computer is to perform is called a _____.
4. Data and programs are typically stored on _____ for future use.
5. Name an operating system for the IBM PS/2 personal computer.
6. Application programs that can be purchased ready to use are called _____.
7. Telecommuting enables workers to use computers at _____.
8. Two computer systems that cannot run the same software are said to be _____.
9. A _____ enables computers to share hardware and software resources.
10. The computer professional responsible for systems development is called the _____.
11. (T or F) Information is processed to produce data that is meaningful, timely, and accurate.
12. (T or F) Operating system software supervises the overall operations of the computer system.
13. (T or F) An icon is a type of packaged program.
14. (T or F) Computer programs are known as software.
15. (T or F) Documentation should include guidelines for using a program.

Solutions

1. input; output
2. central processing unit (CPU)
3. program
4. disk (or another storage medium)

5. DOS or OS/2 (Windows is *not* an operating system, but a graphical user interface for DOS.)
6. application packages
7. home
8. incompatible
9. network
10. systems analyst
11. F—Data is processed and information is produced.
12. T
13. F
14. T
15. T

## ▶ Key Terms

Application, *p. 6*
Application software, *p. 10*
Business system, *p. 14*
Central processing unit (CPU), *p. 6*
Computer literate, *p. 6*
Computer system, *p. 7*
Configured, *p. 8*
Connectivity, *p. 14*
Custom program, *p. 12*
Data, *p. 6*
Disk, *p. 9*
Documentation, *p. 12*
DOS, *p. 11*
Expert system, *p. 26*

Hacker, *p. 20*
Hardware, *p. 7*
Icon, *p. 11*
Incompatibility, *p. 11*
Information, *p. 6*
Information processing, *p. 6*
Input, *p. 6*
Input device, *p. 6*
Multimedia, *p. 26*
Network, *p. 14*
Operating system, *p. 11*
Output, *p. 6*
Output device, *p. 6*
Packaged program, *p. 12*
Personal computer (PC), *p. 6*

Processing, *p. 6*
Productivity tool, *p. 12*
Program, *p. 7*
Programmer, *p. 10*
Software, *p. 10*
Storage device, *p. 6*
Stored-program device, *p. 10*
Systems analyst, *p. 16*
Systems development, *p. 21*
Systems software, *p. 10*
Telecommuting, *p. 27*
User, *p. 6*
User-friendly, *p. 11*
User interface, *p. 11*
Windows, *p. 11*

## ▶ Review Questions

1. List the basic hardware components of a computer system and briefly describe each.
2. Describe the two basic types of software.
3. Explain the term *connectivity* and describe why it is so important in computing.
4. Why is compatibility important and how does that issue relate to computer industry standards?
5. Give some examples of how computers have significantly improved our quality of life. Also give some examples of how computer use has had serious adverse effects on people. Indicate how those adverse effects could have been avoided. Use newspaper or magazine articles for reference if necessary.
6. Indicate why some people have negative reactions to computers and suggest methods that could be used to change these attitudes.

## Multimedia Puts on a Good Show

Can computing help a city get chosen as an Olympic site? Atlanta officials would say yes. They give much of the credit for being selected to host the 1996 Summer Olympics to the multimedia extravaganza they put on for the Olympic selection committee.

Multimedia, a new technology for personal computers, combines text, graphics, animation, high-quality video images, and audio to make presentations and to provide training. With special navigational tools for viewing multimedia presentations, users can interact directly with the program.

Atlanta's program shows the impact multimedia can have on marketing. Developed with the help of the Georgia Institute of Technology, the multimedia presentation program provided the Olympics selection committee with an electronic tour of the city, complete with sights and sounds. The interactive feature enabled the judges to ask questions that were immediately answered on the video screen.

Multimedia is an ideal presentation and educational tool. It has been shown to increase information retention from 20 to 80 percent over simple text presentations. American Airlines uses multimedia to train or retrain thousands of employees in ticketing, cargo, and security procedures.

Some software developers believe the future of multimedia is in the consumer market, potentially as a rival to television. Where the TV viewer is passive, the multimedia viewer is active. Users navigate around presentations and even interact with them, techniques that are not possible with TV. For home reference, Microsoft, the developer of IBM DOS, publishes a dictionary that pronounces words; a book of quotations that features authors reading their works; an analysis of Beethoven's Ninth Symphony, complete with music; and a critical evaluation of major art works, with visual reproductions.

*Multimedia presentations, like the Atlanta show and those illustrated here, are often used by Chambers of Commerce to provide tourists with information about the local sites. The presentations are interactive, enabling users to request the specific type of information they want. The presentations often incorporate videos, graphics, sound, and animation along with text.*

With so many possible applications, why isn't multimedia more widely used? The main problem is the price: to be effectively used for multimedia, a computer system must be fast and have a very large storage capacity. Relatively expensive audio and video hardware and sophisticated software are needed to synchronize images and sound. Another problem with multimedia, as with so many other computing products, is a lack of standards.

As computer manufacturers vie for a share of the multimedia market, prices will begin to decrease. The Apple Macintosh has been the forerunner in multimedia, but IBM is catching up, and so is Tandy. Tandy's 2500SX, which permits recording, manipulating, storing, and playing back digital pictures and sound, is available for multimedia applications for under $3,000.

*Analysis*
1. List three ways that you might use a multimedia system.
2. How might multimedia be used as a presentation or teaching tool for business, education, or home use?
3. Besides price, describe three basic differences between multimedia and TV presentations.

# FROM MICROS TO MAMMOTHS

**A**re the small personal computers you encounter in your daily life *really* similar to the computers the U.S. government uses to manage the enormous federal tax system? The answer is yes. Computers consist of these basic components: input devices; main memory and a central processing unit; output devices; and storage devices that store programs and data on media such as disk. All types of computers have these basic components and all process data in essentially the same way. The desktop PC and larger computer systems that require a full room (or more) for their components use the same basic instructions for processing data.

Chapter 2 covers the fundamentals of hardware, computer processing, and connectivity by answering the following questions:

▶ Why are categorical distinctions among types of computers really artificial boundaries?

▶ How do application areas govern the choice of hardware?

▶ What do users need to know about hardware and connectivity?

 # CLASSIFYING COMPUTER SYSTEMS

## ▶ Types of Computers

Why are categorical distinctions among types of computers really artificial boundaries?

All computers (1) use input devices to read data into main memory, (2) have a CPU that actually operates on the data in main memory, (3) have output devices that print, display, or otherwise create meaningful information for users, and (4) have storage media for holding programs and data for future processing. But computers vary in characteristics such as size, power, and cost. There are four widely used categories for classifying computers. We list them here, from largest to smallest.

1. **Supercomputers.** When it comes to speed, power, and size, supercomputers are the fastest, largest, and costliest of computer systems. They are used mostly in scientific and industrial research, by the government, and by very large organizations for controlling their networks. Some supercomputers can process data from more than 10,000 users at once. A typical supercomputer sells for about $10 million.
2. **Mainframes.** The first computers used in business, beginning in the early 1950s, were mainframes. In mid-sized and large companies, mainframes remain the most widely used computer systems. They occupy entire rooms and often are available to hundreds or even thousands of users who work at input/output devices called **terminals,** which are located at sites away from the main computer's location. See Figure 2.1. Mainframes are very large and powerful computer systems, but they are often so expensive that companies lease them rather than purchase them outright.

**Figure 2.1** *A terminal can be any input/output device not at the same site as the main computer, but most often it is a keyboard/screen device.*

3. **Minicomputers.** Known also as **midrange computers,** minicomputers (or minis), stand midway between micros and larger computers in size, power, and cost. Minis were specifically created as **multiuser systems**—systems that can be shared by many users who access the system using terminals or other input/output devices. For example, all the employees in a small business or a single department within a larger company can use a single mini or midrange system for the bulk of their computing needs. That mini or midrange system can function independently or it can be linked to a larger mainframe or supercomputer.
4. **Microcomputers.** PCs, another name for micros, are used mainly by one individual at a time and are the smallest, least powerful, and least expensive computer systems. They provide users with the ability to increase their productivity by accessing application software or by communicating electronically with larger systems.

Because computers of all sizes are becoming more and more powerful, categories such as microcomputer and supercomputer, and all categories in between, are relative. Supercomputers are simply the fastest, most powerful computers currently available, and microcomputers are at the other end of the spectrum. Today's microcomputers can do the work that it took a room-sized mainframe to accomplish two decades ago; today's supercomputer may well be tomorrow's microcomputer.

As the processing power of computers increases, the lines between categories blur further. The applications best handled by each category of computer are likely to change over time. To market their ever smaller and more powerful computers, manufacturers sometimes introduce new categories. For example, the prefix "super" is often applied to smaller systems, dubbed supermicros or superminis.

New names may lead to new categories, just as minis and micros evolved from mainframes. Even though we use four basic categories of

*With newer technologies emerging, categorical distinctions among computer systems are becoming increasingly blurred.*

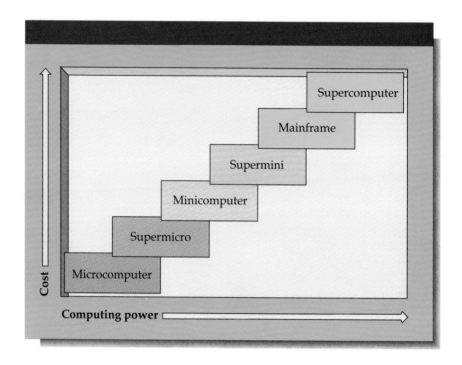

computers in this text, we ask you to keep in mind that these are neither explicit nor consistent distinctions and are not likely to stand the test of time.

Although definitive distinctions do not exist, larger systems are distinguished from smaller ones with regard to the basic factors of size, cost, and processing power. Processing power is related to how much main memory a computer has for processing programs and data, processing speed, and the number of input/output devices each can handle. Let us discuss processing power in more depth.

## ▶ **P**rocessing **P**ower

### MEMORY SIZE

Memory size refers to the primary storage capacity, or **main memory,** available to the CPU. As you work on a computer, each letter, digit, or symbol you enter as data or as part of an instruction is stored in a single storage position called a **byte** of storage.

In larger computers, primary storage capacity is measured in **giga-bytes (GB),** or billions of bytes. Today's micros have main memories ranging up to **megabytes (MB),** or millions of storage positions. In contrast to the latest micros, early PCs had much smaller memories. The main memory of the first Apple and IBM PC computers, for example, was measured in **kilobytes (K).** Each kilobyte equals 1024 bytes, but we typically round a kilobyte to approximately 1000 bytes.

IN A

The CPU and main memory are typically stored in a single unit sometimes called a processor.

## PROCESSING SPEED

Computers process data in speeds measured in fractions of a second. Microcomputer speeds are typically measured in **microseconds,** or millionths of a second. Mini and mainframe computer speeds are measured in **nanoseconds,** or billionths of a second. Supercomputer speeds are measured in **picoseconds,** or trillionths of a second. With each leap in size comes a leap in speed.

The CPU processes data under the control of programmed instructions, the software. To more accurately gauge the processing power of a CPU, computing experts consider both processing speed and memory size in a measurement called **MIPS,** *m*illions of *i*nstructions *p*er *s*econd. The fastest microcomputers operate at 5 to 100 or more million instructions per second. At the other end of the spectrum, some supercomputers operate at thousands of MIPS. More detailed factors affecting the speed and processing power of a computer are discussed in Chapter 4.

## INPUT/OUTPUT DEVICES (PERIPHERALS)

The power of mainframes and supercomputers makes them ideal for the largest networks and for applications required by many users. Although a PC can share the resources in a mainframe or supercomputer network, microcomputers by themselves are mainly single-user systems. The CPU in most micros is designed to handle one user with one set of input, output, and storage devices, or **peripherals,** at any one time. Larger systems can handle multiple users, applications, and peripherals. Yet micros are basically miniatures of larger systems, and they are the computers that you are most likely to have encountered. Thus, we cover here the basics of computer system peripherals from a PC perspective. Keep in mind that the differences among computer categories are essentially differences of degree with regard to size, cost, and processing power. What is true for micros is likely to be true, on a larger scale, for larger computers.

A common input device for PCs and larger systems is the **keyboard,** designed like a typewriter but with additional specialized keys. In many systems, keyboarding is combined with the use of a pointing device, or **mouse.** Both a keyboard and a mouse enable users to enter data and execute instructions. The data entered is visible on the computer **monitor,**

Input/output devices are detailed in Chapter 5, storage devices in Chapter 6, and computer communications in Chapter 12. Appendix A is a tutorial explaining how to interact with microcomputer equipment.

IN A

**UNITS OF STORAGE**

| | |
|---|---|
| Byte | One storage position; used to store a character (letter, digit, or symbol) in data or an instruction |
| Kilobyte (K) | Approximately 1000 storage positions (actually 1,024 bytes) |
| Megabyte (MB) | Approximately 1 million storage positions (actually 1,024,000 bytes) |
| Gigabyte (GB) | Approximately 1 billion storage positions (actually 1,024,000,000 bytes) |

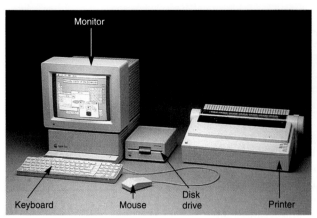

*Figure 2.2* A PC typically has a keyboard, mouse, monitor, printer, disk drives, and a modem, which can be a separate external device or built into the computer.

*Figure 2.3* Color printers are often used to display attractive graphs.

*Figure 2.4* Air traffic controllers rely on information collected from remote locations like airplanes and other control centers.

a video screen that looks like a television. The monitor is an input/output device that displays both inputted data and instructions, as well as computer responses; it can also display output information. See Figure 2.2.

The majority of PC users want to get their information on paper—a report for school, a bill for services, or the family budget. Most output for larger systems—paychecks, inventory reports, sales forecasts—is paper output too. The most common output device is the **printer,** which can print words and pictures on paper in black and white or color. See Figure 2.3.

PC users store their software and data on disks that fit into the computer's disk drives. The CPU controls access to all the data and instructions stored on disk. Disks come in many sizes and may be portable, flexible **floppy disks** or rigid **hard disks** that are mounted permanently in their **disk drives.** Hard disks have much greater storage capacity than floppy disks (also called **diskettes**). The most frequently used floppy disks come in two sizes: 5¼-inch in diameter and 3½-inch in diameter. The 5¼-inch version is older and less durable and has a storage capacity of from 360 K to 1.2 MB. The 3½-inch version is more popular and durable and has a storage capacity of from 720 K to 2.88 MB or more. We discuss disks in depth in Chapter 6.

A device called a **modem** connects the computer system by cable to a standard telephone jack. With a modem, signals from one computer can be transmitted to another over telephone lines. The modem may be built into the computer, as shown in Figure 2.2, or it may be a separate external peripheral connected to the computer by cable. With the proper software and a modem, you can communicate with another PC user or with a computer network anywhere in the world.

The bigger the system, the bigger its CPU. From minis to supercomputers, these larger systems use terminals, which are usually combined keyboard/monitor units, as their main input/output device. These larger systems process much greater volumes of data and instructions than do micros. Many other types of peripheral devices are used for high-volume information processing. Often the system must gather data from remote locations far away from the computer system—the drive-in window at a bank branch, the supermarket aisle, even a national park. See Figure 2.4. We discuss peripherals in more depth in Chapter 5.

Table 2.1 summarizes the four computer categories in order of increasing size, price, and processing power. Computer processing concepts are covered in detail in Chapter 4.

**Micro:** *A Compaq personal computer can be used as a stand-alone desktop micro or connected to other machines in a network.*

**Mini/midrange:** *The VAX is a popular minicomputer manufactured by the Digital Equipment Corporation.*

**Mainframe:** *The IBM ES/9000 mainframe is most often housed in a central computer facility and is accessible to users with terminals at remote sites.*

**Supercomputer:** *The CRAY X-MP/ 48 supercomputer is distinguished by its unique shape and bright colors. The four units shown are processors.*

**Table 2.1** | CATEGORIES OF COMPUTER SYSTEMS

| Category | Price range | PROCESSING POWER | | |
| | | Speed | Memory size | Connectivity |
| --- | --- | --- | --- | --- |
| Micro | From hundreds of dollars to $10,000 | 5–100 MIPS or more | 640 K to 16 MB or more | Essentially single user; can be linked to other systems; high-end PCs may be multiuser systems |
| Mini/midrange | From $10,000 to $100,000 | Nanoseconds; hundreds of MIPS | Hundreds of megabytes to gigabytes | Multiuser |
| Mainframe | $100,000 and up | Nanoseconds; hundreds of MIPS | Dozens of gigabytes | Multiuser |
| Supercomputer | $4 million and up | Picoseconds; thousands of MIPS | Hundreds of gigabytes and up | Multiuser |

▶ **SELF-TEST**

1. Which category of computers is the most powerful?
2. Whatever you type on the keyboard will typically be displayed on a
   _____.
3. What device enables computers to communicate over telephone lines?
4. What computer medium is most often used for permanently storing
   data and instructions?

Solutions

1. supercomputers          3. modem
2. monitor                 4. disk

---

## 2.2  GETTING TO KNOW YOUR HARDWARE

*How do application areas govern the choice of hardware?*

Now we will discuss computer categories in more depth and in the sequence in which they were developed. Mainframes will be discussed first since they were developed first. Remember: Computers of all sizes work on the same principle of input-process-output. They differ mainly in cost, size, processing power (speed, memory size, and the number of peripherals)—factors that determine the applications for which each category is best suited.

### ▶ Mainframes

In the early 1950s the mainframe was the first computer developed for general-purpose use in business. Mainframes remain the most widely used computer systems in medium to large-sized companies where they are the primary computers for large processing applications in business areas such as accounting, sales and marketing, production, and human resources.

A mainframe typically costs $100,000 or more (sometimes much more), and its main memory and CPU, storage, and input/output devices often occupy a large room. Peripherals are connected to the CPU by cables linked beneath an elevated floor in the computer room. Mainframes are operated by a professional computer staff. User needs are handled on a production basis with schedules carefully maintained and controlled. If, for example, payroll checks are prepared by a mainframe, it is likely that a regularly scheduled date and time is allotted for this production run.

Environmental factors such as temperature, humidity, and dust must be carefully set and controlled to keep the mainframe functioning properly. Organizations might expend tens of thousands of dollars to prepare a facility for the hardware and to ensure that the facility is properly monitored. Mainframe computer rooms are usually secured, which means that access is controlled by the computer staff. This minimizes accidents and unauthorized access to equipment, programs, and data.

## WHO INVENTED THE FIRST ELECTRONIC DIGITAL COMPUTER? THE CONTROVERSY RAGES ON

During World War II, the U.S. government was developing new artillery at an unprecedented rate. This created a computational backlog, because the new machines could not be used until range tables were prepared to instruct soldiers how to fire them. Since the calculations necessary for preparing range tables were so extensive, effective use of the weapons was delayed months and sometimes even years. The government was prepared to fund any reasonable project that held a glimmer of hope for this seemingly irresolvable problem.

At the same time, John Mauchly, a physicist at the Moore School of Electrical Engineering of the University of Pennsylvania, had conceived the idea of an electronic digital computer, one that could perform 5000 additions per second—hundreds of times faster than any existing device. Since the Moore School had been under contract to the government for other war-related work, it was relatively easy to obtain a $500,000 contract for Mauchly's proposed device, called ENIAC, an abbreviation for Electronic Numerical Integrator and Computer. Mauchly became principal consultant on the project, and J. Presper Eckert, Jr., a brilliant and energetic young graduate student, became chief engineer.

The ENIAC, developed from 1943 to 1946, and was the first electronic digital computer completed in the United States. It was an enormous device consisting of 30 units and 18,000 vacuum tubes. Because of its speed and reliability, it resulted in a virtual revolution in the computing field. The accompanying illustration shows some of the units of the ENIAC in the Moore School laboratory.

We credit Mauchly and Eckert as co-inventors of the first electronic digital computer completed in the

*The ENIAC was the first operational general-purpose computer. Its components are shown here along with some of the people who helped develop it. J. Presper Eckert is in the foreground (left) and John Mauchly is in the center.*

United States, but you may find that other sources claim priority for a different inventor, John Vincent Atanasoff. Priority issues are not easy to resolve, and it is difficult in many cases to determine which individual or individuals have made the most important contributions. This is so because invention is usually not an isolated act of creativity; rather, it follows an evolutionary path with many significant developments built on each other.

Atanasoff was a mathematical physicist at Iowa State College who developed the Atanasoff-Berry Computer (ABC) in the late 1930s and early 1940s. (Berry was a graduate student who worked with Atanasoff on the project.) The ABC was designed specifically as a special-purpose device that could solve up to 29 simultaneous equations. Atanasoff met Mauchly in 1941 and corresponded with him several times concerning the ABC. Mauchly even visited Iowa State once to see the model being built.

Atanasoff's machine was never fully operational and was designed specifically for a single purpose: to solve systems of simultaneous

equations. Despite these facts, many people claim Atanasoff invented the first electronic digital computer.

Atanasoff's claim to priority was strengthened by a lawsuit filed in 1971 by the Honeywell Corporation against Sperry-Univac. In that suit, Honeywell claimed that the ENIAC patent, held in 1971 by Sperry, was invalid because of the prior invention of Atanasoff's ABC machine. Since Honeywell and other computer manufacturers were paying royalties to Sperry for the right to build machines that used ideas intrinsic to the ENIAC, a significant amount of money was at stake. The suit was settled in 1973 when the judge ruled that the ENIAC patent was indeed invalid for numerous reasons, including Atanasoff's prior invention. Thus, from a legal point of view, Atanasoff's device is seen as a precursor to the ENIAC. Historians, however, are divided over the issue; most believe that Atanasoff's influence on Mauchly was minimal and that the former's device is not really the "first" computer because it was neither a functional machine nor a general-purpose one.

Mainframes are often used as the central computer in organizations that have large networks. In addition to the input/output units located at the same physical site as the CPU, hundreds of remote terminals may be linked or networked to the mainframe by cables, telephone lines, or other transmission media. The terminals can be located from within several feet of the CPU to miles away.

Mainframes, in general, as well as most other types of systems, are said to be **upwardly compatible,** which means two things: (1) the higher the model number, the more advanced the computer and (2) any software that can run on a lower model number can also run on a higher number, although the reverse is not necessarily true. An IBM ES/9000 model 900, for example, has more capability than an ES/9000 model 820. Moreover, any program executable on a model 820 will run on a model 900, but programs that are used on a model 900 may not run on a model 820. We will see that the concept of upward compatibility applies to versions of software as well as hardware: version 2.0 of a software product, for example, is more advanced than 1.0.

## ▶ **M**inis and **M**idrange **C**omputers

**CRITICAL THINKING**

It has been said that many computer manufacturers place obstacles to compatibility by developing proprietary systems or components that differ slightly from the standard. Why might it be in their interest to do this? What can users do to foster the development of standards for hardware and software so that compatibility problems are minimized?

In the late 1960s, when mainframes were at their peak and business functions were being widely computerized, many organizations grew dissatisfied with the concept of one central computer for all their needs. The mainframe was often overloaded, so departments had to wait their turn not only for output but for other application areas to be computerized. The concept of a single facility to satisfy all user needs was not working as effectively as it once did.

Some manufacturers, like the Digital Equipment Corporation (DEC), began to develop minicomputers, which were smaller, less powerful, and less expensive versions of a mainframe that could be used to augment an organization's central computer. Sometimes departments in large companies bought minis to help satisfy their individual needs. In the 1970s and 1980s minis and then superminis were used extensively either as additions to mainframes or as substitutes for them. An accounts receivable department, for example, might have its own mini for all its information processing needs. In other instances, minis were used to **offload** the mainframe for specific tasks. Offload is a term that means reducing one computer's tasks by having those tasks handled by a second computer. An inventory department might use a mini to provide better control of stock and to make predictions about future needs.

Minicomputer capabilities have continued to increase as their cost has decreased thereby making them competitive with mainframes in many application areas. Today, a midrange computer is essentially a device with the power of a mainframe and the cost of a mini. Note that many people use the terms *midrange* and *mini* as synonyms. See Figure 2.5. (The term *mini* as used in this text encompasses both midrange and supermini computers.)

*Figure 2.5 The IBM AS/400 is categorized as a midrange computer, but it competes directly with the VAX supermini manufactured by DEC.*

## ▶ Supercomputers

Supercomputers are the fastest, largest, and costliest computers available. Their speed is in the 120 to 200 MIPS range and is expected to keep increasing. Supercomputers tend to be used primarily for scientific, "number-crunching" applications at large universities and in weather forecasting, aircraft design, nuclear research, seismic analysis, and the space program. All of those applications require rapid analysis of vast amounts of data. Supercomputers are also used in some business environments for controlling very large networks. Prices begin at about $4 million.

Some manufacturers of large mainframes such as Fujitsu, Hitachi, and IBM build supercomputers. One company, Cray Research, specializes in supercomputers and offers extremely sophisticated hardware and processors. Its best-selling Cray-2 sells for approximately $17 million. At these prices, far more supercomputers are leased than purchased outright.

Supercomputers can process data from more than 10,000 individual input/output units or terminals. To do this, however, a supercomputer often needs a smaller computer to coordinate its input and output. The smaller computer, which could be a mainframe or minicomputer, frees the supercomputer for the high-speed, high-volume processing that it does best.

## ▶ Microcomputer Categories

In the late 1970s and early 1980s, when the first micros were offered for sale, smaller firms such as Radio Shack, Commodore, Atari, and Apple

**Supermicro:** *SUN SPARC computers are used as workstations.*

**Desktop:** *The IBM PS/2 is a popular desktop computer.*

**Laptop:** *Laptop computers are often used by people away from the office.*

**Notebook:** *Notebook computers, as their name implies, are the size of a notebook and are very easy to transport.*

**Palmtop:** *Palmtop computers are so small, they can be carried in a purse or a pocket.*

**Table 2.2** | CATEGORIES OF MICROS

|  | Cost | Size | Weight |
|---|---|---|---|
| Supermicro | $7,000–$10,000 | Desktop or floor mounted | 30–70 lbs |
| Desktop | Hundreds of dollars to $5,000 | Desktop | 30–50 lbs |
| Portables |  |  |  |
| Laptop | Hundreds of dollars to $3,000 | Suitcase | 10–15 lbs |
| Notebook | Hundreds of dollars to $3,000 | Briefcase | To 7 lbs |
| Palmtop | Hundreds of dollars to $1,000 | Pocket | Up to 1 lb |

dominated the market. When the microcomputers produced by these companies became very successful, manufacturers of larger systems like IBM and Hewlett-Packard began to develop micros. Today, there are hundreds of micro manufacturers.

Table 2.2 illustrates the main categories of micros. A more in-depth discussion of each type of micro, from largest to smallest, follows.

## WORKSTATIONS: THE SUPERMICROS

A **workstation** is a high-powered supermicro that approaches the processing power of a minicomputer. A workstation can be a multiuser system that can control a small network, or it can be a stand-alone computer used for creating high-quality graphic images. Supermicro use is increasing as more application software is developed for them.

A workstation or supermicro, then, as you would suspect, is a faster, more expensive version of a standard micro. A standard micro has a large set of complex instructions that it can execute, but surprisingly, many workstations have a *reduced* instruction set. Such a workstation is called a **RISC computer** for *r*educed *i*nstruction *s*et *c*omputer. By eliminating complex, infrequently used instructions that can be, if needed, easily performed using a smaller instruction set, these machines are "leaner and meaner." Although RISC-based machines can be used as workstations in a large network or as the central computer in a smaller network, they are likely to become even more widely used for all business applications.

Sun Microcomputer Systems manufactures the most popular RISC-based supermicro called the SPARC, an acronym for Scalable Processor Architecture. IBM's RS/6000 and the NeXt computer are machines that compete directly with SPARC.

## DESKTOP COMPUTERS: THE MIDDLE GROUND

The standard **desktop computer,** which is still the most widely used PC in business, tends to be a single-user device. Advanced operating systems and user interfaces enable the desktop micro to be used for two or more different applications at one time, but most often these applications are under the control of a single user.

*RISC computers can generate sophisticated graphics.*

## LOOKING / BACK

### THE FIRST APPLE AND IBM PCS

Steven Jobs and Stephen G. Wozniak are proof that college dropouts can sometimes go far in this world. In Wozniak's garage, the two young men first built an Apple Computer in kit form in 1977. The Apple Computer Company, which began in that garage, went public several years later thereby making both men multimillionaires.

For nine years, Jobs served in various management positions of Apple, including chairman of the board. As the small company gained prominence in the computing field, he was instrumental in building both the Apple II and Macintosh computers.

Neither Wozniak nor Jobs, however, remained at Apple. Jobs left in

*Wozniak (left) and Jobs holding a board from their original Apple computer.*

1985 to build the NeXt computer, which he hopes will become another revolutionary PC. Jobs introduced NeXt in 1988. Wozniak is a consultant and has his own company as well.

IBM introduced its first personal computer system, the IBM PC, in 1981. Apple, Radio Shack, Commodore, and Atari all had personal computers already on the market. Based on the success of these smaller companies, computer giant IBM hoped to sell 250,000 PCs in total. It sold 15 million units of its original PC. As a result, the microcomputer became the most significant technological breakthrough for business since the telephone.

A decade ago there were fewer than 300,000 micros at work in the United States. By the early 1990s, there were more than 60 million. Currently, one third of all U.S. households have a PC. Worldwide use is estimated at 200 million.

## LOOKING / AHEAD

In terms of applications and processing power, desktop computers are currently positioned between more powerful workstations and smaller, portable microcomputers. As both lower-end and upper-end microcomputers increase in power and decrease in price, today's ubiquitous desktop PC may eventually disappear.

## PORTABLE MICROS: LAPTOPS, NOTEBOOKS, AND PALMTOPS

**Portable microcomputers** are compact and lightweight enough to be transported easily from place to place. Businesspeople use them when they travel or commute to the office, stay at a hotel, visit a branch office, attend a conference, or work at home. Students use them in class, the library, or virtually anywhere—even the beach (but watch out for sand). Portables can be connected to larger desktop PCs or other computers.

Compaq's original 1982 PC was called a portable, but at a weight of 30 pounds, luggable might have been better. Now standard **laptop computers** that weigh in at about 11 pounds are small enough to fit on an airplane tray table or in a small suitcase. At 7 pounds or less, **notebook computers,** which actually look like notebooks, can fit into a briefcase.

More recently, handheld **palmtop computers,** also called picocomputers, which weigh at most a few pounds and which can fit into a pocket or purse, have become popular. The Poqet and Hewlett-Packard palmtops are currently the market leaders. These general-purpose palmtops have much wider use than specialized devices such as the Sharp Wizard, which has limited computing power and is primarily a "personal information manager" with a built-in calculator, clock, and phone directory.

The main objective of portable PCs is to provide the greatest computing power in the smallest area. Most portable computers are almost as powerful as desktop micros and use conventional software. Some are actually components of larger PC systems, which serve as docking stations for the portable when it is home based. See Figure 2.6. Application software and even operating systems are built into some portables. Some

**COMPUTING APPLICATION**

Most micros use electricity as their primary power source. In addition, portables have battery packs that enable them to operate without electricity for several hours or more. The battery packs, which are rechargeable, are fairly heavy, so the computer's portability is reduced. The newer palmtops use standard AA batteries that make them much lighter and enable them to run for days without interruption.

Many portables are equipped with one or two 3½-inch disk drives and sometimes with a hard disk drive as well. Disk drives are, however, quite heavy. To decrease bulk and weight, some portables now use **flash cards** (see accompanying photo) in place of disks. Flash cards, unlike those you may remember from elementary school, are credit-card–

*Flash cards the size of a credit card can store millions of characters of data.*

sized memory cards that fit into the slots of some portables, the way disks fit into disk drives. Originally developed by Toshiba America, these lightweight cards have the potential for replacing hard disks in portables. Because they weigh less

and have faster access times than hard disks, they also increase battery life. Currently, a flash memory card can store from 4 to 16 MB of data, but experts predict that within a few years they will be able to hold 64 MB or more.

The main obstacle to widespread use of flash cards is cost. To be competitive with hard disks, flash cards should sell for approximately $15 per megabyte. They are still far more expensive than that; nevertheless, they are likely to become increasingly popular, especially in situations where speed and portability are the critical factors.

The ability of flash cards to overcome storage capacity and cost concerns will determine whether they are viewed as a "flash" of genius or a "flash" in the pan.

portables are **pen-based systems** that can accept handwritten input. Apple's Newton, a pen-based, palmtop personal digital assistant, has software that understands handwriting. It can also perform numerous functions such as providing travel information and sending faxes.

Laptop slides into expansion base

*Figure 2.6 A laptop computer can fit into a docking station providing the unit with more processing power and making more peripherals available to the laptop when it is home-based.*

*Pen-based computers are often used by a field staff for collecting data.*

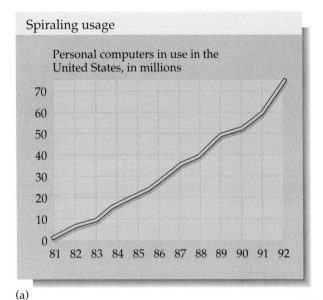

Spiraling usage

Personal computers in use in the
United States, in millions

(a)

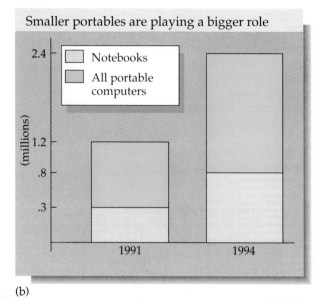

Smaller portables are playing a bigger role

- Notebooks
- All portable computers

(millions)

1991    1994

(b)

(a) *The overall growth of PCs in the
United States.* (b) *The growth of portables.* (c) *IBM's percent of the PC
market.*

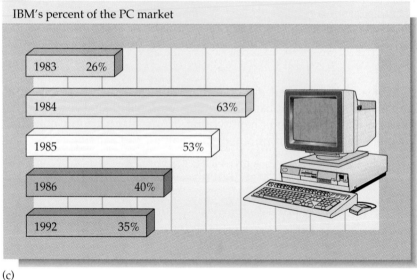

IBM's percent of the PC market

| 1983 | 26% |
| 1984 | 63% |
| 1985 | 53% |
| 1986 | 40% |
| 1992 | 35% |

(c)

## ▶ Apples, IBMs, and Compatibles

Apple's original microcomputers, which preceded IBM PCs by
several years, were in large part responsible for the huge success of the microcomputer. Apple computers are still widely
used in education, particularly in elementary and secondary
schools, and Apple's newer Macintosh computers are viewed by many
as the most user-friendly machines on the market. See Figure 2.7.

The Mac, as the Macintosh is affectionately called, has a graphical user
interface. Icons are selected by pointing a mouse. The Mac's computing

*Figure 2.7 Apple's Macintosh Power-book portable and Macintosh IIsi desktop computer.*

power and user-friendly interface have made it popular with both college students and business users.

At present, most users prefer either the Mac or an IBM or an IBM-compatible, sometimes called a **clone.** An IBM-compatible PC is one that is so similar to the IBM micros that it will run most, if not all, of the software developed for IBM computers.

Although some original IBM PCs are still in use today, IBM's Personal System/2, the PS/2 family of computers (and their compatibles), currently lead the PC market. Compared with the original IBM PCs, the PS/2 computers have more processing power—greater memory capacity and speed—as well as improved features for connectivity. See Figure 2.8. The PS/2 family's model numbers (Models 55, 70, and 95, for example) refer to the overall processing power of the computer. A Model 95 is more powerful than a Model 70, and so on. The IBM PS/1, a more recent entry in the computing field, is a lower-end micro that is designed primarily for home use.

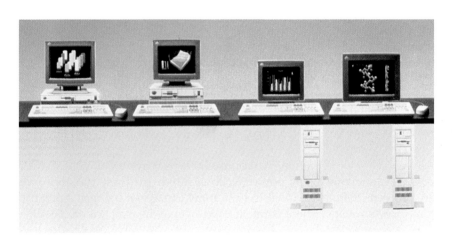

*Figure 2.8 IBM PS/2 models 30, 50, 60, 80; the last two have towers that contain the processor.*

*IBM PS/1 is a lower-end home com-puter with an array of multimedia capabilities.*

Recall from Chapter 1 that operating systems software controls computer processing.

## THE IBM-APPLE ALLIANCE

The competition between IBM and Apple has been one of the computing industry's fiercest rivalries. Facing declining market share, significant inroads by low-cost competitors, and a growing dissatisfaction among users who clamor for compatible products, IBM and Apple have joined forces to develop new PCs. This Apple-IBM joint venture is likely to have a significant impact on the PC market. We anticipate the following results of this alliance.

1. An advanced operating system will be used by both companies' PCs.
2. Apple's user-friendly Macintosh graphical user interface will be integrated into IBM computers, including mainframes.
3. Apple will use IBM's advanced, high-speed CPUs in its Macintosh.
4. The research and development efforts of both companies will be used to develop high-powered multimedia hardware and software.

It remains to be seen if this joint venture will result in standardization, but if it does, IBM and Apple customers will be the biggest gainers.

## ▶ Multitasking on Micros vs Multiprogramming on Larger Computers

As we have seen, classifying computers by type is just a guideline to their cost, size, and processing power. Keep in mind that these classifications are not cast in stone and that today's minis are apt to be most similar to tomorrow's micros. There is one area, however, in which there is still a decided difference between micros and larger systems. Micros are still essentially single-user devices, whereas most larger computers can be shared, at the same time, by many users.

Although micros tend to be single-user devices, they often can run more than one program at the same time. The ability of micros to execute more than one program concurrently is called **multitasking.** A manager may, for example, use a word processing package to create a report and while the report is still "open" (i.e., active), the manager could prepare a budget using a different package that is then "cut and pasted" into the report.

The DOS operating system was not originally designed to provide for multitasking, but other operating systems for IBM computers like OS/2 and UNIX are. In addition, Windows, the popular graphical user interface for IBM micros and their compatibles, permits multitasking with DOS.

The term *multitasking* and the various features of operating systems that enable it to be used will be explained in more depth in Chapter 9. For now, you should know that a micro is essentially a single-user device that can have more than one application running at the same time if it has the proper interface and operating system.

Mainframes and minis, on the other hand, are devices specifically intended to be shared by many users. Their operating systems are sophisticated enough that *different users* can run different applications all at the same time. This multiuser concept is referred to as **multiprogramming.**

Think of mainframes as "mass transportation" devices, with all the features associated with that term; think of micros as automobiles—individualized methods of travel. Mainframes require users to have the appropriate "ticket" for access—a code and a password. Hours of use are determined by the people who provide the service, not the user. But once "on board," you can "leave the driving to them." Micros, on the other hand, are accessible at the user's convenience, but the user is totally responsible for their operation and upkeep.

Recall, however, that many of the features that differentiate computers are becoming less distinct. In fact, this stand-alone, single-user nature of microcomputers is changing. Some multitasking workstations are becoming more like "vans" or "trucks" or "trailers," which make them more diversified and more like "mass transportation" vehicles.

 As we will see in more detail in Chapter 12, many organizations are finding it cost-effective to link, or network, their computer equipment so that hardware and software resources can be shared and computer utilization can be better controlled. In some cases micros are linked to central computers, and in other cases micros are linked to each other. This concept of connectivity, which includes networking and which enables the sharing of resources, means that micros need no longer be predominantly stand-alone devices. If connectivity and networking continue to enhance the computing field, perhaps instead of calling our micros PCs we will call them ICs, for *interpersonal computers.*

Today, connectivity enables computers to perform the following types of activities.

1. Send data, programs, messages, and so on to computers of different sizes and different types.
2. Share resources including hardware such as printers and disk drives.
3. Monitor and control all computer operations to improve overall efficiency.
4. Offload overworked or inoperable computers by rerouting the work flow.

*The IBM RS/6000 RISC Powerserver workstation can be shared by several users.*

▶ **SELF-TEST**

1. A _____ is a high-powered supermicro used for powerful PC processing.
2. What types of computers weigh approximately 1 pound?
3. (T or F) Many portables have the processing power of a desktop micro.
4. Portables often use _____ instead of electricity when operated away from home or the office.
5. Which computers were originally developed to offload the work of mainframes?

Solutions

1. workstation
2. palmtops
3. T

4. batteries
5. minicomputers

## 2.3 CHOOSING AND USING COMPUTER SYSTEMS

*What do users need to know about hardware and connectivity?*

Recall from Chapter 1 that when an organization decides to computerize information processing for its business systems, the systems development cycle begins. Systems development requires the combined expertise of computing professionals and users. Decisions are based not only on the hardware and software available but also on the ways in which the organization uses information. For large production runs such as preparing a payroll, a central mainframe may work best. For other applications, such as developing a departmental budget, microcomputers may be more appropriate.

As smaller computers become more powerful, their applications become more sophisticated. Just as categories and capabilities of micros and larger computers change, so too do the tasks they perform. Many companies are now **downsizing;** that is, they are offloading applications from, say, a central mainframe computer to a smaller system so that the larger machine can be used for centralized applications such as controlling the operations in a network.

### ▶ Information Processing Environments

Downsizing is a growing practice among companies. Smaller, smarter computer systems can make more efficient use of resources that can be distributed throughout a company. Originally, a single, central mainframe served all the separate business systems in a company. As minicomputers and then microcomputers became increasingly powerful and inexpensive, business managers within individual departments began purchasing their own computer systems. They wanted more access to computing power and more control over their own applications. Because of this trend, computer facilities in many organizations became decentralized.

It did not take long, however, for the disadvantages of decentralization to become evident. Computers in individual departments often could not communicate with one another, with computers in other departments, or with central computers. Companies realized that they needed to link their decentralized systems together in order to distribute information and resources throughout the organization. Thus, the computing network was born. Each of these three methods for organizing computer systems—the centralized, decentralized, and distributed processing environments—deserves a closer look. Each environment has its own advantages and disadvantages, and each fosters different degrees of communication between computer users and computer professionals.

## CENTRALIZED PROCESSING

**Centralized processing,** which dates from the 1950s and is still widely used today, serves the computing needs of an entire organization under the control of a single computer department. Centralized processing may not, however, always be the best approach to solving an organization's information processing needs. A single, often overworked, computer system may not offer individual users all the computing power they need. When there are many users, the computer time of each is limited. Moreover, centralized processing is most often controlled by a single computing staff that serves all departments. Such a staff has only limited knowledge of specific user needs in each functional area of the organization. Finally, centralized processing makes it difficult to determine and allocate actual computing costs for individuals and departments. As a result, a company with a centralized environment cannot always effectively assess the benefits or costs of computing for each of its information systems.

*Centralized computing means that one facility is used to satisfy all or most of a company's computational needs.*

## DECENTRALIZED PROCESSING: OFFLOADING TO MICROS, MINIS, AND MIDRANGE COMPUTERS

To better meet the computing needs of individual departments and to allocate resources more effectively, some organizations have separate, decentralized computer facilities for each department or information system. **Decentralized processing** has some advantages over centralized systems. Each department can purchase the precise equipment it needs, hire a staff of computer professionals familiar with its specific requirements, and monitor and control its own computing resources and costs.

A major disadvantage of decentralized computing, however, is that it tends to isolate each information system. There is often no integration or coordination of an organization's data, hardware, software, and professional support. Several departments may use the same data or software for different purposes; one department may need an expensive piece of hardware that it uses only a small percentage of the time. Such duplication of effort and underutilization of equipment occur frequently in decentralized environments.

Decentralization sometimes reduces the ability of the company's top-level managers to obtain information on the organization as a whole. Because the various computer systems do not communicate with one another, effective management of the decentralized environment is difficult.

## NETWORKING COMPUTERS IN A DISTRIBUTED ENVIRONMENT

Top management wants a cost-effective computing environment that integrates the work of all computerized business systems and provides information about the company as a whole so that managers can make more informed decisions. Moreover, computer users, regardless of their department, usually need to share information as well as resources. Recent advances in hardware and software have made it possible for companies of all sizes to derive the benefits of centralized and decentralized environments by using **distributed processing,** which combines the advantages of both while minimizing their disadvantages.

In a distributed environment, each department's on-site, or local, data is processed by hardware and software designed to meet its special requirements. At the same time, a central computer can provide access to remote computing sites located in the departments or elsewhere, assess the cost of each computerized business system, and ensure that

IN A

| Computing Environment | Most Common Computer Configuration |
| --- | --- |
| Centralized | Mainframe oriented |
| Decentralized | Mini or micro based |
| Distributed | Central mainframe or minicomputer networked to PCs |

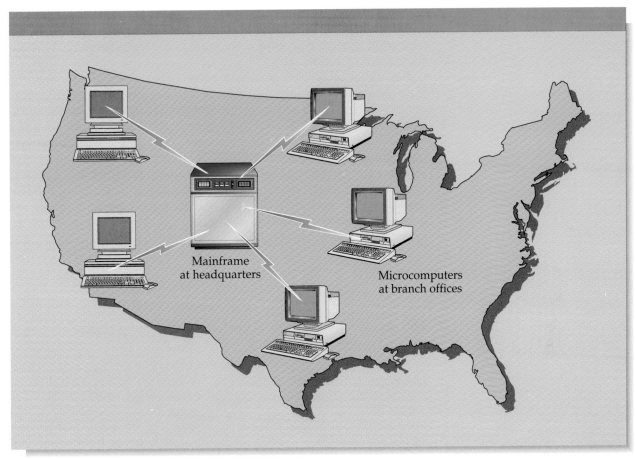

(a)

hardware and software resources are not duplicated. In addition, top-level managers can obtain the kind of integrated information that supports their decision making. As a result, the entire organization works better.

Distributed processing is often used at all levels of computing—from a small company that has only microcomputers linked in a network, to a medium-sized company that has a mini networked to micros, to a Fortune 500 company that has huge mainframe systems linked to minis and micros. See Figure 2.9.

Another advantage of distributed computing is that it is relatively easy and inexpensive for an organization to expand its computing facilities by simply adding micros as the need arises. Micros are now so common as components in distributed systems that their combined hours in use sometimes doubles or triples that of the organization's mainframe.

Distributed systems are not without disadvantages. Networks demand a high level of technical and organizational skill from the computing staff, because the distributed environment must serve all business systems and all levels of computer expertise. As the network expands, strict procedures and design standards must be implemented when hardware or software is added. Finally, because distributed systems typically

(b)

*Figure 2.9* Distributed processing often has micros linked to a large mainframe. (a) *The micros can be in different cities or* (b) *in the next room.*

have so many users (many of them off-site) with access to so much information, computer professionals and business managers must provide a high level of security against unauthorized use and disruption, whether intentional or accidental.

Sometimes organizations decide to use external facilities to augment their computers or to replace them. Selling computer time to organizations, a service provided by some companies, is called **time-sharing.** Companies that specialize in time-sharing can actually provide user organizations with all their computational needs. This is called **outsourcing.** With outsourcing, time-sharing companies supply hardware and software to organizations for a fee and actually run programs as a service, on a regularly scheduled basis. Outsourcing is becoming increasingly popular for many companies that have their own computers but find them inadequate and do not want to spend additional funds to upgrade their facilities.

IN A

### PROCESSING ENVIRONMENTS: ADVANTAGES AND DISADVANTAGES

| Pros | Cons |
|---|---|
| *Centralized Processing* | |
| Fosters standardization of an organization's equipment and procedures | Difficult to assess cost and effectiveness of individual information systems |
| Supervised by a single staff of computer professionals | Business managers tend to rely heavily on the professional computer staff |
| Minimizes duplication of computing resources | Difficult to determine priorities for each department's computer use |
| *Decentralized Processing* | |
| Direct control by users minimizes the communication gap between departments and a central computer staff; computer professionals who better understand a particular department's needs can be hired | Duplication and underutilization of computing resources |
| | Lack of communication within the overall organization |
| | Higher computing costs |
| Response to user needs is more direct; pressure from other departments is minimized | Management control is difficult |
| Assessing the effectiveness of each facility is easier | |
| *Distributed Processing* | |
| Combines the advantages of centralized and decentralized processing | Requires sophisticated hardware and software control |
| Integrates information systems | Requires strict adherence to standards |
| Best method for keeping up with an organization's growth | Because more users have access, computer systems need to be better secured |

## THE MICRO-MAINFRAME MIX

Despite our emphasis on distributed processing and networks, there is a growing misperception that PCs are replacing mainframes and that larger computers will no longer be needed in the years ahead. The fact is, mainframes have been, and continue to be, the backbone of computing in medium-sized and large organizations. The overwhelming majority of the computing needs in these organizations are met by mainframes, just as large transportation systems are the mainstay of urban areas. People who live in urban areas may prefer to use the family car for a Sunday drive or a night out, but they most often rely on mass transportation systems to get to work. Personal computers, like personal cars, may make life easier, but when it comes to providing large numbers of people with transportation (or information), they often cannot do the job.

What is likely to change in the 1990s, then, are the *activities* performed by various-sized computer systems, particularly as more and more companies downsize. As PCs get faster and more powerful, tasks commonly performed today on a mainframe are apt to be offloaded to PCs.

## ▶ The Human Factor in Information Processing: Users and Computer Professionals

## SATISFYING USER NEEDS

Employees working at each level within an organization tend to use computers for different purposes depending on their needs. At the first-line management level, both workers and managers use computers for *operational* purposes: to perform specific tasks such as entering orders, paying invoices to vendors, and so on. Middle managers and the people who work for them use computers to do *tactical analysis;* that is, they use the data inputted at the operational level to make decisions such as when to order new inventory, when to raise a product's price, and so on. At the top management level, computers assist executives in the *strategic planning* that determines long-term policy for the company.

Two different approaches may be used to computerize a business system so that it becomes an effective information system: the traditional approach and the management information system approach. With the traditional approach, information systems are designed to meet the basic needs of each functional area, independent of other departments' systems. Centralized or decentralized computers are often used in companies where the traditional approach to designing information systems is the norm.

With the management information system (MIS) approach, the needs of the overall organization are considered first. We call this top-down processing. The specific needs of functional areas are met secondarily after the information needs of all areas have been integrated. Distributed processing is best used for management information systems.

Traditional information systems are based on the assumption that an organization is the sum of its functional areas, or parts. In other words, the belief is that if each functional area does its work efficiently, the entire organization will run smoothly. Many organizations have used this approach successfully.

Although the traditional approach to information systems is extremely useful in satisfying the needs and requirements of operating staff and managers in functional areas, what do you do if you are a top-level executive and need broad-based sales information across all your company's divisions? How do you get a company-wide sales forecast? How do you analyze your product mix to develop corporate strategies?

These questions point to a fundamental weakness in traditional information systems: even if an information system is effective in meeting specific departmental objectives, the global information needs of top-level executives may not be met. Department managers may be satisfied with the day-to-day information provided by traditional information systems, but top executives need to look at data and trends across a number of functional areas so they can develop business perspectives and create

*Figure 2.10 Each level of management has unique information needs and will access a management information system differently.*

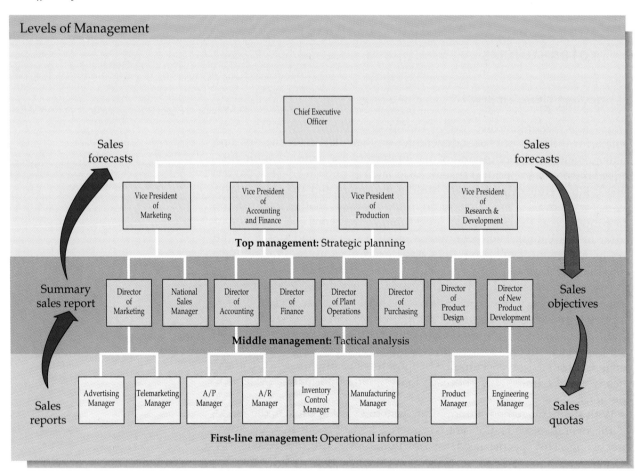

competitive strategies. Traditional information systems are not designed to provide the cumulative, integrated, historically based information that top-level executives need.

Rather than focusing on the business needs of each functional area, an MIS treats an organization as though it were one complete unit with one set of specific corporate objectives, for example, the objective of gaining an increase in market share of 5 percent while making a profit of 14 percent of sales. MIS developers begin by designing a system around the information needed to meet top managers' company-wide goals and then focus on the information needed in each functional area to achieve those goals. In other words, MIS developers view the company as an integrated entity with goals that go beyond the collective goals of all the independent functional areas (Figure 2.10). An MIS depends on a fully integrated database management system to provide needed information to all users.

Both the traditional and MIS approaches are widely used today, but with the availability of packaged database management systems and networks, an effective MIS is now easier to develop and more able to satisfy management needs. Specific types of management information systems are discussed in Chapter 11.

## MIS STAFF: THE PEOPLE BEHIND THE COMPUTER SYSTEM

Centralized and distributed computing facilities are usually maintained by a separate department, whereas decentralized facilities are most often controlled by the departments they serve. In the former case, the computer center's manager may have one of any number of titles (director, manager, or vice president) and the department may be called Management Information Systems, Information Systems, Computer Information Systems, or Information Processing. Regardless of titles, information systems managers are responsible for the entire computer facility and its staff.

Six principal categories of computer professionals are commonly found in computing departments, two of which—programmers and systems analysts—we discussed in Chapter 1. We consider here the personnel in a typical computing department.

1. Systems manager and systems analysts. The systems manager supervises the activities of an organization's systems analysts. Systems analysts are responsible for analyzing existing business procedures, determining basic problem areas or inefficiencies, and designing a more efficient information system. The systems manager assigns specific tasks to individual analysts and evaluates their progress.
2. Programming manager and programmers. The programming manager directs the activities of an organization's programmers. The programmer receives the job requirements from a systems analyst and is responsible for writing, testing, and documenting programs that will be part of the information system as a whole. Some companies also

have programmer analysts who design information systems and write all the necessary programs as well. The programmer analyst is responsible for the entire information system, including analysis and design and all the programming and implementation.

3. Operations manager and operators. Operations managers are responsible for the overall operations of the computer center. They supervise computer operators and data entry operators who enter data and perform control procedures. Operations managers are accountable for the efficient and effective use of computer equipment. An operations manager must ensure that input errors are kept to a minimum and that the computer system is relatively secure from breakdown, natural disasters (earthquakes, fire, power outages), and unauthorized use or misuse.

4. Auditors. Auditors are the accounting and computer specialists responsible for assessing the effectiveness and efficiency of the computer system and for maintaining the overall integrity of each information system's programs and data.

5. Database administrator. The database administrator oversees the structure, organization, and control of all the data used for information processing. The database administrator is accountable for efficient design of the files that contain the data and for implementing proper controls and techniques necessary for accessing them.

6. Network manager. The network manager is responsible for ensuring that computing devices linked to one another are being used effectively and efficiently. The role of the network manager is becoming increasingly important as more organizations are relying on connectivity.

**Common Organizational Structures.**   In small companies, the entire staff of computer professionals may consist of just one or two microcomputer specialists who are responsible for every computer-related function, from customizing software packages and designing the information systems to purchasing hardware. Large companies, however, usually have a department of people as just described. In such companies, computer facilities are usually organized in one of two basic ways: (1) systems analysts reporting to a systems manager and programmers reporting to a programming manager or (2) programmers reporting directly to systems analysts.

The structure on the top of Figure 2.11 illustrates an organization in which programmers and analysts report to different supervisors and work together as peers designing programs for a new system. Under this structure, analysts have less control over the programmers who work on a specific application, but the advantage is that a more open exchange of ideas is likely to occur between the two groups.

The structure on the bottom of Figure 2.11 illustrates an organization in which programmers report directly to systems analysts. In this case, systems analysts are project managers; they supervise programmers, monitor their progress, and evaluate their results. In this instance, there is one overall manager for both systems and programming.

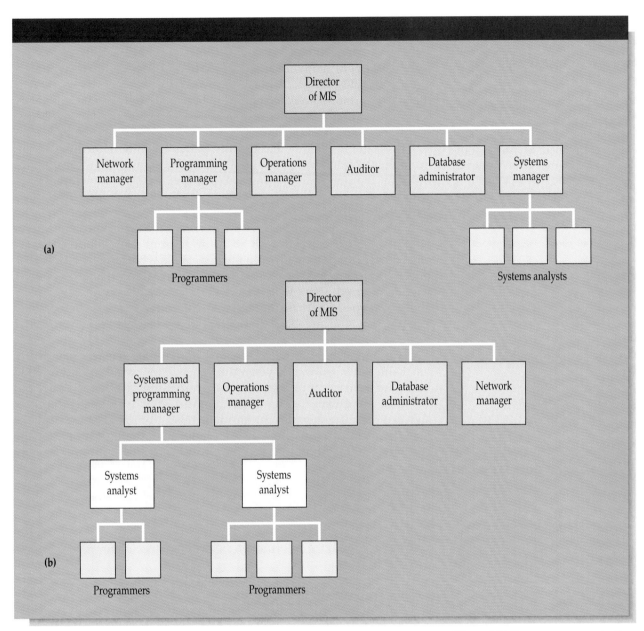

(a)

Programmers

Systems analysts

(b)

Programmers

Programmers

*Figure 2.11 Two common organization structures for MIS departments. When programmers and systems analysts have separate managers, as in the chart on the top, there is more flexibility; but programmers and analysts working in teams, as in the chart on the bottom, makes for better control.*

## ► The Right Time to Buy

In large organizations, computer professionals control the process of selecting computer systems. We discuss this selection process in detail in Chapter 10. Individuals face similar decisions when they buy their hardware. Recall that software drives hardware—you should determine your software needs first and then look at the hardware needed to run that

CRITICAL THINKING

In the early 1980s when microcomputers were new to corporations, computer stores sold approximately 90 percent of all micros. Ten years later, the same stores sell only about 46 percent of all micros. Many customers now shop at department stores or discount houses or purchase PCs through the mail, and many computer stores are merging or going bankrupt. Why do you think this change has occurred?

software. Among the basic criteria used to select computer systems are cost, processing power, connectivity, and size.

When a new computer system becomes available, it is likely to have features that are more advanced or more user-friendly than computers already on the market. Because the hardware is novel, however, it is likely to cost more. Research and development of new products is costly for manufacturers; for buyers, this means higher prices for innovative hardware. Once manufacturers recover their costs, however, and competitors begin to offer similar devices, prices fall, often dramatically. For example, the original desktop IBM PC cost $2500 in 1981. Adjusting for inflation, the same $2500 today will buy you a portable microcomputer with network capability, 35 times the processing power, and 1200 times the storage capacity of the original IBM PC.

If you buy a new product, you will derive the benefits of innovation but at a high price. If you wait for prices to drop, you will save money; but a newer computer with even greater potential benefits—and a higher price—is just around the corner. When laptop PCs weighing 11 pounds were introduced, users who were willing to pay a steep price for portability snapped up these lightweight computer systems. Before they knew it, 7-pound notebook computers that were just as powerful and that cost about the same were available.

If you buy hardware when it is first introduced, you will pay dearly for the benefits it offers. If you wait, you will pay less but outgrow the hardware sooner. People who use their computers only occasionally can live with less power, but users who depend heavily on their computers and use them for complex applications need to upgrade their systems more frequently. If you are a bargain hunter, constantly waiting for the best buy, you may find that you are always shopping but never buying!

## ▶ SELF-TEST

1. What are the three information processing environments?
2. What is downsizing?
3. A distributed processing environment usually uses a group of computers _____ to one another.
4. What are the two approaches to computerizing information systems?

Solutions
1. centralized—one main computer; decentralized—each department with its own computers; distributed—a central computer that can be accessed by PCs or minis in each department
2. offloading applications from a central computer to smaller computers
3. networked or connected
4. the traditional approach in which each department's needs are most important and the MIS approach where the needs of top-level management are most important

## ▶ **C**hapter **S**ummary

Chapter 2 focuses on hardware. How hardware works, types of hardware, and the information processing tasks hardware performs all influence decisions about what computer system is appropriate for an organization or individual.

### 2.1 CLASSIFYING COMPUTER SYSTEMS

Computer systems are classified by size, cost, and processing power. These factors determine the applications for which each type of computer is best suited. **Microcomputers** are mainly single-user systems. **Minicomputers,** or **midrange computers,** are **multiuser systems,** as are the larger **mainframe** computers. Room-sized mainframes may be connected to thousands of users at **terminals** or other **peripherals.** The largest of all computer systems, **supercomputers,** which are used mainly for scientific and industrial research and by the government, often can accommodate as many as 10,000 users at once.

*Why are categorical distinctions among types of computers really artificial boundaries?*

With computers of all sizes becoming more powerful, the boundaries that separate computer categories are not fixed. A supermicro, for example, may be as powerful as a low-end mini. The distinctions between minis and mainframes are becoming blurred. As computers in all categories grow more powerful, the applications they can process grow more sophisticated.

Processing speeds for micros are measured in **microseconds.** Minis and mainframes process data in **nanoseconds** and supercomputers process data in **picoseconds.** In computers of all sizes, **main memory** capacity is measured in **bytes.** The main memory in the early Apple computers was measured in **kilobytes.** Today's PCs have memory capacities ranging up to several **megabytes,** and larger systems operate with **gigabytes** of main memory. Together, processing speed and main memory capacity determine the overall measure of processing power—**MIPS.**

The most common input devices for micros are the **keyboard** and the **mouse,** which enable the user to enter data and instructions to the CPU. A **monitor** displays input or output. **Disk drives** give the CPU access to programs and data stored on **floppy disks** (also called **diskettes**) or on **hard disks.** The most common output device for PCs is the **printer.** With the proper software, computers linked by **modems** and using standard telephone lines can communicate with each other. Terminals are the main input/output device for larger systems. Smaller and smarter peripherals for computers of all sizes are constantly being developed.

### 2.2 GETTING TO KNOW YOUR HARDWARE

Beginning in the 1950s, mainframes were the first general-purpose computers used in business. They remain the most widely used computer systems in medium- to large-sized companies, where they meet com-

*How do application areas govern the choice of hardware?*

puting needs of all the major business systems. With prices averaging $100,000, many companies lease or rent a mainframe rather than buy one. Mainframes are valuable business assets that are closely monitored by computing professionals and maintained in secure, specially designed facilities. Often, mainframes are used as the central computer in a large network.

Mainframe use peaked in the late 1960s when DEC and other companies developed minicomputers in response to organizational needs for more computing power within each functional area. Through the 1970s and 1980s, companies bought increasingly smaller, more powerful, less expensive minis and superminis. These computer systems free up computing time on mainframes by **offloading** applications. Many computers made by the same manufacturer are **upwardly compatible.**

In the United States, the government accounts for more than half of all supercomputer use. Cray Research is the primary supercomputer manufacturer. To operate more efficiently, a supercomputer may be connected to a smaller mainframe or minicomputer. The smaller system handles routine tasks and frees the supercomputer for the complex processing applications it does best.

The earliest microcomputers were introduced about 20 years ago. The first micro to gain wide use was developed by Apple Computer Company. Together with its newer, user-friendly Macintosh, Apple micros are widely used in schools and businesses. Since 1981 IBM has sold 15 million of its original Personal Computers—60 times the number originally forecast—and IBM remains the leader in microcomputer sales. By current estimates, there are more than 100 million micros in use in the United States alone.

Initially, micros were single-user systems, although more recently developed **workstations**—powerful, multiuser supermicros—can control small networks. Many workstations use **RISC** technology, which uses a reduced instruction set that makes them more efficient. Standard **desktop computers** are still the most widely used micros in business, but **portable microcomputers** are also very popular. Compaq introduced its original **laptop** portable in 1982. Ever since, the goal of more computing power in a smaller package has led to **notebook computers** and more recently, **palmtop computers** that weigh a pound or so. Some palmtops are **pen-based systems** that enable the users to handwrite entries. Some portables use **flash cards** in place of disks for storage because they are lighter and use less power.

Among all U.S. microcomputer manufacturers, IBM ranks first with its PS/2 models. Still, more than half of all PCs in the United States are sold by hundreds of companies, each with a small fraction of the total market. The majority of PCs are either IBM or IBM-compatibles called **clones,** however. Once rivals, Apple and IBM are joining forces, a move that may result in greater standardization in the computing industry.

Micros are often used for **multitasking,** that is, processing two or more applications at one time. Larger systems are often used for **multiprogramming** whereby two or more users can run different applications at one time.

## 2.3 CHOOSING AND USING COMPUTER SYSTEMS

When an organization or an individual decides to use computers, the decision is based on the hardware and software available and on the way in which the business uses information. As smaller computers have become more powerful and their applications more sophisticated, more companies are **downsizing** their computing operations.

A generation ago, mainframes were used by businesses in a **centralized processing** environment. Then some organizations moved to **decentralized processing** to better satisfy individual departmental needs. Today, businesses are moving increasingly into **distributed processing** networks to meet their computing needs. Each processing environment has advantages and drawbacks. Regardless of the processing environment, mainframes remain the backbone of information processing in medium-sized and large organizations.

Two approaches to computerizing business systems are possible. In the traditional approach, the needs of each department are considered first. In the management information systems approach, the needs of top-level management are considered first. The computing staff responsible for the design, implementation, and control of information systems consists of systems analysts and systems managers, programmers and programming managers, operations managers and operators, auditors, database administrators, and network managers.

In large organizations, computer professionals control the process of selecting computer systems for a company as a whole, but individuals face the same process when they buy hardware for themselves. Among the basic criteria used to select computer systems are cost, processing power, connectivity, and size. Buying the newest, most innovative hardware may yield benefits, but at a high price. Waiting usually means spending less but outgrowing the system sooner.

Sometimes companies use external facilities for their computational needs. **Time-sharing** organizations will sell computer time to companies. When an organization provides a company with all its computational needs this is called **outsourcing.**

> What do users need to know about hardware and connectivity?

## ▶ **Key Terms**

Byte, *p. 36*
Centralized processing, *p. 53*
Clone, *p. 49*
Decentralized processing, *p. 54*
Desktop computer, *p. 45*
Disk drive, *p. 38*
Diskette, *p. 38*
Distributed processing, *p. 54*
Downsizing, *p. 52*
Flash card, *p. 47*

Floppy disk, *p. 38*
Gigabyte (GB), *p. 36*
Hard disk, *p. 38*
Keyboard, *p. 37*
Kilobyte (K), *p. 36*
Laptop computer, *p. 46*
Mainframe, *p. 34*
Main memory, *p. 36*
Megabyte (MB), *p. 36*
Microcomputer, *p. 35*

Microsecond, *p. 37*
Midrange computer, *p. 35*
Minicomputer, *p. 35*
MIPS, *p. 37*
Modem, *p. 38*
Monitor, *p. 37*
Mouse, *p. 37*
Multiprogramming, *p. 51*
Multitasking, *p. 51*
Multiuser system, *p. 35*

## ► Chapter Self-test

1. The largest type of computer is called a _____.
2. The first computers used in business and the ones most likely to be the central computer in a network for a large or medium-sized business are called _____.
3. _____ are computers that were originally developed to offload mainframes in a large company.
4. (T or F) Micros are usually single-user computers and larger systems are usually multiuser systems.
5. Larger computers differ from small computers in _____.
6. Another term for the primary storage of a computer is _____.
7. Another term for the input/output units of a computer system is _____.
8. A device that enables one computer to communicate with another one over telephone lines is called a _____.
9. When two computers can use the same hardware and software, we say they are _____.
10. A million bytes of storage is called a _____.
11. The most commonly used storage device for saving programs and data is a _____.
12. An IBM-compatible computer is called a _____.
13. With a (centralized, decentralized) processing environment, it is difficult to determine the actual computer costs to attribute to each department.
14. A _____ processing environment attempts to satisfy the needs of each department as well as the needs of the company as a whole.
15. The most difficult information processing environment to manage and keep secure is (centralized, decentralized, distributed).

### Solutions

1. supercomputer
2. mainframes
3. Minicomputers or mid-range computers
4. T
5. cost, size, processing power
6. main memory
7. peripherals
8. modem
9. compatible
10. megabyte
11. disk drive
12. clone
13. centralized
14. distributed
15. distributed

## ► Review Questions

1. List and briefly describe the three alternative computing environments. List at least two advantages and disadvantages of each.
2. Some portables can be purchased as part of a "docking station." The portable can be used as a stand-alone device or as a component of a larger system. Indicate some advantages of such an arrangement.
3. College campuses have computer facilities for their financial and accounting systems, computer science instruction, student registration information, statistical analysis and research, and so on. Review your college's bulletin and catalog and see if you can discover whether your campus has a centralized, decentralized, or distributed computer system. You may find that some computers are centralized, while others, such as those for specialized research facilities, are decentralized.

**PRODUCT ANALYSIS**

**CASE**

### Coming Soon: A Cash Alternative

Your money's no good at the Parris Island PX. Nor is anyone else's. To spare drill instructors the nightly chore of maintaining a cash inventory, the post exchange store at the Marine Corps base in South Carolina stopped accepting money. Instead, the Marines make their purchases with smart cards.

Smart cards are electronically coded with a monetary value that decreases each time the card is used. When the full value has been expended, the card can be thrown away.

At first glance, a smart card looks like an ordinary plastic credit card or bank card. A closer inspection reveals that the smart card is slightly thicker. Sealed inside it are a CPU, memory, and communications capability that make the card a computer. Like a bank card, a smart card is used in conjunction with its owner's personal identification number (PIN), but while an ordinary card identifies an account number, a smart card actually has a cash value.

Developed in France in the late 1970s, smart cards are now widely used in Europe and Japan. In the United States, many credit card companies are

*In France, a Telecarte smart card can be purchased in various denominations and used to make phone calls from any public telephone. When the call is completed, its cost is deducted from the card's balance.*

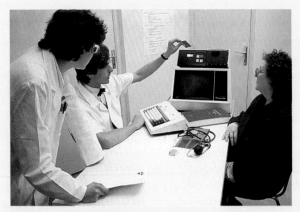

*A patient's medical history can be stored on a smart card.*

reluctant to replace conventional cards with smart cards because of the expense; but several pilot studies, like the one at Parris Island, are underway in which smart cards are being used to purchase groceries, drugs, and cosmetics.

Some state governments are using smart cards in place of food stamps. For 10,000 eligible families in Dayton, Ohio, the Ohio Department of Human Services has equipped 70 food stores with smart card readers that will automatically subtract the amount purchased from each cardholder's balance. The benefit to the government? Instant authorization without long distance expenses.

Some states are thinking of issuing drivers' licenses on a smart card that must be inserted into a vehicle just like the key. Many law enforcement agents believe that such a smart card system will reduce accidents by enabling law enforcers to more closely monitor drivers with poor records, deactivate licenses of individuals with unacceptable driving records, and reduce auto theft.

Note, too, that hospitals are experimenting with a smart card that maintains each patient's medical history.

*Analysis*

1. What benefits might a consumer derive from using smart cards? What benefits do businesses derive?
2. Are smart cards likely to cause changes in consumer spending habits?
3. Do you see any potential dangers in the uses of smart cards?
4. Explain three benefits insurance companies might derive from a driver's license issued on a smart card.

# USING PRODUCTIVITY TOOLS

Hardware oftentimes steals the limelight with its dramatic impact on information processing. But, as you learned in Chapter 1, software makes computers work, regardless of their size, cost, or processing speed. Software helps computer users perform their day-to-day business tasks in the office, on the road, or at home. An **application package** is a type of prewritten software designed for business or personal use. You can purchase packages such as productivity tools off-the-shelf at computer stores, from other retailers, or by mail.

In Chapter 3, you will discover how computer users can derive the benefits of improved productivity by answering the following questions:

▶ Why are application packages called productivity tools so commonly used in business?

▶ What features and functions are commonly included in productivity tools and integrated packages?

▶ What do users need to know in order to choose and use productivity tools?

## 3.1  UNDERSTANDING SOFTWARE

Why are application packages called productivity tools so commonly used in business?

Information processing transforms data—the raw facts—into information. To be useful, information must be timely, accurate, and meaningful: it must serve the user's purpose. Computer systems automate information processing within and among an organization's major business systems. As a result, the functional areas of accounting, production, marketing, and human resources all operate more efficiently.

The driving force behind computing is not hardware; it is software. The experienced computer user selects a computer system not so much for its high-powered processing but for the application areas it serves best. Users must, of course, know how to operate their hardware, but understanding the hows and whys of using software is far more important.

### ▶ Software Makes It Work: A Review

Computer systems operate under the control of programmed instructions, the software. In Chapter 1 you learned that one set of programs, the systems software, controls computer operations and allows users to interact with their hardware. Computer users work with application programs to complete day-to-day business tasks more efficiently, search for the information they need faster, and analyze their options more effectively.

Application software can be purchased as a package, or it can be custom-designed, that is, written specifically for individual users. Both packaged and custom software are used with computer systems of all sizes.

Application packages tend to be more widely available for microcomputers than for mainframes, but many mainframe users purchase or lease accounting packages, financial planning software, and so on. Organizations that are PC-based are apt to have a limited computer staff and are therefore often best served by off-the-shelf packages. Larger organizations with more specific computer needs and more extensive computer staffs often invest in custom software.

One main objective of software—either in the form of packages or custom programs—is to help employees increase their productivity. Regardless of whether users have PCs, larger systems, or distributed networks at their disposal, they rely on software to help them become more productive.

Programs are stored on secondary storage media, such as disks, in the form of program files. The data to be processed by programs is also stored on disk as data files. Sometimes output information as well as input data is created as data files for additional processing later on. Both program and data files must be loaded into main memory (primary storage) for the CPU to operate on them.

**TYPES OF SOFTWARE**

1. Systems software: controls operations of a computer system
2. Application software: transforms raw data into meaningful information to satisfy user needs
   - Packaged: designed for a wide range of users
   - Custom: designed for a specific user's needs

## ▶ The People Who Use Application Packages

Employees at every level have access to computers in organizations these days. Those who use software, particularly productivity tools, fall into three main groups:

1. *Users* who are often business managers, executives, or employees who need computer-produced information to analyze and summarize data and to help them make decisions. These people are commonly referred to more specifically as *end users.*
2. *Software specialists* who tailor the software so that the information produced is in the proper format. These specialists know precisely what the software can accomplish and how it can best be used to satisfy individual needs. Sometimes these specialists are computer professionals who work with end users to obtain the desired output. Sometimes end users are computer proficient enough to do the job themselves.
3. *Data entry operators* who actually enter the data.

Depending on the software and on the application area, these three functions may be performed by separate individuals, or they may be performed by one person. In the first case, managers may make decisions based on information produced by others. The software may have been tailored to their needs by computer professionals and the input entered by data entry operators. Often, however, computer fluent managers who analyze data in different ways to prepare output actually customize the software and enter the data themselves, and then use the results. So in the second case, a single individual wears three different hats when using a software product—that of data entry operator, software specialist, and end user. Such end users are often called power users.

## ► Types of Productivity Tools and Integrated Packages

In this chapter, we focus on a category of application software called productivity tools. These tools are widely used to perform operations that are an integral part of day-to-day business activities. They are most commonly used on PCs, but they also are available on larger systems.

Our goal is to explain why productivity tools are so widely used rather than to teach you how to use specific products. A conceptual understanding of the significance of these tools comes first. Then we recommend you turn to the *Getting Started* tutorials available with this book; they teach you how to use specific packages. These hands-on tutorials assume that you are at a computer and can step through the procedures specified as you read the tutorial. The emphasis in this text, however, is on *why* each type of tool helps to increase productivity not on how to use any specific tool. Our *PassPort* multimedia disk, also available with this text, includes interactive training modules on the productivity tools discussed here.

Many application packages qualify as productivity tools. We discuss four of the main ones here. (Other packages are discussed in Chapter 7.)

### WORD PROCESSING

*Figure 3.1 Word processing software lets users write and rewrite documents easily that can then be processed by electronic page makeup software.*

Employees whose jobs once required many hours a day typing and retyping documents now spend less time at the keyboard because they use electronic **word processing** (Figure 3.1). If you use a standard office typewriter, you must either patch or completely retype your document whenever you need to make a change or correction. Word processing software saves considerable time and energy; it records the words or text electronically and makes them easy to change. Word processing also minimizes the need for retyping every time you want a new version of a document. It allows you to rearrange words, sentences, and paragraphs and insert or delete text with a few simple keystrokes. Word processing is so widely used that the typewriter faces extinction.

A word processing package produces letters, reports, and other text referred to as **documents** that look better and work better, whether their purpose is to inform, entertain, or persuade. Some people believe that by freeing users to concentrate on their writing—what they want to communicate—word processing also makes documents read better. As one professional writer said of her word processing program, "Once I learned it could do the two most time-consuming tasks, inserting and deleting text, I was free to spend my time creating and thinking."

### SPREADSHEET AND GRAPHIC ANALYSIS

The **electronic spreadsheet** package is one of the most important and widely used business tools to come along in the era of microcomputers. In paper form, ledger sheets, **worksheets,** or spreadsheets have always been used by accountants; when produced by an electronic spreadsheet

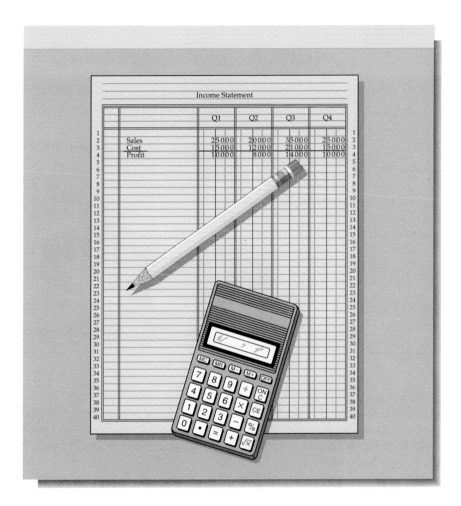

*Figure* **3.2** *The spreadsheet combines three manual tools commonly used for working with numbers: the ledger sheet, the pencil, and the calculator.*

package, they are a powerful analytical tool available to anyone with access to a computer. See Figure 3.2.

Electronic spreadsheets use a column and row format for representing data. The user enters data in the boxes, or **cells,** formed where columns and rows intersect. Formulas can also be entered in cells to carry out mathematical functions.

A common use for spreadsheets is budgeting. Of course it is useful to know how much you will spend in an entire year; but it is also important to have the total amount for each budget category "spread" across 12 months, so you know how much money you need each month.

One reason electronic spreadsheets are so popular is that they will automatically recalculate results when a change to data is made. If you entered a value erroneously, you can reenter that value and the computer will automatically perform all recalculations where the initial value was involved. If you review your budget for the next 12 months and decide you need to reduce your expenses by moving to a cheaper apartment and by not taking a trip you had planned, you could simply make changes to the rent and vacation entries and have the computer generate new totals in seconds.

**Figure 3.3** *Spreadsheet packages display information in column and row format and as graphs for reporting purposes and for enabling managers to perform "what-if" analyses.*

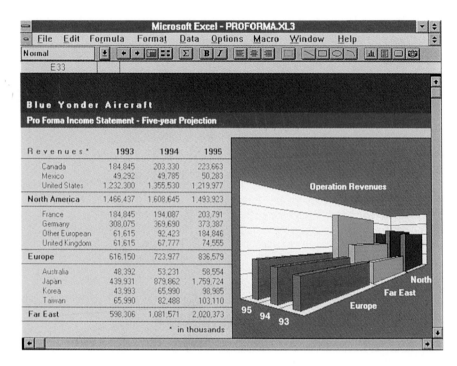

Many users think that the real power of spreadsheet packages lies in the ability they give users to *predict* the effects of a possible or hypothetical change in numbers. What will happen if sales increase by 5 percent? If profits fall by $1 million? What will happen to the family budget if you get that raise?

Having the power to analyze possible changes gives users more control over planning and setting goals. Electronic spreadsheets allow businesses to project the effects of different courses of action on company goals. This "what-if" feature of spreadsheet packages is considered the main factor that launched productivity tools into widespread use in business. In essence, spreadsheets did for software what the PC did for hardware.

Spreadsheets are also capable of graphing results and displaying them pictorially. For instance, a sales manager can compare monthly sales of the top three salespeople during a year by analyzing three columns of numbers. Many people, however, find that looking at a graph that displays the same information is easier and has more impact. Figure 3.3 illustrates the difference between representing the same data in a spreadsheet and in graphic form.

## DATABASE MANAGEMENT SYSTEMS

Walk into almost any office and you will find large numbers of filing cabinets with drawers full of file folders. Storing all this data electronically using an application package not only saves space but makes accessing the data easier and faster.

A concept central to electronic filing—and to a great deal of this

## LOOKING BACK

### HISTORY OF THE SPREADSHEET

The VisiCalc spreadsheet package was the single most important software product of the early 1980s. It has been heralded as the one application package that convinced businesses of the potential of PCs as productivity tools.

Dan Bricklin, a Harvard MBA student, got the idea for an electronic spreadsheet when he saw his professor erasing values from a worksheet he had drawn on the blackboard and trying to do all the necessary recalculations while class was in session. In 1978, Bricklin, with the aid of another Harvard MBA student, Dan Fylstra, and an MIT student, Bob Frankston, developed VisiCalc, an abbreviation for *Visi*ble *calc*ulator. VisiCalc was the first software package to minimize the need for recalculating budgets and schedules by hand.

VisiCalc was initially available for the Apple PCs only; it sold 200,000 copies its first two years. At the time, that was a truly remarkable feat. VisiCalc was considered so appealing that it actually spurred people to buy computers: 20,000 Apple computers were sold primarily because people wanted VisiCalc. This is further proof that software drives the market.

Today there are dozens of spreadsheet packages that include many VisiCalc features.

---

book—is the database. A **database** is a group of related files where a **file** is a major collection of data in a specific application area. For example, all the payroll files, personnel files, and salary history files in a company might be defined as a database. Because they are interrelated, **database files** can be linked together and used in many ways. A manager, for example, can use the personnel and payroll databases to print an address list of all the workers in a specific department and their salaries. See Figure 3.4 for a database illustration.

Traditionally, each business system within an organization has a separate database—one for accounting, one for production, one for sales and marketing, and so on. Each database is accessible to computer users in their respective departments. But separate departmental databases have two drawbacks. First, an organization that uses several databases, each with similar data (say, personnel and payroll files) faces a tremendous duplication of effort. Like paper files, the computer files become bulky, and the advantages of compact, economical storage of data are lost.

Second, since there is no established relationship among the separate databases, it may be difficult to gather important information on the company as a whole. Each department has the advantages of economy and speedy access to its own information, but top-level management may find it difficult to plan organizational goals and long-term strategies. For example, a sales manager may have trouble preparing a company-

*Figure 3.4 A screen in FoxPro's database management system shows records assembled to give information about a customer.*

| SYSTEMS APPROACH | TYPICAL ENVIRONMENT | COMMON PROCESSING FEATURE |
|---|---|---|
| Traditional | Decentralized or centralized processing | Individual database files for each business system |
| MIS | Distributed or centralized processing | Integrated databases in which top-down management needs are considered first |

wide sales forecast, and the marketing department may be unable to easily ascertain what changes are being made to production schedules.

Separate, isolated databases can limit a company's access to information. The newer trend in computing combines data from all the databases in an organization for use by a single management information system (MIS). Databases and management information systems can be as important as hardware and connectivity to an organization. Details on both topics appear in Chapter 11.

A **database management system (DBMS)** is the software used in an MIS. The DBMS creates database files, edits and updates them as needed, and provides reports and responses to inquiries based on data in the database files.

## ELECTRONIC MAIL

**Electronic mail (E-mail)** establishes person-to-person connectivity. E-mail enables computer users to send, store, and retrieve messages by computer at any time of day or night from any location. See Figure 3.5.

*Figure 3.5 Electronic mail enables users to send messages to one another and to reply, forward, print, store, or delete those messages.*

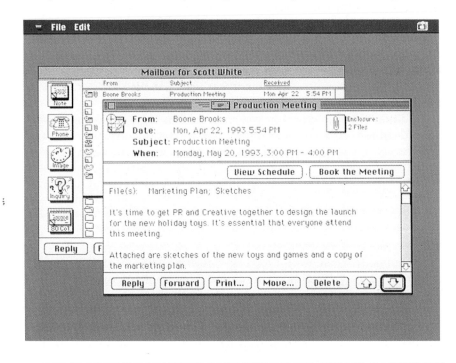

IN A

| TYPE OF SYSTEM | DESCRIPTION |
| --- | --- |
| Computer system | Hardware for information processing |
| Business system | Organized methods for accomplishing business functions |
| Information system | A computerized business system |
| Management information system | An integrated approach so that all of a company's needs are satisfied by a single information system |

IN A
NUT
SHELL

### WHY USE PRODUCTIVITY TOOLS?

*Word processing* speeds up and improves written communication.

Three commonly used word processing packages are Word-Perfect (WordPerfect Corporation), Microsoft Word (Microsoft Corporation), and WordStar (WordStar International Corporation).

*Electronic spreadsheets* enable users to analyze, plan, and set goals.

Three commonly used electronic spreadsheet packages are Lotus 1-2-3 (Lotus Development Corporation), Quattro Pro (Borland International), and Excel (Microsoft

Corporation).

*Database management systems* enable users to integrate information, establish relationships among data elements, extract information, and report on trends.

Three commonly used DBMS packages for PCs are Paradox and dBASE (Borland International) and FoxPro (Microsoft Corporation). There are many others for larger systems.

*Electronic mail*—person-to-person connectivity—computer users are brought closer together.

E-mail packages vary widely de-

pending on the specific application, but cc:Mail (Lotus Development Corporation), Microsoft Mail (Microsoft Corporation), and Beyond Mail (Beyond, Inc.) are common packages for networks.

*Integrated packages* include basic productivity tools and often have additional features as well.

Three commonly used integrated packages are Microsoft Works (Microsoft Corporation), Lotus Works (Lotus Development Corporation), and PFS: First Choice (Spinnaker Corporation).

---

Users can be employees within a company with networked PCs or with terminals that are linked to mainframes. Users can also be subscribers to services that provide e-mail capability to customers.

### DATA FILES CREATED BY PRODUCTIVITY TOOLS

| | |
|---|---|
| Word processing | Document file |
| Spreadsheet | Worksheet or spreadsheet file |
| Database management system | Database file |
| E-mail system | Message file |

## INTEGRATED PACKAGES

Some products combine features of the four productivity tools into a single **integrated package.** Some integrated packages include additional tools such as built-in calendars, notepads, and so on. The way you interact with each productivity tool in an integrated package is the same, so you need learn only one methodology. In addition, you have the ability to easily combine data from two or more tools. A spreadsheet created by the spreadsheet component of an integrated package, for example, can easily be added to a report being prepared by the word processing component.

### ▶ SELF-TEST

1. (T or F) Software should be selected before hardware.
2. (T or F) Most PC users purchase application packages rather than write their own custom programs.

3. (T or F) Productivity tools are a part of systems software.
4. (T or F) Sometimes users customize their software packages and enter data themselves, but sometimes they have software specialists customize and data entry operators key in data.
5. Define and describe four productivity tools.
6. What is an integrated package?

Solutions
1. T
2. T
3. F—They are types of application software.
4. T
5. word processing package for entering, editing, and printing documents; spreadsheet package for representing data in column-and-row format, for calculating automatically, for graphing results, and for determining the impact of potential changes ("what-if" analysis); database management package for creating, editing, and updating files and for producing reports and answering inquiries about the status of those files; e-mail for electronic communication among users
6. An integrated package includes the four basic productivity tools and may have additional features as well.

## 3.2 USING PRODUCTIVITY TOOLS: SHARED FEATURES AND FUNCTIONS

What features and functions are commonly included in productivity tools and integrated packages?

Productivity tools, like most software products, are supplied to users in a package that includes programs on disks. Typically, you can obtain either 5¼-inch disks or 3½-inch disks; sometimes manufacturers supply both. Because most programs provide numerous options, they may require two, three, or more disks. Before purchasing software, be sure you understand what type of hardware you will need to use it. Requirements such as CPU type and size of main memory are usually prominently displayed on the outside of the package.

The software package routinely includes a user's manual or set of manuals. These provide step-by-step procedures for using the product. Most software must be installed, which means it must be configured to run with your specific computer. Nowadays the step-by-step setup procedures are clear and include screen displays to show you what to expect when you install a program and how to respond to the questions asked. If you are using a productivity tool or integrated package that has already been installed, then you can skip installation details and begin by learning how to use the product.

The operating system must be loaded into the computer before you can run an application program. See Appendix A for hands-on details.

### ▶ Loading the Program

All programs must be read, or loaded, into main memory from disks before they can be processed. The user's manual or a separate tutorial

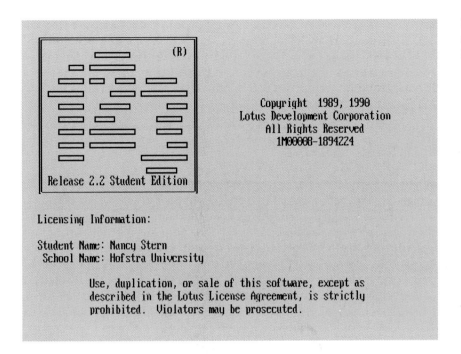

Copyright 1989, 1990
Lotus Development Corporation
All Rights Reserved
1M00008-1894224

Release 2.2 Student Edition

Licensing Information:

Student Name: Nancy Stern
School Name: Hofstra University

Use, duplication, or sale of this software, except as
described in the Lotus License Agreement, is strictly
prohibited. Violators may be prosecuted.

*Figure 3.6* The licensing information specifies the terms under which you can legally use the software.

provides hands-on information about the package and how to load it into main memory.

Once a program has been loaded, an initial screen display introduces the product and provides some licensing information describing your right to use the software. See Figure 3.6 for an example. A message is usually displayed on this screen telling you how to move to the main screen. Typically, you are asked to press a key to continue. After you press the key indicated, a main screen appears. That screen enables you to begin using the product, often by selecting items from a menu.

## ▶ Creating and Retrieving Files

All software products enable users to input data in order to create files. Most often, you begin using a productivity tool by creating a data file. Word processing packages create document files, spreadsheet packages create spreadsheet files, DBMS packages create database files, and e-mail packages create message files. The files created can be displayed or printed, and they can also be saved on disk or another storage medium for future reference or processing. So productivity tools, as well as most software, allow you to create files and retrieve the same files at a later date for future processing.

To save a file you must give it a **filename.** Rules for forming filenames vary, but for most packages a filename should be one to eight characters—letters and digits only. The package adds a three-character file extension, which is separated from the filename by a period; this file extension identifies the file as one created by the specific product. PAY-ROLL.DBF, for example, is a data file created by dBASE, a DBMS product; BUDGET.WK1 is a data file created by the Lotus spreadsheet package. File extensions make it easier to identify files on a disk. All files with a .WK1 extension, for example, are Lotus spreadsheet files. Filenames should be as meaningful as possible to help identify the application area. PAYROLL, for example, is a better name than DATA1, which is not very informative.

## ▶ Status Lines

When a productivity package is loaded into main memory and the main screen is displayed, a status line or lines appear at the top or bottom of a screen. See Figure 3.7. The status line often indicates the time and date, the filename you selected for your file, and the current settings, or **defaults,** for the product. Some packages, for example, start up in uppercase mode; this means that whatever you type appears as uppercase letters. If so, the status line displays CAP or CAPS. To change the setting, or default, you press the Caps Lock toggle key on the keyboard. A toggle key is like an on/off switch: pressing it once changes the setting; pressing it a second time resets the key to its original value. Consult Appendix A for a detailed discussion of the computer's keyboard.

## ▶ Data Entry

When you begin entering data, a blinking cursor on the screen tells you where you are at any time. The status line also indicates the position of the cursor. See Figure 3.8. You can change the location of the cursor by

*Figure 3.7* *This Lotus 1-2-3 status line indicates the date and time of the run, the fact that the default is uppercase mode (CAPS), and that the keypad is in numeric (NUM) mode.*

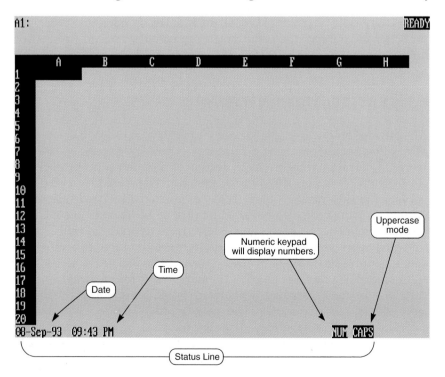

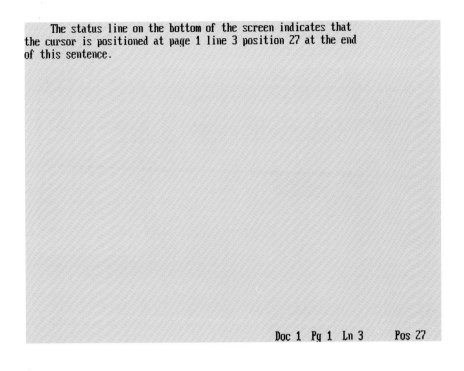

The status line on the bottom of the screen indicates that the cursor is positioned at page 1 line 3 position 27 at the end of this sentence.

Doc 1  Pg 1  Ln 3          Pos 27

*Figure 3.8* The status line on the bottom of this WordPerfect screen indicates the position of the cursor.

using the cursor control keys (↑, ↓, →, ←) to navigate around the screen when you are entering data. There are other cursor control keys as well: PgUp scrolls up 24 lines (which is a page on a screen); PgDn scrolls down 24 lines; Home takes you to the first entry on the screen or the first line of the file; End takes you to the last entry on the screen or file. Some products, particularly word processing and electronic mail packages, provide you with a full, free-form screen so you can enter data anywhere you like. Other products, particularly spreadsheet and DBMS packages, require you to enter data according to more specific data entry rules. See Figure 3.9.

All packages permit you to correct data entry errors. If you realize your mistake immediately, you can always use the Backspace key to delete a character and move the cursor one position to the left. Each time you press the Backspace key, the character at the cursor is erased and the cursor repositioned.

As you type, the keyed data appears on the screen and the cursor moves to the next position. Many packages require you to press the Enter key to actually transmit the data to the computer. Suppose you press the Enter key and *then* realize you made a mistake. To correct errors in data that has already been transmitted to the computer, you typically use the cursor arrows to move back to the error point and then make the required changes. You can replace erroneous characters or insert new characters. The INS, or Insert, key is a toggle key that controls whether your corrections will add a character (insert mode) or replace an existing character with another (replacement mode). Changing *cot* to *cat*, for example, is accomplished by moving the cursor to the *o* and replacing it with an *a* when you are in replacement mode. Alternatively, you can add characters, like changing *cot* to *coat* when you are in insert mode.

*Figure 3.9* *The menus on top of the screen explain how data may be entered in a database file using dBASE.*

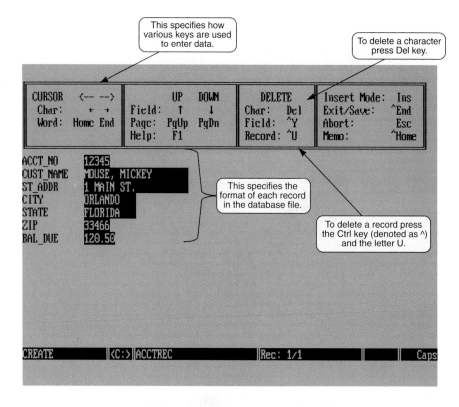

## ▶ **B**asic **C**ommands and **F**unction **K**eys

As noted, you begin using most packages by entering data to create a file. To perform operations such as saving a file, retrieving a file, or printing a file, you must select the appropriate **command.** Commands are most often selected from **menus.** You use the cursor control keys or a mouse to highlight the menu item desired and then select it by pressing the Enter key or clicking in with the mouse. Sometimes there is a main menu that, when selected, provides you with submenu items or pull-down menu items. Most packages also enable you to use **function keys** labeled F1–F10 or F1–F12 to execute some commands. Pressing the F10 function key, for example, may be the same as highlighting the Save command and selecting it. See Figure 3.10.

As you begin to use a productivity tool, you may need help. With most packages, the F1 function key provides **context-sensitive help,** which consists of screen displays that pertain specifically to what you are currently doing in the package. Say you select a file command and then you ask for context-sensitive help by pressing the F1 function key. A screen display will appear indicating file command options. To leave (exit) the help screens, or any other menu item, you usually press the Escape, or Esc, key.

A command common to most productivity tools enables you to define a section of a data file called a **block** and move it, copy it to another

IN A

To get started with any software package, learn how to:

1. Load the program.
2. Name a new file that you will create or retrieve an existing file.
3. Enter a new file.
4. Edit or make changes to a file.
5. Select and execute commands.
6. Save the file.
7. Print the file.
8. Exit the program.

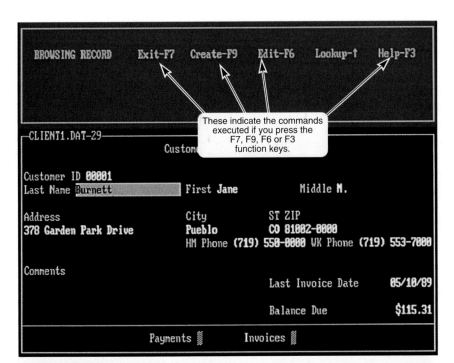

*Figure 3.10* *With this database management system you can exit (or quit) the application by pressing the F7 function key, create a new database file by pressing the F9 function key, edit an existing file by pressing the F6 function key, and get help by pressing the F3 function key.*

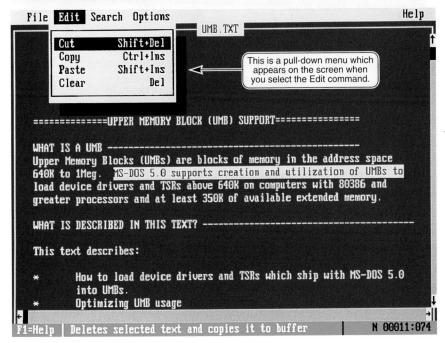

*Figure 3.11* *The highlighted text is called a block. The pull-down menu of the Edit command indicates that the block can be cut (deleted), copied, or pasted (moved) to some other portion of the document. To copy the block, for example, move the cursor to the place where you want it repeated and then press the Ctrl key and the Ins key. The Clear option is used to unblock the text if you decide not to cut, copy, or paste it.*

place in the file or to another file, or delete it. We call this **cutting and pasting** blocks of data. See Figure 3.11.

Another time-saving feature of productivity tools is called the **search and replace** command. Rather than scrolling through a file looking for a specific data item, you can execute a command that will take you directly

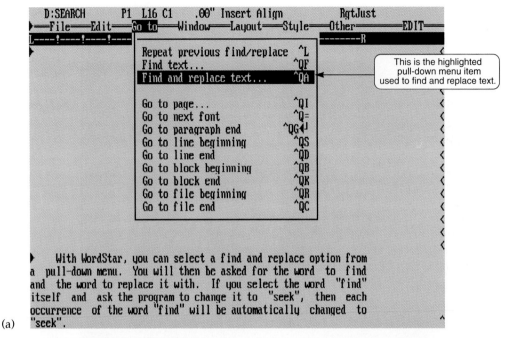

(a)

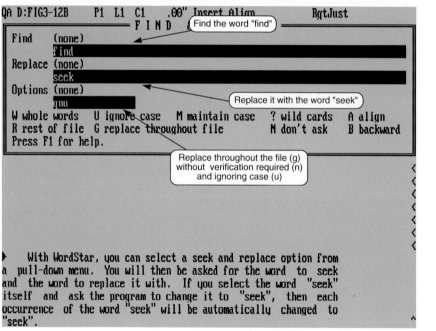

(b)

***Figure 3.12*** *Global find (search) and re-place.* (a) *Selecting the command.* (b) *After the command is executed "find" will be replaced by "seek" and the para-graph will be realigned if necessary.*

to that item. This feature positions the cursor at the item being searched and enables you to change or replace it. In document files, for example, you can find specific terms or topics using the search and replace command without having to read the entire file. In an employee database file you can use search and replace to give all employees who earn less than $30,000 a 10 percent salary increase. A search and replace command can take you to the first occurrence of a data item selected, the last occurrence, or all occurrences—a *global search and replace*. See Figure 3.12.

Commands are available with most productivity tools to format data to be printed. Formatting is used to print headings, set margins, select type fonts, specify page numbers, highlight entries with boldface or italic, and so forth.

## ▶ Macros

Many productivity tools enable users to add customized sets of instructions (called **macros**) to facilitate the creation and use of data files. Macros are usually used to save keystrokes or to make the data entry operation easier. Macros can be inserted in a word processing file, for example, so that it is automatically formatted according to predefined specifications. You might write a macro to establish a file format that you will use to create numerous files, without having to individually select the formatting commands from menus each time. In a spreadsheet file, you might create a macro that automatically produces a graph and prints it at the touch of a key rather than having to select items from several menus.

## ▶ Importing Files

When you import a file, you copy data already created into the file you are currently working on. Perhaps you are working on a word processing document file and decide to add a copy of a letter that you wrote previously. Most packages permit you to do this. Most also provide some compatibility across product lines thereby enabling you to add spreadsheet files to word processing files, for example. See Figure 3.13.

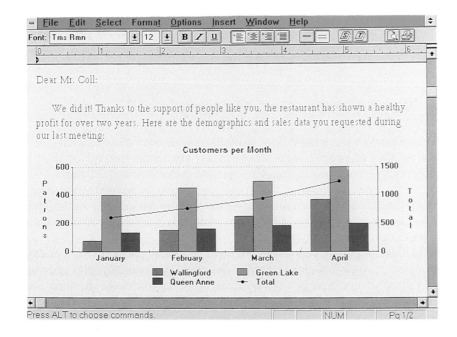

*Figure 3.13* Productivity tools often have multiple uses. Most word processing packages can import a spreadsheet or a database into a document.

### ▶ SELF-TEST

1. Software packages are used to _____ files. To operate on the data, we typically select _____ from _____ or use _____ keys.
2. Most productivity tools enable you to use _____ arrows to move around the screen.
3. What is the term that describes copying a portion of text to other texts?
4. The _____ line usually indicates date, time, name of a file, and default settings.
5. (T or F) Often simple data files can be created by a spreadsheet package and imported into a word processing document.

Solutions
1. create (or edit); commands; menus; function
2. cursor control
3. blocking, or cutting and pasting blocks of text
4. status
5. T

## 3.3 UNIQUE FEATURES AND FUNCTIONS OF PRODUCTIVITY TOOLS

What do users need to know in order to choose and use productivity tools?

The overall look and feel of productivity tools is similar from one type of package to another. Here we focus on why specific tools are so useful. You may find that some of the so-called unique features of each productivity tool are not that unique at all, and what is stated here as pertaining to a spreadsheet package may be available with your word processing package or DBMS. As newer versions of packages are developed, they tend to offer many more features common to most productivity tools.

### ▶ Word Processing Packages

The one use of computers that makes the biggest difference for the greatest number of people, regardless of their particular interest or field of expertise, is word processing. Once people become adept at using a computer for word processing, they pack away their typewriters and invariably wonder how they managed without word processing for so long. It is like a car or copy machine: once you learn how to use it, it becomes a tool you cannot live without.

In this chapter we emphasize word processing packages for general-purpose computers. Some computers are, however, special-purpose word processors; that is, they perform no other function but word processing. Such special-purpose systems are called dedicated computers.

## UNDERSTANDING THE CAPABILITIES

A word processing package is a program or set of programs used to enter, edit, format, store, and print documents. In word processing terms a document could be a letter, report, or any type of text. Documents are created and then stored or saved. Later, they can be retrieved and modified. They can also be printed at any time, with as many copies as you need. All word processing packages make it relatively easy to alter or edit a text on the screen while it is being created or later when you are reviewing it. This minimizes the drudgery of typing because a document does not need to be rekeyed every time changes are made. Making on-screen changes to a document is called **text editing.** You simply use the appropriate cursor arrow keys ($\uparrow$, $\downarrow$, $\rightarrow$, $\leftarrow$, PgUp, PgDn, Home, End) to return to a portion of text that needs to be changed and then make the changes.

Each time you make a change to the document the word processing package automatically reformats it so that it is perfectly aligned. There is no need for using "white out," for cutting and pasting paragraphs to reorganize the document, or for making handwritten corrections. Moreover, you need not use copy machines to make duplicates since you can print as many extra copies as you need.

Organizations use word processing packages to increase productivity by helping employees communicate better in written form. Documents prepared by word processing packages tend to read better because the user does not have to worry about making mistakes. Typos or spelling errors are so easy to correct that users can focus on the message being conveyed rather than on pressing the correct keys. In addition, the user can easily reorganize a document to determine the structure that best conveys the message. Moreover, the message conveyed in the document can be enhanced stylistically by highlighting, formatting, or changing type fonts. As a result, word processing documents have the potential to convey more meaningful messages.

As noted, if you make insertions or deletions in a document the program automatically realigns the paragraphs according to the margin specifications you establish. Margins, line spacing, and page lengths can be set, reset, and changed for different parts of the document. Left margins are always justified, which means that they are precisely aligned. Right margins can be ragged or right-justified, whichever you prefer. See Figure 3.14.

Besides data entry and text editing capability, word processing packages have several other important features.

- Most word processing packages include a spelling checker for finding errors and a thesaurus for providing synonyms. Spelling checkers usually look for spelling errors after a document has been completely entered. If a word is unrecognizable to the package, it will be listed as a spelling error. Correctly spelled words that are similar to the one typed will appear on the screen. See Figure 3.15. If one of the displayed words is the correct version of what you typed, you can replace the misspelled word with the correct one by indicating the

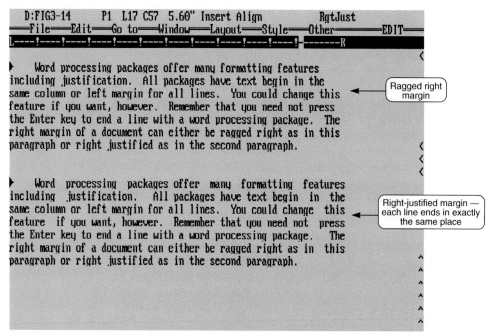

Figure 3.14 *Margins in a document can be ragged right or right-justified.*

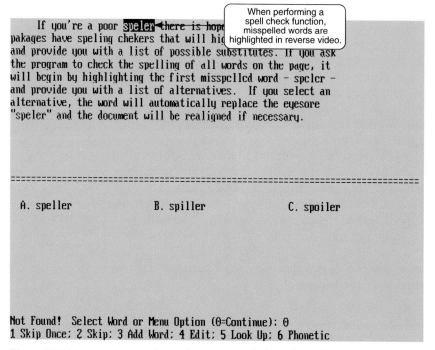

Figure 3.15 *Most word processing packages can check the spelling of words, suggest alternatives for misspelled words, or add unrecognized words from a document to the dictionary so that these words will not be flagged in the future as spelling errors.*

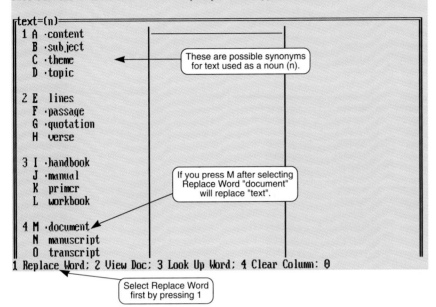

While creating this **text** you may decide that text itself is used too many times in the text. [The thesaurus] can help. If you point the cursor at the word text and then call for the thesaurus a list of synonyms will appear.

> If the cursor is on the t of the word text when you select thesaurus the word text will be highlighted.

```
┌text=(n)════════════════════════════════
  1 A  ·content
    B  ·subject
    C  ·theme              ┌─────────────────────────┐
    D  ·topic              │ These are possible synonyms │
                           │ for text used as a noun (n). │
  2 E   lines              └─────────────────────────┘
    F  ·passage
    G  ·quotation
    H   verse

  3 I  ·handbook
    J  ·manual             ┌─────────────────────────┐
    K   primer             │ If you press M after selecting │
    L   workbook           │ Replace Word "document"   │
                           │ will replace "text".      │
                           └─────────────────────────┘
  4 M  ·document
    N   manuscript
    O   transcript
1 Replace Word; 2 View Doc; 3 Look Up Word; 4 Clear Column: 0
```

> Select Replace Word first by pressing 1

*Figure 3.16* Most word processing packages have a thesaurus from which you can select synonyms for highlighted words. If you select the "replace word" option and then press M for the word "document," the word "text" will be replaced and the page will be reformatted.

word you want and pressing a single key to select it. If your original entry is correctly spelled but is a special term not in the package's dictionary, you can add it to the dictionary so that it won't be flagged as an error in the future. Synonyms from the thesaurus can also be automatically inserted into a text and properly aligned with a few keystrokes. See Figure 3.16. Some word processing packages have grammar and style checkers as well, and even small encyclopedias and almanacs so information can be added to or "pasted" into a document.

- Some word processing packages can create a bibliography, index, and table of contents automatically.
- The text in all word processing files can be blocked so it may be deleted, copied, or duplicated in another place. Copying standardized portions of text into a contract, will, or other document with a word processing package is called **boilerplating** and is a common technique used by legal firms. See Figure 3.17.
- A name file and address file can be merged to produce form letters that look personalized. See Figure 3.18.

The status lines of word processing packages may have date and time, name of file, and defaults, but they are also likely to have the document's current page number, the current line number, and the column where the

## CRITICAL THINKING

Do computers used for word processing actually improve the quality of writing?

Unquestionably computers take some of the drudgery out of writing by minimizing the need for reentering text. Some experts, however, think that the ease with which a document can be revised results in too much drafting and editing. Beyond a few drafts, the quality of one's work does not improve greatly.

Although grammar and style checkers are helpful for catching errors in wording, many people who rely on them find that changes suggested by the package are not always improvements.

Some proponents, however, contend that word processing makes the physical act of writing so much easier that users spend more time being creative. The result is an improved document. Do you agree? Do you see any potential disadvantages to depending on word processing packages?

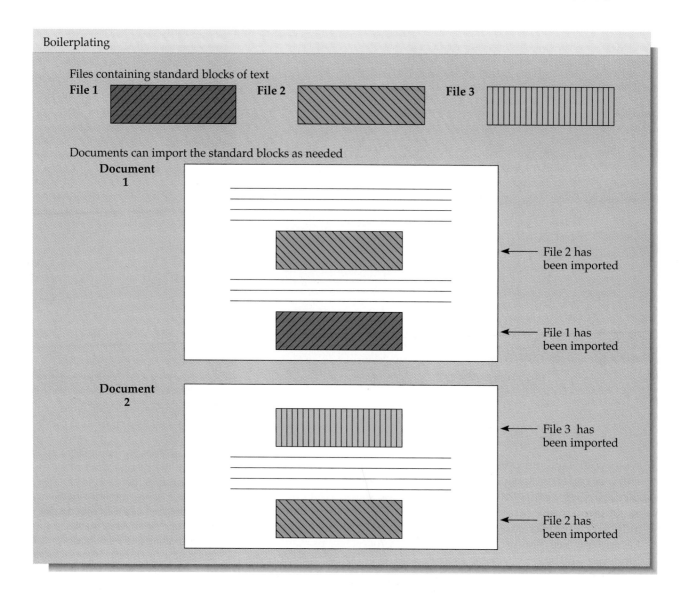

Boilerplating

Files containing standard blocks of text

**File 1**　　　　　　　**File 2**　　　　　　　**File 3**

Documents can import the standard blocks as needed

**Document 1**

← File 2 has been imported

← File 1 has been imported

**Document 2**

← File 3 has been imported

← File 2 has been imported

*Figure 3.17 Boilerplating enables you to import standard clauses, like terms of an agreement, procedures to follow if a problem arises, instructions, and so on, into documents. Each clause can be stored in a separate file and accessed as needed.*

cursor is positioned (where the character you type will appear on the screen). See Figure 3.19.

The page, line, and column numbers on the status line change as you type as does the position of the blinking cursor. Remember that you use the cursor control keys to return to any previous point in a document to make corrections.

## THE FUNCTION KEYS

As we have seen, most productivity tools, including word processing packages, use the function keys to accomplish specific tasks. Typically, pressing a specific function key will save your document file; pressing another function key will center a heading or other text on a line, and so forth. Many packages display the function keys and their commands

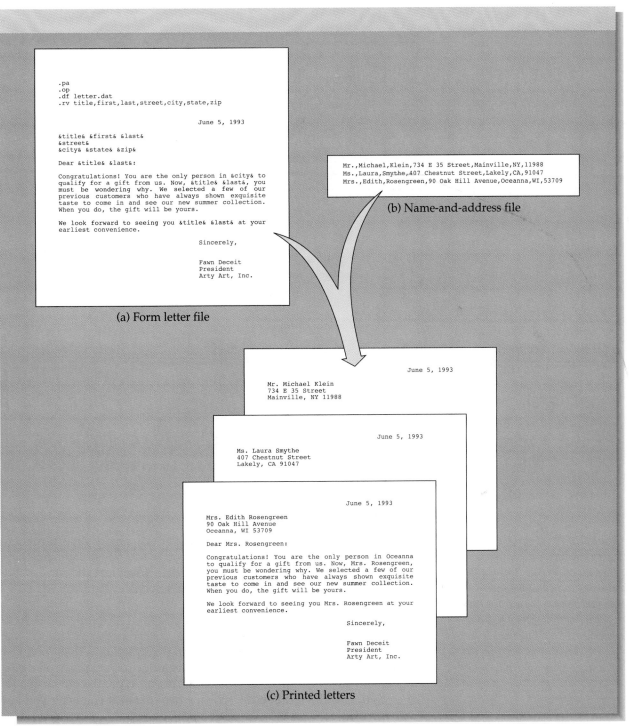

```
.pa
.op
.df letter.dat
.rv title,first,last,street,city,state,zip

                                    June 5, 1993

&title& &first& &last&
&street&
&city& &state& &zip&

Dear &title& &last&:

Congratulations! You are the only person in &city& to
qualify for a gift from us. Now, &title& &last&, you
must be wondering why. We selected a few of our
previous customers who have always shown exquisite
taste to come in and see our new summer collection.
When you do, the gift will be yours.

We look forward to seeing you &title& &last& at your
earliest convenience.

                        Sincerely,


                        Fawn Deceit
                        President
                        Arty Art, Inc.
```

(a) Form letter file

```
Mr.,Michael,Klein,734 E 35 Street,Mainville,NY,11988
Ms.,Laura,Smythe,407 Chestnut Street,Lakely,CA,91047
Mrs.,Edith,Rosengreen,90 Oak Hill Avenue,Oceanna,WI,53709
```

(b) Name-and-address file

```
                                    June 5, 1993

Mr. Michael Klein
734 E 35 Street
Mainville, NY 11988
```

```
                                    June 5, 1993

Ms. Laura Smythe
407 Chestnut Street
Lakely, CA 91047
```

```
                                    June 5, 1993

Mrs. Edith Rosengreen
90 Oak Hill Avenue
Oceanna, WI 53709

Dear Mrs. Rosengreen:

Congratulations! You are the only person in Oceanna
to qualify for a gift from us. Now, Mrs. Rosengreen,
you must be wondering why. We selected a few of our
previous customers who have always shown exquisite
taste to come in and see our new summer collection.
When you do, the gift will be yours.

We look forward to seeing you Mrs. Rosengreen at your
earliest convenience.

                        Sincerely,


                        Fawn Deceit
                        President
                        Arty Art, Inc.
```

(c) Printed letters

***Figure 3.18*** *A name and address file can be merged with a document file to create personalized letters.*

**Figure 3.19** *The status line for the WordStar word processing package.*

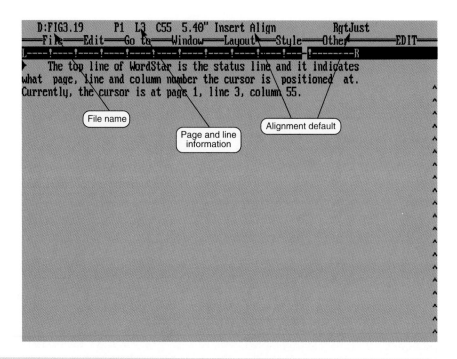

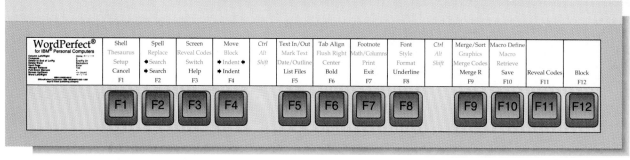

**Figure 3.20** *WordPerfect is a word processing package that uses function keys to execute commands. This is a WordPerfect template that indicates how each function key is used. The template fits on top of the function keys for reference.*

on the screen. Some packages like WordPerfect come with a cardboard template, which is a reference card that you place over the function keys that illustrates the commands executed when you press the corresponding keys. Figure 3.20 illustrates the WordPerfect template.

## ENTERING TEXT IN A DOCUMENT

You begin by loading the word processing package into main memory and then executing the command to create a document. You type a document as you would with a typewriter. As you type, the cursor moves one position to the right on the screen where the next character you key will appear.

Although word processing is very much like typing, there is one important distinction. You do *not* press the Enter, or Return, key at the end of each line as you would press the carriage return key or reset the carriage on a typewriter. Word processing packages automatically proceed from line to line as you key. This saves a considerable amount of time since you do not need to constantly look at the document or listen for a ring that warns you that you are near the end of a line. With all word processing packages, you use the Enter key only when you want to end a paragraph, *not* a line.

If the cursor is near the end of a line and a full word cannot fit on that line, the package automatically performs a **word wrap;** that is, it brings the last word on the current line down to the next line. If the right margin of the document is to be ragged, then blanks appear at the end of the first line. (Look at Figure 3.14 again.) If the right margin is to be right-justified as left margins are, then **microjustification** occurs. This means that the spacing between words on each line is adjusted to make the right margins "flush" as they are on the left. To assure right justification, then, some words may have more spaces between them than others. See Figure 3.21. Sometimes the microjustification required to achieve right justification results in large spaces between words. If you prefer, you can have the computer automatically hyphenate long words rather than simply perform word wrapping. This minimizes the large gaps between words in a right-justified document.

To make corrections, you can use the backspace key to delete to the error point or you can use the cursor control keys to return to the error point and insert or replace characters. Each time you add or delete characters or words, the word processing package automatically reformats so that the document looks perfect.

Word processing packages enable you to type page after page of material. Since a screen displays only about 24 lines of text, you may need to scroll forward or backward to see other parts of a document you are

The cursor arrow keys enable you to move around the text without erasing characters; the backspace key erases as it backspaces.

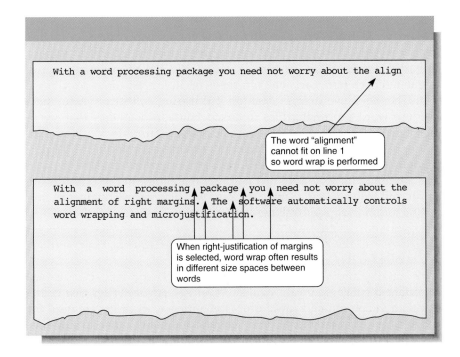

*Figure 3.21 With word wrap, words that do not fit on a line are automatically moved to the next line. For right-justified text, microjustification results in the realignment of words on each line so that they are flush-right. This is done by adding spaces between words.*

**Figure 3.22** *The Find File command with Microsoft Word lists all the files on the designated disk drive and enables the user to open (or read) a file, print it, delete it, copy it, and so on.*

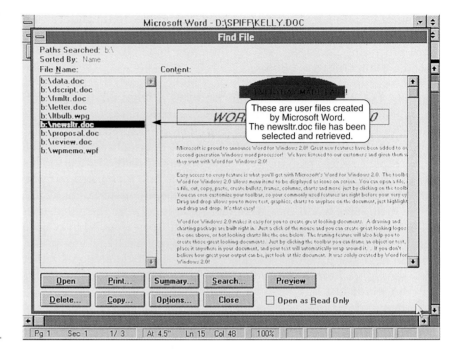

IN A

**NUT SHELL**

**UNIQUE FEATURES OF WORD PROCESSING PACKAGES**

1. Spelling checker, thesaurus, grammar checker, small encyclopedia, or almanac are available.
2. Bibliography, index, and table of contents can be created automatically.
3. Different type fonts, styles, and formats may be used in a document. See Figure 3.23.
4. Personalized letters may be created by merging a document file with a name and address file.

**Figure 3.23** *Most word processing packages can display and print documents using a number of different type fonts.*

entering or editing. Use the PgDn key to scroll forward one page—24 lines—and the PgUp key to scroll back one page.

All word processing packages have similar types of commands, such as retrieving, formatting, and printing. The methods used for executing the commands are, however, package specific. See Figure 3.22 for an illustration.

Many word processing packages enable you to display on a screen just what you would see if the text were printed, that is, a display without formatting codes. This feature is called **WYSIWYG** (wizzy-wig), a tongue-in-cheek term for *what you see is what you get.*

In Chapter 7, we discuss **desktop publishing** software. These packages use word processing files to create printed documents that are of such high quality that they appear to be typeset. Currently, desktop publishing packages are noted for including extensive formatting and printing options to achieve a published look, whereas word processing packages are noted for extensive text editing capabilities. In the years ahead, however, it is likely that a single package will incorporate both word processing and desktop publishing features.

## ▶ E l e c t r o n i c  S p r e a d s h e e t s

Spreadsheet packages create worksheet, or spreadsheet, files that represent data in column and row form. Accounting worksheets are used for budgets, income statements, and ledgers but many other documents, such as schedules and tables, can be structured this way as well.

## UNDERSTANDING THE CAPABILITIES

Spreadsheets are used for reporting, graphing, analyzing, forecasting, or projecting. Spreadsheets enable you to:

1. Prepare worksheets and reports that are formatted properly and are arithmetically correct.
2. Make corrections or changes easily and perform automatic calculations. Numeric data can be changed without affecting the validity of the results. Formulas are automatically recalculated each time a numeric entry used in a formula is changed.
3. Determine the effects of hypothetical changes to data (what-if analysis).
4. Reuse formats or worksheet "shells." An empty worksheet shell can be created that contains labels and formulas but no data. Such shells are called **templates** (not to be confused with the keyboard template that is supplied with WordPerfect to identify how function keys are used). The worksheet templates can be used to create different spreadsheets, each with different data. Consider the budget in Figure 3.24, which was prepared by a spreadsheet package. This budget can be reused in a number of ways.
   a. For Kim Lee's budget next year, using the same formulas.
   b. For distribution to others so they can use the same format for entering their own data. If Jerry Johnson thinks he has the same

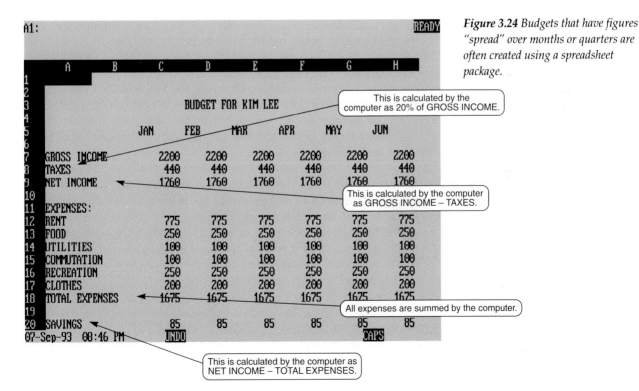

*Figure 3.24* Budgets that have figures "spread" over months or quarters are often created using a spreadsheet package.

**Figure 3.25** *Budgets, like any worksheet, can be used to view the outcome if certain projections are made, or if you want to see the impact of hypothetical changes. When spreadsheets are used for evaluating anticipated changes so that decisions can be made, we call this "what-if" analysis.*

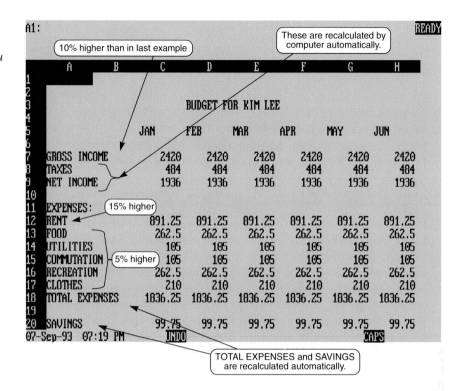

expenses and no others, he can use Kim Lee's spreadsheet format as a template. He can enter his own values for wages, rent, food, clothing and leisure and have the computer generate totals.

c. For projections or what-if analysis. If Kim Lee estimates that her wages will increase by 10 percent next year, that her rent will increase by 15 percent, and that her other expenses are likely to increase by 5 percent, she can use her spreadsheet format as a template to make the necessary changes. See Figure 3.25.

d. Similarly, if Jerry Johnson is considering a new job in a different city, he can enter the new job's wages and estimate his other expenses to see instantly what impact such a change would have on his financial position.

To facilitate reusability, a spreadsheet should include formulas or should *copy* data from other cells where possible. In our budget only one column of values needs to be entered. If you expect all values to be the same for each month, FEB–JUN data would not need to be keyed. Rather you would copy the JAN entries using a copy command. In this way, an actual change, anticipated change, or hypothetical change needs to be made only to the one column. All other cells will then reflect the change.

5. Modify a worksheet as needed. Suppose you like the format of Kim Lee's budget but you have other expenses. You own a car and you have a small life insurance policy. You do not pay rent because you live with your parents. You want your budget to include figures for JAN–MAR only. This does not mean that you must create an entirely new spreadsheet. You can easily modify the existing spreadsheet by deleting the entries for APR–JUN. You can add rows for car pay-

ments, car insurance, parking, gas, and tolls and for life insurance premiums. When changing columns and rows, however, formulas sometimes need to be adjusted as well. See Figure 3.26.

6. Print and graph results. Sometimes data is easier to analyze when it is in graphic form.

Figures 3.27 through 3.30 are sample worksheets created by spreadsheet packages. We illustrate them here just to familiarize you with the

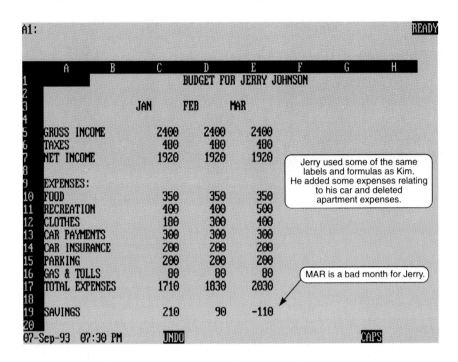

***Figure 3.26*** *You may use an existing spreadsheet's format as a template or "shell" for your own individual needs. Here, Jerry Johnson used Kim Lee's budget as a template and made modifications as necessary.*

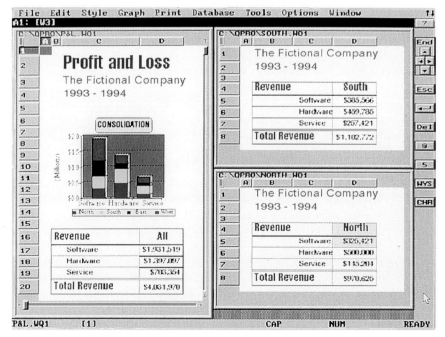

***Figure 3.27*** *A financial statement created by a spreadsheet package.*

*Figure 3.28* *A sales forecast created by a spreadsheet package.*

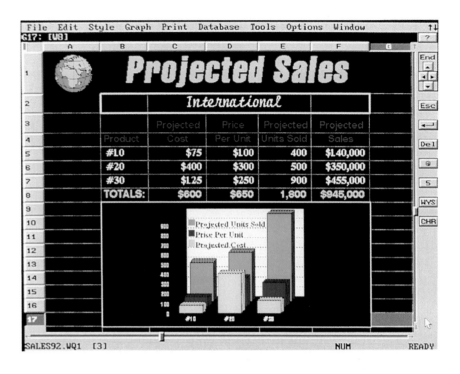

*Figure 3.29* *An income statement created by a spreadsheet package.*

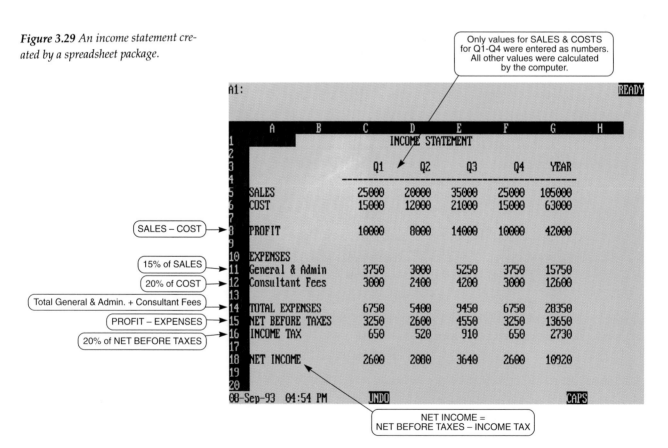

A1: [W23] '                                                    READY

```
              A              B        C        D        E
1                    COPPERSTONE CO. PAYROLL REPORT
2
3
4        Name           F/T or P/T   Check No.  Date     Amount
5
6   Thomas, Andrea       F             29670  15-Jan-93  $600.00
7   Smith, Gregory       P             29671  17-Jan-93  $400.00
8   Harrison, Fred       F             29672  19-Jan-93  $700.00
9   Gotti, James         P             29673  21-Jan-93  $200.00
10  Russell, Jerry       P             29674  23-Jan-93  $125.00
11  Stone, Thomas        F             29675  25-Jan-93  $600.00
12  Shapiro, Myra        F             29676  27-Jan-93  $880.00
13  Bush, Bill           P             29678  29-Jan-93   $95.00
14  Washington, Lamont   F             29679  02-Feb-93  $660.00
15  Harris, Victoria     P             29680  04-Feb-93   $75.00
16  Curtis, Philip       P             29681  06-Feb-93  $175.00
17                                                      ----------
18                                                      $4,510.00
19                                                      ----------
20
07-Sep-93  09:00 PM      UNDO
```

*Figure 3.30 A payroll report created by a spreadsheet package.*

various types of data that lend themselves to being represented in spreadsheet form. Spreadsheets can be used in all of the basic functional areas of a business. In all cases, data is entered and formulas established by the user to enable the package to automatically perform calculations and recalculations if changes are made.

## ENTERING DATA IN CELLS AND USING COMMANDS

We will refer to Figure 3.29 to illustrate how spreadsheets are designed. The worksheet consists of columns and rows. A column is a vertical section identified by letters A–Z, AA–AZ, BA–BZ, and so on. A row is a horizontal section identified by a number from 1, 2, 3, and so on. Data is entered into worksheet locations called cells, which are the boxes formed by the intersection of columns and rows (see Figure 3.31). Cell location B3, for example, refers to a cell in the B column on row 3. The number of cells in a worksheet depends on the package.

You enter identifying labels, numeric data, or formulas in cells. You should always enter a formula when feasible rather than calculating the results yourself. By entering formulas rather than doing calculations yourself, you minimize errors. In addition, any necessary recalculations will be automatic. This significantly reduces the time and drudgery required to check a worksheet, and it minimizes errors.

When you begin, cell location A1 will be highlighted with a shaded rectangle. This shaded rectangle is called a cell pointer and it indicates the active or current cell. It serves as the cursor point. If you enter data, that data would automatically be placed in the cell highlighted by the cell pointer.

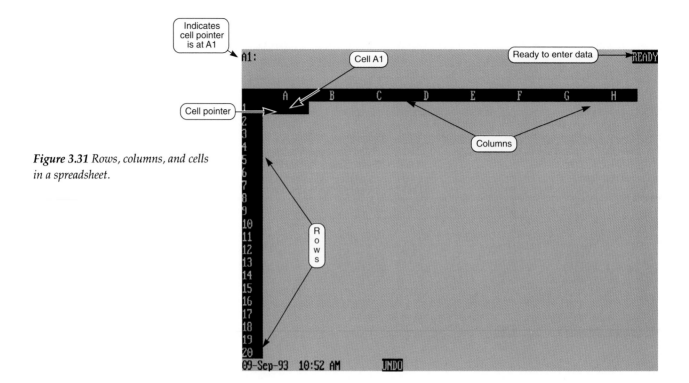

*Figure 3.31* *Rows, columns, and cells in a spreadsheet.*

You may use the cursor arrows keys on a keyboard to move the cell pointer to different locations. In addition, the PgDn key moves the cell pointer down 24 rows (one full screen display), PgUp moves it up 24 rows, Home brings it to cell location A1, and End brings it to the last filled cell location or to the last physical cell location, depending on the package. Many spreadsheet packages also have a "GO TO" function key that enables you to move directly to specific cell locations.

Spreadsheet packages enable you to enter data but they also have commands for operating on that data in a wide variety of ways. Some of the more common commands are discussed next.

**Save, retrieve, and print the spreadsheet.** In addition to the standard formatting commands that set margins, lengths, and so on, a spreadsheet can be printed in compressed format so that more columns appear on a single page. A spreadsheet can also be printed sideways, or in landscape mode, so that the entire spreadsheet appears as one contiguous unit—not in pieces. Moreover, for checking purposes, each cell value or formula can be made to print on a separate line. See Figure 3.32. To print a file, you select the appropriate print command and then choose various options.

**Change the size of cells in individual columns or in all columns.** For example, the first column in a spreadsheet often contains labels that need more characters than cells in other columns.

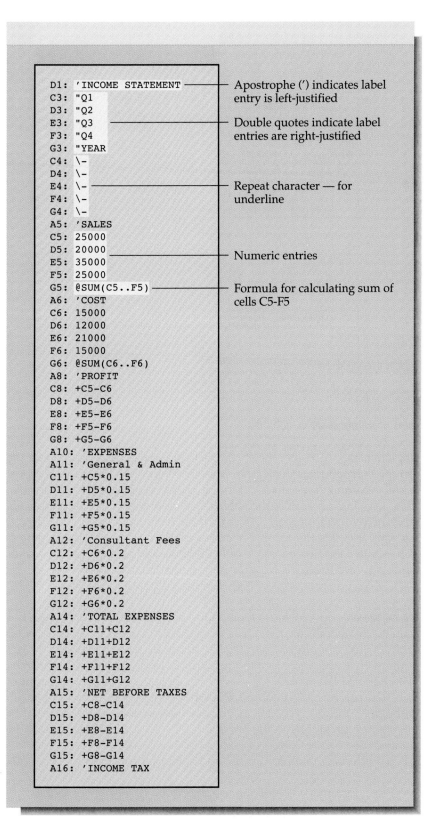

| Cell | Contents | |
|---|---|---|
| D1: | 'INCOME STATEMENT | — Apostrophe (') indicates label entry is left-justified |
| C3: | "Q1 | |
| D3: | "Q2 | |
| E3: | "Q3 | — Double quotes indicate label entries are right-justified |
| F3: | "Q4 | |
| G3: | "YEAR | |
| C4: | \- | |
| D4: | \- | |
| E4: | \- | — Repeat character — for underline |
| F4: | \- | |
| G4: | \- | |
| A5: | 'SALES | |
| C5: | 25000 | |
| D5: | 20000 | |
| E5: | 35000 | — Numeric entries |
| F5: | 25000 | |
| G5: | @SUM(C5..F5) | — Formula for calculating sum of cells C5-F5 |
| A6: | 'COST | |
| C6: | 15000 | |
| D6: | 12000 | |
| E6: | 21000 | |
| F6: | 15000 | |
| G6: | @SUM(C6..F6) | |
| A8: | 'PROFIT | |
| C8: | +C5-C6 | |
| D8: | +D5-D6 | |
| E8: | +E5-E6 | |
| F8: | +F5-F6 | |
| G8: | +G5-G6 | |
| A10: | 'EXPENSES | |
| A11: | 'General & Admin | |
| C11: | +C5*0.15 | |
| D11: | +D5*0.15 | |
| E11: | +E5*0.15 | |
| F11: | +F5*0.15 | |
| G11: | +G5*0.15 | |
| A12: | 'Consultant Fees | |
| C12: | +C6*0.2 | |
| D12: | +D6*0.2 | |
| E12: | +E6*0.2 | |
| F12: | +F6*0.2 | |
| G12: | +G6*0.2 | |
| A14: | 'TOTAL EXPENSES | |
| C14: | +C11+C12 | |
| D14: | +D11+D12 | |
| E14: | +E11+E12 | |
| F14: | +F11+F12 | |
| G14: | +G11+G12 | |
| A15: | 'NET BEFORE TAXES | |
| C15: | +C8-C14 | |
| D15: | +D8-D14 | |
| E15: | +E8-E14 | |
| F15: | +F8-F14 | |
| G15: | +G8-G14 | |
| A16: | 'INCOME TAX | |

**Figure 3.32** *An Income Statement like the one in Figure 3.29 can be displayed or printed in cell-formula mode, with the contents of each cell printed on a single line.*

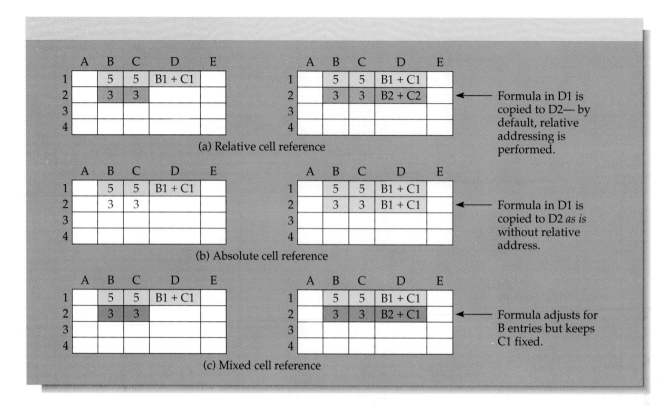

Figure in D1 is copied to D2— by default, relative addressing is performed.

(a) Relative cell reference

Figure in D1 is copied to D2 *as is* without relative address.

(b) Absolute cell reference

Formula adjusts for B entries but keeps C1 fixed.

(c) Mixed cell reference

*Figure 3.33 Relative addressing, absolute addressing, and mixed addressing.*

**Insert or delete rows or columns.**

**Copy formulas.**   Consider the spreadsheet in Figure 3.29. We can enter the formula that subtracts Costs from Sales in cell location B8 and then repeat a similar formula for cells C8 through F8. Or we can copy the formula. When copying a formula, the spreadsheet assumes you want automatic adjustment for columns and rows. So if the formula at B8 is +B5−B6 and you copy it to C8, the computer makes a column adjustment and enters +C5−C6 in C8. This process is called relative addressing. If a copy command is to use *fixed cells* in all formulas, then relative addressing can be overridden; this process is called absolute addressing. See Figure 3.33.

**Use functions.**   Spreadsheets have built-in functions that can be used to evaluate or operate on data. The user does not need to actually enter formulas that are already stored. For example, to find the sum of cell locations E1 to E7 and place the result in E8, you can enter the formula +E1+E2+E3+E4+E5+E6+E7 in cell E8, or you can enter a function in E8 called the @SUM function: @SUM(E1 . . E7). The dots ( . . ) mean "through." You can type this as you see it or you can use the cursor or cell pointer to highlight the block of cells E1 . . E7 that needs to be summed. See Figure 3.34.

Some other common arithmetic and statistical functions are:

@AVERAGE(range)     Finds the average value in a range of values
@MAX(range)         Finds the highest value within a range of values

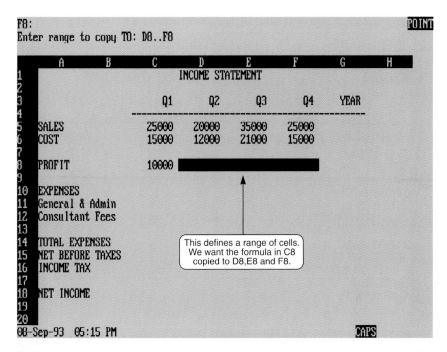

*Figure 3.34* (a) *When copying formulas, you must indicate the range of cells where the copied formula is to be placed. In this case, the formula in C8 will be copied to D8 through F8.*
(b) *The formulas in the C column are copied to columns D through G. This is how the spreadsheet looks in formula mode after all copy commands have been executed.*

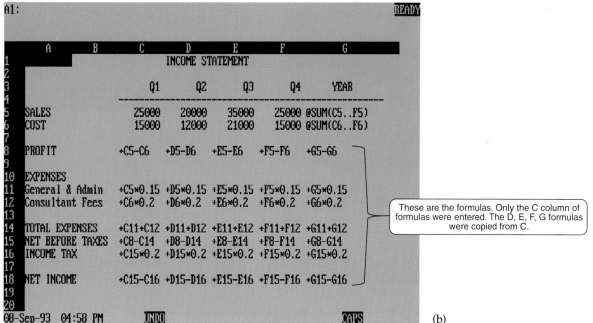

| @MIN(range) | Finds the lowest value |
|---|---|
| @COUNT(range) | Counts the number of items in a range |
| @SQRT(number) | Finds the square root of a number |

Consider the spreadsheet in Figure 3.35. @AVG calculates average grade for the class. @MAX and @MIN indicate the highest and lowest grades.

*Figure 3.35* *Use of functions in a spreadsheet.*

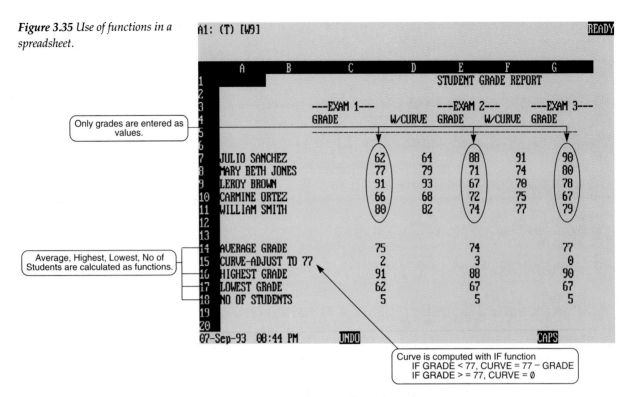

©COUNT counts the number of students.

A useful function for what-if analysis is the @IF function. With this function, you can test a condition and have the computer enter one value in a cell if the condition is met or a different value in the cell if the condition is not met.

Example

@IF (x, y, z)
x = condition being tested
y = operation to be performed if the condition is true or is met
z = operation to be performed if the condition is not true or is not met

Suppose we type @IF(C8=D8,0,1) in cell location F8. If the contents of cell location C8 is equal to the contents of cell location D8, the computer will place a 0 in F8; otherwise it will place a 1 in F8.

Financial functions, mathematical functions, date and time functions, and database functions are also available with most spreadsheet packages. Financial functions are particularly useful because they perform complex operations such as calculating interest rates, balances, and amortizations. The user need only enter the variables and the package will generate the results using built-in functions.

**Graph.** Numeric data in a spreadsheet can be graphed to provide a pictorial representation of the data for analysis or decision making. Graphs are usually in bar, pie, or chart form. Graphs can be displayed, saved, retrieved, and printed. If your monitor or printer has the capability, graphs may be displayed or printed in color. Legends, borders, titles, and other data can be added to the graph.

**Interface with add-in products.** Many spreadsheets are compatible with add-in products that perform specific tasks such as specialized printing or graphing.

**Create database files and functions.** Spreadsheets can be used to create simple database files. The spreadsheet in Figure 3.35, which illustrated the use of functions to help generate student averages, is also a modest database file containing student names and grades. We discuss packages specifically designed for processing database files next.

## ▶ Database Management Systems

### UNDERSTANDING THE CAPABILITIES

A database management system (DBMS) is a set of programs that creates data in database files and enables users to edit and update the data and to inquire and report from the files. DBMS programs allow you to manage data using a computer. You may add, delete, change, sort, or search for data in a database using a DBMS. Your college or university may use a DBMS to store information about you and your courses on a computer. The information in a database is stored in database files on disk rather than in manual file folders. A DBMS allows you to enter and use the information in your database file just as you would use data in file folders, except that the computer quickly performs searches, sorts, calculations, and printing. The examples presented in this section are just illustrations. They could, however, be used by many businesses in their day-to-day operations.

The many uses or applications for a DBMS include:

- Mailing lists (membership and subscription lists).
- Accounting (bookkeeping and accounting information).
- Scientific research (experimental data, scientific journals).
- Business information (customers, vendors, inventories).
- Personal use (record, tape, or book library).
- Library and government databases (scientific, academic, and federal agency publications).

A wide variety of database management systems are available for use not only with micros but with larger computers as well. Micro-based database management systems sell for under $1000, while those for larger systems are much more expensive, mainly because they have far greater capability. Most mainframe-based DBMS products are leased rather than purchased. It is not uncommon, for example, for a highly sophisticated DBMS to lease for tens of thousands of dollars per year or more. Although this seems expensive, in the end it is usually cheaper for an organization to lease a DBMS than developing its own programs.

We will see in Chapter 11 that there are various ways in which data can be organized in a DBMS. For now, you should know that a database management system is used for creating, editing, and updating data and for answering inquiries and producing reports in a timely fashion. A DBMS can be used to integrate or join files so that data can be shared, and help keep access to files secure.

## USING A DBMS

As we have seen, most word processing and spreadsheet packages require you to select commands from menus or use function keys. With a DBMS you may similarly select commands from a menu. Selecting commands from a menu, however, and then subcommands from a submenu or pull-down menu at various levels can be very cumbersome, especially when entries to be extracted from the database need to meet many specific criteria. As users become familiar with the command structure of a DBMS, they tend to prefer keying actual commands rather than selecting items from menus. Most DBMS products offer the user a choice of modes: either selecting commands from a menu or actually typing commands on your own (command mode). See Figure 3.36.

**Entering Data in a Database.** Before a database can be constructed or retrieved you need to know how to structure data. A database file is a

*Figure 3.36 Sometimes a DBMS is command-driven, which means you must type specific commands. Sometimes a DBMS is menu-driven, which means you can select from on-screen menu commands. Often a DBMS, like dBASE, gives you both options.*

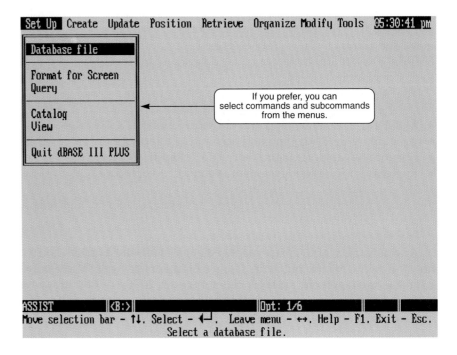

(a) *dBASE III Plus in menu mode.*

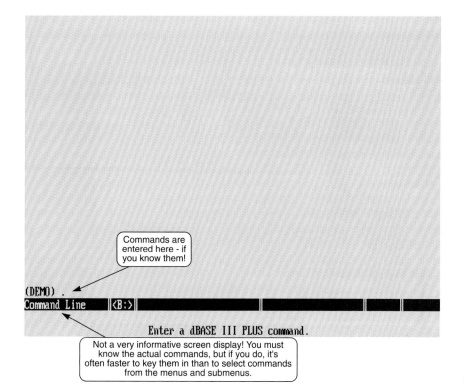

(b) *dBASE III Plus in command mode.*

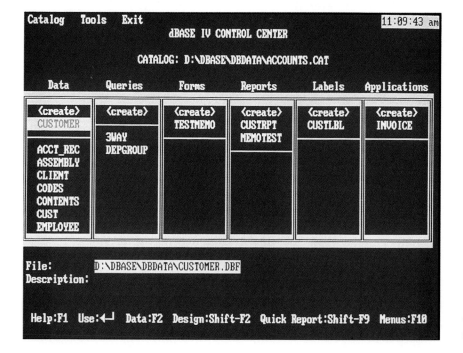

(c) *This is a dBASE IV screen in menu mode.*

**Figure 3.37** *Fields are contained within records, and all records are contained within a database file. Before creating a database file using a DBMS, you must define the format of each record. This is a layout of how fields have been defined for records within an employee database file.*

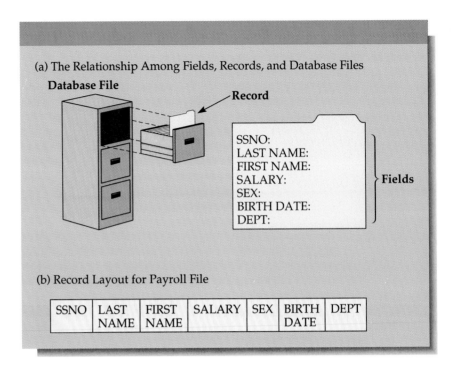

(a) The Relationship Among Fields, Records, and Database Files

Database File

Record

SSNO:
LAST NAME:
FIRST NAME:
SALARY:
SEX:
BIRTH DATE:
DEPT:

Fields

(b) Record Layout for Payroll File

| SSNO | LAST NAME | FIRST NAME | SALARY | SEX | BIRTH DATE | DEPT |
|------|-----------|------------|--------|-----|------------|------|
|      |           |            |        |     |            |      |

collection of information in a specific subject area. Database files differ from what are called flat files in that database files can be joined, or interrelated. We have payroll files, inventory files, accounts receivable files, and so forth. A file is subdivided into **records** and each record is a unit of information pertaining to one item in the file. A payroll file, for example, consists of payroll records; each record pertains to a specific employee. Similarly, an accounts receivable file consists of individual customer records. Each record includes specific elements called **fields.** An employee record within a payroll file, for example, may have a Social Security number field, an employee name field, and a salary field. See Figure 3.37.

Keep in mind that a DBMS is capable of *joining* files by using a key field that appears in both files. Suppose a company has an employee file and a sales file, each with records identified by the Social Security number of the salespeople. The two files can be joined using Social Security number as a key field to determine the commissions of all salespeople based on their sales.

**Creating a Database File.** Before actually creating a database file, you begin by naming it and then specifying the format of records within that file. See Figure 3.38. To specify a format, you indicate the following five characteristics.

1. The sequence in which fields are to be entered in a record. The first field specified is the first one in the record, and so on.
2. Each field's name. Each DBMS has rules for forming field names. Most often, a field name must begin with a letter and contain some com-

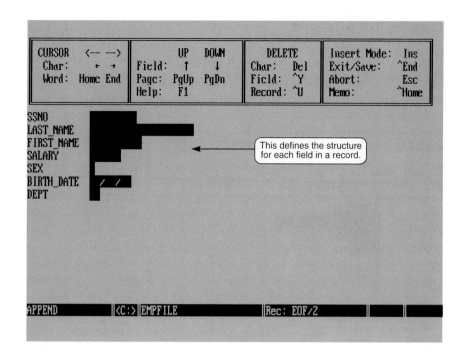

*Figure 3.38* *This is how you would define fields within an employee record.*

bination of letters and digits. Underscores (__) rather than blanks, are sometimes permitted to separate words (e.g., LAST__NAME or LASTNAME is okay, but LAST NAME is not because there is a blank). Rules for forming field names are typically displayed on the screen or are available from a help screen.

3. The field type.
   a. Character: for alphabetic fields or fields that can contain any characters including letters, digits, and symbols, such as an address field.
   b. Numeric: for fields used in arithmetic.
   c. Date: for fields using a date format such as mo/yr, mo/dd/yr, dd/mo/yr.
   d. Logical: for fields designing either/or, yes or no, on or off, (e.g., salaried/hourly or male/female could be designated this way).
4. The width or size of each field. When all records are to be the same fixed length, then each field must be given a size that is large enough for all or most entries. A last name may be 20 characters, for example, or a salary may be 6 integers. Fields can be filled with spaces if each position does not include a significant character.
5. Decimal positions. Typically, the number of decimal positions must be specified if a field has been designated as numeric.

Once the format for records in a database file has been established, you save the format. You can always add fields later on if the need arises. After the format has been saved, you can enter data as input. When you are ready to enter input, the DBMS provides you with an outline of what each record should look like.

**Correcting Data Entry Errors.**   Full-screen text editing is usually available with a DBMS; this means that while you are entering a record and it is displayed on the screen, you can return to previously entered fields using the cursor arrows to add data, delete data, or replace data. The rules for

*Figure 3.39* (a) *An onscreen form (or template) representing field layouts for an employee record.* (b) *Users might find it easier to enter data using this "form" rather than the format shown in* (a). *A DBMS enables you to define your own screen layout for data entry.*

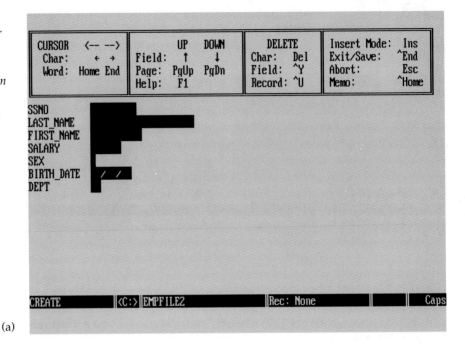

(a)

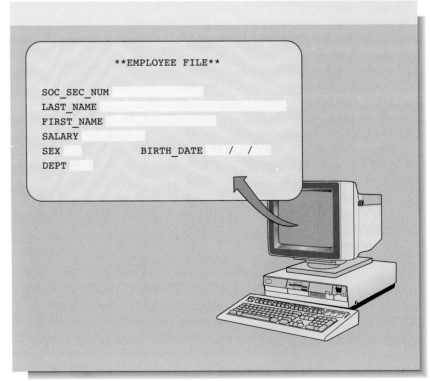

(b)

making corrections are similar to those for word processing packages. Look at Figure 3.38 again.

In some cases, the DBMS shell that enables you to enter data records may not be clear enough. Perhaps the data is to be entered by an operator who is not familiar with the application or with a computer. A DBMS designer can build a screen display that highlights and clarifies the entries to be made and establishes parameters or limits for the user. See Figure 3.39. A salary field, for example, may be established with a range specified so that only salaries from a minimum of $15,000 to a maximum of $125,000 will be accepted. Similarly, other fields, like Social Security number, for example, may be established so that they *must* contain a specified number of digits (e.g., 9). If the user presses the Enter key before nine digits are entered, a message can be displayed. Similarly, some fields can be set up so that the user *must* enter data. Other fields may be protected for security purposes, so what the user enters is not displayed on the screen.

**Executing Database Commands.**   Once you have entered data into a database file, you can save it. A DBMS enables users to browse through a file or display a file to look for errors. The file may be edited or corrected. Users routinely update files by modifying existing records—replacing old values with new ones. Files can also be updated by appending or adding new records and deleting inactive or old records. Most DBMS products also enable the file's structure to be modified by adding or deleting new fields or changing the format of existing fields.

After a file has been created and edited, users can inquire about the status of records. Here are several examples. (Figure 3.40 illustrates the full file used in the examples.)

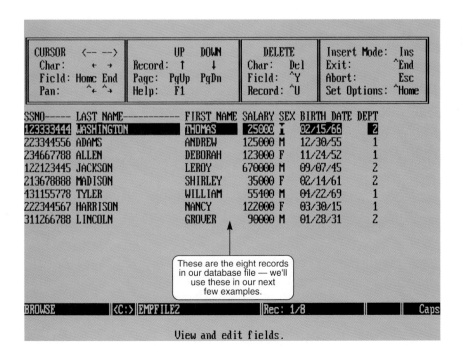

*Figure 3.40* A database file of eight employee records created using dBASE.

*Results of an inquiry: What is the salary of each employee?*

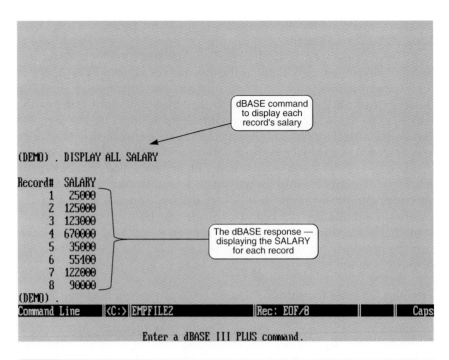

*Results of an inquiry: What is the last name for record 5?*

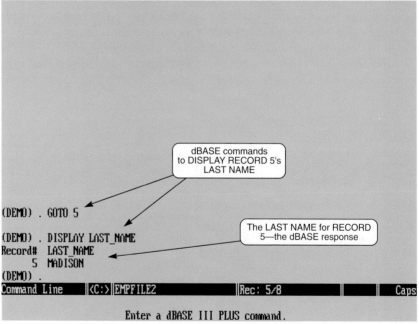

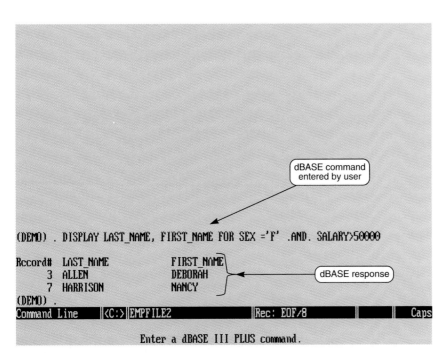

*Results of an inquiry: What are the first and last names of all females who earn more than $50,000?*

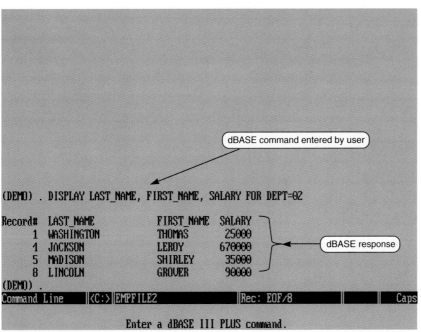

*Results of an inquiry: What is the name and salary of each employee in DEPT 02?*

*Results of an inquiry: What is the total of all salaries for employees in DEPT 02?*

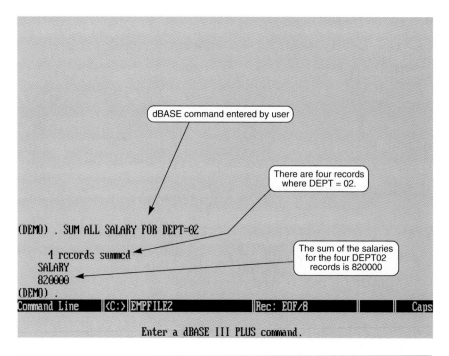

*Results of an inquiry: What is the average salary?*

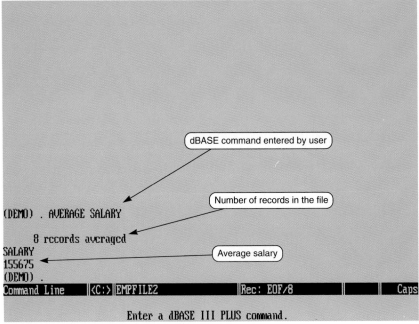

A DBMS can also be used to generate reports. The user specifies, for example, the sequence in which output information is to appear, the actual information desired, the format, the headings, and any totals. See Figure 3.41.

When reporting, as well as when inquiring, data that meets certain criteria can be printed or displayed. Typically, relational operators are used to specify the criteria:

<   Less than
>   Greater than
=   Equal to
<=  Less than or equal to
=>  Greater than or equal to
<>  Unequal to

## Examples

DISPLAY ALL FOR SALARY >= 50000

DISPLAY LASTNAME FOR DEPT = 02

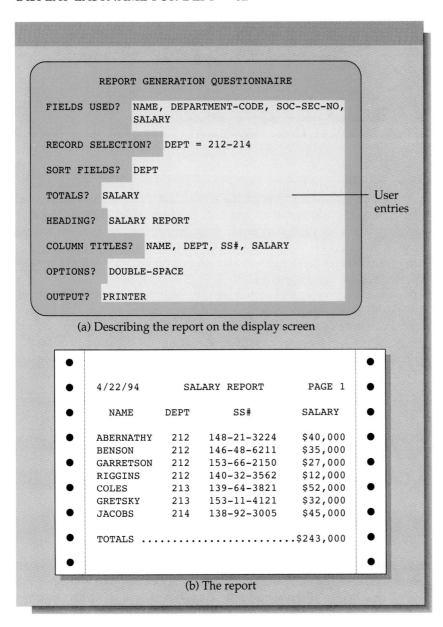

**Figure 3.41** *A DBMS is often used to print reports. First the user fills in answers to questions. Then the DBMS generates the report.*

```
              REPORT GENERATION QUESTIONNAIRE

FIELDS USED?    NAME, DEPARTMENT-CODE, SOC-SEC-NO,
                SALARY

RECORD SELECTION?   DEPT = 212-214

SORT FIELDS?  DEPT

TOTALS?   SALARY

HEADING?   SALARY REPORT

COLUMN TITLES?   NAME, DEPT, SS#, SALARY

OPTIONS?   DOUBLE-SPACE

OUTPUT?   PRINTER
```
— User entries

(a) Describing the report on the display screen

```
4/22/94         SALARY REPORT         PAGE 1

   NAME      DEPT      SS#          SALARY

ABERNATHY    212    148-21-3224    $40,000
BENSON       212    146-48-6211    $35,000
GARRETSON    212    153-66-2150    $27,000
RIGGINS      212    140-32-3562    $12,000
COLES        213    139-64-3821    $52,000
GRETSKY      213    153-11-4121    $32,000
JACOBS       214    138-92-3005    $45,000

TOTALS  ........................$243,000
```

(b) The report

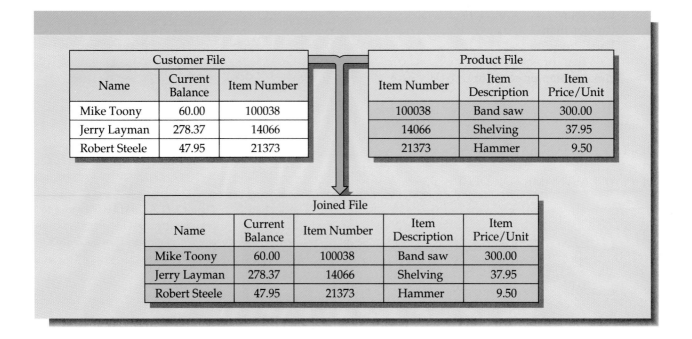

*Figure 3.42 The join feature allows files to be combined on a key field.*

Both inquiries and reports can be generated from joined files in a database. Suppose you want to print the names, balance due, and items purchased by each customer in an accounts receivable file, along with product information for each purchased item, which can be obtained from a separate product file. You would use the item number as the key field in both files. The files can be joined and the required data extracted to generate the report. See Figure 3.42.

Files in a database can be sorted into any sequence for ease of retrieval. Files can also be organized with an index for quick retrieval of specific records. An index enables the computer to look up the location of records by key fields just the way you might look up the location of a book's topic from an index. We discuss indexing in more detail in Chapter 6.

Database management systems are popular for four basic reasons.

1. They make data entry, editing, and updating relatively easy.
2. They enable records within files to be accessed quickly.
3. They enable users to create well-designed reports and to obtain quick responses to inquiries.
4. They enable managers and other users to generate desired output in a timely fashion without the need for a computer professional to write a program.

## QUERY LANGUAGES

One notable feature of DBMS products is that the language used to report from a database file or to answer inquiries is English-like and does not require knowledge of the actual procedures used by a computer to process data. Each DBMS has a **query language,** that is, a method of accessing

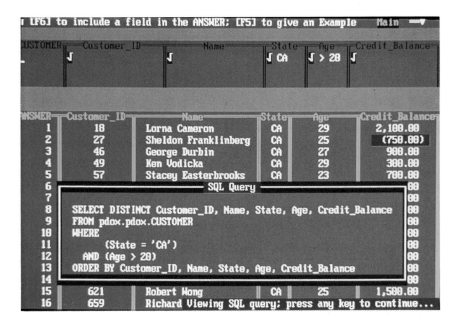

*The query language SQL enables users to obtain data from different databases. In this instance, records for customers from California who are older than 20 are highlighted.*

records quickly and providing users who may not be proficient computer users with necessary information.

A problem with query languages, however, has been that they tend to be different for each package; that is, query languages, like many computer products, are not standardized. As a result, users with knowledge of one query language cannot always transfer that knowledge to other products.

One way in which products get standardized is by persistent user demand. If users tend to buy products that are compatible with others, they can drive manufacturers toward standardization. During the past decade, one query language emerged as a particularly effective, user-friendly language for all types of computers. This query language is called SQL (for *structured query language*). It has become so popular and widely used it is considered a de facto standard—a standard in fact although not formally designated as such. Now most DBMS products have their own proprietary query language but also enable users to make inquiries in SQL. Thus SQL users can make inquiries into database files created by a wide variety of database management systems.

## ▶ Electronic Mail

Electronic mail or e-mail packages enable users to send messages, text, files, graphics, and faxes from one computer to another. Users can communicate with one another using e-mail if they meet one of these conditions.

1. They all have access to one large computer system that has an electronic mail facility.

---

**EVALUATING PRODUCTIVITY TOOLS**

The following factors are important for evaluating productivity tools as well as other software packages.

1. Speed.
2. Cost.
3. Compatibility with existing hardware and other software.
4. Extra features such as the ability to import other files.
5. Quality of the documentation.
6. Ease of learning and ease of use.
7. Error handling.
8. Technical support.
9. Update policy.
10. Online help or tutorials.

## *LOOKING* AHEAD

**E-MAIL TAKES CENTER STAGE**

Word processing, spreadsheet, and DBMS packages have been used for many years. Although the market leader in each category may change, these tools are likely to remain integral elements for improving productivity. Electronic mail, on the other hand, is a relatively new productivity tool. Its success as a major contributor to productivity depends on the degree to which employees—even those who do not otherwise use a computer—learn to adjust to it. Messages are of no value if users don't check their electronic mailboxes! Soon video and sound will be widely available with e-mail, and e-mail will truly be a multimedia productivity tool. In fact, audio and video components are likely to be added to other productivity tools as well for computer-based tutorials and providing help.

2. They all use a service (e.g., CompuServe or Prodigy) that enables subscribers to communicate over an e-mail facility.
3. They are networked within their organization and have a special e-mail package (e.g., cc:Mail, Microsoft Mail, or Beyond Mail).

E-mail messages can be informal and read like verbal messages left on an answering machine or they can be formal documents. The sender can transmit a message to one or more recipients and indicate whether the message is urgent. The message is transmitted when the sender completes it any time that the network is active; similarly, the message can be read by the recipient whenever he or she accesses the network. When users log on to a network, they are told if there is mail waiting. Messages, which can be scanned by subject or by degree of urgency, can be read, saved, forwarded, or responded to. See Figure 3.43 for an e-mail screen display.

*Figure 3.43 A sample electronic mail screen display.*

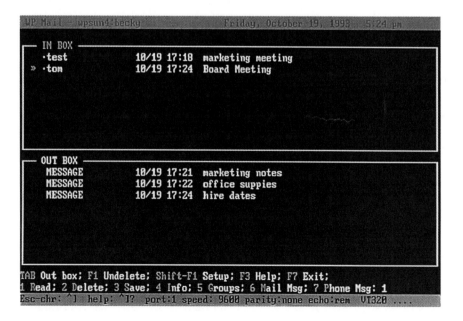

▶ **SELF-TEST**

1. Right margins in a word processing document can be _____ or _____.
2. Sometimes a word that is being typed using a word processing package cannot fit on the current line and is automatically brought down to the next line. What is this process called?
3. Name three types of data users can enter in spreadsheet cells.
4. (T or F) Formulas can be copied from one cell or range of cells to another cell using a spreadsheet package.
5. (T or F) A DBMS can be used to inquire about records in a database file and to report from the database file.
6. Name six criteria often used for evaluating productivity tools.

Solutions
1. right justified; ragged right
2. word wrapping
3. labels; numeric data; formulas
4. T
5. T
6. speed, cost, compatibility, technical support, ease of use, quality of the documentation

## ▶ Chapter Summary

Software is the driving force that makes computers work. **Application packages** are a type of prewritten software designed for business or personal use that can be purchased off-the-shelf. Some of the most important application packages used in business are known as productivity tools.

### 3.1 UNDERSTANDING SOFTWARE AND DATA MANAGEMENT

Software is typically stored on disk and is supplied as program files. Disks can also store data files; these files contain data created by a software product and can be used for future processing.

Software users fall into three basic categories: users who need the output information to perform their jobs, software specialists who help customize software for individual use, and data entry operators who actually key in the input. Power users are those who wear all three hats; that is, they do the job of software specialists and data entry operators as well as analyze output.

The tools most widely used to increase employee productivity are called productivity tools. **Word processing packages** are used for entering, editing, and printing **documents. Electronic spreadsheet** packages are used to create **worksheets** (spreadsheets), which represent data in column and row format and automatically calculate results. Once a format is established, the spreadsheet can be reused with different numeric

> Why are application packages called productivity tools so commonly used in business?

values. Spreadsheets allow users to predict the outcome of hypothetical changes to data and to graph results. **Database management system (DBMS)** software is used for creating, editing, and updating **files** in a database and for inquiring about the status of those files or for reporting from files. **Electronic mail (e-mail)** packages enable computer users to send, store, and retrieve messages at any time. **Integrated packages** combine the features of all four productivity tools.

## 3.2 USING PRODUCTIVITY TOOLS: SHARED FEATURES AND FUNCTIONS

What features and functions are commonly included in productivity tools and integrated packages?

Productivity tools include some common features shared by most software. They create files and enable users to retrieve them if the files need to be changed or reused. Each file is given a **filename** and a file extension that identifies the program that created the file.

The main screen of each productivity tool has a status line containing information such as date and time and current settings, or **defaults,** for the product.

Data is initially entered, or typed, using the keyboard. All packages enable users to make corrections using the cursor arrow keys to return to an error, which can then be corrected. Data is operated on with the use of **commands** that are typically selected from **menus. Function keys** may also be used to execute commands. Sometimes pressing a function key provides the user with **context-sensitive help.**

Typical commands include saving, retrieving, and printing files. A section of a data file called a **block** can be moved, copied, or placed at another point in the file or added to a different file. This process is called **cutting and pasting.** Productivity tools can also be used to find specific items in a data file and to make replacements; this process is called **search and replace.**

Many productivity tools permit you to write special instructions called **macros** to execute a series of commands either repeatedly or whenever the need arises. Many tools also allow files created by one productivity tool to be imported, or added, to files created by another productivity tool.

## 3.3 UNIQUE FEATURES AND FUNCTIONS OF COMMON PRODUCTIVITY TOOLS

What do users need to know in order to choose and use productivity tools?

Word processing packages are used for **text editing** documents, that is, making on-screen changes to documents. In addition, they can format documents, check for spelling, and incorporate standard blocks of text (called **boilerplating**). Most have an electronic thesaurus for selecting synonyms. A bibliography, index, and table of contents may be created automatically and personalized letters may be prepared easily.

Word processing packages automatically perform **word wrap:** they bring words down to the next line if there is no room on the current line. If the space left at the end of a line is excessive, spacing among characters can be adjusted automatically to achieve a more even look—a process called **microjustification.**

Some word processing packages can display text on the screen just as you would see it if printed, even if the text has formatting codes. This feature is called **WYSIWYG** for *what you see is what you get.* Word processing files are also used in **desktop publishing,** where high-quality output is created that looks as if it is typeset.

Spreadsheet packages use locations called **cells** formed where columns and rows intersect for representing labels, numeric data, and formulas. Special functions can be used to evaluate data in cells. Graphic output can also be produced. A spreadsheet shell called a **template** can be created with only labels and formulas (no data); users then create many different worksheets using that shell or template, each with different data entered.

A DBMS creates **database files** consisting of **records.** Each record is a unit of data in a file. Records consist of **fields** of data. Every DBMS has a **query language,** which is a method for inquiring about the status of records.

E-mail message files are similar to files created by other productivity tools. They can be corrected as they are entered and operated on with commands like print, save, and retrieve.

## ▶ C hapter S elf-test

1. What are the four major categories of productivity tools?
2. Name the four files created by each of these tools.
3. A package that combines the features of the four productivity tools and adds some features of its own is called a(n) _____.
4. The intersection of a column and a row in a spreadsheet is called a _____.
5. (T or F) Once a spreadsheet is set up, you cannot insert new rows or columns, so it is important to get it right the first time.
6. @ SUM is an example of a special kind of formula called a _____.
7. (T or F) Some keys on the keyboard are assigned special tasks by each software package.
8. (T or F) All software packages have default settings that assume certain initial values; the user can override such defaults.
9. To end a paragraph in a word processing file, press the _____ key.
10. The _____ keys are used to move the cursor around the screen.
11. (T or F) The structure of a database file can be changed by the user even after data has been entered.
12. Global changes to a file means that _____.
13. A _____ of text can be moved, copied, or deleted from files. The term _____ is used to denote the concept of importing sections of standard text into a current document.
14. (T or F) Records in a database file that meet user-specified criteria can be displayed or printed.
15. (T or F) Electronic mail files can be sent to more than one recipient without having to reenter the message.

Solutions
1. word processing; spreadsheet; DBMS; e-mail
2. document files; spreadsheet, or worksheet, files; database files; message files
3. integrated package
4. cell
5. F
6. function
7. T
8. T
9. Enter
10. cursor control arrow
11. T
12. changes are made to all occurrences
13. block; boilerplating
14. T
15. T

## ▶ Key Terms

Application package *p. 70*
Boilerplating *p. 89*
Block *p. 82*
Cell *p. 73*
Command *p. 82*
Context-sensitive help *p. 82*
Cutting and pasting *p. 83*
Database *p. 75*
Database file *p. 75*
Database management system
   (DBMS) *p. 76*

Default *p. 80*
Desktop publishing *p. 94*
Document *p. 72*
Electronic mail (e-mail) *p. 76*
Electronic spreadsheet *p. 72*
Field *p. 108*
File *p. 75*
Filename *p. 79*
Function key *p. 82*
Integrated package *p. 77*
Macros *p. 85*

Menu *p. 82*
Microjustification *p. 93*
Query language *p. 116*
Record *p. 108*
Search and replace *p. 83*
Template *p. 95*
Text editing *p. 87*
Word processing *p. 72*
Word wrap *p. 93*
Worksheet *p. 72*
WYSIWYG *p. 94*

## ▶ Review Questions

1. What is the purpose of help screens in application packages?
2. What are the benefits of using a word processing package over simply typing a document on a typewriter?
3. What types of page formatting tasks can be performed by most word processing packages?
4. Assume you have created a document in which you repeatedly referred to the date of an upcoming meeting as being March 24. The meeting has been changed to March 28. What would be an efficient way of changing each occurrence of March 24 to March 28?
5. Suppose you are a high-school teacher. What type of productivity tool might you find most useful to maintain student grades? Why?
6. List three tasks that can be performed by a database management system.

7. Based on magazine reviews, brochures from computer stores, manuals, or other information, compare the graphics features of the latest versions of two leading spreadsheet programs. One of these should be Lotus 1-2-3; the other should be either Microsoft Excel or Borland's Quattro Pro. How many kinds of graphs does each offer? What kinds are available in each? (Good sources for reviews include *InfoWorld*, *PC*, *PC World*, and *PC Computing*, which should be available in campus and public libraries.)

## PRODUCT ANALYSIS

## CASE

### Using E-Mail: Neither Rain Nor Sleet Nor Snow . . .

Electronic mail, as we have seen, is used to send, store, forward, and retrieve messages and is used by people networked in an organization or by those who use a subscriber service. But electronic mail has the potential for being more than a read-store-and-forward message system comparable to voice mail on telephone networks. Individuals with different software packages and different computers can use it to exchange messages. It enables businesses to exchange messages with customers, suppliers and other organizations. Advances in e-mail technology allow transmission of more than just text: documents, graphs, spreadsheets, forms, images, voice, and even video messages can be transmitted.

Open Messaging Interface (OMI), from the Lotus Development Corporation, is designed for all these applications. OMI enables users with different e-mail software to send and receive all sorts of information from spreadsheets to schedules and from text to multimedia products by means of a single, standard interface.

Apple and IBM were quick to support OMI and have made it available with their operating systems. Novell, a network company, and Microsoft, developer of Windows, while agreeing to support OMI, will produce their own competitive e-mail interfaces as well. Competition is, of course, healthy for business, but it is not always a benefit to those who want standardization. Advocates of competition point out that when companies vie for market share better products are often produced.

Lotus's cc:Mail for networked e-mail systems supports OMI, as one would expect since OMI is also a Lotus product. cc:Mail is itself a popular package that enables each network to install an electronic "post office." cc:Mail also has very good security procedures; for example, all messages are stored in coded form to minimize the risk of snooping.

As e-mail grows in popularity, certain problems must be resolved such as the complexities associated with different computer architectures, security problems, handling of directory assistance, and effective management and administration of the e-mail system. If OMI becomes a standard, and with it, cc:Mail for actual transmission, we may soon all "be connected" in more meaningful ways.

*Analysis*
1. If you were evaluating e-mail products, what features would you look for?
2. What factors may facilitate development of an e-mail standard?
3. What factors may thwart development of an e-mail standard?

# PART TWO

## HARDWARE ADVANCES THE INFORMATION AGE

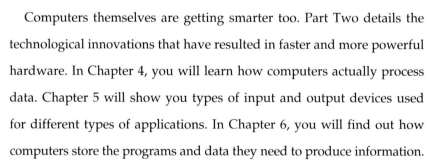

W e have something going for us that our predecessors lacked. Computer technology has made it much faster and easier for us to obtain information, and it has given us new options in the ways we use the information at our disposal. In that sense, computers are making the world smarter. Computers built into everyday products similarly help make the world smarter.

Computers themselves are getting smarter too. Part Two details the technological innovations that have resulted in faster and more powerful hardware. In Chapter 4, you will learn how computers actually process data. Chapter 5 will show you types of input and output devices used for different types of applications. In Chapter 6, you will find out how computers store the programs and data they need to produce information.

Along the way, you will be introduced to some revolutionary new smart and supersmart products—computers that interpret spoken words and read handwritten data, compact disks with very large storage capacities, and other devices that are helping the world grow smarter.

Remember Bob Cratchit in Dickens's *A Christmas Carol?* In the nineteenth and early twentieth centuries, clerks like Cratchit could spend their entire lives copying and adding column after column of figures. Now computers can do the same job more accurately in a fraction of the time. When computers perform routine tasks quickly, they give us more time to do things that really require intelligence, that enable us to be more creative, or that are simply more fun. Smart test bikes, for example, do all the controlling, evaluating, and analyzing while the biker exerts the effort, derives the physical benefits from the exercise, and may have fun as well!

Computers have had a tremendous impact on libraries. In many cases, a computerized system has replaced card catalogs as a source of information about a library's holdings. Special searching techniques enable us to find material on specific topics quickly. Moreover, the contents of a small reference library or a series of journals or books can be stored on a single computer disk called a CD-ROM that can be borrowed from the library just like a book. Although there may always be a place and time for paperback mysteries, you may find it just as enjoyable to access an interactive multimedia mystery story on a CD-ROM and play along as detective.

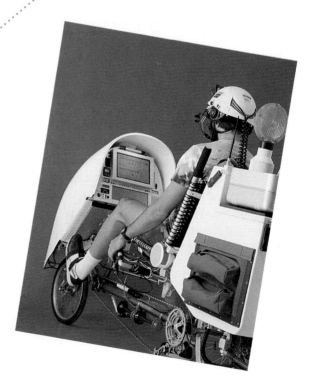

Computers are smarter now than they were just a few years ago. It hasn't been that long since the automated teller machine (ATM), which can read bank cards and approve payments to and withdrawals from a bank account, was regarded as revolutionary. Now a "smart" card can contain a computerized account within itself. Eventually, it may eliminate the need for ATM facilities entirely. Smart cards are becoming widely used as debit cards as well: You "purchase" a card at designated centers for a fixed price and each time you use a service like a phone or copy machine, or purchase a supermarket item, the amount of the transaction is automatically deducted from the card's balance. When you deplete the balance, you simply purchase another card. Smart cards are also used to store medical records, driver information, and so on.

Robots are smart machines that can provide many automated services. They are not only capable of minimizing human effort, but they can reduce the risk of human injury by transporting dangerous products. They can also help the handicapped by using electronic components that, under voice control, can move or position items for the disabled.

To find a smarter world we need not go any farther than our home and our car. Smart appliances range from microwaves—which not only cook to perfection but determine if we set them properly—to sewing machines that can sew any stitch on a garment automatically. Such tasks and many others like them once required constant human supervision or actual manual labor. Smart homes with an array of built-in computerized options from security protection to automatic climate control take much of the burden out of being a homeowner. Cameras are so smart these days that they take better pictures when set to "auto" than some experienced photographers! We can use smart phones to pay our bills or do the shopping. Smart cars with built-in microprocessors are not only safer and more energy efficient, but they can direct us to our destination with an electronically displayed map. These smart devices not only minimize burdensome tasks, they also help improve the quality of life.

# COMPUTER PROCESSING

Regardless of their size, cost, and power, all computers process data in essentially the same way. Micros are simply smaller, less expensive, and less powerful versions of larger systems. Remember that in order to process data, a program must first be loaded into the computer system. The program indicates what type of input is to be read, what processing is to be performed, and what output is to be created.

In Chapter 4 we focus on main memory and the central processing unit, or CPU, of a computer system and answer the following questions:

▶ What properties of the CPU make it the heart of the computer system?

▶ How is data actually stored in a computer?

▶ What factors affect the processing power of a computer?

▶ What are some common methods for computer processing?

## 4.1  HOW THE CPU PROCESSES DATA

### ▶ Overview of Components and Operations

**What properties of the CPU make it the heart of the computer system?**

Chapter 1 introduced a computer system as a group of hardware devices that read data as input, follow programmed instructions to process that data, and produce information as output. A computer system is defined in terms of its central processing unit. The VAX minicomputer manufactured by the Digital Equipment Corporation, for example, has a VAX CPU; a midrange computer from IBM, the AS/400, has a CPU that identifies it as an AS/400.

Peripherals, the input/output devices that are part of the computer system, are linked to the CPU, which controls their operation. Because of the wide variety of hardware available, users are free to set up, or configure, a computer system with the type of input, output, and storage devices that will satisfy their specific needs. For example, one system may be configured with three printers and two disk drives, whereas another may need ten printers and five disk drives. Hardware linked to a CPU can be obtained from the computer manufacturer or from a manufacturer who specializes in producing just input/output (I/O) devices. A larger system may have dozens or even hundreds of input/output devices. A PC is limited to a relatively small number of such devices depending on the number of I/O connections, or **ports,** it has.

The CPU can be linked to peripherals in two ways: (1) by cable if the devices are in the same physical location as the CPU and (2) by communication facilities such as telephone lines if the I/O devices are not at the same local site as the processor.

---

**OPERATIONS TYPICALLY PERFORMED BY A CPU**

1. CPUs control the reading of programs and input files.
   a. The CPU activates input units to read programs and data.
   b. The CPU controls the transmission of program and data files from secondary storage to main memory (primary storage).
2. CPUs process data according to the instructions in a program.
   a. Data can be operated on arithmetically—numbers can be added, subtracted, multiplied, and divided.
   b. Logical tests can be performed on data (e.g., comparing the contents of two fields) to determine a course of action.
   c. Data can be transmitted or copied from one area of primary storage to another.
3. CPUs control the creation of output. The CPU activates an output unit and controls the transmission of outgoing information to that unit.

---

Although CPUs for all types of computers have become much more sophisticated in recent years, the basic operations they perform have remained fairly constant.

Because all computer operations are under the control of the CPU, it is often referred to as either "the brains" of a computer or "the heart" of a computer. Different perspectives about life affect the analogies we use—we prefer to call the CPU the "heart" of the computer! Now let us look at the CPU in detail.

A CPU has the following functions:

1. The CPU interfaces with main memory for storing data and programs.
2. The CPU has a **control unit** that controls each operation.
3. A CPU has an **arithmetic/logic unit (ALU)** that performs arithmetic and comparison operations.

Most often, main memory is physically separate from the CPU, but is on the same circuit board. The control unit and the arithmetic/logic unit of the CPU interface directly with main memory.

Most computers use **integrated circuits,** also called **chips,** for their CPUs and main memory. A chip is approximately 1/16- to 1/2-inch square and about 1/30 of an inch thick. It can hold from a few dozen to millions of electronic components such as transistors and resistors. A single chip or series of chips no bigger than a child's fingernail can contain all of a computer's memory and CPU components. See Figure 4.1.

The CPU of a PC along with main memory is typically contained on a single board called a **microprocessor,** which consists of a series of chips. Figure 4.2 shows an enlarged schematic of a microprocessor chip to give you a sense of the complexity of the circuitry. The CPU of larger systems is stored on a series of boards called processors. We will discuss chips in more detail later in this chapter.

Chips for all types of computers are made from silicon, a sand found in quartz rocks. Silicon itself is considered a semiconductor, which means it is a poor conductor of electricity. A thin sliver of silicon on a chip is coated with an electromagnetic emulsion that is etched in a way that leaves electrical-conducting material behind in paths that form circuits. Silicon chips carry out many operations very quickly; for example, they store and retrieve data, perform calculations, and compare numbers—all in fractions of a second.

*The processor unit of a computer contains two components: the central processing unit (CPU) and main memory. The CPU includes the control unit and the arithmetic/logic unit. Processors for PCs are called microprocessors.*

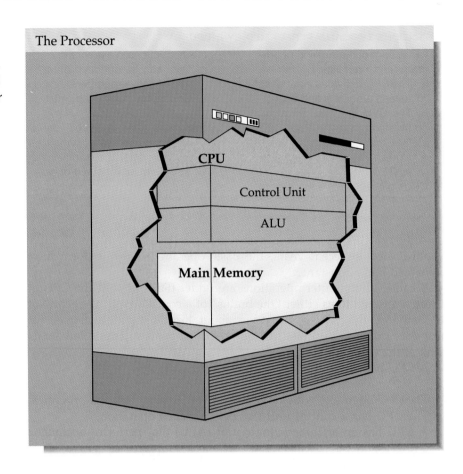

**Figure 4.1** *A chip is a tiny piece of silicon that can consist of millions of electronic elements.*

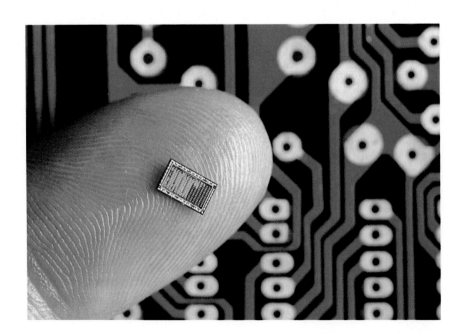

## LOOKING BACK

### TED HOFF: THE HISTORY OF THE MICROPROCESSOR

In 1969, a small Japanese firm called Busicom contracted with Intel, then a small California firm, to build an ordinary calculator that could be programmed. The task fell to Marcian E. (Ted) Hoff. Hoff did more than computerize a calculator. He developed the Intel 4004 chip, which became known as the first general-purpose microprocessor, or "computer on a chip." Intel later became the leading producer of microprocessor chips. In 1982, *U.S. News and World Report* listed 12 Milestones of American Technology. Along with the light bulb, the telephone, the airplane and others, Ted Hoff's microprocessor made the list.

*Ted Hoff developed the first general-purpose microprocessor chip.*

*The Intel 4004—the first computer on a chip.*

(a)

(b)

*Figure 4.2* (a) *A 486 microprocessor chip.* (b) *An enlargement of a microprocessor for the 80486 family of computers. This microprocessor consists of 1.2 million transistors.*

The CPU controls the reading of data into primary storage, the processing of data, and the writing of data from primary storage. Because access to primary storage is controlled by the CPU, we consider some of its features here.

## ▶ Primary Storage or Main Memory

Data and instructions are stored as a series of characters in a computer where a **character** can be a letter, digit, or symbol. Each character is stored in a single storage position of main memory. The storage position is called a byte.

The total primary storage, or number of bytes in main memory, is referred to as the computer's memory size. The primary storage capacity, or main memory, of a computer depends on its category. A supercomputer, for example, has a greater memory size than a mainframe. Similarly, micros have a smaller storage capacity than more powerful computers.

Computer memory sizes are measured as follows:

> Measuring Memory Sizes
> Kilobyte (K) = 1000 (one thousand) bytes
> Megabyte (MB) = 1,000,000 (one million) bytes
> Gigabyte (GB) = 1,000,000,000 (one billion) bytes
> Terabyte (TB) = 1,000,000,000,000 (one trillion) bytes

You may wonder why the main memory of larger computers needs to be so large. It is not only because programs and files are often sizable. Another reason is that most computers are capable of running more than one user program at a given time; this increases the need for very large storage capacities.

Sometimes a computer's primary storage needs to be increased; that is, what was originally considered to be sufficient memory turns out to be inadequate. In such cases, **memory boards** can be added to increase a computer's storage capacity. Each computer type has a range of memory sizes so that it can be configured with one size memory to which storage can be added, up to some established limit.

The main memory of a computer that uses integrated circuits is said to be **volatile,** which means that its contents are lost if the computer loses power or is turned off. That is one reason why data and programs must be saved after processing on an auxiliary storage medium such as disk that is **nonvolatile.**

**TYPICAL MEMORY SIZES**

| | |
|---|---|
| Micros | From 640 K to 16 MB+ |
| Minis/midranges | From hundreds of megabytes to gigabytes |
| Mainframes | From hundreds of megabytes to hundreds of gigabytes |
| Supercomputers | From hundreds of gigabytes to terabytes |

There are two forms of main memory: random-access memory (RAM) and read-only memory (ROM).

## RANDOM-ACCESS MEMORY (RAM)

**Random-access memory (RAM)** is the part of primary storage that is used to store programs and data during processing. The capacity of the computer's memory determines the number and size of programs and data that can be operated on at a given time. When the user quits the application, the memory it took up becomes available for new work.

The term *random-access,* when applied to memory, means that the control unit accesses data directly without the need to search through each storage location in sequence. The speed with which a CPU accesses data from RAM is called the **access rate,** and the speed with which it transfers data into and out of RAM is called the **transfer rate.** We will see that these speeds are two criteria used to evaluate the processing power of a CPU.

## READ-ONLY MEMORY (ROM)

Not all memory in a computer is volatile. When you turn your computer on or load a software program into it, your computer must have some preset instructions available to tell it what to do. These permanent, non-volatile instructions are programmed into **read-only memory (ROM).** Another name for chips that contain ROM is **firmware.** ROM chips have many functions. For example, they provide commands that indicate what the CPU should do when the power is turned on, they check to see that the cable to the printer is connected, and they tell the control unit what each key on the keyboard means. User instructions, on the other hand, are typically stored in RAM, not ROM. See Figure 4.3.

*Figure 4.3 Each RAM chip for PCs has a storage capacity typically in the 1 to 16+ MB range. These are, from left to right, a 16 MB, 4MB, and 1 MB chip.*

Any program, however, *could* be stored in ROM. This would save time because you would not need to load the program by moving disks in and out of the system. ROM, however, tends to be more expensive than the volatile memory chips used for primary storage. In addition, software vendors would have to create new chip circuitry and new ROM chips every time they updated their programs, and users would have to open the computer system's chassis, or case, and replace chips when they wanted to update their programs. Despite these disadvantages, many smaller computers do have some software on ROM. Palmtops, for example, often have word processing and spreadsheet packages on ROM for ease of access.

**PROM, EPROM, EEPROM.** ROM itself has three subcategories called PROM, EPROM, and EEPROM (see Figure 4.4). Each can be custom-made or preprogrammed for the user by the computer manufacturer or software developer. Each can contain programs, as we have seen, or data. For example, an insurance company might have actuarial tables in ROM and an accounting firm might have tax data in ROM.

*Figure 4.4 An EPROM memory chip nestled between a piece of germanium and a piece of silicon from which it is made. Exposing the transparent quartz crystal's "window" to ultraviolet rays will erase the chip's contents so it can be reprogrammed if necessary. ROM, PROM, EPROM, and EEPROM chips resemble each other—but only the latter two have a window for erasing.*

IN A

**TYPES OF ROM**

| PROM | Programmable read-only memory |
| EPROM | Erasable programmable read-only memory |
| EEPROM | Electronically erasable programmable read-only memory |

PROM means *programmable read-only memory*. PROM chips contain instructions and data that cannot be easily changed.

*Erasable programmable read-only memory* (EPROM) chips enable changes to be made to the data or instructions in ROM. To change the contents of EPROM chips, the chips must be removed from the computer. EPROM chips have a transparent quartz crystal covering the circuitry. Subjecting this "window" to ultraviolet rays erases the contents. After the contents of the EPROM chip have been erased, the chips can be reprogrammed and replaced.

*Electronically erasable programmable read-only memory* (EEPROM) is the most advanced form of ROM. Changes can be made to the chips under software control. Thus, there is no need to remove the chips. EEPROM is the most useful form of ROM, but it is also, not surprisingly, the most expensive. It is widely used in point-of-sale systems in which prices and taxes are recorded in read-only memory. When necessary, the information can be re-recorded using a special software package.

We next consider the two main units of the CPU, the arithmetic/logic unit and the control unit, and how registers are used in each.

**CRITICAL THINKING**

What are the advantages and disadvantages of including software on ROM in portable PCs? Hint: Think about factors like weight, compactness, and ease of use.

## ▶ The Arithmetic/Logic Unit

The arithmetic/logic unit (ALU) is the section of the CPU that actually operates on data. All arithmetic and logic operations are executed in the ALU. Arithmetic includes the basic operations of addition, subtraction, multiplication, and division. Logical operations are used to compare two items of data to determine if one is larger than, equal to, or smaller than the other.

## ▶ The Control Unit

The control unit handles the transmission of data into and out of the CPU and supervises its overall operations. Transmission between the control unit, ALU, and main memory occurs on a special electronic path called a **bus.** See Figure 4.5. The speed of a bus and the number of characters that it can handle during a processing cycle are factors that affect the overall speed and efficiency of the computer.

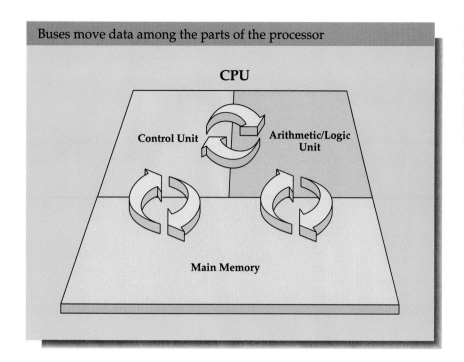

Buses move data among the parts of the processor

**CPU**

Control Unit

Arithmetic/Logic Unit

Main Memory

*Figure 4.5 The bus is an electronic path along which data is transmitted between the main memory and the components of the CPU—the control unit and the ALU. A computer's processing power is dependent on the speed of the bus and the number of characters it can handle in a processing cycle.*

## ▶ Registers and Machine Cycles

To enhance the processing capability of a CPU, the ALU and control unit contain special storage areas called **registers.** Their function is to hold instructions, data values, and main memory addresses of both the instructions and data. There are four basic types of registers.

1. Instruction register—high speed circuits within the control unit that hold an instruction to be executed.
2. Address register—high speed circuits within the control unit that hold the address of data to be processed or of the next instruction to be executed.
3. Storage register—high-speed circuits most often in the ALU that temporarily store data retrieved from main memory prior to processing.
4. Accumulator—high-speed circuits most often in the ALU that temporarily store the results of arithmetic and logic operations.

The processing of a single instruction occurs during a **machine cycle.** It involves accessing data from main memory, using registers in the control unit and ALU to operate on that data, and transmitting results back to main memory. A machine cycle consists of two parts: an **instruction cycle** during which the control unit fetches the instruction from primary storage and prepares it for processing, and the **execution cycle** during which an instruction is actually executed and results produced. See Figure 4.6.

Several basic operations are performed during the instruction cycle.

*Figure 4.6* *A machine cycle consists of two parts: an instruction cycle and an execution cycle.*

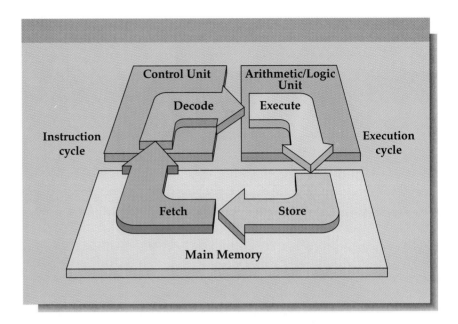

- The control unit fetches the instruction from main memory.
- The control unit interprets or decodes the instruction.
- The control unit places the part of the instruction that indicates the operation to be performed in the instruction register and places the part of the instruction that indicates where the corresponding data is located in the address register.

The basic operations performed during the execution cycle are as follows:

- Using information in the address register, the control unit retrieves the data from main memory and places it in the storage register.
- Using the information in the instruction register, the control unit instructs the ALU to perform the required operation.
- The result of the operation is stored in an accumulator and then transmitted back to main memory.

As you can see, many operations are performed during a machine cycle, but because computers are so powerful, a machine cycle can be as fast as a nanosecond or microsecond.

## ▶ SELF-TEST

1. The _____ is the CPU component that manages the processing of data.
2. Logical operations such as the comparison of two numbers are performed by the _____.
3. (T or F) During processing, data or instructions are held in temporary storage areas called registers.
4. (T or F) RAM is volatile and ROM is nonvolatile.
5. The CPU of a microcomputer together with main memory is called a _____.

Solutions

1. control unit
2. arithmetic/logic unit (ALU)
3. T

4. T
5. microprocessor

## How the CPU Represents Data    4.2

We have seen how data is stored and processed by a computer system. In this section, we consider how data is actually represented within the computer. Computers are capable of storing data and instructions in primary storage as characters, but each character must be converted into a form that permits high-speed processing.

When we refer to the electronic computers of today we usually mean **digital computers,** that is, computers that process data in discrete form as countable numbers. Another category of computers is analog computers; they process entities related to speed, height, or length such as voltage fluctuations or frequencies. A thermostat, for example, is a simple analog computer. In this text we concentrate on digital computers.

All digital computers use some variation of the **binary numbering system** for representing characters, where a character is defined as a letter, digit, or special symbol. Our decimal system is based on 10 digits (0–9); in contrast, the binary numbering system has only *two* digits: 0 and 1. This system is ideal for computer processing because the 1 is used to denote the presence of an electrical pulse or signal in the computer circuitry, and a 0 is used to denote the absence of such a signal. Figure 4.7 illustrates the way digital computers use the binary numbering system.

We begin by considering how binary and decimal numbers can be converted from one to the other. This will help you understand how computers convert data to binary form and then back again. We also look at

How is data actually stored in a computer?

*Figure 4.7* How a computer uses the binary numbering system. 0 is an off state and 1 is an on state.

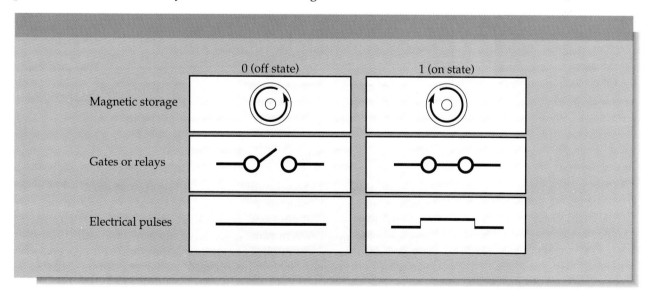

the way the computer actually stores characters internally using a form of binary representation.

## ▶ From Binary to Decimal

Most numbering systems are called positional, because the physical location, or position, of a digit within the number determines the value. For example, in a positional numbering system the number 23 has a different value than the number 32 even though the digits are the same. In positional numbering systems, the *place value* is critical.

Recall that the decimal (base 10) system has the following positional values:

| | | | | |
|---|---|---|---|---|
| $10^3$ | $10^2$ | $10^1$ | $10^0$ | Exponential value of the position |
| 1000 | 100 | 10 | 1 | Decimal value of the position |

A number 1 in the second (10s position) and a 0 in the units position (10) is the number following 9. That is, after we reach 9, there are no more single digits; we proceed to the next position, the 10s position, and initialize or reset the units position with 0. So 10 is the decimal number following 9. In the base 10 system, each position has a value that is a factor of 10. The first position has a value of $10^0$, or 1; the second has a value of $10^1$, or 10; the seventh position would have a value of $10^6$, or 1,000,000, and so on.

The binary numbering system has a base of 2. Thus each position has a place value that is a factor of 2. We have:

| | | | | |
|---|---|---|---|---|
| $2^4$ | $2^3$ | $2^2$ | $2^1$ | $2^0$ | Value of the position expressed as an exponent |
| 16 | 8 | 4 | 2 | 1 | Decimal value of the position |

Any number raised to the zero power is 1; therefore, the units position has a place value of $2^0$, or 1. The adjacent position has a value of $2^1$, or 2 (any number raised to the first power is the number itself). The third position has a value of $2^2$ or $2 \times 2$, which is equal to 4; and so on.

In the binary numbering system, we have only two digits, 0 and 1. To represent the number 2 in binary, we have already, in effect, run out of digits; hence we must initialize the units position to 0 and proceed with the position to the left of the units position—the 2s position. That is, 10 in binary is 2 in decimal.

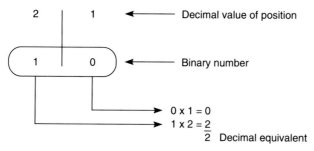

We say, then, that $10_2$ (10 in base 2) $= 2_{10}$ (2 in base 10). In this illustration the subscript represents the base. A 3 in base 2 would be 11; to represent a 4 we must initialize the two rightmost positions and place a 1 in the leftmost or 4s position. Thus, 100 in binary is a 4 in decimal. A 5 would be 101. Notice that the sequence is 0, 1, then proceed to the next position and initialize the previous one (10, 11, 100, and so on):

| Binary | Decimal |
|--------|---------|
| 0 | 0 |
| 1 | 1 |
| 10 | 2 |
| 11 | 3 |
| 100 | 4 |
| 101 | 5 |
| 110 | 6 |
| 111 | 7 |
| 1000 | 8 |
| 1001 | 9 |
| 1010 | 10 |
| 1011 | 11 |
| 1100 | 12 |
| 1101 | 13 |
| 1110 | 14 |
| 1111 | 15 |
| . | . |
| . | . |
| . | . |

Using the binary numbering system, the computer can represent any decimal number with a series of on-off circuits; on is represented by a binary 1 and off is represented by a binary 0.

## DECIMAL EQUIVALENTS OF BINARY NUMBERS

All positional numbering systems have similar structures. To obtain the decimal equivalent of a number in any base, multiply each digit by its positional value and add the results.

### Example 1

$1001_2 = (?)_{10}$.

Find the decimal equivalent of 1001 in binary (represented as $1001_2$), where the subscript denotes the base.

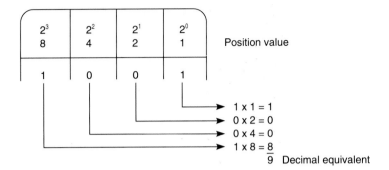

Thus, $1001_2 = 9_{10}$. We can simplify this calculation by eliminating all multiplications where 0 is a factor since the product of each of these multiplications is 0. We have:

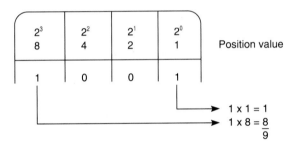

In short, the binary digit with a positional value of 8 and the binary digit with a positional value of 1 are on; the others are off. That is, the 8 bit and the 1 bit are on; **bit** is an abbreviation for *binary digit*.

### Example 2

$1110_2 = (?)_{10}$.

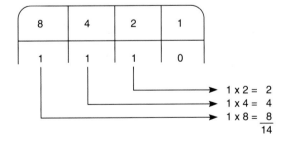

Solution: $14_{10}$

### Example 3

$11101_2 = (?)_{10}$.

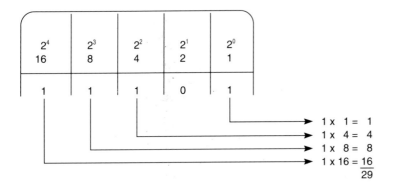

$$1 \times 1 = 1$$
$$1 \times 4 = 4$$
$$1 \times 8 = 8$$
$$1 \times 16 = \underline{16}$$
$$29$$

Solution: $29_{10}$

Thus far we have focused on the way in which binary numbers are converted into decimal numbers. Next, we learn how to determine the binary equivalent of a decimal number.

## BINARY EQUIVALENTS OF DECIMAL NUMBERS

Computers generally represent numeric data in binary form or some variation of this form where digits are indicated by a series of on-off switches or integrated circuits. Keep in mind that numeric data is entered as input in standard decimal form and then converted *by the computer itself* into binary form for processing. Before the processed data is produced as output information, it is again converted by the computer to decimal form unless, for some reason, binary output is preferred.

Converting decimal numbers to binary form is a relatively simple task. We merely use the positional values of binary numbers to find the right combination of digits.

**CONVERSION**

1. Determine the positional, or place, value of each digit.
2. Add the place values for all positions that contain a 1.

### Example 1

$10_{10} = (?)_2.$

In this example we want to determine what combination of 1, 2, 4, 8, 16, 32, . . . will equal 10. First, we do not need to use more than four binary digits to represent $10_{10}$ (10 in base 10), since the fifth positional value is $2^4$, or 16, which is itself greater than $10_{10}$. Hence, we must determine what combination of 8, 4, 2, 1 will equal 10.

There is only one such combination. The numbers $8 + 2 = 10$. Thus our binary equivalent is:

| 8 | 4 | 2 | 1 |
|---|---|---|---|
| 1 | 0 | 1 | 0 |

In order to represent the decimal number 10 in binary form, the 8 bit and the 2 bit are on while the others are off. Thus, $10_{10} = 1010_2$.

Example 2

$(14)_{10} = (?)_2$.

Here again we use four binary digits since the next position has value 16, which exceeds the required quantity. Again, we must determine what combination of 8, 4, 2, 1 will produce 14. There is only one such combination: the 8, 4, 2 bits are on $(8 + 4 + 2 = 14)$, while the 1 bit is off. Thus, $(14)_{10} = (1110)_2$.

Example 3

$(23)_{10} = (?)_2$.

Now we must use some combination of the numbers 16, 8, 4, 2, 1 that will produce 23. That is, we must determine which of these bits are on. The 16 bit must be on, since the 8, 4, 2, 1 bits can produce a maximum decimal number of 15. This means that the 16 bit must be on to obtain a number larger than 15. The 8 bit is off since the 16 bit and the 8 bit combination produces 24, which exceeds the required number. Thus, the 16, 4, 2, 1, bits are on and only the 8 bit is off. We have, then, $(23)_{10} = (10111)_2$.

## ▶ Bits, Bytes, and Words

We have just seen that through a combination of on-off pulses it is possible to represent any decimal digit. These on-off pulses are called bits (for *binary digit*).

Recall that each storage position in main memory is called a byte. If each byte contained four digit bits, representing the decimal numbers 8-4-2-1, it would be possible to represent any of the decimal digits 0 to 9. That is, with 8-4-2-1 we can denote the decimal digits 0 to 9 as well as numbers 10 to 15 (see Figure 4.8). In short, 4 bits in each byte are used to designate a single decimal digit. An "on" bit means that an electrical current is present and an "off" bit means that no current is present.

But what about the representation of alphabetic characters or special symbols? How can they be depicted using binary digits? To represent these characters, the computer frequently uses an 8-bit code with *four zone bits* as well as *four digit bits:*

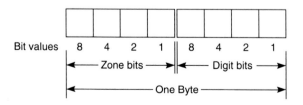

The four leftmost bits are called zone bits. The four rightmost bits are called digit bits.

The smallest unit of data in a computer code is the bit. A group of 8 bits is called a byte. Typically, one character is represented in 1 byte. A

| Decimal Digit | BITS | | | |
|---|---|---|---|---|
| | 8 | 4 | 2 | 1 |
| 0 | 0 | 0 | 0 | 0 |
| 1 | 0 | 0 | 0 | 1 |
| 2 | 0 | 0 | 1 | 0 |
| 3 | 0 | 0 | 1 | 1 |
| 4 | 0 | 1 | 0 | 0 |
| 5 | 0 | 1 | 0 | 1 |
| 6 | 0 | 1 | 1 | 0 |
| 7 | 0 | 1 | 1 | 1 |
| 8 | 1 | 0 | 0 | 0 |
| 9 | 1 | 0 | 0 | 1 |
| 10 | 1 | 0 | 1 | 0 |
| 11 | 1 | 0 | 1 | 1 |
| 12 | 1 | 1 | 0 | 0 |
| 13 | 1 | 1 | 0 | 1 |
| 14 | 1 | 1 | 1 | 0 |
| 15 | 1 | 1 | 1 | 1 |

**Figure 4.8** *The binary equivalents of decimal digits 0 to 15.*

group of consecutive bytes is a **word,** the term for a unit of data that can be processed at one time. The more bytes in a computer's word, the faster it can process data. A computer with a word size of 32 bits can process 4 bytes as a unit, while a faster 64-bit computer can process twice as many bytes as a unit.

Figure 4.9 illustrates the relationship of the three binary units—bit,

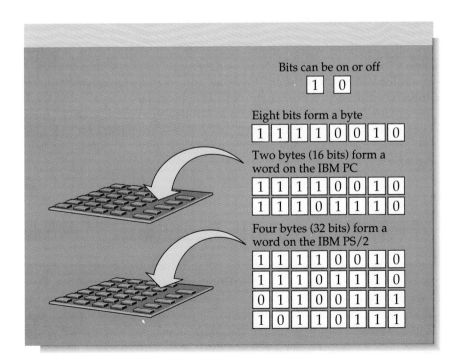

**Figure 4.9** *Eight bits make up one byte, which can represent a character.*

byte, and word. The term *word* in this context should not be confused with its usual meaning. Here, it is a unit of data that corresponds to the number of bits that can be transferred to a register in the CPU's control unit during a single operation. The number of bytes in a word varies from system to system. As noted, the larger the word size, the faster the computer. Word sizes range from 8, 16, 32, 64, to 128 bits. Older, smaller micros have 8-bit word sizes (1 byte); newer micros have either 16-bit (2 bytes) or 32-bit (4 bytes) word sizes. Larger systems have word sizes from 64 to 128 bits.

## ▶ EBCDIC and ASCII

We consider now the two most frequently used computer codes, EBCDIC and ASCII, both of which make use of binary representation. One computer code, **EBCDIC,** which stands for *Extended Binary Coded Decimal Interchange Code* and is pronounced *eb-ce-dick,* is commonly used to represent letters, digits, and special symbols. In EBCDIC, each storage position or byte consists of eight data bits; four are used to specify the zone and four are used to specify the digit.

The four zone bits are used to indicate whether a character is a letter, unsigned number, positive number, negative number, or special character. The four digit bits are used to represent the numbers 0 to 9. For example, 1111 in the zone bits designates a character as an unsigned number; 1100 in the zone bits indicates that the character will be one of the uppercase letters A through I. If 1100 appears in the four zone bits, the digit bits then will indicate which specific letter from A through I is being represented. The digit bits can represent 0 through 9 as 0000, 0001, 0010, 0011, . . . 0101. Figure 4.10 illustrates the EBCDIC code.

EBCDIC is not the only computer code, although it is used by many computers, especially IBM mainframes and their compatibles. **ASCII** is another common computer code widely used by most micros. ASCII stands for *American Standard Code for Information Interchange* and is pronounced *ass-key.* Some computers and terminals use a 7-bit ASCII code; others use an 8-bit ASCII code similar to EBCDIC. These three codes—EBCDIC, 8-bit ASCII, and 7-bit ASCII—are illustrated in Figure 4.11. In all the codes, combinations of binary digits 0 and 1 represent characters.

## ▶ Error Checking with Parity Bits

During processing, data is constantly being transmitted from one part of the computer to another and often from one computer to another. Data is transmitted as electronic impulses, some in the on state and some in the off state, so slight irregularities in the electrical power supply occasionally cause errors to enter the stream of data. One way to verify that

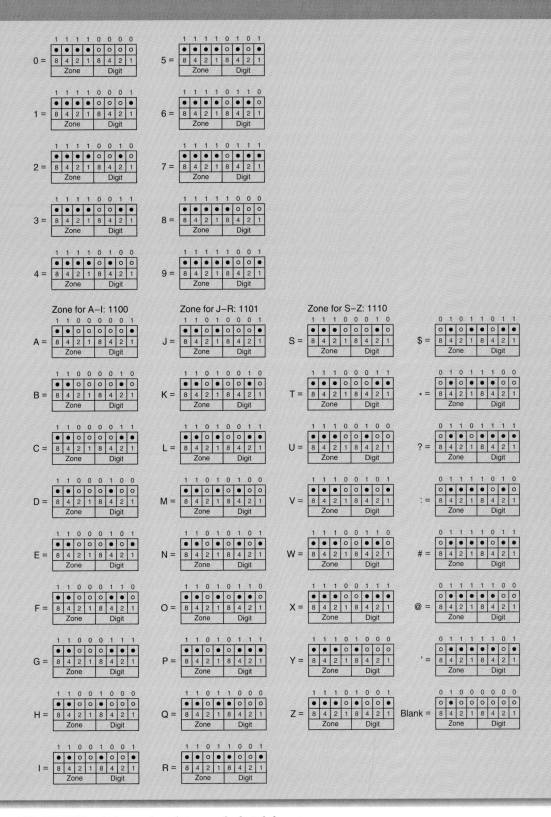

***Figure 4.10*** *The EBCDIC code for numbers, letters, and selected characters.*

*Figure 4.11* *The bit configurations of the EBCDIC, 8-bit ASCII, and 7-bit ASCII codes.*

| Character | EBCDIC | 8-bit ASCII | 7-bit ASCII | Character |
|---|---|---|---|---|
| 0 | 1111 0000 | 0101 0000 | 011 0000 | 0 |
| 1 | 1111 0001 | 0101 0001 | 011 0001 | 1 |
| 2 | 1111 0010 | 0101 0010 | 011 0010 | 2 |
| 3 | 1111 0011 | 0101 0011 | 011 0011 | 3 |
| 4 | 1111 0100 | 0101 0100 | 011 0100 | 4 |
| 5 | 1111 0101 | 0101 0101 | 011 0101 | 5 |
| 6 | 1111 0110 | 0101 0110 | 011 0110 | 6 |
| 7 | 1111 0111 | 0101 0111 | 011 0111 | 7 |
| 8 | 1111 1000 | 0101 1000 | 011 1000 | 8 |
| 9 | 1111 1001 | 0101 1001 | 011 1001 | 9 |
| A | 1100 0001 | 1010 0001 | 100 0001 | A |
| B | 1100 0010 | 1010 0010 | 100 0010 | B |
| C | 1100 0011 | 1010 0011 | 100 0011 | C |
| D | 1100 0100 | 1010 0100 | 100 0100 | D |
| E | 1100 0101 | 1010 0101 | 100 0101 | E |
| F | 1100 0110 | 1010 0110 | 100 0110 | F |
| G | 1100 0111 | 1010 0111 | 100 0111 | G |
| H | 1100 1000 | 1010 1000 | 100 1000 | H |
| I | 1100 1001 | 1010 1001 | 100 1001 | I |
| J | 1101 0001 | 1010 1010 | 100 1010 | J |
| K | 1101 0010 | 1010 1011 | 100 1011 | K |
| L | 1101 0011 | 1010 1100 | 100 1100 | L |
| M | 1101 0100 | 1010 1101 | 100 1101 | M |
| N | 1101 0101 | 1010 1110 | 100 1110 | N |
| O | 1101 0110 | 1010 1111 | 100 1111 | O |
| P | 1101 0111 | 1011 0000 | 101 0000 | P |
| Q | 1101 1000 | 1011 0001 | 101 0001 | Q |
| R | 1101 1001 | 1011 0010 | 101 0010 | R |
| S | 1110 0010 | 1011 0011 | 101 0011 | S |
| T | 1110 0011 | 1011 0100 | 101 0100 | T |
| U | 1110 0100 | 1011 0101 | 101 0101 | U |
| V | 1110 0101 | 1011 0110 | 101 0110 | V |
| W | 1110 0110 | 1011 0111 | 101 0111 | W |
| X | 1110 0111 | 1011 1000 | 101 1000 | X |
| Y | 1110 1000 | 1011 1001 | 101 1001 | Y |
| Z | 1110 1001 | 1011 1010 | 101 1010 | Z |

data has been accurately transmitted would be to transmit it twice and compare the two transmissions, but that would double processing time and costs. Using a **parity bit** is an alternative solution to detecting transmission errors.

The parity bit is a single bit attached to each byte; the computer code itself determines whether the parity bit is a 0 or a 1. There are even-parity

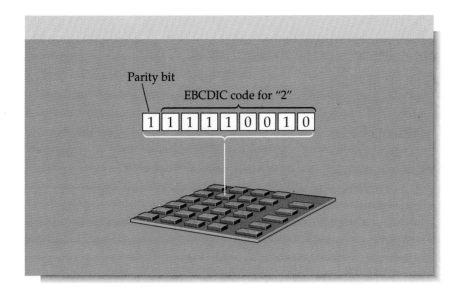

Parity bit

EBCDIC code for "2"

1 1 1 1 1 0 0 1 0

*Figure 4.12 Parity bits are added to each byte to keep the number of on bits even (as shown here) or odd, depending on whether you use an even or odd parity computer.*

and odd-parity computers. In **even-parity** computers, an even number of bits must always be on at any given time; in **odd-parity** computers, an odd number of bits must always be on. With even-parity computers, if the number of 1 bits in any byte is odd, the parity bit is automatically turned on or set to 1 so that there is always an even number of 1 bits on. Also, in an even-parity computer, if the number of 1 bits is even, the parity bit is set to 0. This means that when all the 1 bits are added up, there is always an even number of them. Figure 4.12 shows the EBCDIC code for the number 2, including the parity bit for even-parity computers.

When a transmission is sent to a computer that uses even parity to do error checking, the receiving computer checks to see that there are always an even number of 1, or on, bits. If a byte contains an odd number of on bits, it requests retransmission. Computers using odd parity work in exactly the same way except that the parity bit is used to ensure an odd number of 1 bits.

Parity checking is guaranteed to detect an error only if just one bit is transmitted incorrectly. If, however, 2 bits were transmitted incorrectly, the error would not be detected, because the number of 1 bits would still be even for even-parity computers and odd for odd-parity computers. Although the chance for double transmission errors is very remote, some systems do protect against it. To guard against the possibility of multiple errors, a longitudinal parity can be used. With this technique, a check byte is added to the end of each record or stream of data that is transmitted. Each bit of the check byte is used to preserve the appropriate parity of every bit position in each byte of the record.

Parity checking is most often used to detect errors not to correct them. A number of encoding schemes are now available that both detect and correct single or multiple errors when large volumes of data are transmitted over communications lines. Because they are much more elaborate than parity checks, these encoding schemes require additional processing

IN A

NUT SHELL

**SUMMARY: DATA REPRESENTATION**

1. Computers use some form of the binary numbering system.
   a. Combinations of 0s and 1s represent all characters.
   b. 0 = off state.
   c. 1 = on state.
2. Computers commonly use 8 bits (binary digits) to represent each character.
   a. Each storage position or byte consists of 8 bits: 4 bits for a zone and 4 bits for a digit (8-4-2-1).
   b. An additional parity bit may be used to minimize data transmission errors.
3. Two computer codes are the most common.
   a. EBCDIC—Extended Binary Coded Decimal Interchange Code
   b. ASCII—American Standard Code for Information Interchange (may be a 7- or 8-bit code)

at the receiving end. Their major use is for the long-distance transmission of data to a site where retransmission would be difficult—the transmission of data to a space probe, for example.

Thus far we have described the technical detail of data transmission. Next (and you may give thanks), we will take a look at how data is processed at the operating level.

### ▶ SELF-TEST

1. All computers use some variation of the _____ numbering system to represent data.
2. A character of data is _____.
3. The word *bit* stands for _____.
4. Each _____ of storage holds one character of data.
5. The two most commonly used computer codes are _____ and _____.
6. A _____ bit is used in computer codes for error checking.

Solutions

1. binary
2. a letter, digit, or special symbol
3. binary digit
4. byte
5. ASCII; EBCDIC
6. parity

## 4.3    COMPUTER ARCHITECTURE

One of the most important ways to compare computer systems is to look at processing power—what technology does a computer use to process data and how fast can it operate? Several measurements are used to

**COMPUTING APPLICATION**

If current trends continue, as they are expected to, the cost of primary storage for computer systems will continue to decline. In other words, the cost of memory decreases over time while a CPU's storage capacity goes up, resulting in more power for your money.

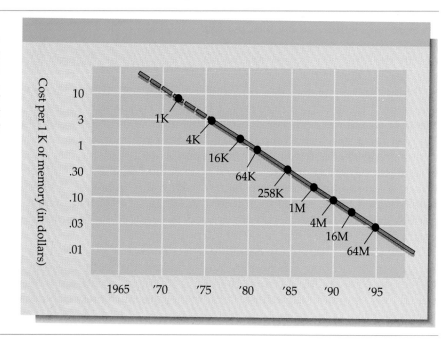

*This graph shows how the cost of memory is declining over time while the chip capacity is increasing.*

define processing power, some of which we discussed in Chapter 2. A relatively small difference in a computer's processing speed may significantly reduce execution time, particularly if the computer is being used for reading and writing many large-volume files.

The following sections describe some of the criteria used for evaluating computer **architecture,** that is, the technology used for processing data. Our emphasis is on microcomputer architecture, but, in general, the same criteria apply to larger computer systems. Keep in mind that differences in types of computers are really differences in power, speed, and size.

## ▶ Chip Technology

The Apple and Macintosh computers use Motorola 68000 microprocessor chips whereas the IBM micros and their compatibles use Intel chips. As we have seen, both main memory and the CPU consist of integrated circuits, or chips. Motorola and Intel are leading manufacturers of high-speed microprocessor or CPU chips that consist of millions of circuits.

The original IBM PC used the 8086 Intel chip; that was followed by the 8088 chip used in later IBM PCs and their compatibles. Computers with 80286 chips are newer, faster, and more efficient; these chips are used in IBM ATs and their compatibles. The IBM PS/2 family of computers and their compatibles also use, on the low end, the 80286 chip, often abbreviated as the "286" chip. In the mid-range, they use 80386 chips, and on the higher end they use 80486 or 80586 chips. Most Intel-based computers today use 80386, 80486, or 80586 chips.

The IBM-Apple alliance is likely to lead to new reduced-instruction set (RISC) chips for use in newer, high-powered workstations.

## ▶ Clock Speed

Every CPU has a clock that generates clock pulses which synchronize the computer's operations. Processing actions occur at each "tick" of the electronic clock. The speed of the clock determines the speed at which the

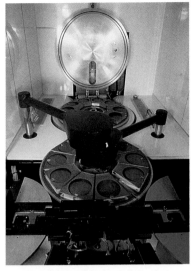

*Semiconductor chip manufacturing device.*

*Inspecting wafers etched with new chips at a Motorola manufacturing plant.*

IN A
NUT
SHELL

**INTEL CHIP DEVELOPMENT**

| Processor | Date Manufactured | Word Size | Instructions per Second | PC Model |
|---|---|---|---|---|
| 8086 | 1974 | 16 | 333,000 | Original PC and IBM clones |
| 8088 | 1978 | 8/16 | 333,000 | Later IBM PCs and XTs, the hard disk version of a PC |
| 80286 | 1982 | 16 | 2,000,000 (2 MIPS) | AT and IBM PS/2 Model 30 |
| 80386 | 1985 | 32 | 15,000,000 (15 MIPS) | PS/2 (Models 55, 60, 70) |
| 80486 | 1989 | 32 | 40,000,000 (40 MIPS) | Workstations and IBM PS/2 (Model 80 and up) |
| 80586 | 1992 | 32 | Up to 100,000,000 (100 MIPS) | Workstations |

## (a) Design features of various microprocessors

| Word size (bits) | Microprocessor chips | Maximum RAM | Sample Microcomputers |
|---|---|---|---|
| 8 (preceded 16- and 32-bit sizes) | Zilog Z-80A, Mostek 6502 | 640K | Radio Shack Personal Desktop, Sanyo MBC/250, Epson QX-10 Apple IIe, Atari 800, Commodore 64 |
| 16 | Intel 8088 (8 bit bus) | 1MB | IBM-PC, XT, Compaq Portable |
| | Intel 8086 | 1MB | Some IBM compatibles |
| | Intel 80286 | 16MB | IBM AT, ITT XTRA 286 |
| 32 | Motorola 68000 (16 bit bus) | 16MB | Radio Shack TRS-80 Model 16B, Corvus Concept, Apple Macintosh |
| | Motorola 68020 | 32MB | Macintosh II |
| | Intel 80386, Intel 80486 | 32MB | Compaq 380, IBM PS/2 Model 80, IBM PS/2 Model 70 A-21, IBM PS/2 Model 95 |

## (b) Clock speeds for sample micros

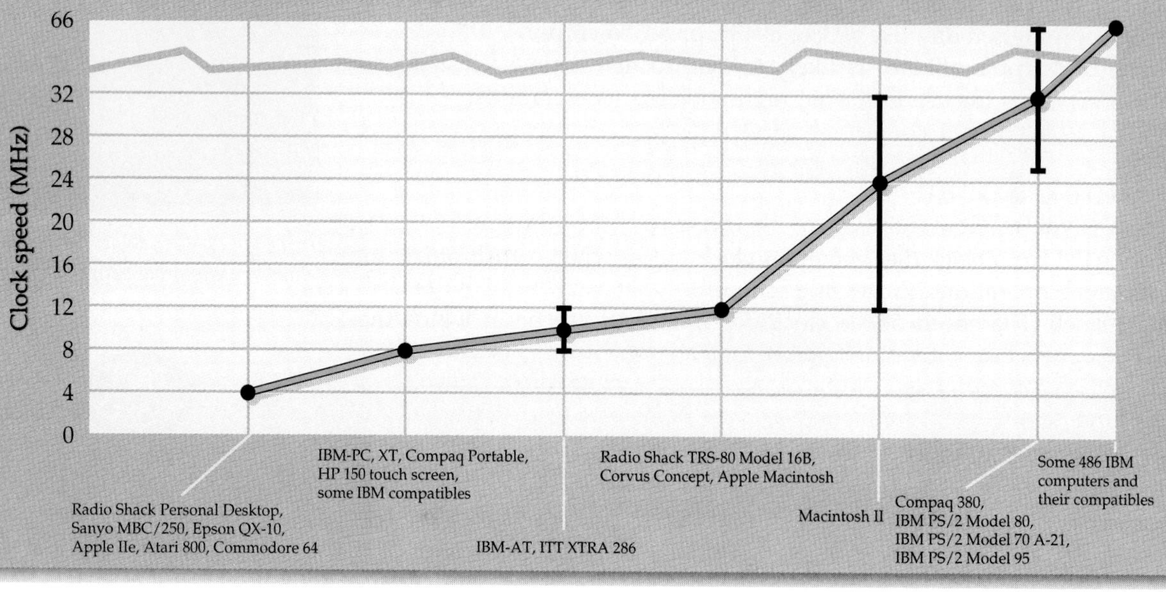

*Figure 4.13* Microprocessors are evaluated on a number of design features that affect speed and capacity. Some of the most critical factors are shown here, along with popular microcomputers that use each type of chip.

CPU can process data. Speed is measured in megahertz (MHz) where 1 MHz is a million pulses per second. Computers with higher clock speeds can process data faster than those with lower clock speeds. Notice in Figure 4.13 that the range in IBM systems varies from 8 MHz for the older IBM PC and IBM XT to 66 MHz or more for the PS/2 Model 95 and higher systems.

What factors affect the processing power of a computer?

## ▶ Processing Speed

Processing speed is the time required to perform operations in the CPU as well as the time required to access data in memory. Both the instruction cycle and the execution cycle determine processing speed. Processing speed is measured in microcomputers in microseconds, or millionths of a second. For example, the older IBM PC family can perform about 20+ million operations per second. Mainframes, minis, and newer PCs operate at speeds measured in nanoseconds, or billionths of a second. At the high end of the scale, processing speeds for supercomputers are measured in picoseconds, or trillionths of a second. The Cray-2 supercomputer can process data at hundreds of millions—or even trillions—of operations per second.

**Coprocessors** are special chips that can be added to or built into micros to speed up certain kinds of operations. One common type is the math coprocessor, which is used to increase the processing speed of mathematical operations for number-crunching applications such as statistical analysis. These are designated as 8087, 80287, or 80387 chips corresponding to the 8086, 80286, and 80386 chips. Many newer 80486 and 80586 chips have math processors built into them.

## ▶ Bus Technology and Word Size

Buses, as you recall, are the electronic tracks on which data moves from memory to the control unit and to the arithmetic/logic unit. The more bytes the bus can handle, the more data passes through and the greater the processing speed. Remember that 1 byte, which stores a character, is equal to 8 bits. Some computers have a word size that is larger than their bus size. A computer with a 32-bit word size, for example, but only a 16-bit bus size, is really limited to processing 16 bits at a time.

IN A

**MEASUREMENTS OF PROCESSING SPEEDS**

| | |
|---|---|
| Microsecond | Millionth of a second (measurement of speed of some microcomputers) |
| Nanosecond | Billionth of a second (measurement of speed of some mainframes and some micros) |
| Picosecond | Trillionth of a second (measurement of speed of some supercomputers) |

IN A

NUT SHELL

**THE M WORDS: MHz, MIPS, AND MEMORY IN REVIEW**

The most widely used measure of a microcomputer's CPU performance is the clock speed, which is measured in megahertz (MHz). One megahertz is a million ticks of a system's clock each second. A 4.77 MHz CPU such as the 8088 in the original IBM PC, for example, has a clock that ticks 4,770,000 times a second.

Most 8088 microcomputers, some of which are still used today, are faster—from 8 to 10 MHz. Man-

ufacturers of clones refer to computers with the faster clock speeds as "turbo" systems.

Note, however, that megahertz refers to processing time, not input/output time. Clock time, then, is not a complete measure of a computer's overall speed.

As we saw in Chapter 2, MIPS, which stands for *m*illions of *i*nstructions *per* *s*econd, is still another measurement of speed. A computer that has a speed of 200 MIPS can

process 200 million instructions per second. MIPS is often considered the most reliable measurement of computer speed. Most manufacturers of mainframes and some manufacturers of PCs use MIPS and nanoseconds to define the processing speed of their computers. PCs process data in the 5 to 100 MIPS range, and larger computers in the hundreds or thousands of MIPS range.

If CPU speed is too fast relative to the rest of the system, wait states may need to be inserted. They prevent the CPU from overwhelming the system by transmitting information faster than the other components can make use of it. A micro with "zero wait states" is a system that has been carefully balanced; that is, the entire computer system can keep up with the CPU.

The speed with which memory chips manipulate data is usually measured in nanoseconds. The time difference between consecutive accesses to memory is also measured in nanoseconds. In both cases, the *fewer* the nanoseconds the faster the chip. A 16-bit CPU with a 16-bit word size, for example, that has zero wait states using 100-nanosecond chips can store or retrieve 16 bits of data at a maximum speed of once every 100 nanoseconds.

## ▶ Main Circuit Boards and Expansion Slots

A microcomputer's microprocessor (CPU and main memory), battery-operated clock, and other circuits are interconnected on a main circuit board sometimes called the **motherboard** (note the sexism!). We prefer to call it a main circuit board. See Figure 4.14. Many micros have an open architecture, which means that the user is able to open the system's cabinet and add components to the motherboard or main circuit board. In such computers, this board has a series of **expansion slots** into which add-on units can be inserted. For example, an enhanced graphics adapter (EGA) board can be purchased and fitted into an expansion slot of the main circuit board of some computers. This greatly increases the graphics capability of the computer. Similarly, random-access memory expansion cards are widely available to increase the primary storage of micros that have an open architecture.

*Figure 4.14* *A main circuit board rests in the system unit, which also houses disk drives. The main circuit board contains the CPU, memory, and the circuitry necessary to process data. Add-on memory boards can be used to increase primary storage capacity.*

## ▶ MCA vs ISA and EISA: An Architectural Battle

Recall that IBM micros and their compatibles use Intel chips. Their bus architecture, however, may differ from computer to computer. The IBM-patented bus architecture in IBM's higher-end PS/2 family of microcomputers is called Micro Channel Architecture (MCA). This architecture is specific to IBM micros and to some other computers whose manufacturers have agreed to pay IBM royalties for using it. IBM-compatible MCA computers are 100 percent compatible, but they tend to be expensive because of the royalty that must be paid to IBM; moreover, devices and boards to be used with such computers also cost more.

First the Industry Standard Architecture (ISA) bus and then the faster Extended Industry Standard Architecture (EISA) bus were designed to compete directly with IBM's MCA bus architecture. In the late 1980s, Compaq and a consortium of eight other top vendors of IBM-compatibles agreed to make ISA and then EISA industry standards. More than 50 vendors immediately pledged support for these standards. Today, most IBM-compatibles are either ISA or EISA machines. While the type of bus architecture affects the speed of a computer it may also determine the type of hardware you can use. Some peripherals designed for MCA computers, which are mostly IBMs, cannot be used with ISA or EISA machines and vice versa.

Intel-based 386 and 486 computers can be either SX, with 16-bit data buses, or DX, with higher performance 32-bit data buses. There are also 386 and 486 SL portables that have been developed specifically for low-power, battery-operated processing.

## LOOKING AHEAD

**COMING SOON**

- The Intel 386 chip will be the minimum technology used in most corporate environments, with 486 computers becoming increasingly popular.
- Continued improvement in data translation, data conversion, and networking will allow incompatible computers to communicate more easily with one another.
- Both MCA (386 and 486 DX) and EISA (386 and 486 SX) computers will thrive.
- RISC workstations will become even more widely used.
- Notebooks and palmtops will become increasingly popular as laptops.

IN A

**SOME SELECTION CRITERIA FOR COMPUTER SYSTEMS**

1. Cost
2. Speed
3. Size
4. Main memory capacity
5. Architecture
6. Number and type of input/output units
7. Software availability (How well suited is the computer for user applications?)
8. Vendor or manufacturer's reputation for quality
9. Vendor or manufacturer's support and service
10. Quality of the documentation or user's manuals

### ▶ Additional Processing Features

Most computers can perform multitasking, which means running more than one application concurrently. Even more sophisticated computers perform multiprogramming, which enables multiple users to share a computer. Many computers—even micros—also have parallel processors; in effect, these are multiple CPUs that permit more than one instruction to be executed simultaneously.

**Cache memory** is a type of memory that is capable of doubling the speed of a computer. It is based on a technique of storing and retrieving the most frequently used data in readily accessible form so that retrieval is made more efficient. The trade-off is that cache memory is very expensive. It is used extensively in minicomputers as well as in some micros, usually for storing the most frequently referenced data and instructions. It also has great potential for supercomputers and larger mainframes. Figure 4.15 shows an enlargement of a cache memory chip.

**Magnetic bubble memory** is often used in addition to, or in place of, integrated circuits because it is nonvolatile: data is not immediately lost when the power is shut off. See Figure 4.16.

*Figure 4.15 An enlargement of a cache memory chip.*

---

**CRITICAL THINKING**

Because there is really more than one 386 or 486 chip architecture for IBM computers and their compatibles, computer people often refer to devices by their chip names rather than manufacturer and model number. "Is yours a 386 SX, 386 DX, or 486 DX2?" is, for example, a common question that prompted one reporter to say, "I suspect that most users do not care whether the data bus is MCA, EISA, or COAT—chip-munks on a treadmill—as long as the job gets done."

What do you think? Do you see any analogies between the MCA-ISA-EISA battle and the video battles between VHS and Betamax?

## ▶ SELF-TEST

1. One megahertz is equal to _____.
2. A nanosecond is _____.
3. A unit of data that corresponds to the number of bits that can be transferred to a register in the CPU's control unit is called a _____.
4. (T or F) The larger the word size, the faster the computer.
5. IBM micros have a bus architecture called _____ which (is/is not) exactly the same as that for Compaq and other IBM compatibles.
6. In addition to megahertz and nanoseconds another term for measuring the speed of a computer is _____.
7. The electronic paths on which data moves between the CPU and memory are called _____.

### Solutions
1. one million clock ticks per second
2. one billionth of a second
3. word
4. T
5. MCA (Micro Channel Architecture); is not
6. MIPS (million instructions per second)
7. buses

*Figure 4.16* Data flow in a magnetic bubble memory. Magnetized domains, or "bubbles"—the blue dots in this photo—flow along channels in a garnet memory crystal. Each bubble can be used to represent a bit of data. Here, the magnetic memory is viewed through a polarizing microscope by a video camera so that bubble motion can be observed. The colors are created artificially by electronic circuitry as a visual aid.

## METHODS OF PROCESSING DATA  4.4

Thus far we have focused on the technical features of a computer. Next we discuss the two primary methods for processing data: in batches and interactively. We also indicate that regardless of the processing methods used, computers typically operate on one record at a time.

What are some common methods for computer processing?

### ▶ Batch Processing

Businesses usually produce all payroll checks for each pay period *at the same time.* This is an example of **batch processing:** holding all data until output is to be produced and then processing the data collectively at one time.

There are a number of ways data is entered before batch processing can be accomplished. In an operation in which input is voluminous, data is often entered on computers or terminals that are not even connected to the main CPU. This type of data entry is called an **offline** operation. For example, payroll information might be keyboarded at several different corporate branch sites in separate offline operations. The disks collected from each site could be transmitted to the computer center at corporate headquarters every Thursday, for example, where they would be merged so that paychecks can be printed on Friday in a batch-processing operation.

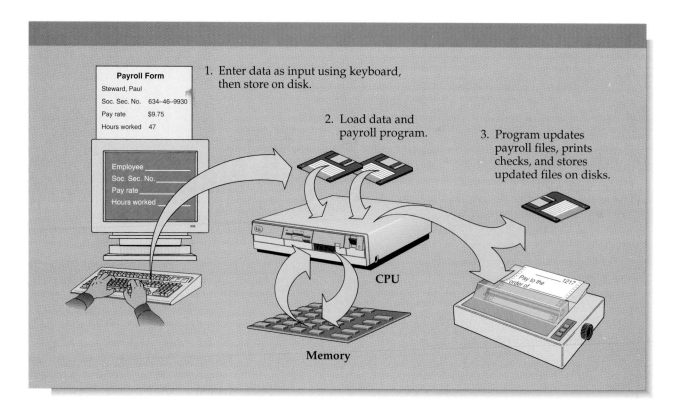

**Payroll Form**
Steward, Paul
Soc. Sec. No.   634–46–9930
Pay rate        $9.75
Hours worked    47

Employee _____
Soc. Sec. No. _____
Pay rate _____
Hours worked _____

1. Enter data as input using keyboard, then store on disk.

2. Load data and payroll program.

3. Program updates payroll files, prints checks, and stores updated files on disks.

Pay to the _____ 1217
order of

CPU

Memory

*Figure 4.17* In batch processing, the computer stores all data until output is needed and then performs all operations at one time.

In a small company that uses microcomputers, the payroll data disks could be created on any microcomputer, then processed in batch mode later. The payroll example in Figure 4.17 illustrates batch processing on a microcomputer.

Batch processing is a good way to make effective use of expensive computer time. First, it is generally more efficient to process the data in a large file all at the same time. Second, there may be a practical advantage to batch processing when preprinted forms such as checks are used for output and have to be specially loaded in the printer.

There are, however, disadvantages to batch processing as well. When data is updated in batch mode, it is less timely; it would be, after all, current only at the time the entire batch is processed. After that, changes are stored, usually on disk, for the next update cycle. Batch processing is not appropriate, therefore, for an application that needs to process or report on current data immediately.

Examples of appropriate tasks for batch processing are producing transcripts of grades at the end of the semester, or producing stock inventory reports at the end of the day. If an inventory manager relies on yesterday's inventory report produced in a batch processing operation, he or she must keep in mind that changes in stock made during the current day will *not* be reflected in the report. In short, if there is no great need for up-to-the-minute accuracy on reports, then batch processing is the most efficient method for producing those reports.

If there is a need to process data as soon as it is transacted or entered, then batch processing would not be suitable.

# ▶ Interactive Processing

It may be that payroll files need to be current only at the end of a payroll period when it is time to produce checks. If so, then the files can be effectively processed in batch mode. On the other hand, airline reservation systems must be updated instantly. Airlines need to know at all times how many seats have been sold so ticket agents will stop selling tickets when a flight is booked. An airline reservations system, therefore, is an example of a system that uses interactive processing (Figure 4.18).

(a)

*Figure 4.18* (a) *An airline reservation system is an example of interactive, or real-time, processing.* (b) *The computer completes each task immediately, keeping all records current and available.*

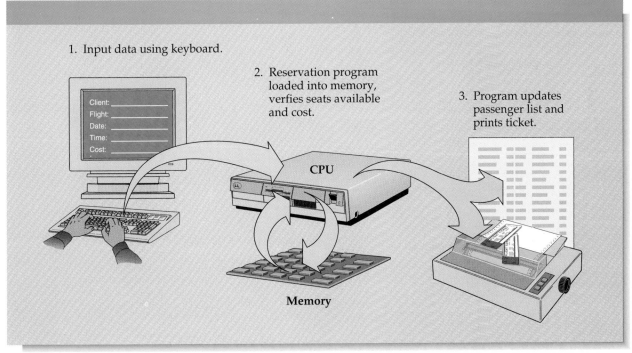

1. Input data using keyboard.

2. Reservation program loaded into memory, verfies seats available and cost.

3. Program updates passenger list and prints ticket.

CPU

Memory

(b)

In **interactive processing** data is processed immediately, as soon as it is transacted, so that updated information can be quickly provided to all users of the system. In airline reservations systems, there are terminals at many sites—in travel agencies, at airports, and so forth. Although the terminals are off-site, at remote locations, they communicate directly and instantly with the central computer via communications lines such as telephones and satellites (see Chapter 12). These systems immediately update ticket information on all flights.

Updating information interactively is called an **online** operation. The person at the remote terminal is said to be "online" with the main computer. For interactive, online processing, the central computer must be linked to all terminals at all times, and a program must also be stored in main memory at all times so that the CPU can process the data being entered from the various terminals.

A form of interactive processing, **transaction processing,** enables a user to input data and complete a transaction on the spot. Figure 4.19 shows how transaction processing is used for telephone sales. The salesperson retrieves names of customers from the customer database and then makes sales calls. When a customer places a new order over the phone, the salesperson first inputs the order information. Then the computer retrieves the customer information from the customer database and processes all data to produce an invoice and a packing slip used by the warehouse for packing and shipping the order. Because updated information is available almost instantly, as with our airline reservation exam-

*Figure 4.19 Transaction processing is a form of interactive processing. Each time a transaction is made, a database is updated and output is generated.*

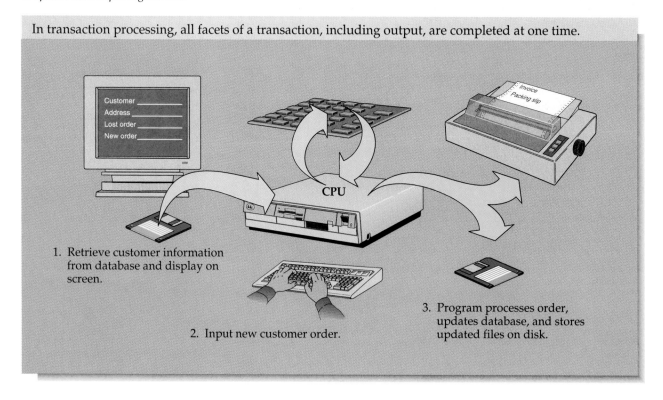

In transaction processing, all facets of a transaction, including output, are completed at one time.

1. Retrieve customer information from database and display on screen.

2. Input new customer order.

3. Program processes order, updates database, and stores updated files on disk.

ple, interactive processing may also be considered **real-time processing.** Real-time processing means that the computerized procedure is fast enough to enable users to input data and then make decisions based on the output.

## ▶ The Main Processing Technique: A Record at a Time

Regardless of the memory technology used by a computer, software is supplied to users on an auxiliary storage medium, usually disk. In order to process data, the program must be read, or loaded into, main memory so that each instruction can be executed. Programs read input data, perform some operations, and produce output information. Input can be entered from a terminal or first stored on disk or other storage device. Main memory then temporarily stores the program, the input, and the output during processing.

Most computers do *not* have the primary storage capacity to store an *entire data file* especially if it is very large. Instead, programs typically read a *unit* of information at a time rather than all input. Suppose, for example, that the program to be executed reads a payroll file, which contains all employee data. The output from the program might be paychecks for all employees. The program is likely to read *only one* employee record at a time, process it, and create a paycheck for that employee. Then it reads the next record and processes it; this procedure continues until all records in the file are read and all checks produced. In this example, a record is the unit of information pertaining to one employee.

In this way, primary storage needs to hold only one record of data. If the payroll file consisted of 10,000 employee records each with 150 characters of data, $10,000 \times 150$ storage positions for input would *not* be required—only 150 storage positions would be needed in primary storage to process each input record.

The input area would be replaced 10,000 times, each time an employee record is read and processed. See Figure 4.20.

Recall that main memory holds programs and data only *temporarily.* Program and data files are stored on auxiliary storage devices like disk because they cannot be permanently stored in main memory, which is volatile. If the power supply is cut off (e.g., there is a power outage), whatever program and data are in main memory are lost.

Because the possibility always exists that data in main memory could be affected by a power failure, data being processed should be saved to disk periodically in case the computer's power is interrupted. Some word processing packages automatically save a document to disk every few minutes or after several thousand characters have been entered. To protect against loss of files, many computers have a battery backup called an uninterruptible power supply. If the system goes "down," the battery kicks in. Computers with magnetic bubble memory or those that operate using a battery are also less susceptible to loss of data since characters

Suppose you go to your bank and make a deposit. A teller keys in your account number and the amount of the deposit. This processing may seem like an interactive application and it may indeed be one, but interactive processing is not necessarily guaranteed. The data entered may go from the teller's terminal to a disk in an offline operation. The disk might be processed daily or even hourly in batch mode. Basically, the depositor has no real way of knowing whether the system is interactive or batch *when a deposit is made.* How can you tell definitively if your bank uses interactive processing? What are the risks of processing transactions in batch mode? What are the benefits?

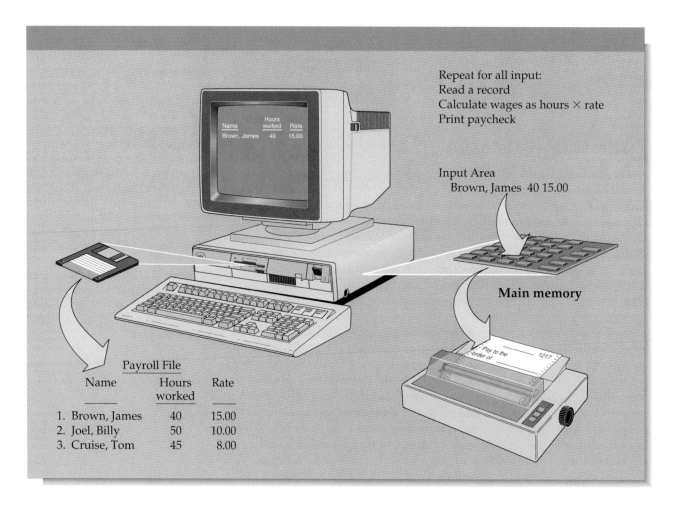

Repeat for all input:
Read a record
Calculate wages as hours × rate
Print paycheck

Input Area
Brown, James  40 15.00

**Main memory**

Payroll File

| Name | Hours worked | Rate |
|------|------|------|
| 1. Brown, James | 40 | 15.00 |
| 2. Joel, Billy | 50 | 10.00 |
| 3. Cruise, Tom | 45 | 8.00 |

*Figure 4.20* Computers read one record at a time and process each record before reading and processing the next one.

in main memory are maintained for a period of time even if the power is lost.

### ▶ SELF-TEST

1. If bills are prepared by computer once a month, we call this a _____ operation.
2. (T or F) When terminals are used to process data then online operations are required.
3. The process of keeping a file current is called _____.
4. (T or F) When batch processing is used to update files, the file is always current.
5. Transaction processing means that _____.

Solutions
1. batch
2. F—Not necessarily.
3. updating
4. F
5. data is processed by computer when it is transacted

# ▶ Chapter Summary

All computer systems consist of various input/output devices, main memory, a central processing unit, and secondary storage. This chapter focuses on the CPU and how it processes data.

## 4.1 HOW THE CPU PROCESSES DATA

A computer system is defined in terms of its CPU. Peripherals, or input/output (I/O) devices, are linked to the CPU, which controls all operations. While large computer systems can have numerous I/O devices, the number of I/O devices a PC can have is limited by the number of I/O connections, or **ports,** it has. The CPU can be linked to peripherals in two ways: (1) by cable or (2) by communications facilities such as telephone lines, if the devices are not at the same physical location as the CPU.

What properties of the CPU make it the heart of the computer system

All computer operations are performed under the control of the CPU. Thus, the CPU is referred to as either the "brains" or the "heart" of a computer. The CPU has three basic features: (1) it interfaces with main memory (primary storage) for storing data and programs; (2) it has a **control unit** for controlling each operation; (3) it has an **arithmetic/logic unit (ALU)** for performing arithmetic and comparison operations.

Most computers use **integrated circuits,** or **chips,** for their CPUs and main memory. The CPU of a PC along with main memory is typically contained on a single board called a **microprocessor.**

Primary storage consists of storage positions called bytes. Each byte can typically store one **character** such as a letter, digit, or symbol. A computer's memory size refers to the number of bytes in the CPU. Sometimes it is possible to enhance a computer's primary storage by adding **memory boards** to increase the storage capacity up to some established limit for that particular type of computer.

The main memory of a computer that uses integrated circuits is said to be **volatile;** that is, its contents are lost if the computer loses power or is turned off. **Nonvolatile** auxiliary storage devices such as disk are used to save data and programs after processing.

There are two forms of main memory: **random-access memory (RAM)** and **read-only memory (ROM).** RAM is that part of primary storage that stores programs and data during application processing. The CPU accesses data from RAM at a speed referred to as the **access rate;** the speed with which the CPU transfers data into and out of RAM is called the **transfer rate.** ROM, also known as **firmware,** refers to read-only memory chips that contain permanent, nonvolatile instructions that have been programmed into them. The three categories of ROM are PROM (programmable read-only memory), EPROM (erasable programmable read-only memory), and EEPROM (electronically erasable programmable read-only memory).

The arithmetic/logic unit (ALU) is the section of the CPU in which all arithmetic and logic operations are performed. The transmission of data between the control unit, ALU, and main memory occurs on a special electronic path called a **bus. Registers** are special storage areas in the ALU and control unit that are used to hold instructions, values, and main memory addresses relating to the instructions and data being processed.

The processing of a single instruction occurs during a **machine cycle,** which consists of two parts: (1) an **instruction cycle** during which the control unit fetches the instruction from primary storage and prepares it for processing and (2) the **execution cycle** during which the instruction is actually executed and the results produced.

## 4.2 HOW THE CPU REPRESENTS DATA

How is data actually stored in a computer?

**Digital computers** process data in discrete form as countable numbers. Internally, all digital computers use some variation of the **binary numbering system** for representing characters, where a character refers to a letter, digit, or special symbol. In the binary numbering system, there are only two possible digits: 0 and 1. In computer systems, the 1 denotes the presence of an electrical pulse or signal in the computer circuitry, and a 0 denotes the absence of such a signal. The smallest unit of data in a computer code is the **bit** (*bi*nary dig*it*)—a single on or off signal. A **word,** or group of consecutive bytes, refers to a unit of data that can be processed at one time.

The two most frequently used computer codes are **EBCDIC** (*E*xtended *B*inary *C*oded *D*ecimal *I*nterchange *C*ode), in which each byte consists of eight data bits, and **ASCII** (*A*merican *S*tandard *C*ode for *I*nformation *I*nterchange), which may be a 7- or 8-bit code. EBCDIC is used by many computers, especially IBM mainframes and their compatibles. ASCII is the code most widely used by micros.

When data is transmitted from one part of the computer to another or from one computer to another, parity bits are used to detect transmission errors. The **parity bit** is a single bit attached to each byte. An **even-parity** computer means that when all the 1 bits in a byte are added up, there must be an even number of them. Similarly, in an **odd-parity** computer, the parity bit is used to ensure an odd number of 1 bits in each byte.

## 4.3 COMPUTER ARCHITECTURE

What factors affect the processing power of a computer?

**Architecture** refers to the technology used for processing data. The word size specifies the number of bits processed by the computer at one time. Generally, the larger the word size, the faster the computer. **Coprocessors** are special chips that can be added to or built into micros to speed up certain kinds of operations. Processing speeds of computers are measured in microseconds, nanoseconds, or picoseconds. The most widely used measure of a microcomputer's CPU performance is the clock speed, which is measured in megahertz (MHz). Another measurement of speed is MIPS (millions of instructions per second).

The term **motherboard** is sometimes used to refer to the main circuit board of a computer that contains the microprocessor, battery-operated clock, and other circuits that are all interconnected. If a micro has an open architecture, that means that the user can open the system's cabinet and add components to the motherboard or main circuit board. In such a computer, the motherboard has a series of **expansion slots** for inserting add-on units.

**Cache memory** is a type of memory that can double the speed of a computer; it is based on a scheme of storing and retrieving the most frequently used data in readily accessible form. **Magnetic bubble memory** is often used in addition to, or in place of, integrated circuits because it is nonvolatile.

## 4.4 METHODS OF PROCESSING DATA

**Batch processing** refers to the storing of all data until output is to be produced and then processing the data all at once. Data entry for a batch processing application is sometimes performed in an **offline** operation. This means that the data is entered on computers or terminals that are not connected to the main CPU. Batch processing may be a good way to make effective use of expensive computer time for some applications, but a major disadvantage of batch applications is that the data is less timely—it is only up to date at the time the entire batch is processed. With **interactive processing** data is processed immediately, as soon as it is transacted. Updating information interactively is referred to as an **online** operation. **Transaction processing** is a form of interactive processing that enables a user to input data and complete a transaction on the spot. **Real-time processing** is a form of interactive processing in which output can be obtained from input being processed quickly enough to affect decision-making.

What are some common methods for computer processing?

## ▶ Chapter Self-test

1. CPU is an abbreviation for _____.
2. All computer systems have the same components: _____, _____, _____, and _____.
3. The CPU copies data from an input device into _____, where it is stored during processing.
4. The part of the CPU that does math and logic functions is the _____.
5. Data moves between the CPU and main memory on an electronic path called a _____.
6. (T or F) If data is stored in volatile memory, it will be lost if the power goes off.
7. Some microcomputers have an internal hard disk that can hold large amounts of data. Is this primary storage or secondary storage?
8. Is the data on an internal hard disk volatile or nonvolatile?
9. RAM stands for _____.
10. Is RAM volatile or nonvolatile?
11. Magnetic bubble memory's advantage over standard microprocessor memory is that it is _____.
12. ROM stands for _____.

13. There are three kinds of ROM memory: _____, which stands for _____; _____, which stands for _____; and _____, which stands for _____.
14. Numbering systems in which the place of a digit within a number impacts the number's value are called _____.
15. The numbering system that uses base 2 is called _____, and the numbering system that uses base 10 is called _____.
16. Two commonly used coding systems are ASCII and EBCDIC. The one used by IBM mainframes is _____; the one used by most microcomputers is _____.
17. The two basic types of processing are _____ and _____. When an entire transaction is completed on the spot, including output, it is a type of interactive processing called _____ processing.
18. Since numbers are frequently represented within the computer as a series of on-off switches, the _____ numbering system is well suited to computer processing.
19. (T or F) All numbers must be entered into the computer in binary form.
20. (T or F) Some numbers can be expressed in base 2 but not in base 10.
21. (T or F) In general, more binary digits are necessary to represent a number than are necessary in the decimal numbering system.
22. $2^2$ = _____.
23. $2^5$ = _____.
24. $2^3$ = _____.
25. $10^2$ = _____.


Solutions
1. central processing unit
2. input devices; the central processing unit and main memory; output devices; and secondary, or auxiliary, storage
3. primary storage or main memory
4. arithmetic/logic unit (ALU)
5. bus
6. T
7. secondary storage
8. nonvolatile
9. random-access memory
10. volatile
11. nonvolatile
12. read-only memory
13. PROM, programmable-read-only memory; EPROM, erasable programmable read-only memory; EEPROM, electronically erasable read-only memory
14. positional numbering systems
15. binary; decimal
16. EBCDIC; ASCII
17. batch processing; interactive processing; transaction processing

18. binary, or base 2
19. F—Decimal numbers as well as binary numbers can be entered as input. Decimal numbers will, however, be converted into binary form or some variation of binary form before they are processed.
20. F
21. T—For example, 16 in base 10 uses two digits but requires five in binary (10000).
22. $2 \times 2 = 4$
23. $2 \times 2 \times 2 \times 2 \times 2 = 32$
24. 8
25. 100

## ▶ Key Terms

Access rate, *p. 135*
Architecture, *p. 151*
Arithmetic/logic unit (ALU), *p. 131*
ASCII, *p. 146*
Batch processing, *p. 157*
Binary numbering system, *p. 139*
Bit, *p. 142*
Bus, *p. 136*
Cache memory, *p. 156*
Character, *p. 134*
Chip, *p. 131*
Control unit, *p. 131*
Coprocessor, *p. 153*
Digital computer, *p. 139*

EBCDIC, *p. 146*
Even parity, *p. 149*
Execution cycle, *p. 137*
Expansion slot, *p. 154*
Firmware, *p. 135*
Instruction cycle, *p. 137*
Integrated circuit, *p. 131*
Interactive processing, *p. 160*
Machine cycle, *p. 137*
Magnetic bubble memory, *p. 156*
Memory board, *p. 134*
Microprocessor, *p. 131*
Motherboard (main circuit board), *p. 154*
Nonvolatile memory, *p. 134*

Odd parity, *p. 149*
Offline, *p. 157*
Online, *p. 160*
Parity bit, *p. 148*
Port, *p. 130*
Random-access memory (RAM), *p. 135*
Read-only memory (ROM), *p. 135*
Real-time processing, *p. 161*
Register, *p. 137*
Transaction processing, *p. 160*
Transfer rate, *p. 135*
Volatile memory, *p. 134*
Word, *p. 145*

## ▶ Review Questions

1. List and briefly describe the components of the CPU.
2. What is the function of primary storage and how does secondary storage differ from it? What do RAM and ROM stand for?
3. Define batch processing and interactive processing.
4. Find out how much memory the computer you use has. Has it been upgraded beyond the amount that it came with originally?
5. Check to see what kind of microprocessor chip your computer uses. You may have to check your computer's documentation. Is it slower or faster than a standard IBM PS/2 in clock speed? in word size?
6. Consult newspapers or journals written five to ten years ago to see if you can find projections regarding computer capability in the 1990s. Compare and contrast the predictions with the current state of the art.

## PRODUCT ANALYSIS

## CASE

### Chipping Away at the Competition: IBM Launches a Multimedia Chip

The IBM PS/2 Model 57SX is a new, fast computer with a new, highly touted, fast 386 SLC chip. In fact, this new 57SX is the fastest performer in its class. Moreover, it is IBM's Ultimedia Model— IBM's vanguard for multimedia products. The computer has an optical disk storage drive with 600+ MB capacity for storing text, images, and sound; a high-quality graphics terminal; and audio capture and playback capability. With this Ultimedia machine, users can interact with all sorts of multimedia products: an encyclopedia, an atlas, a world history guide, Mother Goose's nursery rhymes, Shakespeare's works, and an analysis of Beethoven's symphonies. All these software products provide not only text but animation, graphics, and sound.

When announced, the Model 57SX was quite expensive, with a list price of $5,995. As competing products from other manufacturers become available, *all* of these multimedia computers will be less costly.

The basic Ultimedia computer is available with many add-ons. One is IBM's PS/2 Action Media II Board, which consists of adapters that capture digital video and audio. Another is a PS/2 TV screen, with a speaker, which can monitor and capture live broadcasts from 70 channels. There is also Touch Select, a touch screen that can be added to existing monitors. Such add-on features enable the computer to function as a television and interactive multimedia device as well as a videoconferencing tool.

*A touch screen for IBM's Ultimedia PS/2.*

IBM's Ultimedia adds a new dimension to multimedia for PCs. Undoubtedly, it will spark software developers to make creative, innovative, and exciting products that span the spectrum from education to entertainment. The best is yet to come.

*Analysis*
1. What benefits does multimedia have for businesses?
2. Do you think a $5000 computer with multimedia capabilities can capture the hearts, minds, and pocketbooks, of the conventional PC user?
3. What are the pros and cons of acquiring a new product like this Ultimedia computer when it is first introduced as opposed to waiting for newer, cheaper machines?

# INPUT AND OUTPUT:

# FROM APPLICATIONS TO HARDWARE

We have seen in the previous chapters that computers, regardless of their size, cost, and processing power, operate on data in essentially the same way. The factors that determine how those computers will be used are software, connectivity, and people. In addition, each organization, and each application area within it, needs special computer peripherals for accomplishing its objectives.

Chapter 5 covers the types of input and output devices commonly used in computer systems for business-related applications by answering the following questions:

► How have input devices evolved to meet user needs for error-free source documents?

► How does source data automation actually improve productivity in organizations?

► Considering the criteria that make output information useful, what advantages and disadvantages does each class of output device offer users?

## 5.1   INPUT DEVICES CREATE SOURCE DOCUMENTS AND DATA FILES

### ► A Review of File Processing

How have input devices evolved to meet user needs for error-free source documents?

Most often, computers process data that is organized into database files where a database file is a collection of records in a specific application area. Typically, a master file is created in functional areas such as payroll, accounting, and marketing. Each master file contains all important data pertaining to its corresponding application area. For example, a master payroll file contains salary information about employees, and a master accounts receivable file contains information about customers.

Master files are usually created using a keyboard as an input device; that is, data is first keyed and then stored on disk. We will see, however, that keying operations are not the only ones used to create master files.

After master files are created, they must be updated so they are current. To accomplish this, the computer must read as input any changes

IN A NUT SHELL

| File | Collection of records in a specific application area |
|---|---|
| *Types of files* | |
| Master | Contains the most important data pertaining to a specific application area |
| Transaction | Contains changes to be made to the master file |
| *Update Procedures* | Use transaction data to keep the master file current |

to be made and incorporate them into the master file. Changes to a file are referred to as transaction data. The update procedure may be performed either (1) online, that is, interactively as the change occurs or (2) in batch mode—later on at fixed intervals. With batch processing, transaction data is keyed, saved on disk, and used later at fixed intervals to update the master file.

Up-to-date master files provide managers and the operating staff with the output they need to perform their jobs. As we will see, output is usually produced in the form of printed reports or screen displays, but other types of output are sometimes preferred. Printed reports can be created on a regularly scheduled basis or on demand when the need arises. Regularly scheduled printed output such as checks or invoices are produced at fixed intervals. Printed or displayed output is created on demand when quick responses to inquiries are required.

In general, input is most often keyed and output is most often printed on paper or displayed on a screen. There are, however, many other types of input/output devices besides keyboards, printers, and screens. In this chapter we discuss a wide range of peripherals for computer systems of all sizes, and the application areas that use them. Our discussion covers micro, mini/midrange, and mainframe peripherals and their application areas.

> Input/output units connected to a CPU are types of peripherals.

In business, input data frequently comes from documents such as purchase orders, vendor invoices, or payroll change requests. Such documents are prepared where the original action occurs—at the source of a transaction—so they are called **source documents** (Figure 5.1). For example, the source of a purchase order is the purchasing department; similarly, a payroll change request is likely to originate in the human resources or payroll department.

To increase productivity and to minimize input errors, systems analysts and other computer professionals seek to limit the number of times data needs to be recorded manually. For example, in a company that does not have efficient input procedures, an employee salary raise might involve as many as three inputs: First, the department manager fills out a handwritten form authorizing the raise. Next, the handwritten request

Source document
(bills, payroll
forms, invoices)

Master file
is updated

Printed output
(checks,
statements,
control listings,
reports)

*Figure 5.1 Source documents are often used to update master files so that printed output in the form of checks or statements can be produced.*

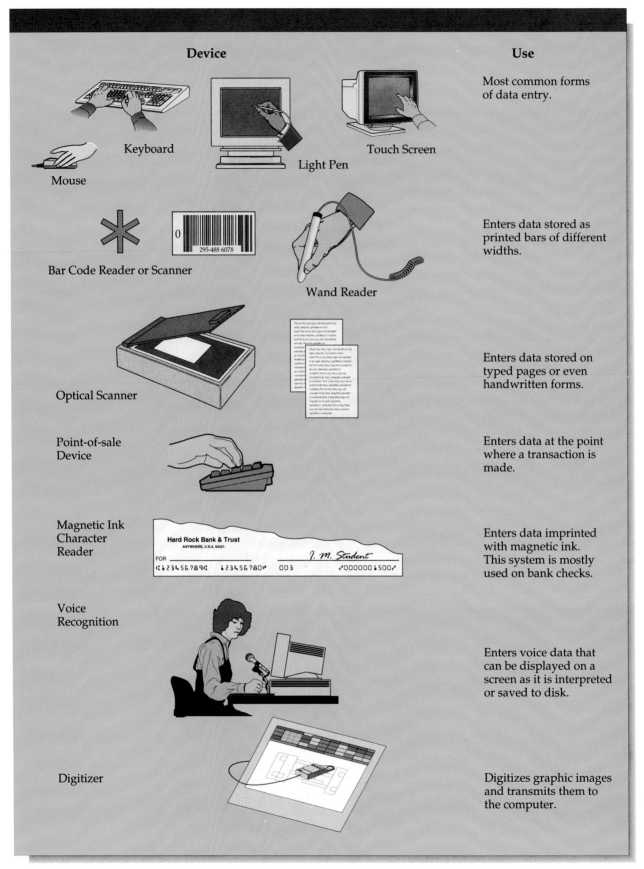

| Device | Use |
|---|---|
| Keyboard, Mouse, Light Pen, Touch Screen | Most common forms of data entry. |
| Bar Code Reader or Scanner, Wand Reader | Enters data stored as printed bars of different widths. |
| Optical Scanner | Enters data stored on typed pages or even handwritten forms. |
| Point-of-sale Device | Enters data at the point where a transaction is made. |
| Magnetic Ink Character Reader | Enters data imprinted with magnetic ink. This system is mostly used on bank checks. |
| Voice Recognition | Enters voice data that can be displayed on a screen as it is interpreted or saved to disk. |
| Digitizer | Digitizes graphic images and transmits them to the computer. |

Hard Rock Bank & Trust
ANYWHERE, U.S.A. 54321

FOR _____  *I. M. Student*

⑆123456789⑆  123456780⑈  003  ⑈000000⑈500⑈

*Figure 5.2 Examples of input devices. Each input device reads in a different form of data for processing by the CPU.*

goes to the human resources department for verification. The human resources department then types up a list of all raises, which is sent to the payroll department where the information is keyed into the computer. In a more efficient computer environment, the originating department enters the salary raise on its own terminal, which is connected to the company's central computer. The human resources department verifies the request electronically, and the payroll department processes the raise without ever reentering the data. If data is keyed only once during the entire process, the risk of input errors is significantly reduced.

Figure 5.2 illustrates basic input devices found in business. Some are used for processing large amounts of data—payroll, order processing, and inventories—whereas others are special-purpose devices, such as supermarket scanners, that are needed in specific application areas where they dramatically improve productivity.

There are two basic types of input devices: those that create a source document along with an input file, and those that read previously cre-

# LOOKING BACK

### THE PUNCHED CARD: DO NOT FOLD, STAPLE, BEND, OR MUTILATE

Herman Hollerith developed the 80-column punched card for storing data for the 1890 U.S. census. See accompanying illustration. He also developed electrical accounting machines that could sort and tabulate the punched-card data. Hollerith's cards and equipment helped pave the way for computers by reducing the time it took to complete a census by 50 percent. His Tabulating Machine Company merged with another business in the 1920s and eventually became known as the International Business Machines (IBM) Company.

Hollerith's census data was recorded on cards in the form of punched holes. These cards, which were the same size as a dollar bill, served as the model for those adopted by the computing field in the 1950s when punched card data became a common form of input. The warning "do not fold, bend, staple, or mutilate" was commonly found on these cards to emphasize how fragile they were. Compare that to today's 3½-inch floppy disk, which can store the equivalent of

(a)                                    (b)

(a) *Hollerith's tabulating machine and* (b) *a punched card, which was designed to be the size of a dollar bill.*

18,000 cards of information or more and has been known to withstand being accidentally washed in shirt pockets!

An exhibit at the Smithsonian Institution features a touch screen station to describe the 1890 census process that used punched cards to record data. The station prompts visitors for information about their age group, gender, and current resi-

dence. The data is then compared to actual 1890 census data, and visitors receive a profile of who they were likely to have been in 1890. A suburban teenage male from Kansas in 1992, for example, would probably have lived on a farm in 1890. At the same time the system gives the profile to the visitor, the information is used to update the person's bar code, which was created when he or she entered the exhibit. The Smithsonian also has on display Hollerith's original tabulating machine.

Recall from Chapter 4 the input-process-output procedure: Data is entered as input, the data is processed by the CPU, and output is created, all under the control of a program.

ated source documents to produce an input file. First, we look at input devices that require a data entry procedure that creates a source document and transmits the data to a CPU in the form of an input file. Next, we consider source data automation, which focuses on techniques other than keying for electronically converting existing source documents to files in machine-readable form. See Figure 5.3.

## ► Keying Devices

When data must be entered into a computer, it is most often keyed by a data entry operator. A single keying operation accomplishes two things: (1) it creates a source document and (2) it inputs the data to a computer. When an airline reservations clerk keys data to create an airline ticket (the source document), that data is also used to update flight information on disk. Similarly, when a clerk keys in a payroll change, that data is transmitted directly to a central computer to update the payroll master file.

Sometimes, however, source documents are created in one procedure, and they are entered as input to a computer in a separate procedure. For example, consider an application in which employees transact their business at a client's premises. These employees may fill out purchase orders that later serve as source documents for the purchasing department. To be processed by computer, the handwritten or typed source documents may need to be keyed in as input to a computer in a separate operation. Independent keying procedures, in which an input file is created, are

*Figure 5.3 Here are some samples of source documents and devices that can be used for entering them as input.*

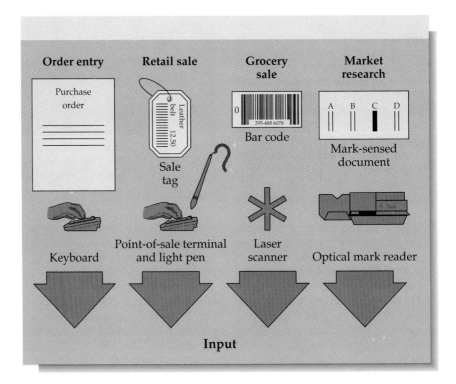

called offline operations. In an offline operation, data entry is not under the control of the main CPU; that is, conversion of source documents into an input file is performed in a separate procedure that keys the data onto disk. Such a procedure results in duplication of effort: first the source document is created at the point of transaction, and later the data is keyed onto disk. Although the procedure may be inefficient, it is sometimes the most practical and inexpensive. We will see later that a method for minimizing duplication would be to provide the field staff with hand-held data collection devices that have a keyboard and can convert the data directly to disk or other machine-readable form as it is being transacted.

In cases where source data needs to be reentered to be read by a computer, the method of input is commonly the keyboard. The keyboard is typically linked to a monitor or video display terminal so that the data being entered can also be viewed on the screen. A combined keyboard/monitor may be a special input/output device called a terminal, which is linked to a central computer, or it may be a microcomputer itself. Data that is entered by means of a keying operation is stored in a transaction file, most often on disk. See Figure 5.4. As we have seen, such a file can be processed in batch mode or online.

The keying operation, which is just like typing, is a labor-intensive activity that tends to be costly and time consuming. Moreover, it can result in numerous errors if the keyed data is not checked. Methods to minimize keying errors are user-friendly screen displays and error-control procedures. Both can be incorporated in the program that accepts the input.

*Figure 5.4* This is a keying operation in which a transaction file is stored on a disk that is later used in batch processing mode to update a master file.

## USER-FRIENDLY SCREEN DISPLAYS FOR REDUCING ERRORS

Selecting entries from a menu minimizes errors and makes it easier for data entry operators to interact with a computer. Consider the following:

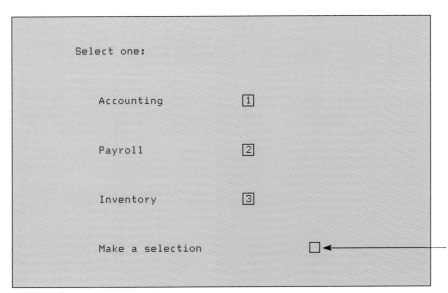

In this main menu, items are displayed on the screen and users select the entry of their choice. To select an accounting application, for example, press 1. The cursor, which is usually a blinking underscore (__), shows you where the value you enter will appear. The statement "Make a selection," which is followed by a blinking cursor, is called a **prompt.** A prompt is a request to supply a response or to input a value.

After an entry is selected from a main menu, the selection process may continue with additional prompts that ask the user to choose more specific entries from submenus. If the submenu appears as a superimposed drop-down menu, it is called a **pull-down menu.** You can use the cursor arrows to highlight an item or command on the pull-down menu. Once you have highlighted an item, you select it by pressing the Enter key. After the required items or commands have been entered, you are typically prompted to key the input.

Figure 5.5 presents examples of user-friendly screen displays. Entries can be highlighted with the use of color, boldface, reverse video (where background and foreground colors are reversed), and a blinking cursor.

Programmers can reduce the risk of input errors and make screens more user-friendly by writing instructions that perform the following actions:

1. Prompt for input with detailed messages: In addition to positioning the cursor at specific points at which data is to be entered, the program can provide clear messages that indicate what the input should look like.
2. Ensure that fields are actually keyed in and are completely filled: For example, a program can ensure that a department number is keyed as two digits by causing any other entry to make the computer beep or wait for an appropriate entry.

*Figure 5.5* (a) *You can select the entry you want from this user-friendly screen display by keying in a number from 1 to 5. (Continued on the next page.)*

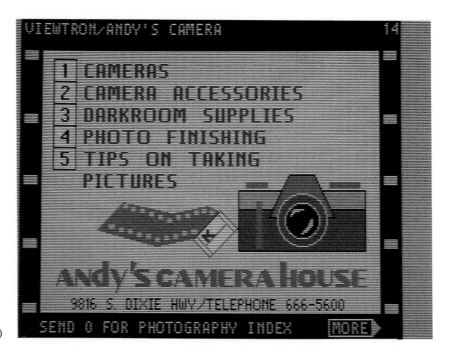

(a)

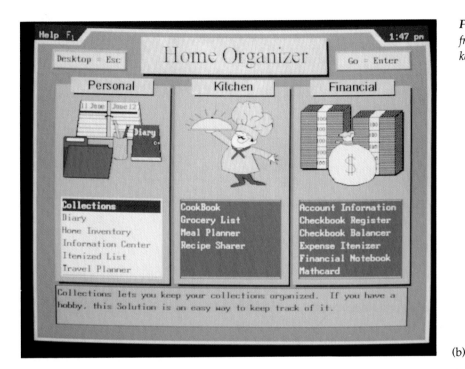

*Figure 5.5* (b) *You can select items from a menu by using the cursor arrow keys to highlight the entry desired.*

(b)

3. Protect sensitive fields such as salaries or passwords from being read by others: Such fields can either remain blank on the screen even when keyed by a data entry operator, or they can appear with special symbols (e.g., #) to mask the values being keyed.
4. Ensure that fields are entered within valid ranges or with valid values: Unit prices, for example, would be accepted only if they fall within price limits established at the company.

## ERROR CONTROL PROCEDURES

Programs that create input files typically include many error-control procedures, in addition to user-friendly displays, to minimize errors. Although errors can be minimized with such procedures, they can never be eliminated entirely. For example, a program can be written to ensure that a salary falls within an acceptable range. But if a transposition error was made in a salary field so that 45000 was entered instead of 54000, it is unlikely that a program could detect the error.

For this reason, *manual verification* by a staff of employees should be part of any error control procedure. A printout called a **control listing** or **audit trail** includes all changes actually made to files. Users compare the control listing to the changes that should have been made. If errors are found on the control listing, the data must be corrected. See Figure 5.6.

Most methods of data verification, even those that are programmed, rely on the human factor. For example, after data for an individual record has been entered, the program may display the data in final form and ask the data entry operator to verify that what is displayed is correct. Well-designed interactive screen displays enable the operator to return to any previously entered data and make corrections if necessary.

You can move from one screen display to another by pressing the PgDn or PgUp key. This is called scrolling.

*Figure 5.6 After this data entry opera-
tor enters inventory changes, an audit
trail is printed and checked by the
manager.*

Even with help from programs in the form of menus, interactive
screen displays, and error-control procedures, keying errors do occur.
Alternatives to keying operations are often used to minimize such errors
and to reduce the cost and time of data entry.

## ▶ **A**lternatives to **K**eying

Instead of using a keying operation, many data entry operators use a
mouse, touch screen, light pen, or even a joy stick for entering input.
Later in this chapter, we will see that the newest data collection systems
accept virtually any form of source document without the need for a separate input procedure.

### MOUSE

A mouse is a small, handheld device that usually contains a ball-type
roller on the bottom and one or more buttons on the top (Figure 5.7).
Apple's Macintosh microcomputer was the first to make widespread use
of a mouse, which is now a popular tool for most micros and many larger
computer systems as well. Because a mouse is easy to use and reduces
the need for typing, it is considered a user-friendly input device.

The mouse is normally used to position a cursor on a screen for selecting choices from a main menu or pull-down menu. You *drag* the mouse
to move the cursor to the item or area desired and then *click* in to select
the item. This selection method is often much faster than using cursor
control arrow keys for positioning the cursor at an entry and then pressing the Enter key to choose it. See Figure 5.8 for an illustration of how
menu items can be selected by a mouse.

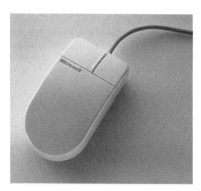

*Figure 5.7 A mechanical mouse.*

A mouse does not eliminate the need to use a keyboard for entering text, although it does reduce some keying operations. In word processing applications, for example, the text is entered using the keyboard, but it may be formatted by using the mouse to make selections from menus that offer choices in type font and page layout. The mouse may also be used to select print options from a menu that offers choices about which pages to print and how many copies are needed. We will see in Chapter 7 that graphics packages make particularly good use of the mouse, which can actually trace or draw patterns.

There are many types of mice. On the underside of the standard mechanical mouse is a ball; as the mouse rolls up, down, left, and right across a flat surface, a signal is sent to the computer that drives the cursor up, down, left, and right, corresponding to the motion of the mouse. An optical mouse is a different type that rolls over a desktop pad with a reflective grid. The optical mouse emits a light as it is dragged, which correspondingly moves the cursor to match the mouse's position on the grid. With both a mechanical and optical mouse, one or more buttons on the top of the mouse are pressed to select, or click in, on the user's commands when the cursor is at the desired position.

Portable computers often use rollerballs or trackballs as pointing devices because they are part of, or can attach to, the keyboard itself. Sometimes these are called mice and sometimes they are simply called pointing devices. A rollerball has rubber-coated control balls for smoother, quieter dragging and clicking. A trackball is a stationary unit that contains a movable ball which, when rotated with the fingers or palm of the hand, moves the cursor on the screen. Both the rollerball and the trackball are often even easier to use than the mechanical or optical mouse. Figure 5.9 illustrates different types of pointing devices.

IN A

*Use your mouse as follows:*
- *Drag* it to position the cursor at an entry so that it is highlighted.
- *Click* the left button to select the highlighted choice.

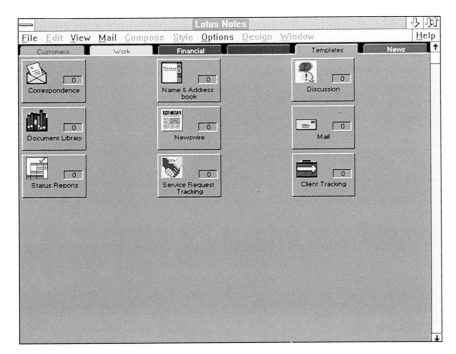

*Figure 5.8 Sample menu items that can be selected by a mouse. You use the mouse to point the cursor at the desired icon and then click in or select the item with the mouse.*

(a)

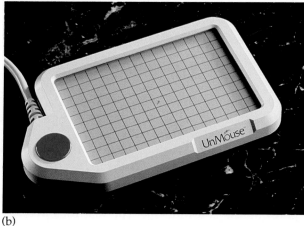

(b)

*Figure 5.9* *There are many different types of mice or pointing devices.* (a) *A BallPoint may be attached to a PC.* (b) *The UnMouse can be used as a standard mouse or pointing device or for drawing graphics.*

Many applications rely on the use of a mouse or other pointing device to select entries represented as symbols, or icons, on a screen. Consider the following prompt: Enter Sex ☐. Instead of requiring the user to enter M (male) or F (female), a program may display icons of a male and a female. The user selects the appropriate sex by pointing with the mouse to the corresponding icon and then clicking in to select it. Icons, such as the ones shown previously in Figure 5.8, can also depict commands that the user may wish to select for performing some task.

Icons create a user-friendly environment from which people can select visual, self-explanatory commands without having to key or remember complex instruction formats. Icons can replace the clutter on a screen, make displays more user-friendly, and make it easier for users to select entries with a mouse, other pointing device, or even a keyboard. Some operating systems like the Macintosh System 7 and OS/2 for the IBM PS/2, and some graphical user interfaces like Windows, make extensive use of icons that are best selected with a mouse.

Although a mouse is well suited for selecting items from a menu and for simple drawing, it is not as useful for artists who require precision to create graphic images. We will see later that a digitizer, or graphics tablet, is another drawing method often used in place of a mouse.

## TOUCH SCREEN

A **touch screen** enables you to select entries and enter choices or commands by simply using your finger to make contact with the screen to highlight the desired item. A touch screen is similar in concept to those buttons on elevators where you select the desired floor by touching the corresponding floor number. Instead of using a mouse to click in on an entry to select it, you actually select the desired entry with a touch of your finger. IBM and other manufacturers make touch screens for PCs as well as for terminals. Some touch screens can simply snap on to existing video monitors. Figure 5.10 illustrates how menu items can be selected from a touch screen.

*Figure 5.10 Items may be selected from a menu by pressing the desired one on a touch screen. Here, presentations from a multimedia show would be selected by touching the screen at the appropriate menu item.*

## LIGHT PEN

A **light pen** works just like the touch of your finger on a touch screen. Instead of using your finger to select items, however, you use a special pen. See Figure 5.11.

## JOY STICK

A **joy stick** is similar to a mouse in that it positions and moves a cursor. It is used primarily for playing games although trackballs are also commonly used for game-playing. See Figure 5.12.

All of the above devices can be used in multimedia applications in which text, video, animation, and graphics are selected for viewing by the user.

Many information systems require source documents to be keyed into a computer. Sometimes, a mouse, touch screen, or light pen is used in place of, or in conjunction with, keying for selecting entries thereby minimizing data entry costs and errors. In the next section, we focus on techniques that minimize the need for manually converting source documents to machine-readable form.

*Figure 5.11 Light pens are used to select menu items by touching the desired item on the screen with the pen. Here, a nurse extracts hospital records for specific patients.*

**Figure 5.12** *A joy stick is often used for playing games or simulating certain actions, such as driving a car or flying a plane.*

▶ **SELF-TEST**

1. A _____ is an originating document that is entered as input to a computer system.
2. (T or F) Most applications use keying devices for entering data into a computer system.
3. What are the two methods used for updating master files?
4. What are the advantages of selecting applications from menus?
5. The file that contains changes to be made to the master file is called a _____ file.
6. Name three alternatives to keying devices that are popular in business.

Solutions
1. source document
2. T
3. online, or interactive, processing; batch processing
4. less keying and fewer errors
5. transaction
6. mouse; touch screen; light pen

## 5.2   SOURCE DATA AUTOMATION REDUCES DATA ENTRY OPERATIONS

In organizations with many branch locations or extensive field staffs, source documents may be created offline (i.e., not under the control of a central computer). These offline operations usually require a clerk or typist to create a source document, or a data entry operator to create a disk file from a source document. Offline data entry operations tend to be less costly alternatives to online data entry, where the data being entered as input is under the direct control of the main CPU and is immediately available to update existing files.

When source documents are created manually, the data from them often needs to be rekeyed into a computer, which results in duplication of effort and which increases the risk for errors. Alternatively, the source document created offline in a manual procedure may be read by special scanners that automatically convert the input to machine-readable form. **Source data automation (SDA)** is the process of computerizing the procedure that converts source documents to machine-readable form. Its objectives are to minimize labor-intensive tasks such as keyboarding and to reduce errors. The most common devices for converting source documents to machine-readable form are optical character readers (OCR), but there are other devices as well. We begin our discussion of source data automation with OCR devices.

> How does source data automation actually improve productivity in organizations?

# ▶ Optical Character Readers

Where large volumes of manually created forms or source documents need to be read by computer, special input devices that physically scan the document and convert it to machine-readable form are more suitable than manual rekeying. **Optical character readers (OCR)** form a class of input devices that can read or scan data without the need for a keying operation. They are widely used with PC-based systems for scanning documents; they are also popular in large organizations where the need to minimize keying is great. OCR input devices include bar code readers, wand readers, optical mark readers, as well as optical scanners that read documents.

## BAR CODE SCANNERS AND WAND READERS

Most grocery stores rely on optical **bar code scanners** or **readers** for their checkout procedures. These devices read, or scan, the zebralike bars that you see on most food packages and other consumer goods. The black-and-white bars of different widths form a code called the **Universal Product Code (UPC)**—a code that identifies the manufacturer of the product as well as the product itself.

The bar code reader is a scanning device that translates the product data into electrical impulses (see Figure 5.13). An electronic cash register at the transaction site uses the UPC information to retrieve the product's price from a computer. The bar code data need not be keyed or otherwise converted to a machine-readable form because the scanner reads it directly, minimizing the time it takes to complete a transaction and reducing data entry errors. In addition, inventory and accounts receivable data can be updated immediately as products are purchased.

You are probably most familiar with bar codes on consumer products in supermarkets or department stores. But bar codes have much wider applicability. Laboratories encode blood samples with bar codes. Facto-

> **CRITICAL THINKING**
>
> When bar code readers are used, item pricing is unnecessary. Although these devices at checkout counters reduce the time it takes to shop, eliminating the price on each grocery item makes it more difficult to comparison shop. As a result, some consumer groups have lobbied to have states pass legislation that requires stores to continue including unit prices on consumer items. Why do consumer groups want such legislation? Why do many stores oppose this legislation? What do you think?

*Figure 5.13 A scanning device at the supermarket checkout counter reads the Universal Product Code on packages. The computer then looks up the price and computes the total cost of a purchase. It also updates inventory records.*

ries use bar code readers for scanning inventory. The New York City Marathon, as well as many other races, has been assigning individual bar codes to runners who must wear them on their shirts. As a runner finishes the marathon, a device scans the bar code to record the runner's name and order of finish. Figure 5.14 illustrates another application for bar codes.

The handheld **wand reader** is a popular scanning device for reading bar codes. See Figure 5.15. Some wand readers can scan data encoded with special OCR typefaces. Wand readers that scan OCR codes are often used as alternatives to bar code readers. The character data scanned is readable by people as well as machines.

*Figure 5.14 Bar codes can be read from Federal Express packages.*

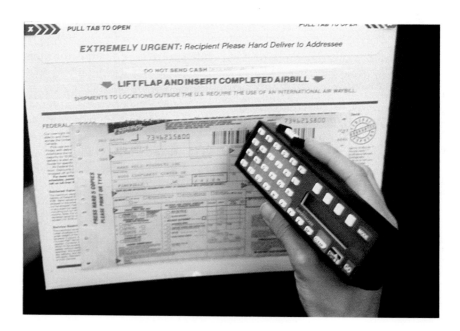

*Figure 5.15 A wand reader scans the UPC from video tapes at a Blockbuster Video store.*

Hospitals, libraries, and factories use wand readers for scanning data. Many retail stores include special OCR coding on their inventory tags. The wand reader can be connected to a point-of-sale terminal or electronic cash register for generating a sales receipt.

## OPTICAL MARK READERS

An **optical mark reader,** sometimes called a mark sense reader, detects the presence of pencil marks on predetermined grids. As a student, you are probably familiar with one type of mark-sense source document: the computer-scored test answer sheet (Figure 5.16). You mark the answers to multiple-choice questions by filling in a square or a circle that surrounds the letter or number of choice. Identifying data such as student

*Figure 5.16 (a) A computer-scored test answer sheet allows the student to fill in answers using a pencil. (b) An optical mark reader is then used to compute the score.*

(a)

(b)

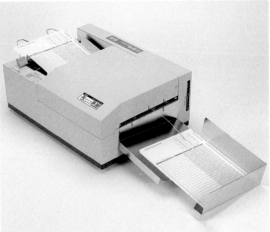

name can also be specified by filling in the circles or squares corresponding to letters.

Other applications of optical mark readers include payment forms and survey or questionnaire forms that request the customer or respondent to fill in answers to inquiries. Grids must be filled in carefully—no stray pencil marks—for data to be interpreted correctly by an optical mark reader.

## OPTICAL SCANNERS FOR TYPED OR HANDWRITTEN DATA

With an **optical scanner,** source documents such as reports, typed manuscripts, or even books can be entered directly to a computer without the need for keying. An optical scanner converts text and images on paper into digital form and stores the data on disk or other storage media. Optical scanners are available in different sizes and for different types of applications. Small handheld units for PCs cost hundreds of dollars and can process a few pages a minute. More sophisticated scanners for larger computers can process hundreds of pages a minute at a cost of thousands of dollars or more, depending on the speed and capability of the device.

The publishing industry is a leading user of optical scanning equipment. Publishers scan printed documents and convert them to electronic databases that can be referenced as needed. Similarly, they may scan manuscripts instead of retyping them in preparation for the process that converts them into books or magazines. Considerable time and money are saved, and the risk of introducing typographical errors is reduced. In addition, publishers who need to reprint previously published articles in different formats may scan the original documents.

Scanners that can interpret handwritten input are subject to even more errors. To minimize mistakes, handwritten entries should follow very specific rules. Some scanners will flag handwritten entries that they cannot interpret or will automatically display for verification all input that has been scanned. (See Figure 5.17.)

Because handwritten entries are subject to misinterpretation and typed entries can be smudged, misaligned, erased, and so forth, optical scanners have an error rate considerably higher than error rates for keyed data. Nevertheless, scanners are widely used by organizations whose

*LOOKING* / *AHEAD*

**PREDICTIONS ABOUT OCRs**
- New OCR devices will allow scanners to read handwriting and poorly reproduced text with improved accuracy.
- Advanced OCR systems will increasingly depend on expert systems to "learn" or decipher the characteristics of new type fonts or handwritten data that may be difficult to read.

*Figure 5.17 Handwritten entries to be scanned must follow precise rules.*

| Rules | Acceptable | Unacceptable |
|---|---|---|
| 1. Make letters big | REDFORD | REDFORD |
| 2. Use block letters | ROBERT | Robert |
| 3. Carefully connect lines | 571 | 571 |
| 4. Close loops | 9086 | 9086 |
| 5. Do not link characters | ROBERT | ROBERT |

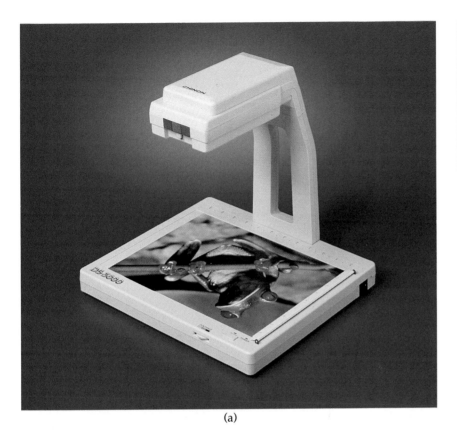

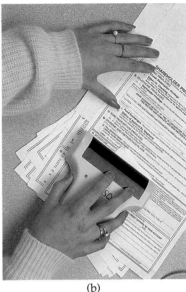

(b)

*Figure 5.18* Scanners can scan images as well as text and can be (a) a desktop unit or (b) a handheld unit.

(a)

documents have been prepared offline and need to be converted to machine-readable form at a later date. Despite the 10% to 20% error rate of some scanning operations, users would rather make corrections resulting from these errors than spend the time and money to rekey documents and risk additional errors. Scanners are becoming increasingly more reliable. Some are sophisticated enough to read not only text but visuals such as photos, illustrations, and graphs. (See Figures 5.18 and 5.19.)

## ▶ Applications Using Data Collection Systems

If salespeople or other field staff employees transact business at the client's premises, the data entry problem is compounded by the need to collect data from many locations or transaction sites. Similarly, in a large store, salesclerks typically complete transactions in their own departments; then data from these transactions needs to be collected before it can be processed. Data collection devices are designed to (1) record data electronically and (2) collect it from various sites.

*Figure 5.19* This scanner is used by law enforcement agencies to scan photos of missing children.

### POINT-OF-SALE TERMINALS

A common input device for data collection with which you may be familiar is the **point-of-sale (POS) terminal** which can be a bar code reader

*Figure 5.20* Point-of-sale terminals are used in retail stores to enter sales information, update inventories, and print customer receipts.

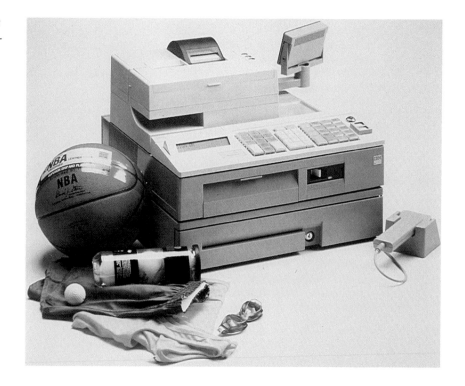

like we discussed previously or a keyboard device. Broadly defined, a point-of-sale system uses remote terminals in retail establishments to enter data at the locations where business is transacted. For example, stores have POS terminals located strategically in many departments (Figure 5.20). At the point of sale, the purchase is recorded and the POS terminal produces a sales slip for the customer. For a purchase made by credit card, the POS terminal transmits the data to the central computer, which verifies the account number and updates the account. The POS terminal also calculates sales totals and may be used to keep track of inventory. Other retail businesses that commonly use POS terminals are fast-food restaurants, supermarkets, and hotels.

A POS terminal can be a keying device, a bar code reader, or any type of data collection device suitable for specific retail applications.

## TELEPHONES, FACSIMILE EQUIPMENT, AND PORTABLE DATA COLLECTION DEVICES

Some computer systems are equipped to accept input data directly from any Touch-Tone telephone. For example, many banks allow their checking account customers to pay bills by telephone. Using a telephone a customer simply responds to prerecorded instructions that request the account number to be entered, the company to be paid (usually identified with a code number), the amount to be paid, and the date on which to make payment. In this case, the phone is simply a remote keying device for data collection. A facsimile machine (fax) can also transmit input directly to a computer over telephone lines.

Portable or handheld keying and scanning devices are available as well. See Figure 5.21. Some of these devices store the data collected on disk in an offline operation and others use the telephone to send input data directly to a CPU in an online operation. A salesperson working at a client's premises (or any remote location not at the same site as the main CPU), for example, can enter orders using a portable keying or scanning device. Some portable devices simply store data for future batch processing. Others generate source documents or transmit data over telephone lines to a CPU that receives the order and updates files.

## PEN-BASED SYSTEMS: THE WRITE STUFF

Pen-based computers are new and exciting data entry units. They are more than keying devices, although they can be used primarily to key data. They are more than optical scanners, even though they can read and interpret handwriting. Pen-based systems are full-blown computers with built-in disk drives. Salespeople who are part of a field staff find them convenient to fill out orders displayed on a screen and store the data on disk. See Figure 5.22. Pen-based systems can also serve as general-purpose computers; input to be entered can be either keyed or handwritten.

A pen system has wider applicability than a system with a touch screen or a mouse because the stylus (or pen) of a pen-based system has the following three features:

*Figure 5.21 Portable keying devices may be used in many types of applications. Here, a law enforcement agent uses a portable keying device to write tickets.*

1. Users can make handwritten movements fine enough to enter not only text but sketches and drawings.
2. Users can insert an entry using a caret (^) to mark the entry point. Text can be marked for deletion by drawing a line through it. The ability to mark text makes a pen more useful than a mouse for some types of applications.
3. Users can actually enter text as handwritten characters.

*Figure 5.22 Pen-based computers can be used to fill out order forms in a supermarket or complete applications for clients.*

## *LOOKING* AHEAD

### INTERACTIVE COMPUTERIZED PHONE SYSTEMS

*We already have:*

- Computerized "receptionists" that lead us through a maze of options that we select with the use of a Touch-Tone phone.
- Computerized direct-marketing machines that dial our phone numbers and deliver a recorded sales pitch. Even if we hang up, the recording ties up the phone until the message is complete.
- Voice recognition equipment used by telephone companies for routing calls and processing requests.

*With increasing frequency we can expect:*

- To order products and make reservations with a Touch-Tone phone.
- To have messages read to us, albeit in a prerecorded monotone.
- To use the digits on a phone to request written information that is then transmitted to us over a facsimile device.
- Automatic dictation to instantly convert a person's voice to computer text.

*Operators are monitoring direct-marketing telephone systems.*

As with optical readers, the problem of high error rates with pen-based systems has yet to be entirely resolved. Even though individual printed characters can be recognized with reasonable accuracy, the normal handwriting of most of us may not always result in an acceptable level of recognition.

Many manufacturers are hoping that pen-based micros will become

*Figure 5.23 Palmtop pen-based system can be used for filling out forms or taking notes.*

the businessperson's primary tool, because these systems can function as general-purpose computers and can store handwritten notes as well. In addition, they allow the pen to work just as a mouse for selecting commands from icons displayed on the screen. In many instances, pen-based systems simply store the handwritten notes without really interpreting them. They can, of course, always be read by the user.

For people who take handwritten notes at meetings, these devices are a real boon. While a computer requires two-handed typing and more of the user's attention, pen-based systems function just like a pad and pencil. The GRiDPAD and the GO computer are the two most common pen-based systems. Palmtop manufacturers like Sony and Poqet have developed even smaller pen-based systems. See Figure 5.23.

 Portable and palmtop pen-based computers make it easier for a field staff to collect data and for individuals to take notes regardless of their location. In so doing, these devices help the world get even smaller.

## ▶ Automation in the Banking Industry

The banking industry has specific information processing needs that are often met by specialized input devices. Some of the input devices used by banks are magnetic ink character readers, automatic teller machines, and debit cards.

### MAGNETIC INK CHARACTER READER DEVICES

When checks are printed for a bank's customers, they contain magnetically encoded digits on the bottom that identify the customer's account and each check number. After the check has been used in a transaction and returned to the bank, it is encoded on the bottom with the amount of the check. Banks use **magnetic ink character readers (MICRs)** to read the magnetic ink numbers printed at the bottom of checks. Figure 5.24*a* is an example of specially encoded bank checks and 5.24*b* illustrates a MICR device.

When magnetically encoded checks are returned to the bank, they can be processed in large batches very quickly by these high-speed MICR devices that read, sort, and store the data on disk or other medium. In the United States alone, billions of checks are processed with MICR devices each day. These units read digits only and some special characters, but not alphabetic characters. Limiting the number of acceptable characters in this way increases the speed of the device.

### AUTOMATIC TELLER MACHINES

The **automatic teller machine (ATM)** is an interactive input/output device in which data entered at the point of transaction can either (1) automatically and immediately update banking records in an online operation or (2) store the transaction and update banking records later

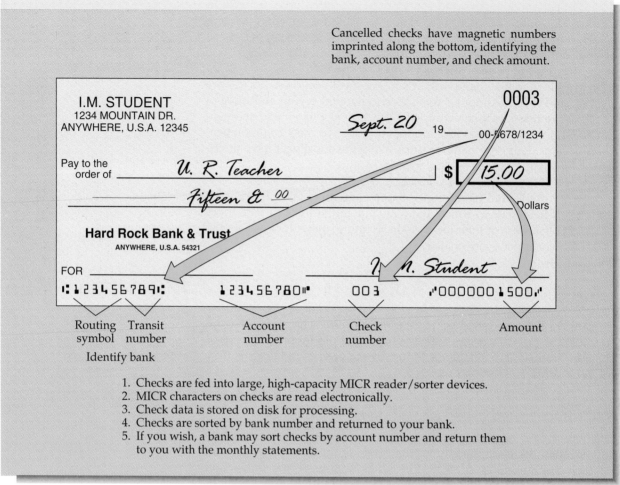

Cancelled checks have magnetic numbers imprinted along the bottom, identifying the bank, account number, and check amount.

I.M. STUDENT
1234 MOUNTAIN DR.
ANYWHERE, U.S.A. 12345

0003

*Sept. 20*   19___   00-5678/1234

Pay to the
order of    *U. R. Teacher*                    $ *15.00*

*Fifteen & 00*                                   Dollars

**Hard Rock Bank & Trust**
ANYWHERE, U.S.A. 54321

FOR _____        *I. M. Student*

⑆1234567891⑆        123456780⑈        003        ⑈0000001500⑈

Routing   Transit          Account        Check          Amount
symbol    number          number         number
Identify bank

1. Checks are fed into large, high-capacity MICR reader/sorter devices.
2. MICR characters on checks are read electronically.
3. Check data is stored on disk for processing.
4. Checks are sorted by bank number and returned to your bank.
5. If you wish, a bank may sort checks by account number and return them to you with the monthly statements.

(a)

*Figure 5.24* (a) *Canceled checks have magnetic numbers imprinted on the bottom identifying the bank, account number, and check amount. An operator encodes the check by keying the amount of the transaction when the check is returned to the bank.* (b) *A MICR check-processing device can process 2400 or more checks per minute.*

(b)

**Figure 5.25** (above) *Automatic teller machines have become an everyday convenience to many people.*

**Figure 5.26** (right) *A debit card with a keypad may be used in bank transactions.*

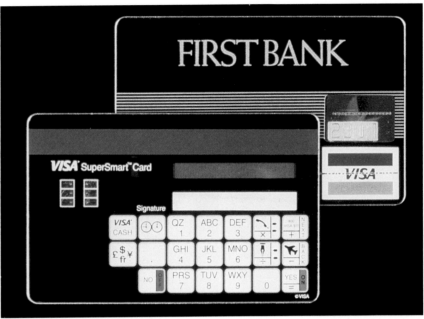

in batch mode. Customers use an ATM to deposit cash or checks, withdraw cash, or electronically transfer money from one account to another. ATMs make banking more flexible because they are usually available 24 hours a day and do not require any intervention from a teller or other bank employee. To protect the customer's funds, the bank provides plastic cash cards that have magnetic strips encoded with account information; the customer inserts the card into the ATM and then keys in a password called a personal identification number (PIN). If the card and PIN are valid and the account is active, the customer is able to proceed with the transaction. See Figure 5.25.

### DEBIT CARDS

A **debit card** looks like a credit card but contains a microprocessor chip with memory. Like credit cards, they are used to make purchases; but with debit cards, transactions are immediately posted to your account and the memory on the card that contains account data is updated to reflect the transaction. Debit cards are a type of smart card that we will discuss in more detail in Chapter 6. Some super smart cards are available with keypads so that you can check the status of your account as well as make purchases. See Figure 5.26.

## ▶ Voice Recognition Equipment

Probably the most user-friendly input device is one that can accept human speech as input and correctly interpret a small vocabulary of spoken words. **Voice recognition** technology uses computers to interpret words and phrases the way people do. For example, a factory worker

(a)

(b)

*Figure 5.27 A voice recognition device can be used (a) by the physically disabled for executing instructions or even for selecting items from a menu and (b) for voice typing.*

can enter inventory data which is then stored on disk, by speaking into a device while opening boxes and analyzing their contents. A laboratory technician can record results of a blood workup by speaking into a voice recognition device while viewing the blood samples in a microscope. A quality control expert can specify the results of an automotive inspection by speaking into a voice recognition device as the inspection is being performed. A security system may use voice recognition equipment to identify authorized personnel based on their responses to computer-generated queries. A voice pattern, like a fingerprint, is a distinctive trait that can uniquely identify an individual. In each case, the voice recognition equipment not only records the input but interprets it as well and stores it in machine-readable form. See Figure 5.27.

Voice recognition devices are most often used in organizations where data entry operators need to use their hands for other operations such as verifying products, stamping cartons, and making handwritten entries. Telephone companies, shop-at-home facilities, and customer service centers rely heavily on this technology. Telephone companies have automated their routing and operator services to such an extent that the need for operator intervention has been greatly minimized and in some instances eliminated entirely. For example, if a taped message announces a collect call, you may be able to decline it by simply saying "no"; the telephone system understands your response to mean that you do not wish to receive the call.

Currently, voice recognition systems exist that can recognize thousands of words regardless of the accent, dialect, or tonal qualities of the speaker. Some can even "learn" the meaning of new words. Some have a high degree of reliability even where there is background noise. But voice patterns differ widely from person to person, so this technology still has a high error rate. As this equipment becomes more reliable, however, its applicability is likely to increase.

Voice recognition devices, like pointing devices, light pens, touch screens, and handheld data collection devices, minimize the need for keying data. This makes them ideally suited for people who do not like to type, whose other tasks prevent them from using their hands, or who have eye-hand coordination problems or other physical disabilities.

## ▶ Digitizers

One fast-growing application of computers today is for drawing illustrations or creating graphic images. Artists, engineers, and designers need specialized equipment to create their designs so that they can be stored, analyzed, and manipulated by the computer. Professional quality illustrations can be drawn with a pen on a sensitized surface called a **digitizer tablet.** As the pen makes contact with the surface, differences in electrical charges are detected, and the image being drawn is stored electronically in the computer. The digitizing tablet contains a grid of sensor wires, and as the pen moves over the grid, it makes contact with specific points on it. In this way, continuous movements of the pen are translated into digital signals. See Figure 5.28.

Digitizer tablets, then, are very practical for converting images into machine-readable format. Small digitizers also function in robots as "eyes" to record shapes and physical properties of objects within their range. The digitized images are compared with those stored in the robot's memory to determine if the robot "recognizes" the object. See Figure 5.29.

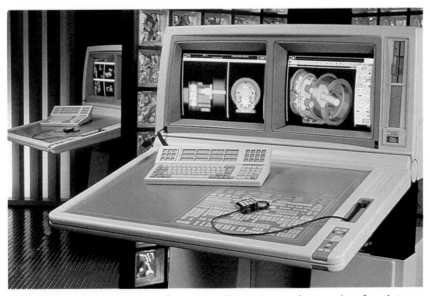

*Figure 5.28 A digitizer is used for drawing illustrations and converting them into machine-readable form.*

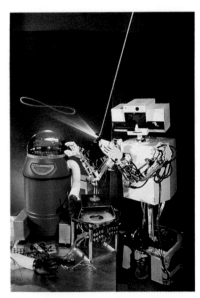

*Figure 5.29 Some robots have digitizers that serve as "eyes."*

▶ **SELF-TEST**

1. (T or F) Offline data entry operations tend to be less costly alternatives to online data entry.
2. Besides keying, the most common devices for converting source documents to machine-readable form are _____.
3. Most grocery stores use _____ readers for their checkout procedures.
4. (T or F) The Universal Product Code on a grocery item or other consumer goods typically includes the price for that item.
5. A _____ system uses remote terminals in retail establishments to enter data at the locations where business is transacted.
6. (T or F) Magnetic ink character readers (MICRs) can read any letter or digit that is magnetically encoded.
7. (T or F) The automatic teller machine (ATM) is an example of an interactive input/output device.

Solutions

1. T
2. optical character readers (OCR devices)
3. optical bar code
4. F—It specifies a code for the manufacturer of the product as well as for the product itself. This data is used to retrieve the price from a computer. To change a price, only the computer entry need be adjusted, *not* the UPC on every product.
5. point-of-sale (POS)
6. F—They can read only digits and some special characters, but not alphabetic characters.
7. T

## 5.3 OUTPUT INFORMATION AND OUTPUT DEVICES

Considering the criteria that make output information useful, what advantages and disadvantages does each class of output device offer users?

We use computers because we expect them to produce some form of useful information, or output. To be useful, output information must meet the criteria of completeness, conciseness, accuracy, timeliness, cost-effectiveness, and relevancy.

In Chapter 1 we discussed the distinction between data and information, and this is a good time to review it. Individual data items—such as today's date or the record of the sale of a box of nails—are typically entered into the computer, which uses application programs to process them in a meaningful way. Each application is designed to produce a particular kind of output, for example, a summary of all sales for a given day. This output, or processed data, is information. Output differs from raw data, or input, in that it can be used for decision making.

If you manage a store's inventory, for example, it is not enough to know how many boxes of nails were sold today. You also need to know how many boxes are on hand at the end of the day, the average number of boxes sold per day, the projected date by which all the boxes of nails will be sold, and how long it takes to restock nails by ordering from your nail vendor. This *information* allows you to decide when to reorder nails.

## ► Types of Output

We use output devices daily, usually without even noticing that a computer program is controlling the application. Many libraries, for example, have converted their card catalogs from drawers stacked with file cards to disk from which specific entries can be displayed on a computer screen. To determine if your library has a certain book, you simply follow a few on-screen instructions. You may type an author's last name or a subject, and the related titles and catalog codes in the library's collection appear on the screen. In this case the computer is producing **soft copy,** or screen display, output. Computers can also produce **hard copy,** or printed output. Some libraries, for example, have the capability of printing a bibliography of titles on a subject. You key in a few parameters and the computer gives you a printed list of all the books that fall within the criteria you set.

There are endless varieties of special-purpose output such as airline tickets, ATM transaction slips, library overdue notices, and a book manuscript from a word processor. Most routine business output, however, can be classified into two categories: responses to inquiries and reports.

### RESPONSES TO INQUIRIES

Inquiries usually involve on-demand searches of a database for a particular piece of information. For example, a human resources department might need to know the date of employment for Lamont Jones, whose Social Security number is 342-00-0228. Or a customer service representative might need to determine whether an item ordered is currently in inventory. Responses to inquiries are usually made interactively with the output either displayed, printed, or perhaps verbally transmitted to the user. See Figure 5.30 for an illustration.

### REPORTS

Printed reports are produced either on demand (unscheduled) or periodically. Special reports may be generated on demand whenever the need arises; usually they are produced in response to a request by management. Periodic reports are printed on a regular basis. Reports can be classified into three groups: exception, summary, and transaction. For example, a marketing manager might notice an unaccountable increase in sales in a geographic area and request a listing of individual orders for that area to determine whether the increase represents a trend. This would be an on-demand **exception report.** An example of a scheduled exception report is a weekly listing of all salespeople whose expense accounts are not within the expected range. Exception reports are usually generated to alert managers to situations that might require their attention.

*Figure 5.30 This clerk uses a keyboard for entering a customer's request or inquiry. The response will be displayed on the screen.*

**TYPES OF REPORTS**

On demand or scheduled
- Exception
- Summary
- Transaction

**Summary reports** are produced periodically—daily, weekly, monthly, quarterly, yearly—or on demand. These include sales summaries, end-of-month inventory listings, a company's financial statements, cost of sales analyses—all the standard working reports needed by an organization's functional areas. Summary reports are used by the operating staff and managers for decision making.

**Transaction reports** contain detailed information of business transactions and are routinely used by the operating staff. Examples of transaction reports include complete listings of payroll checks, orders received, invoices scheduled for payment, and stock transactions.

Most output devices are designed to produce information either as hard copy printouts or soft copy visual displays. Figure 5.31 shows some of the more common ones. Next we will discuss hard copy and soft copy output devices in detail; then we will describe two other forms of output devices: those for audio output and for image processing.

## ▶ Output Devices

### MONITORS

Soft copy screen output is usually associated with some form of interactive processing in which input is entered or a request is made and output is displayed. When performing an interactive inquiry or search, you typically choose an option from a menu; then the screen displays more detailed submenu options; and when your exact request has been entered, the computer retrieves the information you need.

A variety of screen display devices, also called video display terminals

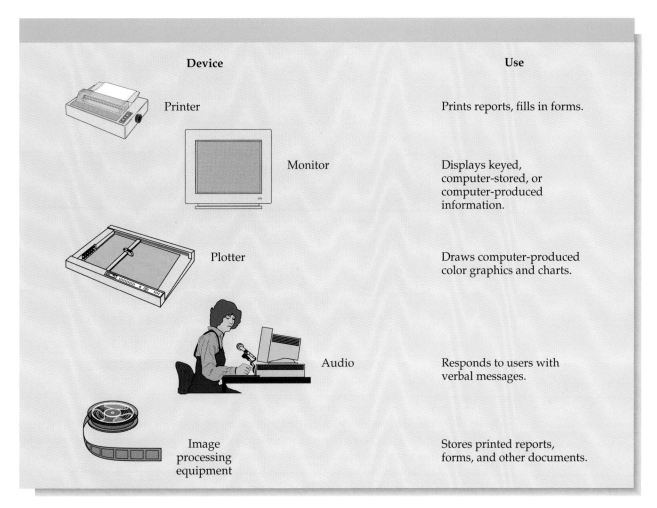

| Device | Use |
|---|---|
| Printer | Prints reports, fills in forms. |
| Monitor | Displays keyed, computer-stored, or computer-produced information. |
| Plotter | Draws computer-produced color graphics and charts. |
| Audio | Responds to users with verbal messages. |
| Image processing equipment | Stores printed reports, forms, and other documents. |

(VDTs), are available, and the technologies used to produce them can be quite sophisticated. For example, early PC monitors or screens were usually either black and white or black and green, but today's monitors can produce high-quality graphics in many colors.

*Figure 5.31 Examples of common output forms and devices.*

**CRTs.**  One common form of display monitor is the **cathode ray tube (CRT),** which is still used extensively with microcomputers and as terminals. They resemble the picture tube in your TV. CRTs contain an electron "gun" that fires a beam of electrons, lighting up tiny points of phosphor that glow for a short period of time. Every character you see on the screen is made up of many of these points of light called **pixels**. A typical CRT, for example, consists of $640 \times 480$ pixels. The gun constantly scans the screen, relighting the pixels so rapidly that the screen characters appear to be glowing continuously. The quality of what you see on the screen is determined by how many pixels your monitor is designed to display. The more pixels, the better the **resolution,** or crispness, of the characters on the screen.

Older or inexpensive CRTs that display only one color are called monochrome monitors, and they are typically either green or amber against a

**Figure 5.32** *On color monitors, each pixel contains three phosphor dots: one red, one green, and one blue. These dots can be turned on in various combinations to display a wide range of colors.*

black background. Color monitors are far more desirable not only because they make viewing text more appealing, but also because they are better for graphic applications. The cost of color monitors has decreased considerably in recent years, which has made them even more popular.

Graphics adapter boards or circuit cards, either built in or added to a microcomputer's main circuit board, are required to create color graphics. Types of adapters include color graphics adapters (CGAs), multicolor graphics adapters (MCGAs), enhanced graphics adapters (EGAs), video graphics arrays (VGAs), and extended graphics arrays (XGAs). Each of these categories represents different standards of resolution, that is, different numbers of pixels and colors that affect the crispness of images and the number of hues available.

Color monitors are often called **RGB monitors** (for *r*ed, *g*reen, *b*lue). RGB monitors have three electron guns—one each for red, green, and blue—and the pixels have a dot of red, green, and blue that can be activated individually or in combination by the electron guns to create many hues and colors. Figure 5.32 shows the high quality of a graphic image displayed on an RGB monitor.

Although CRT screens are well suited for desktop PCs and terminals, portable PCs need screens that are smaller and lighter. Such screens use flat-screen technologies that, in general, do not have the resolution of desktop monitors.

**Flat-Screen Technologies.**  You may have noticed that the monitor on your personal computer is actually deeper than it is wide or tall; this is

*Figure 5.33 An IBM PS/2 model P75 notebook computer with a gas-plasma display screen.*

the shape required for the CRT's electron gun inside. It is not, however, a practical shape or weight for portable computers. Thanks to new flat-screen technologies, portable computers like laptops, notebooks, and palmtops can have high-resolution screen displays. Although most current flat screens are monochrome, color flat screens are available but they tend to be expensive.

One flat-screen technology, electroluminescent (EL) display, is available but it sometimes requires too much power for battery-operated laptops.

The most common flat screen is the liquid crystal display (LCD), in which a current passes through liquid crystals sandwiched between two sheets of polarized material. Characters on the screen are created when crystals arrange themselves so that light does not shine through; the image is dark against a lighted background. An LCD display is used on digital wristwatches and pocket calculators.

Some of the newest laptops use gas-plasma displays, even though they require more power than LCDs. They have very good resolution and graphics capability, and some have color displays as well (Figure 5.33). Gas-plasma displays sandwich a neon/argon gas mixture with grids of vertical and horizontal wires. Pixels are located at the points where horizontal and vertical wires cross.

### The Human Factor: Ergonomics and the Radiation Issue.

**Ergonomics,** or human engineering, is the science related to human-machine relationships. For computer users, ergonomics focuses on the overall effects of sitting at a computer for much of the work day.

*Figure 5.34 Attention should be paid to the comfort and health of employees when designing workstations.*

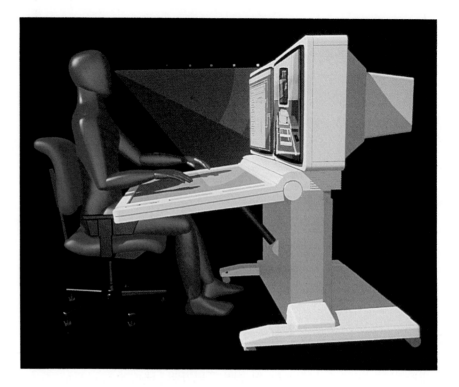

Controversy rages over monitors and their potentially adverse impact on the health of users. Back pain, eye strain, and wrist and hand disorders are relatively minor problems compared to the threat of radiation exposure that some fear. Antiradiation screens can help, but they block electric fields at only low frequencies and they do not block magnetic fields at all. (Some experts consider magnetic fields to be the more serious hazard.)

The issue of whether radiation from monitors is really dangerous has yet to be resolved, so experts advise users to sit at least 18 inches away from their screens and to stay 4 feet away from the sides and back of other monitors in the workplace. To minimize the effects of screen glare, employees who work at monitors should have a 15-minute break every 2 hours.

Organizations can make computer users more comfortable and hence more productive by (1) purchasing adjustable chairs, tables, screens, and keyboards; (2) improving lighting; and (3) minimizing external noise. See Figure 5.34 and Chapter 13, where we discuss ergonomics in more detail.

### IMPACT PRINTERS

Various types of printers are available for hard copy output. They are classified either as **impact** (strike-on method) or **nonimpact printers.** Both kinds are used with all types of computers. Inexpensive impact printers are commonly used with microcomputers and more expensive, high-speed impact printers are used with large mainframes. Nonimpact printers for large and small computers can produce high-quality output faster than most impact printers, but at a higher price. Nonimpact printers include laser, thermal, and ink-jet printers.

**Serial Printers.** Like typewriters, impact printers use some form of strike-on method to press a carbon or fabric ribbon against paper to create a character. At the inexpensive end are **serial printers.** These printers, which are designed for microcomputers or terminals for larger systems, are slow: they print one character at a time. Serial printers are usually designed for feeding paper by either tractor feed or friction feed, although some may include attachments that allow for both methods.

Tractor-feed printers use **continuous-form paper** (Figure 5.35) that feeds through the device without interruption. Continuous-form paper has small holes on either side that fit onto sprockets on the printer which feed the paper through at the required speed. The paper can be preprinted for specialized business tasks. For example, many companies produce their bills and checks on continuous forms which are preprinted with the company logo and the desired format. Pressure-sensitive mailing labels are also available on continuous forms so that they can be printed in batches. Most business forms that go through a computer's printer are some type of continuous form—either standard stock paper or special preprinted forms such as invoices, purchase orders, or shipping labels. These forms are perforated so that they can be separated, and many are chemically treated so that multiple "carbon" copies can be created.

*Figure 5.35* Output is typically printed on continuous forms that are perforated so that the pages can be easily separated.

Friction-feed impact printers feed a sheet at a time through the mechanism as do many nonimpact printers. They are used for high-quality output such as correspondence and reports, often on a company's letterhead paper.

The two types of serial printers are dot-matrix and character printers.

*Dot-matrix Printers.* **Dot-matrix printers** are impact printers that create characters from a rectangular grid of pins. The pins strike against a carbon ribbon to print on paper. The characters are rather crude, but readable. As we will see, line printers as well as serial printers can be of the dot-matrix type. Many offices use a form of dot-matrix printer that is called a near-letter-quality printer because it overprints in a slightly offset pattern that fills in the lines to create much better quality type. Figure 5.36 illustrates output from a standard dot-matrix printer in both draft and near-letter-quality form.

*Character Printers.* Character printers most often use a daisywheel mechanism to print characters. **Daisywheel printers** print fully formed characters from a flat disk that has petal-like projections containing individual characters (Figure 5.37). They are the slowest type of printer, but they produce crisp, letter-quality output. Many offices use daisywheel printers as serial printers for their correspondence because the quality of the output is similar to that of standard typewriter output. The daisywheels themselves are interchangeable so that a variety of typefaces can be used on the same printer. They are limited in their graphics capability, however.

**Figure 5.36** (a) How a dot matrix printer prints characters. The letter E is formed with seven vertical and five horizontal dots. As the print head moves from left to right, it fires one or more pins into the ribbon, which makes a dot on the paper. (b) Printed output from a dot-matrix in draft and near-letter-quality form.

**Figure 5.37** A daisywheel printer uses a revolving, petal-like print head to produce clear, precise letters.

**Line Printers.** At the more expensive end, designed to be used with large computer systems, are high-speed **line printers;** they print one line at a time and also use continuous-form paper. Types of line printers include band printers, chain printers, and drum printers as well as dot-matrix printers previously discussed.

Some line printers use a flexible, stainless-steel print band that is photoengraved with print characters and prints one line at a time. The band rotates horizontally until the characters to be printed are properly aligned. Band printers are popular because they are inexpensive compared to other line printers, produce high-quality output, run at high speed, and have removable bands that allow type fonts to be changed easily.

Chain printers are line printers that have one print hammer for each print position in a line. The chain revolves horizontally past all print

*Figure 5.38* Chain, drum, and band printers. These impact printers all use some form of strike-on method to print. (a) The chain printer hammer strikes as the chain rotates past the paper, while (b) drum printers create lines of type by rotating column sections of the drum. (c) With band printers, the band spins horizontally around the hammer and when the desired character is at the desired position, the corresponding hammer hits the paper.

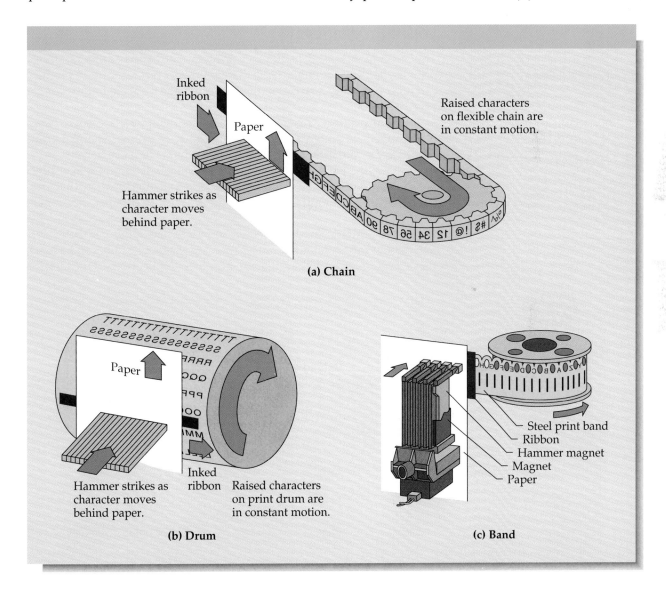

Inked ribbon

Paper

Hammer strikes as character moves behind paper.

Raised characters on flexible chain are in constant motion.

**(a) Chain**

Paper

Hammer strikes as character moves behind paper.

Inked ribbon

Raised characters on print drum are in constant motion.

**(b) Drum**

Steel print band
Ribbon
Hammer magnet
Magnet
Paper

**(c) Band**

positions. As a character on the chain passes the position where it is to print, the hammer presses the paper against the ribbon to produce a character image. Chain printers have two disadvantages: they are relatively expensive and some have chains that are difficult to change.

Drum printers use a cylindrical steel drum embossed with print characters. Each column on the drum contains all the characters, and the columns and drum rotate at high speed to print a line at a time. Many organizations have replaced their drum printers with newer band printers, which are more versatile and tend to last longer. Figure 5.38 shows how the band, chain, and drum print mechanisms work.

The disadvantages of all impact printers (in contrast to nonimpact printers discussed next) are that they are slower, noisier, and more often subject to mechanical breakdowns. Nevertheless, because they are relatively inexpensive, they continue to be popular.

## NONIMPACT PRINTERS

Three commonly used nonimpact printers are thermal printers, ink-jet printers, and laser printers. Note that nonimpact printers cannot produce carbon copies; only a strike-on method can make a visible impression on backup sheets.

**Thermal printers** create whole characters on specially treated paper that responds to patterns of heat produced by the printer. Thermal printers are less popular than ink-jet and laser printers because they are slow; in addition, the paper is expensive and the image deteriorates over time. Newer thermal transfer printers use a heat-and-wax method that produces high-quality output in color and on untreated paper. See Figure 5.39a.

**Ink-jet printers,** for both microcomputers and large computer systems, shoot tiny dots of ink onto paper. Since any color ink can be used, these printers are well suited for graphics applications. Figure 5.39b

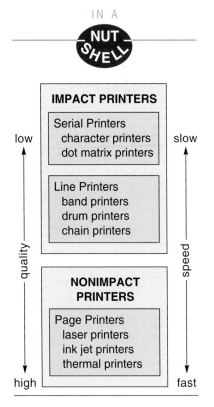

**DESKTOP PRINTERS**

| | Type | Category | Quality | Speed | Cost |
|---|---|---|---|---|---|
| Impact | Dot-matrix | Serial | Draft to near-let-ter-quality | 30 to 500 cps | $100 to $2000 |
| | Character or Daisywheel | Serial | Letter | 10 to 90 cps | $400 + |
| Nonimpact | Thermal | Serial | Near-let-ter-quality | 11 to 80 cps | $200 |
| | Ink jet | Serial | Near-let-ter-quality | 35 to 400 cps | $500 to $2000 |
| | Laser | Page | Letter | 8 to 28 ppm | $500 to $10,000 |

cps = characters per second; ppm = pages per minute; 48 cps = 1 ppm

(a)

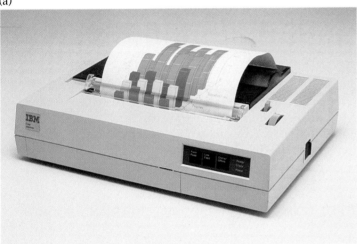

(b)

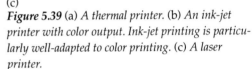

(c)

*Figure 5.39* (a) *A thermal printer.* (b) *An ink-jet printer with color output. Ink-jet printing is particularly well-adapted to color printing.* (c) *A laser printer.*

shows a thermal printer, and an ink-jet printer with examples of its color output.

**Laser printers** were first introduced as high-speed printers for large mainframe systems, but their versatility, high-quality output, and decreasing cost have made them popular for computer systems of all sizes. Laser printers beam whole pages at a time onto a drum; then the paper passes over the drum and picks up the image with toner, like that used in xerographic copiers. At the high-priced end, color laser printers that cost tens of thousands of dollars and produce near-photographic-quality images are being used in the graphics industry for color reproduction of books and magazines. At the lower end, laser printers are available for micros for less than $1000. See Figure 5.39*c*.

One application that has developed largely because of the availability of laser printers for micros is desktop publishing, which uses personal computer systems to produce professional-quality publications. Desktop publishing is discussed in more detail in Chapter 7.

(a)

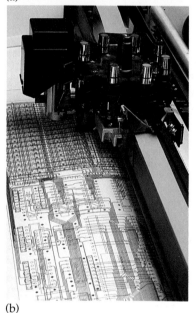

(b)

*Figure 5.40* Plotters can be (a) desktop devices or (b) very large floor models.

## CAPTURING GRAPHIC IMAGES

Graphic images have the visual power to summarize or represent data in a way that is often more meaningful and informative than words alone. In some instances, a graphic image may be the only form that output can take, for example, a customized design of an automobile. Sometimes output is produced graphically because a picture really is worth a thousand words.

Graphic output is usually displayed on a screen and then directed to another medium only if it is needed in hard copy form. Most printers are capable of producing graphics, many even in color. In general, graphic images require far more storage than text does, so that computers used for graphic applications often have more primary storage and auxiliary storage than those used strictly for processing text.

**Plotters** are printing devices specially designed to produce high-quality drawings in color. Pen plotters move pens containing different colors of ink over paper. Electrostatic plotters use electrostatic charges to produce images on paper. Plotters have many applications, particularly for presentation graphics (charts and graphs for business meetings) and engineering drawings. See Figure 5.40.

If the purpose of your output is to make a presentation to a group, you may want transparencies to use with an overhead projector. Transparencies can now be created directly from a screen display. Some printers and plotters will make transparencies if you simply substitute a sheet of acetate for paper when you make your hard copy; sometimes specialized devices are needed to produce transparencies. Also, 35-mm slide makers with a built-in camera can capture a screen display on film by the click of a button. The film is then developed to produce high-quality slides.

## AUDIO OUTPUT USING VOICE RESPONSE UNITS AND SOUND BOARDS

Not all output from computers is visual. **Voice response units** provide verbal responses by means of a voice simulator or a series of prerecorded messages. Some automobiles give you voice messages if you leave your key in the ignition, leave your parking lights on, or trip the security system. In many banks audio response units respond to tellers or to customers at home who need to determine whether an account has funds to cover a check. The teller or customer keys in the account number and the amount of the check using a Touch-Tone phone. The computer then determines whether there are enough funds in the account and selects the appropriate verbal response to "speak" to the teller or to the at-home customer.

Voice simulators are a practical aid for blind people. Figure 5.41 shows a word processing application designed to give audio feedback to typists who cannot visually verify the accuracy of their keyboarding.

Many telephone companies have voice response units for directory assistance. You call an operator who keys the name and address of the person whose number you want; then the voice response unit gives you

*Figure 5.41 A voice response unit for the visually impaired.*

*Figure 5.42 A sound board to create different types of sound.*

the number. Locator services like this have widespread applicability: they can tell customers where the nearest store stocking a desired product can be found—users need only call and key in their ZIP codes; they can indicate the location of the nearest theater that is playing a movie you keyed in; and so on.

Telephone companies also use voice response units often in conjunction with voice recognition equipment for directory assistance and other services. Many other interactive systems are also voice driven. You speak into a voice recognition device and receive a voice response. If the technology really improves, you might not even know if you are communicating with a person or a machine!

**Sound boards,** used extensively with PCs, can generate a wide range of sounds, including music, in addition to voice responses. You may find them in multimedia applications where audio output enhances presentations and the learning process. See Figure 5.42.

## MICROFILM AND OPTICAL DISKS FOR IMAGE PROCESSING SYSTEMS

Many organizations need high-speed devices for recording and storing images of documents for future processing by computer. When data to be stored includes illustrations, photographs, special forms, signatures, and so on, **image processing** systems are used to scan and store the data.

### *LOOKING AHEAD*

**THE DOCTOR IS ALWAYS IN**

Hospitals are experimenting with techniques for creating effective hospital-physician networks. Doctors and their office managers use Touch-Tone phones to obtain information from a hospital and to have the information forwarded to various locations. The system is linked to both a voice response unit that provides the doctors with the facts they need and to a facsimile (fax) machine for transmitting the information to other locations. Physicians can call from their car phones, offices, or virtually anywhere.

*Figure* *5.43* *Using image processing techniques, computers can store, for example, loan applications, stock information, or real estate listings as images.*

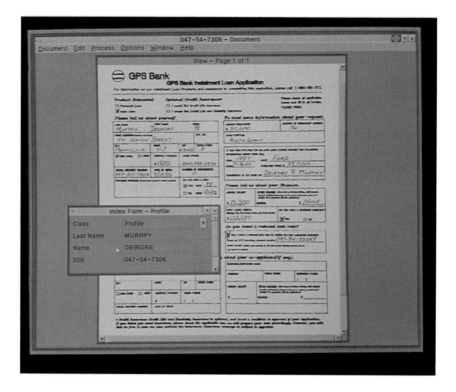

*Figure* *5.44* *Computer output on microfilm.*

Many insurance companies, for example, have image processing systems that scan claim forms and store the data on microfilm or other media. In this way, they are better able to handle a large volume of similar claims, for example, those related to common disasters such as earthquakes and hurricanes. See Figure 5.43. Banks often scan and store credit reports using image processing techniques.

Microfilm and microfiche, collectively referred to as microforms, have been in use for many years to store images and documents. These are miniaturized photographic copies of documents that require a relatively small storage space. See Figure 5.44. Computer output microforms (COM), which can store illustrations as well as text, are one early type of image processing medium.

Optical disks, however, are becoming competitive with film-based systems for storing high-volume data and pictures. Libraries that once used COM now use the newer optical disk technology to store images of newspapers and magazines that they would otherwise be unable to keep because of space limitations. Even University Microfilms International is using optical disk image technologies rather than microfilm for storing some documents. Currently, it offers Business Periodicals Ondisk, a full-text image database that provides access to several hundred business journals on optical disk. (Maybe it is time for University Microfilms to change its name!) Today, many image processing systems store documents on optical disk or other optical media, which we discuss in the next chapter.

▶ **SELF-TEST**

1. (T or F) In computer systems, the word *data* is simply another term for information.
2. Screen display output is referred to as (<u>soft copy/hard copy</u>).
3. Printed output is referred to as (<u>soft copy/hard copy</u>).
4. A(n) _____ report is a listing of all events or data items that fall outside a set of management-determined parameters.
5. (T or F) The more pixels a monitor can display, the better the resolution of the characters on the screen.
6. Ergonomics, or human engineering, is the science that concerns itself with _____ relationships.
7. The two major classifications of printers are _____ and _____.

Solutions
1. F—Data refers to input; information refers to output, or *processed* data.
2. soft copy
3. hard copy
4. exception
5. T
6. human-machine
7. impact; nonimpact

▶ **Chapter Summary**

Information systems rely on input/output devices to meet their computational needs. There are a wide variety of such devices available for specific user needs.

## 5.1 INPUT DEVICES CREATE SOURCE DOCUMENTS AND DATA FILES

Computers process raw data as input and produce information as output. Information is "processed data"—data that has been manipulated, operated on, and formatted in a way that helps users make decisions and take action. Raw data that is entered as input from **source documents** must be entered into a storage medium to be processed. Some source documents must be rekeyed so that they can be read by a CPU; others are already machine readable. Separate keying operations to create an input file are called offline operations.

In business today, data is typically entered via a keyboard and is stored in a file, usually on disk. To minimize errors, a **control listing,** or **audit trail,** may be prepared as a printout so that users can manually check all changes made to files.

Alternatives to keying include several user-friendly input devices. A **mouse,** for example, can be moved around the computer's screen to manipulate the cursor. A mouse is useful for responding to a **prompt** or

*How have input devices evolved to meet user needs for error-free source documents?*

for selecting submenu items, which often appear as **pull-down menus.** Other alternatives to keyboarding include **touch screens** and **light pens.** A **joy stick,** popular for playing games, can also position a cursor. All these devices minimize the need for keying.

## 5.2 SOURCE DATA AUTOMATION REDUCES DATA ENTRY OPERATIONS

*How does source data automation actually improve productivity in organizations?*

**Source data automation** is the process of computerizing the procedure that converts source documents to machine-readable form. A number of devices can read various types of input directly and then convert them to machine-readable form. **Optical character readers (OCRs)** scan data. They include **bar code readers,** which read the **Universal Product Code (UPC)** on merchandise or other types of bar codes; bar code readers can be scanners or **wand readers,** which read bar codes as well as specially typed characters; **optical mark readers,** which read pencil marks made on special forms; and **optical scanners,** which scan text and graphics from typed or handwritten entries.

Applications for source data automation are varied. Data collection systems use **point-of-sale (POS) terminals,** telephones, facsimile equipment, and portable devices for collecting data at the point that a transaction is made. Pen-based systems are ideal for portable data collection. Banks have **magnetic ink character readers (MICRs)** that read the magnetic ink numbers on checks; **automatic teller machines** that act as interactive input/output units; and **debit cards** that maintain transaction records.

**Voice recognition equipment** is perhaps the most user-friendly input device because it interprets spoken messages. Another device growing in popularity is the **digitizer tablet,** which converts illustrations into machine-readable form.

## 5.3 OUTPUT INFORMATION AND OUTPUT DEVICES

*Considering the criteria that make output information useful, what advantages and disadvantages does each class of output device offer users?*

To be useful, output must be timely, complete, concise, and relevant. Standard business output falls into two categories: inquiries and reports. Printed output is either scheduled or produced on demand, usually in the form of **exception reports, transaction reports,** or **summary reports.**

Output hardware includes printers for **hard copy** output and screens for **soft copy** output. Screens are usually associated with interactive output; they present menus of choices from which the user can make selections. The most common kind of screen, or monitor, is the **cathode ray tube (CRT),** which can be either monochrome or color (many color monitors are **RGB monitors**). Each tiny point of light is called a **pixel,** or picture element. The more pixels, the better the **resolution,** or crispness, of the image.

Laptop computers take advantage of flat-screen technologies such as electroluminescent displays, liquid crystal displays, or gas-plasma displays. **Ergonomics,** or human engineering, is a science related to human-machine relationships; it focuses on topics such as the possible adverse effects caused by working with computers.

**Impact** and **nonimpact** printers produce hard copy output. Impact printers can be **serial printers**—slower mechanical devices such as **dot-matrix** and character or **daisywheel printers** for micros—as well as high-speed **line printers** such as band printers, chain printers, and drum printers for mainframes. Both often use **continuous-form paper.**

Nonimpact printers currently in use are primarily **thermal printers, ink-jet printers,** and **laser printers.** The availability of laser printers has led to a whole new industry called desktop publishing. **Plotters** are printing devices specially designed to produce color graphics for presentations and engineering drawings.

Not all computer output is visual. Two forms of audio output are currently available: a **voice response unit** simulates the human voice or plays prerecorded messages in response to input, and a **sound board** plays a variety of sounds including music.

**Image processing** is a new technology that encompasses computer output microform (COM), optical storage, and other high-volume media to capture not only textual output but photos, illustrations, documents, and signatures.

## ► Chapter Self-test

1. What is the difference between data and information?
2. A blinking cursor or an actual message called a _____ signals the user that a computer response is required.
3. A purchase order that must be read by the computer or converted to machine-readable form is called a _____.
4. If a submenu appears as a superimposed drop-down menu, it is called a _____ menu.
5. Input devices that can read printed characters directly from a source document are called _____.
6. Name several ways in which screen output can highlight entries.
7. (T or F) A printout called a control listing or audit trail includes data that a program has found to be erroneous.
8. (T or F) In general, laser printers are faster than line printers.
9. Impact printers that form characters using pins in a rectangular pattern are called _____ printers.
10. (T or F) Daisywheel printers produce letter-quality output.
11. The bar code on consumer goods is called the _____.
12. (T or F) Laser printers use a technology similar to that of copy machines.
13. What are two advantages of impact printers?
14. (T or F) Plotters are used to reproduce photographic images.
15. The computer device that creates output as a microform is the _____ unit.

### Solutions

1. Data consists of raw facts; information is processed data.
2. prompt
3. source document

4. pull-down
5. optical character readers (OCR) or optical scanning devices
6. color; boldface; reverse video; a blinking cursor
7. T
8. T
9. dot-matrix
10. T
11. Universal Product Code (UPC)
12. T
13. They are relatively inexpensive and they can produce multiple "carbon" copies.
14. F
15. computer output microfilm (COM)

## ▶ Key Terms

Audit trail, *p. 177*
Automatic teller machine (ATM), *p. 191*
Bar code reader, *p. 183*
Cathode ray tube (CRT), *p. 199*
Continuous-form paper, *p. 203*
Control listing, *p. 177*
Daisywheel printer, *p. 203*
Debit card, *p. 193*
Digitizer tablet, *p. 195*
Dot-matrix printer, *p. 203*
Ergonomics, *p. 201*
Exception report, *p. 197*
Hard copy, *p. 197*
Image processing, *p. 209*
Impact printer, *p. 202*
Ink-jet printer, *p. 206*
Joy stick, *p. 181*

Laser printer, *p. 207*
Light pen, *p. 181*
Line printer, *p. 205*
Magnetic ink character reader (MICR), *p. 191*
Nonimpact printer, *p. 202*
Optical character reader (OCR), *p. 183*
Optical mark reader, *p. 185*
Optical scanner, *p. 186*
Pixel, *p. 199*
Plotter, *p. 208*
Point-of-sale (POS) terminal, *p. 187*
Prompt, *p. 176*
Pull-down menu, *p. 176*
Resolution, *p. 199*
RGB monitor, *p. 200*

Serial printer, *p. 203*
Soft copy, *p. 197*
Sound board, *p. 209*
Source data automation (SDA), *p. 183*
Source document, *p. 171*
Summary report, *p. 198*
Thermal printer, *p. 206*
Touch screen, *p. 180*
Transaction report, *p. 198*
Universal Product Code (UPC), *p. 183*
Voice recognition equipment, *p. 193*
Voice response unit, *p. 208*
Wand reader, *p. 184*

## ▶ Review Questions

1. Describe two handheld input devices and indicate how they might be used in business.
2. List three ways of detecting input errors.
3. Define the following terms related to screen displays: CRT, pixel, resolution, monochrome, and RGB monitor.
4. Describe three types of flat-screen technologies.
5. For impact printers and nonimpact printers, list at least two advantages and three disadvantages.
6. The U.S. Postal Service hopes to better process the mail by adopting

several new procedures. By 1995, the Postal Service wants 95 percent of the mail to be addressed with bar codes, because bar code readers are more reliable and less expensive than the current OCR systems. The Postal Service hopes to improve or replace its current OCR equipment with more sophisticated equipment that can read addresses unintelligible to the present systems and that can perform more complex routing and checking. Sorting of irregular parcels will be accomplished by machines that can determine the shape and locate the address on the package. A robotic arm, guided by an image processing system, will manipulate the packages. Indicate the benefits of the new equipment that the U.S. Postal Service plans to use.

## PRODUCT ANALYSIS

## CASE

### Pen-Based Computers: The Ready for Prime Time Products

If you were to ask computer gurus to predict the technologies likely to capture the minds and hearts of users by the beginning of the next century (not so far away) most would include pen-based computing near or at the top of the list.

Pen-based computers are already widely used by companies such as United Parcel Service for recording signatures. Instead of signing a paper document acknowledging receipt of a package, customers write directly on the computer screen with a special electronic pen. Many other companies use pen-based computers for displaying documents and forms that can be stored and can record signatures and data. At State Farm Insurance, for example, when claims adjusters visit claimants, they write the information they gather on forms that have been programmed into the machines. If the claim merits it, the adjuster can use a small printer attached to the machine to issue a check immediately, saving time for the claimant as well as the company. The machine stores all the data, which can be transferred to conventional computers for review later.

But pen-based computers are likely to have even wider applicability. They may well replace notepads and even notebook computers in the years ahead. You can write on the screen as you do on a notepad and have your notes—even your doodles—saved for future reference. For those who do not like to type and for those who need to make sketches, pen-based devices are a real boon.

Rather than having digitizers "interpret" the written word (that is, adapting the pen to the computer), new operating systems like GO Corporation's PenPoint and Microsoft's Windows for Pen Computing are trying to make the computer adapt to the pen. Some computers like the GRiDPAD RF pen computer come with wireless network communications capability. In this way, users in the field are able to communicate directly and effortlessly with their home base by means of a radio antenna.

Pen-based portables are likely to change from weighing 5 to 7 pounds and measuring 1-inch thick to being able to fit in a coat pocket. They will function like electronic calendars, address books, and notetakers and be usable for word processing and spreadsheet tasks as well. Prices are expected to fall from $5000 to $1000 in the near future. Predictions are that the number of units sold will increase from just under 300,000 machines in 1992 to a million in 1995.

Most analysts believe, however, that even a volume of 1 million computers will not support the large number of manufacturers that are currently competing in this field and that some high-profile companies may go bankrupt or abandon their plans. On the other hand, manufacturers like Hewlett-Packard and Sony, market leaders in palmtop computers, will expand their product line to include new, pen-based "picocomputers."

*Analysis*

1. State some advantages for businesses in recording data on pen-based computers rather than on traditional, nonelectronic paper forms.

2. Why are pen-based computers more convenient for a field staff than laptop computers?

3. Why might a student prefer to take notes using a pen-based computer rather than a conventional notebook?

4. Suggest some other nonbusiness uses for pen-based computers.

# C · H · A · P · T · E · R · 6

# SECONDARY STORAGE DEVICES

In recent years, computers have become faster, more powerful, and more accessible to individuals and organizations. It is likely that the amount of data and information available in our society will continue to multiply at an ever-increasing rate.

Television shows and movies often provide a futuristic version of what is available to users of large computer systems. In these accounts, the mere click of a few keys brings to the screen an individual's entire life history with photos, fingerprints, and forms such as a driver's license, birth certificate, and marriage license. In another type of movie, scientists scan the records of seemingly thousands of databases to pinpoint diseases, determine drug therapies, locate potential donors for transplants, and so on. Although the widespread availability of such information may not yet be a reality, technologies for storing and retrieving the necessary data are making such uses more feasible.

In Chapter 4 we considered the power of computers and the ways in which the CPU processes data. In Chapter 5 we focused on the wide variety of input and output devices for various application areas. A computer's ability to provide information to users, however, relies heavily on the secondary storage units it has to store programs and data. In this chapter we answer the following questions:

▶ Why is secondary storage a crucial component of a computer system?

▶ Why is disk the main secondary storage medium for most systems, why has it replaced tape, and what other magnetic media are being used?

▶ What advantages do optical devices have when compared with magnetic media for secondary storage?

▶ What are the major ways of organizing data files?

## 6.1   FUNDAMENTALS OF SECONDARY STORAGE

Why is secondary storage a crucial component of a computer system?

In Chapter 4 we saw how data is processed by the CPU. Programs are loaded into primary storage (also called main memory), input data is read, and output is produced as information. But primary storage in most computers is temporary, or volatile, which means that when the power supply is shut off, whatever is in main memory (programs and data) is lost. Storage of programs and data for future processing requires a peripheral device, such as disk, called **secondary storage** or **auxiliary storage.** Secondary storage is *nonvolatile;* that is, all information is saved even after the power is shut off. In this chapter we discuss secondary storage media with storage capacities and retrieval mechanisms that enable fast and easy access of information.

Magnetic units such as disk and, to a far lesser extent these days, tape are traditional storage media for data and programs. Other magnetic media such as flash cards are becoming popular as well. Optical media such as compact disks and magneto-optical disks, though relatively new, have large storage capacities and sophisticated methods of access that enable them to augment or, in some instances, replace magnetic media. See Figure 6.1.

## ▶ Review of File Processing Concepts

Secondary storage units store data that was originally entered using an input device such as a keyboard. Typically, the data is stored in the form of a file. Let us review some file processing concepts before we study specific secondary storage media.

Recall that a file is a major collection of data in a given application area. Within a file, each individual unit of data is called a record. A payroll file, for example, consists of employee records and an accounts receivable file consists of customer records. Each record contains characters organized into fields. A payroll record may have a Social Security number field, name field, salary field, and so forth. In Chapter 11, we will see that database management systems can be used to link or join files so that data from them can be processed in an integrated manner.

Files are processed in either batch mode or interactively. In batch processing, each record in a file is read and processed in sequence from the first to the last record. If a file is routinely processed in batch mode, then it can be organized simply for sequential processing. All storage media can process records in sequence but we will see that tapes, once widely used for secondary storage, can *only* be processed in sequence.

Sometimes records need to be processed interactively. If managers must access or make inquiries about records as the need arises and in no particular sequence, an information system based on sequential access of records will be very inefficient. Similarly, suppose a point-of-sale system updates accounts receivable records as transactions occur—that is, randomly—the records to be processed are not likely to be in sequence by customer number. Disks and optical media can process files randomly but tapes cannot.

## ▶ Criteria for Evaluating Storage Devices

We consider five major criteria for evaluating secondary storage media and drives: the storage capacity, the access time needed to locate data, the transfer rate for data, the cost, and the size of the storage unit itself.

**Storage capacity,** measured in kilobytes (K), megabytes (MB), or gigabytes (GB), indicates the amount of data that the storage medium can hold. The storage capacity for a PC's hard disk may be as much as several hundred megabytes or even a gigabyte whereas the storage capacity for larger disks and some optical media may be as much as hundreds of gigabytes. Only diskettes have storage capacities measured as kilobytes or 1 to 2 MB; all other media have much greater storage capacities.

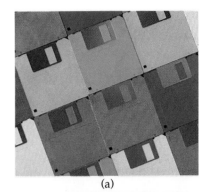
(a)

(b)

*Figure 6.1 Photos of secondary storage. (a) 3½-inch disks. (b) Optical disk.*

### EVALUATING SECONDARY STORAGE MEDIA

| | |
|---|---|
| Storage capacity | How many bytes does it store? |
| Access time | How long does it take to access data? |
| Transfer rate | How long does it take to transfer data to and from main memory? |
| Cost | What is its actual cost and what is its cost per megabyte (or gigabyte)? |
| Size | How much space does it occupy? |

**Access time,** which is the time needed to locate data on a secondary storage device, is measured in thousandths of a second (milliseconds). It varies from 50 to 25 milliseconds for magnetic media, but it is often as slow as 500 milliseconds for optical media.

Data on a secondary storage medium is not available for processing until it is copied from the storage unit to main memory, where the CPU has access to it. **Transfer rate** refers to the speed at which data is transferred (that is, copied) from the secondary storage unit to main memory, and it is measured in megabytes per second. Transfer rates typically range from one to several MBs per second.

---

Note that after a "transfer" operation, the data is still stored on the secondary storage medium. The word *copy* would be a more accurate term.

---

Both access time and transfer rates are far slower than a computer's processing speed, so any technique that speeds up these rates makes a computer more efficient. As noted in Chapter 4, a cache stores frequently accessed data and instructions in a special area that is available for more immediate processing. A cache uses operating system software and innovative technological mechanisms to improve access time and data transfer rates. It has been available for many years on larger systems and is now widely used with microcomputers as well.

The cost of a secondary storage unit directly relates to the preceding three factors. Smaller capacity disk drives for micros may cost from as little as a few hundred dollars to as much as a few thousand dollars; mainframe disk drives may cost tens of thousands of dollars. When a computer system processes large amounts of data, saving even ten thousandths of a second per record can add up to significant amounts of time, a benefit that may more than outweigh a higher price.

The physical size of the storage unit is important because it affects the space requirements for the organization's computer facility. A series of compact disks housed in a desktop unit that stores as much data as several stand-alone or floor-mounted magnetic disk units not only requires less space but is easier to maintain.

### ▶ SELF-TEST

1. (T or F) Data recorded on secondary storage media is nonvolatile.
2. (T or F) When a file is read from secondary storage into primary storage, it is erased from secondary storage in the process.

3. What is the most widely used magnetic storage medium?
4. The time it takes to locate data on a secondary storage device is called
_____.

Solutions

1. T
2. F

3. disk
4. access time

# MAGNETIC MEDIA FOR SECONDARY STORAGE 6.2

In this unit we focus on disks as the main magnetic medium for secondary storage. We include tape concepts as well and discuss some of the newer magnetic storage media.

## ▶ Magnetic Disks and Disk Drives

A magnetic disk, often simply called a disk, is a Mylar film or aluminum platter coated with a magnetic substance such as ferrous oxide. Data is stored in concentric rings called tracks. Each character of data is represented as bits (binary digits) that appear as magnetic fields on the tracks.

Micros use floppy disks (also called diskettes) or hard disks to store programs and data files. Mainframe systems use either fixed disks or removable disk packs; both types consist of a series of disks that operate on data in the same way as microcomputer diskettes, but have greater storage capacity, faster access rates for reading data, and faster rates for transferring data from primary storage to disk and back again. All disks need a peripheral called a disk drive for reading data from the disks and writing to them.

Although mainframe disks were developed first, we will begin with what is probably more familiar to you, the floppy disk. Then we will discuss the types of hard disks for micros and, finally, their mainframe equivalent.

Why is disk the main secondary storage medium for most systems, why has it replaced tape, and what other magnetic media are being used?

### MAGNETIC DISKS AND DISK DRIVES FOR MICROS

**Floppy Disks.** The primary function of floppy disks is to store programs and data files for microcomputer processing. Two sizes predominate today: 5¼-inch and 3½-inch. The 5¼-inch diskettes, which became popular with the original IBM PC, had a capacity from 180 to 360 K, but now they have capacities of from 360 K to 1.2+ MB. Since most typed pages contain approximately 2000 characters, a 1.2 MB 5¼-inch diskette can store the equivalent of 600 typed pages.

The Macintosh computer was the first to use 3½-inch diskettes, beginning in 1984. The IBM PS/2 family of computers also uses 3½-inch disks with a capacity from 720 K to 2.88 MB or more. These diskettes have a

**A "DRIVE"-ING FORCE
IN COMPUTING**

In 1987, IBM introduced the 1.44 MB 3½-inch floppy disk drive for its PS/2, forcing many of its customers to switch to 3½-inch diskettes. Now, a few years later, users may need to "trade up" to higher-density 3½-inch drives that can read 2.88+ MB floppies. IBM has announced that its 2.88 MB diskette drive for 3½-inch floppies will be standard equipment on its PS/2 Model 57SX and other computers as well. Other manufacturers are introducing 3½-inch and other sized diskettes with even greater capacities that require different diskette drives to make use of the added capacity. These disks are likely to cause dissatisfaction with users who are already unhappy about the lack of standards. Why do some manufacturers seem to be insensitive to the problem of compatibility? What can users do to minimize these problems?

rigid plastic casing that provides much better protection than the original, flexible floppy diskettes that actually "flop."

Other sizes of diskettes are available for some types of computers with special disk drives. Although the 3½-inch and the older 5¼-inch disks are still the most widely used, standardization remains a serious industry-wide problem. For example, 1.2 MB 5¼-inch diskettes cannot be read by older diskette drives designed for 360 K floppies. Similarly, older 3½-inch diskette drives designed to read 720 K diskettes cannot read 1.44 MB or 2.88 MB diskettes.

**How Diskettes Store Data.**    Inside a disk jacket, or sleeve, is a thin, flexible plastic disk that has a metal oxide coating capable of retaining magnetic bits of data. The 5¼-inch disks are enclosed in a flexible paper jacket, while 3½-inch disks are enclosed in rigid plastic, which makes them the more durable form.

Figure 6.2 illustrates how data is stored on diskettes. Each diskette contains two surfaces, or sides. On each surface there are a number of tiny concentric circles called tracks, and the tracks are segmented into wedge-shaped sectors. Even though tracks get successively smaller toward the hub of the diskette, each track contains the same amount of data. Data is just recorded more densely in tracks closest to the center.

Most microcomputer diskettes are **soft-sectored;** that is, the sectors are not already defined on the diskettes when you purchase them. Because sector definition differs among operating systems, sectors are defined for the first time when you format, or initialize, your new diskettes. Your computer's operating system contains the program that formats diskettes. Some diskettes designed for specific micros can be purchased already formatted so that you need not bother to format them first.

***Figure 6.2*** *A floppy disk stores data in concentric tracks. The FORMAT command divides the disk into wedges called sectors.*

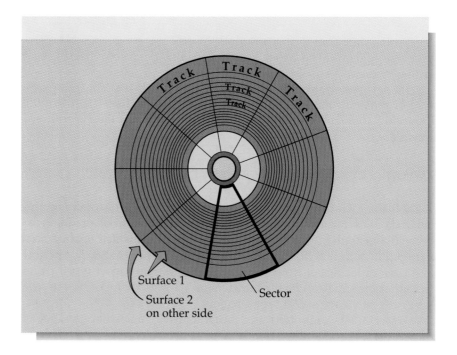

**Taking Care of Diskettes.** Diskettes are fairly durable, but they can be damaged or erased, making your data unusable. Figure 6.3 illustrates five rules for protecting the data on your diskettes.

1. Do not expose diskettes to magnetic fields. Three common sources of magnetic fields that can affect diskettes are telephones, television sets, and copiers. Diskettes can usually pass through X-ray equipment at airports or magnetic sensors in libraries without being damaged, but many people bypass these devices just in case.
2. Keep 5¼-inch diskettes in their paper sleeves to protect the window where the magnetic portion of the diskette is exposed. The diskette's magnetic material can be damaged if it gets scratched or if foreign material such as food or dust gets on it. Store diskettes in boxes to keep objects from being piled on top of them, which may warp them.
3. Gummed labels should be used with diskettes to identify the data on them. On soft 5¼-inch diskettes, write on the label with felt-tip pens, not pencils or ballpoint pens; hard points can press through the jacket and damage the disk. Avoid touching the disk surface itself, because fingerprints can damage it.
4. Do not spill anything on the diskette; do not use any cleaning liquids on it.
5. Do not leave diskettes in heat, sunlight, or in the cold; do not leave them on the dashboard of your car. Disks can become distorted by extremes in temperature, and your data will be destroyed.

Whenever you format a diskette that was used previously, you erase everything that is on it.

With a single command, it is possible to accidentally erase all data on a diskette. For example, the DOS command ERASE *.* deletes all files. To prevent data on diskettes from being erased accidentally, you can write-protect it. Figure 6.4 shows a 5¼-inch diskette with a write-protect notch that can be covered with a gummed tab and a 3½-inch diskette with a built-in write-protect tab that can be positioned to cover the notch. Covering the notch on 5¼-inch diskettes write-protects them so that you cannot write onto them; that is, any instruction to write data on the diskette will result in a "write error." Positioning the tab so that it *does not* cover the notch on 3½-inch diskettes write-protects them. Diskettes containing programs supplied by software developers usually have the write-protect notch permanently covered on 5¼-inch diskettes (often the diskette is supplied with no notch at all). Similarly, 3½-inch write-protected diskettes may have their notch permanently uncovered. This minimizes the risk that users may inadvertently write over an important program.

**How Diskette Drives Access Data.** A **read/write head** is a mechanism for reading data from, or writing information onto, a disk. Diskette drives that process double-sided floppy disks have two read/write heads, one for each side of the diskette. (Older, single-sided disk drives have a read/write head that can access only one side of the diskette.)

Records are stored on diskettes at diskette locations called addresses. A diskette address consists of a surface number, track number, and sector number. When a particular program or data file is to be accessed or read,

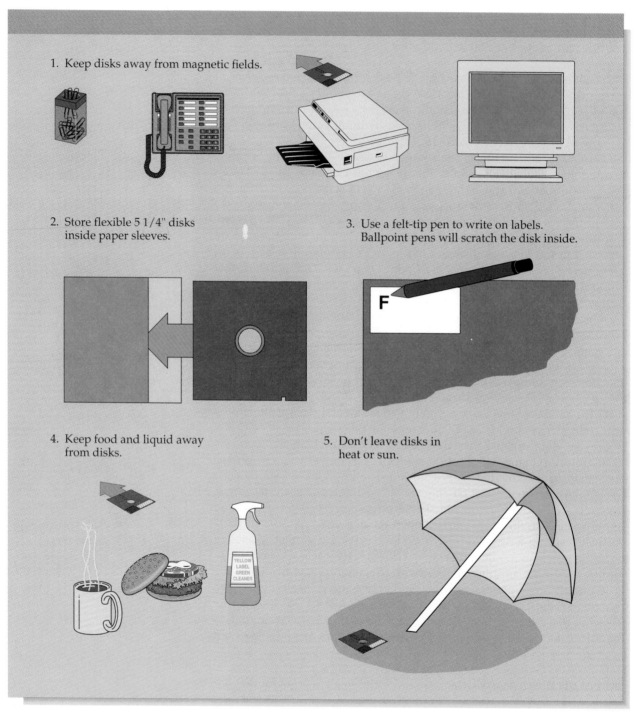

1. Keep disks away from magnetic fields.

2. Store flexible 5 1/4" disks inside paper sleeves.

3. Use a felt-tip pen to write on labels. Ballpoint pens will scratch the disk inside.

4. Keep food and liquid away from disks.

5. Don't leave disks in heat or sun.

*Figure 6.3* *These five simple rules will protect your disks and their data from the most common sources of damage.*

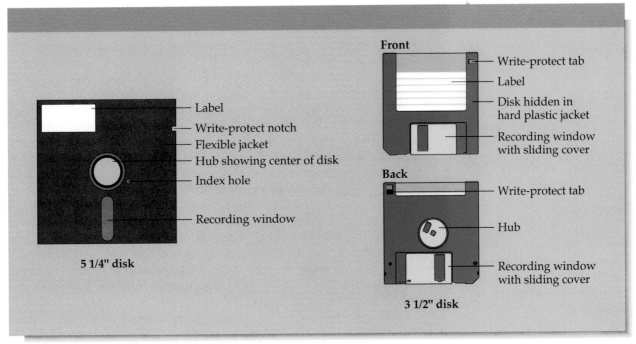

Front

Write-protect tab
Label
Disk hidden in hard plastic jacket
Recording window with sliding cover

Back

Write-protect tab
Hub
Recording window with sliding cover

3 1/2" disk

Label
Write-protect notch
Flexible jacket
Hub showing center of disk
Index hole
Recording window

5 1/4" disk

*Figure 6.4* The 5¼-inch and 3½-inch floppy disks have similar features. However, sliding panels and a hard case give the 3½-inch disk more protection.

the address of the file is looked up from a file allocation table, which keeps track of each file's location. The disk drive then whirls the disk inside its sleeve to locate the correct sector, while the arm moves the appropriate read/write head to the track containing the data. The same thing happens when you write to a disk: the disk drive locates an available surface/sector/track address on which to write the data.

**Hard Drives for Micros.** Microcomputers have one or two floppy disk drives, which may be housed in the system unit or which may be separate external devices. You insert diskettes into these drives as shown in Figure 6.5, which puts the read/write head in contact with the disk so that it is ready for reading or writing data (for 5¼-inch disk drives, close the lever first). When there are two diskette drives in a system unit, the drive on the left or top is usually labeled as drive A, and the one on the right or bottom is called drive B.

Many microcomputers also have a large-capacity internal hard disk, usually called drive C on IBM and IBM-compatible computers, although it can be designated by other letters as well. Macintosh computers identify the drives by icons instead of letters—a more user-friendly approach. Hard disks have a capacity several times that of a diskette; the smallest hard disks hold 20+ MB, while the largest ones currently available hold hundreds of megabytes. Even larger capacities will probably be available soon.

Hard disks are made of a rigid metal substance coated with a metal oxide. Data is stored on a hard disk in surfaces, sectors, and tracks—just as on diskettes. Hard disks are sealed into sterile containers, because the distances from the read/write heads to the disk are so small that even something as tiny as a cigarette smoke particle can affect the mechanism.

*Figure 6.5* Insert a disk into the slot in the disk drive, then close the lever, or gate (if you are using a 5¼-inch disk) to secure it in place. Here, a 3½-inch disk is being inserted into a drive.

*Figure 6.6 Fixed disks, or internal hard disks, are made of a rigid material, and hold many times more data than a floppy disk.*

When foreign substances get between a read/write head and the disk, a **head crash** may occur: the head makes direct contact with the disk and destroys its surfaces. Computer users dread this occurrence because everything on the disk is likely to be lost. We will see later on in this chapter that disks are periodically copied to other disks or other media which are stored as back-ups in case something happens to the originals.

There are two types of microcomputer hard disks. The older, more popular one is called an internal hard disk or a **Winchester disk.** This type of disk is built into the computer's case (Figure 6.6). In the early 1980s, **hard cards** became available. They are circuit boards with hard disks built into them. Because they are boards, they can be added to a micro by plugging them into the computer's internal expansion slots (see Figure 6.7). An *external* hard disk drive could be added to a computer as well. Such a disk drive is often purchased as an add-on peripheral for a computer that has dual floppy diskettes or to augment an existing internal hard disk drive. An external drive means that you need more desk space to accommodate an extra piece of equipment, but the drive has the advantage of being portable; you can unplug it from one computer and move it to another.

Hard disks for micros have many advantages as compared to diskettes. To begin with, the computer's operating system can be copied onto the hard disk. If you have an IBM or IBM-compatible microcomputer, for example, you can start your computer directly from the hard disk without inserting your DOS diskette in drive A. In other words, when you "boot," or turn your computer on, the operating system is loaded automatically from the hard drive.

Another benefit of a hard disk is that you can copy your application

*Figure 6.7 Hard cards are an alternative to fixed hard disks. They can easily be added to upgrade a microcomputer system after it is purchased. Here, the chassis for the computer has been removed to illustrate how a hard card is inserted.*

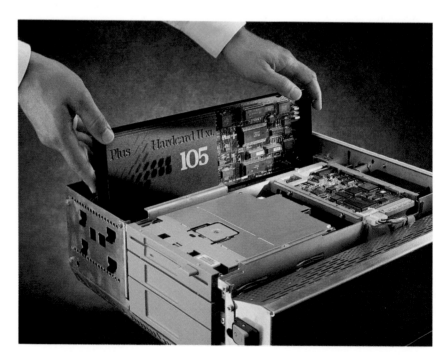

*Figure 6.8* Disk cartridge and drive. This cartridge drive is portable, as is the disk, which stores 90 MB of data.

programs directly to it, thereby eliminating the need to swap large numbers of diskettes into and out of floppy disk drives. For each application on your hard disk, it is best to create a *subdirectory,* which is a separate, labeled area on the disk. Such divisions make it easier to find your way around this large data storehouse and help keep related files together. After data on a disk is no longer needed, it can be erased and written over.

At one time, only mainframes could process large databases because such databases simply would not fit on diskettes. Now that hard disks for PCs have large capacities, many databases can be managed quite satisfactorily on microcomputers. Similarly, hard disks with large storage capacities enable users to store and run more sophisticated programs that require considerable storage.

**Disk Cartridge Drive.**   Although hard drives have the advantage of very large storage capacities, diskettes have the advantage of portability. Data and programs on a diskette can be used with any computer that is compatible with the diskette's format. Data and programs on hard disk need to be downloaded to diskettes to be transported.

**Disk cartridges** accessed by disk cartridge devices combine the advantages of diskettes and hard disks: they have storage capacities comparable to hard disks but they are removable and, thus, are portable. See Figure 6.8. To compete with disk cartridges, some manufacturers have introduced removable hard disks.

To save disk space, many files are compressed, that is, stored in condensed form. Special programs can be purchased that compress files to save space and automatically decompress them when you want to read them. Sometimes programs are provided to users in compressed form to reduce the number of diskettes required. Utility programs must convert compressed programs to usable form before you try to run them.

**CRITICAL THINKING**

Suppose you have a computer at the office with a hard drive and a disk cartridge drive. You have a computer at home with a dual diskette system, but you want to add a storage medium with at least a 40 MB capacity. Would you purchase a hard drive or a disk cartridge drive? Why?

## MAGNETIC DISKS AND DISK DRIVES FOR LARGER SYSTEMS

Larger computer systems use hard disks as their major storage medium. As you might expect, though, disks for the larger systems have far greater storage capacities than microcomputer disks and are larger in size as well. Data on magnetic disks for larger systems is assigned an address just as data on floppy disks for micros. Data is addressed by surface number, track number, and cylinder number, although the *number* of surfaces, tracks, and cylinders is much greater on larger hard disks. A sector on a floppy is similar in concept to a cylinder on a hard disk. See Figure 6.9. A typical micro's disk may have 80 or so tracks, and a disk for a mainframe may have 200 or more tracks.

Because large computer systems need access to enormous amounts of data, a mini or mainframe computer is able to instantly access any disk drive attached to it, and it may have as many as 100 available at one time. Consider, for example, the storage needs of the U.S. Social Security system, which has records on virtually every man, woman, and child in the country.

Most hard disks currently in use for larger systems are fixed disks that cannot be removed from the **fixed-head disk drive.** They are similar to the internal hard disks on microcomputers. Fixed-head disk drives are most often separate, stand-alone peripherals linked by cable to the CPU.

An older type of disk for minis and mainframe computers that is still popular today is a **disk pack.** It consists of *removable* sets of hard disks, typically 14 inches in diameter, mounted together on a center spindle like a group of phonograph records (Figure 6.10). Data is recorded on both sides of each disk, except that the top and bottom surfaces of the disk pack are not used because they are more exposed and susceptible to being damaged. A disk pack consisting of 11 disks or platters, for example, has 20 usable surfaces. Disk packs are being replaced by fixed disks because of the potential for deterioration in data when they are moved on and off the system.

*Figure 6.9 A fixed-head disk device for larger computers.*

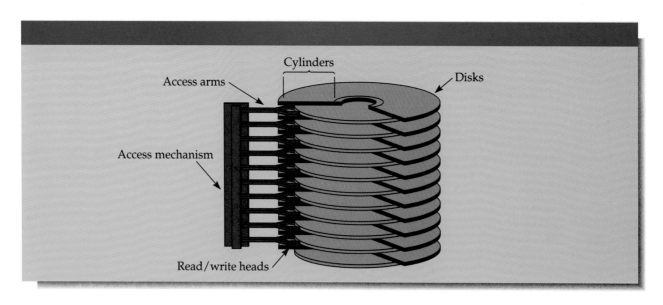

*Figure 6.10* Disk packs are sets of disks mounted together on a spindle. The packs are enclosed in a sterile case that can be easily mounted or removed from the computer system.

## READ/WRITE HEAD DESIGN FOR DISK DRIVES

Disk files can be accessed randomly as well as sequentially by directly activating one of many read/write heads and positioning the head at the appropriate location on the disk. Some disk mechanisms for large systems use moving read/write heads. In this design, all the heads in a stack of disks are attached to a single access mechanism that moves directly to a specific disk address when data is to be read or written. A drive with moving read/write heads is relatively slow, because all the access arms must move together.

Fixed-head disk drives contain one or more hard disks and stationary access arms with separate read/write mechanisms for each of the tracks on the disks. The disk, rather than the head, whirls around, to bring the correct sector to the arm. The correct track of the disk is then positioned at the read/write mechanism for retrieving or writing data, depending on the application.

Some disk devices combine the technologies of both moving- and fixed-head access to produce a high-capacity, rapid-access drive.

## ► Magnetic Tapes and Tape Drives

Although magnetic disk is the principal storage medium today, not long ago magnetic tape held that preeminent position. We consider next some of the reasons why tape is no longer widely used except as a backup medium.

## THE WANING OF TAPE AS A PRINCIPAL STORAGE MEDIUM

A magnetic tape drive is a high-speed device that is very similar in concept to a cassette or tape recorder. The drive can read (play) data from

IN A

**WIDELY USED FORMS OF MAGNETIC DISK**

**Diskettes**
- 5¼-inch—320 K to 1.2+ MB
- 3½-inch—720 K to 2.88+ MB

**Hard Disk**
- Fixed disk
- Removable cartridge
- Disk pack

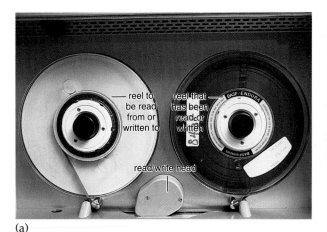

(a)

(b)

***Figure 6.11*** *(a) Magnetic tapes. (b) Magnetic tape drives.*

a magnetic tape and also write (record) data onto a tape by means of a single read/write head. Figure 6.11 illustrates magnetic tapes and tape drives.

Magnetic tape was once used extensively in business as a secondary storage medium, but its popularity has waned in recent years mainly because disks have all the advantages of tape and none of the disadvantages. Disk drives have a series of read/write heads so that the one closest to the data to be accessed can be activated to locate it. This results in faster access time for disks, especially for high-speed, random-access applications. Tapes have a single read-write head and can, therefore, be accessed only sequentially. Thus, their access time is slow; moreover, it is not practical to access records that are not in sequence. In addition, disk records can be read, updated, and rewritten in place, whereas tape records that need to be updated must be written to a new tape. Consider a tape cassette you recorded with your favorite songs on it. If you wanted to add a recording to the middle of the cassette tape, you would need to rerecord the first half onto a new cassette, add the desired record, and rerecord the rest of the tape. Computer tapes need to be processed the same way.

IN A

AN OVERVIEW OF MAGNETIC TAPE

| Type of Tape | Use | Capacity | Price of the Drive* |
|---|---|---|---|
| Reel-to-reel magnetic tape | Larger systems | 200+ MB | $2000+ |
| ¼ to ½-inch cassette tapes | Micros | 40 MB to 5+ GB | $1000 to $4000 |
| 8-mm cartridge tape | Micros | 5+ GB | $7000 |
| Digital audio tape | All sizes of computers | 3+ GB | $2500 to $5000 |

*The tapes themselves usually cost well under $100.

DAT

Cartridge

*Figure 6.12* Cartridge tapes and digital audio tapes, and their respective drives.

## TAPE AS A BACKUP MEDIUM

If tapes are so limited as a storage medium, why do we discuss them at all? First, some organizations still use them for file processing. But more importantly, tapes are popular as a backup medium; they store copies of important files in case the master disks become unusable or are lost. Standard reel-to-reel magnetic tapes often serve as backup media for large computers, while cassettes and cartridges function as PC backup media. Because of their large storage capacity and relatively low cost, digital audio tape can be used as backup for all types of systems. See Figure 6.12.

The contents of a micro's hard disk can be copied to tape in a matter of minutes. Disks for larger systems require a little more time for backup. Some computer systems automatically back up disks to tape at a pre-determined hour of the day or just before the system is turned off.

## ▶ Maintaining Disk and Tape Files

Data is represented on both disk and tape as magnetized bits. These bits of data are extremely small and not visible to the human eye. As a result, large volumes of data can be stored on a relatively small surface area. Data that can be displayed on an 80-character line of a CRT, for example, can typically be stored on $1/20$ inch or less of magnetic tape or disk.

The average tape reel can store up to hundreds of millions of characters. Disks for mainframes have storage capacities ranging from hundreds of millions to billions of characters or more. After a file has been

> **CRITICAL THINKING**
>
> Many PC users do not regularly back up data and programs on their disks. They are simply unwilling to spend the time it would take each day to perform a backup procedure. They know the risks: a disk failure would require them to spend hours or days recreating data files and reinstalling programs. Do you think the risk they are taking is prudent?

processed on disk or tape and is no longer needed, the same disk or tape may be used repeatedly to store other information by erasing and writing over the old file.

## REPRESENTATION OF DATA

**Computer Code.** Data is stored on disk and tape as magnetized bits corresponding to the CPU's own code—either ASCII or EBCDIC. A disk stores the bits that represent a character consecutively along the surface of a track, while a tape uses a series of tracks for representing a single character. See Figure 6.13. Note that the term *track* has different meanings for disk and tape. Tracks on a disk are concentric, with those closest to the center representing the same amount of data, but more compactly. Each track on a tape stores one bit.

**Tape and Disk Density.** Millions or billions of characters can be recorded as magnetized bits on a single magnetic disk or tape. The primary reason for this large storage capacity is the fact that bits are exceedingly small, and hundreds or thousands of them can be placed in an inch or less. The actual number of characters that can be represented in an inch of disk or tape is called its **density.** Since each character is represented by a series of bits in a specific position, disk and tape densities are measured in bits per inch (bpi). Bits on a tape are laid out in parallel tracks so that "bits per inch" is really equivalent to "bytes per inch." The most common tape densities are 1600 and 6250 bpi. Disk densities vary widely. Data on tracks closest to the center of a disk is stored more densely than data on outside tracks. In general, disk densities vary from 6400 bpi to tens of thousands of bpi.

## BLOCKING RECORDS TO MINIMIZE WASTED SPACE AND ACCESS TIME

Disk and tape records are frequently grouped or blocked to save space and access time. **Blocking** means that several actual records (called *logical* records) are grouped together in a block as shown in Figure 6.14. The computer treats one block as a physical record when it reads from and writes to disk and tape. It then segments the block or physical record into its actual (logical) records for processing. This process reduces access time considerably. Thus, blocking of logical records maximizes efficient use of the disk or tape by increasing the speed at which data is transferred to or from the CPU.

In many programming languages, it is relatively simple to instruct the computer that there are, for example, 100-character logical records that are blocked 20. In that case, the computer reads in a block of 2000 characters (100 × 20) and then processes each 100-character logical record within the block in sequence. In short, blocking of disk and tape records decreases access time. Moreover, the handling of blocked disk or tape files is relatively easy for the programmer. Sometimes the blocking of

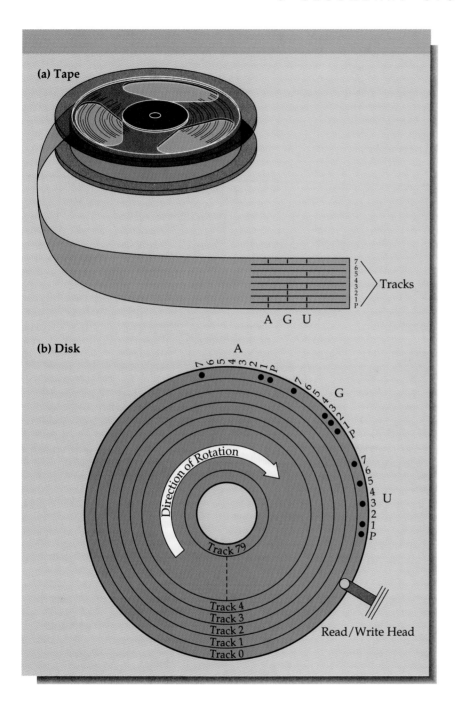

*Figure 6.13* Comparison of how characters are stored on magnetic tape and magnetic disk. (a) This illustrates how bits are recorded on tape tracks. (b) This illustrates how bits are recorded on disk tracks.

disk records is handled entirely by the operating system, which minimizes the need for any extra programming.

## SAFEGUARDING FILES

Most organizations have hundreds or even thousands of magnetic disks and tapes, each utilized for specific applications. These disks and tapes

*Figure 6.14* Blocking of tape and disk records. Here, logical records are grouped eight to a block.

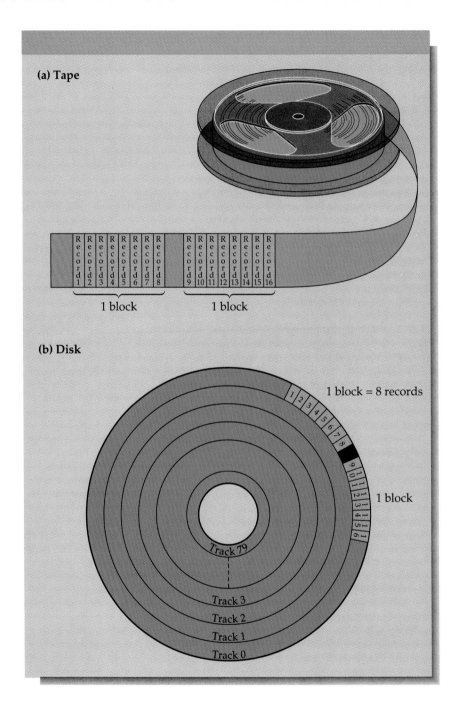

**(a) Tape**

**(b) Disk**

are usually stored in a separate room sometimes called a storage library or media room.

Because data recorded on these media is not "readable," that is, visible to the naked eye, it is often difficult to maintain control of all the disks and tapes. If a master accounts receivable disk were inadvertently written over, or used as output for some other job, for example, the writing of the output would destroy the existing accounts receivable information.

The result could be an expensive and time-consuming re-creation process. Moreover, if there is a fire, theft, or other catastrophe that results in loss of data, many files could be affected. Several control measures have been implemented in most organizations to prevent such occurrences or to reduce the extent of damage should they occur.

**Using External and Programmed Labels.** Gummed external labels are placed on the external surface of each disk or tape (see Figure 6.15) to identify the files on it. These labels are clearly visible to anyone, so the chances of inadvertent misuse of a valuable disk or tape are reduced. The problem with gummed labels, however, is that they sometimes come unglued. Their effectiveness is also directly related to the effort and training of the computer staff. If operators are negligent or distracted, then the labels may be ignored.

To make the identification of disks and tapes more reliable, most programs include a built-in routine that automatically creates a label record

*Figure 6.15 External labels are used to identify magnetic storage media.*

*Figure 6.16* *Here is a media librarian in a cartridge library.*

on each output file. This label is produced as the first record. Such programmed labels are created on output disks and tapes; later, they are checked on the disks and tapes when they are used as input.

**Controlling Access.**   Most companies have access control procedures that permit only authorized personnel to use disks and tapes. Sometimes a media librarian is hired specifically to maintain control of disks and tapes in a library. The result is less misuse and misplacing of disks and tapes. See Figure 6.16.

**Maintaining Backup Files.**   Since files on magnetic media can be erased, damaged, misplaced, or stolen, it is essential to maintain backup copies of all important files. If backup copies are available, the re-creation process, should it become necessary, will not be as costly and time-consuming.

## ▶ Smart Cards, Flash Memory, and RAM Cards: You Can Take It With You!

Newer magnetic media are augmenting disk and tape in specific application areas. We saw in Chapter 5 that a smart card, which closely resembles a credit card, is a piece of plastic that contains a built-in microprocessor and has a memory capacity from 4 K to 3+ MB. Invented in France in 1977, these cards now are used throughout the world for transaction processing. Telephone companies in France sell smart cards of different denominations to consumers. When the consumer makes a call from a pay phone, the smart card is inserted into the phone and the amount of the call is subtracted from the card's balance. When the balance reaches zero, the consumer purchases a new card. In some European countries, people pay for viewing television programs with smart cards.

In Canada and the United States, pilot projects are underway in which drivers pay highway tolls by means of smart cards. When participating truckers in British Columbia, for example, arrive at designated toll booths, they insert their card and the toll is automatically deducted from the card's credit account.

Banks are issuing smart cards to customers for making purchases. The card itself maintains transaction data and keeps track of the customer's bank balance. To use the card, a salesclerk inserts it in a card reader, the owner types in his or her own personal identification number, the transaction is made, and the card is updated. No online service is needed to verify that the card is valid or active as is the case with most credit cards. See Figure 6.17.

Smart cards are being tried in some schools. Students pay a sum in advance to be on a meal plan; the smart card records the cost of each meal and keeps track of the balance available to the student. Access to laser printers in many schools is also controlled by smart cards. You purchase a card with a fixed value and each time you use the laser printer you insert the card in a device that subtracts the price of each page printed. When the value of the card is depleted, you purchase a new one.

*Figure 6.17* *A customer with a smart card pays for purchases.*

IN A

NUT
SHELL

**MEMORY CARDS FOR PORTABLES**

Flash memory cards

RAM cards

Highly reliable, fast access time, very expensive

In comparison to flash memory cards, they have more electrical components, slower access time and transfer rates, and smaller capacities

*This is a flash card, which can be easily inserted in palmtops or picocomputers.*

The U.S. government has begun to replace food stamps with smart cards; the dollar amount to which a recipient is entitled is changed on the card each time he or she makes a purchase.

Every day, new applications for smart cards are implemented. They can store medical and drug records for patients and driver information on an electronic driver's license. They can control access to secure sites: a smart card can store passwords, digital fingerprint data, even photos, to identify individuals seeking access to an area.

As we saw in Chapter 3, the idea behind flash memory is to replace a hard disk with a stack of thin, credit-card-sized memory cards. These are ideal for laptops and notebook computers because they eliminate heavy hard drives and increase battery life. As the capacity of flash memory cards increases and their cost decreases, they are likely to compete directly with hard drives in the PC market.

In place of flash memory cards, some manufacturers of palmtops and other small computers offer RAM cards. These cards are similar in concept, but they are more expensive because they require more electrical components. They also have slower access times and transfer rates, and their current capacities are less than those of flash memory cards. RAM cards are available either with software packages on them or simply as secondary storage.

▶ **SELF-TEST**

1. To increase the access time of data on disk or tape, logical records are often grouped or _____.
2. Why are labels put on disks and tapes?
3. Name one important function of a media librarian.
4. All files should be _____ periodically in case something happens to the original.
5. (T or F) Data recorded on a smart card can be changed.
6. _____ cards are used in laptops as alternatives to heavier hard disks.

*LOOKING AHEAD*

**RAM CARDS**

Small palmtop computers already use credit-card–sized RAM cards in place of diskettes for storing programs and files. As the storage capacity of RAM cards begins to surpass that of floppies and as the cost decreases, these media will soar in popularity, particularly for users of very small computers.

**CRITICAL THINKING**

Some studies suggest that each driver's license will become a smart card that must be inserted into a vehicle just as a key is. The device that accepts the card enables the vehicle—along with the driver—to be monitored. When the police "tag" a car, they can determine the driver's age, driving experience, and driving record. Many law enforcement agents believe that such a system will reduce accident rates. What do you think? Do you see any individual rights violated by such a system?

7. Palmtop computers use ＿＿＿＿＿ rather than flash memory cards to store data and programs.

Solutions
1. blocked
2. to minimize the risk that the disks or tapes will be used for the wrong application
3. To control of access to disks and tapes
4. backed up
5. T
6. Flash memory
7. RAM cards

# OPTICAL STORAGE ALTERNATIVES TO MAGNETIC MEDIA

What advantages do optical devices have when compared with magnetic media for secondary storage?

As the variety of computer applications increases, the need for auxiliary storage devices with greater and greater capacities also increases. Typical hard disks for PCs can store hundreds of megabytes of data or even a gigabyte, and disk packs for mainframes can store hundreds of gigabytes. Even now, the hard disk storage capacity of micros is beginning to approach that of disk packs for larger systems. In the near future, for example, some hard drives for PCs will store well over a GB of data.

In Chapter 5, you learned that optical, or laser, technology is used in scanners and laser printers. It is applicable to auxiliary storage as well. Three types of optical storage media are currently available.

1. CD-ROMs: read-only compact disks
2. WORM CDs: Write-Once, Read-Many compact disks
3. Erasable CDs: erasable compact disks, which use a combined magneto-optical technology

Of the three, CD-ROM is the most widely used as a storage medium. **CD-ROMs** have read-only capability, and they are popular for storing programs and permanent databases. Write-once, read-many disks are not yet standardized and are available in a variety of sizes. Erasable CDs have the greatest potential for augmenting or even replacing hard disks, but they are expensive. Because of their cost, they currently function mainly as a backup medium to replace tapes.

## ▶ CD-ROM Drives: A Most Valuable Player

### ADVANTAGES AND APPLICATIONS

A compact disk with read-only memory is a silver platter, 4.72 inches in diameter. It looks just like a standard audio compact disk and is read by a drive also very similar to that used for audio disks. See Figure 6.18.

*Figure 6.18* CD-ROM drive with a caddy, or case, containing a compact disk. The disk and the caddy are placed in the drive as a unit when information on the disk is to be accessed.

Data on CD-ROM is stored in binary form and is read by a laser beam. The data is stored as microscopic pits on the disk; the presence of a pit represents a binary 1 and the absence of a pit represents a 0.

CD-ROMs can store 650+ MB of data, equivalent to hundreds of floppy disks or more. A single CD-ROM can incorporate the data contained in several full-sized books. The data can be in text form exclusively or can also contain images and sound in document or multimedia files. Figure 6.19 compares a CD-ROM's storage capacity with those of PC disks.

CD-ROMs can be accessed very quickly. The speed of retrieval of CD-ROM drives is much greater than that of most magnetic disk drives. Because they use laser technology, the drives are also more reliable. The CD-ROMs themselves are removable, which makes them far more versatile for data retrieval than hard disks. As the prices for CD-ROM drives and for the disks themselves decrease, this optical technology is likely to become even more widespread.

IN A

**OPTICAL STORAGE AS COMPARED WITH HARD DISK**

**Pros**
1. Larger storage capacity
2. Faster access
3. More reliable
4. Removable

**Cons**
1. Currently most widely available as a read-only medium
2. Both software and hardware are not standardized
3. Still relatively expensive

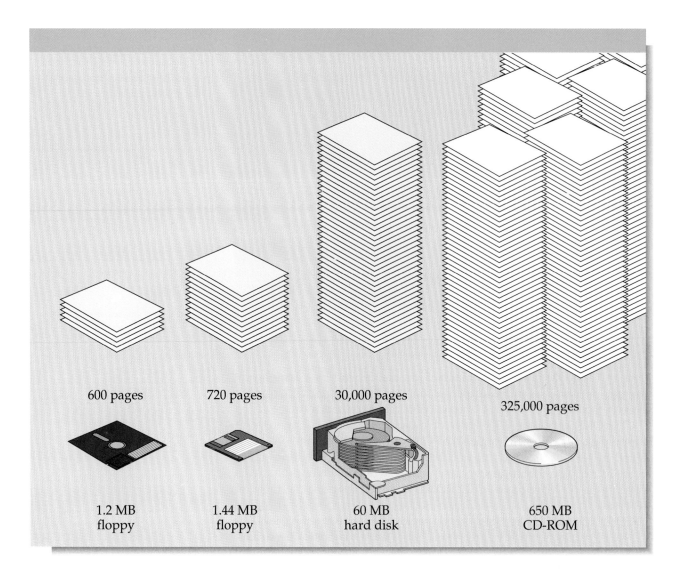

| 600 pages | 720 pages | 30,000 pages | 325,000 pages |
|-----------|-----------|--------------|---------------|
| 1.2 MB floppy | 1.44 MB floppy | 60 MB hard disk | 650 MB CD-ROM |

*Figure 6.19* Comparing storage capacities. Assume that one double-spaced typewritten page is the equivalent of 2 K (two kilobytes) of information. Shown here are the storage capacities in pages of the various types of secondary storage devices.

CD-ROM is used extensively for published databases where mass production of data on a secondary storage medium is needed. The process of creating a database on a CD-ROM is similar to that used for creating an album on an audio compact disk. A master is produced and disk copies are manufactured by stamping them the way audio CDs are stamped. Grolier's encyclopedia, for example, is stored on a single CD-ROM and sells for less than $400. Microsoft's Bookshelf has a CD-ROM with a collection of common office reference tools including a dictionary, thesaurus, almanac, atlas, and encyclopedia. Material from this product can be "cut and pasted" into any document you are working on. Figure 6.20 lists some best-selling CD-ROMs.

Many other publications and collections are available on CD-ROM. Computer Select, for example, contains abstracts and articles from hundreds of computer journals along with computer product and vendor

| New Best-Selling CDs |
|---|

Leading disks, based on number sold in the United States.

**1**   **Grolier Electronic Encyclopedia**

The entire text of the 21-volume Academic American Encyclopedia, more than 9 million words and 1,500 pictures.

**2**   **Microsoft Bookshelf**

A collection of 10 reference works, including the American Heritage Dictionary, Roget's II Electronic Thesaurus, Bartlett's Familiar Quotations and a directory of ZIP codes.

**3**   **Microsoft's Programmer's Library**

Information for programmers.

**4**   **U.S. History on CD-ROM**

The full text of 107 books on U.S. history, with more than 1,000 photos, maps and tables.

**5**   **McGraw-Hill Science and Technical Reference Set**

Science encyclopedia and dictionary of technical terms.

**6**   **Compton's Multimedia Encyclopedia**

Encyclopedia with 15,000 illustrations, with audio renditions of speeches by Martin Luther King, Jr. and John F. Kennedy.

**7**   **PC-SIG Library**

A library of public domain software, including programs for word processing, spreadsheets and games.

**8**   **Mammals: A Multimedia Encyclopedia**

National Geographic disk contains 45 video clips from TV documentaries and sounds of different animals.

*Source: Bureau of Electronic Publishing*

*Figure 6.20* List of some of the best-selling CD-ROMs.

information. Each year, more and more publication services offer a series of journals in specific subject areas on CD-ROM. You may even be able to take some of your library's resources home by checking out CD-ROMs that store thousands of articles or scores of books and that provide the ability to quickly search through the database to locate specific topics.

And the uses of CD-ROM continue to expand. Telephone directories for entire sections of the United States are available on a single CD-ROM. Many companies rely on CD-ROMs for documentation, tutorials, and other company-wide information. Los Angeles County, which has one of the largest libraries in the country, stores its catalog of 5 million titles on a CD-ROM. A search for a specific title takes far less time than it would using a card catalog or microfilm. Accountants in large firms have CD-ROMs containing all of the tax information they need. By accessing a single CD-ROM, job seekers can obtain information about employment

**COMPUTING APPLICATION**

All the world's a stage,
And all the men and women are
merely players:
(*As You Like It,* act 2, scene 7)

Shakespeare is perhaps the most-
quoted playwright in Western litera-
ture. You've probably read some of
the plays he wrote. Now the complete works of Shakespeare, along
with a biography of him, can be
stored on a small, sturdy optical
storage disk.

opportunities throughout the country. Even some software, particularly
graphics packages that use a large amount of storage for representing
images, is available on CD-ROM as well as diskettes (see Figure 6.21).
These are just some of the applications for CD-ROMs. The list is likely
to grow exponentially in the years ahead.

Some CD-ROMs like Grolier's encyclopedia and Microsoft's Bookshelf
are for sale; others with date-sensitive data are available by subscription.
Suppose you subscribe to Computer Select. Initially, you receive
publications for the past 12 months. Each month you receive a new
CD-ROM with the next month's data added. The previous disk can be
discarded or saved as a backup. There is no need for you to integrate the
new data with the old the way you would if the data were in print form.
Moreover, unlike data stored in print form in a library or other central
location, you can access your CD-ROM anytime day or night.

*Figure 6.21 Some graphics packages
like CorelDraw that use a large amount
of storage for representing images are
available on CD-ROM.*

## SOFTWARE REQUIREMENTS

In general, each CD-ROM comes with its own search and retrieval software. The quality of the software is as important as the storage capacity because the ability to retrieve data quickly is essential. Search and retrieval methods typically permit:

- Searches on topics, words, phrases, names, titles, and so forth.
- Users to mark text for copying or printing.
- Use of logical operators (and, or, not) for linkages to make more meaningful searches (e.g., search for "micro" *and* "disk," search for "computer" *not* "laptop").

Since the database is apt to be extensive, the more complete and specific the search, the more useful the product.

Search and retrieval methods make use of sophisticated navigational techniques in which you can move through the database, search for topics, leave bookmarks to return to previous topics, and make requests for animations or additional information. See Figure 6.22.

One problem with CD-ROMs is that the search and retrieval methodology is not standardized, which is one reason it is typically supplied on the CD-ROM itself with the data. As we have seen, it is common in the computer field for newer technologies to suffer from lack of standardization. If the CD-ROM technology prevails, as it surely will, standardization is likely to follow.

Undoubtedly, the software for retrieving data will soon be standardized. Some even predict that the software will become part of the operating system, which will make CD-ROMs even more widely used. In

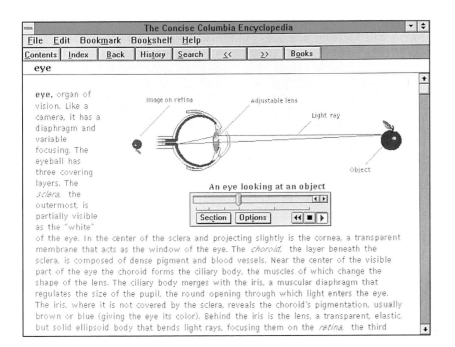

*Figure 6.22 Example of techniques that can be used for searching and retrieving from a CD-ROM for a multimedia application.*

recent years, CD-ROM software and data have been made available on networks, putting large databases online for many users.

CD-ROM drives are still relatively expensive compared to magnetic disk drives. Although many are now available for just a few hundred dollars, new, multimedia computers come equipped with CD-ROM drives. But, remember CD-ROMs have one serious limitation: they are read-only media.

## ▶ WORM Drives: Will They "Worm" Their Way Into Your Heart?

WORM—write-once, read-many—CDs, developed in 1985, are now available in different sizes, but 5¼-inch and 12-inch are the most common. A 5¼-inch WORM CD can store 1+ GB of data and a 12-inch version can store 3+ GB of data. At present, WORM CD drive designs remain nonstandardized and expensive.

WORM disks are used extensively by companies that need to maintain vast archives. Such archives are created once by a user organization and then permanently stored on WORM CDs. WORM drives, like CD-ROM drives, use a laser that changes the physical state of a disk. In contrast, however, WORM drives do not physically pit the surface so they do not lend themselves to mass duplication.

Optical disks such as WORM CDs have made it possible for complete image processing systems to emerge. As we have seen, document management by image processing enables text, graphics, photos, and signatures to be captured, stored, processed, and retrieved. Of course, such systems are quite expensive; they require midrange computer capacity (or more) and cost $200,000+. But the ability for banks, as an example, to store checks, deposits, and withdrawals along with loan applications in an image processing system can actually save money as well as time and storage space. Similarly, insurance companies store their claim applications and insurance policies in such systems.

Optical storage media, like CD-ROM and WORM disks, are a necessary part of multimedia systems as well as image processing systems because of their storage capacity. Nontextual material like photos, signatures, and other graphics require a great deal of storage space.

## ▶ Erasable Magneto-Optical Drives: Doing the Write Thing

Although most storage technologies are either purely magnetic (disk and tape) or purely optical (WORM CDs), erasable CDs make use of combined optical and magnetic principles. They were introduced in 1988 and are called **magneto-optical (MO) disks.** They have several benefits.

- Removability (like floppies and disk cartridges).
- Random-access capability similar to that of hard drives.
- Reliability similar to CD/ROMs.
- Capacity similar to digital audio tape.

The MO drive writes data to a disk as a pattern of magnetized fields by means of both a laser and a magnet. As the disk rotates, the MO drive turns the laser on and off. The laser selectively heats specific spots as they pass, which changes their magnetic polarity. The MO drive reads data by means of the laser only. It interprets these magnetized fields on the reflected light.

MO disks are a good choice as a backup storage medium. Tapes can also be used for backup but tapes need to be converted to disk before data can be accessed randomly. MO disks are "mirror images" of hard disks. Thus, MO drives can read and write randomly, but at a slower rate than hard drives.

MO storage media are also removable, which makes them ideal for situations in which security is an issue or where there is a need for transportability. And MO drives are reliable because the read/write heads do not whirl across the disk as they do with hard drives; they are relatively safe from head crashes, which can destroy a disk if the read/write head accidentally makes contact with it.

The technology does, however, have limitations.

- High cost.
- Lack of a standard size.
- Not as much storage as a hard disk (although there is potential for far greater storage than hard disks).
- Slower access time than a hard disk.

A typical MO disk drive can store 500 MB and costs from $3000 to $5000. A hard drive of similar capacity is approximately half the cost. Although MO disks are not yet standardized, they have the greatest potential for augmenting or replacing magnetic disks, mainly because data can be written, deleted, and rewritten to MO disks. Steven Jobs, founder of

*LOOKING AHEAD*

**BY THE YEAR 2000**

- Storage capacities for all magnetic, optical, and magneto-optical media will increase 30 times, yielding the equivalent of 10 GB on one side of a 5¼-inch CD. Consequently, more search and retrieval and navigational tools will be available with graphics and voice capability to augment and perhaps even replace straight text.
- CD-ROMs may be eclipsed by card-sized read-write optical recording media.
- Optical and magneto-optical storage media will augment rather than replace magnetic disks.
- As networks become more prevalent, they will make available data on optical drives, as well as magnetic disks. The location of the data and the method of access will be transparent (that is, unnoticeable) to the user.

IN A

NUT SHELL

---

**MAGNETO-OPTICAL DRIVES**

| **Pros** | Erasable |
| | Rewritable |
| | Faster than floppies |
| | Reliable like CD-ROMs |
| | Higher capacity than floppies |
| **Cons** | More expensive than hard disks |
| | Not as fast as hard disks |
| | Not as much storage capacity as most hard disks |
| | Not suitable for multimedia applications that need to store sound, video, and graphics images |

## LOOKING AHEAD

### MEDICAL MEMORY CARDS

As an experiment, the U.S. Department of Veterans Affairs in Troy, New York, is testing optical memory cards and read/write devices to store medical records for veterans. If the initial installations are successful, additional test locations will be added. If the system is implemented fully, optical cards may be used by millions of veterans throughout the VA's network of hospitals and clinics.

The hope is that the medical records card will improve health care delivery to veterans while reducing problems caused by inaccessibility to prior records and test results. Patients will carry the optical card and have it updated during each medical visit. In this way, physicians will have immediate access to medical history data, which can provide life-saving information.

Known as the LaserCard, this data storage device is the size of a credit card and can store up to 4.11 MB of data. Medical reports, X-ray images, ultrasound and CAT scans, and other test results can be stored on and retrieved from the card. Access to the card's information can be protected through security codes and software. Also, the patient's photograph, voice print, and signature can be stored on the LaserCard for identification and security purposes.

Apple Computer, bundles his RISC-based NeXt computer with an optional erasable optical disk drive.

## ▶ Networking Compact Disks

 CD-ROM drives are often networked so that many users can access them concurrently. Instead of multiple drives, many systems have CD-ROM servers that stack and retrieve a group of compact disks for large numbers of users (see Figure 6.23). Servers automatically shift from one disk to another without physically replacing disks. Although such devices are most commonly used to store optical or MO disks, they serve the same purpose for tape cartridges.

The District of Columbia Public Library has installed a Pioneer "jukebox" as a server to provide users with access to its three CD-ROMs that contain a U.S. residential and business telephone directory. The appeal of the jukebox is that the librarian does not need to manually insert a different compact disk each time a person seeks information about a geographic location in a different database. A jukebox can access multiple compact disks, sometimes even hundreds of disks. Some servers can make a terabyte (1 trillion bytes) of data available.

**Figure 6.23** *A multiple or stacked CD-ROM unit that can be used as a server.*

## ▶ Multifunction Drives: The Best of Both Worlds

**Multifunction drives** can read or write either WORM CDs or erasable disks. They are comparable in price to erasable drives but they have the added capability of optical WORM disks.

### ▶ SELF-TEST

1. The most common form of optical disk is the _____, which has a vast amount of storage capacity but is limited because _____.

2. CD-ROMs are currently used mainly to store _____.
3. The search and retrieval software for CD-ROMs (is/is not) standardized.
4. WORM disks are used for _____.
5. A device that is capable of stacking compact disks and retrieving data from any one of them quickly is called a _____.
6. Why are some CD-ROMs purchased by subscription?

Solutions
1. CD-ROM; it is a read-only medium
2. large databases
3. is not (yet)
4. write-once read-many applications (such as storing company archives or other data that needs to be recorded only once)
5. jukebox or server
6. If data is date sensitive and newer versions are needed often, then CD-ROMs are typically made available by subscription.

# ORGANIZING DATA FILES

## 6.4

Because disks are still the most widely used storage medium for database files and because high-speed accessing of such files is so important to information systems, we consider next some of the processing techniques commonly used for accessing disk files.

## ▶ Sequential File Organization

We have seen that sometimes files are processed sequentially by reading record 1, then record 2, and so on, until all records have been processed. Records processed sequentially are typically in sequence by a key field such as Social Security number, customer number, or part number. When a file is in sequence by a key field and the only way we need to process the data is in sequence, then sequential files are created either on disk or on tape.

Files that are always processed in batch mode are usually organized for sequential processing. Consider a master payroll file that is accessed once a week for updating. If the changes to the master are in sequence by a key field (e.g., Social Security number) and the master file is also in sequence by the same key field, then sequential file updating is not only feasible, it is most efficient. That is, a program would read one record from each file, compare key fields, and, on a match, update the master file.

Note that the only way to process sequential files is sequentially; if records in these files need to be accessed in a different order, they must be sorted first. For example, the payroll file that is in sequence by Social Security number is fine for updating purposes. But when payroll checks need to be printed, the file is likely to be sorted first, alphabetically by employee name within department so that they can be more easily dis-

What are the major ways of organizing data files?

tributed. Keep in mind that sequential files are almost always accessed in batch mode.

Suppose, however, a manager wants to inquire about the status of individual employee records. Sequential access would be extremely inefficient for such processing. Say the manager needs to know the salary of an employee with a Social Security number of 987-32-6577. The manager could surmise that the record is near the end of the file since the file is in sequence, but that record can only be accessed by reading past all the preceding records.

## ► **R**andom-**A**ccess **F**ile **O**rganization

### INDEXED FILES

If inquiries need to be made from a file in which the records being accessed are in no particular sequence, sequential processing is not the best technique. For example, on an average day, the vice president of marketing may ask for information on 20 salespeople where the requests are in no specific sequence. Similarly, the VP of finance may want to know how many employees in a specific department earn more than $80,000, and the VP of human resources may want to know the names of employees eligible for retirement during the following year. In each case, the requests are random. These users need a technique to access records *directly* without having to read them sequentially.

The indexed method for organizing records in a file allows random access of the records. An **indexed file** is one that is created sequentially but an index is also created that keeps track of the physical location on disk of each record. To each record's key field, the index associates an actual, unique disk address that identifies the record location by its surface number, track number, and sector (or cylinder) number. That index is in sequence and can be "looked up" any time a record needs to be accessed. If you are seeking a record with a key field of 9222, you do not sequentially search the file by reading record 1, seeing if its key field is 9222, then reading record 2, and so on. Rather, the computer "looks up" in the index the disk address of the record with a key field of 9222 and goes directly to the surface, track, and sector on the disk that stores that record. Think of how you might look for a topic in a book. You can sequentially search for the topic by scanning page 1 of the book, then page 2, and so on. Or you can look up the topic in the book's index, find its page number (its address), and go directly to that page. If you have to perform numerous searches on random topics, it is far more efficient to use an index rather than a sequential search.

### DIRECT FILES

Although randomly accessing indexed files is faster than sequentially accessing them when the searches are in no specific sequence, looking for indexed records still requires a search procedure. In a **direct file,** the computer accesses records by converting a key field, through some arithmetic calculation, into an actual address that identifies the surface, track, and sector (or cylinder) number. There is no need to search an index. As a simplified example, assume that in a three-digit key field called Account Number, the first digit provides the surface number and the last two digits provide the track number. This scheme would use 10 surfaces (0–9) and 100 tracks (0–99) for storing the data. Direct file access is faster than indexed access because there is no need to look up an address from an index. But sometimes the direct access method requires more extensive programming, because the programmer must determine the best mathematical formula for converting key fields to addresses.

If the key fields are in sequence, however, and most of the records have consecutive key fields (e.g., 001, 002, 003, and so on), the key field need not be converted to an address at all. That is, the record with a key of 001 may be placed at the first disk location, the record with a key of 002 may be placed at the second, and so on. This is the simplest type of direct file organization. To access a record with a key of 987, the computer goes to the 987th location on disk. Using key fields directly as disk locations is feasible only for records that have key fields with consecutive values (e.g., customer number *not* Social Security number).

## ▶ SELF-TEST

1. When records are always processed by reading the first, then the second, and so forth, the process is called _____ access.
2. When records need to be accessed from a disk in no particular sequence, then _____ processing is required.
3. Disk files to be accessed randomly use either the _____ or _____ method of file organization.

Solutions
1. sequential
2. random
3. indexed; direct

## ▶ Chapter Summary

Every computer system consists of a CPU and various input/output devices. In addition, every system must have one or more secondary storage units to store programs and data for future processing.

### 6.1 FUNDAMENTALS OF SECONDARY STORAGE

When data is processed by the CPU, programs are loaded into primary storage, input data is read, and output is produced as information. Primary storage, however, is usually volatile in nature. A peripheral device such as disk, referred to as **secondary storage** or **auxiliary storage,** is

Why is secondary storage a crucial component of a computer system?

required to store programs and data for future processing. Secondary storage is nonvolatile, which means that all information is saved even after the power is shut off.

There are five major criteria for evaluating secondary storage devices: (1) **storage capacity,** which indicates the amount of data the storage medium can hold and is measured in kilobytes, megabytes, or gigabytes; (2) **access time,** which is the time needed to locate data on a secondary storage device and is measured in thousandths of a second; (3) **transfer rate,** which is the speed at which data is transferred, or copied, from the secondary storage unit to main memory and is measured in megabytes per second; (4) cost of the secondary storage unit; and (5) the physical size of the storage unit.

## 6.2 MAGNETIC MEDIA FOR SECONDARY STORAGE

Why is disk the main secondary storage medium for most systems, why has it replaced tape, and what other magnetic media are being used?

Micros use floppy disks (also called diskettes) or hard disks to store programs and data files. Mainframes use either fixed disks or removable disk packs. All disks use a peripheral called a disk drive for reading data from the disks and writing to them.

Data is stored on a magnetic disk in concentric rings called tracks. On diskettes, the tracks are segmented into wedge-shaped sectors. Most diskettes are **soft-sectored,** which means that sectors are not already defined on a diskette when it is purchased; rather, sectors are defined when the disk is formatted. Diskette drives that use double-sided floppy disks have two **read/write heads,** which are mechanisms for reading data from, or writing information onto, the diskette. Records are stored on diskettes at locations called addresses; an address consists of a surface number, track number, and sector number.

In addition to having one or two floppy disk drives, many micros have a large-capacity internal hard disk. A **head crash** occurs when the read/write head makes direct contact with the disk. In such a case, the data stored on the disk is usually lost. There are two types of hard disks for micros: (1) a **Winchester disk,** which is built into the computer's case, and (2) a **hard card,** which is a circuit board with the hard disk built into it. A hard card can be added to a micro by plugging it into the computer's internal expansion slot. **Disk cartridges** combine the advantages of diskettes and hard disks: they have storage capacities as large as hard disks but they are removable and, thus, are portable.

Most of the larger computer systems have fixed disks that are similar to the internal hard disks on micros. A **fixed-head disk drive** contains one or more hard disks and stationary access arms with separate read/write mechanisms for each of the tracks on the disks. A **disk pack** is an older type of disk common to some minis and mainframe computers. It consists of *removable* sets of hard disks.

The popularity of magnetic tape as an auxiliary storage medium has waned in recent years because disks have all the advantages of tape and none of the disadvantages. Disks are ideal for applications in which data must be accessed quickly and randomly. Tapes, however, can be accessed only sequentially. Tapes function well as a backup medium.

The number of characters that can be represented in an inch of disk or tape is called **density.** Disk and tape records are frequently blocked. **Blocking** means that several actual records (called logical records) are grouped together in a block so that they can be accessed faster.

There are other magnetic media besides disk and tape. A smart card is a piece of plastic that has a built-in microprocessor and memory. A smart card is purchased for a given amount; each time a purchase is made, the amount of the purchase is subtracted from the card's balance on hand. Flash memory is a credit-card-sized memory unit. This type of memory is ideal for laptops and notebook computers because it can replace heavy hard drives and increase battery life. Some manufacturers of palmtops offer RAM cards, which are similar in concept to flash memory cards.

## 6.3 OPTICAL STORAGE ALTERNATIVES TO MAGNETIC MEDIA

Three types of laser, or optical, storage media currently are available: (1) **CD-ROMs** (read-only compact disks); (2) WORM CDs (write-once, read-many compact disks); (3) erasable CDs (erasable compact disks). Of the three, CD-ROM is the most widely used as a storage medium, especially for storing databases. Erasable CDs, called **magneto-optical disks,** make use of combined optical and magnetic principles. A **multifunction drive** can read or write either WORM CDs or erasable disks.

What advantages do optical devices have when compared with magnetic media for secondary storage?

## 6.4 ORGANIZING DATA FILES

The two major methods of organizing data files are (1) sequential file organization and (2) random-access file organization. Sequential files can only be accessed sequentially. Random-access files—either indexed or direct—allow records to be accessed directly without having to read them sequentially. When an **indexed file** is created, an index is established that keeps track of the physical location on disk of each record. This index can be "looked up" any time a record needs to be accessed. With a **direct file,** the computer accesses records by converting a key field, through some arithmetic calculation, into an actual address.

What are the major ways of organizing data files?

## ▶ Chapter Self-test

1. A disk pack consists of a series of platters or disks. How many recording surfaces does each disk platter have?
2. Data is recorded on a disk in concentric _____.
3. (T or F) Because a disk has a series of recording surfaces and numerous read/write heads, it is possible to access disk records more quickly than tape records.
4. A _____ is a direct-access medium common to most microcomputers.
5. A disk is best used for _____ processing in a(n) _____ mode.
6. For direct access of disk files, two methods of file organization are _____ and _____.

7. (T or F) Disks may not be processed sequentially.
8. (T or F) An existing indexed disk record may be altered and then rewritten onto the same physical space on the disk.
9. (T or F) Disks and tapes usually have programmed labels.
10. (T or F) Maintaining control of disk files is easier than maintaining control of tape files.
11. (T or F) It is generally a good idea to copy a master disk file onto a tape for backup purposes.
12. (T or F) Sequential data files are not appropriate for batch processing operations.

Solutions

1. two—except for the first and last disks, each of which has only one recording surface.
2. tracks
3. T
4. floppy disk (or hard disk)
5. random; online
6. indexed; direct
7. F
8. T
9. T
10. F
11. T
12. F

## ▶ Key Terms

Access time, *p. 220*
Auxiliary storage, *p. 218*
Blocking, *p. 232*
CD-ROM, *p. 238*
Density, *p. 232*
Direct file, *p. 248*
Disk cartridge, *p. 227*

Disk pack, *p. 228*
Fixed-head disk drive, *p. 228*
Hard card, *p. 226*
Head crash, *p. 226*
Indexed file, *p. 248*
Magneto-optical (MO) disk, *p. 244*

Multifunction drive, *p. 246*
Read/write head, *p. 223*
Secondary storage, *p. 218*
Soft-sectored diskette, *p. 222*
Storage capacity, *p. 219*
Transfer rate, *p. 220*
Winchester disk, *p. 226*

## ▶ Review Questions

1. What are the advantages of 3½-inch diskettes over 5¼-inch diskettes?
2. How can you protect your micro's diskettes from damage?
3. What are some advantages of optical storage devices over magnetic storage devices?
4. Why are tapes no longer as popular as they once were?
5. Discuss the three principal types of memory cards. Can you think of everyday applications for them?
6. Indicate some possible application areas for compact disks not discussed in the text.

**PRODUCT ANALYSIS**

**CASE**

## CD-ROMs Abound in Diverse Application Areas
..........

Microsoft was the first to release a multimedia business productivity tool, Microsoft Works for Windows, Multimedia Edition. The $199 CD-ROM includes (with Works) digital sound, animation, and pictures in tutorial and reference sections. During the setup phase, a video introduces the program's word processing, spreadsheet, database, drawing, and charting functions as it guides the user through installation. The online tutorial is a collection of more than 40 lessons with multimedia movies, sound, and animation.

Career Opportunities, a new career guide CD-ROM from Quanta Press, is a computer-searchable version of three books: *The Federal Career Guide*, which covers government jobs, *The Occupational Outlook Handbook*, which covers jobs in the private sector, *Your Military Today*, which covers civilian-related military employment. These books, with more than 10,000 pages in printed form, are widely used by career and guidance counselors. The cost for the CD-ROM is approximately $100.

DeLorme Mapping sells its *Street Atlas USA* on CD-ROM. The atlas contains over a million color maps that show every street in every city, town, or rural area in the United States. To find a specific location, you can enter a phone number, zip code, or place name. Any map or portion of a map can be printed or imported to a word processing or graphics package that accepts Windows images. The cost is under $100.

Judging from the growing list of reference works, games, illustrated children's books, software, and other multimedia products that use CD-ROM as the preferred storage medium, we can expect production of these disks and their drives

to continue their upward swing. Multimedia products themselves have no formal standard. Similarly, standards are lacking for CD-ROM drives and their search-and-retrieval techniques. But there are now only a few preferred formats rather than dozens, and standardization is likely to be achieved soon.

### Analysis

1. What are the advantages of CD-ROM as a storage medium compared to conventional hard or floppy disks? What are the disadvantages?
2. Cite some advantages and disadvantages of CD-ROM-based references as compared to printed books.
3. Which reference works would you like to see issued on CD-ROM? How could they be enhanced with multimedia? Would you like to see your textbooks on CD-ROM?

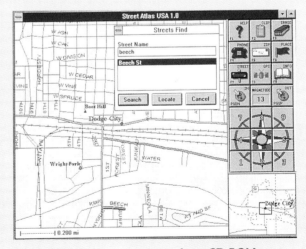

*An illustration of a street map stored on a CD-ROM.*

# PART THREE

# SOFTWARE AND SYSTEMS DRIVE THE INFORMATION AGE

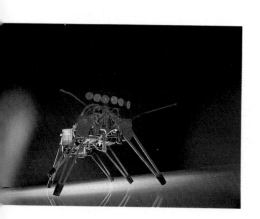

**C**omputers are making it possible for us to explore new forms of creativity. Computers have changed the way we work, have challenged our imaginations, and have provided us with new media for expressing ourselves.

Part Three of this book will tell you about some computer programs designed to help people in the arts, sciences, and business be more creative. Chapter 7 focuses on creative application packages that make charts, illustrations, and published materials more interesting and informative. In subsequent chapters, you will discover some areas in which technology has inspired managers and computer professionals to achieve greater creativity. Chapter 8 deals with custom software, which programmers design specifically for a particular user. Chapter 9, on systems software, describes some of the software elements developed as an interface between computer hardware and computer users that enable people to be more creative. Chapter 10 describes how systems analysts can be more creative by relying on computer-aided software engineering (CASE) tools.

Oils and watercolors, move over! Make room for a new medium—computer art. Now software illustration packages make it possible for artists to use patterns of dots or combinations of lines, arcs, circles, squares, and other shapes to create pictures, exciting graphic displays, and advertising campaigns with the computer. Libraries of art forms called clip art are often made available with packages for people to use as is, to modify, or redesign, as the need arises. Images scanned from other sources can be included and modified for a "collage" effect. Computer art is no longer thought of as a mere gimmick. Schools give courses in this medium and professional computer artists display their work in museums and art galleries.

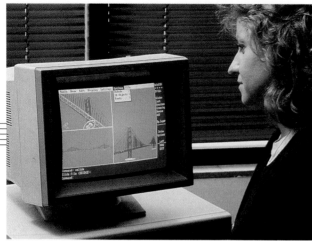

The architects of the ancient world might have produced more than the traditional seven wonders if computers had been available in their time. Today's architects and engineers can use computer-aided design (CAD) packages to automatically compute and display dimensions of buildings and to experiment with designs as well. More precise than other graphics packages, these programs also help users create the complex plans and drawings that are necessary not only in architecture but in related fields like manufacturing and production.

Electronic music is among the most controversial of the new forms of creativity that can be used to generate music or enhance existing compositions.

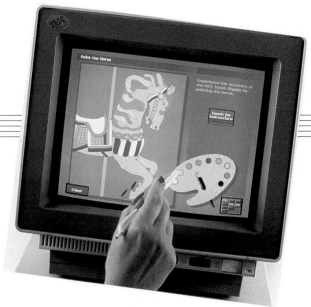

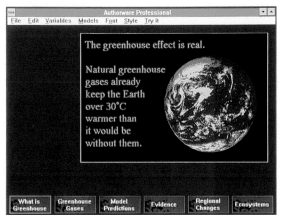

Creative multimedia presentations provide information in an interesting and meaningful way. Audio, video, graphics, and text can all be integrated in a multimedia show. Multimedia as an educational tool brings animated, visually appealing, interactive lessons to the MTV generation.

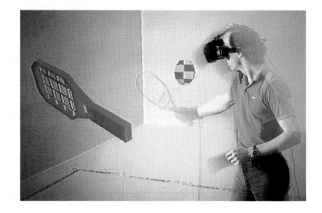

Artificial intelligence is a field of research that explores human thinking and creativity and attempts to simulate those processes. Researchers in artificial intelligence develop games, simulations, and even robots that explore and imitate human thinking. Virtual reality is a creative concept in which an interactive environment is developed that imitates a real-world setting. Using virtual reality concepts and specially designed devices like data gloves, we can learn how to play games such as racquet ball and practice tasks that require special skills such as flying an airplane.

To make virtual reality even more fashionable, some designers have exercised their creative powers by developing chic computer-wear.

# APPLICATION PACKAGES: BEYOND BASIC PRODUCTIVITY TOOLS

In Part Two we looked at the types of hardware that make computerization effective in a wide variety of application areas. Remember, though, software drives hardware, and software needs must be considered before hardware acquisitions are made.

In Part Three we focus on software. We begin with application packages—off-the-shelf software used by many organizations and individuals for all or most of their information processing needs. In this chapter, we answer the following questions:

▶ How have application packages progressed to include even more functions?

▶ What capabilities do today's new "power tools" feature?

▶ How can users make the right choices when selecting application packages?

## 7.1 | A REVIEW OF APPLICATION SOFTWARE

### ▶ Packaged and Customized Programs

How have application packages progressed to include even more functions?

Application software consists of programs that are designed to satisfy specific user needs. User needs exist in various application areas, including those for business, education, and personal use. The following are common application programs for business:

1. A spreadsheet program to create a budget.
2. A payroll program to update a master payroll file.
3. An accounts receivable program to print customer bills.
4. An inventory program to answer inquiries about the quantity on hand for each item in stock.

Application software can be purchased as a package or it can be custom designed specifically for individual users. Both packaged and custom software are used with computer systems of all sizes. Packages tend to be most popular in PC-based organizations, which are apt to have a limited computer staff. Larger organizations with more specific computer needs and a full computer staff often invest in custom software, although they sometimes purchase or lease packages to augment their own software.

### ▶ Basic Productivity Tools Revisited

In Chapter 3, we studied the features and uses of word processing, spreadsheet, database management packages, and electronic mail. All are common tools intended to enhance productivity. Integrated packages (e.g., Microsoft Works, PFS:First Choice, and LotusWorks) include word processing, spreadsheet, database management, and some e-mail func-

IN A

**TYPES OF SOFTWARE**

1. Systems software: to supervise processing
2. Application software: to satisfy user needs. Application software can be:
   • Packaged
   • Custom-designed

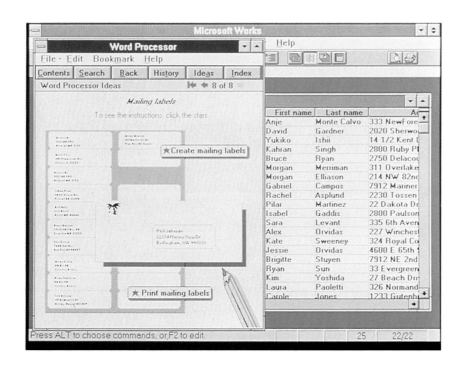

***Figure 7.1*** *User interface from Microsoft Works, an integrated package.*

tions in one software product. The advantage of an integrated package is that it employs one basic type of user interface; that is, the command structure and menu system for all its components are the same. Figure 7.1 illustrates a user interface for an integrated package. Some palmtops, like the Hewlett-Packard and the Poqet, come with ROM-resident packages—a word processor or spreadsheet, for example.

The term *ROM-resident* means the software is actually hardwired into the computer.

## ▶ Additional Productivity Tools

In addition to the four basic tools already discussed, there are many other products designed to increase the productivity of users in an organization. We consider some of the more common ones here.

### DESKTOP ORGANIZERS

Programs called **desktop organizers** have been developed to help regular users of microcomputers eliminate the clutter from their desktops. With a desktop organizer, you no longer need an address or telephone book, a notepad, calendar, calculator, or appointment book. The software package includes all these features and more.

One of the earliest and most well-known of the desktop organizers is SideKick, which is still widely used today. Norton Desktop for Windows is also popular. See Figure 7.2. Most integrated packages include some type of desktop organizer. Similarly, the Windows user interface itself has an icon-based desktop manager. Some palmtop computers, like the Poqet, come with a ROM-resident desktop organizer, which has the advantage of minimizing the need for additional RAM. Many desktop organizers are loaded into main memory and remain there even when

*Figure 7.2 Norton Desktop for Windows is one of the most popular desktop organizer programs.*

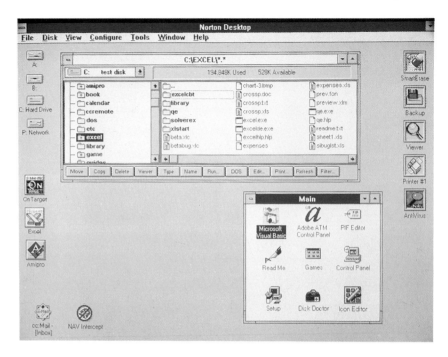

other software is in use; they can be accessed at any time by pressing a combination of control keys. Such programs are called memory-resident or **TSR programs.** TSR means "*t*erminate and *s*tay *r*esident." Once they are loaded, TSR programs are accessible even while other programs are running.

Newer desktop organizers, like so many programs for personal computers, have more capability but also require a large amount of memory. As we will see later, some of these programs have become so capable that they fulfill functions typically performed by project management software such as keeping track of the progress of tasks under the user's control.

## PROJECT MANAGEMENT SOFTWARE AND PERSONAL INFORMATION MANAGERS

As the name implies, **project management software** is for managers who need to keep track of the progress of projects under their control. Like spreadsheet software, project management packages allow you to perform a type of what-if analysis. You can, for example, evaluate a number of different scheduling scenarios before you start a project. Once the project is underway, you can track its progress, reallocate tasks or personnel, or make changes to optimize resources as the need arises. Unlike spreadsheets, however, project management software provides little in the way of quantitative results, except to let you know whether the project is proceeding on time and within budget.

Although project management packages differ in their capabilities, most include certain common features. Among these are **Gantt chart** time lines (Figure 7.3) that graphically show how long projects are scheduled to take and at what points parts of the project development can overlap. Most also enable the user to create **PERT charts** (Figure 7.4), which pro-

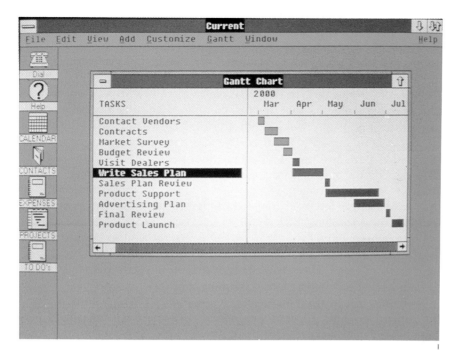

*Figure 7.3* This Gantt chart produced with IBM's CURRENT shows how project management software can help managers schedule and track projects.

*Figure 7.4* PERT charting is a project management technique used to plan large, complex projects. This PERT chart was created with MacProject.

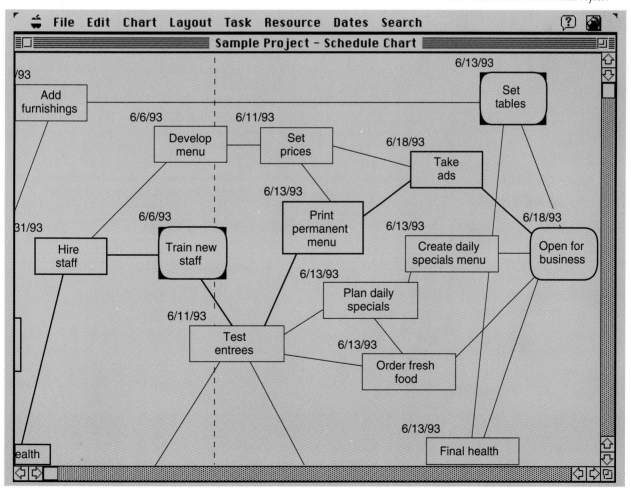

vide a standard approach to planning, reviewing, and evaluating a project's progress. (PERT is an acronym for *Program Evaluation and Review Technique.*) Both charts focus on the critical path in a project, which specifies the series of tasks that must be completed on time to meet a schedule's deadline. If any task within a critical path is delayed, the whole schedule is in jeopardy. Gantt and PERT charts help managers analyze the critical path and track a project's progress. Because systems analysts also depend on these charts, we discuss them again in Chapter 10.

Many project management packages feature on-screen graphics. They may also include an outliner: software that assists writers in developing outlines for documents they are preparing. Once again, such tools do not replace planning and evaluation by managers; rather, they perform some of the more routine tasks, thereby freeing managers for the more important tasks at hand. Harvard Project Manager, SuperProject, and Project Scheduler are among the more common packages.

**Personal information managers** combine some of the features of desktop organizers and project management software for a manager's personal use. Such packages can track projects, resources, dates, and costs for lower-level tasks. They also include notepads, appointment schedules, and calendars. Agenda, Current, and Instant Recall are popular personal information managers. See Figure 7.5.

## COMMUNICATIONS SOFTWARE

In Chapter 2 we saw that communications hardware such as modems and telephone lines can be used to send and receive data from one computer to another. Communications software allows you to set the parameters that enable computers to communicate with one another. Some communications packages common in business are SmartCom, Kermit,

*Figure 7.5 Sample screen display for Current, a personal information manager.*

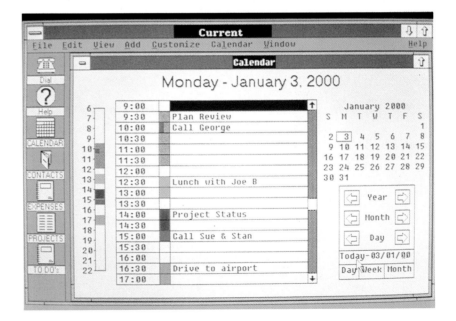

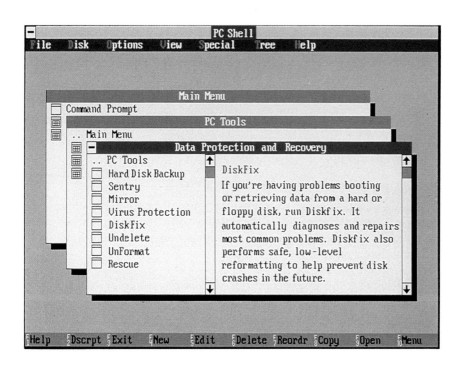

*Figure 7.6* Disk organizer and utility screen display.

and ProComm. We will discuss these packages in detail in Chapter 12. Frequently e-mail packages function in conjunction with communications packages if messages are transmitted over telephone lines or some other communications link.

## DISK ORGANIZERS AND OTHER UTILITIES

**Disk organizers** enable users to manage data and program files stored on their disks. Norton Utilities, PC Tools, and XTree Gold are common examples (see Figure 7.6). One main feature of these packages is the ability to scan all subdirectories on a disk to quickly locate a particular file. Another is the ability to "unerase" disk files or recover data accidentally deleted. This is possible because typically files that are deleted by a delete command are not physically erased; only the *reference* to the file is deleted. The unerase command, then, can call back the reference to a file.

Disk organizers are considered **utility programs,** or utilities, because they perform relatively standardized tasks that are often needed by all or most computer users. Many utilities make more effective use of main memory and disk space and control operations such as sorting of files. Most utilities also provide some form of access control of software and hardware. Some even provide the mechanism for creating backups automatically. Recall that backup copies of program and data files should be maintained in case something happens to the original.

Newer versions of some operating systems now include the common features of disk organizers and other utilities. Some packages such as PC Tools combine features of disk organizers, utilities, and desktop organizers.

### CRITICAL THINKING

It is common knowledge among computer professionals that some of the most popular packages are not necessarily the best. Despite evidence that newer products have better features, companies continue to use and purchase some of the older and staler software. They claim that the cost of a transition, which may include retraining an organization and rewriting applications, outweighs any innovative features. What do you think?

▶ **SELF-TEST**

1. Name the two main types of application software.
2. Name three components of an integrated package.
3. A software package that contains a telephone directory, calendar, calculator, and notepad, among other things, is called a _____.
4. (T or F) Although disk organizers have great capabilities, they cannot "unerase" disk files, because typically files that are deleted are physically erased.

Solutions

1. packaged (off-the-shelf) and custom (specially prepared) software
2. spreadsheet software, word processing software, and database management system software (It usually has e-mail and may have other components as well.)
3. desktop organizer
4. F—Files that are deleted are not always physically erased; typically only the reference to the file is deleted.

## SPECIALIZED APPLICATION PACKAGES: THE POWER TOOLS OF TODAY

*What capabilities do today's new "power tools" feature?*

Application packages frequently perform tasks that would otherwise take users many hours to perform. Such tasks are often prone to errors and are costly, especially when substantial manual labor is involved. We discuss here some of the more commonly used application packages that make processing more efficient and produce more accurate and useful output.

### ▶ Desktop Publishing

Individuals and organizations use **desktop publishing (DTP)** software to design and print documents with a wide variety of type styles and sizes called type fonts. See Figure 7.7. In these documents, text and graphics can appear on a single page. DTP combined with a laser printer enhances the quality of the printed output to the point where the document appears to be professionally typeset—just like this book. DTP products are ideal for creating newsletters, advertising pieces, even full-length texts.

The advantages of desktop publishing for producing typeset-quality documents are similar to the advantages of word processing for preparing manuscripts or documents. Desktop publishing software makes the task of producing output much easier and more efficient. Traditionally, the user who needs printed material submits a typewritten manuscript to a typesetter. The next step is for a designer to determine how the publication will look. The manuscript is then keyboarded using elaborate codes to format the text according to the designer's specifications. If these

***Figure 7.7*** *Aldus PageMaker is a popular desktop publishing package.*

steps are followed, the manuscript will have been keyed twice, once by the authors and once by a typesetter.

Intermediate output is produced next in the form of long strips known as galleys. The galleys are checked by professional proofreaders and then sent to the user to be read again. After all corrections and changes have been made by the typesetter, a further round of proofreading takes place. Finally, revised galleys are cut apart and pasted up in page format, leaving space for artwork. Now we have come to the page stage. The user checks a copy of these pages, called page proofs, not only for any errors in type that were overlooked, but for the acceptability of the layout. All further corrections are typeset and pasted in the pages; depending on the quantity and type of corrections, some pages may need to be completely redone. The final pasteup is sent to the camera department, where plates for the printing press are made. The user checks a proof of this final stage to make certain that everything is in its proper place. Finally, the publication is sent to a press to be printed.

The many steps involved in this traditional method of publishing provide opportunities for errors. Moreover, the process is time consuming, both for the typesetter and the user.

In contrast, desktop publishing software allows the user to control all aspects of the publication process, including designing the publication, setting the type, proofreading, inserting graphics, and producing the final copy. See Figure 7.8. Moreover, the time needed and the cost necessary to produce the document are greatly reduced. Only one typing operation is required to develop the manuscript. DTP packages can utilize text that has been prepared by virtually any word processing package.

With DTP, text and sophisticated graphics can be easily integrated into

*Figure 7.8* Desktop publishing packages can produce typeset quality output with graphics and a variety of type fonts.

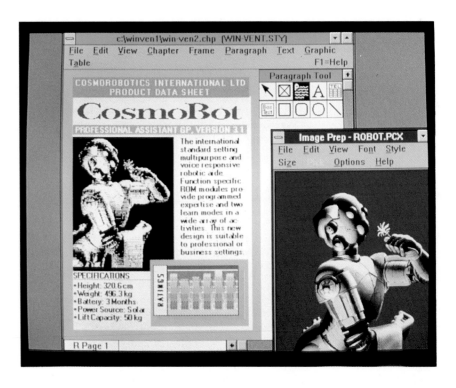

PostScript is a page description language that is used with printers capable of interpreting PostScript codes. The documents created can contain a wide variety of type fonts and graphic images. Because PostScript allows files to be produced on many different printers, it is currently a desktop publishing standard.

a single document. Graphics—ranging from simple lines and geometric shapes to drawings and photographs—can be placed anywhere on the page, enlarged or reduced, and trimmed to fit the available space.

Desktop publishing software also allows complex pages to be formatted on the computer screen in ways not commonly available with most word processing packages. Different typefaces, styles, and sizes can be viewed on the screen just as they will appear when the document is printed. This feature is referred to as WYSIWYG, which, as noted in Chapter 3, is an acronym for *what you see is what you get*. WYSIWYG enables the user to experiment with various screen displays before deciding on a page format. Most DTP packages also include dozens of preformatted page designs, or templates, that can be used as "shells" for creating newsletters, reports, and other documents.

Many desktop publishing packages use a universal code provided in a program called PostScript, developed by Adobe Systems, Inc. PostScript is a page description language that allows users to embed printing codes in documents; the codes tell printers capable of interpreting PostScript how to format each page. The advantage of PostScript is that it is a desktop publishing standard. When PostScript is used, typesetting and formatting codes will always be interpreted in the same way by all printers that support PostScript, including laser printers and phototypesetting machines. For example, if you are using PostScript and choose the typeface called Times Roman for your newsletter, the document produced on a PostScript printer will look the same no matter what printer or phototypesetting equipment is used. This means that you can proof your newsletter on a laser printer, which is relatively inexpensive, and then have the final version produced on more expensive phototypesetting equipment.

The concept of desktop publishing was made popular by a product called PageMaker, developed by the Aldus Corporation for the Macintosh. PageMaker soon had competition from other programs such as Ready-Set-Go! and Quark Xpress. Although desktop publishing was originally used primarily on the Macintosh, it was not long before the Xerox Corporation released Ventura Publisher, the first full-fledged desktop publishing program for IBM microcomputers. Within a few months after Ventura was announced, Aldus introduced an IBM version of PageMaker as well.

PageMaker has remained a popular package partly because it was the first commonly utilized desktop publishing program, and partly because similar versions run on the Macintosh and on IBM PCs. Not only does PageMaker include good page design tools, but it has the ability to integrate graphics easily. Moreover, files created with the IBM and Macintosh versions share a common structure, so they can be used by both systems. PageMaker is easy to learn and best suited for producing short documents and graphic-intensive publications. On the IBM and its compatibles, the use of the Windows graphical user interface is required with PageMaker and most other desktop publishing packages.

Virtually all DTP packages provide a screen that resembles an artist's board into which text and pictures can be placed. Typically, a mouse or other pointing device is used to highlight desired images and to place them in the document.

Many desktop publishing packages do not provide the sophisticated editing features included in word processing packages. Therefore, it is usually preferable to enter the text using a word processing program and then import, or transfer, the text file into the desktop publishing program for formatting. After the text is in the desktop publishing program, it can still be edited, but less efficiently. DTP packages are able to accept documents prepared by a wide variety of word processing packages.

DTP software, like most software, is intended to assist people who design documents, not to replace them or to be a substitute for their creative skills. DTP products have defaults that can be overridden by experienced designers to create truly unique and interesting documents.

## ▶ Graphics Packages

In recent years, businesses have taken to heart the old adage that one picture is worth a thousand words. They are illustrating ideas and information by using programs that interpret information visually (Figure 7.9). **Graphics software** is a general term that refers to programs with tools for drawing, charting, and presenting illustrations. Simple packages can capture screen displays and produce printed copies, film, or 35-mm slides. Some graphics packages convert numeric data into bar, pie, line, and other types of graphs. Some graphics packages also contain **clip art,** a database of graphic displays that you can add to documents. Figure

### LOOKING AHEAD

**DESKTOP PUBLISHING AND WORD PROCESSING ARE LIKELY TO MERGE**

The original manufacturers of desktop publishing products were not, as one might expect, word processing companies. As a result, DTP products still tend to have limited word processing capabilities, and word processing packages still tend to have limited page layout and graphics capabilities. But the distinctions between word processing and desktop publishing are slowly eroding as each continues to adopt features of the other. For now, DTP packages give you greater control over page composition, while word processing packages give you greater control over text editing. In the future, it is likely that one package will satisfy both text editing and page composition needs.

*Figure 7.9* Output produced by a graphics package.

**Figure 7.10** *Clip art available from DrawPerfect's Figure Library can be added to any document or file.*

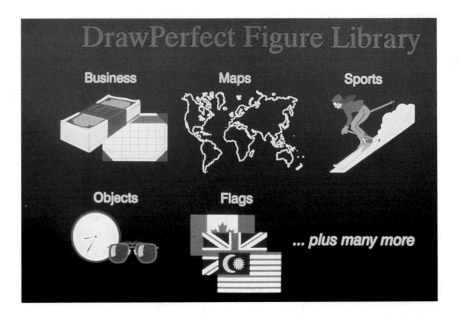

7.10 displays some common clip art. Graphics packages can also produce animated output and three-dimensional graphics.

Graphics software falls into two major categories: (1) presentation graphics programs and (2) illustration graphics programs. These packages differ not only in the types of visuals they produce but also in the ways the graphics are generated. Until recently, separate graphics products were available for different computers; for example, there is apt to be a Mac version as well as an IBM version of these products.

 Now as connectivity increases, computers with different architectures are being linked so that they can share software. Moreover, the IBM-Apple alliance is likely to result in new software developed specifically for the computers emerging from that alliance.

## PRESENTATION GRAPHICS

**Presentation graphics software** is designed to produce graphic representations of data for business presentations. Illustrations can be created as output on a screen, as transparencies for overhead projectors, or as black-and-white or color graphs on paper. Many of these programs allow users to attach devices to their systems that generate or result in high-resolution color slides. For example, you can create a chart or graph on a micro and transmit it via modem to a company that produces high-resolution color slides, which are mailed back to you, to a business associate, or to a client.

Many of the charting programs for IBM micros and their compatibles are similar to the graphics modules of Lotus 1-2-3 and other spreadsheet software, although the former usually allow more choices in graph and chart styles, colors, typefaces, and output devices. As a result, the finished graphs have a more polished, professional appearance than those created using spreadsheet software. Freelance Plus is an example of

**Figure 7.11** *A screen display from Freelance Plus, a presentation graphics package.*

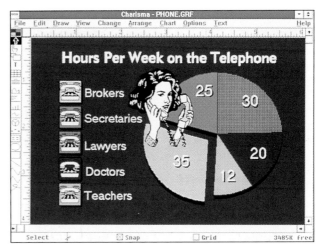

**Figure 7.12** *Micrografx's Charisma has built-in symbols and flexible options, like pie graphs, which help improve the look of presentation graphics.*

graphic and charting software for IBM micros. See Figure 7.11. Power Point is an example of a similar package for the Macintosh. Harvard Graphics and Persuasion are products available for both types of machines. See Figure 7.12.

Generally, presentation packages operate by reading data from a spreadsheet or database file and automatically graphing the data using a selected format. The chart, for example, can then be enhanced with various graphic elements such as special symbols, illustrations, and shading. Presentation graphics and charting packages are relatively limited in their scope, however, compared with the illustration programs we will discuss next.

## ILLUSTRATION PACKAGES

The first Macintoshes featured two built-in **illustration packages:** MacDraw and MacPaint. People were amazed at how easily they could create illustrations with this software. In the 1990s, illustration packages have become increasingly sophisticated. Only recently, however, have business users begun to take this software seriously, largely as a result of the importance that high-quality illustrations have in desktop publishing and in presentations. There are two categories of illustration packages: painting programs and drawing programs.

**Painting Programs.** Painting programs, such as MacPaint for the Macintosh and PC Paintbrush for the IBM (Figure 7.13), create **bit-mapped graphics,** which consist of patterns of dots. Bit-mapped graphics are similar to the output of a dot-matrix printer: each character is actually a grouping of small dots arranged to form desired shapes. The smaller and closer together the dots, the better the quality of the output. On the other hand, the more an image that is bit-mapped is enlarged, the coarser or less clear it becomes.

**Figure 7.13** *PC Paintbrush allows users to create bit-mapped graphics or combine scanned images with original artwork.*

Most bit-mapped graphics are created manually by using a mouse to move the cursor on the screen or by using a tablet that digitizes drawings. Optical scanners can also be used to digitize graphics and photos that already exist on paper. Once a graphic has been scanned, it can usually be edited or refined.

**Drawing Programs.**   As the demand for higher-resolution output has grown, so has the popularity of drawing programs. These programs differ from painting programs in that they use combinations of lines, arcs, circles, squares, and other shapes or objects rather than dots to create visuals. These programs use **vector graphics** as opposed to bit-mapped graphics. Vector graphics can be resized—either enlarged or reduced—without altering their clarity.

Some type fonts are created using bit-mapped graphics but these are not scalable; that is, their sizes cannot be changed easily. Scalable type fonts using vector graphics are more popular today than bit-mapped type fonts.

The more sophisticated drawing programs, such as Adobe Illustrator (Figure 7.14), Aldus Freehand, and Micrografx Designer, offer a great deal of flexibility in creating illustrations. The exact thickness of lines can be specified; objects can be shaded to give them a three-dimensional appearance that was formerly only possible with painting programs, and they can easily be scaled, rotated, duplicated, or revamped for special effects. Micrografx Designer (Figure 7.15), in particular, is a highly sophisticated drawing program with many of the capabilities of the computer-aided design packages that engineers use. We discuss these in the next section.

Drawing programs require more planning, patience, and skill than painting programs. However, large drawings normally take less disk space than large paintings and take less time to print. Painting programs allow for more spontaneity, but they are far less precise.

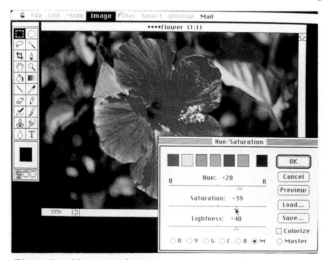

***Figure 7.14*** *Vector graphics programs use computer-generated lines, shapes, and dot patterns. No matter how much an image is enlarged, it remains crisply drawn.*

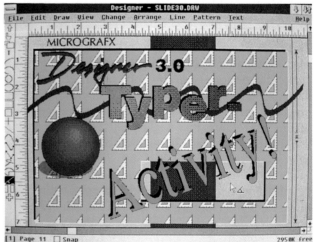

***Figure 7.15*** *Micrografx Designer combines features typically used in computer-aided design programs with those used in illustration packages.*

Most managers use the graphics created by illustration programs but leave the input procedures to data entry operators and the design of the output to computer professionals. In most business and professional settings, the illustration packages are used in graphic design or desktop publishing departments. If a scanner is available, managers may have their company logos or signatures scanned. The logos and signatures can then be electronically integrated into letters, memos, and other documents. Managers also like graphing and charting programs because they make information accessible in attractive and instructional charts and they can produce slides.

## CAD/CAM

**Computer-aided design (CAD)** packages, as the name implies, are used to design products with the assistance of a computer (Figure 7.16). CAD packages are essentially drawing programs, but they offer additional features specifically required by the architects and engineers for whom they were created. CAD programs use objects to create complex drawings, but they allow a degree of precision unavailable in most other graphics packages. For example, they automatically calculate and display the dimensions of an illustration. In addition, they allow you to place objects in precise locations by specifying $x$ and $y$ coordinates. CAD programs also allow you to store a library of symbols on disk. You can insert, scale, and rotate figures as needed.

**Computer-aided manufacturing (CAM)** products help engineers design the manufacturing components in a factory or production facility. CAD/CAM software integrates computer-aided design with computer-aided manufacturing. The products designed in the CAD system are directly inputted to the CAM system.

Because of their complexity, many CAD/CAM packages are used on minicomputer or mainframe computers for designing intricate products such as automobiles, airplanes, or weapons systems. In fact, CAD/CAM packages were once the primary province of larger systems; now they are available for micros as well. (AutoCAD is the most popular package for micros.) Most illustration packages discussed in the previous section were derived from CAD/CAM software.

CAD, CAM, and CAD/CAM packages assist in designing products; they are not a substitute for human skill. Rather, their goal is to provide support to product designers by performing some basic operations, thereby enabling the professionals to focus on the more creative aspects of their jobs.

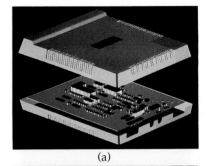

(a)

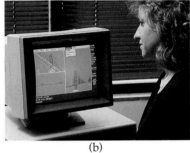

(b)

***Figure 7.16*** *AutoCAD is the most widely used computer-aided design package. It can be used for* (a) *designing chips as well as* (b) *designing bridges.*

## ▶ Statistical Packages

Traditionally, statistical analysis of large volumes of data has been a time-consuming, error-prone task. Because of the computer's speed and accuracy, number crunching was one of its earliest uses. **Statistical packages** such as Minitab, SPSS, SAS, and Systat can perform virtually any statistical operation, such as determining standard deviations and variances,

*Figure 7.17 Analysis performed by a statistical package.*

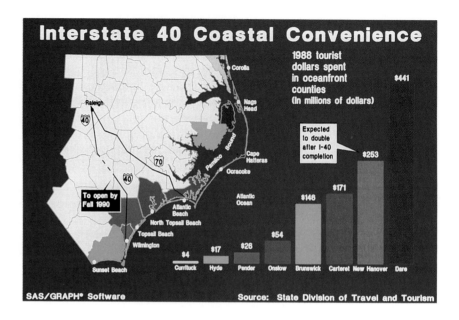

to help managers analyze data (Figure 7.17). Versions of these statistical packages are available for all types of computers from micros to larger systems.

## ▶ Expert System Shells

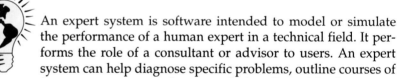

An expert system is software intended to model or simulate the performance of a human expert in a technical field. It performs the role of a consultant or advisor to users. An expert system can help diagnose specific problems, outline courses of action to take, or suggest approaches to a solution. One of the first expert systems to be utilized was a medical diagnosis system called MYCIN developed at Stanford University in the early 1970s. Today, expert systems are used not only for medical diagnosis but for weather prediction, oil exploration, financial planning, newspaper layouts, diagnosing mechanical problems in machinery, and in many other technical areas.

To create an expert system, a systems analyst called a knowledge engineer interviews experts in the specific field and translates their knowledge, called the knowledge base, into a series of rules in the form of if-then relationships. When set up, the expert system begins by asking questions of the user; when the system has enough information, it draws a conclusion by means of a component of the software called an inference engine. In summary, expert systems use:

1. Knowledge in the form of a database.
2. Rules in the form of if-then relationships.
3. Human interaction: users respond to queries.
4. An inference engine to draw conclusions.

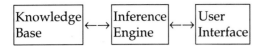

Expert systems are best suited for providing advice or support to the decision maker. They are not substitutes for human expertise, because human factors such as intuition, creativity, and experience are not easily built into such systems.

Expert systems are nonprocedural; that is, the designer of the system does not write a sequence of steps to be executed as is done in many programming languages. Rather, an expert system is rule based, which means that the designer writes a set of rules that people typically follow under specified circumstances. The rules are written in the form of IF (conditions are met) THEN (conclusions or actions to be taken) statements.

Examples

1. IF Student__attendance > 30 and Midterm > 89 and Final > 87
   THEN
      Grade = A
2. IF Temperature > 100.3 and Lung__infection = Yes
   THEN
      Diagnosis = pneumonia

Expert system shells have been developed as generic expert systems. The shells enable users to enter their own knowledge base and inferences to form application-specific expert systems. An expert system shell has an established human interface in the form of dialogs and displays and an inference engine in the form of rules. The knowledge base for these shells can be supplied by the users themselves or by other technical experts.

Expert systems and shells are capable of probabilistic reasoning; that is, even if there is uncertainty or incompleteness of data, predictions can

## LOOKING AHEAD

### THE NERVOUS SHOCK ADVISOR

Knowledge engineers at the University of British Columbia working with IBM have built an expert legal system that provides attorneys with advice on legal cases involving nervous shock, emotional distress, and emotional suffering. The system, called the Nervous Shock Advisor, advises lawyers about whether people who say they have suffered emotional distress have a viable claim. The system bases its conclusions on judgments reached in previous court cases.

After asking the attorney for specific facts about the case, the Nervous Shock Advisor:

- Searches a legal database and determines whether the claim is valid.
- Lists the factors used to arrive at its conclusion and presents a confidence level value for each factor.
- Supplies references to relevant court cases that either support its conclusion or go against it.

- Gives references to cases that demonstrate the arguments that the defendant (that is, the opposing side) might use to present his or her side of the case.

If the system determines that the plaintiff has no case, it tells the lawyer what elements are lacking.

The system was designed to help lawyers prepare a case by presenting the basic elements that support successful litigation.

be made. In addition, expert systems allow the user to obtain explanations about how conclusions were reached and why specific data was necessary. At any point in an analysis, the user can interrupt the consultation and ask why certain information was needed and how a conclusion was reached.

In business, expert systems are used for many purposes.

- Evaluating stocks.
- Determining seating capacity and airplane utilization for various airlines.
- Marketing and planning to help establish prices, provide sales forecasts, and make profitability estimates.
- Diagnosing equipment failure.

VP-Expert and GURU are expert system shells that can be used with PCs as well as larger computers. In Chapter 11 we will see how expert systems function in decision support systems and executive information systems.

## ▶ **M**ultimedia and **A**uthoring **P**roducts

Multimedia, which essentially merges the capability of the PC with a TV, is fast becoming one of the most significant application areas for micros. Some main uses of multimedia software are for making dynamic presentations by providing information or computer-based training in an interactive and exciting manner that makes use of video, sound, animation, and graphics as well as text. Multimedia software tools use a *hypermedia* navigational technique incorporated into a wide variety of products. Hypermedia itself is based on *hypertext* navigation which was text-based but incorporated innovative mechanisms for interacting with a computer.

**Hypertext** software is a dynamic approach to navigating, or moving, through a database where information is linked together and is accessible in any form desired, regardless of its location. With hypertext, some links lead to other links, which are further linked to other topics, and so forth. Suppose you are interested in information about display terminals. You can go to a reference book, look up the topic in the index, and then read the pages cited. This would be a basic hypertext search. But the pages to which you were referred may also discuss menus, prompts, icons, and mice. These subjects might be helpful as well and might themselves be cited in other places in the book. It would be difficult to navigate through the book looking for all topics that relate to display terminals.

By using software that contains hypertext components, you can select a topic, read about it, and then choose subtopics from a menu. The context-sensitive help provided by many software packages has hypertext tools to enable users to find the levels of help they desire. As an author using hypertext software, you can build connections between ideas and concepts and structure your ideas in a number of meaningful ways.

The basic concept behind hypertext is not new. Think of an encyclopedia. An article in an encyclopedia often ends with a series of subtopics that relate to the article. Each subtopic may also have reference points,

IN A

**EXPERT SYSTEMS AND HYPERTEXT**

Expert systems are tools that bring an expert's knowledge to individuals who need to diagnose problems, troubleshoot operations, or plan a course of action. Hypertext is often part of such systems. Hypertext navigates users through material to clarify topics and to analyze the rules that are being applied to particular situations.

Hypertext is ideal for navigating through help menus. Typically, when you use help menus, you want to go from main topics to more detailed ones and jump around to see related information. This type of browsing is made much simpler with hypertext links.

both to subtopics of information specifically related to it and to more general topics. Using a computer, however, it is easier to "page up" and "page down" to specific screen displays than to flip through the volumes of an encyclopedia.

**Hypermedia** improves on the hypertext concept by linking together not only text but graphics, sound, animation, and even video. The major benefit of computerized hypermedia is that readers do not need to know the physical location (analogous to a page number) of any data. They can simply select the links they desire. Suppose you are at your computer reading about activities at your college or university from a manual available online. You come across the term *physical fitness* and it is highlighted, which means that more information is available. You can move the cursor to this item or use your mouse to click in on it. The screen will be cleared and an animated description of how to stay fit will appear. From here, you can select information about your school's exercise equipment, and a video may be played demonstrating how to use the equipment.

Some hypermedia products allow you to interact with them. For example, you can test your understanding of a topic or you can enter values to see how they would affect results. Such interactive techniques make hypermedia tools ideal for online tutorials and other computer-based training applications. Many software packages have hypertext or hypermedia features added on for navigating through the package or for getting online help. QuickBASIC and QBASIC (supplied with DOS 5.0 and higher), for example, are two such products.

Hypermedia techniques include:

- Paging or navigating through a lesson that may include text, graphics, video, animation, and sound.
- Leaving bookmarks to return to specific pages for reference.
- Going directly to any new concept without having to sequentially scroll through a text.
- Returning to previous menus.
- Taking tests at any point and getting results immediately.
- Viewing a map of all linkages to get an overview of the structure.

## LOOKING BACK

### THE BEGINNINGS OF HYPERMEDIA

Theodor (Ted) Holm Nelson first created the concept of hypertext in 1964. He used the term to describe documents that can be accessed in any manner without the need to sequentially read through them. Hypertext remained an unrealized concept, however, until 1987 when Apple created a version of hypertext called HyperCard. HyperCard was bundled with every Macintosh sold between 1987 and 1990. Claris Corporation now markets HyperCard as a separate product.

*Photograph of Theodor (Ted) Holm Nelson, creator of the hypertext concept.*

## IN A NUTSHELL

| Hypertext | Provides sophisticated navigational techniques for interacting with and viewing text |
|---|---|
| Hypermedia | Provides sophisticated navigational techniques for interacting with and viewing text, graphics, video, animation, and sound |
| Multimedia Product | Incorporates more than one medium such as text, graphics, video, animation, and sound |
| Authoring or Multimedia Software | Employs hypermedia to create sophisticated presentations and to provide computer-based training |

*Multimedia screen display for a package that provides information about Beethoven's works, along with actual recordings of his symphonies.*

## LOOKING AHEAD

**HYPERMEDIA PREDICTIONS**

1. Hypermedia tools will be used by increasing numbers of professionals as part of their desktop systems and for database processing.
2. Computer-based training will continue to make extensive use of hypermedia tools.
3. Hypermedia concepts will be built into the operating system, thereby creating an environment that makes the system easier to use and more flexible.

A multimedia software product called PassPort is available with this text. Still other software enables users to develop their own hypermedia linkages among databases and user interfaces. HyperCard is perhaps the most well known tool. Introduced in 1987, it was originally supplied (or bundled) with the Macintosh but is now sold separately.

The uses of hypermedia tools are varied:

- Help systems, online tutorials, and computer-based training.
- Authoring programs to build presentations, training courses, and exhibits.
- Personal information managers to provide reference links between related pieces of information (e.g., to tie together notes, phone book entries, and calendar entries about a client before a meeting).
- Application generators to link data from different files.
- Database management for joining files and generating graphics, video, animation, and sound, if appropriate.

Separate hypermedia tools for linking databases and navigating through them continue to be popular, but mainly with individuals who are interested in utilizing their personal resources more effectively. For creating dynamic presentations and computer-based training tools, however, multimedia or authoring tools with hypermedia components are far more powerful. ToolBook and Authorware are products that enable users to develop software that includes text, graphics, video, animation, and sound along with hypermedia tools for linking and interacting with these media (see Figure 7.18). Multimedia is a concept likely to further revolutionize the computing field, and authoring products will help educators, salespeople, and others to present their ideas more effectively. Authoring or multimedia tools with hypermedia components are also being used to create databases with photos, documents, and videos along with text and to enable users to access the databases using a combination of media.

Computer-based training is currently the major application area for these tools. Authoring or multimedia products that contain hypermedia

*Figure 7.18 Authorware screen displays developed for (a) a training tutorial on security for American Airlines and (b) a tutorial for training medical personnel.*

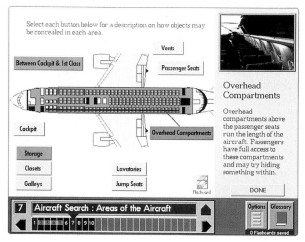

(a)

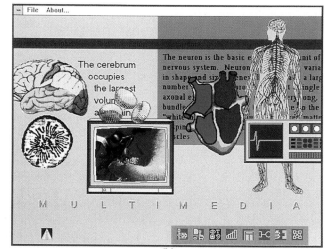

(b)

techniques have been developed to teach people how to fly an airplane, perform a medical procedure, or perform any number of tasks.

Authoring software really has two parts: (1) a program that creates the software and (2) a separate runtime system for using the products developed. A runtime version of ToolBook, for example, may be bundled with Windows for IBM PCs so that any ToolBook product created by an author is accessible to people who have a copy of Windows. The PassPort software that accompanies this book can be read by those who have the runtime version of ToolBook.

## ▶ CASE Tools

So far we have discussed some of the many software products available to users. But when systems analysts set out to analyze existing business information systems and design more efficient, computerized ones, they have traditionally relied on paper and pencil. Virtually no software packages have been available to help them do their jobs. The situation is analogous to the proverbial shoemaker who makes shoes for everyone but his or her own children.

Finally, times are changing. **Computer-assisted software engineering (CASE)** is a category of productivity tools used by systems analysts to build information systems. As we will see in Chapter 10, integrated CASE tools help to effectively design elements of new systems. Because of their graphics component, CASE tools alleviate the need to hand draw graphic representations of systems specifications.

CASE tools, like most of the software we have discussed, are designed to assist, not to replace, people. CASE tools help the systems analyst design the system; they are *not* intended to fully automate the process. Actually, CASE consists of tools that help to increase the productivity of people who develop systems. In this regard, CASE tools are similar to the CAD/CAM tools used by architects, engineers, and other designers.

## ▶ Horizontal and Vertical Business Packages

**Horizontal packages** refer to software that is applicable to many different types of companies, from small to large. For example, a particular accounting package may be used by a small boutique as well as a large department store chain or a fast-food franchise. In contrast, **vertical packages** are designed to meet the highly specialized needs of a specific industry or business.

### ACCOUNTING PACKAGES: A HORIZONTAL APPLICATION

Some small businesses function well using spreadsheet packages for all of their financial and accounting needs. Other businesses, however, need software that is specifically designed to computerize the overall accounting function. A typical accounting program consists of several modules that work interactively. The three most commonly used modules are those that manage the general ledger, accounts receivable, and accounts payable functions. Depending on the nature of the business, inventory or payroll modules may also be added. Other common features of accounting packages include a systems manager program that integrates the modules, specialized report writers, and charting and graphing routines. See Figure 7.19.

A good accounting program includes error-detection procedures and extensive audit trails that enable users or auditors to trace transactions from the general ledger stage through to individual accounts. Such a program should also provide automatic year-end closings, that is, create complete financial statements that summarize the activity for the year.

Accounting software comes in entry-level, midrange, and high-end configurations that are aimed at small, medium-sized, and large businesses, respectively. In other words, horizontal accounting packages are designed for computer systems from micros to mainframes, and they are priced to reflect their complexity. Some software publishers have a line of accounting software and upgrade policies that make it possible to start out with one version and move up to a more sophisticated version as the need arises. Dac-Easy Accounting, Insight Expert, and SBT (Figure 7.20) are examples of popular microcomputer accounting packages.

In most cases, an accountant or clerk enters data. In larger businesses, networked versions of accounting programs make it possible for several people to enter data or to handle specific duties, such as billing and writing checks, from different workstations.

Although the modules of an accounting program come ready to run,

**Figure 7.19** *An accounting package can be used for completing income tax returns.*

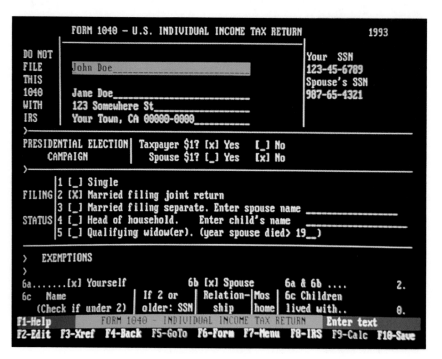

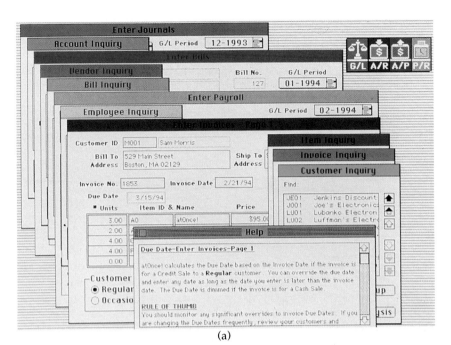

(a)

*Figure 7.20* (a) *An accounting package like this one allows small businesses to computerize their accounting procedures.* (b) *This is a diagram of the steps involved in computerizing accounting procedures.*

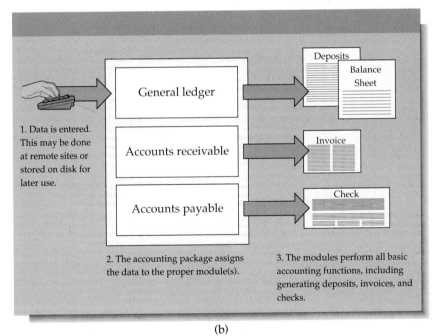

1. Data is entered. This may be done at remote sites or stored on disk for later use.

2. The accounting package assigns the data to the proper module(s).

3. The modules perform all basic accounting functions, including generating deposits, invoices, and checks.

(b)

they usually can be tailored to suit the needs of a particular business. Most packages automatically produce statements, invoices, and paychecks, although a certain amount of formatting is necessary to match the actual output required with the specific forms provided.

Packages such as the accounting software discussed here can be used in a wide variety of organizations. Other types of horizontal packages include payroll, inventory, and sales management software.

*Figure 7.21* A vertical application for hospital use includes maintaining and reporting on patient data.

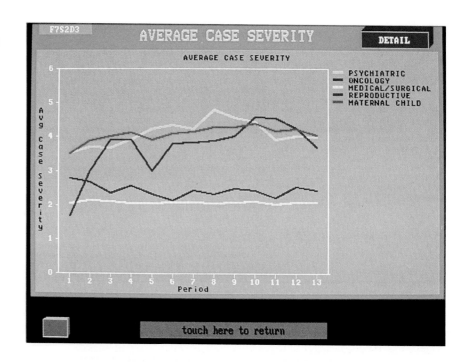

## MEDICAL PACKAGES: A VERTICAL APPLICATION

Many vertical packages have been developed to meet the specialized needs of the medical profession (see Figure 7.21). One example is software used to perform the business tasks in optometrists' offices. The software might schedule appointments, maintain patient records, send bills, and keep track of employees' work schedules. It is designed to take into account the specific needs of optometrists, as compared with other groups of professionals such as lawyers, or even more closely related groups such as dentists.

Keep in mind that there are horizontal and vertical packages for both PCs and larger systems. In fact, all types of software packages discussed here are available for both micros and larger systems. Many types were designed originally for mainframes, but versions for micros soon followed. Today, most micro-based software is off-the-shelf, whereas both custom and packaged software are common with mainframes. Because PCs lend themselves to individual use by people with little or no computer background, packaged software is ideal. More sophisticated users in mainframe-based companies tend to rely more heavily on custom software.

IN A

### SPECIALIZED APPLICATION SOFTWARE

All of the following packages are available for IBM and IBM-compatibles; most are also available for the Macintosh. Some packages have both DOS and Windows versions for the IBM, but others are only available with *either* DOS or Windows. Some are available with OS/2 as well, which is another IBM operating system.

| | |
|---|---|
| Integrated packages | Microsoft Works (Microsoft Corp.)<br>Enable (Software Group)<br>PFS:First Choice (Symantec)<br>LotusWorks (Lotus Development Corp.) |
| Desktop organizers | SideKick (Borland International, Inc.)<br>Norton Desktop for Windows (Symantec) |
| Project management | Harvard Project Manager (Software Publishing Corp.)<br>SuperProject (Computer Associates)<br>Project Scheduler (Heizer Software)<br>MacProject II (Claris Corp.)—for the Mac |
| Personal information<br>managers | Agenda (Lotus Development Corp.)<br>Instant Recall (Chronlogic Corp.) |
| Communications | SmartCom (Hayes Microcomputer Products, Inc.)<br>Crosstalk (Crosstalk Communications/DCA, Inc.)<br>ProComm (DataStorm Technologies, Inc.)<br>Kermit (public domain) |
| Disk organizers and<br>other utilities | Norton Utilities (Symantec)<br>PC Tools (Central Point Software, Inc.)<br>XTree Gold (XTree Co.) |
| Desktop publishing | PageMaker (Aldus Corp.)<br>Ventura Publisher (Xerox Corp.)<br>Ready-Set-Go! (Letraset Graphic Design Software) |
| Presentation graphics | Freelance Plus (Lotus Development Corp.)<br>Harvard Graphics (Software Publishing Corp.)<br>Power Point (Microsoft Corp.)<br>Persuasion (Aldus Corp.) |
| Illustration | MacPaint, MacDraw (Claris)—for the Mac<br>PC Paintbrush (ZSoft Corp.)<br>Adobe Illustrator (Adobe Systems, Inc.)<br>Cricket Draw (Computer Associates International, Inc.)<br>CorelDRAW (Corel Systems Corp.)<br>Designer (Micrografx, Inc.) |
| CAD/CAM | AutoCAD (Autodesk Inc.)<br>Claris CAD (Claris Corp.) |
| Statistical | Minitab (Minitab, Inc.)<br>SAS (SAS Institute Inc.)<br>SPSS (SPSS Associates Inc.)<br>Systat (SYSTAT, Inc.) |
| Expert system shells | GURU (MDBS, Inc.)<br>VP-Expert (Wordtech Systems, Inc.) |
| Multimedia and<br>authoring software | Toolbook (Asymetric Corp.)<br>Authorware (Authorware, Inc.)<br>HyperCard for the Mac (Claris Corp.) |
| Accounting | DacEasy Accounting (DacEasy, Inc.)<br>Insight Expert (Peachtree Software)<br>SBT (SBT Corp.)<br>Accounting Software (OPEN SYSTEMS, Inc.) |
| Medical systems | (Medicus Systems Corp.)<br>(Accumedic Computer Systems, Inc.) |

▶ SELF-TEST

1. Packages that can produce typeset-quality output with text and graphics appearing on a single page are called _____.
2. (T or F) Most word processing packages have the same capability as desktop publishing software when it comes to formatting text on the computer screen.
3. Hypermedia allows you to link not only text but _____.
4. (T or F) A horizontal package is one that is useful in a broad range of organizations.
5. (T or F) A vertical package is one that is designed to meet the highly specialized needs of a specific industry or business.

Solutions
1. desktop publishing (DTP) software
2. F—Desktop publishing software allows you to view different typefaces and type styles and sizes on the screen just as they will appear when the document is printed.
3. graphics, sound, animation, video
4. T
5. T

# 7.3    CHOOSING AND USING SOFTWARE

Thus far we have discussed some of the more widely used software packages. In this section, we consider what users need to know when selecting specific products.

How can users make the right choices when selecting application packages?

## ▶ The Make or Buy Decision

Users along with computer professionals need to decide whether to "make or buy"—whether to acquire existing software or to develop custom software for any given application. Many factors should be considered before making such a decision. Consider first the benefits of off-the-shelf software:

- Packaged software is less expensive than custom software. The development costs and the time it takes to complete a top-notch product are considerable; but the manufacturer sells each package for a fraction of its total cost in anticipation of a large number of sales. Thus, an off-the-shelf package that cost millions of dollars to develop may be sold for hundreds of dollars to thousands of people. As a result, both users and developers benefit.
- Packaged software is immediately available, already tested, and thoroughly documented. Users need not wait for development and testing.
- Packaged software is typically supported by features such as tutorials,

IN A

## TO MAKE OR BUY SOFTWARE?

| | **PROS** | **CONS** |
|---|---|---|
| **Packaged Programs** | 1. Immediately usable on acquisition<br>2. Widely tested<br>3. Less expensive for each user<br>4. Well documented with numerous support features. | 1. Likely to meet most, but not all, of a user's requirements<br>2. After acquisition, user is dependent on outside support (e.g., telephone hot lines) rather than having programmers available if modifications are needed or problems arise |
| **Custom Programs** | 1. Specifically designed to satisfy individual user needs<br>2. More easily modified if the need arises<br>3. Developers readily available to support implementation and modification if needed | 1. More expensive to develop and maintain because costs are not shared among many users<br>2. Takes more time to implement |

documentation, manuals, and hot line telephone numbers that provide technical support.

Although application packages have such benefits and some are quite flexible, they rarely satisfy all of an individual's needs. Since such products are designed for many types of users, they cannot easily be individualized. On the other hand, they are likely to be more useful for a greater number of users.

Although we use the terms *make* or *buy* when determining whether to acquire packages, a great deal of mainframe software, particularly the more expensive types, are apt to be *leased* rather than purchased. The user pays an annual fee for the right to use the product. Each year, the product is upgraded and the new versions are made available.

## ▶ Versions of Software

Popular software products are updated with some frequency. Sometimes the new versions have only modest changes and sometimes the changes are significant. Version numbers provide information about the level of the update. Version 2.0, for example, is a significant improvement over 1.0, whereas version 2.2, which has the same integer as 2.0, is likely to have only minor improvements. Software products, like hardware products, are upwardly compatible. A file created using a product with version 1.0 will typically be usable with all newer versions, but files created under newer versions may not be usable with older ones.

When acquiring software, be sure you get the most recent version. Ask about the upgrade policy as well. Some companies sell newer versions to current users at greatly reduced prices.

# ▶ Evaluating Software Products

## CRITERIA

The most important factor in evaluating software is, of course, how well the product meets your needs. Remember, though, to consider these additional factors in evaluating application packages.

1. Compatibility with existing hardware and software.
   - Can it be run as is with existing equipment?
   - Can files from other programs be read, or imported, into the package?
   - Can files from the new package be written, or exported, to files created by other programs?
2. Speed.
3. Quality of documentation
4. Ease of learning.
   - Are online tutorials available?
   - Are the help menus helpful?
5. Ease of use.
   - Are pull-down menus available?
   - Are icons available for selecting commands?
6. Error-handling ability.
7. Technical support.
   - Are there hot lines?
   - Is telephone support available 24 hours a day?
   - Is technical support free?
   - Are telephone costs free?
8. Upgrade policy.
   - When new versions of the software become available, can users of the previous versions purchase the product at a discount?
   - Can data created using older versions be used without change?
9. Cost of the package.

When you need to evaluate software products, consider the following:

## CHECK REVIEWS IN PUBLICATIONS

Many magazines like *PC World, PC Week,* and *InfoWorld* provide periodic reviews of software products. There are also technical publications like the Seybold series and *DataPro* that specialize in analysis of hardware and software.

---

**CRITICAL THINKING**

Software users realize the importance of technical support. Some software companies provide free telephone support (800 numbers) for a fixed period of time (e.g., 90 days); when the fixed time period has lapsed, they require the user to dial a long distance number or a 900 number for continued support. How do you think the companies enforce this? Do you think the reduced telephone costs are worth the goodwill they lose by making customers pay for calls?

## PERFORM BENCHMARK TESTS

**Benchmark tests,** or performance tests, can help you determine the efficiency of a product. These tests involve running various programs and measuring the time it takes for the computer to perform the tasks. You can enter the same data into a variety of products and compare the results. Based on the criteria most important to you, you can select the product that best meets your needs.

## CHECK OUT THE MANUFACTURER

When it comes to software development, reputation is extremely important. It is wise to consult other users of the product. Sometimes manufacturers will supply a list of satisfied customers with whom you can speak.

# ▶ Where and How to Acquire Software

## THE MARKETPLACE

As with hardware, there are numerous sources for acquiring application packages; Table 7.1 lists the most common. Recall that typically the manufacturer produces the product but a separate vendor or retailer may sell it (you can usually purchase software directly from the manufacturer as well).

**Table 7.1** | WHERE TO GET APPLICATION PACKAGES

|  | Pros | Cons |
|---|---|---|
| Mail order | Tends to be inexpensive since the mail-order house has very little overhead | Technical support from the vendor is minimal (although the manufacturer may provide technical support). |
| Discount stores | Often as inexpensive, or almost as inexpensive, as a mail-order house | Very little support is provided. |
| Computer, electronic, or retail stores | Tends to be moderately expensive (list price or a little less) | Technical support may be available if personnel are familiar with the product. |
| Directly from manufacturer | List price | Technical support from the manufacturer is typically available to all users regardless of the source of acquisition, but manufacturers put their customers on a mailing list for upgrades. |

*A computer store is a good place to go to get information about software packages.*

## SHAREWARE AND PUBLIC DOMAIN SOFTWARE

Some software packages are expensive. To spend $500 or more for a micro-based productivity tool, for example, is not uncommon. Some mainframe packages cost hundreds of thousands of dollars to purchase; others are leased at hefty annual fees. With this in mind, be aware that there are packages in virtually every computing category that can be obtained for little or no cost.

**Public domain software** consists of noncopyrighted programs that developers make available free of charge. **Shareware** is software that can be obtained without cost, but the developer asks the user to pay a small fee to help share handling and packaging costs and perhaps even a small usage fee. A widely used communications package called Kermit, for example, is in the public domain.

Some shareware and public domain programs are really quite good— desktop managers, utilities, and games are among the most popular. Major computer magazines typically include ads from mail-order houses indicating how such products can be obtained; usually you need to pay distributor's costs of a few dollars. Also, electronic bulletin boards and subscriber services such as CompuServe or Prodigy provide lists of products that can be downloaded to a microcomputer at no charge. Computer clubs often provide shareware and public domain software as well.

The main disadvantages of most shareware and public domain software are (1) they are prone to viruses, which we discuss in the next section, and (2) they frequently have inadequate documentation.

## ▶ The Human Factor: Security and Safety

## LICENSING AND COPY PROTECTING SOFTWARE

Most software that is sold or leased is accompanied by a licensing agreement that specifies how the product should be used. When the program is first loaded into the computer, the licensing agreement asks for confirmation that the user agrees to its terms.

Licensing agreements indicate the number of copies users are legally permitted to make. Some licenses explicitly permit users to make as many copies of the software as they need. Others ask the user to make a single copy for backup purposes only. Still others permit copies to be made, but ask that only one be used at a given time; that is, you can make one for home, one for the office, and one for school, but you should only use one at a time. The license prohibits someone from using your office copy while you are using your copy at home.

If an organization has many users who need access to a product at the same time, the organization may be able to obtain a **site license.** With a site license, the manufacturer or vendor agrees to sell or lease the rights to a fixed number of copies of the software for a set price. Site licenses are particularly useful in organizations that have networks.

Some software manufacturers enforce their licensing agreements by **copy protecting** their software. Copy-protected disks contain some programmed feature that limits the number of copies that can be made. Sometimes a hardware feature is used instead of software for copy protection. In such a case, the hardware device must be connected to the computer for the software to run. Most software manufacturers, however, do not copy protect their software; rather, they rely on the user's honesty and integrity to adhere to the licensing stipulation.

Making copies of software in violation of the licensing agreement is not only dishonest, it is illegal. In fact, some organizations have actually been sued for such violations, and the software manufacturers typically win such lawsuits. Despite existing laws and efforts by some manufacturers to have them enforced rigorously, it is estimated that software "piracy" costs the computing industry over $2 billion per year!

From a practical point of view, it is fairly easy for individual users to make extra copies of software—especially software that is not copy protected—for themselves or others. Even if the software is copy protected, other packages are available that have been designed to override copy-protection features. Moreover, the likelihood of an individual being sued for copyright infringement is remote.

The issue becomes one of ethics rather than legality. Illegally (or unethically) copying software is not much different from illegally using someone else's property. The main difference is that when you copy software illegally, you are less likely to get caught. Illegal copying of software is not unlike duplicating licensed videos or copying pages from a book.

## COMPUTER VIRUSES

Hackers are computer-proficient hobbyists who take pride in violating systems, breaking codes, or otherwise using computers in unauthorized ways. News stories relate tales of individuals who successfully gain access to systems, sometimes just for fun and sometimes for more malevolent reasons. Often they are caught and punished, but sometimes a crime is not even realized for months or years. Although we may be amused by some of the antics of hackers who gain unauthorized access to computers, the government views them as criminals. Indeed, sometimes they pose a real threat to data security and integrity, and even to society as a whole.

Some hackers have moved from breaking into systems to wreaking havoc with software. They add some instructions to operating systems or application software that can not only destroy the product but also "infect" every file on disk. These **viruses** have been known to cripple entire computer systems for long periods of time. As a computer user, you should be aware of the danger of computer viruses just as you are aware of the danger of any infectious disease. Take precautionary steps to minimize the risk to your system. One practical step you can take is to avoid copying other people's files. You do not know where they have been and you do not, therefore, know whether they carry a virus. Although this may sound like a lesson in health education, it is relevant to computing. Many organizations have not only increased security to

**CRITICAL THINKING**

On June 28, 1990 Lotus won a court victory over Paperback Software, the producer of VP Planner, a clone of Lotus's best-selling spreadsheet package Lotus 1-2-3. The ruling protects the menus and command structures of Lotus 1-2-3 and, more importantly, it considerably expands the scope of copyright protection for all software. In the wake of its victory, Lotus sued Borland International charging Borland with copyright infringement for its product Quattro Pro. Do you think software developers should be able to copyright menus or screen displays?

**COMPUTING APPLICATION**

Viruses abound and just as soon as a new one is introduced, an anti-virus program for it is marketed. It might be more efficient if the hackers who create and spread the viruses would develop a "vaccine" along with it. Maybe someday they will.

Viruses, like any infection, can be prevented if people are careful and always protect themselves. Treat your disks as you would your body, like a temple. Do not bring in anything unless you know where it has been. If you copy your friend's software, do you know where it originated? Always use protection—in the form of an anti-virus program. Get tested often to prevent the spread of the disease. And—most importantly—use common sense.

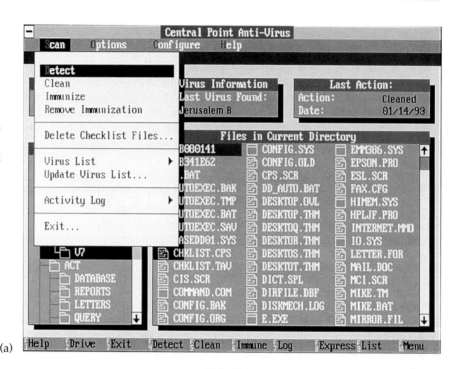

(a)

(b)

*Anti-virus program screen displays.*
(a) *This screen display shows how you would detect a virus.* (b) *This screen display shows how you would remove a virus from your system.*

prevent viruses but they have purchased *anti-virus* programs—software designed to detect viruses and eliminate their threat. Organizations and individuals with their own computers should consider the following strategy suggested by the National Computer Security Association, Washington, D.C., to prevent PCs from being infected by a virus.

1. Back up disks frequently. Maintain two or three sets of backups. Be aware that if a virus is "timed" to go off after a three-month period, for example, it could also be on your backup disks. If a virus is detected, your hard disk should be reformatted and files reinstalled. This recovery procedure can, however, be time consuming, especially if you have many programs on your hard disk.
2. Test new software on a specially designated "test" PC. If there is a virus present, testing on a test PC will ensure that it is not copied to and shared among working PCs throughout your office.
3. Use a virus detector like VirusScan.
4. Before running files downloaded from subscriber services or publicly accessible bulletin board services, test them for viruses.

Ethical issues in computing including those related to software will be discussed again in Chapter 13.

## ▶ SELF-TEST

1. (T or F) Off-the-shelf packages are generally more expensive than custom software.
2. (T or F) Version 2.0 of a software product is a significant improvement over 1.0, whereas version 2.2 is likely to have only modest improvements over 2.0.
3. A test that helps to determine the efficiency of a software product is called a _____ test.
4. Software that is available for minimal cost to anyone and that may be freely copied is called _____.
5. (T or F) Making copies of software in violation of the licensing agreement is illegal.
6. A _____ is a set of instructions that when added to an operating system or application program can destroy the product and even infect every file on disk.

Solutions
1. F
2. T—Version 2.2 has the same integer as 2.0.
3. benchmark
4. shareware or public domain software
5. T
6. virus

▶ **C**hapter **S**ummary

### 7.1 A REVIEW OF APPLICATION SOFTWARE

How have application packages progressed to include even more functions?

Systems software supervises overall processing; application software satisfies user needs. Application software can be purchased or leased as a package or it can be custom-designed, that is, written specifically for individual users. Integrated packages include word processing, spreadsheet, database management, and some e-mail functions—the four basic productivity tools. An integrated package employs one basic type of user interface; that is, the command structure and menu system for all its components are the same. A ROM-resident package is software that is hardwired into the computer.

**Desktop organizers** typically include features such as on-screen calculators, electronic card files, notepads, and automatic dialing from the program's phone directory (if a modem is attached). Some desktop organizers are **TSR programs** (*t*erminate and *s*tay *r*esident), which means that when they are loaded into main memory, they remain there even though other software is in use.

**Project management software** allows users to set up schedules and allocate personnel and resources for projects. The project's progress can be monitored, and personnel and resources reallocated as needed. These packages allow you to create Gantt and PERT charts. **Gantt chart** time lines graphically show how long projects are scheduled to take and at what points parts of the project development can overlap. **PERT charts** provide a standard approach to planning, reviewing, and evaluating a project's progress.

**Personal information managers** combine features of project management software and desktop organizers for a manager's personal use.

Communications software allows the user to set parameters that allow computers to communicate with one another.

**Disk organizers** enable users to manage data and program files on their disks. A major feature of these organizers is the ability to scan all subdirectories on a disk to facilitate quick access to a particular file. Files can also be "unerased." A disk organizer is an example of a **utility program,** which is software that performs relatively standardized tasks that are often needed by all or most computer users.

### 7.2 SPECIALIZED APPLICATION PACKAGES: THE POWER TOOLS OF TODAY

What capabilities do today's new "power tools" feature?

**Desktop publishing (DTP)** software integrates text and graphics in documents and creates sophisticated page layouts that are professional looking and of typeset quality.

**Graphics software** refers to programs with tools for drawing, charting, and presenting illustrations. **Clip art** is a database of graphic displays that can be added to documents, printed, or modified. The two major categories of graphics software are presentation graphics programs and illustration graphics programs. **Presentation graphics software** produces graphic representations of data for business presentations. Painting programs and drawing programs are types of **illustration packages.** Painting programs create **bit-mapped graphics,** which consist of patterns of dots. Drawing programs create visuals by combining lines, arcs, circles, squares, and other shapes, rather than dots, to produce **vector graphics.**

**Computer-aided design (CAD)** packages are highly sophisticated drawing packages that engineers and architects use to create complex drawings. **Computer-aided manufacturing (CAM)** packages help engineers design the manufacturing components in a factory or production facility.

**Statistical packages** perform analysis of data, such as determining standard deviations and variances.

An expert system is software designed to model or simulate the performance of a human expert in a technical field.

**Hypertext** software allows a user to navigate, or move, through a database where information is linked together and accessible as desired, regardless of its physical location. **Hypermedia** improves on the hypertext concept by linking together not only text but graphics, sound, animation, and even video. Multimedia and authoring tools use hypermedia for dynamic presentations and computer-based training.

**Computer-assisted software engineering (CASE)** tools help systems analysts build information systems.

A **horizontal package** meets a specific business need for organizations of all sizes. A **vertical package** is designed to meet the highly specialized needs of a specific industry or business.

## 7.3 CHOOSING AND USING SOFTWARE

Users, along with computer professionals, need to decide whether to acquire off-the-shelf software or to develop custom software for any given application. **Benchmark,** or performance, **tests** can be used to determine the efficiency of a software package.

How can users make the right choices when selecting application packages?

**Public domain software** consists of noncopyrighted programs that developers make available free of charge. **Shareware** is software that can be obtained with little or no cost; often the developer asks the user to pay a small fee to help share handling and packaging costs.

Licensing agreements indicate the number of copies users are legally permitted to make. With a **site license,** the manufacturer or vendor agrees to sell or lease the rights to a fixed number of copies of the software for a set price. Some software manufacturers enforce their licensing agreements by **copy protecting** their software to limit the number of copies that can be made.

Hackers are computer-proficient hobbyists who use computers in unauthorized ways. Some hackers introduce **viruses** into systems by adding instructions to operating systems or application software that can destroy the product and infect files on a disk.

## ▶ Chapter Self-test

1. (T or F) Desktop publishing allows you to create documents that are similar in quality to typeset documents.
2. (T or F) Editing is usually easier to do in a desktop publishing package than with word processing software.
3. What are the two types of graphics used in drawing packages?
4. Graphing and charting programs are commonly referred to as "business graphics" or _____ graphics.
5. What do we call specialized drawing software that helps architects and engineers create complex designs?
6. (T or F) Communications software is simplified word processing software that can be used to write short letters and memos.
7. (Horizontal/vertical) packages are developed to meet a common need in many kinds of businesses, whereas (horizontal/vertical) packages are designed to meet a range of needs of a particular business or industry.
8. (T or F) PageMaker is an example of a vertical package.
9. (T or F) The purpose of desktop organizers is to provide an interface between the user and the operating system.
10. What is the name for software packages that allow users to integrate text and graphics to produce professional-quality publications?
11. (T or F) CAD programs use bit-mapped graphics.
12. What do we call software that can be used freely by anyone, without charge?

Solutions
1. T
2. F
3. bit-mapped graphics; vector graphics
4. presentation
5. computer-aided design (CAD) programs
6. F
7. Horizontal; vertical
8. F
9. F
10. desktop publishing
11. F
12. public domain software

## ▶ Key Terms

Benchmark test, *p. 287*
Bit-mapped graphics, *p. 271*
Clip art, *p. 269*
Computer-aided design (CAD), *p. 273*
Computer-aided manufacturing (CAM), *p. 273*

Computer-assisted software engineering (CASE), *p. 279*
Copy protection, *p. 288*
Desktop organizer, *p. 261*
Desktop publishing, *p. 266*
Disk organizer, *p. 265*
Gantt chart, *p. 262*

Graphics software, *p. 269*
Horizontal package, *p. 279*
Hypermedia, *p. 277*
Hypertext, *p. 276*
Illustration packages, *p. 271*
Personal information manager, *p. 264*

## ► Review Questions

1. Suppose you are a manager and want to acquire a desktop publishing package. What sources would you use to select three packages that are likely to satisfy your needs? Prepare a list of questions you would ask vendors who sell these three products.

2. Suppose you are a sales manager and wish to computerize your sales records. Prepare a list of questions you would ask your staff to determine whether to purchase software from (1) a mail-order firm, (2) a discount software house or electronics company, or (3) a traditional retail store.

## PRODUCT ANALYSIS

## CASE

### Show Me: Evaluating Presentation Graphics

How would you help colleges decide which courses to offer? At New York's State College of Optometry, administrators consult line graphs that compare potential student enrollments with costs. WordPerfect Corporation's DrawPerfect software produces the graphs.

Illustrations used commercially are known as business graphics, or presentation graphics. Besides graphs, they include charts, maps, and general artwork. Presentation graphics are usually produced as works on paper, as slides, or as transparencies for overhead projectors.

Because of its built-in graphics capability, the Macintosh computer was once the undisputed champion of computer-generated presentation graphics. Now, with Mac under challenge by new software for IBM and compatibles, and with new programs available for Mac itself, it's getting harder to decide which graphics package to choose. Experts recommend considering these factors: cost, ease of use, editing capabilities, speed,

*All presentation graphics packages are capable of producing high-quality visual displays in bright colors.*

and quality of output. To judge output quality, examine the number and variety of charts a program offers, the colors it provides, and the images and symbols it includes.

You may have to sacrifice one factor for another. For example, some programs, including Aldus

Corporation's Persuasion for Windows, produce high-quality graphics, but they may be slow. Think about which features are most important to you.

Also consider becoming a desktop Walt Disney. The development of multimedia has literally added new dimensions to presentation graphics. Now you can choose a program that includes animation (motion), video, and sound. The results can be compelling, and some experts predict that multimedia programs like Gold Disk's Animation Works and Paracomp's Action will soon be more popular than traditional graphics software.

*Analysis*

1. Explain why businesses and institutions might want to use presentation graphics.
2. List some criteria to evaluate presentation graphics packages. Which do you consider most important and why?
3. Suggest some appropriate uses for multimedia presentation graphics. Then think of situations where you believe traditional computer-generated presentation graphics would be just as effective.

# Developing Custom Software

**G**etting computers to accomplish the tasks users want done requires four basic components: hardware to enter and process data, and to produce the necessary information; software to drive the hardware; people to control the overall operations; and connectivity to enable all components to interact with one another effectively.

Users and computer professionals first try to acquire off-the-shelf, or packaged, software to accomplish the needed tasks. Such software is often readily available, inexpensive, and well documented. But sometimes people need specially prepared software with features that are not available as a package. In this chapter we consider some of the main programming languages and their features, and we answer the following questions:

▶ Why is there a need for custom programs when packages abound and who develops such software?

▶ What are the steps involved in software development and why is the process called a cycle?

▶ What benefits do standardized program development techniques offer both the software developer and the user?

▶ How have generations of programming languages evolved to enhance the software development process?

## THE SOFTWARE DEVELOPER

Why is there a need for custom programs when packages abound and who develops such software?

When an organization decides to have software specifically developed for its needs rather than to purchase or lease packages, the company's requirements are likely to be unique; that is, modifying existing packages will not suffice. In such a case, either company employees or outside consultants need to develop the software.

### ▶ In-house Software Developers — Analysts, Programmers, and Users

Organizations with an in-house computing staff often have their own employees develop software. An organization's own staff is familiar with company policy and operating procedures. Moreover, as computing professionals, they have the expertise to develop, implement, and document software.

In most medium-sized to large organizations, systems analysts supervise software development undertaken by programmers. The systems analyst and the future users of the software work closely with programmers to develop a clear understanding of each program's purpose.

The systems analyst focuses on user needs and determines not only how these needs can be met, but also on how the new software can be integrated efficiently into information systems. Since *users* are the people most knowledgeable about the tasks that the software must perform, their needs must be considered first. Users, however, are not computer professionals and may not even be computer proficient, so they do not always know how to define their computing needs. To ensure effective computerization, the systems analyst serves as a kind of liaison between users who understands business problems and programmers who actually develop the software.

In some companies, a computer professional called a **programmer analyst** may serve as both programmer and systems analyst. This person possesses programming and systems analysis skills and is responsible for integrating new software into an information system. Similarly, users at smaller companies sometimes take on an added role of assisting developers or even doing some program development themselves if they are computer proficient.

## ▶ Work-for-hire Consultants

A company may need custom programs, but may not have an in-house computing staff. Even if it has an in-house computing staff, the staff may be committed to different projects or may lack technical expertise in a particular area. In such instances, freelance programming consultants, specialized software development "houses," or outsourcing firms that provide outside services may be needed.

One main reason for using outside software consultants is that they have expertise in a particular application area. Some developers may specialize in horizontal software, which means that they have specific expertise in an area such as payroll, accounting, or inventory. Other developers may specialize in vertical software, which means that they have specific expertise in a type of business such as production, accounting, or retail sales. If an outside consultant has expertise in the area being computerized, the software developed is likely to better suit the needs of the company.

Another reason for hiring outside consultants is that it is often less expensive than assigning the work to an in-house staff. The cost of the project is negotiated in advance, and overhead and fringe benefits are not usually added to the price.

## ▶ SELF-TEST

1. The two ways in which application programs can be obtained are by _____ and _____.
2. Who develops custom programs?
3. Name the three categories of employees who determine program specifications.

IN A

**THE STORY OF SOFTWARE**

1. Operating system software
   • Controls the overall operations of the computer
   • Used for managing and monitoring computer activities

2. Application software
   • Used for satisfying specific user needs.
   • Available off-the-shelf in packaged form.
   • Designed as custom programs for individual users.

**CRITICAL THINKING**

A major complaint of some users is that the custom software does not really meet their needs. Can you think of measures that could be taken to minimize the risk that software might prove to be unsatisfactory? What clauses might you include in a contract with freelance programmers to improve the chances for success?

Solutions
1. purchasing packages; developing custom programs
2. in-house programmers or work-for-hire programmers
3. the user, systems analyst, programmer (Sometimes a programmer analyst wears two hats, that of a programmer and systems analyst.)

IN A

**IN-HOUSE VS WORK-FOR-HIRE SOFTWARE DEVELOPMENT**

| **In-house Developers** | **Work-for-hire Developers** |
| --- | --- |
| 1. Programmers are familiar with the company but not necessarily with the application area. | 1. Programmers are hired based on their familiarity with a specific application area or with the type of company. |
| 2. Because programmers are employees, the company has better control of the development process. | 2. The price for the software is set in advance, typically on a contract or fixed-fee basis. |
| 3. After programs are implemented, programmers are usually still available to answer queries or make modifications if the need arises. | 3. Once a program is accepted, it may be more difficult to track down the developer if modifications are necessary. |

# 8.2  SOFTWARE DEVELOPMENT CYCLE

*What are the steps involved in software development and why is the process called a cycle?*

All programs should be designed in a systematic and scientific manner. We refer to the design steps as the **software development cycle.** Figure 8.1 illustrates the steps in the cycle, which are as follows.

1. Develop the program specifications.
2. Design the logic to be used in the program.
3. Code the program and translate it into machine language.
4. Test the program until it is fully debugged.
5. Install, or implement, the program.
6. Maintain the program.
7. Document the program.

Software development is considered a cycle because the process is apt to be repeated. After programs are written and used for a period of time, they may begin to lose their effectiveness, or users may find that their

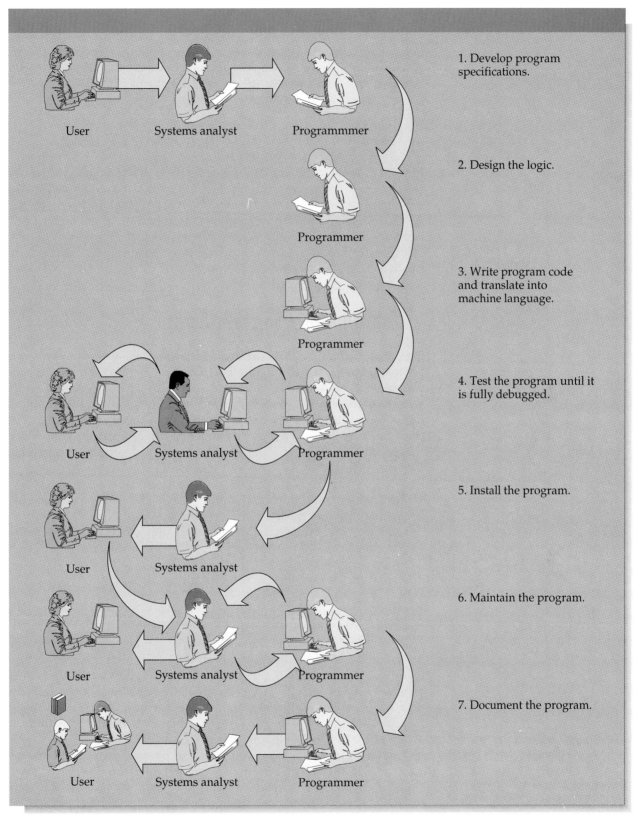

1. Develop program specifications.

2. Design the logic.

3. Write program code and translate into machine language.

4. Test the program until it is fully debugged.

5. Install the program.

6. Maintain the program.

7. Document the program.

User

Systems analyst

Programmmer

Programmer

Programmer

User

Systems analyst

Programmer

User

Systems analyst

User

Systems analyst

Programmer

User

Systems analyst

Programmer

*Figure 8.1* *The development of well-designed programs follows these seven steps, known as the software development cycle.*

needs have changed. When these situations occur, the development cycle is repeated and new software is produced to meet the changing needs. Now we will detail each of the cycle's seven steps.

## ▶ Develop the Program Specifications

First, the tasks to be accomplished by the software must be defined clearly. Does this seem self-evident? You would be astounded at the amount of software that is written without a clear understanding of user needs. In many cases, the programmers simply did not define the problem to be solved in a precise way. An important first step, then, is to have software developers and users agree on program specifications that indicate what the software is to accomplish.

## ▶ Design the Program Logic

Once the problem is clearly defined by the user and systems analyst, and is described as a set of program specifications, the programmer or software developer can begin to design a program. First, developers create an algorithm, which is similar to a recipe: It is a sequential listing of all the steps needed to obtain desired output from the available input. The steps must be logical; that is, they must be listed in the order in which they are to be performed. For example, here is an algorithm for preparing a customer invoice.

1. Read the account number, the unit price of the item purchased, and the quantity purchased.
2. Calculate the bill by multiplying the unit price by the quantity purchased.
3. Print the account number and the total bill.
4. Repeat the process for all customer invoices.

Each of these steps accomplishes a given task or tasks; collectively they meet the program's requirements.

In addition to planning the logical steps in a program, the programmer should include error-control procedures. For example, our sample algorithm will multiply the unit price by the quantity purchased. A full program should include procedures that first ensure that the numeric data necessary for performing calculations has been entered and that it has reasonable values. In this case, the unit price should be within the actual range of acceptable unit prices (e.g., < 500 and > 2.50).

A number of problem-solving tools can be used to plan the overall logic of a program. The three most common tools are flowcharts, pseudocode, and hierarchy charts. We begin with flowcharts, which were once the most popular planning tool but have since been replaced in many organizations with a combined use of pseudocode and hierarchy charts.

Sometimes programmers "cut corners" at the planning stage. In their enthusiasm to get started, they may decide not to use a planning tool. When this happens, the chances for an effective software solution to a problem are reduced.

## FLOWCHARTS

A **flowchart** is a pictorial representation of the logic flow to be used in a program. It illustrates the major elements of the program and how they will logically integrate. A flowchart is to a program what a blueprint is to a building. Before architects begin to build a building, they draw a blueprint to ensure that all components fit together effectively and efficiently. For the same reasons, many programmers choose a flowchart as their problem-solving tool before writing a program. As with architectural blueprints, the diagrams should be discussed with users before any actual development work begins to minimize misunderstandings that may result in dissatisfaction later. The flow lines in a flowchart depict the logical flow of instructions in a program. Examine the flowchart in Figure 8.2, which shows the process for calculating an employee's gross pay. The program developed using this flowchart will read data, transfer control to a subprogram that calculates the gross pay, and print the results.

Figure 8.3a illustrates a flowchart template, which contains flowchart

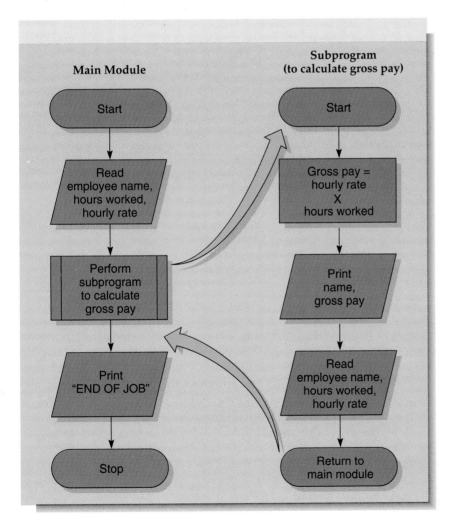

*Figure 8.2* Dividing a program into modules, or subprograms, for specific procedural tasks simplifies program structure. These modules can then be used to build other programs. In this flowchart, a gross pay is being calculated.

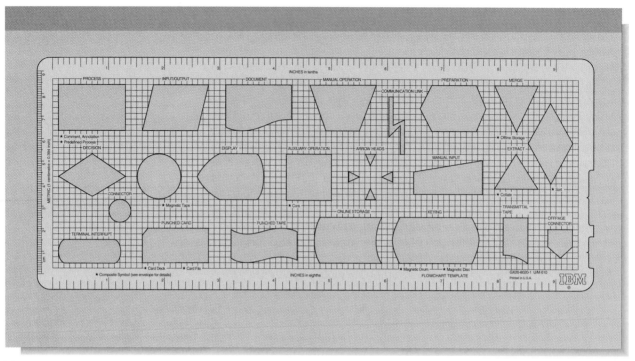

(a)

*Figure 8.3* (a) *A flowchart template.* (Continued on the next page.)

symbols. Figure 8.3*b* lists and describes each of the symbols. Each symbol either denotes a particular operation or identifies a program unit called a **subprogram** or **module** that will execute a series of operations. The programmer writes a notation inside each symbol.

## PSEUDOCODE

The use of flowcharts as a planning tool has waned in recent years because flowcharts for large, complex programs are often cumbersome to draw and difficult to understand. Also, it is difficult to make modifications to a flowchart without completely redrawing it. Finally, because a flowchart is frequently very long, the logical structures can be difficult to follow. For these reasons, programmers are now more likely to use an alternative design tool called **pseudocode** (literally, "false code"), which consists of English-like statements (as opposed to symbols) to plan a program's logic. Pseudocode need not indicate *all* the processing details, but it should carefully describe the overall *flow of program logic*. Pseudocode is popular because it can easily represent all the programming structures that programmers need and because its English-like terms are easy to learn and understand.

Figure 8.4 illustrates pseudocode for depicting program logic. Compare the flowchart in Figure 8.2 to the pseudocode; both are describing the same program logic, but in different ways. A programmer commonly uses one or the other as a planning tool, depending on the preferences of the organization. The programs illustrated throughout this chapter will use the logic described in these figures as their basic starting point.

While flowcharts use *symbols* to plan and illustrate logic, pseudocode uses *words*.

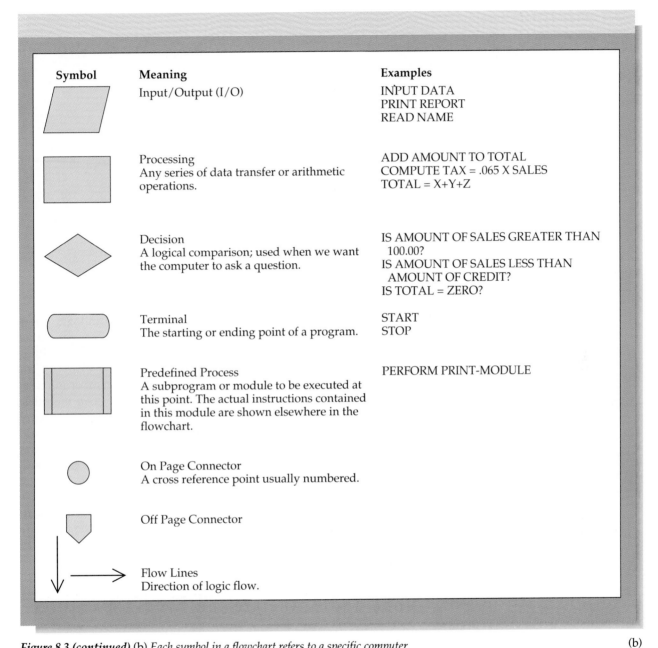

| Symbol | Meaning | Examples |
|---|---|---|
| | Input/Output (I/O) | INPUT DATA<br>PRINT REPORT<br>READ NAME |
| | Processing<br>Any series of data transfer or arithmetic operations. | ADD AMOUNT TO TOTAL<br>COMPUTE TAX = .065 X SALES<br>TOTAL = X+Y+Z |
| | Decision<br>A logical comparison; used when we want the computer to ask a question. | IS AMOUNT OF SALES GREATER THAN 100.00?<br>IS AMOUNT OF SALES LESS THAN AMOUNT OF CREDIT?<br>IS TOTAL = ZERO? |
| | Terminal<br>The starting or ending point of a program. | START<br>STOP |
| | Predefined Process<br>A subprogram or module to be executed at this point. The actual instructions contained in this module are shown elsewhere in the flowchart. | PERFORM PRINT-MODULE |
| | On Page Connector<br>A cross reference point usually numbered. | |
| | Off Page Connector | |
| | Flow Lines<br>Direction of logic flow. | |

*Figure 8.3 (continued)* (b) *Each symbol in a flowchart refers to a specific computer operation.*

(b)

*Figure 8.4 In pseudocode, English words are used to express program logic.*

**START**
 READ Name, Hours, Rate
 PERFORM subprogram to calculate Pay
 PRINT Name, Pay
**STOP**

*Figure 8.5 Hierarchy charts break a large task down into smaller tasks, which then become subprograms, or modules.*

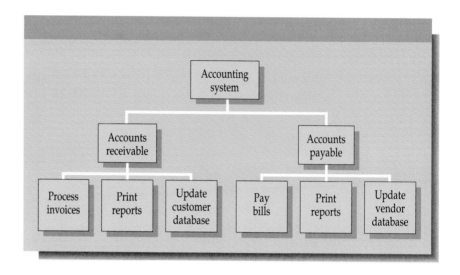

## HIERARCHY CHARTS

Flowcharts and pseudocode are tools for designing program logic. **Hierarchy charts,** sometimes called **structure charts,** illustrate how programs are segmented into subprograms, or modules, and how the modules actually relate to one another. Figure 8.5 is a hierarchy chart for an accounting system. Each box represents a major subprogram, or module, in the system. The accounting program is subdivided into two modules: accounts receivable and accounts payable. The next level in the hierarchy chart represents separate modules within each subprogram. Each of these modules may then be divided further so that complex hierarchy charts can consist of many levels. Note, however, that a hierarchy chart does not focus on the detailed design elements for each module. Rather, it helps to ensure that all program components fit together logically.

In summary, programmers typically draw a flowchart or write pseudocode to design the program logic. For larger programs, they prepare a hierarchy chart to keep track of how modules interrelate in the overall design.

## ▶ Code and Translate the Program

The planning tools described in the previous section are used to develop an acceptable program design. Once the design and the logic are agreed on, the programmer writes, or codes, the instructions in one of a wide variety of programming languages. The programming language that is selected depends on the resources available, the expertise of the programmer, and the application. As you will learn later in this chapter, there are many programming languages, each best suited for a particular set of tasks.

To actually be executed, however, a program must be in **machine language,** the computer's own internal language. Each type of computer has its own machine language that is designed to be as efficient as possible.

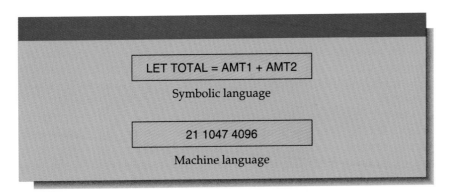

*Figure 8.6* Machine language code uses actual machine addresses and operation codes so that there is no need for translation.

The one commonality among machine languages is complexity: they all use actual storage addresses and complicated operation codes (Figure 8.6) to process data.

Because of the complexity of machine languages and the fact that they are different for each type of computer, most programs are *not written* in machine language. They are written instead in symbolic languages, such as BASIC or COBOL, which are much easier for programmers to use. **Symbolic languages** use instructions, such as ADD or +, instead of complex operation codes. They allow the programmer to assign actual names to storage locations.

A program written in a symbolic language is not, however, executable in that form. It cannot be executed until it has been first translated, or converted, into machine language. The computer itself performs this translation process by means of a translator program. This translator reads a symbolic program as input and converts it to output, which is the machine language equivalent. The symbolic program is called the **source program,** and the translated program in machine language is called the **object program.**

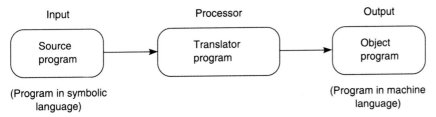

## ▶ Test the Program Until It Is Fully Debugged

**Debugging** means finding and correcting all logic and coding errors, or "bugs," in a program. Debugging begins even before the program is executed. All programs should first be **desk-checked.** This is the process in which the programmer manually traces through the program, from beginning to end, visually checking for coding errors, called **syntax errors,** which can be simple typing mistakes or violations in the rules of the language. Most syntax errors can be located by carefully desk-checking a program. Keying AD instead of ADD, for example, may cause a syntax error. If syntax errors are not caught before the program is entered into the computer, the language's translator program will generally find them and print an error message. Keep in mind that programs cannot be fully translated into machine language until all syntax errors have been corrected.

The first step, then, in the debugging process is to eliminate all syntax errors. But programs without syntax errors are not necessarily completely correct. The program may be coded perfectly but still generate incorrect output or no output at all. Incorrect output is typically the result of logic errors. A **logic error** may occur because of a mistake in the sequencing of instructions or because the wrong instructions were used. Sometimes mistakes in logic are so severe that they result in run-time errors, which mean that the execution of the program is terminated. The test of a program's validity is to make sure it runs and to verify that the output is correct.

**Program testing** is crucial in pinpointing logic errors. A program with a logic error may produce correct results most of the time, but incorrect results when some unanticipated input is entered. For example, a payroll program may correctly calculate paychecks for employees who work up to 40 hours per week, but it may incorrectly calculate paychecks involving overtime pay. A logic error causes this program to process data incorrectly when hours exceed 40. Such a logic error will be detected only if test data includes situations requiring overtime pay.

All logic errors must be detected and corrected before a program is implemented. The following four techniques help to eliminate logic errors.

1. Recheck the logic.
   Is there a flaw in the logic? Does the logic of the actual program correspond to the logic depicted with the programming design tools (flowchart or pseudocode and hierarchy chart)?
2. Prepare test data with great care.
   Make certain that the test data used as input during the debugging phase incorporates all possible types of input, that the program includes tests for specific conditions, and that the test data includes all realistic values. Programs must be written to anticipate any conceivable condition and to process data accordingly. If not, then Murphy's Law is sure to apply: If it is possible for something to go wrong in a program, eventually it will go wrong.
3. Compare computer output with manual output.
   Using the test data, manually compute the results expected from a program run. Compare actual computer output to the expected output. If there is a discrepancy between what should happen in a program and what actually does happen, then the problem must be found and resolved. Whenever an error occurs, the program must be corrected, retranslated, and tested again to ensure that it produces correct output. A program normally requires many test runs before it is fully debugged.
4. Perform a structured walkthrough.
   For long or complex programs, it is often helpful to have a program-

*Programmer checking output from a test run.*

ming team manually "walk through" the logic of a program to ensure that the sequence in which modules are executed is correct and to verify that the program will run efficiently.

Testing a program with all types of input and including many error-control routines minimizes the risks that errors will go undetected.

## ▶ Implement the Program

After a program has been thoroughly tested and debugged, it is ready to be implemented. Typically, custom programs are implemented so that they can run on a regularly scheduled basis. A payroll program, for example, may need to be run weekly, whereas a program that produces customer bills might be run monthly.

A program is usually implemented as part of an overall, integrated information system. See Figure 8.7. An accounting information system, for example, is likely to have several programs *all* of which will require an integrated implementation process. We discuss implementation techniques for information systems in Chapter 10.

## ▶ Maintain the Program

Studies have shown that only about one-quarter of a programmer's time is spent in developing new software. The remaining three-quarters is spent maintaining existing software. Software maintenance falls into two broad categories: (1) correcting errors and making the software easier to use and more standardized and (2) making modifications because of changing needs.

***Figure 8.7*** *A systems analyst, programmer, and user gather to discuss the implementation of a pilot version of the firm's new software.*

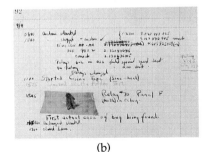

Increasing the ease of use of a program and eliminating even minor bugs improve user satisfaction. Many businesses hire **maintenance programmers** whose main responsibility is to make such improvements to existing software. If a program was designed properly initially, these types of modifications will be small and can be performed whenever time is available.

All organizations have changing needs, and software is continually being modified to meet those needs. For example, an accounting department may need to have a program modified to incorporate new accounting procedures or changes in the tax laws. Often, users may want the software to perform additional tasks that were not in the original specifications. Thus, new modules may need to be developed to enhance existing software.

## ▶ Document the Program

Documentation, which explains every facet of a program to the user, should be prepared on an ongoing basis—as the software is being developed, tested, and implemented. Some documentation is built into the program itself as comments, but most documentation takes the form of printed user manuals. Some parts of the manual explain how to use the program; other parts are written for the technical staff and explain the actual methodology of the program in case it needs modification (Figure 8.8).

*Figure 8.8 A complete software package or custom program includes disks, user manuals, and detailed documentation.*

## ▶ Software Development: Art or Science?

Programmers systematically follow the previously described steps in the program development cycle when they develop custom software. Such a step-by-step procedure suggests that the process of software development is basically scientific. In fact, those who focus on the scientific and technical aspects of programming refer to program development as **software engineering.**

But many computer professionals still refer to the "art," rather than the "science," of programming. They believe that there are elements in the process that go beyond the systematic, technical ones. Most people believe that to develop good software, programmers need to be creative, to communicate well, to make decisions based on experience, and to use their intuition—all nonquantifiable and nonscientific elements.

Applying both the science and art perspectives to programming may seem incompatible. But proponents of both views agree that techniques used to systematize aspects of the development process combined with a creative approach to the subject are apt to make programs easier to write, read, maintain, and modify.

## ▶ SELF-TEST

1. What two program design tools are used specifically to describe the logic to be included in a program?
2. A program design tool used specifically to interrelate modules in a program is called a _____.
3. Why are programs typically written in a symbolic language rather than machine language?
4. A program written in a symbolic language must be _____ before it can be run.
5. Finding and correcting errors in a program is called _____.
6. A rule violation in a program is called a _____ error.
7. How are logic errors in a program typically detected?

### Solutions
1. flowcharts, pseudocode
2. hierarchy chart (or structure chart)
3. Machine language is cumbersome and requires knowing complex operation codes and keeping track of actual storage addresses.
4. translated
5. debugging
6. syntax
7. By executing the program with test data

# PROGRAMMING TECHNIQUES FOR STANDARDIZING SOFTWARE DEVELOPMENT

## 8.3

In recent years, techniques have been developed to help standardize programming. These techniques, which are now used widely, minimize major differences in the way programmers approach problem solving. Programs that are standardized are easier to code, debug, maintain, and modify. We describe next the most commonly used techniques for standardizing programs.

What benefits do standardized program development techniques offer both the software developer and the user?

## ▶ Modular Programming

In modular programming, each segment of a program is written as an independent series of steps that is often called a module, routine, subroutine, or subprogram. These program segments are each called in, or executed, by a main module. Review Figure 8.2, which has two modules, a main module and a subprogram module.

Each component of a modular program accomplishes a specific task and can be written and tested independently. Indeed, some modules can even be used in more than one program. A module that evaluates and prints errors, for example, may be reusable in several programs.

## ▶ Structured Programming

**Structured programming** is a design technique that integrates, or ties together, program modules in a systematic way. Structured programs have a main module from which all subordinate modules are executed. There are no branch points (called "GO TOs") that make the logic difficult to follow. All program steps are executed using just four logical control constructs: sequence, selection, iteration (looping), and Case. See Figure 8.9 on pages 314 and 315.

### SEQUENCE (Figure 8.9a)

Each instruction in a program is executed in sequence—as it appears—unless another logical control construct is used.

### SELECTION (Figure 8.9b)

Instructions can be executed *selectively*. IF a given condition is true or is met, THEN specific instructions or modules will be executed. IF the condition is false or is not met, THEN a different set of instructions is executed:

IF condition
THEN
      ← statements to be executed if the condition is met
ELSE
      ← statements to be executed if the condition is not met

Another term for this selection control structure is the IF-THEN-ELSE structure.

### ITERATION OR LOOPING (Figure 8.9c)

A module or series of modules can be executed from another module. Module B, for example, can be executed from module A either once or repeatedly. Iterative techniques are executed in most languages with a DO or PERFORM loop. We may say, for example, DO (a module) 100 TIMES. Or we may say DO (a module) WHILE CTR < 100. If CTR begins at 0 and is incremented by 1 each time through the loop, then the module would be executed 100 times.

### CASE (Figure 8.9d)

With the Case logical control construct, modules or series of modules are executed, depending on the contents of certain fields either entered as input or computed. For example, a program may display a menu and ask a user to SELECT an item from it:

```
┌─────────────────────────────────────────────────────┐
│                                                       │
│        PROGRAM OPTIONS                                │
│                                                       │
│     ╭───╮                                             │
│     │ 1 │            Payroll                          │
│     ╰───╯                                             │
│                                                       │
│     ╭───╮                                             │
│     │ 2 │            Human Resources                  │
│     ╰───╯                                             │
│                                                       │
│     ╭───╮                                             │
│     │ 3 │            Accounting                        │
│     ╰───╯                                             │
│                                                       │
│     ╭───╮                                             │
│     │ 4 │            Sales                            │
│     ╰───╯                                             │
│                                                       │
│     ╭───╮                                             │
│     │ 5 │            Inventory                        │
│     ╰───╯                                             │
│                                                       │
│                                                       │
│   Enter Selection: ____                               │
│                                                       │
└─────────────────────────────────────────────────────┘
```

The Case structure selects a course of action depending on the contents of a specific field. That is, a payroll module will be executed if 1 is entered, a Human Resources module will be executed if 2 is entered, and so on.

To software developers, Case has two different meanings. As discussed in Chapter 7, CASE—computer-assisted software engineering—is a tool to help build information systems. Here we focus on Case as a type of logical control construct.

In summary, structured programs utilize the four logical control constructs to indicate the order in which instructions or modules are executed regardless of the programming language being used. The structured programming technique helps to standardize the logic used in all programs.

## ▶ Top-Down Programming

Top-down programming means that proper program design is best achieved by developing major modules before minor ones. In a top-down program, the main module is coded first, followed by intermediate and then minor ones. By coding programs stepwise in this top-down manner, the general organization of a program is given primary attention while details are left for minor modules, which are coded last. Top-down programming is analogous to designing a term paper by developing the outline first. Your outline gets increasingly detailed only after you have established the main organization or structure. See Figure 8.10.

## The Four Logical Control Constructs:

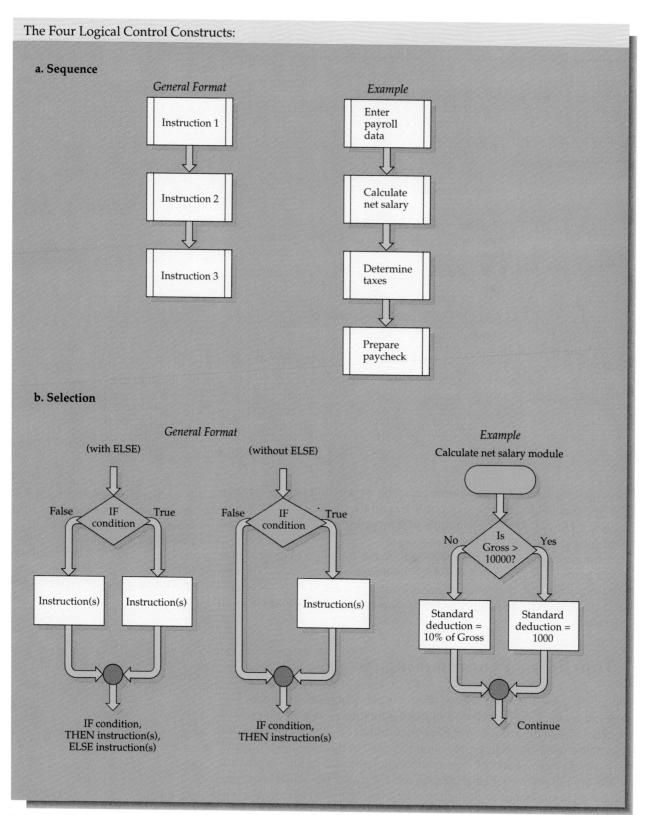

**a. Sequence**

*General Format*

Instruction 1

Instruction 2

Instruction 3

*Example*

Enter payroll data

Calculate net salary

Determine taxes

Prepare paycheck

**b. Selection**

*General Format*

(with ELSE)

False — IF condition — True

Instruction(s)    Instruction(s)

IF condition,
THEN instruction(s),
ELSE instruction(s)

(without ELSE)

False — IF condition — True

Instruction(s)

IF condition,
THEN instruction(s)

*Example*

Calculate net salary module

No — Is Gross > 10000? — Yes

Standard deduction = 10% of Gross    Standard deduction = 1000

Continue

*Figure 8.9* *The four logical control constructs: sequence, selection, iteration (or looping), and Case.*

# The Four Logical Control Constructs:

## c. Iteration or Looping

*General Format*

*Example*

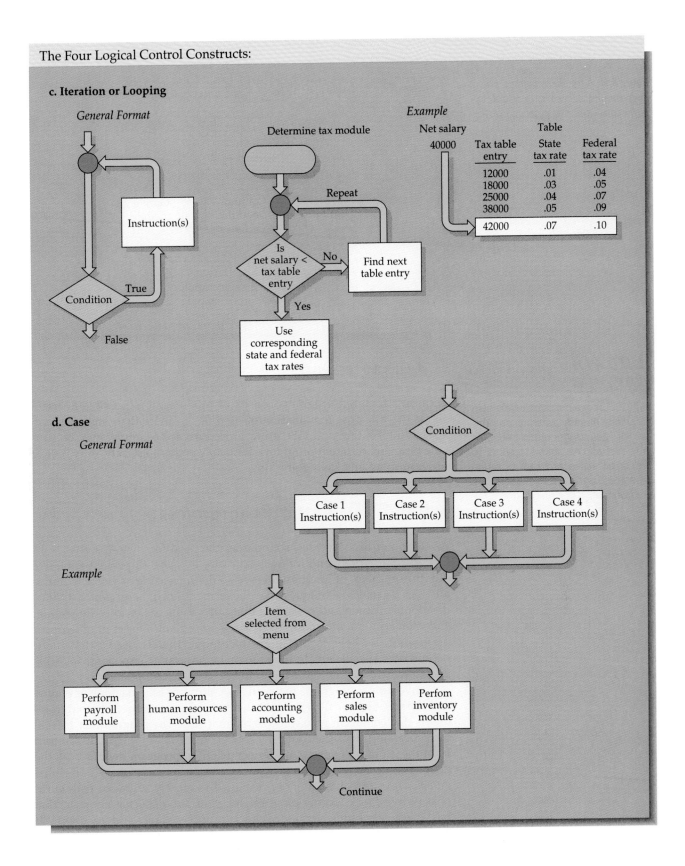

## d. Case

*General Format*

*Example*

**Figure 8.10** *A top-down approach to programming where a main module executes subordinate modules and so on.*

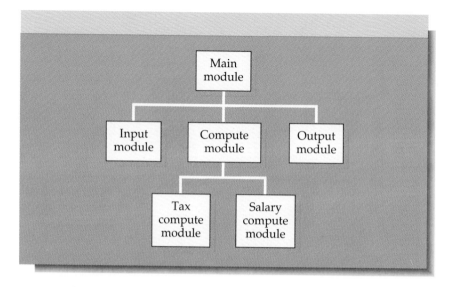

**LOOKING** *AHEAD*

Many industry experts believe that in the years ahead software companies will sell segments of reusable code that can be linked together to form a cohesive program in much the same way that Lego blocks are interconnected.

## ▶ Reusable Code

Because structured programs consist of modules, it is possible to use a single module or a combination of modules in more than one program. An editing routine or a tabulating procedure, for example, may be suitable for many different programs. **Reusable code** can significantly reduce programming and debugging time.

## ▶ Object-Oriented Programming

As computer use increases, so too does the need for custom software. In fact, the overall demand for such software is rising 12 percent annually, but the number of programmers is only increasing 4 percent annually. As a result, techniques like those mentioned here, which reduce development time and cost by making programs easier to write, debug, and maintain, are becoming even more important. Object-oriented programming is likely to become a technique that is used extensively, because it is specifically designed to make program components reusable and to reduce the time it takes to develop those components.

Conventional programs focus on the computer as a machine or engine and data as the raw material that the computer processes. The programmer is the technician who controls the machine. The programmer lists all the processing steps the computer must take to obtain the needed output from the input. In contrast, an **object-oriented program** defines both the data and the set of operations that can act on that data as one unit called an *object*. An object is an entity designed to closely resemble real-world objects. In a check-writing program, for example, a check is an object that has these attributes: amount, check number, date, and recipient. It responds to these instructions: write, cash, sign, and record.

Reusability is achieved because objects belong to classes and objects within a class have the same format and respond to the same instructions as all other objects in the class. If a check belongs to a document class, then it inherits all attributes from the document class and can respond to all instructions written for that class. **Inheritance** is a major feature of object-oriented programming. As another example, a horse is an object belonging to the class of mammals. It "inherits" the characteristics of a mammal (body hair, live birth, nursing its young, and so on). However, it also has characteristics that distinguish it from other mammals, such as its size and shape, the way it moves, and the kinds of sounds it makes.

When a programmer creates a new object, he or she only needs to add the object's new features; the inherited ones are already there and need not be restated. To see how inheritance makes the programmer's job easier, assume you are writing a space-war game. Both sides—the Federation and the Ferengi—have fighting spaceships, but of slightly different types. In addition, each side has nonfighting ships, such as space shuttles and cargo barges. The object *ship* has certain characteristics: *x-y* coordinates, shields, warp speeds, and loyalty (Federation or Ferengi). The object *fightingship* has everything *ship* has, plus photon torpedoes. The object *shuttlecraft* has everything *ship* has except shields and warp speeds. There is no need to redesign ship attributes each time a ship is used; new attributes to make fightingship or shuttlecraft need only be added to ship attributes.

The major goals of object-oriented programming are to improve programmer productivity and increase software reusability, thereby reducing the cost of software development and maintenance.

Object-oriented programming focuses on the data to be manipulated rather than on the procedures that do the manipulating. The main challenge is to be able to define a software system in terms of data types, or classes and subclasses, and to be able to describe the properties of each class or subclass.

Object-oriented programming incorporates the assumption that certain aspects of data can be contained in the program itself and, indeed, can be treated by the programmer as fixed. The concept is similar to "real-world processing" by humans. A person who drives a car need only know how to perform certain operations on the car (e.g., steer, accelerate, brake, and so on). The fixed aspects of a car (e.g., how the carburetor works, how the engine works) are of no real concern to the driver when driving. Object-oriented programming attempts to model programming after such real-world concepts. The programmer defines certain objects (e.g., an engine of a car) and uses them in a program without focusing on how they function. In this way, programmers need not duplicate code that can be the same from one program to another (e.g., an engine can be used in more than one type of car).

Many programmers agree that object-oriented programming can greatly reduce the time needed to implement new software. In addition, because new software builds heavily on existing objects, the code is more likely to be reusable and error-free. The next few years will determine whether the full potential of object-oriented programming is as great as many computer professionals believe it to be. If it is, expect tremendous improvements in the speed of software development and the quality of the final product.

▶ **SELF-TEST**

1. A self-contained program segment that can be written and tested independently and even reused in other programs is called a _____.
2. What are the four logical control constructs used in a structured program?
3. Programs in which major modules are coded stepwise before minor modules are said to use _____ programming techniques.

Solutions
1. module (subroutine, subprogram, routine)
2. sequence, selection, iteration, Case
3. top-down

## 8.4  FIVE GENERATIONS OF PROGRAMMING LANGUAGES

How have generations of programming languages evolved to enhance the software development process?

Traditionally, types of programming languages have been categorized chronologically by "generations," each with specific features. Even though newer generations may have features that are viewed as superior to those of older generations, sometimes older generation languages are still uniquely suited for specific tasks. You will see, however, that programs are now rarely written in a first- or second-generation language. Most are written in a third- or fourth-generation language. Fifth-generation languages currently are more significant in their potential than in their actual use.

### ▶ Machine Language: The First Generation

Machine language, as we have seen, is the computer's internal language, which executes directly without translation. Machine languages are referred to as first-generation programming languages because they were the earliest type developed. Initially, in the 1940s and early 1950s, all programs had to be coded in these languages.

Programming in machine language, however, is time consuming and is conducive to making mistakes. Also, machine language is different for each type of computer; if an organization decides to acquire a new computer, all programs must be in the new computer's machine language to be executed. Thus, we say that machine languages are wholly computer dependent and are therefore nonstandard. Because of the complexity and widely disparate formats of machine languages, few programmers actually code in them today.

But, as we saw in the last section, all programs must be in machine language to be executed, that is, actually run. What programmers do is write programs in other languages, which need to be translated by the computer into machine language for execution.

## ▶ Assembly Language: The Second Generation

In the 1950s, when computers were first used commercially, the complexity of machine language programming paved the way early on for a second generation of languages called **assembly languages.** In assembly language, the complex operation codes required for execution can be assigned easily remembered names such as ADD, SUB, and MULT. Also, the actual storage addresses where data is located can be defined with names such as AMT1 and AMT2 for ease of reference.

Aside from being able to name operations and storage addresses, assembly languages are very much like their corresponding machine language. This means that to be a proficient assembly (or machine) language programmer, you need to understand the machine's architecture, that is, how it physically processes data. Moreover, since each type of computer has its own individual architecture with its own machine and corresponding assembly languages, the structure of one such set of machine language instructions may be totally different from that of another set. Assembly languages, therefore, like machine languages, are *computer dependent.* We say that assembly language programs are not **portable:** you cannot run an assembly language program written for one category of computers on another type of computer unless they have the same architecture.

Programs written in assembly languages have special codes that make them easier to write than programs written in machine language. But these programs will not execute unless they are translated into machine language by a special program called an **assembler.** An assembler reads the assembly language program as input and then converts it, as output, into a machine language version called the object program.

Despite the complexity of assembly languages, they are still used for some applications today. Because they are so similar to machine language, they result in very efficient code. When maximizing the efficient use of the computer is a major goal of a program, such as is the case with systems software, assembly language is still favored.

## ▶ High-Level Languages: The Third Generation

Computer use in businesses grew dramatically in the 1950s as did the need for programmers and application software. Machine and assembly language programming, however, was just too difficult for many people, slowing down the development process. Computer manufacturers, as well as user groups, began to develop third-generation languages (3GLs) that would be both easier to program in and portable. If users decided to upgrade their equipment or acquire more current hardware, they would not need to revise all their software.

These languages are called high level because they are relatively easy to learn and not at all like machine language; rather, they are more like the English language. High-level programs, however, require a computer-based translation process that is very complex. In general, the easier it is to program, the higher the level and the more complex the translation process. Most translator programs for high-level languages are called compilers, but some are called interpreters. We discuss both of these types of translators later in this chapter.

High-level languages, like their predecessors, are called **procedural languages.** This means that the program must specify the *precise set of instructions* necessary to accomplish a given task. We will see that many programs written in newer fourth- and fifth-generation languages are **nonprocedural;** that is, they need not follow precise rules. Think of ordering a piece of pie in a restaurant. In a procedural language, you need to specify the ingredients, how to bake the pie, how to serve it, and so on. In a fourth- or fifth-generation nonprocedural language, you can simply say, "Get me a slice of apple pie."

The most commonly used third-generation languages, in order of their development, follow. These are by no means the only ones; there are hundreds of them, some with a very extensive user base. Those discussed here, however, have had the greatest impact.

## FORTRAN

In the 1950s, most of the people actually writing programs were scientists or engineers. The types of problems they wanted to solve required a great deal of computation. It is not surprising, therefore, that the first widely used high-level language was scientifically oriented. **FORTRAN,** an acronym for *For*mula *Tran*slator, was developed by IBM in the 1950s and is the oldest high-level language. The fact that it is still used today attests to its impact on the field.

Although FORTRAN is ideal for the complex math of scientific and engineering applications, it is *not* well suited for typical business applications that require rather simple arithmetic operations but a large volume of input/output operations. Although originally developed for large mainframe systems, FORTRAN has been implemented on microcomputers in recent years. Figure 8.11 shows a simple FORTRAN program. This program inputs hours worked and hourly rate and calculates weekly wages. We will illustrate the same program in different third-generation languages so that you can see the main features of each language.

## COBOL

During the 1950s, the business community began to realize that computers could solve many of its information processing needs. But FORTRAN was not ideally suited for business processing. Consider the procedure for preparing a bill. The number of steps involved may not be large or involve complicated math, but the customer base may be so big that the input/output procedures are quite complex.

In 1959 a group of computer professionals formed an organization called CODASYL (*Co*nference on *Da*ta *Sy*stems *L*anguages) and held a

```
C  ***                        PAYCHECK PROGRAM                        ***
C  ***                                                                ***
C  *** This program calculates an employee's paycheck based on the   ***
C  *** number of hours the employee worked and base pay per hour.    ***
C  ********************************************************************

program Paychk

character * 12 Name
real Gross, Hours, PayRat
C
C  Prompt the user for the employee's name, hours worked, and rate of
C  pay per hour.
C
print*, '       PAYCHECK PROGRAM'
print*
print*
print*, 'Enter the employee''s name:  '
read*, Name
print*, 'Enter the hours worked:'
read*, Hours
print*, 'Enter the hourly pay rate:'
read*, PayRat
C
C  Calculate gross pay.
C
Gross = Hours * PayRat
C
C  Print the results of the paycheck calculations for this employee.
C  Then quit.
C
print*, 'Employee Name          ', Name
print*, '   Hours Worked         ', Hours
print*, '   Pay Rate             ', PayRat
print*, '   Gross Pay            ', Gross

stop
end
```

*Figure 8.11* This FORTRAN program calculates each employee's paycheck amount.

series of meetings to establish guidelines for the development of a business-oriented language. The objectives of this language were to be machine independent, easy to maintain, and English-like. The language developed was **COBOL,** an acronym for *Common Business Oriented Language.* It was released in 1960.

In the 1960s, the American National Standards Institute (ANSI) was charged with the task of developing standards for major programming languages. The first ANSI version of COBOL was approved in 1968. All major computer software manufacturers agreed to adhere to this standard. As a result, COBOL is portable. COBOL programs can run on many different kinds of computers with only minimal changes—an important feature for large businesses that need a variety of hardware.

A second version of ANSI COBOL was released in 1974. This version further standardized the language and made it even more efficient. However, both the 1968 and 1974 versions of COBOL needed some modifications to be totally structured, which would make them more standardized. In 1985, ANSI released a long-awaited version that formalized COBOL's structured programming methodology. Most companies have implemented this new structured COBOL, and COBOL remains the most widely used language for business programs developed for mainframes. It has been estimated that 70 to 80 percent of all mainframe applications are still coded in COBOL and many micro-based applications are written in COBOL as well. The constant predictions of its impending demise seem to be greatly exaggerated. Figure 8.12 shows a structured COBOL program that can process any number of input records.

## SYMBOLIC LANGUAGES THAT HAVE BECOME LESS WIDELY USED: PL/1 and RPG

In the early 1960s, many computer professionals believed that a single language should be developed to meet the needs of the business and scientific communities. PL/1, an abbreviation for *Programming Language/1*, was designed to satisfy this need. PL/1 combines the major advantages and features of COBOL and FORTRAN. Released in 1966, it was originally designed to be used on the IBM System 360 family of mainframe computers, but today there are many versions of PL/1 that can run on a variety of computers, including micros. PL/1 is best used in organizations that require both scientific and commercial applications. For example, an engineering firm that has one large computer for both engineering and business applications might use PL/1. In recent years, PL/1's popularity has waned, largely because the language is quite complex and newer languages with more features have since been developed.

RPG, an abbreviation for *Report Program Generator*, was also developed in the 1960s as a language that enabled users to produce their own reports. In concept, RPG was a precursor to more recent languages that use English-like structures to generate printed output from databases.

## BASIC

During the 1960s, many people believed that languages such as FORTRAN, COBOL, and PL/1 were difficult to learn. In addition, these languages were batch oriented and not really intended for newer, interactive methods of processing. In the early days, the programmer submitted both the program and the test data to the computer center for execution in batch mode at some later time. As terminals became popular in the 1960s, these batch methods for executing programs were viewed as slow, inefficient, and limited in applicability.

At the same time, two professors at Dartmouth College, John Kemeny and Thomas Kurtz, wanted to teach students in nontechnical disciplines to write interactive programs on large time-sharing systems. They cre-

```
00101 IDENTIFICATION DIVISION.
00102 PROGRAM-ID. SAMPLE.
00103 ENVIRONMENT DIVISION.
00104 INPUT-OUTPUT SECTION.
00105 FILE-CONTROL. SELECT EMPLOYEE-DATA    ASSIGN TO DISK.
00106               SELECT PAYROLL-LISTING ASSIGN TO SYSLST.
00107 DATA DIVISION.
00108 FILE SECTION.
00109 FD   EMPLOYEE-DATA              LABEL RECORDS ARE STANDARD.
00110 01   EMPLOYEE-RECORD.
00111      05   EMPLOYEE-NAME-IN      PICTURE X(20).
00112      05   HOURS-WORKED-IN       PICTURE 9(2).
00113      05   HOURLY-RATE-IN        PICTURE 9V99.
00114 FD   PAYROLL-LISTING            LABEL RECORDS ARE OMITTED.
00115 01   PRINT-REC.
00116      05                         PICTURE X(21).
00117      05   NAME-OUT              PICTURE X(20).
00118      05                         PICTURE X(10).
00119      05   HOURS-OUT             PICTURE 9(2).
00120      05                         PICTURE X(8).
00121      05   RATE-OUT              PICTURE 9.99.
00122      05                         PICTURE X(6).
00123      05   WEEKLY-WAGES-OUT      PICTURE 999.99.
00124 WORKING-STORAGE SECTION.
00125 01   ARE-THERE-MORE-RECORDS     PICTURE XXX VALUE 'YES'.
00126 PROCEDURE DIVISION.
00127 100-MAIN-MODULE.
00128      OPEN INPUT EMPLOYEE-DATA
00129           OUTPUT PAYROLL-LISTING.
00130      READ EMPLOYEE-DATA
00131           AT END MOVE 'NO ' TO ARE-THERE-MORE-RECORDS.
00132      PERFORM 200-WAGE-ROUTINE
00133           UNTIL ARE-THERE-MORE-RECORDS = 'NO '.
00134      CLOSE EMPLOYEE-DATA
00135           PAYROLL-LISTING.
00136      STOP RUN.
00137 200-WAGE-ROUTINE.
00138      MOVE SPACES TO PRINT-REC.
00139      MOVE EMPLOYEE-NAME-IN TO NAME-OUT.
00140      MOVE HOURS-WORKED-IN TO HOURS-OUT.
00141      MOVE HOURLY-RATE-IN TO RATE-OUT.
00142      MULTIPLY HOURS-WORKED-IN BY HOURLY-RATE-IN
00143           GIVING WEEKLY-WAGES-OUT.
00144      WRITE PRINT-REC.
00145      READ EMPLOYEE-DATA
00146           AT END MOVE 'NO ' TO ARE-THERE-MORE-RECORDS.
```

*Figure 8.12* This is an excerpt from a COBOL program. Note that the COBOL program is different from the others—it operates on any number of data items, whereas the others just operate on one set of data.

**CRITICAL THINKING**

Computer professionals often make a distinction between "programming" in languages such as BASIC and COBOL and "using" application packages such as Lotus 1-2-3 and dBASE. Indicate the ways in which writing a program differs from using an application package.

ated **BASIC** (*B*eginner's *A*ll-purpose *S*ymbolic *I*nstruction *C*ode); the acronym is far more suitable than the full name! BASIC is easy to learn and is appropriate for small businesses with a limited programming staff. Because BASIC is widely implemented on microcomputers—the type of computer most common in schools from elementary to the college level—it is the language students are likely to learn first. Figure 8.13 shows a short BASIC program that, as our previous programs, calculates an employee's net pay.

Although BASIC is used mainly on micros, it is available on mainframes as well. One problem with BASIC, however, is that there is no standard that has been embraced by users as the one to follow. Even on IBM micros and their compatibles, the versions abound. In addition, mainframes have versions that are not entirely compatible with the micro versions.[1]

## LANGUAGES DESIGNED SPECIFICALLY FOR STRUCTURED PROGRAMMING: PASCAL AND MODULA-2

**Pascal.** In the mid- and late 1960s, the concept of structured programming to make programs easier to code and debug became a priority

[1] *Getting Started with Structured BASIC,* available with this text, focuses on QBASIC and BASICA, versions of BASIC used on IBM and IBM-compatible PCs.

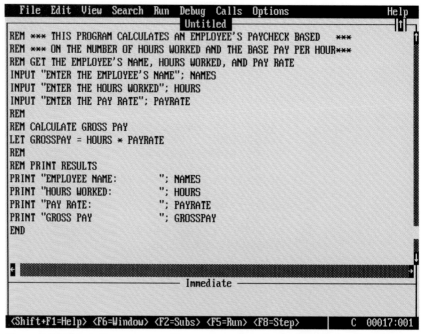

**Figure 8.13** *This is the same payroll program written in BASIC. Notice that this version of BASIC does not number lines. Some versions of BASIC require line numbers while others do not.*

among computer scientists. As a result, many computer educators came to believe that structured programming techniques should be taught to computer students from the beginning. In 1971 Niklaus Wirth, the main proponent of structured programming, developed **Pascal** to meet the need for an easy to learn, highly structured language. Figure 8.14 contains a short Pascal program. Wirth named Pascal after the seventeenth-century mathematician Blaise Pascal, who developed the first mechanical calculator.

Many computer scientists embraced Pascal as a major improvement over languages such as COBOL and BASIC, which were, at the time, essentially nonstructured. Because Pascal was designed to be a truly structured language, it became the introductory programming language for computer science students at most universities. Pascal was not, however, intended to be powerful enough for major business applications; that is, it cannot handle large quantities of business data nearly as efficiently as languages such as COBOL. But it can perform complex mathematical operations, so it remains popular with engineers and scientists.

IN A

**BASIC, COBOL, AND PASCAL: THE BIG THREE**

| Language | Features | Limitations |
|---|---|---|
| BASIC | Conversational; interactive<br>Easy user interface and simple diagnostics<br>Free-form—no grammar or spacing rules | No real standard—programs written in one version are apt to need modifications to run under another version<br>Some versions are slow and inefficient |
| COBOL | Very effective for complex input/output<br>Instructions and data names are English-like | Tends to be verbose, requiring a large amount of writing<br>Not suitable for mathematical or scientific applications |
| Pascal | Structured<br>Lends itself to object-oriented programming<br>Can result in very efficient code | Weak input/output capabilities |

**Modula-2.** Niklaus Wirth created Pascal to be primarily a teaching language. As its use spread to business, its shortcomings became more apparent. Wirth then developed **Modula-2** as an expansion and improvement over Pascal. Introduced in 1980, Modula-2 is better suited for handling the large quantities of data that are processed in business applications. Because Modula-2 retains the original emphasis on structured programming concepts that were first introduced in Pascal, and because it has commercial applicability as well, some universities have begun using it in computer science courses. But relatively few translators are currently available, so its future in both schools and business remains unclear.

```
program Paycheck (input, output);

{ *** This program calculates an employee's paycheck based on  ***
  *** the number of hours the employee worked and the base pay ***
  *** per hour.                                                ***  }

var
   Name : string;
   Hours, PayRate, GrossPay : real;

begin   { Paycheck }

   { Prompt the user to enter name, hours worked and hourly rate. }
   write ('Enter the employee''s name: ');
   readln (Name);
   write ('Enter the number of hours worked: ');
   readln (Hours);
   write ('Enter the hourly pay rate: ');
   readln (PayRate);

   { Calculate gross pay.}
   GrossPay := Hours * PayRate;

   { Print the results of the paycheck calculations for this employee.
     Then quit. }

   writeln ('Employee Name:      ', Name);
   writeln ('Hours Worked:       ', Hours:8:2);
   writeln ('Pay Rate:           ', PayRate:8:2);
   writeln ('Gross Pay:          ', GrossPay:8:2);

end.     { Paycheck }
```

**Figure 8.14** This Pascal program also calculates employee pay.

## C: THE HIGH-LEVEL ALTERNATIVE TO ASSEMBLY LANGUAGE PROGRAMMING

The **C** language was developed in 1972 by Dennis M. Ritchie at Bell Laboratories. C incorporates the advantages of both assembly language and high-level languages and is therefore often referred to as a "middle-level" language. It is a structured language that uses high-level instruction formats, but it also allows the programmer to interact directly with the hardware, as in assembly language. These combined capabilities make C well suited as the main language for writing operating systems that require extremely efficient code. In addition, instructions written in C, unlike those written in assembly languages, are portable. The UNIX operating system, which we will discuss in the next chapter, was written in C.

The C language is more difficult to learn than other structured languages like Pascal. Even so, because of its power and wide implementation on microcomputers, it is popular among systems programmers for developing systems software and utilities. Figure 8.15 shows the employee pay program we have been illustrating written in C.

## ADA

In 1978 the U.S. Department of Defense, dissatisfied with the languages available at the time, held a design competition to select a programming language standard for its software. As the world's largest purchaser of computer hardware and software, the department realized it could save billions of dollars in development by standardizing its software language. The winning language was named for Augusta Ada, the Countess of Lovelace, who designed what we would call "programs" for computing engines originally conceived by Charles Babbage in the nineteenth century.

**Ada** is a general-purpose language based on the structured concepts first used in Pascal. It is extremely powerful and sophisticated. Learning the language well enough to take advantage of its full potential can take

IN  A

## LANGUAGES

| Features | Ada | BASIC | COBOL | FORTRAN | Pascal, Modula-2, C, and C++ |
|---|---|---|---|---|---|
| Scientific | X | X | | X | X |
| Business | X | X | X | | |
| Procedure-oriented | X | X | X | X | X |
| Standardized | X | | X | | X |
| English-like | | X | X | | X |
| Interactive | X | X | | | X |

```
/***                              PAYCHECK PROGRAM                       ***/
/***                                                                     ***/
/*** Program Paycheck calculates an employee's paycheck based on the ***/
/*** number of hours worked and base pay per hour.                       ***/
/*********************************************************************/

main()
{
char    Employee_Name[40];
float   Gross_Pay;
float   Pay_Rate;
float   Hours_Worked
int     Temp;
char    c;
/* -------------------------------------------------------------- */

    /* Prompt the user for the employee's name, hours worked, and rate
    of pay per hour. */
printf ("                               PAYCHECK PROGRAM\n");
printf ("Enter the employee's name: ");
    /* read characters into name array, one at a time  */
for (Temp = 0; (Temp < 40) && ((c = getchar()) != '\r') && (c != '\n');
    Temp++) Employee_Name[Temp] = c;
Employee_Name[Temp] = '\0';      /* put in end of string character */
printf ("\n");                   /* write a new line to screen     */

printf ("Enter the number of hours worked: ");
scanf ("%f", &Hours_Worked); /* read number of hours from standard input*/
printf ("Enter the hourly pay rate: ");
scanf  ("%f", &Pay_Rate);  /* read pay rate from standard input        */

    /* Calculate gross pay. */

Gross_Pay = Hours_Worked * Pay_Rate;

    /* Print the results of the paycheck calculations for this employee.
          Then quit. */

printf ("\n\n");
printf ("Employee Name            %s\n",    Employee_Name);
printf ("    Hours Worked         %8.2f\n", Hours_Worked);
printf ("    Pay Rate             %8.2f\n", Pay_Rate);
printf ("    Gross Pay            %8.2f\n", Gross_Pay);

}
```

**Figure 8.15** *This C program is not as readable as the others, but its translation to machine language is easier for the computer.*

# LOOKING BACK

## THE FIRST COMPUTER AND THE FIRST PROGRAMMER

*Charles Babbage (1791–1871).*

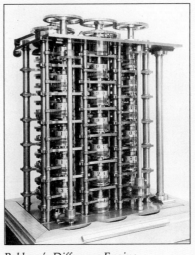

*Babbage's Difference Engine.*

*Augusta Ada (1815–1853).*

Charles Babbage, a nineteenth-century Englishman, is frequently considered the father of the modern computer. Although he did not actually build an operational computer himself, his ideas became the basis for modern computational devices.

In 1822, Babbage began work on a device called the Difference Engine, which was designed to automate a standard procedure for calculating the roots of polynomials. The calculations were used for producing astronomical tables that were required by the British Navy for navigational purposes. Despite his foresight, Babbage did not complete his original project. Instead, he abandoned the Difference Engine to work on a more powerful device, the Analytical Engine, which was remarkably similar in concept to twentieth-century digital computers.

The Analytical Engine was designed to use two types of cards: one, called operation cards, to indicate the specific functions to be performed, and the other, called variable cards, to specify the actual data. This idea of entering a program (or set of instructions) on cards, fol-

*Babbage's Analytical Engine.*

lowed by data cards, is one method used by the first generation of modern computers for implementing the stored-program concept.

Babbage conceived of two main units for his Analytical Engine.

1. An area he called a *store* within the device, in which instructions and variables would be placed. Today we call this the *memory* of the computer.
2. An area he called a *mill* within the device, in which arithmetic operations would be performed.

Today we call this the *arithmetic/logic unit.*

Lady Augusta Ada Byron, the Countess of Lovelace and daughter of the poet Lord Byron, worked closely with Babbage in the design of programs for the Analytical Engine. She wrote a demonstration program for the Analytical Engine, prompting many to refer to her as the first programmer. The programming language Ada, discussed here, was named for her.

```
-- ***                        PAYCHECK PROGRAM                        ***
-- ***                                                                ***
-- ***   This program calculates an employee's paycheck based on the  ***
-- ***   number of hours worked and base pay per hour.                ***

package Paycheck_Program is
   procedure Paycheck;
end Paycheck_Program;

with Text_IO;                    -- Text_IO is a standard Ada package used
                                 -- to control text input and output.
package Paycheck_Program body is

   Employee_Name  : string (1..12);

   Gross_Pay,
   Hours_Worked,
   Pay_Rate       : real;

------------------------------------------------------------------------------
procedure Paycheck;

begin    -- Paycheck

-- Prompt the user for the employee's name, hours worked, and rate of
-- pay per hour.

   Text_IO.Put ("                               PAYCHECK PROGRAM");
   Text_IO.New_Line;
   Text_IO.Put ("Enter the employee's name: ");
   Text_IO.Get (Employee_Name);

   Text_IO.Put ("Enter the number of hours worked: ");
   Text_IO.Get (Hours_Worked);

   Text_IO.Put ("Enter the hourly pay rate: ");
   Text_IO.Get (Pay_Rate);

-- Calculate gross pay.

   Gross_Pay             := Hours_Worked * Pay_Rate;

-- Print paycheck information for this employee. Then quit.

   Text_IO.Put ('Employee Name         ');
   Text_IO.Put (Employee_Name);
   Text_IO.New_Line;

   Text_IO.Put ('   Hours Worked       ');
   Text_IO.Put (Hours_Worked);
   Text_IO.New_Line;

   Text_IO.Put ('    Pay Rate          ');
   Text_IO.Put (Pay_Rate);
   Text_IO.New_Line;

   Text_IO.Put ('    Gross Pay         ');
   Text_IO.Put (Gross_Pay);
   Text_IO.New_Line;

end Paycheck;

end Paycheck_Program;
```

*Figure 8.16* *This is a sample of Ada programming, which is particularly suited for real-time processing.*

several years. Figure 8.16 shows the program we have been illustrating that determines an employee's net pay as it could be written in Ada.

Much of the software developed by the Department of Defense is used in **embedded systems,** which are computer systems built into other systems. Computers that are placed on aircraft, for example, are embedded systems. These systems are most commonly used in real-time processing where the computerized process must interact quickly enough to respond immediately. For example, navigational equipment on an aircraft must use real-time processing to continually respond to new input and feedback so that its output is not only correct but timely, and therefore immediately usable. Because Ada is well suited for real-time processing, its use in business is growing. It has been applied effectively to the automation of factory and office tasks.

## OBJECT-ORIENTED PROGRAMMING LANGUAGES

SmallTalk, developed in 1972 by Alan Kay at Xerox's Palo Alto Research Center, is one of many languages specifically designed to enable users to implement object-oriented programming (OOP). In object-oriented programs, a programmer uses objects instead of the operation codes and data names or symbolic addresses that are common to most languages. Two other object-oriented languages popular for developing graphical user interfaces, multimedia, and database management systems are **C++** and object-oriented Pascal, modifications of C and Pascal, respectively.

An object in a program can be a dialog box, a window, or a menu. Operating systems such as OS/2 and graphical user interfaces such as Windows can be considered object oriented because they make use of these types of objects. If a window with scroll bars and dialog boxes is to be a component of a program, for example, the programmer can simply use the windows created by a graphical user interface without even knowing how these were created.

## INTERPRETERS AND COMPILERS

Third-generation languages use translators called compilers or interpreters, which are more sophisticated than assemblers. An **interpreter** translates a program written in a high-level language one statement at a time as the program is actually being run on the computer. Each statement is translated and executed before the interpreter proceeds to the next statement. This process continues until the end of the program is reached. A **compiler** translates the entire source program into machine language in one process, thereby creating an object program. Another program, referred to as the linking loader or linkage editor, prepares the object program for execution.

Most high-level programming languages use compilers, but some languages, for example BASIC, also have interpreters. Interpreters do not take up as much space in the computer's primary storage, but they are slower than compilers. Compilers are capable of creating an object pro-

## TYPES OF TRANSLATORS AND THEIR FEATURES

*Assembler*

- Uses symbolic operation codes and storage addresses, which are easier to remember than the codes of machine language
- Resembles machine languages in all other ways (Each machine language has its own corresponding assembly language.)
- Requires programmers to understand the machine language of the computer
- Requires a translation process

called an assembly to convert the program to machine language
- Results in very efficient code
- Used for developing operating systems, utilities, and background programs where efficient use of the CPU is most important

*Compiler*

- Is the most common type of translator program
- Translates the entire symbolic program into machine language in one cycle

- Translates each symbolic instruction written by the programmer into machine language instructions

*Interpreter*

- Translates and executes each instruction as it is read
- Translates a program each time it is to be executed (Compiled and assembled machine language code can be saved so that the translation process need not be repeated.)

gram that can be stored in executable form; so if the program is to be run again, it need not be retranslated each time. Thus, programs that are to be run on a regularly scheduled basis are nearly always written in high-level languages that can be compiled as opposed to languages that require interpreters.

## ▶ Fourth-Generation Languages

Recall that first-, second-, and third-generation languages are all procedural languages because the programmer must write each step and must use logical control structures to indicate the order in which the instructions are to be executed. Fourth-generation languages (4GLs), on the other hand, are nonprocedural languages. This distinction can be compared to the way in which you might instruct someone to cook a meal. The nonprocedural method is simply to state the needed output: fix a meal of chicken, rice, and salad. The procedural method, on the other hand, involves specifying each step—from preparing the shopping list to washing the dishes.

A nonprocedural language is easier to code, but it gives you less control over how each task is actually performed. For example, if you simply state, nonprocedurally, "wash the dishes," the dishes might be washed by hand or in a dishwasher; the decision typically would be beyond your control. When you use nonprocedural languages, remember that the instructions are easier, but the methods employed and the order in which each task is carried out are left to the program itself.

Instructions for 4GLs do not focus on *how* to perform a function but on *what* is actually to be done; the software itself generates the required operations. As a result, 4GLs sacrifice computer efficiency so that programs are easier to write. They require more computer power and processing time than their procedural counterparts. As the power and speed of hardware increase and the cost of the hardware decreases, the need for emphasizing efficient code becomes less important. The result is the blossoming of user-friendly 4GLs.

Because fourth-generation languages have a minimum number of syntax rules, users who may not have been trained as programmers can learn to write application programs in these languages as the need arises. Time is saved and professional programmers are free to focus on more difficult tasks. Fourth-generation languages, which are used widely on both mainframes and micros, are divided into three basic categories: query languages, report generators, and application generators.

## QUERY LANGUAGES

**Query languages** allow users to retrieve information from databases by following simple syntax rules. For example, you might ask the database to locate all customer accounts that are more than 90 days overdue. Examples of query languages are Structured Query Language (SQL), Query-By-Example (QBE), and INTELLECT. Look at the following example of SQL for querying an employee database and increasing salaries of some employees by 1000; the operations performed are fairly straightforward.

### SQL Example

UPDATE EMPLOYEE
SET SALARY = SALARY + 1000
    WHERE JOBCODE = 3 OR 6

This increases salaries of employees with a job code of 3 or 6 by $1000.
    Query languages typically have the following two features.

1. Echo back for verification, where a query is restated in the language's standard format:

### INTELLECT Example

USER: HOW MANY PROGRAMMERS DO WE HAVE?
INTELLECT: COUNT EMPLOYEES WITH JOB = PROGRAMMER
ANSWER: 25

2. Query languages can perform trapping so that if a query requires an extensive amount of computer time, the computer will notify you.

### INTELLECT Example

USER: WHAT IS THE AVERAGE SALARY FOR THE COMPANY?
INTELLECT: PRINT AVERAGE SALARY
              THE NUMBER OF RECORDS TO RETRIEVE IS 15,326.
              YOUR REQUEST IS RELATIVELY EXPENSIVE TO
                  ANSWER.
              HIT THE ENTER KEY TO CONTINUE PROCESSING OR
                  ENTER A NEW REQUEST

IN A

**FEATURES OF 4GLS**
- Easy to learn, understand, and use even by those with little computer training
- Convenient for accessing databases
- Focuses on maximizing human productivity rather than minimizing computer time
- Nonprocedural
- Available as packaged software that is then used to develop custom applications

SQL has become the de facto standard for query languages and is now part of many database management systems.

## REPORT GENERATORS

**Report generators** produce customized reports using data stored in a database. The user specifies the data to be in the report, how the report should be formatted, and whether any subtotals or totals are needed. For example, you might ask the system to create a list, arranged by account number, of all the company's customers located in Oklahoma. Often, report specifications are selected from pull-down menus, which makes report generators very user-friendly. Examples of report generators are Easytrieve Plus and R&R Report Writer.

## APPLICATION GENERATORS

A user can access a database with query languages and report generators but generally cannot alter the database with these tools. **Application generators** create programs that allow data to be entered into a database. The program prompts the user to enter the needed data. It also checks the data for validity. MANTIS and ADS are examples of application generators.

In summary, fourth-generation programming languages are suitable for writing short, simple programs. They do not require the training of a professional programmer. They do have a major limitation: Because they are nonprocedural, the person generating the program does not have as much control over the specific processes used as he or she would with high-level languages such as COBOL or Pascal. Chapter 11 covers query languages, report generators, and application generators in more depth.

## ▶ Fifth-Generation Languages

Fifth-generation languages (5GLs) are also nonprocedural languages. They are most often used to access databases or to build expert systems. In concept, 5GLs are intended to be **natural languages,** which resemble as close as possible normal human interaction. The user need not employ any specific vocabulary, grammar, or syntax when making a query or issuing a command. Artificial intelligence techniques that enable computers to duplicate or imitate the functions of the human brain are part of 5GLs. These techniques help the computer interpret requests or commands. Currently, 5GLs are still in their infancy; only a few are available commercially. Expert systems developed using fifth-generation languages can help predict the weather, diagnose diseases, and determine where to explore for oil.

LISP, a 5GL, was developed in 1958 by John McCarthy at MIT. Although it is one of the oldest programming languages, it has been used extensively in one of the newer technologies: artificial intelligence research. Prolog, another 5GL, was developed in 1972 in France by Alain

*Figure 8.17* *An excerpt of a Prolog program.*

```
Predicates
    likes(person, thing).
    dislikes(person, thing).
    angers(thing, person).
    healthy(thing).
    unhealthy(thing).


Clauses
    likes(walter, chocolate).
    likes(steve, chocolate).
    likes(diana, chocolate).
    likes(earl, chocolate).
    likes(karla, chocolate).
    likes(wendy, jogging).
    likes(zelda, jogging).
    likes(bruce, alcohol).
    likes(zelda, alcohol).
    likes(walter, salads).
    likes(diana, salads).
    likes(wendy, salads).
    dislikes(isaac, chocolate).
    dislikes(wendy, chocolate).
    dislikes(bruce, chocolate).
    dislikes(walter, jogging).
    dislikes(steve, jogging).
    dislikes(diana, jogging).
    dislikes(earl, jogging).
    dislikes(isaac, jogging).
    dislikes(bruce, jogging).
    dislikes(walter, alcohol).
    dislikes(diana, alcohol).
    dislikes(steve, alcohol).
    dislikes(earl, alcohol).
    dislikes(karla, alcohol).
    dislikes(isaac, alcohol).
    dislikes(wendy, alcohol).
    dislikes(steve, salads).
    dislikes(earl, salads).
    angers(chocolate, zelda).
    angers(jogging, karla).
    unhealthy(chocolate).
    unhealthy(alcohol).
    healthy(jogging).
    healthy(salads).


Goal:angers(chocolate, zelda).
True
Goal:healthy(alcohol).
False
Goal:unhealthy(vodka).
False
Goal:


Goal:likes(steve, chocolate).
True
1 Solution
Goal:likes(zelda, chocolate).
False
1 Solution
Goal:


Goal:likes(Who, chocolate).
Who = walter
Who = steve
Who = diana
Who = earl
Who = karla
5 Solutions
Goal:
```

Language Generations

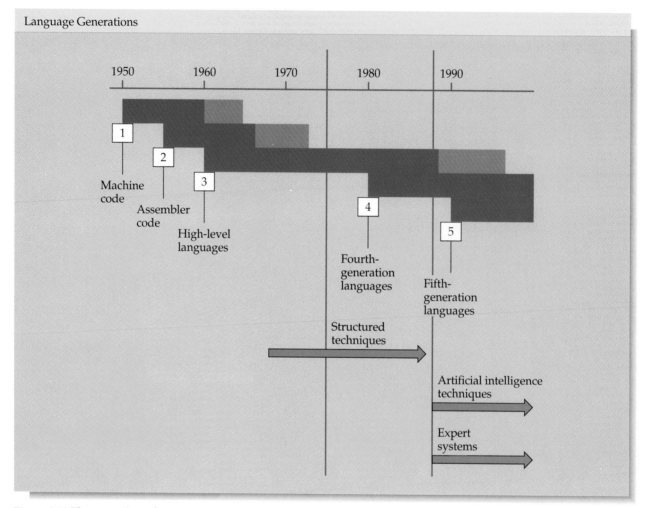

***Figure 8.18*** *The generations of programming languages.*

Recall from Chapter 7 that an expert system includes a knowledge base and an inference engine designed to enable the computer to simulate the decision-making process of an expert.

Colmerauer and Philippe Roussel. It quickly became popular throughout Europe as it improved and expanded. There are several implementations of Prolog for microcomputers. Figure 8.17 illustrates a Prolog program. The clauses in Figure 8.17 define a database of information. The predicates indicate rules. The goals indicate queries that the computer answers based on the rules and the contents of the database. As noted, 5GLs are appropriate not only for developing expert systems, but also for making natural language inquiries from databases.

Currently, most expert or knowledge-based systems are coded either in LISP or Prolog although some are written in C or C++ as well. Recent efforts to improve artificial intelligence languages have attempted to combine the best features of LISP and Prolog. Fifth-generation languages are likely to have great impact in the near future.

See Figure 8.18 for a review of the five generations of programming languages.

## ▶ SELF-TEST

1. (T or F) A program written in a high-level language is more user-friendly than one written in an assembly language.

2. (T or F) Most third-generation languages are portable, which means they are not machine dependent.
3. A language commonly used for business applications, particularly on mainframes, is called _____.
4. A high-level language initially designed for students in an interactive environment is _____.
5. What are nonprocedural languages?
6. Name two ways in which fifth-generation languages are typically used.

Solutions
1. T
2. T
3. COBOL
4. BASIC
5. They are languages designed for noncomputer professionals to obtain information from the computer without necessarily specifying the precise steps or sequence in which operations are to be performed.
6. for designing expert systems; for accessing databases

# ► Chapter Summary

## 8.1 THE SOFTWARE DEVELOPER

Organizations sometimes find that off-the-shelf software does not completely fulfill their needs. One alternative is to have software specifically developed to accomplish the required tasks. In most medium-sized to large organizations with an in-house computing staff, systems analysts supervise programmers who undertake software development. In smaller companies, a **programmer analyst** may serve as both programmer and systems analyst. Some companies hire consultants such as freelance programmers, specialized software development "houses," or outsourcing firms.

*Why is there a need for custom programs when packages abound and who develops such software?*

## 8.2 SOFTWARE DEVELOPMENT CYCLE

The term **software development cycle** refers to the steps involved in creating a program. These include (1) developing the program specifications, (2) designing the logic to be used, (3) coding the program and translating it into machine language, (4) testing the program, (5) installing, or implementing, the program, (6) maintaining the program, and (7) documenting the program.

The three most commonly used tools for planning the logic of a program are flowcharts, pseudocode, and hierarchy charts. A **flowchart** is a pictorial representation of the logic flow to be used in a program. Each flowchart symbol denotes either a particular operation or a series of operations to be performed by a program unit called a **subprogram** or

*What are the steps involved in software development and why is the process called a cycle?*

**module.** An alternative design tool is **pseudocode,** which consists of English-like statements instead of symbols. **Hierarchy charts** (sometimes called **structure charts**) illustrate how programs are segmented into subprograms (or modules) and how the modules relate to one another.

A program must be in **machine language,** the computer's own internal language, in order to be executed. Most programs are written in **symbolic languages,** which use instructions such as ADD or + instead of complex operation codes. To be executed, a symbolic program, also called the **source program,** must be translated into machine language. The translated program is referred to as the **object program.**

**Debugging** a program means finding and correcting all logic and coding errors, or "bugs." **Desk-checking** is the process in which a programmer manually traces through a program visually checking for **syntax errors,** which are coding errors. A program without syntax errors, however, does not necessarily produce correct output. There may be **logic errors,** which are errors that occur because of mistakes in the sequencing of instructions or the use of wrong instructions. **Program testing,** or executing a program with different sets of data, is a technique used to pinpoint logic errors. A **maintenance programmer** is a computer professional who modifies existing programs to make them more current or efficient.

**Software engineering** is a name sometimes given to the program development cycle by those who focus on the scientific and technical aspects of programming.

## 8.3 PROGRAMMING TECHNIQUES FOR STANDARDIZING SOFTWARE DEVELOPMENT

What benefits do standardized program development techniques offer both the software developer and the user?

**Structured programming** is a program design technique that integrates program modules in a systematic way. A structured program has a main module from which all subordinate modules are executed. There are no branch points. All program steps are executed by means of just four logical control constructs: sequence, selection (IF-THEN-ELSE), iteration (looping), and Case. In a top-down program, the main module is coded first, followed by intermediate and then minor modules.

**Reusable code** refers to a module or combination of modules that can be used in more than one program. Object-oriented programming is a technique designed to make program components reusable and to reduce the time it takes to develop those components. An **object-oriented program** defines both the data and the set of operations that can act on that data as one unit called an *object*. **Inheritance** refers to the fact that all objects within a class share the same attributes.

## 8.4 FIVE GENERATIONS OF PROGRAMMING LANGUAGES

How have generations of programming languages evolved to enhance the software development process?

Machine languages are referred to as first-generation languages because they were the earliest type developed. They are wholly computer dependent and thus nonstandard. They are highly efficient, but they are not user-friendly: they make use of complex operation codes and reference actual machine addresses that store data.

The second generation of programming languages are **assembly languages.** These languages use symbolic instruction codes and symbolic names for storage areas but are similar to machine languages in other ways. Assembly language programs require a translation process by which a program called an **assembler** converts an assembly program into machine language. Assembly language programs are not **portable;** that is, they only run on computers that have the same architecture.

Third-generation languages are more symbolic and easier to use than first- or second-generation languages. They are also portable. These languages are called high-level because they are relatively easy to learn and not at all like machine language; rather, they resemble the English language. High-level programs require a complex translation process to convert the source program into machine language. High-level languages, like their predecessors, are called **procedural languages;** this means that the program must specify the precise set of instructions to accomplish a given task. Some of the most commonly used third-generation languages are **FORTRAN, COBOL, BASIC, Pascal, Modula-2, C, C++,** and **Ada.** Much of the software developed by the U.S. Department of Defense is written in Ada and is used in **embedded systems,** which are computer systems built into other systems.

An **interpreter** translates a program in a high-level language one statement at a time into a machine language as the program is being run on the computer. A **compiler** translates an entire source program into machine language in one process.

Fourth-generation languages are **nonprocedural languages;** that is, they need not follow precise rules. Programs written in these languages are easier to code but give users less control over how each task is actually performed. They are designed so that users as well as programmers can easily access databases. **Query languages** allow users to retrieve information from databases by following simple syntax rules. **Report generators** produce customized reports using data stored in a database. **Application generators** create programs that allow data to be entered into a database.

Fifth-generation languages, which build expert systems, are intended to be **natural languages**—those that resemble as close as possible normal human interaction.

## ▶ Chapter Self-test

1. (T or F) Programs must be coded before the program specifications are determined.
2. In large information processing departments, a _____ usually oversees each new project, whereas a _____ does the actual coding of the program.
3. A programming tool called a _____ uses special symbols to plan the program logic, while _____ uses English words to plan the logic.
4. Today, second-generation languages, also called _____ languages, are often used to develop systems software.

5. (T or F) In structured programming, programmers attempt to avoid using iteration.
6. _____ errors are grammatical mistakes in writing a program; _____ errors are caused by incorrect or incomplete processing steps.
7. Programming languages that are _____ can be executed on many different computers with minimal changes.
8. The language _____ has the advantages of both assembly languages and high-level languages and is often used in systems programming.
9. Programs written in a _____ language can be executed without first being translated.
10. (T or F ) The programmer who uses the top-down approach divides a program solution into smaller and smaller parts.
11. A translator called a _____ translates and executes programs written in a symbolic language one statement at a time; in contrast, a translator called a _____ translates the entire source program into an object program that may be executed at any time.
12. What is the language most commonly used for business programs that need to access large files of data?
13. What was the first widely used high-level language for scientific and mathematical applications?
14. Which language did Niklaus Wirth develop to teach structured programming techniques to students?
15. (T or F) Fourth-generation languages such as SQL are often used to query databases.
16. (T or F) Programs are tested only after the installation and conversion process is completed.
17. What languages are most commonly used in artificial intelligence and expert systems?

Solutions
1. F
2. systems analyst; programmer
3. flowchart; pseudocode
4. assembly
5. F
6. Syntax; logic
7. portable
8. C
9. machine
10. T
11. interpreter; compiler
12. COBOL
13. FORTRAN
14. Pascal
15. T
16. F
17. Fifth-generation languages

## ▶ Key Terms

## ▶ Review Questions

1. Describe the steps in the software development process.
2. What is structured programming and why is it so important today?
3. What is the difference between source and object code?
4. What is debugging?
5. Describe the differences between compilers, assemblers, and interpreters.
6. Why is documentation important?

### PRODUCT ANALYSIS

### CASE

#### OOP! Watch Out for This New Programming Concept

Object-oriented programming (OOP) has become a buzzword, but it does not always mean the same thing to everyone. To programmers, it means a component approach to software so that reusability is facilitated and reliability and consistency of design are achieved. To users, it means that what you ask for you can easily obtain.

Users are hoping that OOP techniques will not only improve custom software but enable them to actually customize off-the-shelf software. The expectation is that users will be able to restructure programs with menu choices that rearrange blocks of code as needed. OOP also means that it will be easier to add a wide variety of plug-in modules to existing programs thereby increasing their functionality.

According to Jim Manzi, CEO of Lotus Development Corporation, "object-oriented programming will be the most abused phrase in the industry over the next three to five years."[1] Instead of viewing applications as one complete structure, we will be looking at components or objects— "software Legos."

Bill Gates, CEO of Microsoft, is also very interested in the future of object-oriented program-

[1]Flynn, M.K. (1992) "An object by any other name," *PC Magazine*, **11** (3), 29.

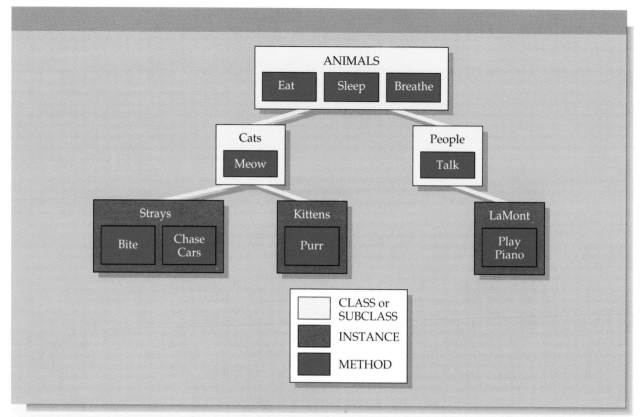

*Object-oriented programming enables procedures or methods to be combined with data to form objects. The ability of objects to inherit class characteristics facilitates the development of reusable code (supplied here).*

ming, which he defines as "using indirect dispatching so that you can perform an operation without having to understand the underlying form of the data."[2]

Some people, especially hardware developers, are more philosophical about OOP. Michael Dell, CEO of Dell, sees object orientation as "just another evolution in the user interface, like multimedia. It's all part of getting communication with

PCs to be more like the way we communicate with each other."[3]

The next few years should determine whether OOP is likely to be the major software trend of this generation or, as Dell predicts, just another step in the evolutionary process of software development.

*Analysis*

1. How does object-oriented programming differ from traditional programming?
2. What are OOP's benefits?
3. Can you think of any obstacles to using OOP?

[2]*Ibid.*, p. 29.

[3]*Ibid.*, p. 29.

# CHAPTER 9

## SYSTEMS SOFTWARE

**W**hether application software is purchased off-the-shelf or custom-designed for an individual user, it is the driving force in a computer environment. But before the application programs can be run, a computer requires a set of control programs. These control programs supervise overall processing and establish an interface between the computer and the user. It is systems software that provides the control and interface.

In this chapter, we discuss systems software by answering the following questions:

▶ What functions do operating systems perform and how are they accessed by users?

▶ What are some common operating systems for micros?

▶ What does the portability of the UNIX operating system and the availability of network operating systems mean for the computing field?

▶ What are some common mainframe operating systems?

## SYSTEMS SOFTWARE: FUNCTIONS AND FEATURES

What functions do operating systems perform and how are they accessed by users?

### ▶ What Systems Software Actually Does

Application software today is much more sophisticated and diverse than programs were only a few years ago. Software packages are available to perform tasks as diverse as creating typeset-quality publications that contain complex graphics or keeping track of daily appointments. If no package can manipulate data in ways that a user desires, then custom products can be developed.

Not only must application software perform complex tasks, it must also be user-friendly. As application programs become easier to use, so too does the systems software that includes the operating system and acts as an interface between us and the hardware. The systems software that has become available along with the growth of micros is not only user-friendly, but it also is capable of running several applications concurrently.

The most important demand we make of the systems software for our computers is that it allow us to use our time as efficiently as possible. Of late, systems software is becoming more diversified in the services it provides. Some types can provide a detailed accounting of how computer resources are being used. Some have antiviral programs built in for protection, along with other utilities that make it easier to use the computer system.

The operating system is the main component of systems software, but,

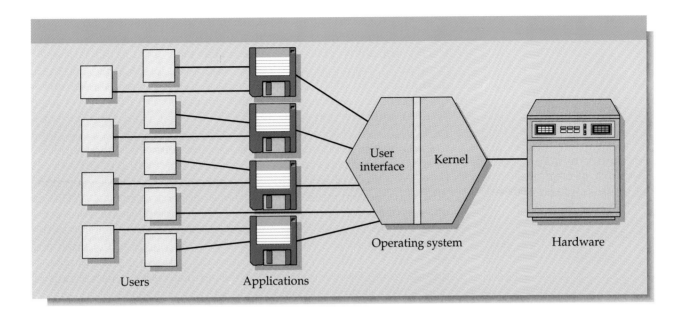

Users          Applications

*Figure 9.1* An operating system consists of a user interface that accepts user requests and interprets the various activities or applications to be performed, and a kernel that controls the execution of these activities.

as we will see, there are other components as well. Operating systems have two basic functions: to manage the computer's resources efficiently and to execute the user's instructions. The part of the operating system that manages the computer's resources—including the CPU, primary storage, and peripheral devices—is commonly called the **kernel** (or the **supervisor**). It is the kernel that monitors the keyboard—it determines when a key has been depressed and what action to take. Similarly, the operating system controls the transfer of data from secondary storage to main memory and back again.

The **user interface,** or operating environment, is the part of the systems software that permits you to communicate with the hardware, for example, to instruct the system to execute a particular application package or to save a file. On larger systems, on some micros, and on networked systems, the user interface controls access through user IDs, passwords, and access codes. Figure 9.1 illustrates how the parts of the operating system interface with the user and the computer hardware.

Operating systems, as well as systems software in general, are designed to maximize the efficient use of the computer's resources. Systems software is written by **systems programmers**—software developers with knowledge of computer architecture. Systems programmers write instructions that use as little RAM as possible so that there is more main memory available for application software.

As you would expect, systems software for micros is less sophisticated and has fewer capabilities than similar software for larger systems. The systems software for a large computer may manage many terminals at different sites and allocate resources to multiple users. On the other hand, systems software for a PC is usually intended for single users. In addition, systems software for a micro may include one or two translator programs (e.g., for BASIC), whereas systems software for larger systems may have numerous translators.

Because it needs to control and maximize the efficient use of hardware, systems software must be written for each computer's architecture. Hence, such software is not often portable, or usable on, other types of computers. Systems software for the Macintosh, for example, cannot be used as is on an IBM PC. Even systems software for an IBM PC sometimes cannot be used as is on an IBM-compatible PC. Mainframes have systems software that is dramatically different from such software for PCs.

Connectivity is so important in to-day's world because it enables computers with different architectures and different systems software to communicate effectively with each other and to make use of each other's resources.

In contrast to application software, systems software is often supplied by the computer manufacturer or a vendor, along with the hardware. If the price of the hardware includes the systems software, we say it is **bundled** with the computer. If you prefer a different operating system or other systems software programs that are compatible with your computer but are not bundled with it, or if you want a newer version of the operating system you currently have, you can purchase the programs separately. As with any packaged software, outlets for such purchases include computer manufacturers, stores, or mail-order houses. Prices of an operating system or other systems software components vary widely. DOS for IBM PCs or compatibles costs less than $100 while OS/2 can cost several hundred dollars. UNIX, another operating system, varies in price from hundreds of dollars to thousands of dollars depending on the computer. Operating systems for mainframes typically cost thousands of dollars.

Because systems software is designed to be as efficient as possible, it must be written in a programming language that best utilizes a computer's architecture. For this reason, most systems software was once written almost exclusively in a computer's assembler language. More recently developed systems software programs, however, are written in the C programming language, because C permits direct addressing of a computer's memory and it is portable. The newest systems software is often written in C++, an object-oriented version of C, that is capable of providing graphical user interfaces.

A multitude of operating systems are currently available as part of systems software. Some of these operating systems, such as DOS and the Macintosh operating system, are designed to be used with specific microcomputers. Others, such as IBM and IBM-compatible mainframe operating systems, can be implemented only on large computers. Still others,

IN A

**TYPES OF SOFTWARE**

| | |
|---|---|
| Systems software | The programs that enable the computer to process data quickly and efficiently; consists of many different types of programs. |
| Operating system software | The part of systems software that actually controls computer operations; consists of programs that monitor and supervise computer processing. |

such as UNIX, are applicable to all levels—microcomputers, minicomputers, midranges, mainframes, and even supercomputers. UNIX, in fact, is available not only for different sizes of computers but also for different "platforms," that is, computers developed by different manufacturers. Its use on DEC superminis, for example, as well as IBM mainframes and PCs, makes UNIX viable as a candidate for a general-purpose, standardized operating system or as the main operating system in a networked environment. Many people expect—or hope—it will become the standard operating system for all computers.

## ▶ How Operating Systems Maximize Processing Efficiency

One of the primary purposes of an operating system is to ensure that a computer's resources are used as efficiently and effectively as possible. In this section we discuss some of the ways this is accomplished.

### MULTIPROGRAMMING AND MULTITASKING

Most larger computer systems are capable of running many programs concurrently by means of a technique called multiprogramming. With multiprogramming, several application programs are placed in the computer's primary storage at the same time and the CPU, under control of the operating system, divides its time between these programs. See Figure 9.2. The operating system enables the CPU to execute one program for a brief period of time and to then switch to another, and so forth, until each program is completed. New programs are then loaded into available portions of main memory, and the multiprogramming process is repeated. All of these tasks are performed in such a way that users may not even know that other people are running programs at the same time.

On computer systems intended for interactive use, the operating system allows the CPU to juggle its time among various users and respond to requests quickly. In this way, numerous users have access to a CPU, all at the same time, and none of them is adversely affected by the fact that they are operating in a multiuser environment.

When a computer system performs multiprogramming operations, it must divide primary storage into separate areas. Each separate area in primary storage in which an application is placed is called a **partition.** An operating system with multiprogramming capability ensures that partitions are kept separate, so that one application will not interfere with the others that are being processed concurrently. Generally, such an operating system also assigns priorities to the various tasks submitted to the CPU, in order for important tasks to be executed before those of less urgency. For example, the requests of upper-level management are often assigned a higher priority than those of data entry personnel; similarly, large, routine accounting jobs may be assigned a lower priority than a simple query to a database that needs to be handled quickly.

Multiprogramming is accomplished through a series of **system inter-**

IN A

**SPECIFIC FUNCTIONS PERFORMED BY AN OPERATING SYSTEM**

- Works with ROM to boot the computer.
- Performs diagnostic tests to ensure that the components are functioning properly.
- Controls access to the computer.
- Provides an interface between the user and the computer.
- Manages data and controls transfers between secondary storage and main memory.
- Activates peripherals as needed.
- Makes utilities and other systems software available.

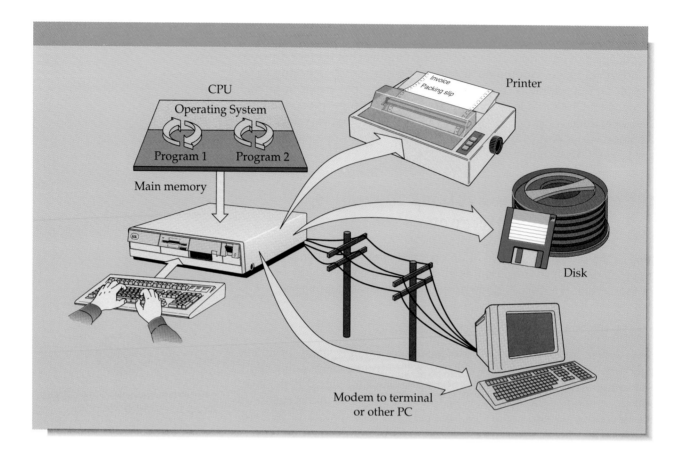

*Figure 9.2 An operating system with multiprogramming capability enables one or more users to communicate with one or more programs and one or more peripherals.*

**rupts** which cause execution of a program to be temporarily suspended when resources and devices are being used by other programs. Although it may look as if programs are executed continuously from start to finish, in fact, the operating system constantly interrupts these programs to effectively use existing resources.

Once confined exclusively to mainframes, multiprogramming is becoming increasingly common on smaller computers. Originally, the ability of larger computers to perform multiprogramming was the one characteristic that separated them from micros. As the speed and capacity of micros increase, however, this distinction is beginning to fade.

Multitasking is really a variation of multiprogramming that was implemented first on high-end microcomputers and now is widely available on most computers. Multitasking allows *one user* to access *several programs* at the same time. You can tell the computer to print a word processing file, sort a database, and recalculate data in a spreadsheet; all operations will be performed concurrently if the operating system allows multitasking. Figure 9.3 illustrates how multiprogramming and multitasking are achieved.

In summary, multitasking permits a single user to perform many tasks all at one time. Multiprogramming, however, is usually applied to situations in which several users want to access different programs and data—or even the same programs and data—at the same time.

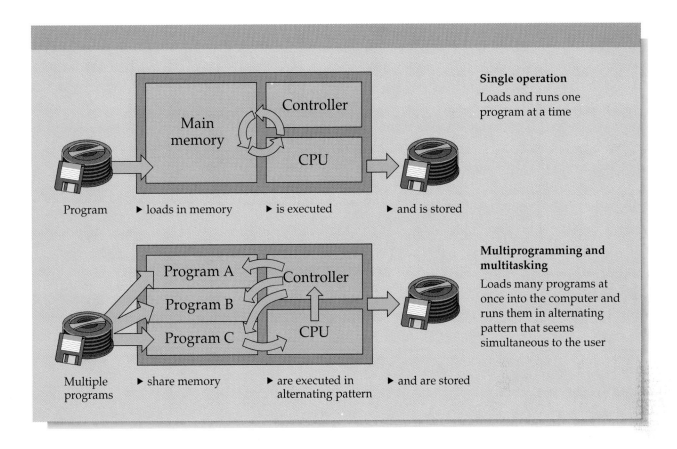

**Single operation**

Loads and runs one
program at a time

Program ▸ loads in memory ▸ is executed ▸ and is stored

**Multiprogramming and
multitasking**

Loads many programs at
once into the computer and
runs them in alternating
pattern that seems
simultaneous to the user

Multiple ▸ share memory ▸ are executed in ▸ and are stored
programs                         alternating pattern

## MULTIPROCESSING

**Multiprocessing** involves linking two or more CPUs to optimize the handling of data (Figure 9.4). While one CPU is executing one set of instructions, another CPU can be executing a different set. This technique differs from multiprogramming, which executes only one program at a time but switches quickly among the different programs currently in memory. In multiprocessing, the system can actually execute several programs simultaneously because parallel processors or multiple CPUs are being used.

## VIRTUAL MEMORY AND THE "VIRTUAL MACHINE" CONCEPT

**Virtual memory,** sometimes called **virtual storage,** enables the computer system to operate as if it has more main memory than it actually does. An application program is segmented into a series of modules (called pages) that are stored outside main memory on a high-speed, direct-access device such as a disk. When the CPU is ready to execute a specific page, the operating system moves that page from secondary storage into main memory and moves a page in main memory back to secondary storage. This process, which is referred to as **swapping,** is illustrated in Figure 9.5. Swapping enables very large programs to be executed in a relatively small area of main memory because the entire program is not loaded in at the same time. Virtual memory is common on larger sys-

*Figure 9.3 Multitasking, a variation of multiprogramming, allows a user to access several programs at the same time. Multitasking is for single-users; multiprogramming is performed in a multi-user environment.*

*Some operating systems permit several applications to be running at the same time. Each application appears in a separate window.*

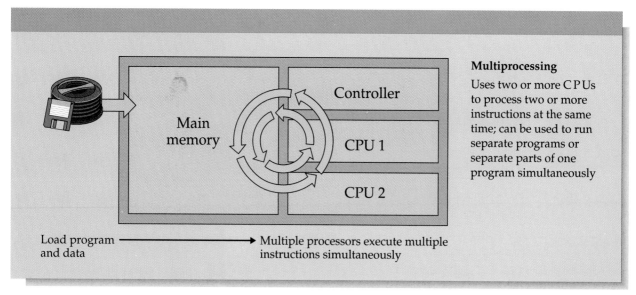

**Multiprocessing**

Uses two or more CPUs to process two or more instructions at the same time; can be used to run separate programs or separate parts of one program simultaneously

Load program and data → Multiple processors execute multiple instructions simultaneously

*Figure 9.4* Multiprocessing enables a computer to actually run two programs simultaneously—using two processors.

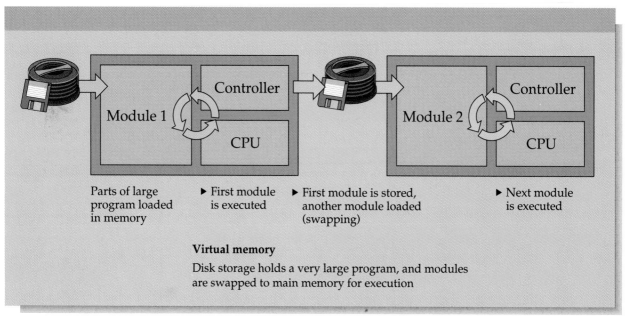

Module 1 Controller CPU

Module 2 Controller CPU

Parts of large program loaded in memory

▶ First module is executed

▶ First module is stored, another module loaded (swapping)

▶ Next module is executed

**Virtual memory**

Disk storage holds a very large program, and modules are swapped to main memory for execution

*Figure 9.5* In virtual memory, disk storage supplements the computer's main memory, and parts of a large program are swapped back and forth.

tems, and is becoming available on many microcomputer systems as well.

Virtual memory is distinct from *real memory*, which is actual RAM. Recall that cache memory is memory set aside for the most frequently used data. An operating system that supervises virtual memory as well as cache memory can significantly improve the overall efficiency of a computer.

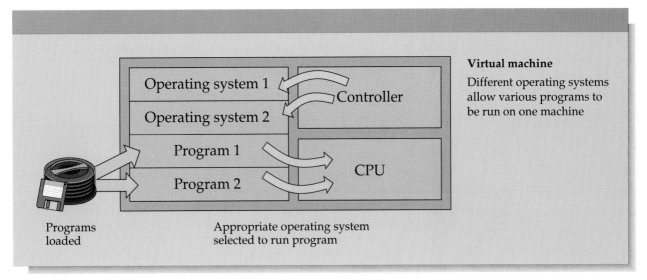

**Figure 9.6** *A virtual machine has a second operating system, so one computer can act like two.*

The concept of a **virtual machine (VM)** takes virtual memory one step further. The real machine, usually a mainframe, simulates a number of virtual machines, each capable of having its own operating system (Figure 9.6). So even though in reality there is only one computer system, it operates on data as if there were a number of separate systems. The CPU automatically chooses the appropriate operating system for each application program. It appears to an individual user as if an entire CPU and its peripherals are dedicated completely to his or her specific needs. Because the concept of virtual machines allows a computer system to execute several operating systems simultaneously, it provides a great deal of flexibility. For example, several application packages that each require a different operating system can be executed on the same hardware.

## ▶ Other Tasks Performed by Systems Software

### MEMORY MANAGEMENT

Systems software controls and manages the use of main memory. **Memory management,** a component of systems software, specifically refers to four tasks.

1. Allocating memory to programs.
2. Protecting memory so that one program does not have access to the storage space used by another.
3. Giving higher priority to some programs.
4. Making the most effective use of a computer's memory.

More advanced memory managers produce audit trails that track programs, the storage they use, the devices they access, and the time it takes them to run. Such information helps in scheduling, allocating, and monitoring computer resources.

## INTERFACING WITH TRANSLATORS

Translator programs are sometimes provided as part of systems software. Even if they are separate, the systems software controls how they access source programs, translate them, and prepare them for execution. Recall that the three types of translators are called assemblers, compilers, and interpreters; compilers are the most common.

Compilers and assemblers convert the entire *source program* written by an application programmer into an *object program,* which is the machine language equivalent of the source program. If there are no syntax errors, the program is ready to run. But the object program must be linked to the CPU; that is, it must be assigned designated primary storage space so that it can run. See Figure 9.7. Any special routines that the program needs must also be linked to it. Special functions such as square root computations or input-output error routines are typically linked to an object program by the systems software. The **linkage editor** is a systems software program that performs the necessary operations.

A program that uses an interpreter as a translator does not normally need a linkage editor, because the program is executed directly, one instruction at a time. The disadvantage of interpreting a program, however, is that the entire program cannot be stored in machine language

*Figure 9.7 A linkage editor places programs into a partition before execution. It links the programs to the CPU for execution.*

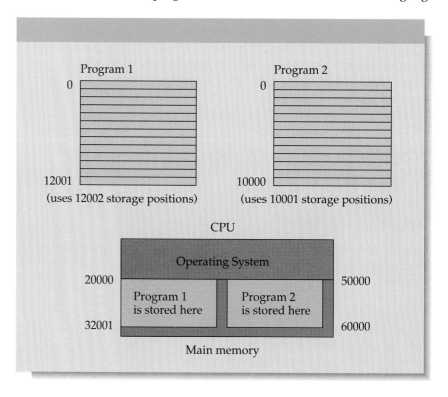

form and then linked as necessary; instead, the program must be translated again each time it is run.

## PERFORMING UTILITY FUNCTIONS

A utility is a systems software program that performs "housekeeping" tasks commonly required by many different types of application programs. Such tasks are the same regardless of the application area, so computer manufacturers often bundle utilities with systems software so that users do not need to write their own programs or buy additional software. In this section we discuss some tasks performed by utilities. Keep in mind that operating systems may perform some essential functions very well, but their utilities may be limited. If they are, you may need to purchase separate utilities.

**Sorting.**   In many applications, files must be sorted into sequence by key fields. Sometimes a payroll file, for example, may need to be in sequence by Social Security number; other times the sequence required may be by last name or department number. Often, multiple sorts are necessary: the file may need to be accessed by department number and within department by last name and then first name. In other words, all records need to be in alphabetic order within department. Sort utilities can perform single or multiple sorts on any fields specified. They can also sort into ascending sequence (from low to high) as well as descending sequence (from high to low).

**Spooling.**   One function of systems software is to establish a queue (a waiting line) for processing programs. Each program in a queue is executed according to a priority system established by the computing center. Output from application programs that have been queued is generally created on disk, because a disk can be accessed—read from or written to—very quickly in batch mode. The output data is transferred at high speed to printed form in an offline operation called **spooling.** Figure 9.8 shows how spooling is performed. Spooling, which increases the efficiency of the system, is usually controlled by systems software, but sometimes application software includes spooling techniques. Input, as well as output, can be spooled to increase efficiency.

In a single-user environment, the DOS PRINT command accomplishes spooling. It establishes a temporary print area called a **buffer** where a queue of files wait to print. The PRINT command feeds the printer a file at a time in background mode while other programs can be run. In a multiuser environment, spooling enables output from programs being executed at different terminals to be queued and printed in a sequence established by the operating system.

**Text Editing.**   Sometimes users must create special files that the systems software needs to interface with the computer. For example, you might need to instruct the operating system to establish buffer areas if you want output spooled. The buffer area would be created in a special systems file. A word processing package could be used to create such a file, but

*Figure 9.8 Spooling directs output to be printed to a disk or buffer area where the transfer of data can be completed very quickly; the actual printing then can be performed while the CPU is doing other things.*

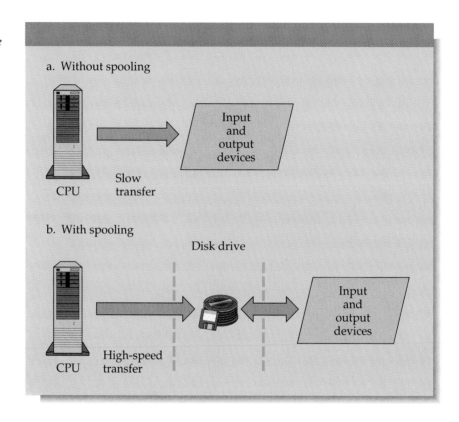

IN A

**NUT SHELL**

**PRINCIPAL FEATURES OF SYSTEMS SOFTWARE**

Systems software provides users with the most computer capability for their applications. It typically consists of:

- An operating system that interfaces with ROM to boot (start) the computer. The operating system controls the overall operations of the computer. It consists of a kernel, or supervisor, and a user interface, or operating environment.
- A memory manager to maximize the efficient use of primary storage.
- Program translators—compilers, assemblers, interpreters—and their user interfaces.
- Utility programs for sorting files, printing files in batch mode, text editing, and so on.

typically word processing packages include special formatting or control characters that are not understood by systems software. For that reason, systems software often comes with its own basic **text editor** for creating the simple files the operating system needs for controlling overall processing.

**Using Device Drivers.**   **Device drivers** are special utility programs that enable application programs to receive data from, and send data to, specific hardware devices. When you acquire a software package for your PC, you typically need to install it before you actually run it. Installation means, among other things, selecting the appropriate device drivers that will enable you to use the program. When you are installing a software package, you will be asked some hardware-specific questions such as the type of computer, monitor, disk drives, and printer that you are using. Each time you select a piece of hardware, a device driver is added to your systems software to enable the package to interact with it.

The process of adding device drivers for each software package you install is not very efficient. It would be much better if the systems software automatically selected the device drivers needed for all your applications programs. Newer versions of operating systems do just that.

**Performing Data Compression and Decompression.**   One way to save space on a disk is to code data so that it is in compressed form. Some operating systems automatically compress data when files are saved and decompress the data when the files need to be read again.

## EXECUTING BATCH FILES WHEN STARTING UP

Systems software enables you to establish a file that will always be executed immediately after the computer is turned on or after you log on. You may want this file to contain a set of program names that you always want executed before you do anything else. Many systems call this an AUTOEXEC.BAT file for "automatically executed batch file." This file can display any defaults or parameters you want to know about, such as date, time, number of current users, and amount of memory available. This start-up file can turn off default displays such as log-on messages, help menus, or listings of directories if you prefer not to see them each time. It can automatically execute some programs immediately, for example, a virus test program, a personal information manager, or a specific utility.

Since the systems software executes this batch file automatically, you can include commands in this file that will customize the user interface to best suit your needs. You can also use this file to load in any programs you want without having to key in commands each time you start a computing session. Batch files are typically created by the system's text editor or by a word processor that can create straight ASCII text.

## MAINTAINING SUBDIRECTORIES AND A FILE ALLOCATION TABLE

When you boot up or log on to a computer system, you are typically in the main directory, called the **root directory,** of the default drive. But if all program and data files were in this root directory, it would be difficult to find them or to maintain order, especially if the default drive is a hard drive or fixed disk with millions of storage positions. Files, then, are typically stored on disks in **subdirectories** where each subdirectory contains related files. A subdirectory is like a tab in an address book—it enables you to quickly locate items in a particular section. Address books have tabs that are alphabetic; similarly, computers have subdirectories that include files of a particular type. See Figure 9.9.

Figure 9.9 shows 11 subdirectories. PAINT, INFO3, and SAMPLER contain their own files, DBSAMPLE has its own two subdirectories, and so on. The PAINT subdirectory contains all PAINT program and data files, the 123 subdirectory contains all Lotus 1-2-3 files, and so forth. Without subdirectories, all files would be in the root directory and the command to list the directory would list *all* files. Some operating systems, graphical user interfaces, and utilities enable you to view the contents of files in subdirectories in a more useful and accessible manner. See Figure 9.10.

Systems software for all sizes of computers enables you to establish subdirectories and to use them effectively. It also sets up a **file allocation table** for disk drives that permits fast access of files within subdirectories. The file allocation table contains the disk address for each file and is searched, like an index, when you look for a file. When you erase or delete a file from a disk, the file is not actually erased—it is the *reference* to the file in the file allocation table that is eliminated so that it is no longer accessible. Since it is possible to accidentally erase or delete files, many operating systems, user interfaces, and utilities have an "unerase"

### LOOKING AHEAD

**NEW FEATURES FOR OPERATING SYSTEMS**

1. Printers differ widely in their capabilities. Typically, they need to be installed (or set up) for each program or package. Operating systems of the future will include features so that printers, as well as other devices, can be installed automatically.

2. The user interface will become standardized so that the way you access operating system commands will be the same for most systems.

3. The operating system will control the ways in which data and programs are exchanged among computers.

4. More utilities will be bundled with systems software. Virus detection and protection programs, programs that convert files from one format to another, and desktop organizers are just three of the many add-ons being supplied with newer operating systems.

***Figure 9.9*** *How subdirectories are displayed with DOS.*

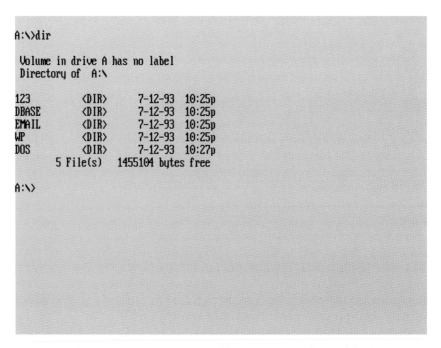

***Figure 9.10*** *A more user-friendly display of subdirectories.*

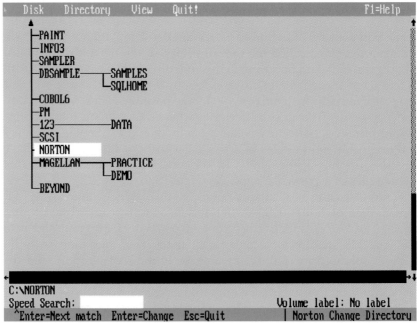

command that finds the original reference to the file in the file allocation table and restores it so that it is accessible again.

## ▶ SELF-TEST

1. What do we call the type of processing whereby multiple CPUs optimize the handling of data?

2. Name two types of memory controlled by an operating system that maximize the efficient use of computer resources.
3. What is the term used for producing output using a temporary print area called a buffer where a queue of files can be stored while they wait to print?
4. A program that can create and edit simple files is called a _____.
5. Why are subdirectories used?

Solutions
1. multiprocessing
2. virtual memory, cache memory
3. spooling
4. text editor
5. to place related files together in an area that is easily accessible

# MICROCOMPUTER OPERATING SYSTEMS AND GRAPHICAL USER INTERFACES

The microcomputer world is dominated by two families of operating systems: the DOS and OS/2 operating systems used with IBM microcomputers and their compatibles, and the Apple Macintosh operating system. The IBM-Apple alliance will produce a new operating system called the Pink operating system to be developed by Taligent, a joint venture of both IBM and Apple, which will combine the best features of both families.

What are some common operating systems for micros?

## ▶ DOS: PC-DOS and MS-DOS

The disk operating system IBM initially chose for its personal computer is known by the acronym PC-DOS (Personal Computer Disk Operating System). It was developed by Microsoft Corporation, which also offers a generic version called MS-DOS (Microsoft Disk Operating System) for IBM-compatible computers. We will refer to both of these operating systems simply as DOS.

DOS was introduced in 1981 when the first IBM PC was unveiled. To date, over 80 million copies have been sold and there are literally tens of thousands of applications written for DOS-based computers.

DOS tells the computer how to format, read, and write information on either floppy disks or hard disks. It manages peripheral devices such as the printer and the keyboard. It also controls the execution of software. In addition, it establishes several parameters, such as the number of files that can be contained in a disk directory, the number of bytes of memory that can be on a disk, and the number of bytes of memory usable by a program.

To boot an IBM or IBM-compatible microcomputer, you place DOS either in the A drive for dual diskette systems or in the C drive for hard disk systems. (Each disk drive of an IBM PC or compatible micro is assigned a letter.) DOS loads the COMMAND.COM file, which performs

## LOOKING BACK

**DOS VERSIONS**

*DOS 5.0 is a recent version of DOS.*

| Version | Date | Features |
|---|---|---|
| 1.0 | 1981 | The original version; provides date and time stamping for each file created, has a simple line editor and some utilities, and includes a BASIC translator |
| 2.0 | 1983 | Provides support for subdirectories and color and handles more functions |
| 3.0 | 1984 | Provides support for high density 5¼-inch disks and hard disks up to 32 MB; adds network support |
| 3.3 | 1987 | Provides support for IBM PS/2 computers |
| 4.0 | 1988 | Includes a menu-driven user interface shell; provides support for hard disks over 32 MB |
| 5.0 | 1990 | Provides Windows interface and better memory management; uses less RAM; permits easy upgrading from lower DOS versions |

diagnostic tests on hardware and prompts for date and time. You then see an A> or C> prompt, depending on which drive has the operating system software in it. For most versions of DOS, operating system commands are entered at what is called the command line—the line with the disk drive prompt. For example, to see the names of the files stored on the disk in drive A, type DIR at the A> prompt (A> DIR) and press the Enter key.

DOS has been updated many times to take advantage of technological improvements. Each new version of DOS is assigned a version number. The higher the number, the more sophisticated and more recent the version. For example, when DOS 2.0 was released, it was a major improvement over DOS 1.0. DOS 2.1, on the other hand, contained minor improvements over 2.0.

Through the 1980s, DOS was essentially a command-driven operating system that was not at all user-friendly. You needed to type precise commands such as COPY A:*.* B: to copy all files from the A drive to the B drive. Moreover, DOS was essentially a one-task-per-machine type of operating system—it did not lend itself to multiprogramming. Compared to Apple's Macintosh operating system, it seemed antiquated. See Figure 9.11.

DOS 5.0, however, brought users the most significant update in years. It was the first version of DOS to take significant advantage of the extended memory beyond 640 K, which is now available on 80286, 80386, and 80486 computers. Extended memory is controlled by disk caches; DOS 5.0 automatically recognizes caches so that there is no need for a formal installation procedure.

Despite its advances, DOS 5.0 is the first version of DOS that needs *less* RAM than its predecessors, actually about 5 K less. Unlike most of the older versions of DOS that required you to type specific commands, DOS 5.0, as well as DOS 4.0 before it, allows you to select commands from a menu if you prefer (see Figure 9.12). In this respect, DOS 4.0 and 5.0 are more user-friendly than their predecessors. DOS 5.0 is also the

**COMMON DOS COMMANDS (FOR ALL VERSIONS)**

| Command | Function |
|---------|----------|
| DATE | Allows current date to be set or changed |
| TIME | Allows current time to be set or changed |
| FORMAT | Initializes diskettes |
| VER | Displays the DOS version number |
| DIR | Displays any disk's directory |
| TYPE | Displays the contents of a file |
| COPY | Copies files |
| DISKCOPY | Formats a disk and copies all files from one disk to another |
| CHKDSK | Checks for disk's available space and specifies whether there are faulty files on the disk |
| RENAME or REN | Renames files |
| DEL or ERASE | Deletes files |
| MKDIR or MD | Creates new directory |
| CHDIR or CD | Changes the current directory |
| RMDIR or RD | Removes empty directories |

Appendix A provides a hands-on DOS tutorial.

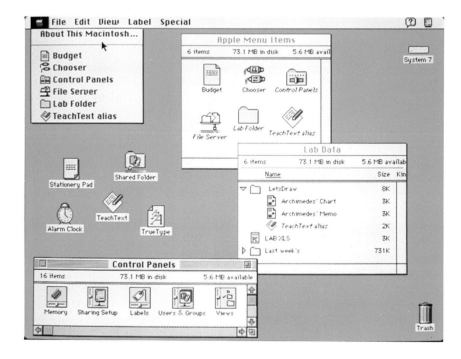

*Figure 9.11* The Macintosh operating system—with its user-friendly screen displays.

*Figure 9.12* *DOS 4.0 and 5.0 have a*
*user-friendly shell with features that*
*were unavailable in earlier versions,*
*such as pull-down command menus.*
*This illustrates the DOS 5.0 Help pull-*
*down menu.*

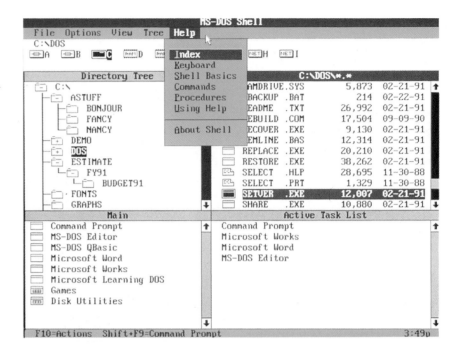

first version available separately through retail PC stores; previous versions were bundled with the computer.

A disadvantage of DOS 4.1 and lower versions was that if you had a hard disk and had to reinstall the operating system, you had to reformat the disk and reload all files—a time-consuming and tedious task. DOS 5.0 allows you to upgrade a previous version of DOS *without* having to reinstall it.

Additionally, DOS 5.0 has other advantages for users. It offers online help and enables applications to be launched by using a mouse. Newer versions will have these features as well. DOS 5.0 performs tasks that were previously available only with DOS add-on systems software packages like Norton Utilities. With previous versions of DOS, if you needed to find a file but didn't know what subdirectory it was in, you had to change to each subdirectory, then type DIR to see what was in the individual subdirectory. If you have many subdirectories, this is a tedious process. DOS 5.0 can search subdirectories for specific files with a single command. Also, UNDELETE, like Norton's UNERASE, can restore erased files.

DOS once had a very basic text editor called EDLIN, but it was difficult to use. In DOS 5.0, the "clunky" EDLIN was superseded by a new mouse-driven, full-screen text editor called EDIT with cut and paste capabilities, clip art, and pull-down menus. DOS 5.0 also provides an improved version of the BASIC programming language. PC-DOS 4.1 and lower versions included BASICA, and MS-DOS has GWBASIC (similar to BASICA). With DOS 5.0, you receive a version of Microsoft's QuickBASIC, called QBASIC, which has a much better interface, translator, and help menus. (*Getting Started with Structured BASIC* is a supplement to this text that includes coverage of QBASIC.)

## ▶ DOS with Windows

Throughout the years, a number of improved user interfaces have been created in an attempt to make DOS easier to use. These improvements include software features that are more graphic than text oriented. Graphical user interfaces use icons (i.e., symbols) to represent various objects. Two enhanced user interfaces that work in conjunction with DOS are Microsoft Windows and Desqview. In both of these interfaces, each application is opened in a window and several windows can be opened at once, allowing you to switch from one application to another. We focus here on Windows because it is so popular.

Windows is not an operating system per se but an operating environment or graphical user interface (GUI). That is, it operates under the control of DOS and it provides a kind of bridge between the user and DOS— a responsive and user-friendly bridge. Many people believe that Windows used in conjunction with DOS makes an IBM micro as user-friendly as a Macintosh.

Windows frees you to work as you would at your desk; you can, for example, spread out several "windowed" documents to reference and work on simultaneously. This feature enables you to perform some multitasking operations not previously available with older versions of DOS. The most recent versions of DOS and Windows enable programs to access more than 640 K of memory, which was once a limitation of IBM micros.

Windows has pull-down menus from which you select commands. To select a command, use the cursor keys to highlight it and press Enter, or use the mouse to point to it and then click on the entry. With Windows, then, there is no need to memorize operating system commands.

Because Windows for the IBM is not an actual operating system but an operating environment, DOS must be loaded in first when the computer is turned on. With the Mac, the Windows interface is actually part of the operating system so that no other program is required for starting up. There is, however, one advantage to the IBM version: Windows for the IBM is supplied with a number of desktop programs such as Write, a word processor, and Paint, a graphics tool. The Mac counterpart to these two products, MacWrite and MacDraw, must be purchased separately.

One primary objective of Windows is to permit the user to perform multitasking, that is, running more than one application concurrently. As noted, Windows also includes a number of desktop programs all of which can be opened and run concurrently. With multitasking, there is no need to leave or "close" one application in order to load or "open" a second application. The concept is analogous to a desk that has several elements (e.g., a calculator, calendar, phone book) available at the same time. It is not uncommon for a person who is preparing a budget to suddenly find the need to call someone to make an appointment before returning to the budget. With multitasking, the spreadsheet for the budget, along with a calculator, calendar, and phone book are available to the user at the same time.

The following 10 desktop programs are among those supplied with Windows.

1. CALC.EXE puts a calculator in a window for you to use.
2. CALENDAR.EXE, an appointment calendar, keeps track of appointments, "beeps" you if you have an appointment while you are online, and displays days of any year.
3. NOTEPAD.EXE provides notepads for writing brief notes to yourself.
4. CARDFILE.EXE establishes index cards that are automatically alphabetized. People use this feature as an address and phone book.
5. CLOCK.EXE displays the time in either analog or digital form depending on your preference.
6. SPOOLER.EXE permits you to do background printing at the same time that you are performing other tasks.
7. PAINT.EXE displays graphics.
8. WRITE.EXE is used for word processing.
9. CLIPBRD.EXE enables you to save a portion of any application so that it can be "pasted," or copied, to another application. A full spreadsheet or a portion of a spreadsheet, for example, can be stored in a clipboard and pasted to a document prepared by a word processor. The clipboard serves as a temporary holding area for transferring information from one application to another.
9. TERMINAL.EXE is a relatively simple communications program that enables uploading of data from a micro to a mainframe as well as downloading of data from a mainframe to a micro. Windows has an autodial feature that enables you to look up a phone number from a CARDFILE and automatically dial the number using TERMINAL.EXE if you have a modem.
10. CONTROL.EXE enables you to change settings on the clock, modem, and so on.

Any of these Windows programs can be run either alone or in conjunction with others. By selecting an icon, you can run the application represented by the symbol at any time. To select the icon, you point to it with a mouse and then click in. See Figure 9.13.

A wide variety of applications are designed specifically to run in conjunction with Windows. Microsoft Word, a word processing package; ToolBook, a hypermedia authoring tool; Aldus PageMaker, a desktop publishing package; and CorelDRAW, a graphics package, are all Windows applications, which means they were specifically designed to run under Windows. In addition, many software packages like Lotus 1-2-3 and WordPerfect have Windows versions. See Figure 9.14.

Applications that run under Windows have been developed to take advantage of Windows features and to work with other Windows applications in a multitasking environment. They are generally more graphical in their presentations and use of icons. Windows also provides a memory management system that interfaces more efficiently with applications.

Non-Windows applications can often be used in a Windows environ-

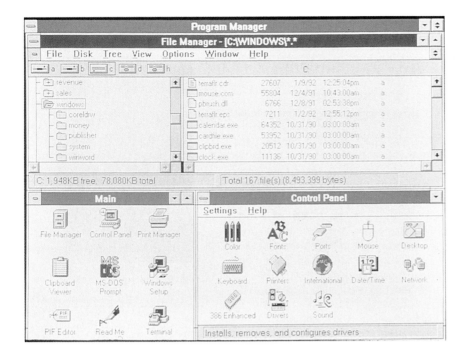

*Figure 9.13 Selecting icons from Windows.*

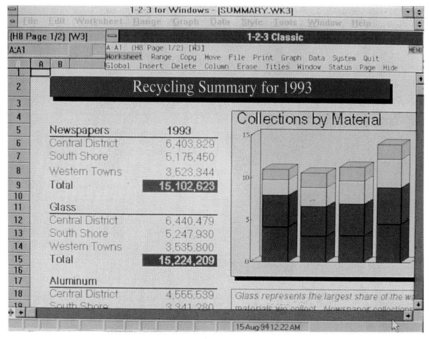

*Figure 9.14 Lotus 1-2-3, as well as other packages, have special Windows versions.*

ment, even though they were not specifically designed for that purpose, but sometimes they cannot be active along with another program. Users need to experiment to find out how well given applications work in the Windows environment if they are not specifically designed for it.

In addition to having multitasking capability, a user-friendly screen display, and a set of desktop applications, Windows permits users to size and position windowed applications to suit individual tastes and needs.

IN A

**WHY USE WINDOWS FOR IBM MICROS AND THEIR COMPATIBLES?**

- Instead of typing in cryptic commands, you can simply use a mouse to select icons that transmit messages to the computer.
- You can run more than one application at a time.
- You have at your disposal desktop applications such as a built-in calculator, clock, calendar, and so on which make your computer simulate a real desktop.
- You may need it to run many of your application packages.
- You can easily copy or move text and graphic data from one application to another.
- Many different type fonts are available with Windows.
- Your hard disk becomes an extension of main memory, enabling

you to effectively use more than 640 K of storage, even if your computer's primary storage capacity is only 640 K.
- You can display programs and data in windows that can be sized, moved to a different place on the screen, overlaid on top of other displays, or "tiled" next to one another. This provides visual features that text-based programs simply cannot match.
- You can easily group tasks and programs into logical categories and identify them with an icon for easy access.
- You can use your mouse not only to select objects, but also to drag them to different locations on the screen. For example, if you want a

*An innovative ad for a Windows product.*

wider column in a spreadsheet, you can drag it and size it any way you want.

Another advantage is its ability to move text or graphic data from one application to another easily and efficiently by means of its clipboard feature. Newer versions of Windows include pen and multimedia support along with many utilities and electronic mail facilities.

# ▶ OS/2

In 1987, as the computing world listened attentively, IBM announced a new line of personal computers, the PS/2 (Personal System/2) series, and its new operating system, OS/2, also developed by Microsoft. Although the initial release of OS/2 still had a text-based user interface, it was soon followed by a more graphic interface known as Presentation Manager.

OS/2 overcomes many of the limitations of DOS 4.1 and lower versions. For example, with OS/2, programs can use more than 640 K of RAM, which was the original size limitation for programs run under DOS. It also allows multitasking so that several application packages can be run at the same time. Each application runs in its own window; you can switch between windows and copy data back and forth.

Presentation Manager, in fact, is very much like Windows for DOS; that is, the original OS/2 plus Presentation Manager has many of the

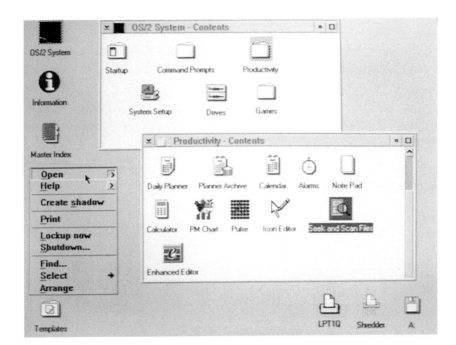

*Figure 9.15* OS/2 version 2 screen display.

features of DOS plus Windows, in addition to some extra capabilities. The newest version of OS/2 has a new interface called the Workplace Shell. IBM tends to promote the OS/2 environment, but Microsoft, the developer of DOS, Windows, and OS/2 promotes DOS with Windows. Some products (e.g., Aldus PageMaker) that were originally developed for Windows also have OS/2 versions. Currently, versions of OS/2 are marketed by both IBM and Microsoft. See Figure 9.15.

## ▶ Macintosh Operating System

Unlike the IBM PC family, the original Macintosh always provided a graphical, rather than a text-based, interface between the user and the system. The Mac operating system is also unlike the original DOS in that there never was a need to memorize a variety of commands; the Macintosh presents such commands in a menu. This approach proved to be so popular that the IBM world, first with Microsoft Windows and more recently with OS/2, adopted a similar look for its interfaces.

When you first turn on a Macintosh, you see a "desktop" with icons representing various files. See Figure 9.16. Related files can be placed in "folders," which are similar to subdirectories. Finder, which manages a single application and MultiFinder, which manages multiple applications, are the Mac's graphical user interfaces that allow you to open and manipulate the files on the desktop. Most often, the actions needed to perform a specific function are obvious. For example, if you want to delete a file, you use the mouse to place the file in the trash can. You select additional commands from pull-down menus, which are displayed when you select a main menu item.

### LOOKING AHEAD

**OS/2 VS DOS PLUS WINDOWS: THE BATTLE CONTINUES**

IBM is running a major campaign to promote OS/2 while Microsoft is promoting Windows. IBM, in fact, has taken over responsibility for further development of OS/2. For one thing, IBM significantly reduced the one-time license fee (under $200 for first-time users, under $100 for DOS and Windows users). To further heat up the battle, Microsoft is planning to develop further versions of OS/2 that may *not* be compatible with version 2.0, which IBM supports. Chances are both Windows and OS/2 will survive, further reducing the potential for the standardization that so many users seek.

*Figure 9.16 On a Macintosh, items are selected from menus. To select an entry, use the mouse to position the cursor on the menu item. Click in with the mouse button. Then release the button to execute the command.*

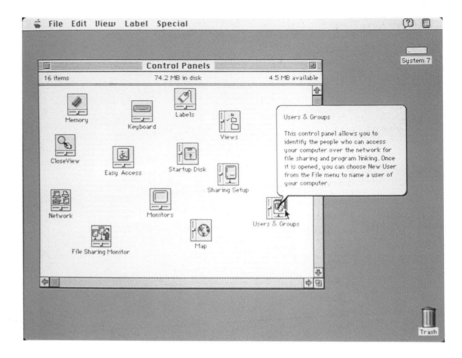

## LOOKING AHEAD

### THE IBM-APPLE ALLIANCE

Taligent, a joint IBM-Apple venture, plans to develop an object-oriented operating system that will employ reusable building blocks of program code. Taligent will develop objects, which include program modules that can be built into the Mac operating system, AIX which is UNIX for the IBM, OS/2, and the Pink operating system designed specifically for the new IBM-Apple power PC computers. So the objects will be compatible with a number of different computers.

The graphics capabilities of the Macintosh are very popular with publishers, designers, journalists, and educators. Its acceptance in business and industry, however, has been slow, largely because, until recently, Mac could not run DOS applications. In addition, the original Macintoshes, unlike PC-compatible micros, did not allow for easy expansion. Most DOS-based computers have expansion slots that allow you to customize the system to meet your specific needs; in contrast, adding more peripheral devices to the early Macintoshes was a difficult task. The newer Macintoshes, however, such as the Macintosh II, have expansion slots, and special circuit boards can be added to allow them to run DOS software.

The Mac's newest operating system, version 7, requires 2 MB RAM—the operating system uses over 1 MB of RAM all by itself. And most, but not all, of Mac's software will run on it. This version is specifically designed for facilitating multitasking. MultiFinder, which was once optional, is an integral part of System 7. Version 7 includes these additional features.

- The trash can no longer empties when you start up an application or shut down the system. For safety's sake, you must empty it deliberately.
- You can now navigate around in a window using the keyboard as well as the mouse.
- A "Balloon Help" system is available whereby you select an icon on the menu bar at the top of the screen. When Balloon Help is on, balloons appear that explain everything your cursor touches. This help feature is very useful for novices but can be quite distracting for experienced users who are likely to keep it turned off most of the time.

# ▶ Pen-Based Operating Systems

As we saw in Chapter 5, pen-based computers are becoming popular for collecting data at customer sites or in the field and for taking notes at business meetings. Pen-based computers have their own operating systems; we discuss the two most important ones next.

## PENPOINT: THE GO OPERATING SYSTEM

With traditional mouse or keyboard interfaces, invoking a command is a two-step process: getting to the right place with the mouse (or cursor keys) and then clicking in or keying the command. If you are using a GO computer with a PenPoint operating system, you just handwrite the command in the appropriate place. The following commands are available: ? for help; ^ for insert; and X for delete.

Whereas other graphical user interfaces depict a "desktop" as the primary metaphor for a computer, GO shows a "notebook." The notebook screen is subdivided into pages, each of which roughly corresponds to a disk file. The initial page is the table of contents; you can create tabs or page numbers for each item in the contents. Then you use a "pen tap" to get to specific pages; that is, you actually tap the pen on the page number desired. See Figure 9.17.

IBM and NCR, as well as GO, have hardware compatible with the PenPoint operating system. Moreover, WordPerfect Corporation and Borland International make software that can be run with the PenPoint system.

## WINDOWS FOR PEN COMPUTING: THE MICROSOFT PEN-BASED OPERATING SYSTEM

Microsoft manufactures Windows for Pen Computing as a pen interface for computers that use their Windows product. While PenPoint requires the user to know Windows first, Windows for Pen Computing was developed to be used by anyone, even a novice. Both PenPoint and Windows for Pen Computing can interface with DOS and both require 4 MB of RAM and an 80386 processor or higher. GRiD Corporation manufactures pen-based notebook computers that can use either operating system.

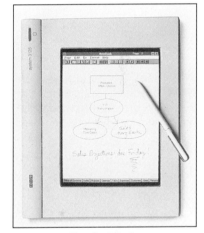

**Figure 9.17** *Pen for Windows screen display.*

## ▶ SELF-TEST

1. Name and describe the two versions of DOS for IBM computers and their compatibles.
2. What is the most popular graphical user interface used with DOS?
3. Name another IBM operating system that has its own graphical use interface.
4. What micro has always had a graphical user interface that makes it seem very user-friendly?

5. (T or F) Windows helps IBM micros perform multitasking more effectively.
6. Name two pen-based operating systems.

Solutions
1. PC-DOS is for IBM micros and MS-DOS is for IBM compatibles.
2. Windows
3. OS/2
4. Macintosh
5. T
6. PenPoint, Windows for Pen Computing

# 9.3 OPERATING SYSTEMS THAT FACILITATE CONNECTIVITY

## ▶ UNIX — An Operating System for All Categories of Computers

What does the portability of the UNIX operating system and the availability of network operating systems mean for the computing field?

UNIX was developed by AT&T's Bell Laboratories in 1969 for use on minicomputers and is a registered trademark of AT&T. Its development is interesting because, unlike the other operating systems discussed in this chapter, UNIX was designed by a small group of programmers as a simple operating system with a limited set of instructions. Originally, it was used primarily in research and development by experienced programmers.

UNIX has two advantages. Unlike most operating systems, it is available on many different types and sizes of computers. Its portability stems from the fact that it was written in the programming language C rather than in an assembly language. In addition, UNIX was one of the first operating systems designed to provide smaller computers with multiprogramming capability.

As more sophisticated microcomputers are developed to support multitasking and multiuser environments, UNIX is becoming the operating system of choice. Microsoft has a version of UNIX called XENIX for microcomputers, IBM supports a version called AIX for its computers, and Apple's version is called A/UX. There are UNIX operating systems for the NeXT, Sun RISC workstations, and other computers as well. Because of the variety of implementations and its popularity among programmers (many of whom were trained to use it on university computer systems), UNIX is now widely available in business and industry and is expected to gain even more popularity in the years ahead.

The original goal of UNIX was to build an interactive programming environment that had features to help programmers develop software more efficiently. For example, UNIX provides a wide variety of utility programs called tools. The user interface is contained in a **shell,** or sep-

**Table 9.1** | COMMON UNIX COMMANDS

| UNIX Command | Description |
| --- | --- |
| pwd | Lists the current directory |
| ls | Lists files and subdirectories in current directory |
| cp | Copies files or directories |
| mv | Renames a file |
| mkdir | Creates a subdirectory |
| rmdir | Removes a subdirectory |
| tput clear | Clears the display screen |
| lp | Queues and prints data files |
| cat | Displays contents of a text file |

arate software module, and is not part of the operating system itself. There are a number of commonly used UNIX shells.

A major complaint about UNIX is that it is not particularly user-friendly. Its commands are often cryptic and difficult to remember (see Table 9.1). However, many computer manufacturers are now supplying user-friendly shells to make these systems easier to use. Another major complaint is that there are many versions of UNIX, all slightly different.

Because the UNIX operating system is available on a broad spectrum of computers, it is becoming widely used in networks where many different types of systems are linked to one another.

## ▶ Network Operating Systems

Special network operating systems like Novell NetWare for IBM and Mac computers and AppleShare for Mac networks not only perform standard operating system tasks but also monitor shared resources so that effective utilization of all hardware and software is achieved.

Table 9.2 reviews the various types of operating systems software for microcomputers.

## ▶ SELF-TEST

1. Why is UNIX such a popular operating system?
2. What are some disadvantages of UNIX?
3. What does IBM call its version of UNIX for IBM micros?
4. What type of operating system is Novell NetWare?

Solutions
1. UNIX can be used on a variety of computers; that is, it is portable.
2. It is command driven and not particularly user-friendly; there are different versions that are not compatible.
3. AIX
4. It is a network operating system designed to enable resources to be effectively shared among different computers.

---

**CRITICAL THINKING**

Suppose your organization had a number of IBM or IBM-compatible PCs and you were asked to standardize with a single operating system. What questions would you ask users before making your decision?

**Table 9.2** | A REVIEW OF OPERATING SYSTEMS SOFTWARE FOR MICROCOMPUTERS

| System | Features |
|---|---|
| Macintosh | The first operating system to have a user-friendly interface, called the Finder, which allows the user to select commands from pull-down menus. Objects such as files are represented by icons. A multitasking version called MultiFinder is now available. |

*Systems for IBM Micros and Compatibles*

| System | Features |
|---|---|
| DOS 1.0–4.1 | First operating system for IBM and IBM-compatible PCs and PS/2s. It is command driven; that is, commands are entered without benefit of menus or prompts. It also has strict memory limits. DOS 4.0, 4.1 and higher include an optional command menu shell, mouse support, direct support of expanded memory, and support for hard disks larger than 32 MB. |
| DOS 5.0+ | An operating system with multitasking capability, memory management beyond 640 K, and some extra disk-handling features. It provides for easy upgrade from previous versions of DOS. |
| Microsoft Windows: A Graphical User Interface for DOS | Allows several programs to be open at a time, each in its own window. Windows 3.0, 3.1, and higher have a true multitasking environment and eliminate the 640 K RAM limitation imposed by DOS 4.1 and lower versions. |
| OS/2 | IBM's operating system introduced with the PS/2 family or micros. PS/2s can use DOS with Windows, the original OS/2 with Presentation Manager, which is a graphical user interface similar to Microsoft Windows, or OS/2 version 2 with the Workplace Shell. |

*The UNIX Alternative*

| System | Features |
|---|---|
| UNIX for PCs | IBM's AIX and Apple's A/UX are UNIX operating systems for PCs. Uses standard commands and is available on a wide variety of computers of all sizes. IBM's AIX is also the standard operating system for IBM's midrange AS/400. |
| Network operating system | Novell NetWare and AppleShare are operating systems designed to more effectively share resources in a networked environment. |

# COMMON MAINFRAME OPERATING SYSTEMS AND THEIR INTERFACES

## 9.4

Because mainframes run large programs and are used for time-sharing applications, their operating systems commonly have a variety of capabilities. Multiprogramming, multiprocessing, and virtual memory allow them to operate at peak efficiency. In this section, we will discuss the operating systems originally created for IBM's S/360 and S/370 families of mainframes and now used on many types of computers. Although we use IBM examples, these capabilities are typical of all mainframes and minicomputers, including popular models from Digital Equipment Corporation and Unisys.

IBM has always designed computers with the business customer in mind. Therefore, when it developed the S/360 family of computers in the mid-1960s, the idea was to make them upwardly compatible. In essence, this means that if an organization buys a small mainframe and then expands to the point where a larger system is needed, the application software and operating system that ran on the old machine will also work on a new one in the same family. The organization saves the time and money that would otherwise be needed to convert or modify the software. If a user has an ES/9000 model 820 and decides to trade it in for an ES/9000 model 900, all peripheral devices as well as software can still be used. It is important to realize, however, that these computers are not necessarily downwardly compatible. If a larger model in a family of computers is traded in for a smaller model, software may need to be modified.

All machines in the S/360 family had the same type of computer architecture; that is, they shared CPU design features so that data is processed in the same way on all systems. In the 1970s, this architecture was carried into IBM's new line, the S/370 family. Today, there are many computers that use this architecture and can run the same operating systems.

Typically, the command language required for interfacing with mainframe operating systems is not very user-friendly. Job control language (JCL), as it is called on many computers, includes a relatively complex set of commands. When the IBM and IBM-compatible PCs were first unveiled, they were criticized because the command language for the DOS operating system was too much like JCL and not enough like the Apple methodology.

We discuss now some of the more common mainframe operating systems and their interfaces.

What are some common mainframe operating systems?

## ▶ MVS

Multiple virtual storage (MVS) is the high-end operating system for IBM's batch-oriented mainframe systems. MVS provides for a maximum of 16 processors for multiprocessing. It carefully manages the use of virtual storage to create the illusion that primary storage is considerably larger than it actually is, and it can process many large applications efficiently and simultaneously in a multiuser environment.

## ▶ VM

As previously discussed, a virtual machine (VM) operating system is designed to provide each user with a complete, simulated machine devoted solely to his or her needs. Each simulated machine can run a different operating system.

## ▶ TSO

TSO stands for Time Sharing Option. It is an operating system that, as the name implies, permits numerous users to share time on a computer.

## ▶ CICS and CMS: Communications Monitors

**CICS** is an abbreviation for IBM's Customer Information Control System. It is a general-purpose supervisor and data communications monitor that also provides database management capabilities. CMS, Conversational Monitoring System, is another IBM innovation that has become popular in recent years. CICS and CMS can be interfaced with an IBM operating system and application programs written in any one of a number of programming languages, including COBOL and assembler. Thus, strictly speaking, they are not full operating systems per se.

CICS and CMS can be configured for each specific installation. They enable resources to be distributed to each workstation or terminal as needed. Some of the features provided by CICS and CMS include

- Task management: handles priority scheduling, transaction monitoring, and synchronization.
- Program management: provides multiprogramming capability.
- Terminal management: handles formatting of data, interfacing with the system, queuing, and so on.
- File and data management: enables authorized users to update files, other users to query files, and so on.

## ▶ SELF-TEST

1. What is upward compatibility?
2. Are computers generally downwardly compatible?
3. (T or F) IBM's job control language includes a relatively complex set of commands.
4. (T or F) CICS can be interfaced with an IBM operating system to monitor data communications and provide database management support.

### Solutions

1. When a computer in a series is expanded or upgraded, all software and hardware used with the previous CPU will be compatible with the new CPU.
2. No
3. T

4. T

# ▶ **C**hapter **S**ummary

Software drives hardware. In this chapter we focus on systems software that controls the overall operations of the computer and ensures that application programs are executed properly.

## 9.1 SYSTEMS SOFTWARE: FUNCTIONS AND FEATURES

**Systems software** includes the operating system and acts as an interface between users and hardware. The operating system, which is the main component of systems software, has a **kernel,** or **supervisor,** which monitors resources; it also oversees the running of user programs. The **user interface** is the part of systems software that permits you to communicate with the hardware in an operating environment.

What functions do operating systems perform and how are they accessed by users?

Systems software is written by **systems programmers** who are software developers capable of writing efficient code for computers with a specific architecture. Systems software can be purchased separately, but it is usually **bundled,** that is, supplied with the hardware by the manufacturer or vendor.

Systems software uses several features to maximize computer efficiency. It controls multiprogramming, which **partitions** a computer's primary storage into separate areas so that several programs can be entered and run simultaneously. By means of a series of **system interrupts,** execution of some programs can be temporarily suspended so that others can use the resources and devices of the computer.

Systems software controls multitasking, which enables several applications to be active at the same time. Systems software also controls **multiprocessing** whereby two or more CPUs are linked so that different instructions can be run simultaneously.

Some systems software uses **virtual memory,** also called **virtual storage,** techniques that enable a computer to operate as if it had more primary storage than it actually does. With virtual memory, an application program is segmented into a series of pages; **swapping** techniques move the pages from secondary storage into main memory and back again. The **virtual machine** concept enables one real machine to operate as if it had a number of virtual machines each capable of having its own operating system.

Other principal tasks performed by systems software include **memory management,** which allocates and controls the effective use of a computer's memory; interfacing with translators; and performing utility functions. **Spooling** is a utility function that enables data you want printed to be stored in a temporary print area called a **buffer.** The buffer establishes a queue of files to be printed and prints them while other processing is being performed. Text editing is another utility function whereby a **text editor** creates simple files. Two other tasks performed by systems software are executing batch files when a computer is turned on and maintaining a **root directory,** which is a main directory, and **subdirectories** for organizing files and a **file allocation table** for quickly accessing files on a disk. Systems software also enables you to use **device drivers,** which are special utilities needed for interfacing with certain types of hardware such as a sound board or CD-ROM drive. Systems software also has a **linkage editor** that enables the computer to store a program and any external modules needed in main memory so that it can be executed.

## 9.2 MICROCOMPUTER OPERATING SYSTEMS AND GRAPHICAL USER INTERFACES

*What are some common operating systems for micros?*

IBM micros use the PC-DOS operating system and IBM-compatibles use the MS-DOS operating system. Windows is a graphical user interface that can be used with these DOS operating systems to provide a more user-friendly environment, to effectively manage a computer's resources, and to run programs that actually require the Windows environment. IBM's OS/2 with its Presentation Manager graphical user interface is an alternative to DOS with Windows.

The Macintosh, which has an operating system with a graphical user interface built in, popularized the concept of user-friendly interfaces. Pen-based systems have their own operating systems such as PenPoint by GO and Windows for Pen Computing by Microsoft.

## 9.3 OPERATING SYSTEMS THAT FACILITATE CONNECTIVITY

*What does the portability of the UNIX operating system and the availability of network operating systems mean for the computing field?*

UNIX is an operating system that can be used on a wide variety of computers. Its user interface called a **shell** is separate from the operating system and is nonstandard. UNIX is expected to grow in popularity.

Network operating systems like Novell NetWare and AppleShare are also widely used where different types of computers share resources.

## 9.4 COMMON MAINFRAME OPERATING SYSTEMS AND THEIR INTERFACES

*What are some common mainframe operating systems?*

Mainframe operating systems have a variety of capabilities. Some of the common systems are multiple virtual storage (MVS), VM for virtual machine, and TSO for Time Sharing Option. **CICS,** Customer Information Control System, is a popular interface as is CMS (Conversational Monitoring System).

## ▶ Chapter Self-test

1. (T or F) To carry out multiprocessing, a computer system must have two or more CPUs.
2. With virtual memory, a technique called _____ is used to move program modules from secondary storage to main memory as they are needed.
3. (T or F) The UNIX operating system was originally designed to be used on mainframes.
4. Both Windows and the user interface for the Macintosh use _____, which are symbols representing various objects or functions.
5. (T or F) Windows is a complete operating system for IBM and IBM-compatible PCs.
6. What is the graphical user interface for the Mac called?

7. (T or F) Some applications can only be run in a Windows environment.
8. (T or F) UNIX is an operating system that can run on a wide variety of computers.
9. The _____ is the part of the operating system that allocates computer resources.
10. _____ permits more than one program to be active in a CPU at the same time.
11. The version of DOS used on IBM-compatible micros is called _____.
12. (T or F) With virtual machines, more than one operating system can be used at the same time.

Solutions

1. T
2. swapping
3. F
4. icons
5. F
6. Finder or MultiFinder

7. T
8. T
9. kernel
10. Multitasking
11. MS-DOS
12. T

## ▶ Key Terms

Buffer, *p. 353*
Bundled, *p. 346*
CICS (Customer Information Control System), *p. 372*
Device driver, *p. 354*
File allocation table, *p. 355*
Kernel, *p. 345*
Linkage editor, *p. 352*

Memory management, *p. 351*
Multiprocessing, *p. 349*
Partition, *p. 347*
Root directory, *p. 355*
Shell, *p. 368*
Spooling, *p. 353*
Subdirectory, *p. 355*
Supervisor, *p. 345*

Swapping, *p. 349*
System interrupt, *p. 347*
Systems programmer, *p. 345*
Text editor, *p. 354*
User interface, *p. 345*
Virtual machine (VM), *p. 351*
Virtual memory, *p. 349*
Virtual storage, *p. 349*

## ▶ Review Questions

1. Explain the differences between multiprocessing, multiprogramming, and multitasking.
2. Explain the differences between virtual memory and cache memory.
3. What is a memory manager?
4. What is a linkage editor?
5. What features does Windows add to a DOS operating environment?
6. Under what conditions would you change the standard operating system for your PC from DOS to UNIX?

## PRODUCT ANALYSIS

## CASE

### Is Now the Right Time for QuickTime?

Apple Computer Inc. has gone a long way toward ushering in the multimedia age by providing sound, animation, and video capabilities for the Apple Macintosh with QuickTime, its operating-system-enhancement software. Mac owners with a 68020 or higher microprocessor can import video clips and edit, create, and view "movie" files using the QuickTime operating system extension and about $1000 worth of additional hardware.

Apple is hoping to make QuickTime a multimedia standard that can be used by other operating systems as well. This is likely to spur the already revolutionary growth in multimedia products. Microsoft is currently developing a version of its Windows graphical user interface that will have QuickTime capabilities.

QuickTime enables users to create low-cost, portable, digital video for multimedia applications, but, so far, the image quality does not meet TV broadcast standards. Because it is software-based, QuickTime's video-compression scheme permits you to play back digitized video, stored as QuickTime movies, at about 15 frames per second, compared with 30 frames per second for full-motion, real-time video. QuickTime applications use a great deal of memory. So the price of computers that can run these applications—with all the requisite hardware like a CD-ROM drive (to store videos) and a video disk player—is still quite high.

Software developers have begun to offer products compatible with QuickTime. Gold Disk Inc., for example, has its Surpass presentation package which, for under $400, lets users integrate sound, animation, and QuickTime "movie" files into business presentations. Users can prepare dynamic documents with sound effects and video capabilities by means of QuickTime-compatible word processing packages. Many developers are also supporting IBM's Ultimedia standard along with QuickTime.

Although Oscar-quality videos are not expected

*A video disk player often used for multimedia applications in a QuickTime environment.*

in the near future, the ability of a real estate firm to store a video of a house for sale, or of an e-mail package to transmit video, is eagerly awaited.

### Analysis

1. QuickTime is a revolutionary product. Based on other developments in the computing field, do you think it will become an immediate standard or are competing products likely to be developed?

2. If you were thinking about purchasing QuickTime for multimedia applications, what questions would you have regarding its capabilities? How would you go about comparing QuickTime with IBM's Ultimedia standard?

3. Suppose you have an IBM microcomputer and you are interested in multimedia applications. Would you look for ways to enhance your computer or would you purchase a separate Mac or IBM for that purpose? Explain your answer.

# SYSTEMS ANALYSIS AND DESIGN:
# A CASE STUDY APPROACH

**C**omputerized business systems called information systems integrate hardware, software, people, and the concept of connectivity so that information produced is accurate, timely, and meaningful. Design of these systems is usually supervised by systems analysts who work closely with users and other computer professionals to produce an effective set of procedures. In this chapter we consider how systems analysts analyze current procedures and then design more efficient ones by answering the following questions:

▶ What skills must systems analysts bring to their study of the systems development life cycle and to the analysis, design, and implementation of new information systems?

▶ Beginning with the problem definition, what analytical tools do systems analysts use to create new information systems?

▶ What part do systems design tools play in the building of effective information systems?

▶ How are new information systems approved and implemented?

## 10.1    THE ROLE OF THE SYSTEMS ANALYST

Every business consists of a series of interrelated functional areas that accomplish an organization's goals. No matter how large or small a business is—whether it is a yacht-building firm or a mom-and-pop grocery store—it consists of functional areas that are organized to achieve business objectives. A yacht builder, for example, might need these four functional areas:

1. Purchasing to order building materials.
2. Production to build the yachts.
3. Marketing to sell the yachts once they are built.
4. Finance and accounting to manage cash flow.

Each of these functional areas consists of a set of procedures, or methods, that employees use to complete their tasks or achieve their goals. For example, employees in the purchasing department might have systems for checking the quality of materials, negotiating with vendors, and ordering supplies.

The procedures used to check products in and out of inventory in a warehouse (Figure 10.1) and provide daily summary reports also constitute a business system.

## ▶ **M**aking **B**usiness **S**ystems **M**ore **E**fficient

Managers plan, organize, and control business systems on the assumption that if each system's functional area works efficiently, the entire organization will run smoothly. To keep organizations running efficiently, managers hire systems analysts to examine their procedures and systems and to recommend how to make them more efficient.

Systems analysts design **information systems** that use computers to improve the efficiency of existing business systems. An information system (IS) is a combination of the computer hardware, software, and networked facilities people need to perform business functions. This chapter focuses on traditional information systems, which are computerized business systems for functional areas. In the next chapter, we focus on management information systems, which are designed to provide output to managers on a company-wide basis—across functional areas.

Analysts examine business systems for two reasons: to improve a current system or to create an entirely new one. Management may be dissatisfied with an existing system, computerized or manual, and may call on analysts to make it more efficient. Dissatisfaction with an existing system often results from high costs, high error rates, output that is not delivered on a timely basis, a need to be more competitive (e.g., to provide online services to customers), and lack of security.

When managers discover that computers can perform a task that was previously impractical to perform manually, or was too complex to do efficiently, they may ask analysts to design a new information system. For example, marketing managers who discover that computers can perform complex statistical analyses on customer demographic data may ask analysts to build a marketing information system to help them forecast future sales.

Any new system should effectively solve existing company problems and "cater" to the user, that is, produce complete and concise, accurate,

What skills must systems analysts bring to their study of the systems development life cycle and to the analysis, design, and implementation of new information systems?

**Figure 10.1** *Automated inventory procedure makes information processing more efficient.*

IN A

**NUT SHELL**

Information should CATER to its users by being:

- **C**omplete
- **A**ccurate
- **T**imely
- **E**conomically sound
- **R**elevant

*t*imely, *e*conomically sound, and *r*elevant output.[1] A new information system may also result in many nontangible benefits:

- Faster response time in answering inquiries from customers, which leads to more efficiency and better public relations.
- Greater employee satisfaction resulting in lower turnover of staff.
- More accurate delivery promises to customers.
- Better availability of stock and fewer out-of-stock situations.
- Improved quality of products and services.
- More efficient use of resources and personnel.
- Better management control.
- Greater flexibility in dealing with a changing business environment.
- Improved ability to handle growth.

## ▶ In-House Analysts vs Outsourcing

Systems analysts are basically problem solvers. The solutions they design may or may not involve computers; that decision depends on the business needs of the organization they are evaluating. For example, analysts generally recommend that computers replace the routine and repetitive business systems that require speed and precision, such as those in payroll or accounts receivable. In some cases, however, they may determine that a procedure is best done primarily or entirely by people, for instance answering customers' questions. See Figure 10.2.

[1] Fitzgerald, Jerry, and Fitzgerald, Ardra. *Systems Analysis and Design,* 3rd ed. New York: Wiley, 1987.

*Figure 10.2 Systems analysts work closely with employees on all levels to assess the needs and potentials of an information system.*

Systems analysts may be employees of the organization or outside consultants. Analysts who are employees have a long-term relationship with their company that helps them understand the current operating environment and in turn helps them create a more successful system. Their in-depth knowledge of company procedures and their relationships with other employees may enable them to solve business problems more effectively than outside consultants.

When an organization uses outside services to satisfy some of its needs this is called *outsourcing*. Companies may hire analysts on a contract basis when they need specific expertise that is not available within the organization. For example, an airline manufacturing company that produces a significant amount of documentation might hire a systems analyst with desktop publishing expertise to help analyze its current documentation system and suggest more efficient ways to create maintenance and training manuals.

Because outside consultants have no ties to internal departments, or people that might bias their analysis, they are often able to see real or potential problems better than those deeply involved in the operating environment. If political controversies exist, outside consultants may be better able to remain objective enough to focus on the business system without being influenced by power struggles.

Whether analysts are employed by a company or hired as consultants, they possess similar skills and go about their job in similar ways. Their role is essentially advisory: they evaluate a business system and recommend to management how the system can be improved. The decision to proceed with a new system, however, rests with management.

## ▶ Job Requirements

To be effective in designing information systems, analysts must combine technical knowledge of how computer systems operate with an understanding of how business systems work. Analysts must also possess good communication skills because part of their job is to serve as liaison between software developers and users. Systems analysts are usually experienced computer professionals. Typically, they have an MBA, or an undergraduate business degree, and several years of business experience, often as application programmers.

## ▶ Interfacing with Key Users

Because many users today are computer proficient, their role in the systems analysis and design process has changed dramatically, particularly in PC-based computer environments. Managers often ask users who have a strong interest and technical expertise in computing to help develop information systems for their work areas. Called key users, these people are intimately familiar with business problems in their own functional area. They also have an understanding of how computers can best be used, so they act as on-the-spot problem solvers. Key users often need

### LOOKING AHEAD

**OUTSOURCING ON THE RISE**

An increasing number of businesses are outsourcing, that is, using outside consultants for the analysis, design, and implementation of their information processing needs. Their hope is that outsourcing will be cheaper and more efficient than maintaining an in-house staff. Design of an information system as well as implementation and regularly scheduled computer runs may all be performed by outside firms.

### LOOKING BACK

**"EFFICIENCY EXPERTS"**

In the 1950s, systems analysts were often called efficiency experts. Armed with their clipboards, *they* determined what systems needed revising—not management; sometimes those recommendations included eliminating a large number of jobs. Many efficiency experts were accused of callousness in regard to their recommendations. Today, management determines the systems to be revised, and analysts are more sensitive to the sometimes negative image associated with the term *efficiency expert*. As a result, changes in an organization are being made with less fear and resistance on the part of users.

to learn the techniques of systems analysis and design to assist them in solving business problems quickly.

Many users experience some anxiety when a new information system is put into place. Even if the new system is clearly for the better, users may fear that they will be held responsible for an existing system's flaws, lose their jobs in the transition, be forced to surrender their familiar routines and their status in the organization, or be unsuccessful in using the new system. For a new system to be successful, analysts and key users must be able to gain the confidence of the staff by convincing them that their cooperation is vital and that a new system will, in the end, make their jobs easier. Sometimes reassuring users that their positions are not in jeopardy is enough to gain their support. Simply asking employees to offer suggestions for improving a system also helps alleviate apprehension because their input actively involves them in the project's development. Users can also contribute valuable insights into the needs of the organization.

Throughout this chapter, we will build on the following case study to reinforce general concepts in a specific situation.

Margaret Cotham is an administrative assistant in the MBA office at Metropolitan Graduate School (MGS). Her supervisor asked her to design an information system for downloading student data files from the campus minicomputer to the department's three micros. Such a system could help the office track student progress through the MBA program, schedule future classes, and in general make it easier to compile student statistics. The chairperson of the MBA program decided that he did not have enough money to hire a systems analyst as a consultant, and because several microcomputer database and communications packages were advertised to be user-friendly, he asked Margaret, as a key user, to design the information system. Margaret thought computer systems were interesting and felt that the assignment was a good way to get a promotion, so she eagerly accepted the task. She quickly realized, however, that she was not sure about how to design a new information system. The first thing she needed to do was analyze the current set of procedures as objectively as possible. Before undertaking such an analysis, Margaret needed to understand the life cycle of business systems.

## ▶ Understanding the Systems Development Life Cycle

Whether entirely new information systems are created or existing ones are simply improved, each system passes through four basic stages known as the **systems development life cycle:**

1. Investigation and analysis.
2. Design and development.
3. Implementation.
4. Operation and maintenance.

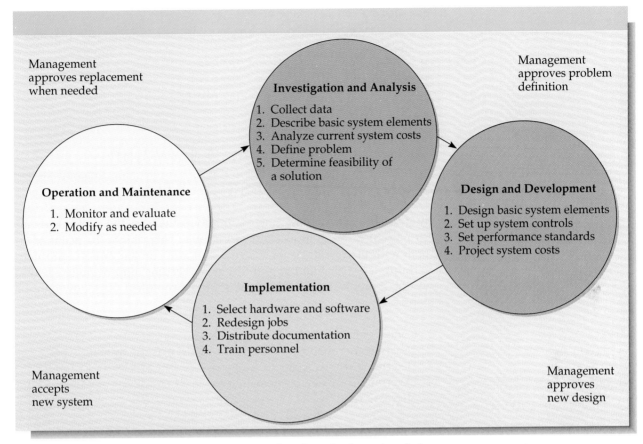

*Figure 10.3* The life cycle of a business system moves from investigation and analysis through design and development, implementation, and then operation and maintenance. Eventually, the business system needs to be replaced with a new system and the cycle is repeated.

The term *life cycle* is appropriate because, like living organisms, business systems are born (planned and analyzed), grow (are designed and implemented), mature (are operated and maintained), and eventually die or are replaced. During its lifetime, a system must constantly be modified and refined to ensure that it satisfies user needs even if business objectives change. The systems analyst is responsible for overseeing the four stages of the life cycle.

Figure 10.3 provides a detailed schematic of the steps involved in the systems development life cycle, which are discussed in the next section.

## ▶ SELF-TEST

1. Give several tangible reasons why analysts are asked by management to examine an existing business system.
2. A systems analyst could be an outside consultant or _____.
3. The term _____ means that a company uses outside services for its computer needs.
4. (T or F) Users should not be involved with the analysis or design of business systems because they are not objective.

Solutions
1. Current procedures are too costly, inaccurate, time consuming, and labor intensive.
2. an internal staff member
3. outsourcing
4. F

# INVESTIGATING AND ANALYZING EXISTING BUSINESS SYSTEMS

Beginning with the problem definition, what analytical tools do systems analysts use to create new information systems?

Analysts begin designing new or improved systems by first analyzing basic problem areas in existing procedures. Then they present management with the results of their analysis in a document called a **problem definition,** which highlights those areas needing improvement. Before writing a problem definition, analysts must complete the following four steps.

1. Collect data about the existing system.
2. Describe and analyze the elements of the existing system.
3. Determine current costs.
4. Determine if a new system is feasible. If so, devise possible design alternatives.

The problem definition must be approved by management before a new design is undertaken.

> In the MBA office, Margaret Cotham, the key user who is serving as a systems analyst, needs to write a problem definition that specifically describes the current business system, including costs and any flaws in the system. Her report should outline in broad terms if a new system is feasible and, if so, how she would redesign the old system to eliminate current problems. Because the purpose of the problem definition is to present alternatives rather than a fully defined solution, Margaret needs her boss's approval of the problem definition before she formally begins to design a new system.

## ▶ Collecting Data About the Existing System

Analysts begin the problem definition phase by gathering as much information as they can about existing procedures and basic problem areas (Figure 10.4). Generally, they use a combination of several methods for collecting data.

*Figure 10.4 Analysts must collect data about an existing system from the users themselves.*

## REVIEWING WRITTEN POLICIES, PROCEDURES, MEMOS, AND REPORTS

Analysts often begin by studying all written documents—organization charts, written procedures, and operations manuals—to determine how the business system was originally designed to function. By comparing documents and written procedures to what is actually practiced, problem areas become identifiable. The differences between written procedures and actual practice often help pinpoint the areas where analysts should focus attention. Analysts also sift through all policy statements, memos, and reports to ascertain how information is currently moving through the company.

*Analysts carefully review all written documents as a first step in understanding a system.*

At MGS, Margaret began by reading the following documents.

- The school's organization chart.
- The school catalog, which outlined degree requirements and formal registration processes.
- Lists of all classes taught in the MBA department.
- Office procedure manuals for tracking student progress.
- All student registration reports.
- All form letters the MBA staff sent to students.
- All MBA department reports regarding students.

Analysts review forms carefully but they recognize that the written records tend to focus on how things *should* be done not on how they *actually* are done. Because what she read was often out of date or did not match what she knew to be common procedures in the office, Margaret quickly realized that she could not depend solely on formal documentation to get a sense of current procedures. As a result, she began to observe employees as they worked to find out how procedures really were carried out.

## OBSERVING EMPLOYEES AT WORK

Analysts observe employee activities to objectively examine actual work procedures. They select the employees to be observed, set a time for the observation, and inform the employees that they will be observed.

Employees may be uncomfortable when they know they are being watched. To be effective, analysts need to be unobtrusive about their observations and convey the message that the quality of people's work is not being questioned. Analysts should do all they can to gain support by letting employees know that their cooperation will improve the new design effort and that one objective is to improve overall job satisfaction in the user department. During the observation, analysts learn the tasks actually performed and the sequence in which they are performed as well.

## SAMPLING

Sampling is another technique for obtaining data about large systems. Suppose you want to determine how often a computer room is left unlocked. You would not want to spend 24 hours a day, 7 days a week, determining what percentage of the time the room is left open. Instead, you select representative periods of the day over many days to make an estimate. Sampling enables analysts to make predictions in a fraction of the time that would be required for continuous observation.

After all observations and sampling are complete, analysts usually decide that they still need more specific information. The best method for gathering additional information is to interview key employees.

## INTERVIEWING EMPLOYEES

Analysts desire to gain the confidence of employees and encourage them to speak freely during an interview so that they can gather as much information as possible about the existing system. Of course analysts should already be familiar with the system before interviewing begins to avoid wasting time. During interviews, analysts ask questions such as these.

- What do you do in your job? What functions do you accomplish and which are the most important? How much time do you spend on each function?
- What do you do that could be delegated to someone at a lower level? To whom?
- What other tasks could you be doing if you were given the proper authority, responsibility, and resources? Would you want to do any of these tasks?

- What problems do you face in doing your work and what solutions can you suggest for these problems?

## PREPARING AND ANALYZING EMPLOYEE QUESTIONNAIRES

In some cases a large number of people are involved in the system under study, thereby making it difficult to talk to all key personnel. In other situations analysts suspect that employees might be reluctant to be honest in an open interview. To overcome these problems, analysts prepare a questionnaire either as an alternative to interviews or as a precursor to the interview process.

Written questionnaires can supplement information obtained from documents, observations, and interviews. By means of questionnaires, analysts can evaluate how superiors and subordinates communicate with each other, employee attitudes about current systems, and the overall usefulness of current systems. Questionnaires are also practical for gathering large amounts of statistical data. However, developing a questionnaire with the proper mix of questions to obtain quantitative and qualitative data can be difficult, and evaluating the results can be time consuming.

By examining documents, observing, sampling, interviewing, and evaluating questionnaires, analysts begin to determine how effectively current systems achieve business goals. In general, when you are gathering information, get to know your subjects as well as you can. Know which are more powerful within the organization, which are considered to have the most integrity, and so forth. Remember that the interview is likely to be the best method for gathering information.

## ▶ Describing the Elements of an Existing System

Often the best way to analyze a system is to break it down into its seven components.

1. Objectives.
2. Constraints.
3. Output.
4. Input.
5. Processing.
6. Controls.
7. Feedback—methods used to evaluate performance.

Figure 10.5 illustrates these components of a system and how they relate to one another. Analysts examine them to see how they work and to identify problem areas. Later, if a new system is designed, each of these components will be modified as the need arises.

*Figure 10.5 Breaking a business system down into its seven elements helps analysts examine the system's effectiveness and identify problems.*

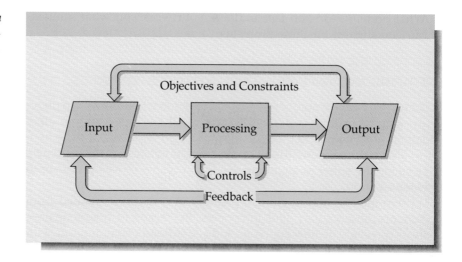

Once Margaret had gathered data, she was prepared to describe and analyze the current MBA office system in terms of its components.

## OBJECTIVES

A common objective in companies is reduced costs. Being able to say to managers "I can provide you with 95% of what you want for 50% of the current system's cost" is a very persuasive argument for effectively modifying existing systems and restating business objectives.

By the time analysts have finished collecting information, they generally have a good idea of the system's original objectives. Then they look at how the current system actually supports those objectives. They also consider appropriate new goals so that they can begin to create a new system design if it proves feasible to do so. For example, if a department store chain has as its goal improving customer service, an analyst may begin to think about designing an online accounts receivable system that enables customers to inquire about their balance while they are purchasing an item.

Margaret found that the MBA program's long-term objectives are to allow for a 25% increase in student enrollment and the hiring of four new professors during the next five years, to maintain a high quality of service, and to make registration procedures as easy for students and staff as possible. To analyze whether the current system meets the objectives, and to design a system that meets *new* objectives, Margaret next needs to look at the constraints, or limitations, placed on the existing system.

## CONSTRAINTS

Every system has its own unique constraints, which are the limitations placed on it. The most common are legal, budgetary, and equipment constraints.

**Legal.** Laws affect business operations at the local, state, and federal levels. Businesses need licenses, they must pay taxes and file tax reports, and in general, they must obey laws. Before undertaking an analysis of input, processing, and output, an analyst must understand the legal constraints that affect the company.

Legal constraints limit how much analysts can modify systems. For example, employers are required by law to withhold various federal, state, Social Security, and local taxes from payroll checks. Because federal and local governments dictate what the W-2 forms look like, how many copies there should be, and when they must be sent to employees, the part of the payroll process that produces these reports cannot be modified.

**Budgetary.** Managers commonly impose budgetary constraints on systems thereby limiting the time and money that can be spent on them. A manager may say, for example, that an accounts receivable system must be operational within one year, should not cost more than $100,000 to design, and must cost less than $25,000 a year to operate. Budgetary constraints clearly have a major impact on a system's design; sometimes analysts find that the existing system is deficient partly because the original budgetary constraints were too restrictive.

**Equipment.** Computer hardware and other equipment already in use in a company constitute a constraint. Existing business systems were designed with equipment constraints in mind, and new information systems must consider such constraints as well. If additional equipment is needed for a new design, analysts must determine whether a substantial change to the existing computer system is justified.

In summary, analysts examine existing objectives and constraints when they analyze a current system. Later, when they design new systems, they determine whether the objectives and constraints are still applicable or whether new ones are needed. After objectives and constraints are considered, outputs, inputs, and the processing needed to convert input to output are evaluated.

## OUTPUT

During both the analysis and design phases of their work, analysts consider output requirements *before* input and processing. This is so because the needs of the users—that is, the outputs that will be produced by the system—are the most important elements in the design. Only after output needs have been determined can input and then processing procedures be evaluated.

## INPUT

After determining the output derived from a system, analysts examine all the incoming data needed to produce the output. In an accounts receivable system, for example, incoming data can be in the form of cur-

*Figure 10.6 Processing operations can vary widely. A banking system, for example, needs to provide teller receipts and ATM transaction records as well as detailed check logs, customer balance statements, and balance sheets for all operating levels at the bank, from the teller to top management.*

rent sales figures, sales quotas, and proposed goals that are used to evaluate progress. It can also be in the form of information from the field about what competitors are doing, the status of retail dealers, and so on.

## PROCESSING

After studying the existing output requirements and input data, analysts inspect the types of processing operations that are being performed on data to obtain the desired results. See Figure 10.6. To fully understand an existing system, an analyst must understand all procedures and the ways in which various computations are made. For example, assume a purchasing clerk needs approval from management before making a major purchase. The analyst needs to examine the manager's decision-making process to see if the clerk could make the same decision or if the decision could be made more efficiently some other way.

## CONTROLS AND FEEDBACK

When systems are designed, **controls** are developed to minimize errors. Controls include techniques for verifying that the data entered is correct and for cross-checking calculations.

Because errors occur even with the best of controls, techniques are also needed to evaluate performance. These techniques help pinpoint errors in the system and indicate how they are handled once they are discovered. **Feedback** is the process of periodically evaluating a system to determine how well it meets user needs. Analysts need to know all current procedures for adjusting and correcting systems when feedback shows that errors have occurred. For example, they need to know what happens when a paycheck is issued for an incorrect amount. The analysts must also know the procedure for voiding the check and issuing a new one. In addition, they must know how appropriate adjustments are made, if necessary, to the employee's year-to-date figures for earnings, federal tax withheld, Social Security tax deducted, and so on.

> A system is defined in terms of its seven components each of which is reevaluated when the analyst designs a new system.

Margaret found that the secretaries in the MBA program were using a personal computer to develop a database of graduates' names and addresses based on program records. Several years ago, MGS's development staff, which solicits funds for the school, installed a sophisticated desktop publishing system, which they linked to the registrar's computers. The development office was now creating the same database as the secretaries, but in booklet form and more quickly and accurately. Nobody had informed the department secretaries! Margaret realized instantly that this was a major problem area.

## ▶ Using Structured System Charts to Describe the Existing System

Several tools help analysts depict and evaluate the components of a system. Four common techniques for analyzing systems are the structured analysis methodology, data flow diagrams, system flowcharts, and automated design tools such as CASE.

### STRUCTURED ANALYSIS

**Structured analysis** is a top-down method of systems analysis used to describe a system. It is analogous to the structured technique used by programmers to plan the logic in a program. By means of this structured technique, analysts first identify the top-level function of a complex system, then analyze it and break it down into secondary-level components, and, finally, identify, analyze, and subdivide all lower-level components. Breaking a system into smaller and smaller components makes analyzing large systems easier.

### DATA FLOW DIAGRAMS

Another tool available to analysts for depicting a system is called a **data flow diagram.** This diagram focuses on the flow of data through a system—where it originates and where it goes. Figure 10.7 illustrates the standard symbols used in data flow diagrams. The process symbol shows what is done to data in the current system—whether it is filed, printed out, forwarded, and so on. The source symbol indicates where data has

*Figure 10.7 These are the standard symbols used in a data flow diagram.*

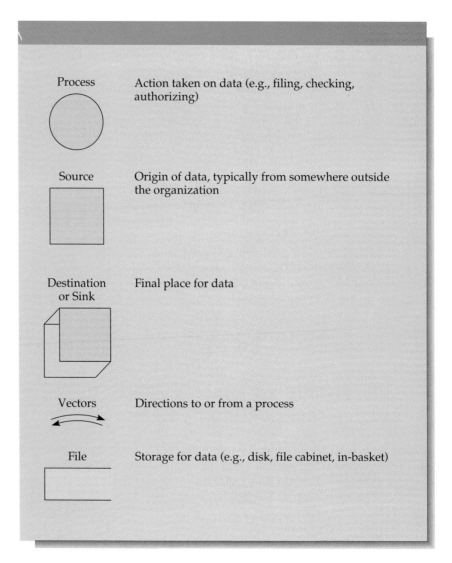

| | |
|---|---|
| Process | Action taken on data (e.g., filing, checking, authorizing) |
| Source | Origin of data, typically from somewhere outside the organization |
| Destination or Sink | Final place for data |
| Vectors | Directions to or from a process |
| File | Storage for data (e.g., disk, file cabinet, in-basket) |

come from. A destination, or sink, symbol shows where data is going, for example, to a recipient. Vectors illustrate the direction of flow. Storage for the data is indicated by the file symbol.

At MGS, a student's course record may be sent by the MBA office (source) to the registrar (sink). A file symbol indicates that the data is stored—in a filing cabinet or on a computer disk. Figure 10.8 is a data flow diagram depicting how a student registers for classes at MGS.

## SYSTEM FLOWCHARTS

Analysts also need to represent the information flow within the total system in order to depict elements of the system. The **system flowchart,** like

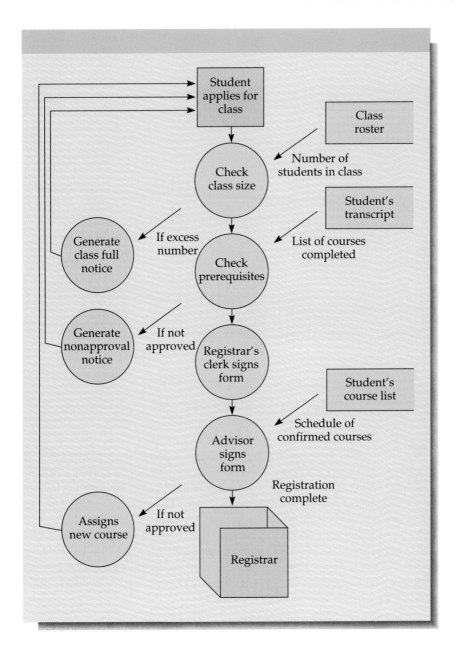

*Figure 10.8* This data flow diagram shows how a student registers for a class at Metropolitan Graduate School. The necessary databases are indicated on the right.

its more detailed counterpart the program flowchart, shows relationships among inputs, processing, and outputs, in terms of the information system as a whole.

Figure 10.9 illustrates the symbols commonly used in system flowcharts. Analysts draw flowcharts by means of plastic templates or special automated programs. Figure 10.10 is a system flowchart for a payroll system. Note how relatively easy it is to understand the overall processing involved by reading such a flowchart.

A data flow diagram focuses on the flow of data in a system whereas a system flowchart illustrates the relationships among system elements.

*Figure 10.9 These are the commonly used symbols in a system flowchart.*

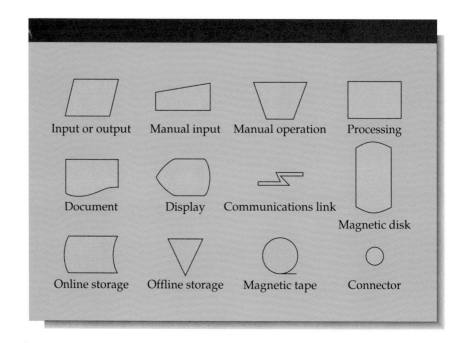

## AUTOMATED DESIGN TOOLS SUCH AS CASE

CASE, an acronym for computer-aided software engineering, is a set of software tools that can help analysts as they evaluate an existing system and, as we will see later on in this chapter, as they design a new one. CASE tools actually assist in the development of data flow diagrams and system flowcharts.

Keep in mind that no definitive rules exist for analyzing business systems. Each business activity must be assessed for its value to the total system. As a rule of thumb, well-defined, independent procedures are easiest to analyze. In contrast, procedures that interact with each other need to be broken into smaller tasks.

IN A

**HINTS FOR SYSTEMS ANALYSTS**

- *Do not overlook the obvious:* Errors may be high, for example, simply because users do not have calculators.
- *Do not overlook the forest for the trees:* Patching small problems over and over again might be expedient, but fixing the overall

structure may, in the end, be more prudent. Putting buckets under leaks is okay once or twice, but eventually the roof needs to be replaced.
- *Determine if a problem really exists:* Sometimes the main problem with an existing system is that the

user's expectations are unrealistic. Other times the problems initially cited by management are only symptoms of a much larger problem. Be objective in evaluating existing procedures to ensure that a new system will solve the real problems.

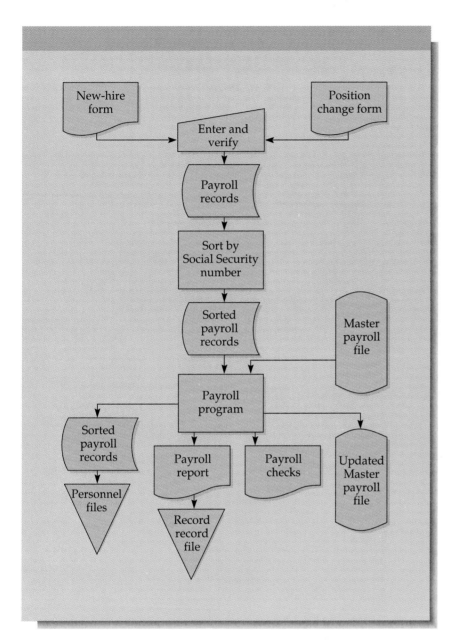

***Figure 10.10*** *This system flowchart shows the process for updating a company's payroll records.*

## ► **U**ndertaking the **F**easibility **S**tudy

After the data has been collected and the current system has been described and analyzed, the analyst undertakes a **feasibility study.** This study determines if, in fact, the current problems can be resolved and if a solution is feasible given the cost and time constraints established by management. If the analyst believes a solution is feasible, he or she prepares design alternatives for recommendation to management in the form of a problem definition. If no design is feasible, the analyst states this in the problem definition.

## ▶ Developing Alternative Design Strategies

Once the current system has been described and analyzed, and the feasibility of developing a solution to the problem has been established, analysts generally outline several broad design alternatives for the new system. At this stage in the design process of information systems—

*Figure 10.11 Here are five design alternatives for maintaining MBA records at the Metropolitan Graduate School.*

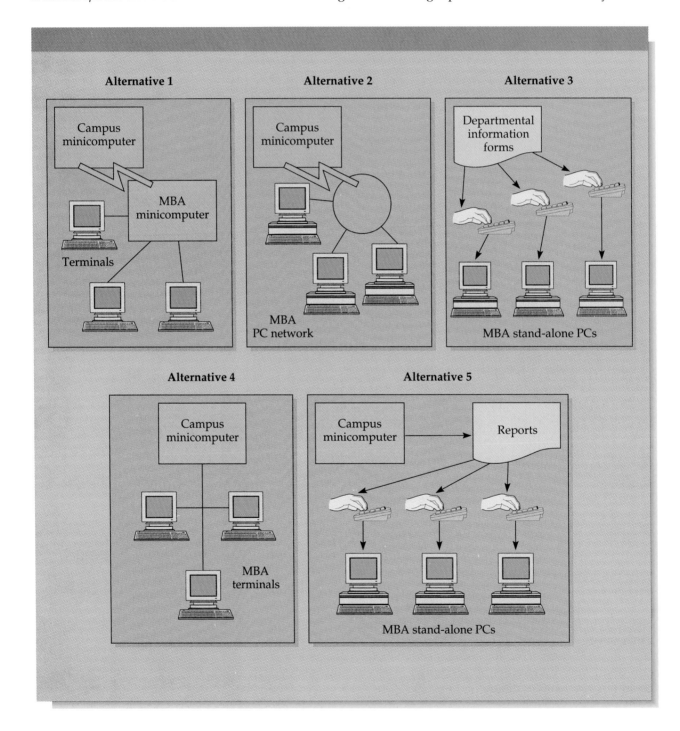

especially large ones that interact with other systems—analysts usually describe for management the trade-offs between a new system's cost and its potential benefits. Often, the most desirable system is the most expensive. Because analysts make recommendations, not final decisions, they provide management with several design alternatives to help them decide whether to build extremely effective systems at a high cost or to build systems that will cost less but may not be as effective.

Margaret might suggest five design alternatives to her boss (Figure 10.11).

- *Alternative 1:* Purchase a new minicomputer.
- *Alternative 2:* Link three existing personal computers into a network and download data from the campus minicomputer.
- *Alternative 3:* Update and maintain student data records for the department, independent of other campus records.
- *Alternative 4:* Purchase terminals linked to the campus minicomputer.
- *Alternative 5:* Keep doing what they have always been doing: receiving hard-copy reports from campus computers and manually entering data as needed into personal computers for further analysis.

At this stage of the analysis phase, the analyst only describes, in general terms, alternative design strategies. After an alternative is selected by management, the analyst will begin the design phase. One way to outline design alternatives is simply to ignore the costs and determine the best information system imaginable. Even though some alternatives may be economically impractical, this technique usually stimulates innovative ideas. Moreover, the process itself may suggest affordable design alternatives.

For each alternative design, analysts prepare detailed system flowcharts or data flow diagrams of the proposed system. The output, input, and processing requirements for each alternative are described along with control and feedback procedures. System flowcharts and data flow diagrams, then, are helpful in describing the new system as well as the existing one. Once again, CASE tools can help prepare charts and diagrams.

## ▶ Providing Cost-Benefit Analyses for the Design Alternatives

After outlining design alternatives, analysts estimate the cost of designing, implementing, and operating each of them. The most important factor in obtaining management's approval for a new design alternative is to demonstrate that the new design will result in a cost benefit. Performing a **cost-benefit analysis,** which compares the costs of the existing system to costs of a proposed system, is an integral part of an analyst's job.

To obtain a complete picture of the financial benefits of a proposed system, analysts compare the overall effects of the current and proposed systems on employee productivity and on the quality of goods and services. They measure these effects by means of both quantitative (numeric) and qualitative (descriptive) evaluations.

Here is a typical way of determining the annual cost (quantitative evaluation) of a new system:

$$\text{Annual cost} = \frac{\left(\begin{array}{l}\text{Initial}\\\text{development cost}\end{array}\right) + \left(\begin{array}{l}\text{Implementation}\\\text{cost}\end{array}\right)}{\text{Estimated life of system in years}} + \begin{array}{l}\text{Annual}\\\text{operating}\\\text{cost}\end{array}$$

The initial development cost consists of a one-time, nonrecurring capital investment in (1) anticipated hardware acquisitions and setup fees for the new design and (2) anticipated systems and programming costs for the new design.

Implementation costs include (1) development of facilities for new hardware—space, power, air conditioning, cabling, preparation, and so forth, (2) development of test procedures, (3) employee training, (4) development of backup systems, and (5) conversion costs—costs associated with converting from the current system to the new one.

Operating costs are the recurring expenditures required to operate the system on an ongoing basis. These costs consist of (1) hardware and software maintenance, (2) telephone and other communications links, (3) space, (4) overhead—security, insurance, taxes, and utilities, (5) operating staff labor costs, and (6) supplies.

Typically, annual costs for all alternative designs are estimated to illustrate the differences among several systems being considered.

Cost-benefit analyses usually project the costs of each new design alternative for a period of three to five years (Figure 10.12). After that, cost estimates are apt to need revision, or the system itself may need to be replaced.

Another method for comparing costs of the current system to those of proposed systems is called **break-even analysis.** A proposed system has nonrecurring development and implementation costs, so it might be years before the system begins to be cost-effective. By means of break-even analysis, systems analysts determine the year at which these nonrecurring costs will be absorbed and the new system will begin to cost the same as, or less than, the old one.

Figure 10.13 compares the cost of a proposed system to that of the current one. Initially, the cost of the proposed system is much higher, but by the third year the system hits a break-even point and begins to be less expensive than the old system.

Qualitative evaluation, the other measure of cost effectiveness, assigns a "soft-dollar" value to the benefits of current and proposed systems. Soft-dollar savings consider improvements in business processes that cannot easily be measured in dollars and cents. Typical benefits that an organization may receive from an upgraded information system are improved customer relations, better internal communications, improved

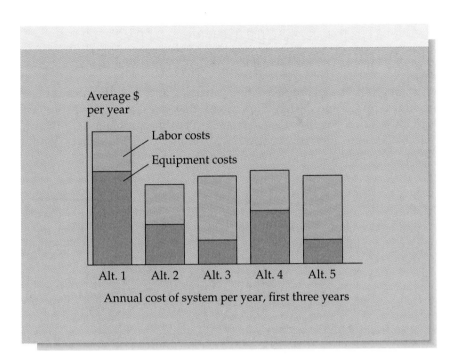

*Figure 10.12* Cost comparison chart for the five MBA department alternatives.

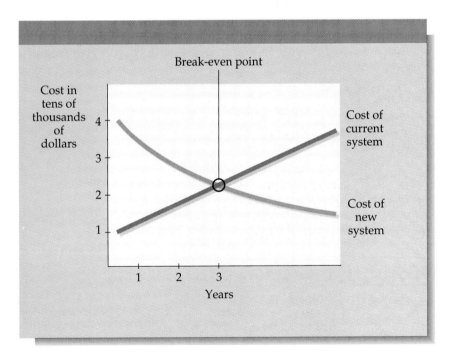

*Figure 10.13* Break-even analysis shows a new system reaching the break-even point in year 3.

task delegation, higher level of employee satisfaction, or a decreased need for travel. Such soft-dollar savings actually do result in a better financial position, but they are difficult to quantify because they are indirect. For example, by how much will sales increase if customer satisfaction is improved?

**STEPS IN SELLING A NEW SYSTEM DESIGN TO MANAGEMENT**

- Define the problem in a problem definition. Be sure the problem definition is:
  1. Nontechnical.
  2. Clear and concise.
  3. Free of spelling or grammatical errors.
- Prepare for presentation of the problem definition.
  1. Notify people in a letter indicating when the presentation will occur.
  2. Discuss the problem definition, prior to presenting it, with key people who are apt to be supportive. Ask them for advice.
  3. Use flip charts, overhead transparencies, slides, and other visuals where feasible.
- Make the presentation.
  1. Know in advance who will be attending your presentation and know something about each person.
  2. Dress for success.
  3. If you are using visuals, prepare in advance and make a trial presentation.

## ▶ Obtaining Management Approval for a Design Alternative

After analysts have completed their analysis and have mapped out, in general terms, some design alternatives, they present a formal problem definition to management. Management uses the problem definition to select a design alternative. The costs outlined by the analyst for the design selected become a constraint on the new system.

In the case of MGS, Margaret's boss decided to approve the previously outlined alternative 2—to link the MBA program's three personal computers into a network and download data from the campus minicomputer. At that juncture, Margaret began designing the new system.

## ▶ SELF-TEST

1. What are the seven basic components of any system?
2. What are three common types of constraints?
3. Describe five basic methods of collecting data.
4. What are two design tools commonly used to depict elements in a system?

Solutions
1. objectives, constraints, output, input, processing, controls, and feedback
2. legal, budgetary, and equipment
3. reviewing procedures manuals and other documents, interviewing employees, making observations, designing and evaluating questionnaires, and sampling
4. system flowcharts and data flow diagrams (also structured analysis and automated design tools)

## 10.3 DESIGNING A NEW SYSTEM

After the analyst evaluates the existing system, determines the feasibility of a solution, and discusses possible design alternatives, management selects a new design. Analysts then begin the design stage by preparing a model of the new system using system flowcharts, data flow diagrams, and other design tools.

## ▶ Prototyping a System

What part do systems design tools play in the building of effective information systems?

The systems design process requires a lengthy period of development, and the needs of users may change during that time. **Prototyping** enables

*Figure 10.14* Users and analysts can test a prototype using a computer.

analysts to provide users with all essential systems elements very quickly, before all of the interfaces and software modules have been designed. For instance, an analyst might create an on-screen menu or interactive display for users to try out, and then modify it to incorporate their suggestions—all before the system is actually implemented. See Figure 10.14.

Prototyping is a relatively new systems design tool in which a new information system, or a part of it, is simulated by means of a model constructed with a fourth-generation programming language. The result is a working model, although it is not intended for online production. Prototyping is one of the best methods for getting users to view the new systems design and to identify any additional needs or changes that can be made to improve its effectiveness. See Figure 10.15.

The 4GL software can create preliminary files of data, provide interaction among the files, perform processing activities, provide output, and so forth. Languages like RAMIS, FOCUS, and NOMAD are often used for prototyping because of their embedded database management systems, screen generators, and links to other database packages. Suppose you are designing a system to prepare purchase orders. With a 4GL, you can develop a prototype for a system that will prepare these purchase orders on a micro. But first users test the procedures you designed by interacting with the prototype. A number of iterations will normally be necessary for the procedures to work satisfactorily.

Even before a new system is fully designed, criteria for evaluating its performance should be devised so that management will be able to measure its effectiveness. Performance standards need to be related to the overall objectives and the key characteristics of the system. For example, if a 10% increase in revenue is a goal, then performance criteria should include an assessment to see if this increase occurs. Performance criteria that result in meaningful feedback should answer the following types of questions:

*Figure 10.15* *Developing a prototype requires several steps.*

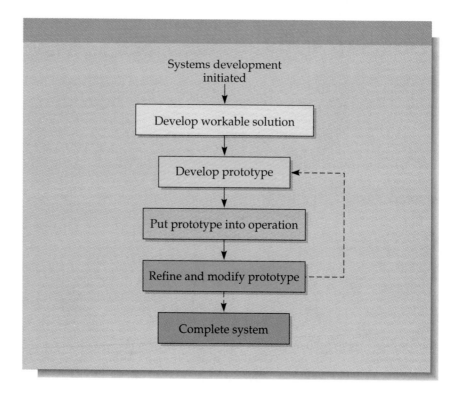

**DEVELOPING PROTOTYPES**

**Pros**

- Speedy design of a model
- Ability to be responsive to needed changes
- Involvement of users in the design and development process

**Cons**

- Lack of understanding by users who do not always realize that the full design is apt to be more complex and take more time to develop
- Cost

- Does the system meet the specified goal?
- Is processing time at an acceptable rate?
- Is the cost appropriate?
- Is a better product or service produced?
- Has productivity increased?
- Are there fewer errors?
- Is there adequate security?
- Are there fewer breakdowns and delays?
- Is documentation adequate?

Prototyping allows analysts to begin an iterative process of refining the system to meet user needs before any design elements become final. If the prototype is unsatisfactory, it can be changed quickly and easily. Consider the following three advantages of prototyping a system:

1. It enables users to interact easily with a model of the system. Such interaction helps analysts correct misunderstandings about user needs and basic design mistakes.
2. It makes the system easier to change if the need arises.
3. It makes implementation easier because users take an active role in the design process; consequently, users have a better understanding of how the system will work in practice.

A prototype can, however, be expensive and difficult to manage and control.

# ► Using CASE — An Automated Design Tool

CASE is a systems analysis productivity tool intended to help analysts evaluate existing systems and design structured, efficient, and well-documented new systems. It is a tool for building information systems. If integrated with a graphics package, for example, CASE tools alleviate the need to draw by hand graphic representations of an existing system's specifications. Similarly, CASE tools assist the systems analyst in designing a new system. They do *not*, however, fully automate the systems development process. Analysts must still control the overall process; CASE tools are used to increase their productivity.

Several principal features characterize CASE tools:

- Automatic construction of charts such as data flow diagrams and hierarchy charts.
- Ability to integrate other productivity tools such as project managers, cost-benefit analysis tools, and spreadsheets.
- Quality assurance capability to check for consistency and completeness of a design.
- Ability to share diagrams and data with other systems.
- Rapid prototyping for timely generation of screen displays and output.

Index Technology Corporation's Excelerator was the first CASE product for IBM PCs and is the current market leader. It is best used to automate the early phases of the systems development life cycle. Excelerator enables analysts to automatically diagram entire systems, from conceptual overviews down to individual data records. Excelerator uses a structured design technique—a top-down "explosion" feature—that allows analysts to start with an overview of the system, progress to finer levels of detail, and then explode the whole into different types of graphs and diagrams. Figure 10.16 is an example of an Excelerator data flow diagram.

To appreciate how helpful CASE tools can be, suppose Margaret Cotham needs to determine long-range class enrollments. She decides to begin by analyzing enrollment trends in all business courses at MGS over the past 50 years. Even if she had 10 people to help her, if they worked by hand, they would all be sitting at desks a long time, and it would be difficult to coordinate their work. CASE tools can help identify course names and enrollments and will automatically produce an organized, integrated index of courses. Margaret can choose from many packages for the micro market.

IN A

**BENEFITS OF CASE TOOLS**

1. Increased productivity
2. Improved quality assurance
3. Better documentation
4. Facilitates standards (though they are still too limited)
5. Elimination of redundancy because global changes can be made easily
6. Sharing of data flow diagrams and data dictionaries by more than one system
7. Ability to pinpoint inconsistencies in systems design

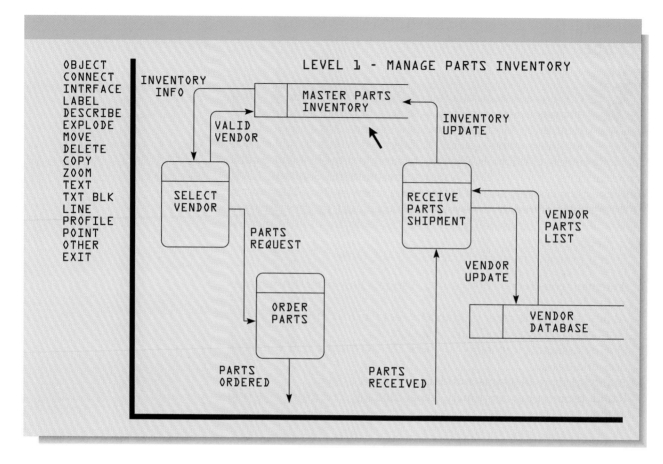

```
OBJECT                              LEVEL 1 - MANAGE PARTS INVENTORY
CONNECT
INTRFACE        INVENTORY
LABEL             INFO                     MASTER PARTS
DESCRIBE                                   INVENTORY                INVENTORY
EXPLODE         VALID                                               UPDATE
MOVE            VENDOR
DELETE
COPY
ZOOM
TEXT
TXT BLK         SELECT                     RECEIVE
LINE            VENDOR                     PARTS                    VENDOR
PROFILE                                    SHIPMENT                 PARTS
POINT                                                              LIST
OTHER                       PARTS
EXIT                        REQUEST                        VENDOR
                                                           UPDATE

                                ORDER                              VENDOR
                                PARTS                              DATABASE

                     PARTS                          PARTS
                     ORDERED                        RECEIVED
```

*Figure 10.16 Excelerator is an automated design tool that uses structured design techniques. An Excelerator screen display is shown here. Analysts start with an overview of the system and progress to finer levels of detail.*

Functional capabilities of CASE products are built around a **data dictionary,** which records and maintains the contents of files and the properties of data elements. CASE tools also provide a mechanism for controlling changes to data description specifications and checking the specifications for consistency and completeness. See Figure 10.17.

CASE tools have graphics capabilities for segmenting a system into components and drawing data flow diagrams and structure charts. See Figure 10.18. In addition, some CASE tools even generate limited program code. This reduces the programming effort required to transform the specifications into working systems. CASE tools also help to prepare documentation.

## LOOKING AHEAD

**MORE CHANGES FOR CASE**

- CASE tools will be able to contribute to the *entire* systems development life cycle.
- CASE will be used to generate source code, probably in COBOL.

- Currently, the main obstacle to widespread use of CASE tools is a lack of standards. CASE tools are often incompatible with each other and do not interface prop-

erly with other software products. Eventually, a *de facto* standard will emerge as it typically does with software and hardware.

| NO. | FIELD NAME | DESCRIPTION | FORMAT* (size & type) | CODED FIELD | DEPT | R – Overdue List | R – On-Loan List | R – Best Seller List | DB – Customer Database | DB – Book Database | DB – New Titles Database | DB – Extended Loan | DB – Multimedia |
|---|---|---|---|---|---|---|---|---|---|---|---|---|---|
| 1 | TITLE | Book title | A (150) | | Acquisitions | X | X | X | | X | X | X | X |
| 2 | ISBN | Int'l Std Book No | N (9) | | Acquisitions | | | X | X | X | X | X | X |
| 3 | YRPUB | Year of Publication | N (2) | | Acquisitions | X | X | X | | X | X | X | X |
| 4 | AUTHOR | Author | A (25) | | Acquisitions | X | X | X | | X | X | X | X |
| 5 | PUBL | Publisher | A (25) | | Acquisitions | | | | | X | X | X | X |
| 6 | LIBCARD | Customer Card No | N (6) | X | Circulation | | | | X | | | | |
| 7 | DUEDATE | Due date | N (6) | | Circulation | | | | X | | | | |
| 8 | LNAME | Last Name of Customer | A (20) | | Circulation | | | | X | | | | |

*A is alphanumeric (any character). N is numeric.

*Figure 10.17* Some companies use CASE tools to maintain an up-to-date data dictionary with descriptive information for all data elements. These data elements are cross-referenced to appropriate files, reports, and source documents.

## ► Designing Components of the New System

While the prototype is being developed, the analyst begins the detailed design of all components of the new system with the assistance of CASE tools where feasible. Recall that there are seven components: objectives, constraints, output, input, processing, controls, and feedback. Analysts designing a new system evaluate each of these components and make modifications as necessary.

### OBJECTIVES AND CONSTRAINTS

Based on the results of discussions with management, analysts begin by defining objectives and constraints for the new system. These may include some of the objectives and constraints of the existing system, but they are also likely to include new elements.

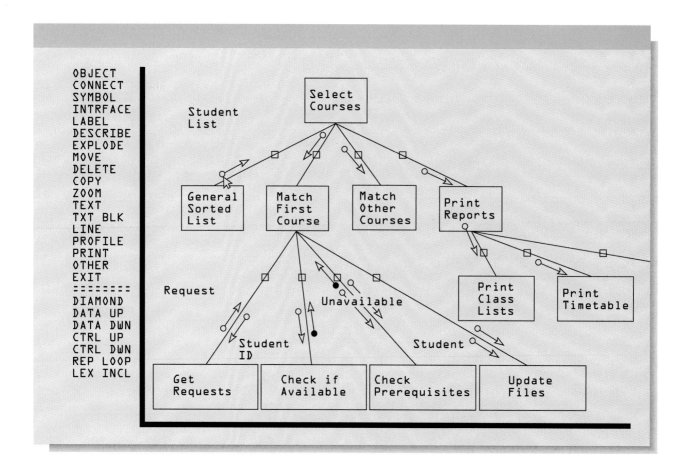

**Figure 10.18** *A structure chart produced by Excelerator.*

Because the MBA program's long-range goal is to improve administrative services, Margaret and her boss agree that the new information system should meet three new objectives:

1. Students should be able to register for all their classes *in one hour.*
2. The administrative staff should be able to plan the next semester's courses *within the first week* of a new semester.
3. Advisors should be able to determine a student's matriculation status *within 15 seconds.*

Margaret and her boss also agree that she can only spend two months building the new information system and no more than $3000 on hardware and software. When the system is completed, she will spend 25% of her time maintaining the system and training users.

## OUTPUT DESIGN

Just as analysts considered output before input in analyzing the existing system, they should design output as the first component for a new system. Designing output first helps ensure that users' needs will be satisfied. Analysts review all the reports generated by the current system and discuss with users any additional reports or changes needed from a new design. The design of new output affords the analyst the opportunity to give users exactly what they need.

> At this stage Margaret sat down with her boss and designed all the new forms and computer screens needed in the new system.

## INPUT DESIGN

After new outputs have been agreed upon, analysts and users determine what new input will be required and what other resources will be needed to create the desired output. Sometimes business systems need to be entirely redesigned to ensure accurate, timely input.

> Margaret's boss wanted the new system to generate reports indicating
>
> - All professors teaching during any semester.
> - All professors who teach a particular course.
> - All courses a professor has taught over the years.
>
>   Although the campus minicomputer could easily provide the first two requests, getting a list of courses that all professors have taught over the years was more difficult. Margaret created a set of procedures that ensured proper input; in this case, the faculty secretary was required to
>
> - Retrieve the data from file cabinets in storage.
> - Create a database on the personal computer.
> - Update the database every semester.

Input is stored in database files. When the analyst designs a database file, he or she defines record descriptions, fields within the records, and the size and type of those fields. All the data used by the system is described in the data dictionary, which can be created using a CASE tool. Design of input also includes establishing screen formats and dialogs for data entry.

## PROCESSING REQUIREMENTS

Analysts decide whether batch or online procedures are best suited for processing the data. Whatever processing method is selected, appropriate software and hardware are necessary to convert input to output.

   Most analysts use or augment software and hardware that already exists in the organization. Before acquiring new software, analysts must decide whether to purchase it or to have custom programs written, either by in-house programmers or by software consultants who specialize in designing specific kinds of software. Chapter 7 discussed how analysts decide whether to "make" or "buy" software.

Analysts initially attempt to design new information systems by using the computer equipment already in place in the organization. Frequently, a new design may require additional computers or peripherals. If the new design requires its own large computer system, or if it requires the organization's current computers to be upgraded, then the following procedures must be followed:

- Prepare a request for proposal.
- Evaluate the proposals from vendors.
- Select a vendor.
- Make preparations for installing the new system.

**Prepare a Request for Proposal.**   Analysts prepare a document called a **request for proposal (RFP)** to obtain specific technical information and cost bids from vendors and to ask for information about the vendors themselves. A successful RFP includes two parts: (1) the description of the organization's needs, often called a **needs analysis,** and (2) a request for information regarding the vendor and the equipment proposed by the vendor. To provide a thorough description of a proposed company's computer needs, an RFP must contain the following elements.

- A description of the company that includes its main business, its locations, number of employees, and other information about departments or groups who will use the computer system.
- A description of what a new computer system should accomplish.
- The terms and conditions under which the procurement will be made, such as a fixed price, cost plus incentive for early delivery, warranty requests, and so on.
- A budget that provides the vendor with a general idea of what the company plans to spend.
- The organization's schedule for development, implementation, training, and start-up of the proposed system.
- An outline of the proposed computer system's specifications.

The RFP also serves as a formal request for information about the vendor. Vendor information requested in an RFP includes

- Specifications in the form of technical manuals, sample screen formats, and so on.
- Financial viability of the vendor, in the form of annual reports, performance records, and length of time in the business.
- Available support, specifying maintenance and training programs and including frequency of training, background of instructors, and promptness and thoroughness of technical support.

In addition, an RFP should request a list of current users of the computer system proposed by the vendor, along with a brief description of

---

**CHECKLIST OF ITEMS TO BE CONSIDERED BY AN RFP**

*Rating*
*Factor*

_____ How does the hardware perform?

_____ What is the cost of hardware (purchase or lease)?

_____ What are the installation requirements and costs?

_____ Do software products come bundled with the hardware (i.e., at no extra cost)?

_____ What training, software, and other technical services are provided?

_____ What maintenance is provided?

_____ What type of warranty does the equipment have?

_____ How thorough is the documentation?

_____ What is the delivery schedule? Is there a penalty clause for late delivery?

_____ Are there conversion costs?

each client's application areas. This information should include the client's business and the length of time the computer system has been installed. An RFP should also request samples of documentation and manuals so the company can judge the quality and thoroughness of these items.

**Evaluate the Proposals from Vendors.**   Analysts prepare criteria for evaluating proposals received from vendors so that they can make comparisons. Often evaluation criteria for proposals take the form of a weighted checklist based on required systems features and the vendor's ability to support the customer.

The cost of operating each proposed computer system is a crucial factor in rating competitive bids. In addition, intangible factors such as the vendor's reputation, anticipated installation date, support to be provided, and so on, must also be considered.

**Select a Vendor.**   After evaluating responses to the RFPs, analysts are ready to recommend a specific computer system. They must also recommend whether the system selected should be purchased, leased, or rented. Figure 10.19 indicates the principal advantages and disadvantages of these three methods of acquisition. Hardware can be obtained directly from a manufacturer or from a company that specializes in configuring computer systems. Such companies are called OEMs for *o*riginal *e*quipment *m*anufacturers or VARs for *v*alue-*a*dded *r*eseller.

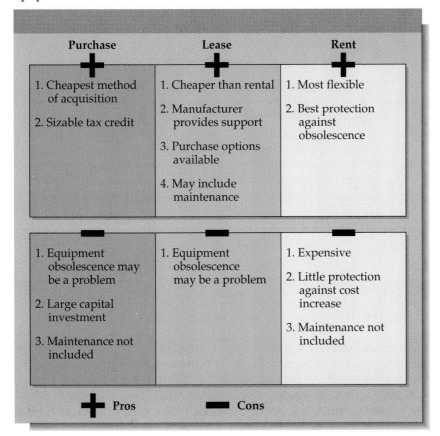

*Figure 10.19 Advantages and disadvantages of the principal methods of acquiring computer equipment: purchase, lease, and rent.*

Once analysts and users have reviewed all the bids, they make a written recommendation to management. The recommendation highlights the reasons for selecting a particular computer system and a method of acquisition. After a computer system is ordered, the analyst develops and supervises conversion and implementation plans. In all cases, decisions about major hardware purchases should be made after software needs have been determined. Software choices should ultimately determine which hardware is to be acquired or used.

**Make Preparations for Installing the New System.**    During the implementation phase, before any new hardware arrives, the users and systems analysts must determine the site where it will be installed and, if necessary, prepare the site. Some computers, for example, require more air conditioning or a greater power supply than is normally provided in a standard office. The systems analyst finalizes the site requirements and oversees the schedule for preparing the site.

### CONTROLS AND FEEDBACK

After all output and input have been designed, and software and hardware have been selected, analysts evaluate what controls are needed to ensure the quality of output. Controls consist of manual as well as computer audit trails to guarantee the reliability of information. Feedback procedures also need to be developed to help evaluate the effectiveness of the new system.

Margaret had to use existing computer facilities when she designed the new system. First, she identified the data she wanted from the campus minicomputer; then she created periodic update schedules for downloading this data to the department's personal computers. To ensure data integrity, she decided to have one of the clerks in the MBA office check every 20th MBA record each month. Margaret also created backup procedures to protect the department's computer system against the possibility of a hard disk failure. To obtain consistent feedback from the system, Margaret planned to meet with users once a month to discuss problems and new ideas and to suggest better ways to use the system.

## ▶ The Role of Users in Designing a New System

Experienced analysts schedule frequent meetings with users to review the system as it is being developed. Unfortunately, not all relevant points can be anticipated. An iterative process of creating, reviewing, revising— then reviewing and revising again—is essential to produce the best system possible and to incorporate all needed data, user features, and business functions. Sometimes users feel that little progress is being made because of the repetitive nature of the design process. Analysts must assure them and their managers that iteration is a part of any design process, that the schedules and cost estimates provide for that iteration, and that the need for revision does not mean a lack of planning or skill on anyone's part.

Users should also work with analysts to establish the acceptable limits for key system characteristics such as response time, report runtime, report costs, overall system usage cost, processes the system will have to handle concurrently, and so on. As users become more knowledgeable about their choices, they will be better able to balance the trade-offs offered them. When analysts give users the option of adding or deleting a feature, they must be sure to provide an estimate of the resulting effect on the system as a whole. Inherent performance trade-offs can be evaluated by asking questions such as: "What am I sacrificing (or gaining) by taking away (or adding) this feature?"

Once an information system that satisfies business needs has been designed, analysts implement the system so that it can be used on an ongoing basis.

## ▶ Monitoring the Progress of the New Design

During the design phase, several tasks are undertaken concurrently, but some can only be begun after others have been completed. In addition, some tasks are performed by the analyst, while others require the participation of programmers, users, or vendors. A programmer could begin to write a program even before the analyst selects hardware, but the programs cannot be fully tested by the user until the hardware is in place. Project management tools help analysts determine how to schedule interrelated tasks and to keep track of their progress. See Figure 10.20.

## ▶ SELF-TEST

1. (T or F) Output should be designed before input.
2. A _____ defines and describes data in a database.
3. If an additional computer system is needed for a new design, the analyst must prepare a _____ to obtain technical information and bids from vendors.
4. _____ enables a new system or part of a system to be tested before the full design has been finalized.
5. An automated design tool used to assist in building information systems is called _____.

Solutions

1. T
2. data dictionary
3. RFP—request for proposal

4. Prototyping
5. CASE

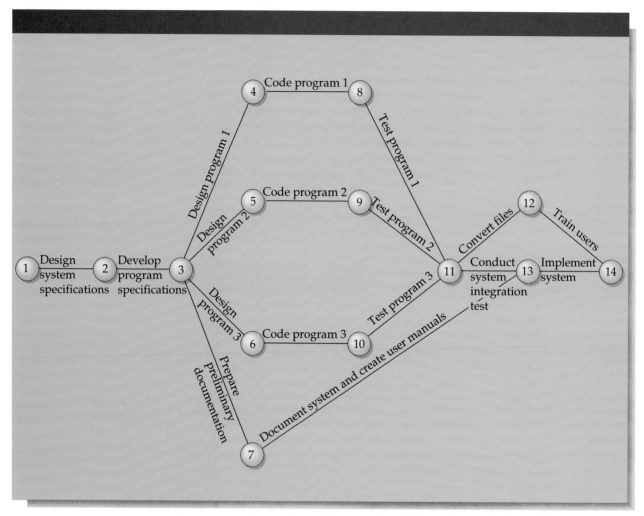

**Figure 10.20** *A PERT chart can be used for the design, development, testing, and implementation of information systems. In this chart, lines represent activities and circles represent important points when activities have been completed or new ones can be begun. One advantage of PERT charts is that they illustrate what specific activities must be completed before others can begin.*

## 10.4 IMPLEMENTATION

### ▶ Obtaining Management Approval for Implementation

How are new information systems approved and implemented?

In most instances, analysts make another presentation to management after the entire set of procedures has been designed and all programs have been written or acquired. This presentation includes

- A detailed description of the new system.
- An analysis of the actual design costs and the operating costs of this new system as compared to the costs estimated in the problem definition.
- A plan for converting to the new system.

If management approves the actual design, the analyst can continue with the final phase, implementation. Recall that managers typically approve a new design alternative as outlined in the problem definition because they are not satisfied with the existing system. They may not, however, approve implementing a new system if the analyst's plans are unacceptable for some reason (e.g., if original cost estimates differ significantly from actual costs).

## ► Implementing the New System

After receiving management approval, analysts implement the new system. A new information system is likely to require changes to existing files and to the media on which files are stored. The process of creating computerized files for a new system is called **file conversion.** Controls such as the following must be incorporated during this process to ensure the integrity of the new files:

- Comparing record counts and batch totals of key fields before and after conversion to verify that all of the data has been converted correctly.
- Comparing and checking randomly selected records before and after conversion.
- Testing the information system with the new files to verify that all file conversions have been completed successfully.

## ► Redesigning Tasks Performed by Users

To reap the full benefits of the new system, analysts usually advise managers about the need to restructure the jobs of some employees. Every new job description should make use of an employee's skills, maintain individual autonomy insofar as possible, and provide a degree of job satisfaction.

## ► Types of System Conversions

In Chapter 8, we discussed the ways programs are implemented in information systems. Similar methods are used to convert to new information systems. As with program implementation, the four conversion alternatives are direct conversion, parallel conversion, phased conversion, and pilot conversion. See Figure 10.21.

**Direct conversion** occurs when a company simply stops using its old

*Analysts work closely with users to help them get started with a new system. Documentation should be thorough and easy to understand.*

*Figure 10.21 Techniques for converting from one system to another.*

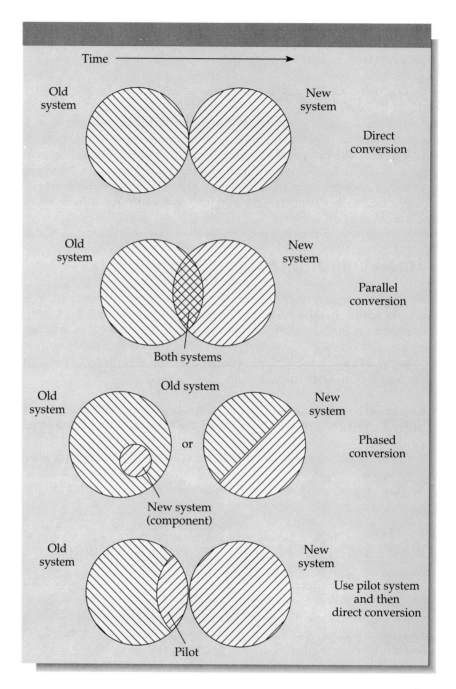

**ANALYZING AND DESIGNING INFORMATION SYSTEMS**

*Define the problem.*

- Collect data about the existing system.
- Describe the elements of the existing system.
- Use structured system charts to describe the system.
- Undertake a feasibility study.
- Devise possible design alternatives.
- Prepare cost-benefit analyses for design alternatives.
- Obtain management approval for one design alternative.

*Design the new system.*

- Create a prototype while designing new components.
- Select and/or develop software.
- Select hardware.
- Monitor progress of the new design.

*Implement the system.*

- Obtain management approval for implementation.
- Implement system.
- Redesign jobs if necessary.
- Prepare and distribute documentation.

system and begins using the new one; there is no overlap between systems. If a sufficient number of prototypes have been tested, direct conversion may be an efficient way to implement the new system. The risk is, however, that something unexpected may occur and the company's business may slow down, or even stop, while the problem is being solved.

In **parallel conversion,** the old system and the new system operate simultaneously for a period of time. Output from both systems is compared to make sure the new system is functioning properly. When the new system is operating satisfactorily, the old system is discontinued. Parallel conversion is a slow but reliable method.

**Phased conversion** is a gradual implementation. It is particularly appropriate when a large, complex system has been designed in modules that can be run independently. As each module is implemented and refined, it is added to the others in the system. For example, a company might implement the order processing module, then the inventory management module, and finally the accounting module—each module should run effectively before the next is introduced.

**Pilot conversion** refers to implementation of the entire system in one part of the company, perhaps a single department or a single division. This approach allows the analyst to work out any problems that develop while the scale of implementation is small and manageable.

## ▶ Documenting the System

Once the system is functioning properly, analysts provide a complete record of the precise procedures and techniques it uses, as well as technical specifications for all the hardware and software used. This record is called a **documentation package.** It is usually prepared during the analysis and design stages and finalized during implementation. Because documentation describes all the facets of a new design, it is similar to a procedures manual (although it may consist of several components). If a problem occurs after the system is operational, analysts and users can consult the documentation, which, if it is complete, should provide a solution. Figure 10.22 lists typical elements in a documentation package.

The analysis, design, and implementation of a new information system is a complex project that involves the creativity of many people, including managers and system users. The time and cost for involving these people are usually justified by the increase in profitability, productivity, and job satisfaction that can result from a well-designed information system.

*Figure 10.22 A documentation package typically consists of four elements: logical design, physical design, programming, and operations and procedures.*

| Logical design elements | Physical design elements | Programming elements | Operations and procedures |
|---|---|---|---|
| • Output specifications | • Database and file layouts | • Top-down structure charts | • User options |
| • Processing procedures | • Processing procedures | • Pseudocode and flowcharts | • Data entry procedures |
| • Systems and program logic | • Input formats | • File and record layouts | • Data control procedures |
| • File specifications | • Output formats | • Code specifications | • Computer operations |
| • Input specifications | • File conversion plan | | |

▶ **SELF-TEST**

1. The process of creating computerized files for the new system is called _____ .

2. Name the four types of conversions.
3. A new system is fully described in the _____ package.

Solutions
1. file conversion
2. direct conversion; parallel conversion; phased conversion; pilot conversion
3. documentation

---

▶ **C**hapter **S**ummary

### 10.1 THE ROLE OF THE SYSTEMS ANALYST

What skills must systems analysts bring to their study of the systems development life cycle and to the analysis, design, and implementation of new information systems?

Every business consists of a series of interrelated functional areas that accomplish the organization's goals. To keep organizations running efficiently, managers hire **systems analysts** who examine business systems and recommend how they can be improved. Systems analysts are basically problem solvers, and the **information systems** they design may or may not involve computers. Analysts can be company employees or outside consultants; *outsourcing* is the term for using outside services to satisfy a company's needs. As information needs increase, key users often use systems analysis and design techniques to help them solve business problems.

Business systems pass through four basic stages known as the **systems development life cycle:** (1) investigation and analysis, (2) design and development, (3) implementation, and (4) operation and maintenance.

### 10.2 INVESTIGATING AND ANALYZING EXISTING BUSINESS SYSTEMS

Beginning with the problem definition, what analytical tools do analysts use to create new information systems?

Analysts begin designing new systems by first understanding the basic problem areas in existing procedures and by presenting their results in a **problem definition.** To write a problem definition, analysts (1) collect data about the existing system, (2) describe and analyze the elements of the system, (3) determine current costs, and (4) devise possible design alternatives if a new system is feasible. The problem definition is the means by which management approval is obtained for a design alternative. Analysts combine several methods for collecting data about the current system: reviewing written policies, procedures, memos, and reports; observing employees at work; sampling; interviewing employees; and preparing and analyzing employee questionnaires.

Perhaps the best way to analyze a system is to segment it into its seven component parts: objectives, constraints, output, input, processing, **controls,** and **feedback.** Analysts examine these components to see how they work and to isolate any problem areas. Later, when a new system is designed, each of these components is modified as the need arises. Analysts use several techniques to help them diagnose and evaluate these seven system components. Four common tools are **structured analysis, data flow diagrams, system flowcharts,** and automated design tools such as CASE.

After analyzing and describing the existing system in a problem definition, analysts undertake a **feasibility study** to determine if a new design is possible given constraints established by management. If a solution is feasible, several broad design alternatives are outlined and the cost of each is estimated. To measure costs, analysts choose from two basic methods: **break-even analysis,** which indicates when the new system will start to be cost-effective, and **cost-benefit analysis,** which compares the cost of an existing system to the cost of a proposed system.

## 10.3 DESIGNING A NEW SYSTEM

After analysts have completed a formal problem definition, they present their analysis to management for approval. Once management decides on a new design, analysts prepare a model, or prototype, of the new system using a 4GL to simulate the essential elements of the system. A structured analysis process requires long planning and design periods, and during that time the needs of the user often change. **Prototyping** enables analysts to have users try out parts of a proposed system so that there will be fewer changes when the entire system is implemented.

CASE tools assist the analyst in designing a structured, efficient, and well-documented new system. They help produce a **data dictionary** that records and maintains the contents of files and the properties of data elements. The new design is defined in terms of the seven basic system components: objectives, constraints, output, input, processing, controls, and feedback.

As part of the design process, software is either purchased or developed. If it is to be developed, either in-house programmers or consultants will be used.

If the new system requires major changes in hardware, analysts prepare a **request for proposal (RFP)** to obtain specific technical information from vendors and to ask for information about the vendor itself. The two parts of a successful RFP are (1) the description of the organization's needs, often called a **needs analysis,** and (2) a request for information about vendors themselves.

Once all seven components of the new system have been designed, management must approve the system. The analyst then implements the system.

## 10.4 IMPLEMENTATION

Implementing the new system usually requires a **file conversion** (i.e., the process of creating computerized files), redesigning tasks performed by users, and converting to the new system by employing one of four approaches. **Direct conversion** occurs when an organization stops using

*What part do systems design tools play in the building of effective information systems?*

*How are new information systems approved and implemented?*

its old system and begins using the new system with no overlap. In **parallel conversion,** the old and new systems operate concurrently, and the output is compared at various stages to make sure the new system is running correctly. When it is, the old system is discontinued. **Phased conversion** involves introducing one module of a large system at a time; **pilot conversion** means the system is used in only one part of the company until all the problems are solved.

Once the system is functioning properly, analysts provide a **documentation package** that details the procedures and techniques used in the new system as well as the technical specifications of the hardware and software.

## ▶ Chapter Self-test

1. What is the document, prepared by the analyst, that defines in detail all aspects of the existing system?
2. The _____ must work closely with users when creating a new system design.
3. (T or F) Preparing a cost-benefit analysis for a proposed system is usually the responsibility of a cost accountant.
4. Bids from _____ must be compared during a feasibility study.
5. (T or F) The systems analyst's role in an organization is essentially advisory.
6. (T or F) A new design must be based on the existing system's objectives, which cannot be altered in the revised system.
7. (T or F) Legal constraints can generally be modified in the new system.
8. (T or F) If an analyst suggests a new form of output in the system design, the user should not question it because the analyst is more qualified to decide what is best for the system as a whole.
9. (T or F) Systems analysts should always design systems so that computer equipment replaces all manual operations.
10. (T or F) A systems flowchart depicts the relationships between inputs, processing, and outputs for the system as a whole.
11. An analyst must evaluate the way an existing system meets its _____.
12. Suppose that in the current system a payroll check is computed incorrectly. The procedures for correcting the error are part of _____.
13. Name four methods of collecting data about an existing system.
14. The basic inadequacies of the existing system are described in the _____.
15. A _____ is a document that analysts send to vendors to solicit technical information about computer systems.

Solutions
1. problem definition
2. systems analyst

3. F—It is the responsibility of the systems analyst.
4. computer vendors
5. T
6. F—Objectives can, and frequently do, change.
7. F—Legal constraints cannot be changed.
8. F—Designing output is a joint task of users and analysts.
9. F—New designs can include both manual and computerized components.
10. T
11. objectives
12. controls and feedback
13. review documents, observe employees, design and distribute questionnaires, interview employees
14. problem definition
15. request for proposal

## ▶ Key Terms

Break-even analysis, *p. 398*
Controls, *p. 390*
Cost-benefit analysis, *p. 397*
Data flow diagram, *p. 391*
Data dictionary, *p. 404*
Direct conversion, *p. 413*
Documentation package, *p. 415*
Feasibility study, *p. 395*

Feedback, *p. 390*
File conversion, *p. 413*
Information system, *p. 379*
Needs analysis, *p. 408*
Parallel conversion, *p. 414*
Phased conversion, *p. 415*
Pilot conversion, *p. 415*
Problem definition, *p. 384*

Prototyping, *p. 400*
Request for proposal (RFP), *p. 408*
Structured analysis, *p. 391*
Systems development life cycle, *p. 382*
System flowchart, *p. 392*

## ▶ Review Questions

1. Briefly discuss four methods of gathering data about business systems. Which method do you think is most important?
2. What are the seven components of a business system?
3. Describe four tools used to analyze systems.
4. Briefly describe two common ways analysts measure the cost and benefits of business systems.

## ▶ Chapter Case Study Problems

1. Do you think Margaret should purchase software or hire someone to write software for the MBA program's new information system? Explain your answer.
2. Which of the five possible design alternatives that Margaret provided would have required an RFP? Write a brief RFP for one of the alternatives.

3. The MBA office staff consists of an executive director (Margaret's boss), an administrative assistant (Margaret), a program director, a faculty chairperson, a faculty secretary, and a receptionist. If Margaret and the faculty secretary will maintain the new computer system, do you think their jobs should be redesigned? If so, briefly describe how you would change their job titles and descriptions.

4. Draw a data flow diagram for the registration process in your school. Can you see areas for improvement? If so, what are they?

## PRODUCT ANALYSIS

## CASE

### Selecting a Vendor*

You are Phil A. Mignon, the information systems (IS) manager for the White Mare Steak House, a chain of some 100 company-owned restaurants that is growing at the rate of 15% a year. As IS manager you are responsible for home-office computing, mostly accounting systems, central purchasing systems, and inventory systems that are very old. The computer on which they run is very old as well, but it is working adequately. Unfortunately, your growth has made the existing system inadequate for current needs. An upgrade is needed immediately.

You and your department have narrowed the choices down to two very different alternatives. The first is the easiest: acquire the latest and next bigger model (almost twice as big and costing $500,000) from your current vendor. Although this will support all current programs and would be simple to convert to, it has some drawbacks. The technology is still not very advanced. It will not support some features that your company will want soon, such as interactive point-of-sales systems, interface to food co-op buying system, and decision support tools. Furthermore, it is unclear if your vendor, who is known as "Old Reliable" in the business, will ever get them. They are not known as pioneers. They are known for superior inexpensive support and training to which you can attest. You have never had a service complaint and have used their training extensively. If you go with this system, it will be the biggest offered by your

vendor, although they have always added to the high end of their line.

The other choice is a vendor who is a pioneer. Their system is equal in speed and cost to your vendor's system, but it is in the middle of a full range of computers offered by this vendor. They are smaller than "Old Reliable" but are growing faster. Their rapid growth has meant that they have occasionally dropped the ball in servicing new accounts, and their technology is so new that there usually is no formal training for a while. The computer you have tentatively selected has many advanced features that you would not get by upgrading with your current vendor including decision support systems and communications interface. They do not currently have interactive point-of-sales systems but promise to have it in nine months. Their reputation is that they always deliver new functions on time, though it may take some time to get all the bugs out. The biggest obstacle to selecting this system would be the conversion of existing programs to work on the new system. You know that some functions, a few important ones, can never be converted. An outside consulting firm will do as much as can be done in one big effort for $300,000. You have also looked at having your staff do the work all in-house, though this would take six months if everyone worked at it full time. Changing vendors has many implications, mostly negative in your opinion. Your people are trained in the skills of your current vendor and you know it would be easier to hire more of the same skills than to get employees knowledgeable in the new vendor's technology. On the other hand, you are not so sure that your

*From Wysocki, Robert K., and Young, James. *Information Systems: Management Practices in Action*. New York: Wiley, 1990, pp. 71–73.

staff would not find it more professionally rewarding to go with a more progressive vendor. Both vendors are lobbying aggressively for the business.

*Analysis*

1. Which vendor would you recommend? Why?
2. Are there any other strategies that should be considered?
3. What are the most important considerations in your decision?
4. What risks would each approach invite?
5. Should this be an IS call or should top management make the decision?
6. Under each strategy, what would a good acquisition approach be (e.g., buy-lease-rent)?
7. How much should the IS professionals be involved in this decision?

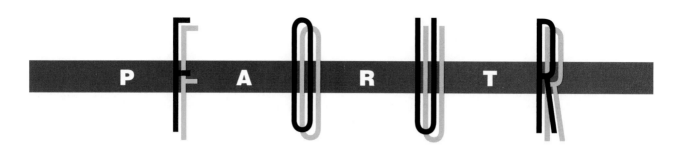

# PART FOUR

## CONNECTIVITY UNITES THE INFORMATION AGE

I f you want to stay in touch—even when you get away from it all—then computers can help. In the old days, it was relatively easy to escape from society and lead a life of seclusion, but with that luxury came some anxiety because you could not be reached, even in an emergency. Today virtually every corner of the world is reachable by some sort of communication system. Even scientists temporarily stationed in remote, uninhabited Antarctica are equipped with communications devices so that they can keep in touch with a home base. Nor is space travel a private retreat. If you have ever watched a NASA broadcast, you know how closely the astronauts are observed. In a very real sense, computers are bringing us closer together.

Part Four discusses issues related to connectivity. In Chapter 11, you will learn about computerized databases and management information systems, which can store and process vast amounts of information that help make the world more connected. Chapter 12 deals with networking—the way computers themselves are connected to one another, both within an organization and outside it. Finally, Chapter 13 raises issues that have great significance in the information age: With the ease of collecting and distributing information, how can individuals and organizations protect their privacy and ensure that their databases are secure?

Do you feel out of touch when you are away from your office? A modem will enable you to access information through a telephone line or via a wireless network. Computers can be connected to one another by cable, telephone lines, satellites, microwave relays—even radio waves—so that we can combine and use their power and resources, no matter where the hardware is physically located.

In 1860 the pony express offered a fast mail delivery service. It took about eight days for a letter or package to travel approximately 2,000 miles. Nowadays it takes only seconds to transmit and receive messages and other information by computer. Vast networks of computers collect, monitor, and process data, often bringing together users from all parts of the world. E-mail allows us to send and retrieve all sorts of data, including documents, graphs, charts, pictures—even video images. Using e-mail networks both within an organization and outside it, users can communicate with their office no matter where they are and also have the ability to access external databases with vast amounts of information.

But with ready access comes the potential or threat of illegal or unethical use. Virtually every day lawsuits are brought against organizations that use computers to invade people's privacy or provide inaccurate information that adversely affects an individual's ability to get a job, credit, or buy a house. The courts also deal with people who commit computer crimes for financial gain or with hackers who infect computers with viruses just for the challenge it provides. Illegal uses are resolved in the courts, but unethical uses can only be controlled by an informed and computer-proficient society that places a high value on the rights and responsibilities of individuals.

The telephone, which was patented in 1876, can scarcely be called a new device. Yet today many new applications depend on this age-old communication link. Direct dialing provides voice, data, and even video access to almost any place on earth. Touch-Tone phones have made it possible for organizations to bypass human operators and electronically access information, process college registrations—and even help immigrants begin the process of applying for U.S. citizenship.

Network television provides information and entertainment to people throughout the world. High-definition TV makes available even higher quality images and sound which can be further enhanced by computer. Interactive TV connects consumers to a host of information services, and will perhaps revolutionize the way we shop and transact business.

# DATABASES AND MANAGEMENT INFORMATION SYSTEMS

**R**ecall from Chapter 2 that there are two kinds of information systems designed by systems analysts: traditional systems that focus on satisfying the operational needs of each department and management information systems that focus first on providing top-level management with immediate access to data and second on satisfying operating needs. In the previous chapter, we discussed traditional information systems and how they are designed. In this chapter, we look at management information systems.

Regardless of whether organizations have traditional information systems or management information systems, they typically have databases to store the data and database management systems to access and manipulate the data. We concentrate in this chapter on database management systems and their use in management information systems by answering the following questions:

▶ How do the format and features of a database affect the usefulness of a database management system?

▶ How can access to databases improve the quality of information for management decision making at all levels of an organization?

## 11.1 DATABASE MANAGEMENT SYSTEMS: THE DRIVING FORCE BEHIND INFORMATION PROCESSING

How do the format and features of a database affect the usefulness of a database management system?

A database is a collection of related files. For example, the accounting system in an organization contains database files with records on all sales, customers, purchases, vendors, budgets, and financial plans. Similarly, the payroll system has database files with information about employees and their salary history. In a traditional information system, database files provide the operating staff with information to perform day-to-day operations. In management information systems, however, the primary purpose of databases is to provide information to top-level managers on a company-wide basis.

A software package called a database management system provides users with the ability to join, manipulate, or otherwise access the data in any number of database files. Each functional business area may have database needs that are totally independent or that overlap with those of other functional areas. For example, the marketing department requires access to information on sales and customers as well as product information and current inventory levels. The manufacturing department needs access to files relating to purchases of raw goods and the names and addresses of vendors as well as inventory data. A database management system (DBMS) enables users to access and cross-reference data from different files and different application areas easily and efficiently. Some database management systems are better suited for traditional information systems and others are better suited for a top-down management information system (MIS).

You were introduced to databases for microcomputers in Chapter 3 and to the way data is stored in Chapter 6. Now you will see how DBMS software is used to create, edit, update, and report from an organization's database files.

In most large companies, database management systems run on mainframes, midrange, or minicomputers and are accessed by terminals or micros. The terminals or micros in each application area are connected, or networked, to a host computer that maintains the database and provides access to each user. Small businesses, however, often use a DBMS developed for micros, where each user station controls access to its own files. Whether large or small, most companies buy commercially available DBMS packages, because it would take thousands of hours, or more, to develop these powerful productivity tools. A DBMS, whether it was designed for mainframe or micro use, or for a traditional system or an MIS, can be customized to meet the specifications of users.

One of the principal features of a DBMS is ease of use. Data entry personnel, managers, and the operating staff can learn—without any technical training—how to access data from a database by means of a DBMS. In other words, it is not necessary to know the specifics of the database programs or to understand how data is interrelated in a database to access, edit, or update the data.

In a management information system, database files are frequently joined, and networks allow access to the data. Traditional information systems have less of a need to interrelate data from different systems and to connect data among departments.

## ▶ Database Structures

### HOW DATA IS ORGANIZED AND RETRIEVED IN A DATABASE

First, let us review the data hierarchy concepts introduced in Chapter 3. You may also want to reread the section in Chapter 6 that deals with data hierarchy. Figure 11.1 is a graphic representation of the relationship of fields, records, and files in a database. The text that follows expands on this terminology and explains the role of the computer professional who administers the database.

**Database.**   An organization may have more than one database, each of which consists of related files. The records and fields within files can be joined or otherwise interrelated for query purposes. An MIS is the type of system most likely to need information linked from numerous database files. A school, for example, may have a database containing the names and authors of all the books in its library, a short description of each book, a list of books checked out, a list of books on order, and a list of students who are eligible to borrow books. Each list may be in a separate file; the composite group of files makes up the library's database.

The same school might have another database containing information about its employees, including salaries, dates hired, home addresses, year-to-date payments, year-to-date deductions, amounts paid to the IRS, and any other information needed to process the payroll. It is likely that the year-to-date payroll and tax deduction information would be in one file, while the rest of the employee information would be in another file. Having the two files, each containing different payroll information, is more efficient than one master file for this reason: Several different func-

IN A

**HIERARCHY OF DATA**
Database
   File
      Record
         Field
            Character

*Figure 11.1* (a) *A database consists of files that can be linked.* (b) *The hierarchy of data in a database is illustrated here.*

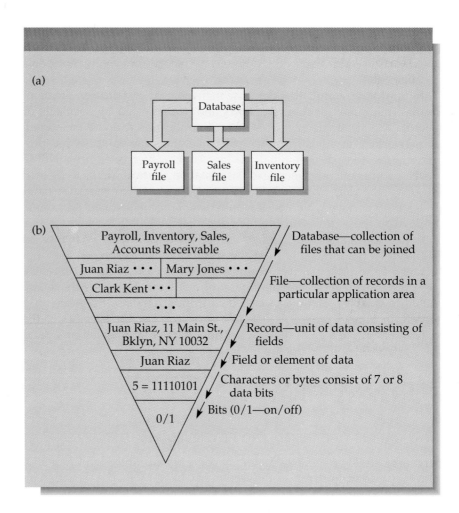

tional groups can access employee data—accounting and payroll as well as the human resources department, for example—and they each may need different data. If a master file contained *all* employee data, that file would be very large, and retrieving data from it could be quite time consuming. Very large files also are far more difficult to access in a multiuser environment or for an MIS.

**Database File.** A database file, often called simply a file, is a collection of records used in a given application (e.g., payroll or accounts payable). A file usually contains many records, each with the same structure. A payroll file, for example, may consist of many payroll records, each with a similar format.

**Record.** A record is a collection of fields that represents one entity within a file, such as an employee record in an employee payroll file or a customer record within an accounts receivable file (see Figure 11.1). All the records in a database file generally have the same structure; that is, each record contains the same fields and the fields hold the same type of information. The contents of the fields for each record, however, are different.

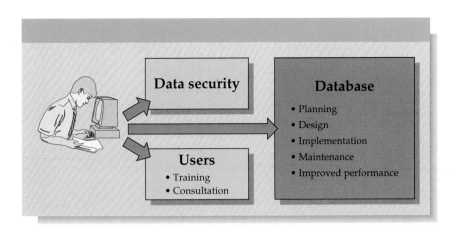

*Figure 11.2* A database administrator's duties include ensuring data security, controlling the database life cycle, and supporting user needs.

**Field.**   A field is a unit of data within a record (see Figure 11.1). For example, salary and number of dependents claimed would each be a field in a payroll record. Customer name and telephone number fields would be in an accounts receivable file consisting of customer records. A *key field* is one that uniquely identifies each record. Social Security number is likely to be a key field in a payroll file and part number is apt to be a key field in an inventory file.

**Database Administrator.**   Database applications are designed to be used by managers and other users who need output for decision-making purposes or for performing day-to-day jobs such as answering inquiries, updating files, and preparing reports. A computer professional called the **database administrator** manages the overall use of databases in an organization. You might consider the database administrator the equivalent of a head librarian who is responsible for the books and the operation of the library. The database administrator is responsible for the databases themselves, the integrity and validity of the data, security of the information, and the operation and maintenance of the DBMS. Some of the database administrator's duties are illustrated in Figure 11.2.

## FLAT FILES AND FILE MANAGEMENT SYSTEMS

File management systems, which have been widely available for years, are not true database management systems, because data in one file cannot be linked easily to data in another file. Despite this limitation, file management systems are often very useful for storing simple data files on a computer, especially in traditional information systems. For example, you might use a file management system (sometimes called a "file manager") to store your personal address book or a small payroll file. Such systems are too limited, however, for most true database or MIS applications where files need to be linked in some way. Symantec's Q&A, PFS:File from Software Publishing, and Reflex from Borland International are three examples of microcomputer file management programs (Figure 11.3).

*Figure 11.3 A file management system can be used to create and maintain individual files.*

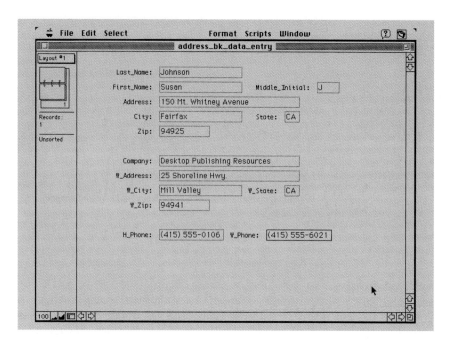

File management programs are generally inexpensive and easy to use, but usually they are limited to some maximum number of records, which may be too small for larger applications. There also may be limitations on the size of records or the number of fields permitted within each record.

File management programs create flat files, which means that the files cannot be linked to other files without the use of a customized application program. Flat files are useful in a traditional system but not in an MIS, which often requires linked files. To retrieve data from flat files, you can access the data sequentially when you need to inquire about the status of all or most records. Such files can be sorted into different sequences depending on the application and then accessed sequentially. Or, the files can be created with an index so that they can be accessed randomly to answer inquiries or perform updates.

True database processing requires more than sequential and random access: it requires files to be linked when the need arises. This is particularly true for an MIS or for traditional systems that rely on data from many sources. A DBMS, rather than a file management system, enables files to be joined. Four basic database structures can be used by a DBMS for interrelating files and records: hierarchical databases, network databases, relational databases, and object-oriented databases.

## HIERARCHICAL DATABASES

A **hierarchical database** is organized like a tree planted upside down—with the roots at the top. In Figure 11.4, for example, the root field (the top field in the diagram) is the Business Department. It is linked to its corresponding courses. One branch from the Business Department root field contains the Introduction to Marketing course, another contains the

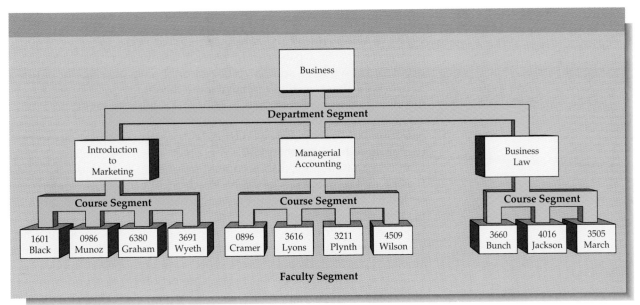

Faculty Segment

*Figure 11.4 Segments of data in a hierarchical database are organized into levels, where each level is increasingly detailed. Each segment can have only one upward path.*

Managerial Accounting course, and the third contains the Business Law course.

Each data item or group of data items shown in the inverted tree diagram is called a segment, which is similar to a file of records. You could consider the segments to be arranged like a family tree. Parent segments (Departments, for example) appear above the child segments (Courses) in the diagram. Each parent segment can have more than one child, but a child can only have one parent. This is called a one-to-many relationship. Each segment lies on a hierarchical path, from the root segment to the branches to the lowest-level child, and a given segment cannot appear on more than one path.

In the hierarchical structure shown in Figure 11.4, faculty members teach courses in only a single department. If a faculty member taught both Business Law and Introduction to Marketing, the hierarchical model would not be totally effective, because the same faculty name would have to appear in two different segments. That violates the rule that a given segment cannot appear on more than one path. Similarly, if there were a Managerial Accounting course in both the Business Department and the Law Department, a hierarchical database model such as the one described would not be ideal.

Certain types of data lend themselves to hierarchical representation. For example, if a retail establishment has a series of stores and each store has its own unique sales staff, then a hierarchical database structure could be used to store salesperson data. There would be no risk that data in one segment might also appear in another segment.

An example of a hierarchical database management system for mainframes in large organizations is IMS/VS from IBM. The database can be accessed by commands in the IMS/VS query language or by a custom program written in a third-generation language such as COBOL.

A root field in a hierarchical database is like a root or main directory on a disk, and a segment in a hierarchical database is like a subdirectory on a disk.

## NETWORK DATABASES

Network and hierarchical databases are similar in the way they organize data according to a parent-child type of relationship. In a hierarchical database, as we have seen, a child can only have one parent, but in a **network database,** a child can have more than one parent. Consider our Business Department root field in Figure 11.4 with its segments. Professors who teach in different areas can be handled easily in a network database. Similarly, salespeople who work in more than one location can have two or more branch (parent) offices in a network sales database. A child with no parent at all is also permitted in a network database. So if Professor Kim Lee in the Business Law Department were on leave, she could be linked to the department segment without being linked to an intermediate course segment.

Figure 11.5 shows the department/course/faculty example for a network database. A network DBMS can create more complex relationships among types of data and thus is suited to more types of applications. Users are limited, however, to the connections that were originally defined by the application's developer. One disadvantage of both hierarchical and network database models is that relationships among elements must be determined when the system is designed; if there is a need to make changes to those relationships later on because different information is required, then the database must be restructured.

The most popular network database model was developed by CODA-SYL (Conference on Data Systems Languages), a standards group that also helped shape the COBOL language. Many commercial products use the CODASYL network database model. One such product is TOTAL from Cincom. Its data manipulation language (DML) is used to access records in a CODASYL database. DML commands were designed so that they can be "embedded" in application programs written in COBOL, FORTRAN, or other third-generation languages.

*Figure 11.5 Segments of data in a network database can have multiple relationships to parent segments on a higher level.*

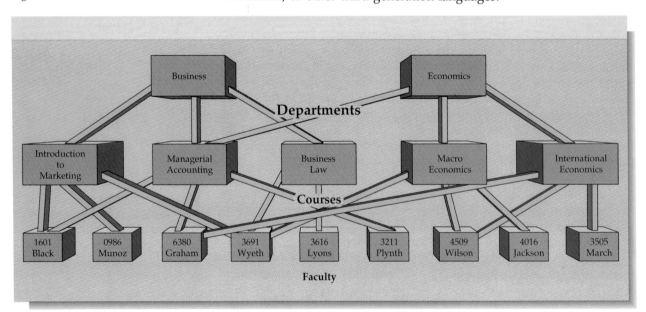

## RELATIONAL DATABASES

**Relational databases** are the most common type of database structure for all levels of computers, from micros to mainframes, and for most types of systems, from traditional to management information systems. In a relational database, key fields within records can be used to link, or join, any number of files. Whereas hierarchical and network database management systems establish the relationships among data elements when the database is being designed, a relational database allows virtually any type of linkage or relation among data elements to be established as the need arises. This flexibility is one important reason why relational databases are so popular.

Many DBMS packages based on the relational database model present files in table format: the records are represented conceptually as rows and the fields as columns (Figure 11.6). Data is presented this way because it is often more easily visualized in tabular form. The computer, however, does not actually store files in table form but as a sequential stream of records. In addition, the records are not necessarily stored in the order in which they appear in a table. Relational databases are designed so that they can display data in table form in any sequence desired.

As we noted, a major advantage of a relational DBMS is that it allows linking, or "relating," several database files. For example, the payroll department needs employee addresses only once a year, when W-2 forms

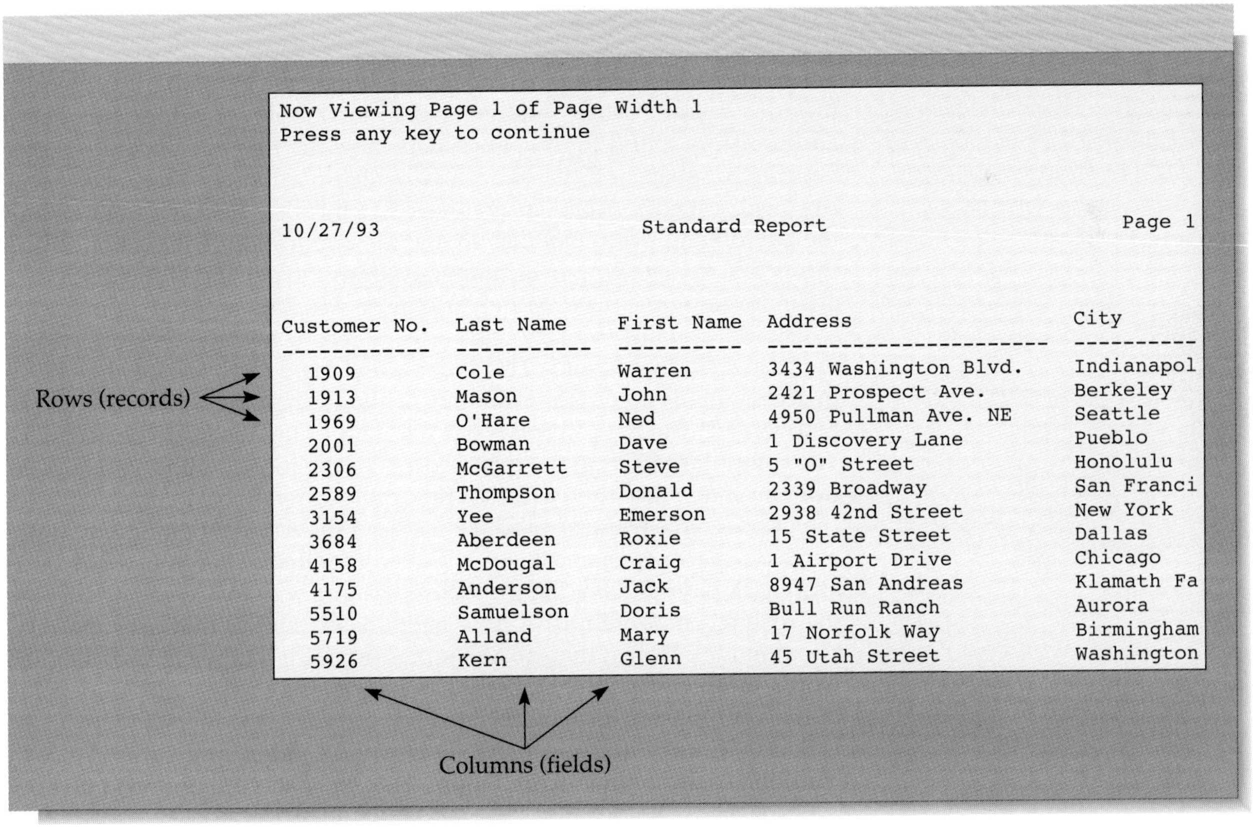

*Figure 11.6 A relational database usually presents data in table format, as shown in this screen from a dBASE IV database.*

```
Now Viewing Page 1 of Page Width 1
Press any key to continue


10/27/93                    Standard Report                      Page 1



Customer No.  Last Name   First Name  Address                  City
------------  ----------  ----------  -----------------------  ----------
    1909      Cole        Warren      3434 Washington Blvd.    Indianapol
    1913      Mason       John        2421 Prospect Ave.       Berkeley
    1969      O'Hare      Ned         4950 Pullman Ave. NE     Seattle
    2001      Bowman      Dave        1 Discovery Lane         Pueblo
    2306      McGarrett   Steve       5 "O" Street             Honolulu
    2589      Thompson    Donald      2339 Broadway            San Franci
    3154      Yee         Emerson     2938 42nd Street         New York
    3684      Aberdeen    Roxie       15 State Street          Dallas
    4158      McDougal    Craig       1 Airport Drive          Chicago
    4175      Anderson    Jack        8947 San Andreas         Klamath Fa
    5510      Samuelson   Doris       Bull Run Ranch           Aurora
    5719      Alland      Mary        17 Norfolk Way           Birmingham
    5926      Kern        Glenn       45 Utah Street           Washington
```

Rows (records)

Columns (fields)

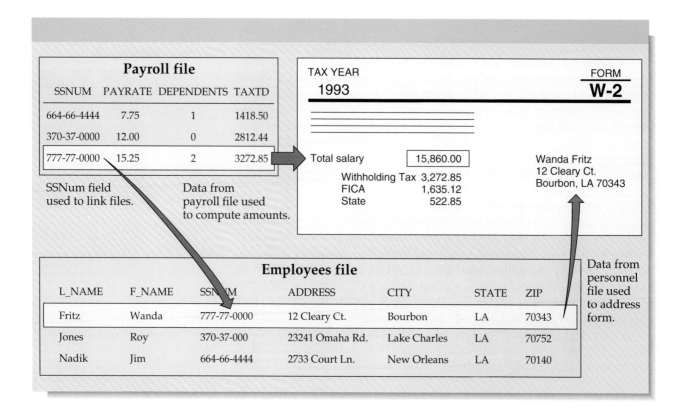

**Payroll file**

| SSNUM | PAYRATE | DEPENDENTS | TAXTD |
|-------|---------|------------|-------|
| 664-66-4444 | 7.75 | 1 | 1418.50 |
| 370-37-0000 | 12.00 | 0 | 2812.44 |
| 777-77-0000 | 15.25 | 2 | 3272.85 |

SSNum field used to link files.

Data from payroll file used to compute amounts.

| TAX YEAR | FORM |
|----------|------|
| **1993** | **W-2** |

Total salary 15,860.00

Withholding Tax 3,272.85
FICA 1,635.12
State 522.85

Wanda Fritz
12 Cleary Ct.
Bourbon, LA 70343

**Employees file**

| L_NAME | F_NAME | SSNUM | ADDRESS | CITY | STATE | ZIP |
|--------|--------|-------|---------|------|-------|-----|
| Fritz | Wanda | 777-77-0000 | 12 Cleary Ct. | Bourbon | LA | 70343 |
| Jones | Roy | 370-37-000 | 23241 Omaha Rd. | Lake Charles | LA | 70752 |
| Nadik | Jim | 664-66-4444 | 2733 Court Ln. | New Orleans | LA | 70140 |

Data from personnel file used to address form.

*Figure 11.7* To send W-2 forms, a relational DBMS retrieves salary information from the payroll file and then uses the SSNUM field to locate and retrieve the corresponding employee address from the personnel file.

are mailed. To save space and access time, the payroll file typically includes Social Security numbers but not employee addresses. These addresses are found in a separate personnel file that also includes Social Security numbers and that is accessed only occasionally. The Social Security field, called SSNUM in Figure 11.7, functions as a key field to link the payroll and personnel files so that the application that generates W-2 forms can retrieve employee addresses from the personnel file. Both files are indexed on the SSNUM field. Recall from Chapter 6 that an index for a disk file contains the key field for each record and the disk address of the corresponding record. This index provides a fast way for the DBMS to access the desired data randomly without scanning a file from beginning to end. The user supplies the key field of the record to be accessed. The computer looks up the disk address of the record with that key field from an index and then accesses the record directly.

Suppose you want to produce a screen display containing employee names, departments, and taxes withheld to date so that you could visually check payroll data. Figure 11.8 shows one way to access and display the required data with dBASE, a micro-based DBMS that uses the relational model. Notice that dBASE's programming language uses English words in abbreviated sentences. The names assigned to files and fields in this example are also abbreviated but are easy to understand: SSNUM is Social Security number, PAYIND is payroll index, and so on. We will consider each command in Figure 11.8 so that you understand how dBASE accesses the database.

```
.  SELECT 1
      Selects an initial file work area.
.  USE EMPLOYEES
      Opens the EMPLOYEES personnel file as file 1.
.  INDEX ON SSNUM TO EMPIND
      Indexes on SSNUM field and creates an index file called EMPIND.
.  SELECT 2
      Selects a second file work area.
.  USE PAYROLL
      Opens the PAYROLL file as file 2.
.  INDEX ON SSNUM TO PAYIND
      Indexes on SSNUM field and creates an index file called PAYIND.
.  SET RELATION TO EMPLOYEES INTO SSNUM
      Relates SSNUM for both files.
.  GO TOP
      Goes to the top of the first record in the linked files.
.  DISPLAY ALL FIELDS SSNUM,TAXTD,ENAME,EDEPT
      Displays fields where SSNUM in EMPLOYEES file = SSNUM in
      PAYROLL file.
```

- The SELECT command assigns a file work area. Each file in use must have its own work area. The command in Figure 11.8 specifies work area 1.
- The USE command opens, or readies, a file for access and assigns it to the previously SELECTed work area. The EMPLOYEES personnel file is here assigned to work area 1.
- The INDEX command creates an index using the key field SSNUM and instructs the database to place the index in a file named EMPIND, an abbreviation for employee index.
- A second work area is specified for the PAYROLL file, and it is indexed similarly (with SELECT/USE/INDEX).
- SET RELATION instructs the system to relate the currently SELECTed file, which is PAYROLL, with the EMPLOYEES personnel file and specifies the key field to use, which is SSNUM. This command links the two files.
- The GO TOP command tells the database to go to the top of the list created from the two related files, that is, to the first record in the linked files.
- The DISPLAY command tells dBASE to create a screen display, and ALL tells it to display all records. FIELDS specifies which fields in the records to display—in this case, the SSNUM and TAXTD (tax to date) fields in the payroll file and the ENAME (employee name) and EDEPT (employee department) fields in the EMPLOYEES personnel file.

The resulting table would look like the one in Figure 11.9. It contains all the data needed for inquiry purposes. The data in the table cannot be edited directly, however, because it is not a formal file; rather, it is a

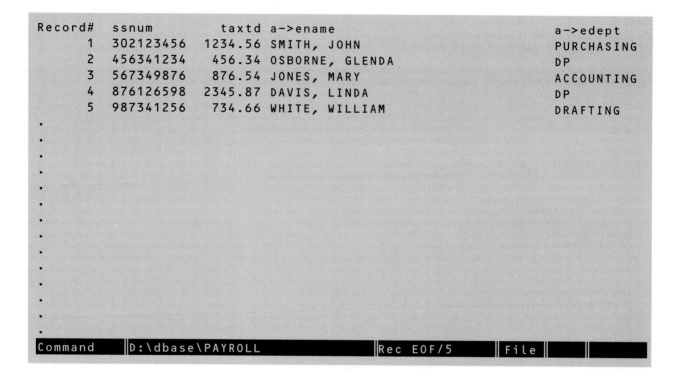

```
Record#   ssnum        taxtd  a->ename                    a->edept
      1   302123456  1234.56  SMITH, JOHN                 PURCHASING
      2   456341234   456.34  OSBORNE, GLENDA             DP
      3   567349876   876.54  JONES, MARY                 ACCOUNTING
      4   876126598  2345.87  DAVIS, LINDA                DP
      5   987341256   734.66  WHITE, WILLIAM              DRAFTING
      .
      .
      .
      .
      .
      .
      .
      .
      .
      .
      .
      .
```

| Command | D:\dbase\PAYROLL | Rec EOF/5 | File |

**Figure 11.9** *This is the linked file created by the program in Figure 11.8. It can only be viewed or printed; it cannot be edited.*

**Figure 11.10** *Here, the IRS uses Social Security numbers to compare individual reporting of bank interest income with bank records.*

linked relation of two files that is temporarily stored for purposes of providing needed output.

Let us take a look at another application for a relational DBMS: how the IRS might set up files to verify that taxpayers are declaring all their interest income (Figure 11.10). The IRS has a file of data from bank records as well as a file of data from income tax returns submitted by each taxpayer. The bank file consists of customer records with fields for customer name, bank account number, Social Security number, total deposits for the past year, and total interest earned. The taxpayer file contains records that include fields for taxpayer name, Social Security number, reported income, and reported interest earned from bank deposits. The Social Security number is the key field used to link these two files.

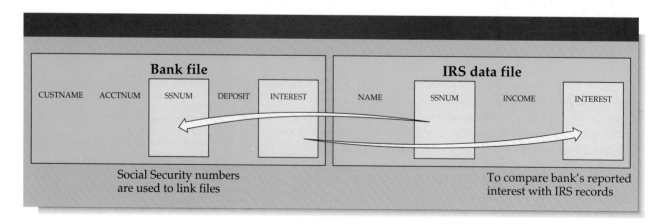

Linking the two files enables the IRS to compare each taxpayer's total interest earned for the year with the reported interest earned. In this way, any returns in which reported interest is less than actual interest may be flagged.

## OBJECT-ORIENTED DATABASES

Most database management systems today use the relational model, but object-oriented databases are likely to gain considerable ground in the next few years. Object-oriented database management systems use objects as elements within database files. An object consisting of text, sound, video, other images such as documents and forms, or graphics can be integrated into one database record. Objects in an object-oriented DBMS can also mix differently structured records alongside one another. Perhaps most importantly, objects in a database inherit characteristics, or attributes, from their parents; in this way, attributes need only be defined once—at the highest level.

Consider an automobile inventory application in which objects contain information about cars and car parts, including prices, suppliers, transaction data, and customer information. The database includes text descriptions as well as color images of car parts. The object-oriented DBMS can display a "tree" depicting all of the objects and their hierarchical relationships to each other. For example, specific types of cars inherit parts such as a motor, chassis, and so on from major classes of cars. Color can be used in any way desired; items displayed in red, for example, could mean out of stock. By means of an object-oriented DBMS, car parts can be viewed, combined, assembled, and so on.

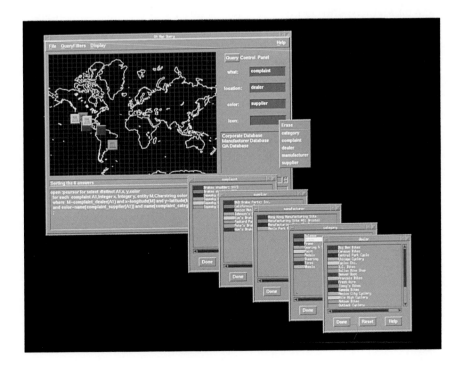

*An illustration of how different forms of data can be integrated in an object-oriented database.*

Object-oriented systems are becoming very popular and are likely to have a considerable impact on the computing field in the years ahead, especially as multimedia techniques improve. The ability to display a video or a photo—even sound—along with textual data on an object can be very useful.

**Table 11.1** | DATABASE MANAGEMENT SYSTEMS FOR MAINFRAMES

| Product |
|---|
| Relational |
| Oracle |
| DB2 |
| Ingres |
| Hierarchical |
| Focus |
| IMS/VS |
| RAMIS |
| Network |
| Adabas |
| IDMS |
| TOTAL |

**Table 11.2** | POPULAR DATABASE MANAGEMENT SYSTEMS FOR MICROS

| Product | Manufacturer |
|---|---|
| dBASE IV | Borland |
| R:BASE | Microrim |
| FoxPro | Microsoft |
| Paradox | Borland |
| Oracle | Oracle |

Table 11.1 lists some of the better-known database management systems currently available for mainframes. Table 11.2 includes a similar list for micros. There are many packages available for all categories of computers.

## ▶ Components of DBMS Software

Database management systems enable users to establish and use databases for a wide range of customized applications. There are six basic components in a DBMS (see Figure 11.11): (1) data dictionary, (2) data definition language, (3) data manipulation language, (4) utilities, (5) application generators, and (6) report generators.

### DATA DICTIONARY

Many database management systems include a data dictionary, described in Chapter 10, which specifies the features of the data, how data can be accessed by users, who has access to specific parts of the database and their passwords, and so on. The data dictionary is typically maintained by the database administrator. A data dictionary helps to minimize errors because as data is entered, the dictionary checks it to make sure it is within specified parameters (e.g., a salary might be required to be within a set range of values).

### DATA DEFINITION LANGUAGE

The **data definition language (DDL)** describes in detail the technical specifications for the elements in the data dictionary and the relationships among them. Each DBMS package has its own DDL.

### DATA MANIPULATION LANGUAGE

Database management packages have some form of **data manipulation language (DML)** that allows users to create custom-designed applications. Many DMLs are unique to a specific product. These languages, which are also called query languages, are classified as fourth-generation languages because they enable users to request data from a database file or update data in a database file. Query languages use simple English words such as APPEND, MODIFY, or DELETE and are easier to learn than third-generation languages such as COBOL or Pascal. With 3GLs,

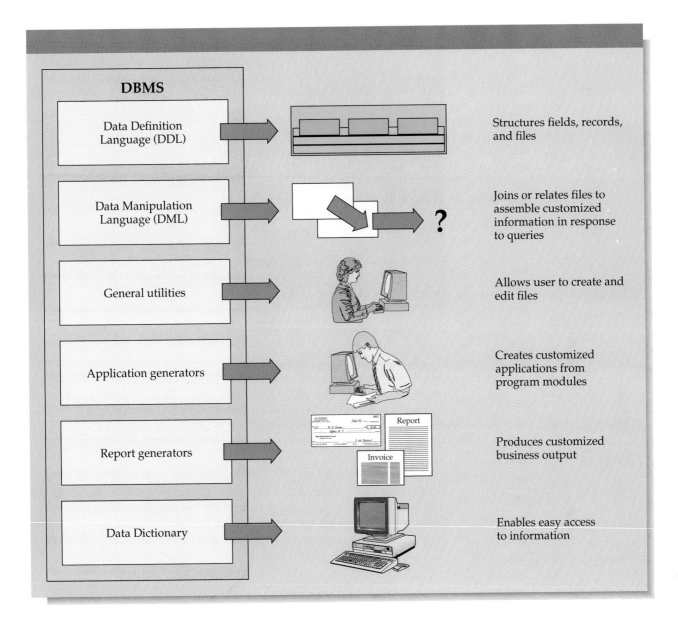

**DBMS**

| | | |
|---|---|---|
| Data Definition Language (DDL) | | Structures fields, records, and files |
| Data Manipulation Language (DML) | | Joins or relates files to assemble customized information in response to queries |
| General utilities | | Allows user to create and edit files |
| Application generators | | Creates customized applications from program modules |
| Report generators | | Produces customized business output |
| Data Dictionary | | Enables easy access to information |

the programmer must indicate the precise procedures to be followed; with query languages and other 4GLs, the user need only issue English-like commands.

A query language that has become a standard for data manipulation languages is **SQL** (*Structured Query Language*). Some database management systems, like dBASE and R:BASE, have their own data manipulation languages but have added SQL capability in their most recent versions to make them more useful to people who know SQL. Other query languages include QBE (Query-By-Example) and QUEL (Query Language).

Many database management systems also allow instructions written in third-generation procedural languages such as COBOL and Pascal to

*Figure 11.11 The six components of a database management system allow organizations to set up and use their databases for a wide range of customized applications.*

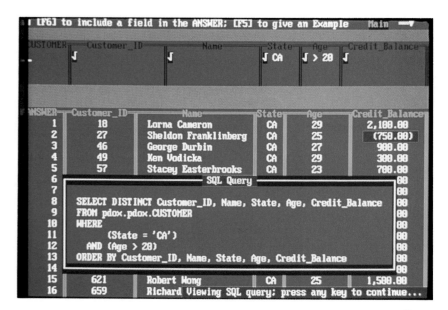

*An SQL screen display that reports on the status of specific records in a database.*

be used in designing applications. The query language for the DBMS is embedded within the procedural language. This permits application designers to go beyond the limitations of the package's own data manipulation language when they must design large and complex applications.

### UTILITIES

Utilities are the components of a DBMS that allow you to maintain the database by editing data, deleting records, creating new files, and so on. Utilities enable users to control the input procedure by establishing ranges for data items entered, types of acceptable data, and so on. They

## LOOKING AHEAD

### USING NATURAL LANGUAGE TO QUERY A DATABASE

In the future, you will be able to use a "natural query language" to query a database over the phone or on a computer terminal and receive your answer in conversational English. A natural query language enables you to use standard English without following any specific programming rules. It is as natural as speaking to another person. Here is a fictitious example of an interactive dialog be-

tween a user at a terminal and a computer. The computer's responses are in italics.

- How much does John make?
- *John who?*
- Smith.
- *I've got two John Smiths, one in Purchasing and one in Sales.*
- The one in sales.
- *$40,000 plus commissions.*
- How much was his commission in

1993?
- *$32,456.67.*

If you are a science fiction fan, you are probably familiar with the concept of natural language interfaces. They are likely to be in full use for database management systems by the year 2000, if not sooner. Some current query languages have begun to approach this level of natural communication.

can also help create user-friendly screen displays for data entry or data retrieval.

## APPLICATION GENERATORS

The **application generator** is the component of a DBMS that allows users to create applications without actually writing programs. It is really a collection of program modules. A user requests specific tasks and the application generator selects the appropriate program modules.

## REPORT GENERATORS

The report generator makes it easy to ask for and design hard copy output in the form of reports and graphs. It permits users to define row and column heads, to generate report headers identifying the full report, page headers at the top of each page, and so forth. In summary, DBMS report generators enable users to create readable and attractive reports on short notice and with little computer expertise.

As you learned in Chapter 7, application generators and report generators are also regarded as fourth-generation programming languages because they permit people without programming experience to develop computer applications. Moreover, users need only learn English-like commands, rather than program logic, to have the computer execute procedures.

## ▶ Issues for the Database Administrator

A DBMS is used to create, edit, update, and report from database files. The relative ease with which data can be manipulated using a DBMS sometimes results in errors; for example, unauthorized users may gain access or data entry workers may make errors. So the use of a DBMS actually increases the need for security and for minimizing the risk of entering invalid data. The database administrator is the computing professional who must address these issues.

## SECURITY

Database security refers to the measures that protect databases against unauthorized access. Most organizations have hardware and software controls that protect and monitor overall computer activities. In addition, many database management systems offer their own security software to help minimize unauthorized access and to prevent destruction of files.

Security measures are often extremely complicated and difficult to implement; nevertheless, they must be as comprehensive as possible, especially for highly sensitive data (Figure 11.12). Regardless of the type of information system and DBMS, security measures are necessary to minimize risks. It is unrealistic, however, to expect such measures to be

IN A NUT SHELL

**FEATURES OF A DBMS**

1. Many different people can use the same database files, often at the same time. There is no need to duplicate database files when several people require access or when data needs to be linked.
2. Users with little or no computer expertise are able to store, retrieve, update, operate on, or report from database files.
3. Users from different functional areas can access each other's data. For example, the linking of manufacturing and marketing data might enable a production department to obtain sales data, otherwise unavailable, to help plan its manufacturing operations. A DBMS also enables managers in an MIS to access company-wide data from numerous databases.

*Figure 11.12* *The control room for a NASA flight receives data from public weather systems and secret on-board control systems. Complex information transmitted to users scattered around the world makes data security a major concern.*

able to eliminate *all* risks.

The security offered by various database management systems ranges from minimal to excellent. Most have log-on security, which prevents unauthorized users from accessing the DBMS. The database administrator defines which files, which records, and which fields within records each user or department can access. In addition, the administrator may assign various access levels that define who can read files, update records, delete records, or add data. Most DBMS products can protect a file so that it is only readable by the person who "owns" or shares it. Data in a DBMS is often protected by encoding it in a special way, a technique called **encryption.**

The more users that have access to a DBMS, the greater the security risk and the greater the need for monitoring file access. Database management systems designed originally for mainframes tend to have the best security because they were intended to provide access to many users.

In addition to the security offered by a DBMS, any network that connects database users should have its own security procedures. Some examples are log-on security, restricted access to programs (e.g., those in a database management system), and restricted access to database files. If no network security is available and several users have access to the same computer or to other users' files, different protection measures must be established. For example, databases can be stored on removable storage media so that they can be maintained in a secure place, or a separate encryption program could be written.

## DATA INTEGRITY

Maintaining **data integrity** means ensuring that a system is uncorrupted by invalid data. Corrupted data can come from many sources.

- The storage medium itself might be corrupted by exposure to a magnetic field. Do not leave a disk near a copying machine, a telephone, or a television.
- A user might inadvertently enter a command that incorrectly changes data. For example, your intention may be to change a date in one record, but you state the command ambiguously and as a result the date is changed in all or part of the file.
- A virus may have invaded your system.

Despite all efforts, simple data entry errors will inevitably occur. A DBMS can never eliminate all of them, but it can succeed in minimizing them. For example, the DBMS cannot find an invalid date such as 11/30/93 when it should be 11/29/93 or a price entered as $12.00 instead of $12.50. It can, however, flag clearly invalid entries such as a date of 11/31/93 (November has only 30 days). Similarly, it can flag a negative price as an error.

The cost of recovering or restoring files from corrupted data can be very high, especially if many records are affected. The database administrator is responsible for training users in good practices, ensuring that applications are designed to protect data integrity, and controlling access to limit the risks of corrupting data. In addition, the administrator implements feedback and control mechanisms to check the reliability of the database on a periodic basis. The database administrator also participates in the selection and evaluation of the database management system.

## SELECTING A DBMS

Several factors should be considered when an organization chooses a database management system:

- Compatibility with existing hardware and software.
- Type of database models—relational, hierarchical, or network.
- Suitability of the DBMS for specific applications.
- Purchase or lease price and maintenance costs (many mainframe DBMSs can only be leased, not purchased).
- Response time for queries, indexing, sorts, and so on, given the existing hardware and the size of the files.
- Number of simultaneous users permitted by the DBMS.
- Restrictive limitations on database, file, or record sizes.
- The number, type, and quality of query languages and/or programming languages that can be used.
- Capability and ease of use of the application generator and report generator.
- Security features.

## ▶ SELF-TEST

1. In relational databases, records are often displayed as _____ in a table and fields are often displayed as _____.
2. (T or F) A file manager is generally more powerful than a relational database.
3. In a hierarchical database, how many parents does a child have?
4. (T or F) Object-oriented database management systems use objects to store graphics, video, and even sound as part of a record.
5. What are two key issues a database administrator faces?

Solutions
1. rows; columns
2. F
3. one
4. T
5. security and integrity of databases

## 11.2 MANAGEMENT INFORMATION SYSTEMS

## ▶ Facilitating Decision Making at All Management Levels

How can access to databases improve the quality of information for management decision making at all levels of an organization?

Throughout this book we have emphasized that information is data processed in such a way that it can be used as a basis for decision making. To be useful, information must be complete and concise, accurate, timely, economically justified, and relevant.

A business system whose primary objective is to provide useful information to managers from the top levels on down is referred to as a management information system. An MIS may use not only the data in an organization's own databases but also data from external database services such as company profiles and stock analyses. The principal goal of an MIS is to deliver to managers the timely and relevant information that they need for effective planning and managing.

### HOW AN MIS DIFFERS FROM A TRADITIONAL INFORMATION SYSTEM

All managers need information to help them make decisions and to assist them in achieving their business objectives, but the kind of information required differs at each level of management. For example, the day-to-day operational information that a line supervisor requires may not be of value to a vice president responsible for long-range planning. An MIS integrates all of an organization's information, from the highest organizational level to the operating level, so that it is capable of satisfying the needs of top-level management first and then those of the operating staff.

A senior manager of a major food manufacturer complained about the company's traditional information systems to a vice president. She said

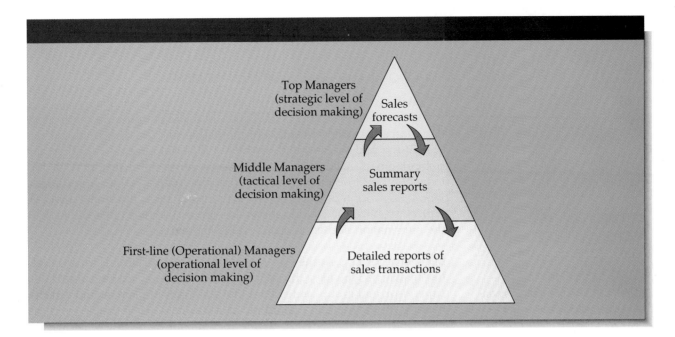

*Figure 11.13* A top-down MIS approach focuses on information to meet the needs of high-level managers first. Reports for lower levels of management can then be generated from the same data.

that although she had all the *data* she could use about product sales in each department, she still did not have the *information* she needed—a comparison between last year's total cold cereal sales and a major competitor's total sales. As a senior manager, her job was to quickly detect trends and business patterns in the organization and in the industry as a whole. To get the comparative information she needed, she had to sift through 700 pages of reports and two journal articles to find and add up columns of numbers! Information systems that focus primarily on day-to-day operations were of little use because they did not provide her with broadly based information. A well-designed MIS would solve the problem by focusing on managers' needs first.

The traditional approach to designing information systems, discussed in Chapter 10, treats each functional area or business system as a separate unit. Analysts design operational-level systems based on the assumption that if each functional area within an organization operates efficiently, the organization as a whole will run smoothly. Although these traditional operational-level systems are designed to satisfy the requirements of lower-level managers and operating staff, they often do not provide the information top-level managers need.

In contrast, the MIS approach focuses on the organization as a whole with one set of specific corporate objectives that originate from top management. The primary objective of an MIS is to help meet those objectives. The MIS approach assumes that if the system meets the information needs of top managers, more detailed information will "trickle down" the organization to meet the needs of lower-level managers. For instance, if the main objective of an MIS is to provide top managers with sales forecasts, middle managers in each functional area should be able to obtain summary reports from the data that was used to compute the sales forecasts. Similarly, first-line managers can receive transaction reports, using the same data but in a more detailed way (Figure 11.13).

Such an approach is often referred to as a top-down approach because it is designed to satisfy top-level needs first and foremost.

## FUNCTIONS AND LEVELS OF MANAGEMENT

We saw in Chapter 2 that an organization consists of functional areas that work together to meet the overall goals of the organization. Typical functional areas, or departments, are marketing and sales, manufacturing, accounting and finance, and research and development—all necessary components of a business. Organizations consist of a hierarchy of top managers, middle managers, and first-line managers, or supervisors, who work within or integrate the activities of these functional areas. A typical organization chart is shown in Figure 11.14. Next, we will look at the information needed at each level in more detail.

**Operational Level.**    At the lower levels of the organization chart are first-line managers who have titles such as office manager, accounts receivable supervisor, and group leader. First-line managers implement and directly oversee the day-to-day operations of a business. Their major concerns may be to meet daily or weekly production and marketing schedules, to maintain inventory records, or to monitor the progress of workers. In

*Figure 11.14 Within a typical organization, information flows vertically down organizational lines as well as horizontally among departments.*

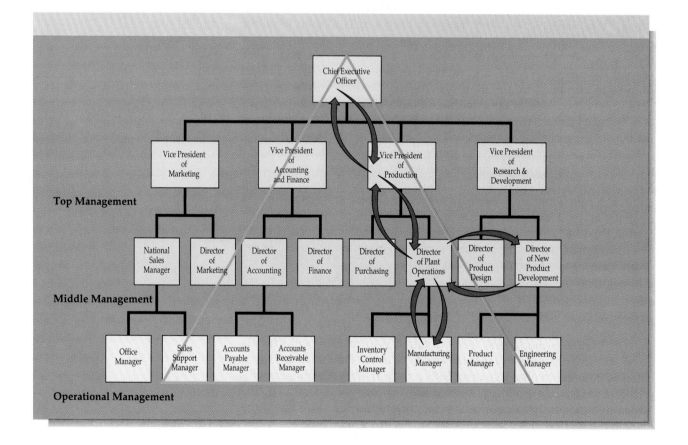

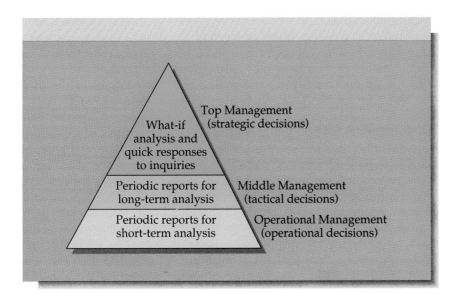

*Figure 11.15 Each level of management has its own information needs. First-line or operational managers generally send information up the organizational line; middle managers communicate up and down the line; top managers generally communicate across functional lines.*

general, their jobs are more structured, routine, and focused on short-term rather than long-term objectives.

To accomplish their jobs, operating-level managers need current, detailed, internal information most often produced by transaction processing. First-line managers generally send information vertically within functional lines (Figure 11.15). For example, in the cold cereal division of a food manufacturer, the product managers need periodic reports that show the number of cases of their cereal sold each month in each sales region for the past 12 months, as well as a listing of each sale made in each reporting period. This information gives them the support they need to design strategies for increasing sales or correcting sales problems and to prepare reports for the director of marketing.

**Middle-Management Level.**   Middle managers receive information from managers below and above them and use it to implement the strategic plans of top management and to monitor current operations in their area. Typical titles for middle mangers are national sales manager, director of research, and director of finance.

To develop specific plans for achieving the overall strategic plans outlined by top managers, middle managers most often perform fairly structured activities such as formulating and managing budgets, developing training programs, and monitoring sales. Generally, they rely more on internal than external information, do a great deal of quantitative analysis, and require less detail than first-line managers. Middle managers need summary information that provides just enough detail for them to describe recent business activities in comparison to other activities, for example, to compare this month's sales with last month's sales.

As shown in Figure 11.14, information at the middle-management level moves both horizontally and vertically. For example, the director of marketing for cold cereals needs to report how all of the division's cereals have sold across the nation. She gathers sales information from each cereal's product manager. She also requests reports on how competitors' cold cereals sold during the same period and reports about her company's current market share for each cereal and for cold cereals collectively. This middle manager then uses the information to help develop strategies with the product managers, and makes recommendations to the division's vice president.

**Top-Management Level.**    Top managers are chief executive officers, chief financial officers, and vice presidents of functional areas or divisions. They formulate the strategic plans to guide a firm toward its long-range goals, to establish performance objectives, and to coordinate the activities of the entire organization to achieve these goals.

Top-management tasks vary greatly and require more decision making than middle-management tasks. For example, top managers establish financial goals for the firm, approve new markets and products, and evaluate potential mergers and acquisitions. Clearly, the decisions that top managers make have the greatest effect on the organization, although the effect may not be felt for years. To make strategic decisions, top managers need information that is in summary, rather than detail, form, is directed toward the future, and relates to external as well as internal factors.

The various vice presidents of the cold cereals division, for example, must make decisions on what products to develop, which products are not profitable and should be dropped from the product line, and what sales target will be both aggressive and achievable. To accomplish these

*Image processing is becoming an important component of management information systems.*

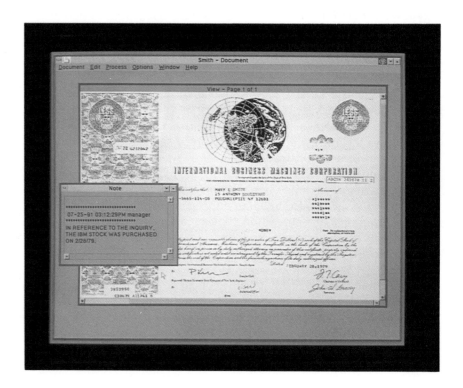

goals, top management needs not only summary reports from the middle managers in their division but also immediate access to news of competitors' product development, long-range predictions of the cost of grains and other raw materials, marketing analyses of customers' changing preferences, and so on.

In summary, a manager's level determines what kind of information he or she needs. To be effective, an MIS must provide information appropriate for each level of management. It does so by providing top-level management with the information it needs and then using that information in a more structured and detailed manner to satisfy the needs of lower-level personnel.

## ▶ MIS Hardware

In large-scale management information systems, a mainframe, midrange, or minicomputer typically serves as a host computer in a distributed processing network. Managers and other personnel access the system through various terminals, PCs, and workstations linked to the host. An MIS, then, is usually implemented using a distributed computer facility. See Figure 11.16.

*Figure 11.16* MIS hardware typically includes a mainframe as a host, network architecture, and interactive graphics terminals or micros. This equipment provides maximum access to programs and databases.

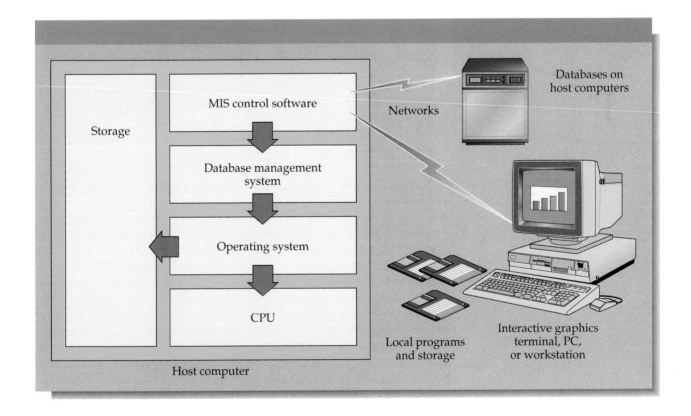

## ▶ Specialized Management Information Systems

Three types of management information systems—decision support systems, executive information systems, and expert systems—are growing in popularity for business applications.

### DECISION SUPPORT SYSTEMS

A well-designed MIS provides whatever information managers need in the form most useful to them. But typically the information supplied by an MIS to all levels of management is *structured* information. In general, structured information requires managers to know in advance what they want the system to provide.

A **decision support system (DSS)** goes beyond providing well-designed structured reports to managers. A DSS is a *flexible* information system that allows top-level managers to access both corporate and external databases and to create their own reports and applications, even their own specialized databases. With a DSS, a manager is able to address problems that are not structured and problems that may not have been anticipated when the system was designed.

The five goals of a decision support system are to

1. Specifically address the decision-making needs of the top levels of management.
2. Address problems that were not previously thought about when the management information system was developed.
3. Make available to the decision maker analytical tools for financial planning and forecasting.
4. Enable decision makers with only a minimal amount of computer expertise to use the system, that is, to make interaction as "natural" as possible.
5. Enable decision makers to access corporate data in any way they want and to perform what-if analysis with ease.

Assume that you are a customer service manager for Analyze!, a major software vendor that sells more than a hundred different software products. Top management decides that Analyze! has come on hard times and therefore should concentrate only on its most profitable products. Top management wants you to reduce service on products that are not doing well, that is, those products that in your judgment require more customer service resources (such as staff time) than they are worth. To help you decide which products warrant a cut in support level, you need to determine which bring in the most sales revenue and which require the most telephone support with customers. Once you have this data, you can analyze it to determine which products do not bring in enough revenue to justify their level of customer support. If a product is expensive to support but is a best-seller, you will want to continue to support it. But if a product is both expensive to support and does not sell well, you will probably recommend a change in the amount of support.

**CRITICAL THINKING**

Think of some situations in business where unanticipated needs for information from an MIS might develop.

The Analyze! managers are fortunate: their company's systems analysis group designed the management information system to provide them with a number of flexible decision-support tools for obtaining and analyzing such data. These tools are based on fourth-generation languages and are *relatively* easy to use. We stress the word *relatively* because although 4GL tools are much simpler to use than procedural programming languages (3GLs), considerable training and experience may still be required to use them effectively. The standard types of 4GL tools available to the Analyze! managers allow them to interact with the company's database and to analyze data in the following ways.

- Modeling—to develop a simulation, or model, of the functional areas of the organization using a computer.
- Statistical analysis—not only to obtain basic statistics but to determine risks through risk analysis and trends through trend analysis.
- Forecasting—to make predictions.

**Financial Planning Languages.**   **Financial planning languages (FPLs)** are the most common tools used for modeling, performing statistical analyses, and forecasting. You now have a month's data about Analyze! product support phone calls stored in the customer support database. You have also used the DSS's query language to retrieve product profitability data from the corporate database. So you are prepared to analyze product data to find out which products are too expensive to support. The company's FPLs will provide you with sophisticated mathematical, statistical, and forecasting methods for analyzing data. Figure 11.17 is a screen from the FPL program called IFPS developed by Execucom. IFPS (*Interactive Financial Planning System*) is a 4GL commonly used for modeling, statistical analysis, and forecasting for decision-making purposes.

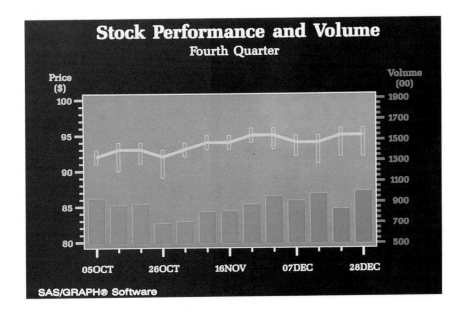

*Financial analysis tools help to develop decision support systems.*

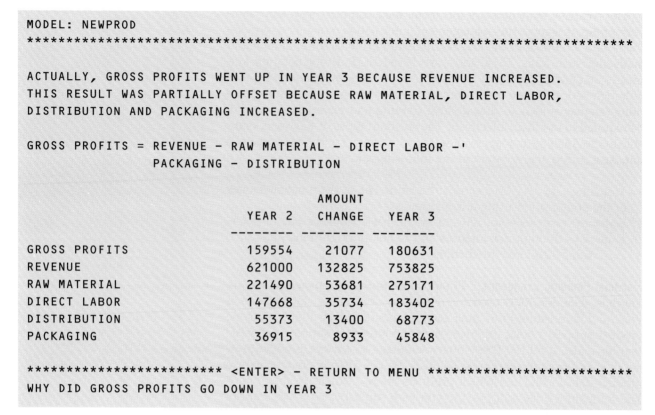

```
MODEL: NEWPROD
******************************************************************************

ACTUALLY, GROSS PROFITS WENT UP IN YEAR 3 BECAUSE REVENUE INCREASED.
THIS RESULT WAS PARTIALLY OFFSET BECAUSE RAW MATERIAL, DIRECT LABOR,
DISTRIBUTION AND PACKAGING INCREASED.

GROSS PROFITS = REVENUE - RAW MATERIAL - DIRECT LABOR -'
                PACKAGING - DISTRIBUTION

                               AMOUNT
                    YEAR 2     CHANGE    YEAR 3
                    --------   --------  --------
GROSS PROFITS       159554      21077    180631
REVENUE             621000     132825    753825
RAW MATERIAL        221490      53681    275171
DIRECT LABOR        147668      35734    183402
DISTRIBUTION         55373      13400     68773
PACKAGING            36915       8933     45848


************************ <ENTER> - RETURN TO MENU **************************
WHY DID GROSS PROFITS GO DOWN IN YEAR 3
```

*Figure 11.17* IFPS, a financial planning software package, provides managers with both the financial information they need and the ability to perform analysis.

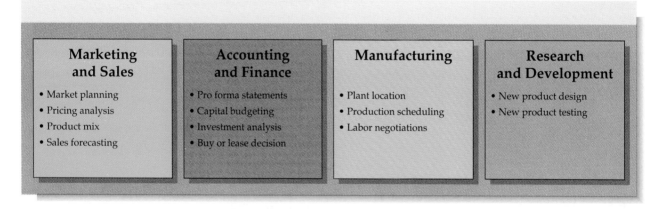

| Marketing and Sales | Accounting and Finance | Manufacturing | Research and Development |
|---|---|---|---|
| • Market planning<br>• Pricing analysis<br>• Product mix<br>• Sales forecasting | • Pro forma statements<br>• Capital budgeting<br>• Investment analysis<br>• Buy or lease decision | • Plant location<br>• Production scheduling<br>• Labor negotiations | • New product design<br>• New product testing |

*Figure 11.18* These are common business uses for FPLs in the four functional business areas. FPLs enable managers to do the what-if analyses that are so common in business.

Some common uses for FPLs in different functional areas are shown in Figure 11.18. FPLs enable managers to perform what-if analyses by asking questions such as: "What if the price of raw materials increased 20% next year?" "What if interest rates increase 2% next month?" "How sensitive is net income to changes in sales price?" Financial planning languages have more sophisticated what-if capabilities than the spreadsheets discussed in Chapter 3.

By using FPLs to set up a financial model of the relationship between product profitability and the cost of customer support, the customer service manager can calculate which products do not bring in enough revenue to justify their level of customer support. You might, for example, use the decision support system's FPL for quantitative analysis to construct bar charts that compare the amount of support time with profitability for each Analyze! product. You may find that five of the products require a level of support that is disproportionate to their profitability, while three other products are borderline. You then might incorporate the bar charts in a report listing your recommendations. The report generator helps you format a professional-looking report, perhaps even in color, for your manager. As this example illustrates, managers can use DSS tools to create, store, retrieve, organize, summarize, and manipulate data to create information that enables them to be effective and productive at their jobs.

**Other DSS Tools.**   Decision support systems designed for managers include a wide range of tools in addition to FPL packages for quantitative analysis. Some produce high-quality graphics that quickly display charts and can accompany text drawn from different internal and external sources to produce reports that help managers make decisions (Figure 11.19).

*Figure 11.19 Metaphor, a decision support system, can process and display information from a variety of sources. This sales graph, for instance, updates itself whenever it is retrieved or printed in a report.*

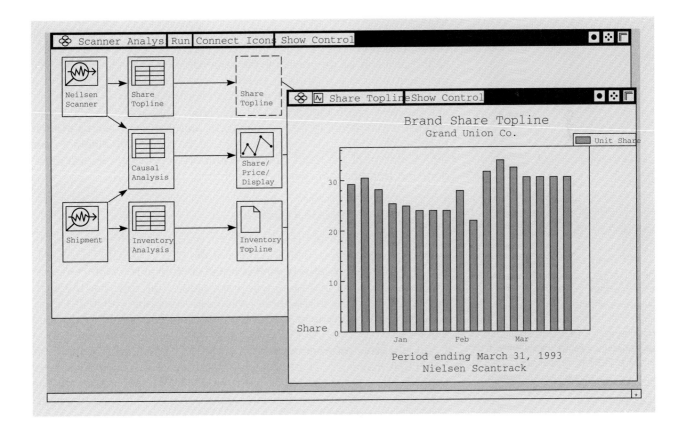

**COMPUTING APPLICATION**

Decision support systems help physicians make diagnoses. The physician enters the symptoms and provides an initial evaluation; the decision support system analyzes the evaluation, and suggests alternative diagnoses and medical tests that could be used to verify a diagnosis.

Decision support systems are also often used in training pilots to improve their decision-making capabilities. A pilot in training interfaces with a computer as if it were an actual airplane. He or she has use of joy sticks and other control mechanisms for piloting the "aircraft." The computer presents a set of situations or circumstances that require

*Decision support systems help doctors and pilots make decisions.*

the pilot to make a decision, and the decision support system analyzes and evaluates that decision. The evidence is that such techniques help to make better pilots.

For example, the vice president of marketing wants to determine whether any sales regions performed poorly during the previous month. He selects a menu option called January's Performance and views a summary chart listing all sales regions; problem regions are highlighted in red. He selects one of the highlighted regions to view a detailed report containing more specific sales information as well as a textual analysis of the problem as provided by the regional sales manager. If the vice president notices a disturbing trend in several regions, he can build a financial model using the system's FPL to verify his analysis of the trend and create a graph that illustrates the trend. This graph can be incorporated into a memo to district managers, and the memo can be printed in color. The district managers who receive the memo will obtain a clear representation of the trend, and communication between the vice president and first-line managers in the field will be enhanced.

## EXECUTIVE INFORMATION SYSTEMS

A DSS provides tools to the organization's managers so they can develop their own applications. One weakness of the DSS approach, however, is that the tools are relatively sophisticated and require some computer expertise. Top-level managers who have neither the time nor the inclination to learn how to use these tools need something different if they want to apply the power of the computer to their needs as decision makers.

An **executive information system (EIS)** is a custom-designed DSS for individual managers. The EIS tends to be used at the highest management levels, whereas a DSS is used mainly by middle managers. The basic distinctions between decision support systems and executive information systems follow.

IN A

**NUT
SHELL**

A DSS provides managers with a broad range of data and tools for accessing data, but training is required to use it effectively. A DSS is designed to be flexible enough to permit changes and to add applications as needed. Note, however, that while a DSS is reasonably easy to use, it does require some training.

- A DSS is typically designed generically for middle-level managers and is used by many managers for different purposes. An EIS is usually designed for the unique needs of a single, high-level executive and takes his or her skills and needs into account.
- A DSS, while relatively easy to use, requires some training before a manager is effective at tasks such as building applications or creating a financial model. An EIS requires no computer training: the analyst designing the system creates the needed models and menus so that the executive is free to simply ask for exactly the information required to make corporate decisions.
- Because a DSS is developed generically for a number of managers, it is much less expensive to develop than an EIS, which is designed for a single executive (or for a small group of executives).

*Executive information systems are customized for each executive.*

Executive information systems use the same tools as decision support systems, but computer professionals design the systems so that they are customized for individual executives. An EIS is usually implemented on very sophisticated minicomputer or microcomputer workstations, but the systems analyst creates a turnkey system—one that requires little or no computer knowledge on the part of the user (Figure 11.20). Four design factors are essential for an EIS system.

**An EIS must not be too technical.**   An EIS should present information to executives in a way that hides the technical communication links between all the hardware and software that might be accessed to compile a report. For example, if a report combines information from an external database such as the Dow Jones News/Retrieval System, and from an internal database such as payroll, the EIS should graph the information without the executive being concerned about the specific details of where the information came from (unless he or she is interested in the source).

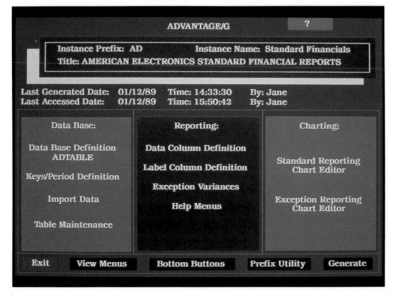

*Figure 11.20 This Pilot executive information system allows the user to access customized reports, update data, and generate standard or custom charts from a simple menu.*

*Executive information systems provide top management with the type of information they need in the form that suits them.*

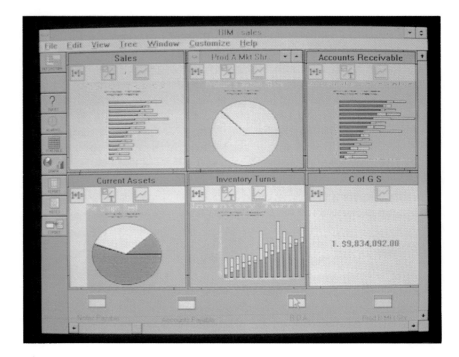

**An EIS must be individualized.**   Menu options should focus on information or tasks that are of specific interest to the executive, and the options should be expressed in words and terms that he or she uses frequently. Executive information systems often use individualized databases as well: subsets of the corporate database, databases developed from industry statistics, sources outside the company, and online database services such as CompuServe discussed in the next chapter.

**An EIS must evolve with the executive.**   Each executive has an individualized style of decision making that is based on his or her training and experience. An effective EIS provides only the information the executive is likely to use when making decisions.

Typically, the initial step in building an EIS is taken by the executive. He or she requests a system that will provide information on six or seven issues of particular importance, for example, changes in stock prices, information about competitors, news items on a special topic, or particular internal reports such as production forecasts. The systems analyst responds by designing a simple, one-level system that provides those six or seven menu choices and the information in an easy to understand form.

As the executive becomes accustomed to accessing this information, he or she discovers more desirable features that the analyst can add to the system. Often these become second-level menu choices. For example, information about competitors might evolve into three lower-level screens, one that compares the sales of each leading product with those of each competing product, a second that compares advertising budgets of each leading product with those of their competitors, and a third that summarizes news items about competitors.

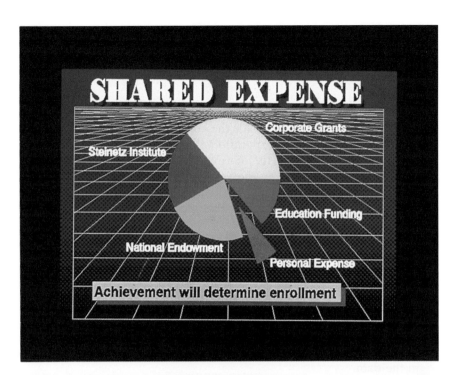

*Statistical analysis is a common use of an executive information system.*

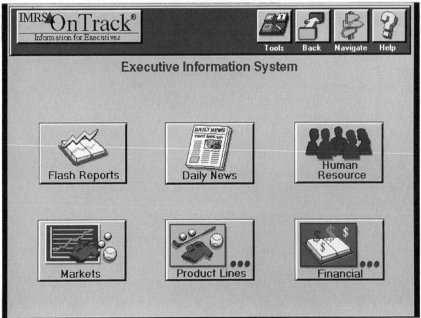

*This is how a customized executive information system main menu may appear.*

**An EIS must be relevant, complete, and clear.**   An EIS should contain only information that is relevant for a specific executive, and the information should be displayed in comparative forms, where possible, such as in ratios, exception reports, and historical perspectives. Extraneous or irrelevant information impedes a manager's ability to use the system effectively and efficiently.

## EXECUTIVE INFORMATION SYSTEMS AREN'T JUST FOR MAINFRAMES ANYMORE

A recent study revealed that 60% of all sites surveyed had implemented an EIS on a desktop PC, workstation, or a network of PCs. The benefits cited included lower cost, less dependence on general management information systems for development of applications, and faster response time.

In addition, the presentation style of an EIS must be tailored to the executive's preferences. For example, the analyst should choose the type of display method with which the executive is most comfortable—numeric tables, bar graphs, scatter graphs, or pie charts.

**An EIS in Practice.** To see how a high-level EIS might operate in practice, let us look at a system devised for the chief financial officer (CFO) of a large consumer products corporation (Figure 11.21). When this CFO turns on his workstation in the morning, the EIS software activates the communications link between the workstation and the mainframe and connects the workstation to the "command center" mainframe system. A menu then appears on his screen that enables him to:

- Read memos, reports, and messages that have come in over the electronic mail system since he last logged on.
- Review selected financial data that he has marked for close scrutiny.
- Review external data, such as economic indicators, competitive information, or financial markets, that are downloaded automatically to the EIS database.
- Analyze sales and financial results with a wide range of "push-button" statistical tools that can explore ratios, trends, and relationships in the data.
- Review reports generated by existing corporate information systems that have been linked to the EIS at the mainframe level.
- Select and download corporate data to microcomputer disks in forms readable by popular spreadsheet packages.

*Figure 11.21 A typical executive information system assembles data from various sources and makes it available for use at the executive's computer.*

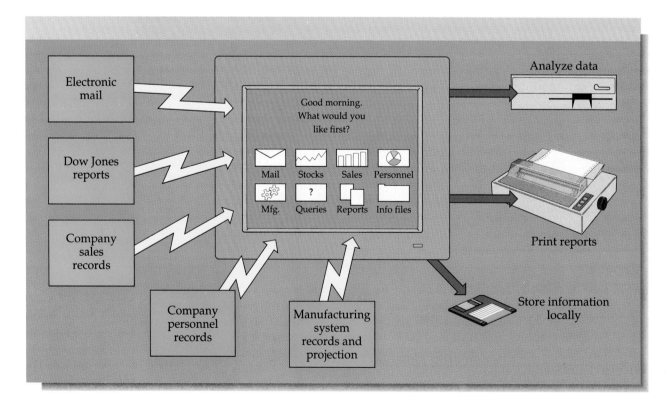

- Access personnel data to keep tabs on who's who in the organization and how each functional area is performing.
- Track the progress of key projects and development schedules.

## EXPERT SYSTEMS

Theoreticians have debated for years about whether machines will ever be able to think like people. Regardless of the various points of view on this subject, no one doubts that artificial intelligence—simulated human decision making—in the form of expert systems is beginning to play an important role in running companies. Expert systems consist of a database and software that simulate the knowledge and analytical ability of an expert in a particular field.

For example, analysts at the American Express Company (AMEX) built an expert system that uses a computer to quickly determine customer credit limits and to approve requests for additional credit. The system helps the company provide better service to customers by allowing its staff to approve credit more quickly. Because the American Express credit card has no fixed spending limit, it had been difficult for the staff to determine appropriate levels of credit for each customer. Each time a customer made a large purchase, a merchant telephoned AMEX to authorize the charge. An AMEX employee had to search through as many as 13 databases for more information about the customer and then make a judgment call. The expert system, called Authorizer's Assistant, now performs that search and makes recommendations to the credit employee, who makes the final authorization decision. The entire process takes only seconds (while the merchant is on the phone); it had previously taken as much as half an hour.

**Uses for Expert Systems.**   Expert systems are best suited for problems that need to be solved repetitively and that require some decision making. The best applications for expert systems are often those in which employ-

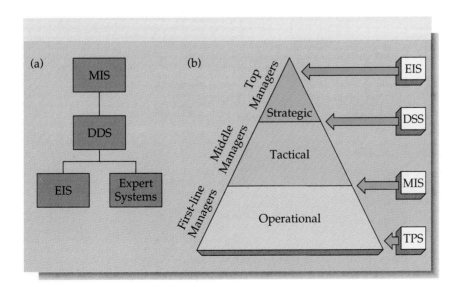

(a) *Relationship of types of information systems.* (b) *How information systems best suit the needs of various levels of management (TPS stands for transaction processing system and is a type of traditional information system).*

IN A

## COMMON APPLICATION AREAS FOR EXPERT SYSTEMS
- Diagnosis
- Planning
- Monitoring
- Instruction
- Interpretation
- Control

ees who are highly trained, well paid, or have very specific expertise cannot always be available on site to make critical decisions quickly. Although expert systems are expensive to develop, the cost must be weighed against the cost of keeping highly trained decision-makers readily available at widely scattered locations.

There are other ways in which expert systems help solve business problems.

1. *Time limits:* Complex analyses that need to be done quickly in order to be useful are good candidates for expert systems. If AMEX employees had half an hour to process a credit request, an expert system would not be necessary. Because a merchant requires an answer in seconds, however, AMEX's expert system delivers a definite advantage. Another example is the expert systems that have been developed for medical diagnosis where time can be a critical factor. When a patient exhibits an unusual set of symptoms, a physician may call on an expert system to diagnose an illness and to identify appropriate tests or treatment.

2. *Limited number of experts:* Repetitive but important tasks that can only be done well by a few experts are good candidates for expert systems. For example, Honeywell built an expert system to help field service technicians diagnose problems on commercial air conditioning systems. Although the technician's personal ability could range from average to excellent, the expert system ensured that service quality was uniformly high. Expert systems also help keep costs down if increased volume requires more experts. In addition, the knowledge of skilled experts is not lost if they leave the organization.

3. *Consistent decisions:* Tasks that require employees to make consistent decisions and remain alert over long periods of time, sometimes under

*Expert systems in business help users determine whether a client is a good credit risk.*

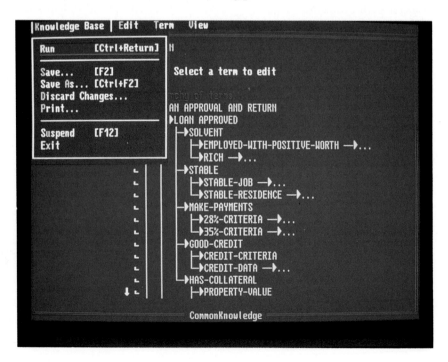

difficult circumstances, are good candidates for expert systems. For example, N L Baroid, an oil drilling services company, created MUD-MAN to analyze the drilling fluids, or "muds," that are pumped down shafts to facilitate drilling. On deep or difficult wells, an on-site engineer often has to sample and analyze more than 20 parameters such as viscosity, specific gravity, and silt content at least twice a day. MUDMAN provides analytic consistency and also enables Baroid to provide better service than its competitors. MUDMAN correctly diagnosed a mud contamination problem in the North Sea that human experts had misdiagnosed for more than a decade; such success naturally had a positive effect on company sales. See Figure 11.22.

**Components of an Expert System.**   An expert system has four basic components: a knowledge base, an inference engine, subsystems, and a user interface (Figure 11.23).

The **knowledge base** is the heart of the system. It translates the knowledge from human experts into rules and strategies and is developed by a computer professional called a **knowledge engineer.** Unlike a database, which consists of static relationships among fields, records, and files, a knowledge base is always changing as it reflects the advice of human

*Figure 11.22* Oil drilling and production, which often take place in isolated and remote locations like this platform in the North Sea, make extensive use of expert systems.

*Figure 11.23* The principal components of an expert system are the knowledge base, the inference engine, the subsystems, and the user interface.

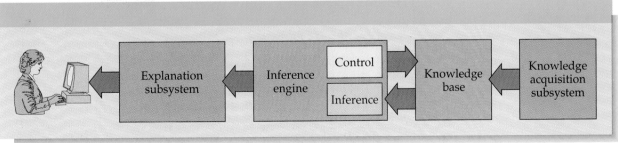

experts. In fact, as more information is supplied, the basis for making decisions or the decisions themselves may actually change.

The knowledge engineer encodes knowledge by means of a variety of approaches. The most common way is to use rules that express knowledge in an IF-THEN format: IF a patient's symptoms are lung infection, fever, and a cough, THEN he or she has an 80% probability of having pneumonia. Expert systems often assign probabilities, because like human experts, they cannot be 100% sure. The person who obtains the computerized results must weigh the risk of delaying treatment against the risk of making the wrong diagnosis.

The **inference engine** is the software that draws conclusions. It examines existing facts and rules to make its conclusions. The inference engine also adds new facts if it finds them consistent with present information and rules. For example, if it noticed that most of the patients meeting the criteria for pneumonia also shared another symptom, this symptom would be added to the knowledge base. In addition, the inference engine controls the way the knowledge base is searched. A search can be a time-consuming process if the knowledge base is large and complex.

Two subsystems assist knowledge engineers in updating the knowledge base and explaining to users how a recommendation was made. The knowledge acquisition subsystem helps the knowledge engineer define and encode the expert's problem-solving ability, and it also allows the engineer to easily insert knowledge in the system or delete it if the need arises. The explanation subsystem describes to users why the system has chosen to ask a certain question or how it has reached certain conclusions.

Ideally, expert systems should communicate information with a **natural language interface.** This type of interface lets users conduct dialogs with the computer that seem as natural as talking to another human being.

**Steps for Developing an Expert System.**   Nontechnical managers with the proper tools can build a small-scale expert system. Sometimes the knowledge of experts in the company can be incorporated into the database developed for the expert system. Large expert systems require a team of knowledge engineers and generally a year or more to develop. Devel-

*Figure 11.24 The five phases of development for an expert system.*

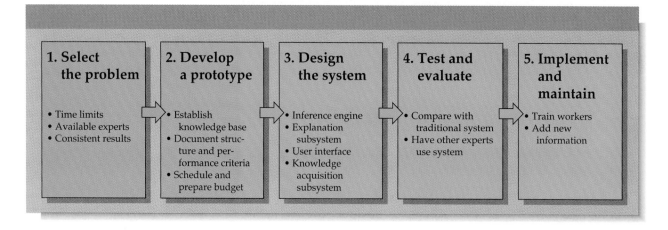

| 1. Select the problem | 2. Develop a prototype | 3. Design the system | 4. Test and evaluate | 5. Implement and maintain |
|---|---|---|---|---|
| • Time limits<br>• Available experts<br>• Consistent results | • Establish knowledge base<br>• Document structure and performance criteria<br>• Schedule and prepare budget | • Inference engine<br>• Explanation subsystem<br>• User interface<br>• Knowledge acquisition subsystem | • Compare with traditional system<br>• Have other experts use system | • Train workers<br>• Add new information |

opment consists of five phases that parallel the steps in the systems development life cycle (Figure 11.24).

1. *Define the problem.* To avoid wasting development time and money, knowledge engineers first identify a suitable subject for an expert system. Good opportunities for expert systems require expensive or rare experts make fast decisions consistently over a long period of time.
2. *Develop a prototype.* A prototype is a small-scale model of an expert system. During this step, knowledge engineers learn everything about the problem they can from books and reports, and they help the human experts convey their knowledge about solving certain tasks. Knowledge engineers also select the best tools for building the expert system. The most flexible design approach is to use one of the artificial intelligence programming languages such as LISP or PROLOG. Alternatively, the engineers may choose a commercially available expert system shell such as VP-Expert or Guru (PC products); they then enter the decision-making rules to create a knowledge base. Knowledge engineers develop a detailed design document that estimates the num-

## LOOKING BACK

### EVOLUTION OF INFORMATION SYSTEMS

This graph provides a historical view of the evolution of types of information systems from the 1950s through the 1990s. As you can see, expert systems are a relatively recent innovation.

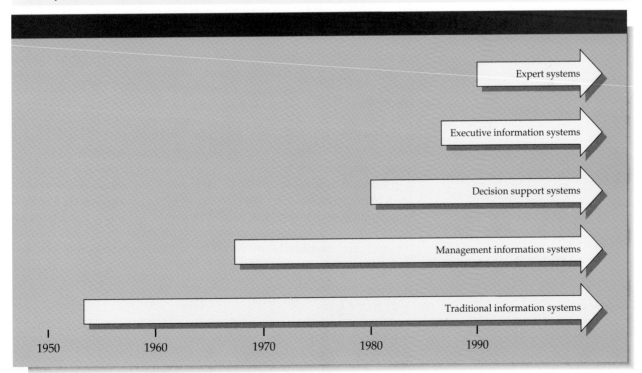

## *LOOKING AHEAD*

### THE NERVOUS SHOCK ADVISOR

Knowledge engineers at the University of British Columbia working with IBM have built an expert legal system that provides attorneys with advice on legal cases involving nervous shock, emotional distress, and emotional suffering. The system, called the Nervous Shock Advisor, advises lawyers about whether people who say they have suffered emotional distress have a viable claim. The expert system bases its conclusions on judgments reached in previous court cases.

After asking the attorney for specific facts about the case, the Nervous Shock Advisor:
- Searches a legal database and determines whether the claim is valid.
- Lists the factors used to arrive at its conclusion and presents a confidence level value for each factor.
- Supplies references to relevant court cases that either support its conclusion or go against it.

- Gives references to cases that demonstrate arguments that the defendant (that is, the opposing side) might use to present his or her side of the case.

If the system determines that the plaintiff has no case, it tells the lawyer what elements are lacking. Nervous Shock Advisor was designed to help lawyers prepare cases by presenting them with the basic elements that support successful litigation.

ber of rules to be included, a more precise statement of performance criteria, and a detailed schedule and budget for the entire project.

3. *Design the complete system.* Now the knowledge engineer and the expert fine-tune the knowledge base by creating additional rules that are capable of handling the more subtle aspects of the problem. At this point, the knowledge engineer begins to turn development over to the experts and to monitor the project rather than actively participate in it. In turn, the expert, with all the insight and experience gained during the development process, starts to implement the expert system.

4. *Test and evaluate the system.* Once the knowledge engineer and expert believe the system is complete, they test it. Results obtained should be evaluated according to the performance criteria specified during prototyping. For example, a medical diagnostic system's recommendations can be evaluated by comparing diagnoses with bacterial culture tests performed later. Testing may result in further refinements of rules entered into the knowledge base. Other experts may also be invited to experiment with the system in other working situations.

5. *Implement and maintain the system.* After the first four steps have been completed, it is time to integrate the expert system into the workplace and provide training for prospective users. Maintenance of the system is an ongoing process. A major benefit of expert systems is that knowledge engineers can continue to add new information or modify existing information. As a result, expert systems have much more flexibility and are eventually more accurate than information systems developed using more traditional approaches.

### ▶ SELF-TEST

1. A business system whose primary objective is to provide useful information to managers from the top level down is called a _____.
2. (T or F) One basic difference between a DSS and an EIS is that the EIS is simpler to use.

3. Name four basic design requirements for executive information systems.
4. What are the five steps for developing an expert system?
5. What kinds of tasks are best incorporated into expert systems?

Solutions
1. management information system
2. T
3. it requires no technical knowledge; it is individualized; it evolves with the executive; information is relevant, complete, and just what the user needs.
4. select the problem; develop a prototype; design the complete system; test and evaluate the system; implement and maintain the system
5. those performed by highly trained and well-paid decision makers; those that require decisions to be made very quickly

## ▶ Chapter Summary

A database management system (DBMS) provides users with the ability to create, edit, update, and report from database files. Database management systems are used in both traditional and management information systems (MIS). An MIS uses a DBMS primarily to provide top-level management with company-wide information; only after management needs are met do operating staff needs—the major concern of traditional information systems—get addressed.

### 11.1 DATABASE MANAGEMENT SYSTEMS: THE DRIVING FORCE BEHIND INFORMATION PROCESSING

Data in a database is stored in files that contain records; each record stores individual units of data called fields. Database management systems can join, or link, files in a database; in contrast, file management systems have flat files that cannot be linked.

A **database administrator** is the computing professional who manages the database and protects it from unauthorized access and poor database practices.

The four database structures are hierarchical, network, relational, and object-oriented. A **hierarchical database** has a tree structure with branches that are viewed as segments. "Parent" segments can have "child" segments, but a child segment can belong to only one parent segment, which limits the applicability of this kind of database. A **network database** is similar, but a child can have many parent segments, which enables records to be linked to numerous files. With both of these types of databases, however, the relationship among elements must be known in advance. In a **relational database,** which is the most common database form, key fields of records in different files can be linked to create a table that relates the files. Relational databases are more flexible than hierarchical or network databases. **Object-oriented databases,** which use

How do the format and features of a database affect the usefulness of a database management system?

objects as elements within database files, can combine text, graphics, sound, video, and other images and have great potential for the future.

Database management systems typically include six components: (1) a data dictionary that defines relationships among elements, (2) a **data definition language (DDL),** which defines the technical specifications of the database, (3) a **data manipulation language (DML)** (or query language) that allows users to create custom applications, (4) utilities for performing basic database functions, (5) an **application generator** for creating applications without writing programs, and (6) a report generator for creating custom reports. Some systems also have their own proprietary DDLs. **SQL** (Structured Query Language) is a standard query language used with many database management systems.

To keep databases secure, database administrators sometimes use **encryption** techniques. They also must focus on **data integrity** to ensure that the database is not corrupted by invalid data.

## 11.2 MANAGEMENT INFORMATION SYSTEMS

How can access to databases improve the quality of information for management decision making at all levels of an organization?

Management information systems are designed according to the top-down approach. Rather than focusing on the business needs of each functional area, the top-down approach views an organization as though it were one complete unit with one set of specific corporate objectives.

A manager's level in the organization dictates what kind of information he or she needs. Broadly speaking, lower-level managers generally require information derived from operational-level business systems. Middle-level and top managers use **decision support systems (DSSs)** to meet their quantitative and analytical needs; a DSS is often designed to be used by managers across all functional areas. Top managers may use a specialized form of DSS called **executive information systems (EISs).** These systems are individually tailored to deliver specific financial, reporting, and planning information needed by a particular executive.

A DSS provides middle managers with specific tools, such as **financial planning languages (FPLs),** designed to solve specific problems or develop business applications. DSS software is typically stored on a host mainframe or minicomputer, which managers access through workstations.

An EIS has four basic design requirements: (1) it must be easy to use, (2) it must be individualized, (3) it must evolve with the executive, and (4) it must provide information that is relevant, complete, and clear.

Expert systems, another type of specialized MIS, consist of a database with software that processes and distills the knowledge of an expert in a particular field. Expert systems can apply expertise without bias and tell users what assumptions were made to make a decision and what line of reasoning was used. An expert system consists of four components: the **knowledge base,** the **inference engine,** two subsystems (the knowledge acquisition subsystem and the explanation subsystem), and the human interface (usually a **natural language interface**). Although nontechnical managers with the proper tools can build a small-scale expert system using traditional systems design and development methods, large systems require a team of **knowledge engineers** and take more time to develop. They require five development steps: (1) define the problem, (2) develop a prototype, (3) design the complete system, (4) test and evaluate the system, and (5) implement and maintain the system.

## ▶ Chapter Self-test

1. (T or F) Operational-level systems analysis focuses on the top-down approach to designing information systems.
2. (T or F) In a company that has implemented an MIS, information systems for individual departments usually function independently.
3. What does SQL mean?
4. (T or F) The database administrator is responsible for maintaining the data dictionary.
5. (T or F) It is usually better to write your own database management system than to buy one.
6. (T or F) A data dictionary contains technical information about the data stored in each record and how to access the information.
7. DBMS stands for _____.
8. What do we call the computer professional who builds expert systems?
9. What types of tasks are well-suited for expert systems?
10. (T or F) In hierarchical databases, each parent segment can have many children segments; this is called a one-to-many relationship.
11. (T or F) A file manager is generally more powerful than a relational database.
12. In a hierarchical database, how many parents does a child have?
13. (T or F) A top-down management information system uses separate databases for top management and operational-level departments.
14. What do we call a DSS specially designed for executives?
15. (T or F) When designing an MIS, it is important to make the integrated system flexible enough to meet the changing needs of an organization.
16. Name three kinds of reports typically provided by a DSS.
17. (T or F) Advanced DSS tools for analyzing data are so easy to use that middle managers do not require training.

### Solutions
1. F—An MIS uses a top-down approach.
2. F—Information from various departments is combined to form the MIS database.
3. Structured Query Language
4. T
5. F
6. T
7. database management system
8. knowledge engineer
9. those that need to be performed quickly and repetitively
10. T
11. F
12. one

13. F—The same databases are used, but different kinds of information are generated as appropriate for each level of decision making.
14. executive information system (EIS)
15. T
16. periodic reports, exception reports, special reports
17. F—Use of advanced DSS tools requires considerable training.

# ▶ Key Terms

Application generator, *p. 443*
Database administrator, *p. 431*
Data definition language
  (DDL), *p. 440*
Data integrity, *p. 445*
Data manipulation language
  (DML), *p. 440*
Decision support system (DSS),
  *p. 452*

Encryption, *p. 444*
Executive information system
  (EIS), *p. 456*
Financial planning language
  (FPL), *p. 453*
Hierarchical database, *p. 432*
Inference engine, *p. 464*
Knowledge base, *p. 463*
Knowledge engineer, *p. 463*

Natural language interface,
  *p. 464*
Network database, *p. 434*
Relational database, *p. 435*
SQL, *p. 441*

# ▶ Review Questions

1. Why is a file manager not a true database management system?
2. What are the major differences between relational, hierarchical, and network databases? What are the advantages and disadvantages of each?
3. Describe the three levels of management. In general, what kind of information is most useful to managers at each level? Explain your answer.
4. Explain the roles of the four major components of an expert system: the knowledge base, the inference engine, the two subsystems, and the human interface.
5. Your mother bakes the best chocolate cheesecake in the world. You would like to build a cheesecake business based on your mother's baking skills. Give three reasons why her baking ability is a good candidate for an expert system. Illustrate your reasons with three specific examples of how personal judgment and expertise might be reflected in an automated recipe for chocolate cheesecake.
6. Your chocolate cheesecake expert system and your company are doing well. You have bakeries in two locations that serve six food distributors and a fleet of five trucks that serve 50 local restaurants. You have 30 production employees, 10 front-office and clerical workers (who handle all accounting on two desktop micros), and 2 outside sales representatives. Your business grosses close to $1 million per year and nets almost $100,000 before taxes. However, your sales representatives and drivers have reported declining orders in the past few months because of growing competition. You figure you need an advantage to hold your market share, or perhaps you need to add some new dessert products.

   Briefly describe the design requirements for a DSS that could help improve the business. What kind of information do you need? In what form? From what source? What tools would you use? Hardware? Software? With what other systems, if any, should your DSS communicate?

7. Your college has hired you as a consultant on expert systems and wants you to examine its administrative procedures to pinpoint good opportunities for expert systems. Briefly discuss two good opportunities at the college and explain your rationale for choosing them.

8. In what situation do you think a network database would be better than a hierarchical or relational database?

9. Make a list of all the database management systems you can find advertised in computer magazines; include their prices. Identify the kind of database model of each—relational, hierarchical, network, or object-oriented.

## PRODUCT ANALYSIS

## CASE

### Touch-Tone Eases College Registration

Now you can register for college from the comfort of your own home—if you attend the University of Oregon, San Jose State, or one of the other schools currently using Touch-Tone course registration systems. With Touch-Tone registration, students electronically enroll in the classes of their choice by pressing buttons on their phones in response to "voice" instructions.

For example, at California's San Jose State University (SJSU), students who call the TOUCH-SJSU registration system are greeted electronically and prompted to enter a term code: 2 for spring or 4 for fall. Then they are asked to key in their Social Security number and a personal identification number (PIN) that has been assigned to them. To add a class, the student presses 2 and the five-digit code for that class. To drop a class, the student presses 3 and the code.

The system can also delete from class lists the names of students who have not paid their tuition. The university estimates that in its first semester of use, TOUCH-SJSU saved more than $60,000 in computer costs alone, not to mention savings in labor and student wear-and-tear.

At the University of Oregon, the Touch-Tone registration system, named Duck Call after the school's mascot, began operating in May 1991. Before that, registration had always taken two full

days, adding up to a total loss of eight teaching days per year (a quarter system). Another inconvenience was that registration had always been held on the two days before each quarter began, which made it difficult for administrators to make scheduling changes because professors were not readily available. Now registration proceeds at a more leisurely pace. Students can use Duck Call 14 hours a day for several weeks before the new quarter begins, and faculty members and administrators have more time to make adjustments to schedules when necessary.

The registration procedure with Duck Call, which takes each student only a few minutes, provides university administration with statistical information that can be used for making decisions on class size and growth of students' majors. Developed by the Periphonics Corporation of Bohemia, New York, as was TOUCH-SJSU, Duck Call can handle up to 32 simultaneous phone calls.

*Analysis*

1. What uses can you envision for Touch-Tone telephones in business application areas?

2. What types of reports can the Touch-Tone system generate for the university administration to help them make decisions?

3. Cite positive and negative implications of Touch-Tone systems.

# NETWORKS

**W**e have seen how hardware, software, and people work together to create effective information systems. With connectivity, such systems can be made available to a wide variety of users who may be employees within a single organization, people from different organizations, or any individuals who need access to central databases.

In this chapter, you will learn how connectivity is the cornerstone for the Information Age by answering the following questions:

▶ What type of communications linkages contribute to connectivity so that an organization's resources can be distributed and shared?

▶ How is connectivity achieved in various facets of an organization's operations?

▶ What specifications and protocols must be provided to computers by communications software?

▶ What types of network configurations can be used to achieve connectivity?

▶ What other technologies have emerged that help make the world more connected?

## 12.1  COMMUNICATIONS AND CONNECTIVITY

### ▶ Sharing Resources Is the Goal

 Connectivity—the technologies that enable computers to pass data, voice messages, and video electronically to one another—is the backbone of the Information Age. We live in a time when being able to get the right information quickly to the right place often means the difference between success and failure.

By means of communications facilities, people can combine the power and resources of computers no matter where the hardware is physically located. The communications lines, or links, that connect these devices may be cables, or, for wider-area communications, they may be telephones, satellites, microwave relays, or radio waves.

When trainers for Olympic athletes in colleges and universities around the country seek broad-based physiological information for their athletes, they use computers in their offices to tap into a specialized sports database located in Colorado. Similarly, salespeople with small, inexpensive microcomputers in Iowa access the power and resources of a multimillion dollar mainframe facility in New York through a telephone link. Immediate pricing estimates and inventory information enable them to complete their sales quickly. Some real estate appraisers have doubled their earnings simply by accessing a national electronic database of public and private real estate records to do research and analysis that once took them hours.

Such capabilities are possible because of advances in data communications that enable computers to work together no matter where they are located. Computers near each other, either in the same room or building, can send data directly to one another through cables or telephones. Computers stationed at a considerable distance from each other use a special data communications technology called **telecommunications** that can transmit data via communications facilities such as satellites. Highly advanced communications technologies now quickly send—to almost anywhere in the world—not only textual data but also photographs, illustrations, and video images.

The main feature of communications applications is that computers and input/output devices can be in different rooms, different buildings, or even in different geographical locations, and still communicate with each other. Keep in mind that the term *connectivity* as used in this text has a broad meaning: it refers to the linking of all equipment such as telephones, fax machines, and televisions as well as computers.

> What type of communications linkages are used to achieve connectivity so that an organization's resources can be distributed and shared?

## ▶ Communications Hardware

### A REVIEW OF NODES AND HOSTS IN A NETWORK

A network is the type of configuration that enables devices to communicate with one another. Often, one or more central computers interface with a variety of input/output devices at remote locations. In such a network, each device is called a node. A node may be an input/output device or a computer. Some networks have a series of nodes linked to a central computer. In this case, the central computer is called the host. Other networks have a ring of computers that communicate with one another where there is no need for a host computer. See Figure 12.1.

Nodes in a network can be "intelligent terminals," that is, they can have their own computing power. Intelligent terminals may be workstations or higher-end PCs, or they may be standard desktop micros. If your school's computing center has a **file server,** which transmits software like

**Figure 12.1** *A node can be a computer or terminal in a warehouse.*

**Figure 12.2** *A node can be a desktop PC or a workstation in an office. In this illustration, a university's PCs access a library network.*

a spreadsheet package or a DBMS to PCs, then the host is the file server and the nodes are the PCs. See Figure 12.2. In other networks, terminals with no actual computing power, called "dumb" terminals, may be nodes. Point-of-sale systems in retail establishments use dumb terminals to transmit accounts receivable and inventory data to a host. A dumb terminal can really be any type of input/output unit that is not located at the same site as the host, but usually it is a keyboard/monitor unit. In larger networks, minis, superminis, midranges, or mainframes linked to even larger mainframes or supercomputers may serve as nodes.

## COMMUNICATIONS CHANNELS

The linkages between nodes and a host (if there is one) in a network are called **communications channels.** The simplest type of channel is a direct cable. When devices are connected by cables, we say they are hardwired. A common alternative to cables is the telephone line. By means of a modem, nodes connected to a telephone can communicate with another node and/or the host, each of which must also have a modem linking it to a telephone line. So any two computer devices located anywhere in the world that have access to telephone lines can communicate with one another. For faster communications over longer distances, satellite and microwave lines, as well as specially prepared or "conditioned" telephone lines, are used. Wireless communications via light beams or radio waves is the newest technology.

The types of communications linkages that are available today include (1) hardwired cables, (2) telephones, (3) microwave stations, (4) satellite stations, and (5) radio or infrared waves. To share resources in a wide variety of areas, often more than one type of linkage is used.

**Hardwired Cables.** Hardwired terminals are directly linked to a CPU or host by cable. Terminals are commonly hardwired when they are rela-

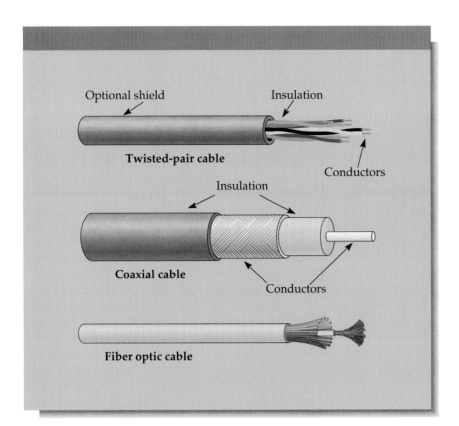

***Figure 12.3*** *Three common types of cable: twisted-pair cable, coaxial cable, and fiber optic cable.*

tively near the host and their locations are not expected to change. Because moving a hardwired terminal requires rewiring the cable, it is best to hardwire only when devices are likely to remain at fixed locations.

A principal advantage of hardwired terminals is that they have immediate access to a central processor as soon as they are turned on. There is no need, as with a telephone line, to "dial up" the computer. Networks may be hardwired with three basic types of cable: twisted-pair cable, coaxial cable, and fiber optic cable.

Twisted-pair cable is the typical telephone wire used in your house, and it is the most common type of hardwired cable for small networks. It consists of bundles of pairs of copper wires that are twisted to give them physical strength (Figure 12.3). Twisted-pair cable is relatively inex-

IN A

---

**HARDWIRED COMMUNICATIONS CHANNELS**

*Twisted-pair cable*

- Most common type of hardwired cable for small networks
- Inexpensive
- Least reliable because it is subject to "noise" on the line resulting from electrical interference

*Coaxial cable*

- Used for high-quality data transmission
- More expensive than twisted-pair cables
- Sturdy
- High speed

*Fiber optic cable*

- High speed
- Highly reliable
- Transmits signals by light impulses rather than electrical impulses
- Not subject to electrical interference

**Figure 12.4** *Bundles of threadlike glass fibers in a fiber optic cable carry encoded light beams to transmit voice and data messages virtually without interference.*

pensive and has low maintenance costs. A major disadvantage of this type of wiring for communications, however, is that it is highly susceptible to electrical interference (called "noise") both from within and outside the system. Noise is a major source of transmission errors. For protection from interference, shielded twisted-pair wiring is available at a slightly higher cost.

A **coaxial cable** is used in place of standard twisted-pair cables for high-quality data transmission. Although it is more expensive than twisted-pair cable, coaxial cable is sturdy enough to be laid without the wiring conduits or mechanical support elements that twisted-pair cable wiring requires. If conduits for twisted-pair cables are *not* already in place, coaxial cable may be cheaper to install and more flexible to use. Illustrated in Figure 12.3, coaxial cable consists of a central cylinder surrounded by a series of wires that transmit data at high speeds. Coaxial cable is commonly laid under the floor or in the ceiling of computer centers. It is so sturdy that telephone companies often bury it underground or lay it across sea bottoms to provide high-quality phone transmission.

**Fiber optic cables** are highly reliable communications channels. Data can be transmitted at very high speeds with a relatively low error rate. While standard cables transmit signals electrically in the form of moving electrons, a fiber optic channel transmits by means of light impulses that travel through clear, flexible tubing half the size of a human hair. Unlike wire cables, fiber optic cables are not subject to electrical interference. Technological innovations continue to drive down the costs of installing, using, and manufacturing fiber optic cables, so they are becoming competitive with traditional cabling. Most long-distance telephone companies now use fiber optic cables. See Figure 12.4.

**Telephones for Data Communications.**   Standard telephones commonly connect computers and terminals that are separated by long distances. With telephone technology, nodes can be located virtually anywhere in the country, or even in the world, and still have access to a host computer. Salespeople can call in and place orders from the field and send transaction data directly to a central processor. For example, a salesperson uses his or her terminal or micro to "dial" the host computer's phone number; if the computer line is free, the salesperson has direct access to the host.

Telephone lines do have several disadvantages as a transmission medium. They are slower and have higher error rates than hardwired cables because they were specifically designed to handle voice transmission signals, not computer signals. In addition, as we all know, long-distance telephone rates are expensive.

To send computer data, which is in digital form, over the phone, users need additional interface equipment such as a modem and, perhaps, a communications controller to convert the signals.

*Modems.* Data in a computer is formatted as digital signals—on-off electronic pulses. Because telephone lines were designed to transmit the human voice, they transmit data as analog signals, that is, as continuous waves, not discrete pulses (see Figure 12.5). For communication between computers to take place over a telephone line, the digital signal, or pulse,

Analog data transmission
(wave signals)

0 1 0   1 0 1 0   1 0

Digital data transmission
(pulse signals)

**Figure 12.5** *Analog signals are transmitted in wave form and digital signals in pulse form.*

must be converted to an analog signal, or wave, before it can be transmitted. After traveling over telephone lines, the analog signal must then be converted back to a digital signal so that it can be used by the receiving computer. See Figure 12.6.

The process of converting a digital signal to an analog signal is called modulation. Demodulation is the process of converting the analog signal back to a digital signal. The device that accomplishes both modulation and demodulation is a modem, short for *modulator-demodulator*. There are two basic kinds of modems: direct-connect modems and acoustic couplers. As the name implies, direct-connect modems are attached directly to computers and, as shown in Figure 12.7, they can be either an internal device on a circuit board inside the computer or an external device in a unit separate from the computer. Both internal and external modems work in the same way. They connect to the phone line, or jack, with a standard telephone wire.

If you are using a telephone without a jack (e.g., a pay phone), an **acoustic coupler,** shown in Figure 12.8, will allow you to transmit and receive computer data over telephone lines. The acoustic coupler has two cups into which a telephone handset is placed. The acoustic coupler transmits the computer's data through the mouthpiece and receives data through the earpiece of the handset.

An acoustic coupler is an older interface that is not as common today as direct-connect modems. Still, it is useful for transmitting data from locations that have internal phone systems where there is no phone jack, for example, hotels or other business establishments. And public telephones, which are used frequently by field staff for communicating with a host computer, also have no phone jacks. Sometimes acoustic couplers are built into a terminal or microcomputer, thereby enabling the device itself to be used in conjunction with a telephone handset. A salesperson, for example, who routinely obtains rate information from the central office or transmits orders to the central office from a pay phone would benefit from an acoustic coupler built into his or her PC.

We will see that the speed of transmission for direct-connect modems and acoustic couplers is measured in bits per second (bps). Roughly speaking, these devices can transmit and receive from 240 to hundreds of thousands of characters per second.

IN A

**TYPES OF MODEMS**
- Direct-connect
  1. Internal—on a board, fits into a slot
  2. External—separate unit, plugs into the computer
- Acoustic coupler: external—either a separate unit or part of a micro; handset of telephone, rather than telephone wire, fits into it

*Figure 12.6 Telephone lines currently transmit only analog, or wave, signals. Modulator-demodulator units (modems) convert digital signals to analog form so that data can be transmitted over phone lines. A modem at the receiving end converts the analog signals back to digital form.*

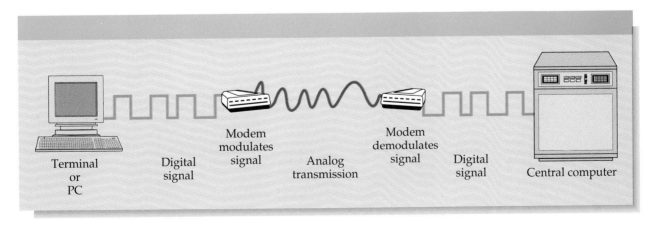

Terminal or PC — Digital signal — Modem modulates signal — Analog transmission — Modem demodulates signal — Digital signal — Central computer

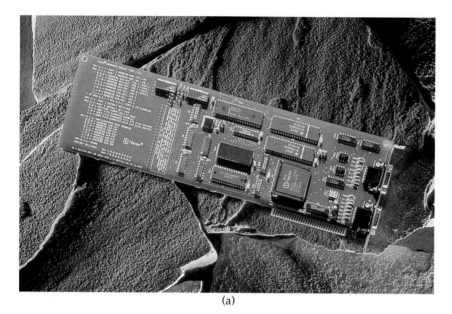

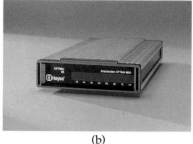

(b)

(c)

(a)

*Figure 12.7* (a) *This internal modem on a circuit board slips into one of the expansion slots on a micro, and a telephone cord plugs into it to complete the connection.* (b) *This external modem plugs into its own power outlet.* (c) *A WorldPort modem can be carried in a purse or pocket and is commonly used with portable computers because it is small and compact. When modems are used, communications software controls the transmission of data.*

*Communications controllers.* When PC users communicate with hosts or other devices by means of data communications links such as telephones, all they need is a modem. But if an application calls for collecting messages from several devices at one location for batch transmission across communications lines, more powerful devices with additional capabilities are more efficient than modems. Multiplexers and front-end processors, discussed next, provide control and monitoring functions and have built-in modems as well for transmitting a high volume of data over telephone lines.

A **multiplexer** is a hardware device that collects messages from many nodes at one physical location and transmits them in batch mode at high speeds over a single communications channel, as illustrated in Figure 12.9. Similarly, a multiplexer can be used for message switching, which means that it can receive a collection of responses from a host CPU and transmit each response back to the appropriate node. Multiplexing minimizes two major sources of inefficiency. First, most interactive commu-

*Figure 12.8* *A telephone handset, cradled in an acoustic coupler, provides the connection between a computer modem and the telephone lines.*

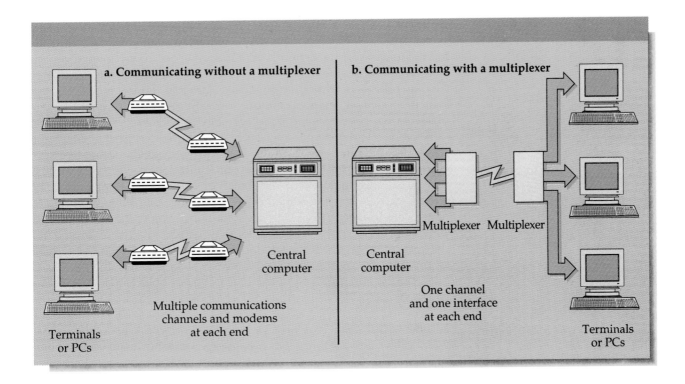

**a. Communicating without a multiplexer**

**b. Communicating with a multiplexer**

Central computer

Central computer

Multiplexer  Multiplexer

Terminals or PCs

Multiple communications channels and modems at each end

One channel and one interface at each end

Terminals or PCs

nication is intermittent: you enter data, then wait for a response, and so on. During those wait states, the communications channel is not active. If the channel uses a long-distance telephone line, these delays can be very expensive. A multiplexer can maximize the efficient use of the channel by batching transmissions from many users. Second, without multiplexing, each time a node is added to the network a new channel or communications link is required. With multiplexing, new devices can simply be connected to the multiplexer, which is itself connected to the communications channel. A department store with several branches, for example, does *not* have each POS terminal linked to its host at a central office. Rather, each POS terminal is linked to a multiplexer at the branch office, and all transmissions to the host are controlled by that multiplexer. The result is a considerable saving of telephone costs and CPU time.

When many terminals are connected directly to a central computer, the host must spend an inordinate amount of time monitoring and coordinating the flow of data rather than processing that data. For example, the host needs to keep track of which terminals are sending data; it must check data and coordinate message switching; it might need to prioritize transmissions, and so on. While it is performing these tasks, actual processing of applications is suspended. **Front-end processors** are specialized micros or minis that offload the activities performed by the host computer so that it can run more effectively. Front-end processors ensure that data is routed appropriately and that it is free of errors; they also perform some of the housekeeping and control tasks that would otherwise be performed by the host.

*Telephone carriers.* In 1968, the Federal Communications Commission (FCC) handed down the now-famous Carterfone decision, which

*Figure 12.9 For some applications, each terminal has its own modem and telephone line to connect it to a central computer. Alternatively, a multiplexer can combine transmissions so that many terminals can send data over a single line.*

required AT&T to allow independent equipment manufacturers to use public telephone networks. By 1972, competing companies were permitted to launch their own communications satellites. Today, a wide variety of companies provide many different types of services using telephones for networking. In addition to switched lines that connect telephones via switching centers, many telephone companies offer **value-added services:** extra services beyond those normally provided for voice messages.

A leased telephone line is one such value-added service that telephone companies provide for a fixed fee. It is a private line dedicated to a specific organization for its individual communications needs. A leased line may handle digital data only, or it may be capable of handling both voice and digital data just as a standard telephone line does. When leased lines have been designed specifically for data transmission, they produce less static and fewer transmission errors than regular telephone lines—and they are more secure from wiretapping and other security risks. Most importantly, the central processor is always accessible through the leased line, and the line usually transmits data at faster speeds than a standard telephone line.

**Microwave and Satellite Transmission.** Most networks use either hardwired cables or telephones for networking. Some, however, transmit and receive data over very long distances by microwave signals. Microwave networks are usually more expensive, and sometimes less reliable. They tend to be used where cables are not practical, for transmission across waterways or highways, for example, or in sparsely populated areas or over rough terrain.

Microwave and satellite signals travel in a straight line. Therefore, they require transmission stations to redirect them around the earth's curved surface. The stations boost the signals and then transmit them again. Microwave and satellite transmissions also require interfaces to convert analog signals to digital form.

*Microwave stations.* A microwave station transmits data, such as radio

*Figure 12.10* (a) *Microwave transmission towers send signals which are relayed in space.* (b) *Microwave transmission towers also receive signals sent from other stations. Stations are used to amplify signals and transmit them directly to other stations.*

(a)

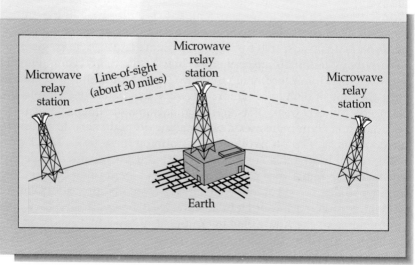

(b)

(a)

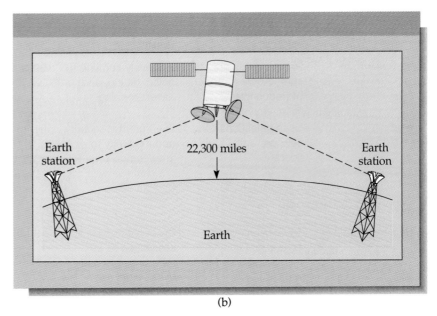

Earth station    22,300 miles    Earth station

Earth

(b)

signals, through the air rather than through wires. Microwave stations primarily transmit data at high speeds over very long distances. Normally, the stations are placed at high points—on mountaintops and on tall buildings—where they can transmit to other stations without interference. You may be familiar with the dish antennas of microwave stations that are typically located on the roofs of buildings or on hilltops (Figure 12.10). More than half of the standard telephone transmissions make use of microwave technology.

*Satellite stations.* Communications satellites in space, orbiting tens of thousands of miles above the earth, also serve as microwave relay stations (Figure 12.11). They orbit around the equator at a speed that makes them appear stationary to microwave transmitters on the ground. These satellites are used for high-volume data transmission as well as for television broadcasting and telephone transmission. A satellite can beam transmissions to other satellites, which relay signals back to stations on earth. Hundreds of satellites are currently in orbit.

*Figure 12.11* (a) *Satellite receiving dish.* (b) *Satellite stations orbit around the equator tens of thousands of miles above the earth.*

**Other Wireless Transmission.**   Networks that use radio or light waves to connect PCs and other devices such as printers move us one step closer toward full connectivity. Motorola was one of the first companies to introduce this technology through a product called Altair, which is intended to provide wireless desktop connectivity for network-linked devices within a building. Some pen-based computers, like GRiD, can be purchased with wireless network features.

The primary benefit of wireless networks is that they minimize the high cost of cabling as well as high labor costs associated with installation, maintenance, and moving. In addition, the fact that wireless networks are portable is a major benefit and a feature that helps make the world smaller. Organizations

**Table 12.1** | WIRELESS NETWORK TECHNOLOGIES

| Type | Features | Benefits | Speed* | Applications |
|---|---|---|---|---|
| Spread-spectrum radio | Radio signals are spread over a range of frequencies | Relatively immune to noise, fading, and eavesdropping | 900+ MHz | OK for e-mail and print sharing but not fast enough for frequent file transfers |
| Infrared | Uses reflections off ceilings, walls, and floors | Even greater security and immunity to interference | Up to 20 Mbps | Ideal for niche applications (e.g., links to highly sensitive life-support monitoring equipment that could be disturbed by radio signals) |
| 18-GHz microwave | 18-GHz channels consist of two segments, each 10 MHz wide | System's radio links are limited to 50 feet; units are relatively expensive (about $3000 per unit) | 15 Mbps | Intended to be used with standard networks |
| New spectrum allocation (Apple)† | Range of 150 feet or so | Apple proposes that 40 MHz be reserved for data transfers of about 2 GHz | | |

*MHz = megahertz; Mbps = million bits per second; GHz = gigahertz.
†Pending FCC approval.

that lease office space may not want to invest in a network that requires substantial cabling. Reporters covering a major news event may need a network that can be set up quickly, without the need for cables. People like traders on financial exchange floors or data collection employees have more freedom of movement if they can use wireless, handheld computers. The primary disadvantage of wireless networks is their cost, which is sometimes twice the price of conventional network stations. A second problem is interference.

The four major types of wireless network technologies are described in Table 12.1. Wireless networks are still relatively new and hence non-standardized. This makes it difficult, at the present, for one wireless network to communicate with another. Recall that new technologies often suffer from such lack of standards.

### ▶ SELF-TEST

1. (T or F) Microcomputers and minicomputers cannot be used as terminals in a network.
2. (T or F) A multiplexer can reduce the overall cost of transmitting data over communications lines.
3. (T or F) Remote terminals can be placed strategically at different locations, but they must be in the same building as the computer.
4. (T or F) Terminals can only be used for online, or transaction, processing.

5. Networks use _____ placed strategically at key locations to enter input and/or receive output.

Solutions

1. F
2. T
3. F

4. F
5. terminals, PCs, or nodes

## COMMON APPLICATION AREAS FOR NETWORKS

**12.2**

Although there are a variety of application areas for networks, we will focus on the following: distributed processing, accessing external subscriber services and other networks, electronic mail, and telecommuting. Connectivity is achieved by using networks for transmitting computer information and for conducting other office functions as well, such as those performed by networked fax machines or voice-mail systems.

### ▶ Distributed Processing

The transmission of computer power throughout an organization from a central facility to each user site is called distributed processing. The most common distributed systems have micros, minis, midranges, or terminals linked to a host computer, usually a mainframe, in order to improve productivity and to provide users with immediate access to files. Many business tasks such as receiving customer orders and sending merchandise can take several days to complete when manual (uncomputerized) procedures or batch procedures with a central computer are used instead of distributed systems. The two most common distributed processing activities are (1) remote data entry and inquiry and (2) remote job entry and time-sharing.

*How is connectivity achieved in various facets of an organization's operations?*

#### REMOTE DATA ENTRY AND INQUIRY

In remote data entry and inquiry applications, nodes serve as input devices for entering transaction data, that is, data needed to update a master database file. Entering data on a terminal located where a transaction actually occurs, such as in point-of-sale systems in fast-food restaurants or supermarkets, is called **remote data entry.** Remote data entry applications have a host that may not be physically at the same site as the terminals or nodes. See Figure 12.12.

Remote data entry systems can be designed for either interactive or batch processing. Recall from Chapter 4 that in interactive processing the computer reads input data as it is entered and uses it to update the master files immediately. In batch processing, the computer stores the data and processes it all together at a scheduled time. In a batch system, the data entered is first stored in a file on a secondary storage medium such

*Distributed processing enables users at remote sites to do processing locally and to access a central computer as well.*

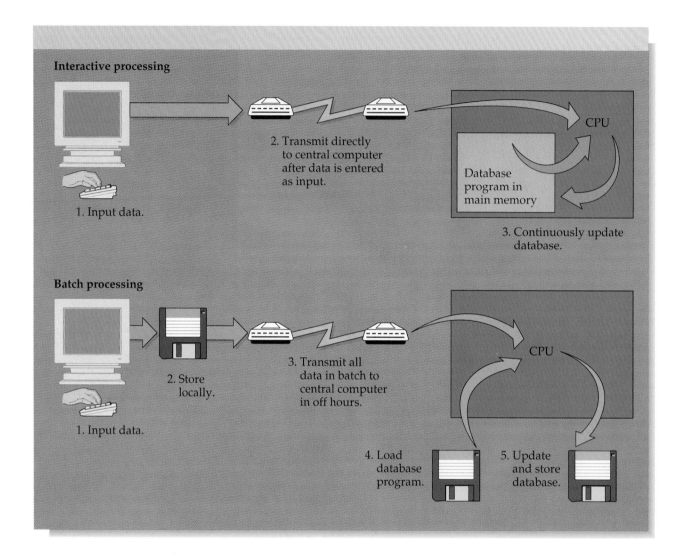

Interactive processing

1. Input data.

2. Transmit directly to central computer after data is entered as input.

Database program in main memory

CPU

3. Continuously update database.

Batch processing

1. Input data.

2. Store locally.

3. Transmit all data in batch to central computer in off hours.

CPU

4. Load database program.

5. Update and store database.

*Figure 12.12* *Remote terminals and communications equipment can be used in both interactive processing and batch processing to interface with a central computer.*

as disk. The computer then processes the entire file at some later time. Batch processing makes more efficient use of a computer than interactive processing for three reasons:

1. A high-speed auxiliary storage device like a disk drive can transmit data to a CPU much faster than a person can key it in using an online terminal.
2. Data can be transmitted later in the day, after standard working hours, when transmission costs such as telephone charges are cheaper.
3. The database files to be updated, along with the update program, do not need to be online at all times; this makes the central computer available for other applications.

Systems analysts who design remote data entry systems consider factors such as cost, speed, and security when they decide whether to use interactive or batch processing. For example, a department store's accounts receivable system often processes transactions immediately. Processing in this manner creates a charge slip that is the customer's receipt and keeps data such as the customer's available credit up-to-date at all times. On the other hand, interactive processing of an accounts receivable master file for a small organization may be too expensive; it might also be more prone to security problems because employees at specific locations would always have access to the master file. In this instance, batch processing may be preferable.

Remote terminals or micros may also be used to inquire about the status of records in a file. Organizations that process data online need to request information about data stored in a database file linked to a central computer. Stockbrokers, for example, frequently query a central database of stock information when they want to quote a stock price to a customer. To get a price, the broker keys in a stock code at a terminal or micro on his or her desk. The host computer receives this code immediately, accesses the price from the database, and transmits the information back to the stockbroker in seconds or even a fraction of a second.

A display screen and keyboard are almost always essential for inquiry purposes—even for simple queries. Sometimes a printer is also needed to produce hard-copy output. Businesses generally use remote inquiry systems when customers want immediate responses to requests or when managers need information immediately for making decisions. Connectivity enables the responses to inquiries to be transmitted to other devices such as laser printers for high-quality output or fax machines for delivery to other locations.

*Figure 12.13* This stockbroker and his client are working with an information system to retrieve stock prices and other information. The same system can be used to buy or sell stocks and keep brokerage records.

Typically, systems with remote data inquiry capability require database files to be up-to-date at all times. Remote data inquiry devices are also commonly used for remote data entry. For example, the stockbroker who queries the database for a stock price also needs to buy and sell stocks. Thus, remote data entry and remote inquiry are often part of the same system (Figure 12.13).

### REMOTE JOB ENTRY AND TIME-SHARING

In remote *data* entry systems, the program that processes the data must already be stored in the host's main memory whenever data is transmitted. In remote *job* entry systems, the program is loaded along with the data; that is, it is either supplied at the remote site *along with* the data or it is accessed by the host and made available to the node on request.

In **remote job entry** applications, users run programs from terminals or micros. They use terminals or micros either (1) to enter both programs and data files, which are then processed by a central host or (2) to access programs and data files that are stored at the same site as the host for a production run such as producing bills or checks. In these instances the host computer must be capable of running more than one program concurrently in a multiprogramming environment.

Students who write and run programs from terminals located throughout a university are operating in a remote job entry environment (Figure 12.14). They can enter their own programs at the remote site or access programs from the host. Engineers who have terminals or micros linked to a host for solving equations, creating designs, and obtaining other mathematical results are also operating in a remote job entry environment. In each case, the user has access to his or her own set of programs and data.

A node in a remote job entry system commonly consists of a keyboard, monitor, disk drive for loading data or programs, and a printer. A user at a remote job entry station might send a program and data from a local disk drive to a host at another location for processing. The host then transmits the output back to the printer at the node (Figure 12.15). Similarly, users may upload files—send data and programs to the host for storage or processing—or download files—copy files stored at the host site to a disk drive at their station. For example, if your micro is a node, you can write a program and create data files and then upload them to the host. The host then executes and debugs the program. When the program is running properly, you can download the final version and its output onto your hard disk or diskette.

*Figure 12.14 Students who use library terminals to access a university mainframe for writing and running programs are interfacing with a remote job entry system.*

Time-sharing enables users, often from different organizations, to independently access a large CPU while the operating system controls the overall processing of all programs. Users have access to the CPU remotely, or they may physically bring their data to the central site. Because the host computer is so fast, it appears to the users at each organization that all the instructions within different programs are being executed simultaneously. Actually, by interleaving instructions from various programs, a CPU executes only one instruction at a time, but at very high speeds. If parallel processors are used, then multiple programs may, in fact, be executed simultaneously.

A potential danger of time-sharing is that one user will monopolize the system at the expense of others. Thus, operating systems must allocate computer time and resources in a way that is equitable to all users. **Time-slicing** is one common method whereby a small "slice" of computer time is allocated to each user. When the allotted time is used up,

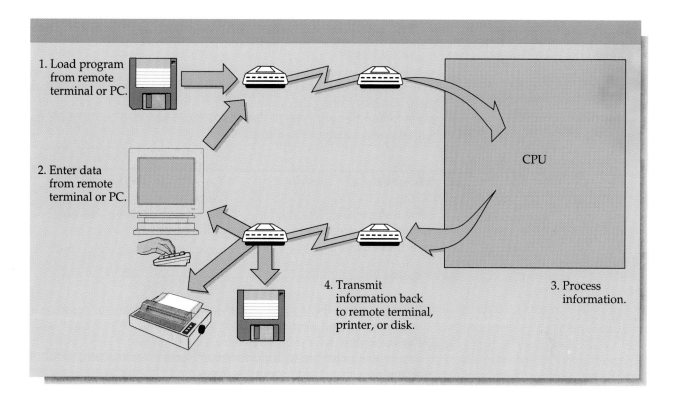

1. Load program from remote terminal or PC.

2. Enter data from remote terminal or PC.

CPU

4. Transmit information back to remote terminal, printer, or disk.

3. Process information.

the CPU transfers control to another user's program and puts the first program in a wait state for a short time. In this way, many programs can be executed at the same time, and because large computers execute instructions at very great speeds, users may not even notice the wait states.

Time-sharing is a popular outsourcing vehicle for companies that need computing power but either cannot afford to maintain their own systems or need additional computing resources. These companies rent computing time and use resources from companies that own large systems and specialize in providing computing services to others. Some time-sharing firms provide programming and systems support to their clients as well. Time-sharing does, however, have disadvantages:

- When a user wants to access the system, the computer may be too busy to handle the request.
- Security and privacy can be problems.
- Costs may be high if usage is high. Total costs depend on the amount of time the CPU is used, plus the cost of transmission.

In place of time-sharing, some organizations purchase relatively inexpensive minis, midranges, and micros to meet their computing needs. Although these computers do not have the capability of larger systems, they are far less expensive and more adaptable to a smaller company's needs. In addition, they are under the user's control and are less prone to security problems.

*Figure 12.15 In remote job entry applications, workers use terminals to send programs as well as data to the central computer, which often outputs the information to a screen, a printer, or local storage media such as disks.*

## ▶ Accessing Information from External Services

A computer, modem, and telephone line enable any user access to a variety of databases and other resources. For a fee, **subscriber services** offer access to hundreds or even thousands of databases. Here are some of the better-known subscriber services.

| *General* | *Specific* |
|---|---|
| CompuServe | Lexis/Nexis (legal) |
| Prodigy | WestLaw (legal) |
| Genie Service (GE Network for Information Exchange) | Business (Dow Jones News/ Retrieval) |
| America Online | |

Access to a subscriber service requires you to

1. Enroll or subscribe, that is, pay a start-up fee and obtain passwords, log-on codes, and documentation.
2. Pay a monthly fixed-rate service fee.
3. Pay connect charges to the subscriber service for the time you are online as well as for any extra services.
4. Pay the telephone company for connect time. Most subscriber services provide access to Telenet, Tymnet, or some other wide area telephone service so that you can communicate with it using a local telephone number; with some, however, you must make a long distance call.

*Dow Jones News/Retrieval screen display.*

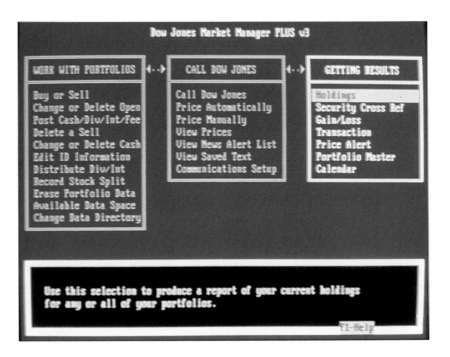

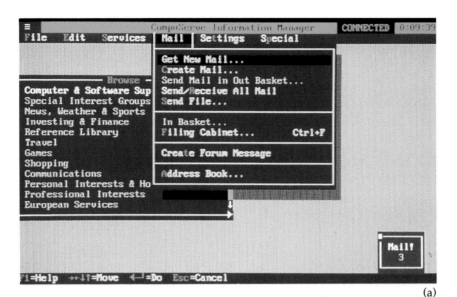

*Figure 12.16* (a) *A CompuServe screen display.* (b) *A Prodigy screen display.*

IN A

**NUT SHELL**

*General subscriber services enable users to*

- Bank at home.
- Make reservations for hotels, airlines, and car rentals.
- Access stock information and make transactions.
- Shop from catalogs.
- Obtain information from professional and personal databases (sports, travel, news, movie reviews).
- Communicate electronically with others who subscribe.
- Become a member of a special interest group in order to receive new information and communicate with others who have similar interests.
- Download shareware or public domain software to your micro for a small fee or sometimes even for free.

CompuServe is a text-oriented, combined command- and menu-driven subscriber service that has been available for many years. Prodigy, a more recent joint venture between Sears and IBM, is a graphically oriented and completely menu-driven service. Figure 12.16 illustrates the different interfaces for these services. CompuServe and Prodigy are currently the market leaders; each has more than a million subscribers. Prodigy is cheaper primarily because it accepts and displays advertisements.

*Figure 12.17 A menu from a bulletin board service.*

In addition to general subscriber services, there are specialized international and national networks of research and academic organizations. Internet and Bitnet, two of the largest such networks, provide members with information on recent publications, advances in specific fields, upcoming conferences, and so on (more on this later in the chapter). Free bulletin board services are also widely available, some for special interest groups such as Mac users, IBM users, or WordPerfect users, or for members of various clubs or societies. See Figure 12.17. These electronic bulletin boards enable users with similar interests to communicate with one another, keep track of recent innovations in specific areas, and upload and download files.

## ▶ Electronic Mail

Electronic mail (e-mail) is the transmission of memos and messages over a network. Users send messages to individual recipients or "broadcast" messages to groups of users on the system. If the recipient is online when the message is being transmitted, a beep will announce that mail has arrived. If the recipient is not online, the next time he or she logs on, a message will indicate that there is mail waiting. Recipients can read, reread, reply to, forward, delete, or save messages. "Folders" can be established so that all mail from and responses to specified individuals or groups of individuals can be stored separately.

Electronic mail has the potential for greatly influencing the ways in which people communicate. For one thing, people need not play "telephone tag" trying to track down each other. Messages can be as detailed as necessary and can include spreadsheets, charts, other documents, and so on. Records of messages sent and delivered can be retained as "ticklers" or to help evaluate the effectiveness of the exchange. People can take time to structure a message so that what is transmitted is exactly what is intended—verbal messages are not always as effective in this regard.

To send or receive e-mail, you must be connected to a network. If the network is active 24 hours a day, you can transmit and receive messages at any hour. Moreover, you can transmit messages to people who may be far away but who have access to the network over telephone lines. If groups of people use the same network—either by accessing their own company's computer or by using a subscriber service, for example—messages can be transmitted over local phone lines with minimum telephone costs, even if other users are not at the same location.

Connectivity, which makes people better able to share computing resources with one another, is greatly enhanced by e-mail. This means of electronic communication is available not only to employees within a company, but to anyone who makes use of subscriber services, electronic bulletin boards, or other public networks. One problem with e-mail is lack of cross-communication: users may have access to many e-mail services, none of which permits communication with another. E-mail software such as cc:Mail by Lotus is designed to ease this problem. It enables users to establish one set of IDs and passwords and a set of folders that can be called in to communicate across disparate e-mail services.

**CRITICAL THINKING**

In what ways does e-mail *improve* communication between people and in what ways does it *impede* effective communication?

## ► Telecommuting

Telecommuting is the use of computers to access office databases, programs, electronic mail systems, and so forth while away from the office. Managers, professionals, and many other types of employees can work effectively at home or on the road, almost as if they were in the office. Telecommuting has the potential for improving the quality of life of employees by increasing leisure time and by enabling workers to do their jobs on a schedule that better suits their individual needs. It has societal benefits as well. Telecommuting can save energy and decrease pollution and traffic congestion. Studies predict that by the year 2000, 42% of the work force will be telecommuting for part of their workweek.

*Telecommuting from a hotel.*

 The common application areas for networks are not mutually exclusive. An organization may use data communications for remote data entry, for inquiring about the status of records in a database file, and for accessing a subscriber service. Connectivity, in its most global sense, relies on multiple uses of networks.

## ► SELF-TEST

1. A device called a _____ makes programs and data available to nodes on a network.
2. (T or F) Remote data entry systems can only be used for interactive processing.

3. (T or F) In remote job entry applications, the host computer works in a multiprogramming environment.

4. _____ is the transmission of memos and messages over a network.

5. (T or F) Telecommunications is the use of computers to access office databases, programs, and so on by employees while they are away from the office.

Solutions

1. file server or host
2. F—They can also be designed for batch processing.
3. T
4. Electronic mail (or e-mail)
5. F—The term is *telecommuting*.

# 12.3 CONTROLLING DATA FLOW WITH COMMUNICATIONS SOFTWARE

What specifications and protocols must be provided to computers by communications software?

Communications software provides computers with **transmission protocols,** the rules and procedures for exchanging information between computers. These protocols enable computers to communicate with one another. The software controls transmission by indicating the (1) speed of transmission, (2) direction of data flow, (3) method of transmission, (4) number of bits in the computer code, and (5) type of parity, if any.

## ▶ Speed of Transmission

Transmission speeds set by communications software indicate how fast data can travel accurately across specific communications channels. Different types of channels can handle data efficiently only at certain speeds. Transmission speed is related to the band width of a channel. There are three types of band widths—narrow band (which is rarely used now), baseband, and broadband—which determine the capacity of a channel to transmit data. Just as you would not drive 80 miles an hour over a rocky, pot-holed road, you would not send data through narrow band lines at extremely high speeds.

IN A

**SPEEDS OF TRANSMISSION LINES**

| Type of Line | Example | Characteristics | Range of Transmission Speed |
|---|---|---|---|
| Narrow band | Teletype | Very slow | Up to 150 bps |
| Baseband (voice-grade or midrange) | Telephone | Most commonly used, some noise | 300 to 19,200 bps |
| Broadband (wideband or high speed) | Leased lines, microwave, satellite, fiber optics | More expensive, least noise | 20,000 to 300,000+ bps and above |

The speed at which data is sent is commonly expressed as a **baud rate,** measured in bits per second (bps). Note that bps stands for the number of bits (not bytes) sent through the line per second. Most modems and acoustic couplers operate at 1200, 2400, 9600, 14,400 or more bps, roughly equivalent to 120, 240, 960, and 1440 or more characters per second. The computer code for just a character itself typically requires seven or eight bits. Sometimes start and stop bits are added along with a parity bit to control and regulate transmission. In all, a transmission may require 10 or so bits per character. Hence, we say that a 9600 bps modem transmits approximately 960 characters per second.

The speed of the communications line and the baud rate of the modem determine the maximum transmission rate. It is advisable to select a modem with a baud rate similar to the capacity of the transmission channel. It would not be prudent, for example, to use a modem with a baud rate of 9600 bps for transmitting data over a narrow band; similarly, it would be inefficient and unnecessarily slow to use a 1200 bps modem to transmit data over broadband channels.

## ▶ Direction of Data Flow

Traffic signs direct cars to move in only one of two directions on a street; similarly, data moves only in specific directions through communications channels. Electronic impulses can move in one of three ways: using sim-

*Figure 12.18 Transmission protocols allow one-way (simplex), alternating (half-duplex), or full two-way (full-duplex) transmission.*

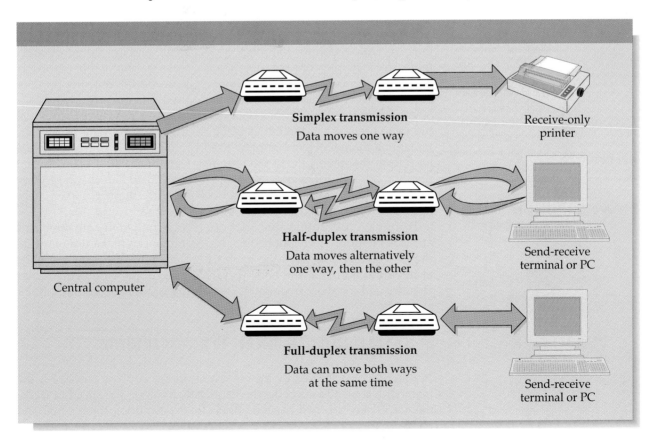

**Simplex transmission**
Data moves one way

Receive-only printer

**Half-duplex transmission**
Data moves alternatively one way, then the other

Send-receive terminal or PC

**Full-duplex transmission**
Data can move both ways at the same time

Send-receive terminal or PC

Central computer

*Figure 12.19 Receive-only terminals that use simplex lines have limited applications, such as displaying flight information at airline terminals.*

IN A

**TYPES OF CHANNELS**

1. Simplex— permits transmission of data in one direction only (e.g., from computer to printer); rarely used now
2. Half-duplex—permits transmission of data in two directions but not at the same time (analogous to CB transmissions)
3. Full-duplex—permits transmission of data in two directions at the same time (e.g., most baseband and broadband transmissions)

plex, half-duplex, or full-duplex communication channels. See Figure 12.18. Communications software sets the transmission protocols that indicate the way data will flow over a communications channel.

**Simplex lines** allow data to flow in one direction only, like a one-way street. A simplex line functions with a device that only sends or only receives data from a CPU but does not do both; a printer, for example, is a receive-only device that could obtain its messages over a simplex line. An airline monitor that displays departure and arrival information might use a simplex line because data is always transmitted in one direction only—from the CPU to the monitor (Figure 12.19). But simplex lines are clearly very limited and are therefore used infrequently.

A **half-duplex line** permits data to move in two directions, but not at the same time. When the line is being used to transmit data from a terminal to a main CPU, it cannot be used simultaneously to transmit data back from the main CPU to the terminal. Data moves first one way and then the other, but never at the same time. Half-duplex channels work like CB radios, which can send and receive voice messages alternately, but not at the same time.

By using a **full-duplex line,** data can be transmitted in both directions at the same time. A telephone line, for example, can make use of a full-duplex channel: Similarly, the main CPU transmits messages to a node at the same time that the node is transmitting to the CPU. Full-duplex channels are the most frequently used channels in data communications applications.

## ▶ Serial and Parallel Transmission

Another factor specified by the communications software package is the method of transmission. Like the baud rate, it affects the speed of transmission. There are two basic methods for transmitting data: serial and parallel.

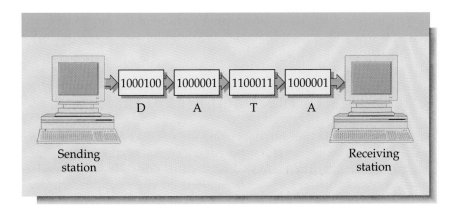

*Figure 12.20 Serial transmission.*

## SERIAL TRANSMISSION

In **serial transmission,** each bit is transmitted one at a time in sequence over a single channel. See Figure 12.20. Initially, most peripherals communicated with computers in serial mode through a standard serial interface called the RS-232C interface, which attaches to modems. Most serial transmissions today use an enhanced version of that interface called the RD-422.

There are two types of serial modes for sending data: asynchronous and synchronous. **Asynchronous transmission** means that one character at a time is transmitted. The transfer of data is controlled by start and stop bits. This is the least expensive method of transmission and is often used with narrow or low-end voice band channels. **Synchronous transmission** enables blocks of characters called packets to be transmitted in timed sequences. A stop bit indicates the end of data. Synchronous transmission is not only much faster than asynchronous transmission, but it is also more widely used.

## PARALLEL TRANSMISSION

**Parallel transmission** is a faster method of transmission in which all bits are transmitted simultaneously. See Figure 12.21. Parallel transmission is

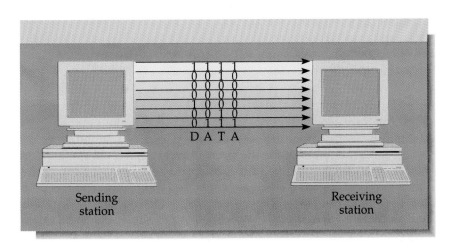

*Figure 12.21 Parallel transmission.*

more expensive than serial transmission because of the large number of cables needed and is usually limited to communications over relatively short distances.

## ▶ Data Bits in the Computer Code

Computers typically transmit data using the ASCII code which, as noted in Chapter 4, is an abbreviation for American Standard Code for Information Interchange. There are two versions of this code, a 7-bit and an 8-bit version. In order for two computers to communicate with one another, the communications package must include a parameter indicating which ASCII version—7-bit or 8-bit—is being used by each computer.

## ▶ Parity

In Chapter 4 you learned that parity bits are added to computer codes to minimize the risk of transmission errors. Even-parity computers require each character being transmitted to have an even number of bits on at all times. If the character being transmitted uses an odd number of ASCII bits, then the parity bit is automatically turned on to ensure that an even number of bits are being transmitted. If the character being transmitted uses an even number of ASCII bits, then the parity bit is automatically turned off so that an even number of bits is, in fact, transmitted. Some computers use even parity and some use odd parity; other computers do not use parity bits at all. The type of parity—odd, even, or none—must be specified by the communications software used for interfacing with another computer.

The number of characters that actually get transmitted per second is only partly determined by the baud rate. The actual number of characters transmitted per second depends also on the computer code, parity, and method of transmission being used. Consider, for example, an 8-bit code with parity and one stop bit. This type of transmission requires 10 bits per character. In this instance, a baud rate of 2400 bps would mean a transmission of 240 characters per second. If no parity were used, or both a start and stop bit were included, or the code were 7-bit, then the number of bits per character might not be exactly 10.

## ▶ Software and Standards

A number of communications software packages enable computer devices to communicate with one another over telephone lines. They are used not only for setting the transmission protocols but also for storing phone numbers, log-on codes, passwords, and so on. SmartCom is probably the most common package, but ProComm and Kermit (a public domain package that is often available through subscriber services and

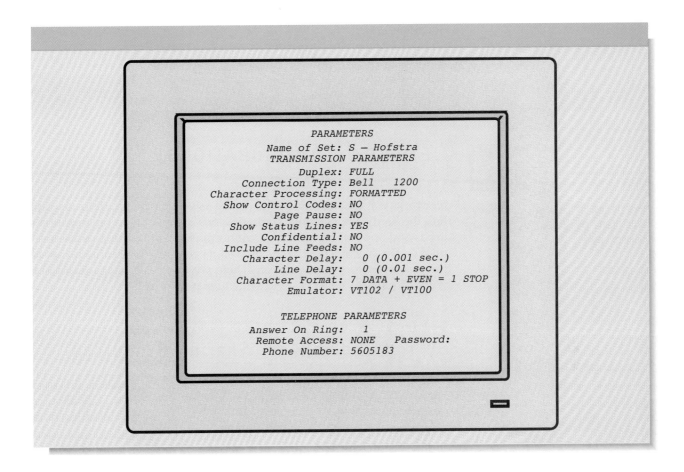

```
                    PARAMETERS
            Name of Set: S — Hofstra
            TRANSMISSION PARAMETERS
              Duplex: FULL
     Connection Type: Bell   1200
 Character Processing: FORMATTED
   Show Control Codes: NO
          Page Pause: NO
    Show Status Lines: YES
         Confidential: NO
    Include Line Feeds: NO
      Character Delay:   0 (0.001 sec.)
          Line Delay:   0 (0.01 sec.)
     Character Format: 7 DATA + EVEN = 1 STOP
            Emulator: VT102 / VT100

            TELEPHONE  PARAMETERS
      Answer On Ring:   1
       Remote Access: NONE    Password:
        Phone Number: 5605183
```

bulletin boards) are widely used as well. See Figure 12.22 for an illustration of a SmartCom screen display.

In a move toward standardization, the International Standards Organization (ISO) in Geneva, Switzerland has defined a set of communications protocols called the **Open Systems International (OSI) model.** The model has been endorsed by the United Nations but has not yet become a fully recognized standard.

*Figure 12.22 Sample parameters set by the SmartCom communications software package.*

### ▶ SELF-TEST

1. The speed at which data is transmitted over communications channels is expressed as a _____.
2. (T or F) A 9600 bps modem transmits approximately 960 characters per second.
3. (Simplex/half-duplex/full-duplex) channels are the most frequently used ones in data communications applications.
4. The two basic methods for transmitting data are serial transmission and _____.
5. (T or F) Computers typically communicate with one another using the EBCDIC code.

Solutions
1. baud rate, or bits per second (bps)
2. T
3. Full-duplex
4. parallel transmission
5. F—They typically use the ASCII code.

# 12.4 NETWORK CONFIGURATIONS

What types of network configurations can be used to achieve connectivity?

Networks consist of computer hardware as well as the programs used to link the hardware. Network configurations depend on an organization's needs and application areas. Full connectivity of office equipment—telephones, fax machines, printers, as well as computers—can be achieved through a network configuration. There are two basic categories of networks: local area networks and wide area networks.

## ▶ Local Area Networks (LAN): The Promised LAN for Sharing Resources

A **local area network (LAN)** is the most common configuration. It is used when computer devices are in relatively close proximity to one another. Although some LANs can connect devices as far apart as 50 miles, most connect devices within several thousand feet of one another. Most often, these LANs have coaxial or fiber optic cables for linkages, but telephone lines or wireless radio waves could be used.

LANs enable organizations to share resources such as software, hardware, and data. They also help schedule, supervise, and monitor the processing of data from remote locations. LANs used in this way have a file server, which is linked to each station or node. As we have seen, this file server can be a RISC-based microcomputer, itself a workstation, or a mainframe, midrange, or minicomputer depending on the complexity of the jobs it must perform.

## ▶ File Servers and LANs

### SHARING SOFTWARE

In some organizations, all or most stand-alone PCs run the same software products. As PCs proliferate, the need for the software increases. Software manufacturers and vendors often provide site licenses, which permit one software package to be shared by many users. Obtaining a site license is usually less expensive than purchasing individual copies of the software for each user.

One way to enable users to share software once a site license has been acquired is to put the software on the file server. Users can access or download programs as they need them. In this way, a single copy of the

IN A NUT SHELL

**PHYSICAL COMPONENTS OF A LAN**

1. *Nodes*, which may be input/output devices or micros.
2. *File server* that stores the data and software and controls access to resources
3. *Network cables* or links such as telephone lines or wireless radio waves that connect nodes to a host or file server. LANs usually employ coaxial cables, either baseband or broadband (see Table 12.2).
4. *Interface cards* inserted in an expansion slot of the nodes that enable the devices to communicate with other devices.
5. *Cable interface unit* in a separate device that enables signals to be sent and received on the network cables.

**Table 12.2** | COMPARISON OF BASEBAND AND BROADBAND LANs

| Characteristics | Data Transmission | Example |
|---|---|---|
| *Baseband (voice-grade or midrange)* | | |
| Low cost<br>Medium speed<br>Lower band width<br>(means less<br>capacity) | Baseband LANs consist of a *single path* over which text, graphics, voice, and video data can pass, but *only one* type of data can pass at a time. They can transmit 300 to 19,200 bits per second. | Telephone |
| *Broadband (wideband or high speed)* | | |
| More expensive<br>High speed<br>Higher band width<br>(means greater<br>capacity) | Broadband LANs consist of several paths, enabling transmission of many different types of data simultaneously. Broadband LANs can also connect devices over longer distances than baseband LANs. They are used for cable TV. | Leased lines, microwave lines, satellite lines, fiber optic cables |

software stored on the file server can be used by all stations or nodes, even at the same time.

Site license agreements vary widely. Some manufacturers permit unlimited use of a product, whereas others are far more restrictive. (Refer back to Chapter 7 for more information.)

## SHARING HARDWARE

In microcomputer systems, the printer is typically a device that is used less frequently than the CPU, keyboard, or CRT. Users usually print only after all processing has been completed. Thus, if an organization has numerous PCs and each has its own printer, the printers are often underutilized.

A LAN permits several PCs to share a printer. The output from a group of micros is stored, queued, and then printed. Moreover, output can be directed to virtually any printer on the network, so if one or more is inoperable ("down"), users at any specific PC are not at a disadvantage. For systems with a limited number of relatively expensive laser or color printers, a LAN can help to distribute these printer resources equitably. Other devices such as a modem or plotter can be shared by micros on a LAN as well.

In addition, a LAN enables computers with different architectures and operating systems to communicate with one another. An important benefit of a LAN in organizations that have both Apple Macintosh and IBM micros is the sharing of resources it allows among the two environments or platforms. In principle, incompatible computers and input/output devices can be connected to each other by means of a LAN.

### SHARING DATA

A LAN enables multiple users at remote stations to enter data, inquire about records in a database file, and update database files, depending on the application. In distributed processing applications, for example, many users typically have access to databases, all at the same time. The LAN software can control and monitor access to ensure that only designated users and devices can retrieve specified data. It provides a measure of security by minimizing the risk that unauthorized personnel will gain access to a database. The LAN can also alert authorized users if data is in the process of being altered as they are working on it or, alternatively, it can prevent changes to files currently being accessed by others.

### SUPERVISING AND MONITORING ACTIVITIES

LANs maintain records on user activities, software and hardware use, and so forth. Such information assists decision makers in determining whether resources are being utilized effectively or whether additional resources are needed.

LANS make it possible to control the overall processing of data by minimizing the use of auxiliary storage devices at local sites. Since data and programs can be stored on the LAN, many networks do not read to, or write from, local disk drives. This reduces the risk that users will violate copyright laws by illegally downloading software. It also helps reduce the risk of viruses (which are designed to destroy files) being uploaded from a floppy disk to a central computer. A LAN can provide automatic backup and recovery as well as minimize security risks. LANs often have virus protection programs as well. As we saw in Chapter 7, the threat of a virus is a major problem in organizations where data and programs are shared.

In general, there are two basic techniques for using a file server. In the conventional method, the server mainly downloads files to PCs, which perform the processing. With the **client-server** method, the file server does as much central processing as is possible before downloading, in an effort to improve overall efficiency.

*File servers enable software and hardware to be shared by many users.*

## ▶ LAN Software

LAN software interfaces with application software and controls resources. This software must contain an operating system or operating system interface that enables a variety of different programs to be used on the LAN. LAN software also contains communications programs that permit all devices to communicate either with the file server or with each other. In addition, the software contains utilities for monitoring and supervising hardware and software use. Currently, Novell is the leading developer of LAN software.

Installing and controlling hardware and software on a network can be fairly complex. Many organizations employ a network manager or administrator who is responsible for establishing the network, supervising its implementation, and monitoring its activities.

## ▶ Network Topologies: Star, Bus, Ring

The specific type of network configuration is called the **network topology.** The topology differs depending on how the network will be used. The three types of network topologies—ring, star, and bus—are illustrated in Figure 12.23. Each topology has specific features.

1. Ring
   - This topology is the standard for LANs that use file servers.
   - It also can be used to connect a series of devices where there is no central computer.
   - Nodes are linked to each other as well as to the file server.
   - A message transmitted from one node to another must pass through the ring from node to node until it reaches its destination.

2. Star
   - All devices can access a host but not necessarily each other.
   - Typically, there are no difficulties if one node is down—it is simply bypassed.
   - The central computer (the host) monitors all processing.
   - This topology is ideal for networks where branch offices need to communicate with a main office.

3. Bus
   - This topology is truly interactive.
   - Nodes share the same bus, or channel, for transmitting to other nodes or hosts.
   - *Ethernet,* a popular LAN that interconnects PCs via coaxial cable, has a bus topology.
   - Nodes can access a host as well as each other.

Networks that use a file server to enable users to share resources will most likely use a *token* ring topology. IBM's **token ring network** uses twisted pair cables for transmission and has become a de facto standard in the industry. A "token" is a special signal that moves from node to node around the LAN. Only one token on the network is available at any given time. When a user at a node on the network wants to transmit or receive data from the file server, it first captures the token; then it completes its transaction. After the transaction is complete, the token is released back to the network for use by other nodes. Think of the tokens as dump trucks revolving around a ring—some are empty and some are full. Some will be dumped at the central site and some must first pick up a load.

Often networks are used by larger organizations for distributed processing; nodes process data at the local level as well as transmit and

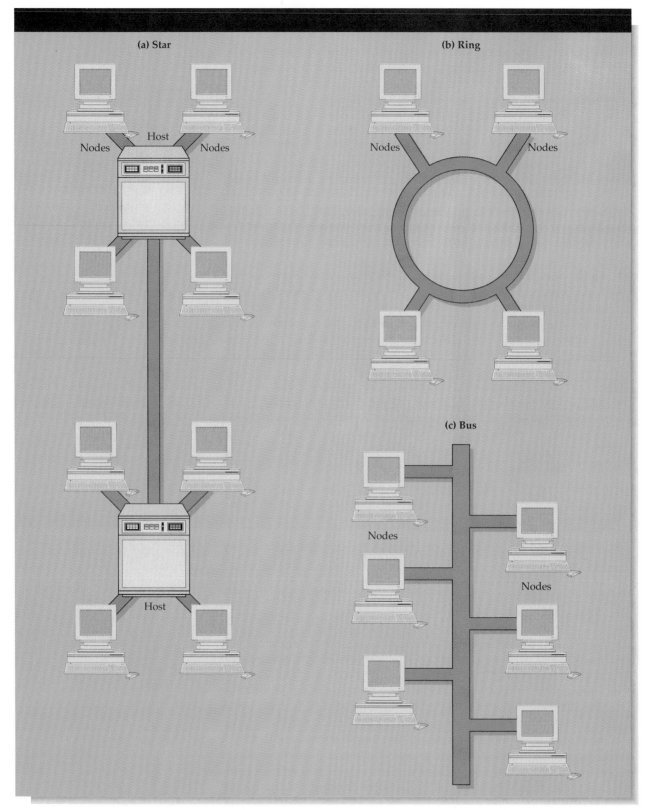

**Figure 12.23** *A comparison of star, ring, and bus networks. (a) A star network is most often used with terminals (or PCs) and hosts. (b) In a ring network, all computers are connected in a continuous loop. Data flows around the ring in one direction only. (c) Bus networks are commonly used in Ethernet systems.*

receive data from a host computer. Large-scale database management systems are typically accessed by means of networks for distributed processing applications. Such applications are likely to use a star or a bus technology. Networks in which a central computer is accessed by terminals primarily for remote data entry are apt to use a star topology.

## ▶ Wide Area Networks (WANs)

Our discussion of LANs has been fairly detailed because that is the type of network you are most likely to encounter at school or at the office. If local area transmissions and transfers of files are not sufficient, however, **wide area networks (WANs)** are required.

### FOR TRANSMISSION OVER GREATER DISTANCES THAN LANS

As you may suspect, WANs are similar in concept to LANs except that the technology permits transmission over greater distances. A WAN typically uses microwave relays and satellites so that individuals at nodes can communicate with a host or with each other over long distances, even around the world. Commercial WANs widely available in the United States include Tymnet and Telenet, which link users to subscriber services. Organizations rent or lease private telephone lines from Tymnet and Telenet and then provide shared resources to computer users at a relatively low cost.

MasterCard's worldwide, private WAN is called Banknet and consists of 14 switching centers, 8 in the United States and 6 in other countries. One major application area for Banknet is electronic funds transfer (EFT). Banks around the world that are MasterCard members settle their accounts daily by using the Banknet WAN to electronically transmit transaction data rather than by creating a paper trail of checks, deposit slips, withdrawal slips, and so forth.

### FOR NETWORKING LANS

Sometimes a WAN is simply a network of LANs. A department store, for example, may have a LAN at each branch store; in addition, the LANs at all stores may be connected to the main office by means of a WAN. Sometimes a WAN simply permits a large number of nodes at different locations to communicate with each other.

### GATEWAYS AND BRIDGES CONNECT LANS TO WANS

LANs linked to WANs require a special device, usually a computer, along with special software. The term **gateway** describes the technology and hardware that connects the two types of networks. Gateways are sophisticated enough to connect nodes and LANs that use different tech-

---

**CRITICAL THINKING**

Do you think profit-making organizations should have access to Internet?

---

*LOOKING* / *AHEAD*

**GLOBAL NETWORKING**

1. The distinctions between LANs and WANs are fading as global networking becomes more popular.
2. The trend toward very sophisticated network management capabilities will grow.
3. Networks will result in more "downsizing"—smaller computers networked to more sophisticated file servers.
4. Wireless networks will enable the world to be even more connected.

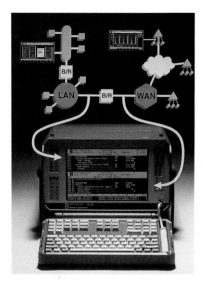

*Figure 12.24 LAN gateway.*

# LOOKING AHEAD

**A SUPER NETWORK**

The National Research and Education Network (NREN) is a proposed super network based on Internet that will link educational institutions, scientists, and businesspeople to supercomputers across the nation. The $3 billion funding for this project has been approved by Congress. When implemented, this network is likely to bring people in all fields closer together and will make available to them a wide variety of resources.

nologies; that is, they can interpret and convert each LAN's data format and transmission protocol. Gateways are often so user-friendly that they are transparent: a user can access another network without even knowing that it is another network. See Figure 12.24. A **bridge** is similar. It consists of hardware and software that connect LANs together. When a bridge is being used, a message can be sent from a node on one LAN to a node on a different LAN.

National and international WANs like Bitnet and Internet consist of hundreds of local networks used by industry, the government, and universities. These WANs make use of bridges and gateways to provide high-speed transmissions virtually around the world. Bitnet, an acronym for the catch-phrase "*Because It's Time NET*work," began in 1981 as a communications link between the City University of New York and Yale University. It has grown to be an extensive network of several hundred sites, mostly at universities, in dozens of countries. Through gateways, connections can be made to a wide variety of additional networks such as ARPANET, which is the network of the U.S. Department of Defense's Advanced Research Projects Agency; CSNET, which is also used by scholars to communicate with each other; and Internet, which is an international network of research and academic institutions sponsored by the National Science Foundation.

Researchers, students, and members of the academic community communicate with one another over the vast Internet network and access databases in numerous subject areas. Once a U.S. Department of Defense research project, Internet now connects 350,000 host computers on 5000 networks in 35 countries. Its total user base is estimated to be over 3 million people.

Through Bitnet and Internet, you can send a message, a file, or database to someone at another participating university. You need to know the recipient's ID and node name (the name assigned to his or her school). Use a terminal or micro linked to your school's mainframe, log on in the usual way, and access the Bitnet or Internet network as specified by your institution. Most schools use their electronic mail facility to provide access. Thus, when you log on, your computer will tell you if you have mail waiting. Bitnet and Internet also provide electronic news in a number of different subject areas and provide access to thousands of databases.

## ▶ SELF-TEST

1. (T or F) A LAN benefits organizations that have both Macintosh and IBM micros because it enables resources to be shared among the two environments.
2. (T or F) All networks must have a host or file server.
3. (T or F) A wide area network can consist of a network of LANs.
4. (T or F) It is possible to connect nodes and LANs that have different technologies.
5. A (gateway/bridge) can be used to send a message from a node on one LAN to a node on a different LAN.

Solutions
1. T
2. F—A ring network connects a series of devices where there is no central computer.
3. T
4. T—This can be accomplished with a gateway.
5. bridge

# CONNECTIVITY LEADS TO A SMALLER, SMARTER, AND MORE CREATIVE WORLD

**12.5**

In the previous sections, we considered connectivity in relation to computerized application areas for information processing. As we approach the twenty-first century, computerized devices are likely to be used in a more integrated manner to help people in their businesses and in their personal lives as well. Connectivity is the key to that integration. In this section, we discuss other technologies and application areas that will make the world more connected in the years ahead.

What other technologies have emerged that help make the world more connected?

## ► Facsimile Machines

A **facsimile machine (fax)** enables us to transmit virtually any document to any location over telephone lines. The sender uses a telephone to dial the receiving fax machine's phone number and then feeds the document through the sending fax machine. The receiving fax machine produces a copy of the document.

Facsimile machines have a scanner that reads and digitizes a document. The document itself can contain illustrations and photos as well as handwritten or typed text. The digitized document is converted into analog form and transmitted over telephone lines. At the receiving end, the analog signals are converted back to digital form thereby producing a copy of the document.

The number of fax machines for both business and personal use has increased dramatically during the past few years. See Figure 12.25. Fax machines are popular because they can be programmed to (1) transmit at off-peak hours when phone rates are lower, (2) transmit to a number of different locations (e.g., each sales office of a company), and (3) accept documents from designated senders only, so that the risk of receiving a "junk fax" is reduced.

Some application areas are already predominantly fax-based; that is, they rely on telephones along with fax machines to communicate with clients. For example, potential customers dial a designated number for information about items. An answering machine instructs them on how to select a specific item—a sales brochure, for example. Typically, the customer is instructed to key specific digits using a Touch-Tone phone.

(a)

(b)

**Figure 12.25** (a) *Office fax machine.* (b) *Public fax machines.*

**Figure 12.26** *Fax board for PCs.*

The customer then keys in his or her fax number and the system immediately faxes the information requested. This is called a fax-back system. As phone charges decrease and mail charges increase, fax and fax-back systems for providing information to customers are likely to become more popular.

Some computers have **fax boards** that capture any document or screen display stored by the computer and transmit it via a modem either to another computer with a modem or to a fax machine. See Figure 12.26. Some e-mail and subscriber services enable users to create documents on a PC, upload them to the host, and have them faxed to a receiving party who has either a computer or a fax machine. Fax boards in PCs originated in 1986. They are often preferable to fax machines for several reasons:

- Security and privacy is better maintained—no one but the sender and receiver sees a copy of documents.
- Junk fax can simply be deleted without ever being printed.
- A PC can store incoming faxes in background mode while other processing is being performed and keep a log of faxes sent and received.
- The amount of paper generated and stored in offices is reduced because faxed documents can be stored on disk rather than in hard copy form. This may facilitate the trend toward a paperless office, which is a goal in many organizations.

The current sales figure for PC fax boards is about $20 million as compared to $4 billion for stand-alone faxes.

Most fax boards are internal computer devices, but some companies sell external fax boards for use with portable computers. Fax boards are best used to send *computer-produced* documents. If data is not in a computer file or on a storage device (e.g., a book page, photo, or drawing), it must be scanned (or retyped) and stored before it can be transmitted by fax board.

*Networked Fax Machines.*   Stand-alone office fax machines, like copy machines, require a staff to feed, monitor, and oversee operations. Many companies are now integrating fax, computer, and network technology to cut costs, save time, and avoid the inconvenience associated with fax transmissions. Users transmit their computer-produced document to a network-based "fax server" which sends faxes, from numerous users, in batch mode. The PC user who has access to a network-based fax server does not have to wait for documents to be printed and then wait on a separate fax line to transmit them. Instead, documents generated on a PC may be uploaded to a fax server for transmission to a recipient.

Fax servers reduce the need for multiple phone lines. Whereas each stand-alone fax machine or fax board typically has its own phone line, a network-based server can queue documents to be faxed and transmit them, in batch mode, over one phone line. Fax servers, like all fax machines, can be programmed to transmit documents that are not time sensitive at off hours when the cost is cheaper and the lines are less congested.

But most of the benefits of network-based faxing are outward bound. To date, the network technology to permit fax servers to automatically route *incoming* faxes to the appropriate PC recipient is still very expensive. In the future, however, we can expect fax servers to be able to inexpensively scan the name of a recipient and transmit the document directly to that person's computer.

## ▶ Cellular Telephones and Radio-Frequency-Based Modems

A wireless device available to the general public with many of the same features as private radio networks is a cellular telephone. A cellular telephone uses radio waves to communicate with a local cell assigned to an individual geographic location. Cellular phones are often used in cars, and the newest ones have modems that permit transmission of computer messages from a laptop or other portable computer. See Figure 12.27.

IBM recently announced a portable PC that can communicate with larger computers via radio or cellular telephone hookups. The notebook-sized computer, called the PC Radio, is aimed at service technicians, salespeople, police, and other mobile workers. Users of the PC Radio will be able to transmit information to larger systems from virtually any location.

Portable modems are alternatives to cellular telephones with modems. Data collection services can be improved by use of a standard telephone, portable modem, and a PC. For example, computerized vending machines hooked to telephones could signal suppliers for refills, "smart" courier pickup boxes could notify a dispatcher if a package is deposited, and alarm systems could phone security if someone enters restricted premises.

In the near future, wireless transmissions from PC to host by means of radio waves are likely to be common. ARDIS, an acronym for *Advanced Radio Data Information System*, is the largest commercial radio network for PCs, but it is not yet available to individuals, only to

*Figure 12.27 Cellular phones—* (a) *standard and* (b) *wrist-sized.*

(a)

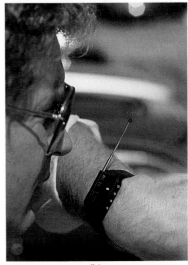

(b)

Fortune 1000 companies and businesses with more than 500 employees. It serves 8000 U.S. cities and soon may be marketed as a more reliable and efficient alternative to communications based on cellular telephones.

## ▶ Smart Phones

Does the rotary dial telephone seem like a dinosaur to you? Now some telephone manufacturers are hoping to make the Touch-Tone telephone a memory too. The caller who has a **smart phone** can automatically pay the heating bill by pushing a button, order a pizza by pushing another, and find out what is on sale at the local supermarket or department store by pushing a third button. See Figure 12.28.

Smart phones contain computer chips that can be programmed for many advanced features and monitors that can visually display data. They have modems and built-in fax capability as well.

AT&T, Northern Telecom, and other telephone companies supporting smart phone development believe that these devices will encourage consumers to shop and bank at home. For many years, subscriber services have offered consumers the ability to shop, bank, and retrieve data from databases while at home. But consumers have been slow to use this technology.

*Figure 12.28 A smart phone can pay bills, do the shopping, and provide us with a variety of information services.*

The new smart phones, however, are expected to make banking and shopping services more convenient. Because they are telephones and do not require a separate computer, they seem more user-friendly. Many people believe that telephones may be better suited than computers for home shopping because, unlike the PC, they are already found in almost all homes and people are intimately familiar with them. Smart phones are less likely to intimidate users and they fit more comfortably into the average living room! Developers of the smart phone admit, however, that what they are really doing is disguising a computer to look like a telephone. They hope that the simplicity, price, and convenience of a smart phone will encourage people to use it the way subscriber services are used.

Some of the telephone services offered with the smart phone, such as Caller ID which displays the number of the caller, are designed to spur interest as well. For a cost of $150 to $200, users can have enhanced phone services as well as shop-at-home capabilities.

## ▶ High-Definition Television

High-definition television (HDTV) has the potential for converting TVs from a passive, receive-only home unit used exclusively for entertainment purposes, to an interactive device that brings a wide variety of services and information into the home. Technically speaking, HDTV, as defined by the U.S. government, is a system that provides wide-screen pictures with twice the resolution, or sharpness, of ordinary TVs and sound as clear as that on a compact disk. In an effort to minimize the proliferation of noncompatible units, the government has established a competition to determine a standard for HDTV broadcasting. Six companies are competing and the estimated date for determining the winner is mid-1993.

Currently, HDTV technology is used for improving computer images and video for CAD/CAM and other industrial applications. Standard workstations cannot project graphic images onto a large screen without a significant loss of resolution, unless the image is first converted into 35-mm slides. In contrast, HDTV not only projects a high-resolution image on a large screen, but it also enables computer users to manipulate those images. For computer-aided design applications, then, HDTV is ideal.

Because HDTV digitizes all signals including text, graphics, and sound, it has great potential as a fully computerized device. Integrated digital databases that store video and audio images as well as data and text can be transmitted over the TV and used in multimedia presentations. Interactive dialogs between user and TV could bring all sorts of information to the home and literally change the way we learn and how we use information.

In anticipation of HDTV, Commodore International has introduced a multimedia compact disk system called CD TV. It looks like a CD player and connects to the TV and home audio system to become an interactive, educational, informational, and entertainment center. A handheld, wireless, infrared remote control unit provides access to a library of stored multimedia titles. Of the 50 or so titles currently available, there are encyclopedias, maps, the *Guinness Book of World Records*, and Disney software, with interactive versions of classics like *Cinderella* and *The Tale of Peter*

*Research is currently being undertaken on high-definition TV at MIT's Media Lab.*

*Rabbit*. Self-improvement multimedia titles in sports, cooking, gardening, and so on are available, as well as electronic games.

## ▶ Videoconferencing

 **Videoconferencing** systems enable full-motion video and sound to be transmitted over telephone lines. Sound, captured by microphones, and images, captured by cameras, are digitized, compressed, and transmitted to the receiver. See Figure 12.29. The systems include recorders and receivers along with compression/decompression units called codecs, which are similar to modems in that they enable video and sound signals to be transmitted over phone lines but in compressed, digitized form.

Although expensive, videoconferencing equipment can result in a considerable savings in travel expenses for a company and in wear-and-tear on employees. Time-shared videoconferenced facilities are available to organizations at an hourly rate. The cost for such services a decade ago was $2000 per hour; now it is about $50 per hour. Some companies are experimenting with picture phones that allow video conferencing right at your desk. Desktop computers may have tiny video cameras, miniature microphones, and video software that can connect you to video networks.

Text, video, and graphic images as well as sound are being transmitted with greater frequency over phone lines. Transmission standards are needed to ensure compatibility and to improve efficiency. Many telephone companies offer Integrated Services Digital Network (ISDN) as a suggested standard for the digital transmission of voice, video, and data over telephone lines. We discuss this standard in more depth in the next

*Figure 12.29* *Videoconferencing systems transmit full-motion video and sound over telephone lines.*

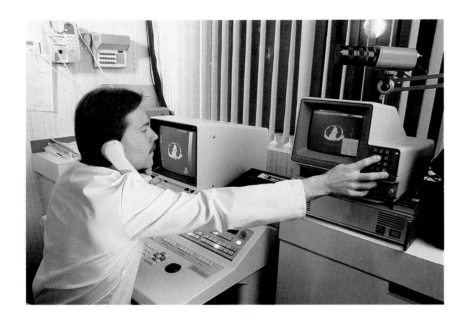

*An experimental image transfer system is capable of transmitting displays of all types over telephone lines.*

chapter as we summarize the reasons why standards are so important in the computer field.

▶ **SELF-TEST**

1. (T or F) Computers can send messages to facsimile machines if they have fax boards.
2. (T or F) With a smart phone, you can shop at home.
3. (T or F) HDTV has the potential to a make a TV function like a computer.

Solutions
1. T
2. T
3. T

---

▶ **C**hapter **S**ummary

Data communications allows us to combine the power and resources of computers no matter where the hardware is located. Connectivity, which brings the world closer together, is accomplished through different types of networks.

## 12.1 COMMUNICATIONS AND CONNECTIVITY

Connectivity involves a combination of technologies that enable computers to transmit data, voice messages, and video electronically to each

What type of communications linkages contribute to connectivity so that an organization's resources can be distributed and shared?

other. When computers are located near one another, cables or telephone lines connect the systems. When computers are a considerable distance from one another, a special communications technology called **telecommunications** (or teleprocessing) is required. Connectivity refers to the linking of all types of equipment—telephones, fax machines, and televisions as well as computers—so that resources in a wide variety of organizational and personal areas can be distributed and shared.

A network is the type of configuration that enables devices to communicate with one another. In some networks, remote devices called nodes are linked to one another; in other networks, nodes are linked to a central computer called a host. A **file server** is a special host computer that makes programs and data available to nodes on a network. **Communications channels** are the linkages between nodes and/or hosts in a network. Types of communications linkages include hardwired cables, telephones, microwave stations, satellite stations, and wireless networks. Three types of cable can be used for hardwired channels: twisted-pair cable, **coaxial cable,** and **fiber optic cable.** When telephones are used for communications, modems are needed to convert computer data, which is in digital format, to an analog format for transmission, and vice versa. Two basic kinds of modems are the direct-connect type and the **acoustic coupler,** which has two cups into which a telephone handset is placed.

A **multiplexer** is a device that collects messages from numerous nodes at one physical location and transmits them collectively at high speeds over a single communications channel. A **front-end processor** is a microcomputer or minicomputer that helps offload the activities performed by a host computer so that it can run more efficiently.

Many telephone companies offer **value-added services,** such as leased telephone lines, which are extra features beyond those normally provided for voice messages.

## 12.2 COMMON APPLICATION AREAS FOR NETWORKS

How is connectivity achieved in various facets of an organization's operations?

Distributed processing refers to the transmission of computer power throughout an organization from a central facility to each user site. Common distributed processing activities include (1) remote data entry and inquiry and (2) remote job entry and time-sharing. **Remote data entry** means that terminals or PCs are used for entering data at the places where transactions occur, such as in point-of-sale systems; the terminals or PCs are not physically at the same site as the central computer, or host. **Remote job entry** means that users write or run *programs* from terminals or PCs. Time-sharing involves the sharing of a large computer by many users—often from different organizations—who typically access the computer by means of terminals or PCs at various locations. **Time-slicing** is a time-sharing method used to allocate a small "slice" of computer time to each user.

Networks are used in other application areas as well. **Subscriber services** allow a user with a computer, modem, and telephone line to access a wide variety of databases and other resources. Electronic mail *(e-mail),* the transmission of memos and messages over a network, is a growing business application. Telecommuting is the use of computers to access office databases, programs, e-mail systems, and so forth while away from the office.

## 12.3 CONTROLLING DATA FLOW WITH COMMUNICATIONS SOFTWARE

**Transmission protocols,** procedures that are part of communications software, set the speed at which data can travel accurately across communications channels. The **baud rate,** expressed in bits per second (bps), is the speed at which data is sent.

Simplex lines permit transmission of data in one direction only. **Half-duplex lines** permit data to move in two directions, but not at the same time. With **full-duplex lines,** data can be transmitted in both directions at the same time. With **serial transmission,** each bit is transmitted one at a time in sequence over a single channel. There are two types of serial transmissions: **asynchronous transmission** means that one character at a time is transmitted, and **synchronous transmission** enables blocks of characters called packets to be transmitted in timed sequences. With **parallel transmission,** each bit of a character is transmitted over a separate channel. The **Open Systems International (OSI) model** is a set of communications protocols that may become an international standard.

*What specifications and protocols must be provided to computers by communications software?*

## 12.4 NETWORK CONFIGURATIONS

A **local area network (LAN)** connects devices that are in relatively close proximity to one another, typically within a range of 50 miles. LAN software controls and monitors computer and data access, ensuring that only designated users and devices can read specified data. One technique for using a LAN is called the **client-server** method; with this method, a file server does as much processing as possible before downloading.

The term **network topology** refers to the type of network configuration used in a data communications system. IBM's **token ring network** is a topology that has become a de facto standard in the industry; it allows only one node at a time to transmit or receive data from the file server.

A **wide area network (WAN)** uses microwave relays and satellites to enable users at nodes to communicate with a host or with each other over long distances around the world. The term **gateway** describes the technology and hardware that connects LANs to WANs. A **bridge** consists of hardware and software that connect LANs.

*What types of network configurations can be used to achieve true connectivity of office equipment?*

## 12.5 CONNECTIVITY LEADS TO A SMALLER, SMARTER, AND MORE CREATIVE WORLD

A **facsimile machine (fax)** scans documents, and **fax boards** capture computer screen displays or files. The documents, displays, or files are then transmitted to either computers or other fax machines. Cellular telephones and radio-frequency-based modems permit people in the field to communicate with the home office. **Smart phones** have features that make them function as home computers. **High-definition television (HDTV),** a system that provides wide-screen pictures with twice the resolution of TVs and high-quality sound as well, has the potential for con-

*What other technologies have emerged that help make the world more connected?*

verting TVs into interactive computers that bring many services and information into the home. **Videoconferencing**, which can transmit full-motion video and sound over telephone lines, enables people at different locations to see and hear one another and to communicate interactively.

## ▶ Chapter Self-test

1. The term _____ refers to electronically transmitting data from one location to another by means of communications channels.
2. (T or F) Using terminals at remote locations avoids manual transmittal of data, which can be very time consuming.
3. A _____ in a computer is used to send messages to a facsimile machine.
4. What kind of transmission waves do wireless LANs use?
5. A _____ distributes resources in a network.
6. Immediate online processing of data is required only when files must be kept _____ at all times.
7. Entering both a program and input from a disk at a remote location is called _____.
8. What term describes a technique that enables several businesses to rent computer time from a service organization?
9. Most simple data communications systems use _____ or _____ as a data communications link.
10. _____ cable is the fastest but most expensive communications link available for data transmission.
11. High-speed data communications use _____ stations and _____ stations above the earth.
12. The speed of a communications channel is called the _____ rate.
13. When transmission is permitted both to and from a CPU over the same communications line but *not at the same time*, the line is called _____.
14. What is the device that converts signals in digital form to analog form for transmission over telephone lines?
15. What is the device that can collect messages from numerous terminals and transmit them collectively over a single communications line?

Solutions
1. connectivity
2. T
3. fax board
4. infrared or radio
5. file server or host computer
6. current
7. remote job entry
8. time-sharing
9. a standard voice-grade telephone line; a cable
10. Fiber optic
11. microwave; satellite

12. baud
13. half-duplex
14. modem or acoustic coupler
15. multiplexer or front-end processor

## ▶ Key Terms

Acoustic coupler, *p. 479*
Asynchronous transmission,
  *p. 497*
Baud rate, *p. 495*
Bridge, *p. 506*
Client-server, *p. 502*
Coaxial cable, *p. 478*
Communications channel,
  *p. 476*
Facsimile machine (fax), *p. 507*
Fax board, *p. 508*
Fiber optic cable, *p. 478*
File server, *p. 475*
Front-end processor, *p. 481*

Full-duplex line, *p. 496*
Gateway, *p. 505*
Half-duplex line, *p. 496*
High-definition television
  (HDTV), *p. 510*
Local area network (LAN),
  *p. 500*
Multiplexer, *p. 480*
Network topology, *p. 503*
Open Systems International
  (OSI) model, *p. 499*
Parallel transmission, *p. 497*
Remote data entry, *p. 485*
Remote job entry, *p. 488*

Serial transmission, *p. 497*
Simplex line, *p. 496*
Smart phone, *p. 510*
Subscriber service, *p. 490*
Synchronous transmission,
  *p. 497*
Telecommunications, *p. 475*
Time-slicing, *p. 488*
Token ring network, *p. 503*
Transmission protocol, *p. 494*
Value-added service, *p. 482*
Videoconferencing, *p. 512*
Wide area network (WAN),
  *p. 505*

## ▶ Review Questions

1. Briefly discuss three major ways network technologies are used in a distributed computer system.
2. List seven major communications links for sending data between computers. Briefly discuss two advantages and disadvantages for each.
3. Describe two common hardware devices used for sending data over the telephone system.
4. Briefly explain how multiplexers and front-end processors reduce communications costs and integrate the use of terminals.
5. List and describe three common configurations for networks.
6. How many computer networks are used on your campus? What types of networks and configurations? How are they being used? Is there access to a WAN? If so, why is it being used?
7. Assume that you are a member of a five-person research team that will produce a report on the status of acid rain in the New England states. Each member of the team is located on a different university campus. What kind of computer network will be most useful to help the group do the research and prepare the report if each member has a terminal or networked microcomputer? If all five members were on the same campus, what kind of configuration would the network have? What software would you need? How would you use the network to help prepare the report?

## Building a Network without Reinventing the Wheel

Consider the accompanying ComputerLand ad and answer the questions that follow.

### Analysis

1. From the ad, can you tell what user concerns about networks ComputerLand has addressed and answered?
2. What services is ComputerLand attempting to sell with this ad?
3. Explain the meaning of the claim "Building a

network without re-inventing the wheel."
4. Provide an analysis of the strengths and weaknesses of the ad. Remember that there are no right or wrong answers. The quality of your answer will be determined by how well you make your points.

*ComputerLand ad for networks.*

# MAKING INFORMATION SYSTEMS PRIVATE, SECURE, AND MEANINGFUL

Throughout this text, we have seen that effective computerization has many advantages for individuals as well as organizations. But sometimes computer use needs to be controlled or monitored to protect an individual's rights, an organization's files, and the proper relationship between the individual and the organization.

We will explore the issues of privacy, security, and meaningfulness by answering the following questions:

▶ What personal, legal, and ethical issues are raised by the proliferation of information systems and computer networks?

▶ Why should security be an integral component of information systems and computer networks?

▶ How do information systems and computer networks affect the quality of life?

## PROTECTING THE PRIVACY OF USERS

What personal, legal, and ethical issues are raised by the proliferation of information systems and computer networks?

Privacy and security issues raise legal as well as ethical questions. Where breaches in privacy or security result in violations of a law, legal issues are involved. Where breaches result in a violation of a commonly accepted standard of behavior, but do not break an existing law, ethical issues are involved. Any society that promotes social responsibility needs to be concerned about both the legal and ethical behavior of people.

The problems associated with keeping a network secure so that it protects people's right to privacy need to be addressed seriously if connectivity is to be accepted widely and used effectively. The more accessible a network is, and the more options available on it, the greater the risk. As networks proliferate, which they will in the years ahead, and as more and more people have access to them, the risks are likely to increase as well.

Because the entire field of connectivity is so new, there are very few laws to deal with violations of privacy. State governments and the federal government, however, are becoming increasingly sensitive to the issues and are beginning to enact appropriate legislation.

### ▶ Privacy Issues Relating to E-Mail

With 12 million employees in the United States currently using computers for e-mail, the potential for policy disagreements and lawsuits with regard to privacy issues is great. Currently, no federal law addresses the rights and obligations of e-mail users, and state laws are often inadequate.

Many companies have been taken to court over privacy issues relating to e-mail. Because established policies are not in place and clear-cut laws do not exist, employees and employers often find themselves in disagreement as to what privileges e-mail users should have. Consider the following case, which illustrates how a lack of laws that specifically address computer issues can frustrate people who believe their rights have been violated. A class-action suit was filed in California against Epson America, Inc. The company fired an e-mail administrator because he alleged that the company intercepted employee's e-mail messages and that the interception was a violation of privacy. The case was dismissed on the grounds that e-mail does not fall within the state's wiretapping laws.

In an effort to minimize e-mail abuse, Prodigy and other subscriber services limit the number of e-mail messages that subscribers can send or charge extra for exceeding a fixed number of messages. Some even state that using e-mail for mass mailings to others on the network is grounds for membership cancellation. Naturally, many users object.

In addition, Prodigy has a policy of screening messages before they are placed in "forums," which are special-interest user groups. Some people believe that a subscriber service's e-mail facility should be afforded the same protection as the United States mail. They believe that e-mail users should have the freedom to send virtually anything, even if it is offensive to some. Prodigy and others reject this notion and think that e-mail services should have the same status as newspapers; that is, they bear some responsibility for what is printed.

## ▶ Privacy Issues Relating to Database Access

Privacy concerns have become even more widespread as the use of computers for storing public access databases increases. Because of the proliferation of large databases, it is becoming easier for companies to gather information on individuals and organizations, information that might not otherwise be readily available or easy to compile. For those reasons, many individuals and consumer groups have sought to enact laws that would limit access to computerized databases.

Consider reporting agencies that have access to credit information for large numbers of individuals. For a fee, they provide organizations with an individual's credit history. The potential for violations is very great. For one thing, the credit searches performed are not always accurate. As with any data captured by computer, it could be obsolete or it could simply be wrong. Correcting such data can take a long time, and in the interim a person's credit rating and chances for getting a loan could be seriously affected.

The *Privacy Journal* recently published articles about 200 people who lost their jobs or suffered in other serious ways because databases containing credit information were incorrect. TRW, Equifax, Trans Union Credit Information, and other credit reporting agencies are now required by law to provide any person, on request, with their own credit history, free of charge. Now you can know in advance what the report will reveal to others, and you have the opportunity to make corrections. Perhaps this

**CRITICAL THINKING**

The controversies concerning a person's first amendment rights have been both frequent and heated. Should pornographic material and discriminatory comments sent over networks be censored? Should individuals always be free to exchange views with one another the way they can over a telephone or by mail? Junk faxes and junk e-mail also pose a problem. Some users want legal protection from unsolicited messages sent over networks. What do you think?

Caller ID is a telephone service that reveals a caller's number on a display screen. Privacy advocates say Caller ID could divulge an unlisted phone number, which is protected information. Caller ID advocates favor the technology because it gives those receiving calls an opportunity to screen callers. Enhanced Caller ID systems could compound the privacy issue because advanced systems can link a caller's telephone number to databases. So companies could use the Caller ID numbers to create mailing lists. Do you think there should be laws enacted to limit how Caller ID is used?

change will reduce the impact that inaccurate credit histories have on people's lives.

In addition to the risk of inadvertent errors, we need to be concerned about deliberate invasions of privacy. Hackers have gained access to the credit histories of large numbers of individuals. In addition, medical and legal histories as well as other personal records may be accessible by those who unscrupulously or illegally gain access to databases.

Several recent indictments illustrate how real the threat to individual privacy is. For example, indictments were brought against police officers who sold criminal histories from the National Crime Information Center (NCIC) databases. Other indictments were brought against several employees of the Social Security Administration who were bribed by "information brokers" to perform computer searches through the records of thousands of individuals. The Social Security Administration has earnings records for approximately 140 million workers. The market for improperly obtained information from the NCIC and the Social Security Administration databases includes private investigators and creditors who are trying to locate people, lawyers who are deciding whether to bring lawsuits against certain individuals, and employers who are deciding whether to hire, fire, or promote prospective or actual employees.

Sometimes organizations put together profiles on people based on information compiled from many sources. Such information can reveal personal habits or spending patterns that might otherwise not be available. Lotus Development Corporation recently terminated development of a CD-ROM product (called Lotus MarketPlace: Household CD-ROM) that was to make available to companies a database of names, addresses, and life-style profiles on 80 million Americans. Lotus received so many complaints and such bad publicity about this database that it decided it would be prudent to simply terminate the project. There are other companies, however, building products that use confidential credit data to create mailing lists.

Minimizing the problems associated with invasion of privacy is not easy. One mechanism, of course, is to enact laws. We discuss next legislative measures enacted and planned to alleviate some of these problems, but passing laws is just one method to protect people's rights. Public awareness of privacy issues and pressure placed on information firms by an informed society are equally important.

## ▶ Privacy Legislation

The Fair Credit Reporting Act of 1970 gives individuals the right to review and correct credit reports. It also prohibits credit agencies from sharing personal information with anyone except those who have a "legitimate business need." Privacy advocates are not satisfied, however. They say the law fails to clearly define the term *legitimate business need*, so they call for clarification of the 1970 act.

Sometimes people need protection from government organizations as well as credit agencies. The Privacy Act of 1974 restricts the way the federal government can use information about its citizens. The law allows some data matching from different databases at different agencies, but the information must be used in a way that is consistent with the purpose for which it was originally collected—whatever that means! The Right to Financial Privacy Act of 1978 is more specific: it establishes strict procedures for federal agencies that seek to examine an individual's bank account.

A Code of Fair Information Practice for automated personal data systems was proposed in Congress in 1973, but it never was enacted. Although the code has been adopted by many information-collecting businesses, privacy advocates would like to see it written into law. The code includes these points.

- There can be no personal data record-keeping systems whose existence is kept secret from the public.
- There must be a way for individuals to find out what information about them is in a database and how it is used.
- There must be a way for individuals to prevent information that was obtained for one purpose from being used or made available for other purposes without their consent.
- There must be a way for an individual to correct a record.

The following regulations, international and national, have been proposed to protect the use of information.

- Regulations, proposed by the European Community, attempt to control the types of data that international corporations can collect. The regulations are designed to avoid disputes between countries with conflicting rules about data use. Because many European countries have stricter privacy rules than the United States, the European Community guidelines could force U.S. businesses that deal with customers abroad to change their own practices.
- The Data Protection Act, currently under review by Congress, would create a federal data protection board. If enacted, the board would serve as an ombudsman for citizens concerned with the abuse of information. The board would examine complaints, petition federal agencies, and advise policymakers on privacy matters involving technology. It would also provide information about international laws to protect data.

## ▶ SELF-TEST

1. (T or F) Several federal laws specifically address the rights of e-mail users.
2. (T or F) Credit reporting agencies are now required by law to provide individuals with their own credit histories, free of charge.
3. (T or F) Federal agencies can share information about U.S. citizens without any restrictions or limitations.
4. (T or F) Under the law, personal record-keeping systems may not be kept secret from the public.

Solutions

1. F
2. T
3. F—The Privacy Act of 1974 allows some data matching, but the information must be used in a way that is consistent with the purpose for which it was originally collected.
4. F

## 13.2 MAKING INFORMATION SYSTEMS AND NETWORKS MORE SECURE

**Why should security be an integral component of information systems and computer networks?**

The existence of large databases that include information about us brings up important social and organizational issues which may require legal action and the use of security measures. We have just analyzed one such issue: privacy. People need assurance that their personal information, such as employment and credit history, will be used appropriately. More laws need to be passed and enforced to protect privacy.

Security is another issue, one that is more of an organizational concern, although not exclusively so. Businesses need safeguards that protect computer systems and their data from damage or unlawful use. First, security measures are needed to protect hardware, software, and data from natural disasters such as fire, flood, and earthquakes (Figure 13.1). Second, security measures are also needed to guard against computer crime, which can take the form of sabotage and espionage as well as theft.

Computer crime has become a costly threat for organizations ranging in size from small businesses to multinational and networked corporations. It is a threat for the federal government as well. We will focus on computer crime and measures that organizations use to protect them-

*Figure 13.1 Backup copies of databases and custom programs stored away from the main office allow companies to recover quickly from natural disasters and other situations that can destroy computers and their data. When the recent Los Angeles earthquake occurred, those companies that had backup copies of files were able to reopen quickly.*

selves from such crime; these methods also help to protect data from natural disasters.

# ▶ What Is Computer Crime?

One recent study of 283 businesses and government institutions found that more than half are victims of computer crime each year. Records show that while a bank robber armed with a gun steals an average of $1600 from a bank, the white-collar criminal armed with a computer steals an average of $100,000! These statistics for white-collar crimes may, in fact, be low, because many organizations such as banks, fearing a loss of customer confidence, do not report all the crimes that occur. The statistics may also be low because many crimes go undetected.

Computer crime can be as relatively "innocent" as the unauthorized use of computers for personal purposes, for example, for creating greeting cards or calendars or for playing computer games. On the other hand, it can be as serious as using computers to send corporate financial assets to a private Swiss bank account.

Computer crime is difficult to detect and even more difficult to prevent. Detection and prosecution are hampered because (1) it may take many months or even years before the crime is discovered, (2) it is difficult to gather evidence and prove culpability, (3) the laws governing computer crimes are not as clear-cut and well-tested as other types of laws, and (4) often organizations like banks, credit card companies, and investment houses are reluctant to report the crime. **Computer crimes** can be separated into four types.

1. Theft of computer time.
2. Tampering with programs or data.
3. Theft of data and assets.
4. Illegal copying of software.

## THEFT OF COMPUTER TIME

As we have seen, theft of computer time may be as relatively innocent as a student doing a term paper on a computer at work or as serious as someone stealing thousands of dollars of processing time for personal profit. Sometimes an employee will moonlight as a software developer and do programming at his or her employer's computer site—often on company time! Most people would view this as unethical, but it is also, strictly speaking, a theft.

## TAMPERING WITH PROGRAMS OR DATA

Perhaps you have seen the movie *Sneakers* about criminals who steal computer files or the classic 1983 movie *War Games* in which an amiable teenager changed his grades in the high school computer by using a modem at home and then almost caused World War III by "breaking into" a Department of Defense computer. See Figure 13.2. Unfortunately, such actions are all too common. Sometimes the crime is committed for

(a)

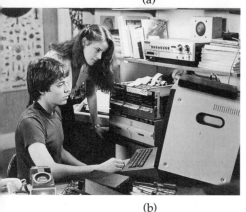

(b)

*Figure 13.2* (a) *River Phoenix, Robert Redford, Dan Aykroyd, and Sidney Poitier use computers and computer codes in the movie* Sneakers *to help the United States maintain its competitive edge.* (b) *A young Matthew Broderick and Ally Sheedy in the movie* War Games *break into their school's computer and change their grades.*

profit or gain, and sometimes just for fun. In 1989, a Cornell University student broke into the Internet international computer research network and sabotaged files in thousands of computers. The perpetrator, whose father was, ironically, a computer security expert, received three years probation and a $10,000 fine and had to perform 400 hours of community service.

Newspapers frequently print stories about hackers who break into public and private databases for the technical challenge involved. Hackers have even planted computer viruses that tie up CPUs by commanding them to do such time-consuming tasks as attempting to calculate the precise value of pi, thereby crippling enormous data networks. As we saw in Chapter 7, a virus is a self-replicating computer code that winds its way through a system, possibly transferring itself to other systems or disks. It can destroy data and programs, cause the system to crash, or simply send mischievous messages to the user. Some hackers infect systems for fun while others engage in industrial espionage.

There are over 600 known viruses. The *Joshi* virus, for example, changes the hard disk drive's partitions so that it gains access to, and damages, the system. *Stoned* is a virus that infects the default drive and any floppies put into the machine. Another type of virus is the *Jerusalem* virus, which adds itself to a program repeatedly until the program is too large to be loaded. Another virus is called a "logic bomb" because it destroys all files that are run when the computer shows that the date is a Friday the thirteenth. You may also have heard of the infamous Michelangelo virus, which has a trigger date of March 6—the birth date of the famous artist.

Any of these viruses can be "caught" from an infected program that is uploaded to the system by disk. The best protection against viruses, as with all computer crime, is to impose hardware and software controls to prevent their spread. Many programs are available that not only detect but rid a system of a virus. Despite the proliferation of viruses, however, a recent survey revealed that only 78% of computing sites use **antiviral software** as protection.

The problem with viruses is apt to get worse before it gets better, especially as the capacities of computers increase. A virus can slowly erode the integrity of a file or an entire storage device without anyone knowing it. In other cases, a virus can encrypt data, and when the time is right, transmit it to an unknown receiver, for example, a corporate raider. For those of you with personal computers, we strongly recommend that you always use a virus protection program when you boot up. Some operating systems, utilities, and desktop managers now come bundled with such software. We will discuss other methods of protection later in this chapter.

## THEFT OF DATA AND ASSETS

Legally called embezzlement, computer theft often involves a trusted employee who cannot resist the temptation to steal. All too often, the theft is amazingly easy to carry out. For example, the chairman of the board and some of the executive officers of the now infamous Equity Funding Corporation—a publicly held mutual fund and insurance company—used terminals to enter insurance policies for nonexistent people. By entering bogus data over a period of years, they greatly increased the company's apparent assets. Of the 97,000 insurance policies maintained by the computer, almost two-thirds were fictitious policies with a face value of $2.1 billion! Because the company appeared to be more profitable than it actually was, the stock of Equity Funding was greatly inflated; consequently, the officers, who were large shareholders, were able to sell their shares at considerable profits. The fraud went undetected because auditors consistently accepted as beyond question the computer printouts that listed policyholders. The crime was uncovered only after a former employee revealed the scheme. It became a classic case of how easy it is to use a computer fraudulently if proper controls have not been implemented.

Although most computer thefts are committed by current or past employees, industrial espionage by wiretapping to access another company's files is not only feasible, but relatively easy to achieve by means of communications links like telephones. As more and more companies access external databases using telephone lines, the risks of wiretapping increase as well.

## ILLEGAL COPYING OF SOFTWARE

Are you "stealing" when you make a copy of word processing software for a friend? The law says you are. Yet many normally law-abiding people who would not dream of shoplifting, see nothing wrong with making a copy of a $500 word processing package and giving it to a friend, despite the fact that such an action is in violation of the U.S. Copyright Law. **Bootlegging of software,** or the making of unauthorized copies, is clearly unethical as well as illegal, yet it is so widespread that estimates suggest there may be as many as 10 illegal copies of a program for every legitimate copy sold.

To prevent bootlegging, or "software piracy," software vendors sometimes sell **copy-protected software,** which means that the programs cannot easily be copied to other disks or can only be copied a limited number of times, generally twice. Copy-protected software is becoming rarer, however, as vendors respond to complaints from legitimate users that copy protection is a nuisance. Copy protection can make it difficult to do legitimate copying, such as creating backup disks or recovering from hard disk failure. In fact, the lack of copy protection is often a selling feature for many packages.

Ironically, software piracy may become less of a problem in the future, if viruses abound. Any experienced computer user will be more likely to load into his or her computer only those programs that come packaged with a warranty from the manufacturer, because a program that has "been around" is more likely to be infected.

## ▶ Legal Concerns

Because computer crime is on the rise, many of the laws to protect organizations and individuals from such crimes need to be clarified or revised.

## LEGISLATION TO CONTROL COMPUTER CRIME IS LIMITED

Legislators have been trying for years, without much success, to enact laws at the federal level to curb computer crime. The major stumbling block is the lack of legal definitions for *property* and *value* as they relate to computerized information.

One way to help clarify laws is to have the judicial branch of government rule on key cases. But companies are reluctant to prosecute because a trial might draw attention to the weaknesses in their computer's security system. Prosecutors are also reluctant to take computer criminals to court because computer crime laws are so vague that it is difficult to build and win cases.

Because the federal government has not enacted effective laws in this area, many states are beginning to pass stronger legislation that protects companies from crimes such as computer theft and deliberate destruction of data.

## RIGHTS OF HACKERS MAY NEED PROTECTION TOO

*Figure 13.3 Former members of "Legion of Doom," an organization that believes in protecting the rights of computer users, even hackers, now own a computer security company called Consec Data Security.*

The Electronic Frontier Foundation was formed by Mitch Kapor, a developer of Lotus 1-2-3, and Grateful Dead lyricist John Perry Barlow. This organization looks at security and protection in a different way: it seeks to protect the computer user who in some instances is the computer abuser! It lobbies, for example, for laws to encourage freer use of public computer networks, such as computer bulletin boards. It also assists in the legal defense of individuals it believes to be unjustly charged with computer crimes. The foundation's goals are to protect the rights of users, including hackers, to access public networks.

Although hackers are sometimes guilty of using the property of others, the foundation feels that not all are guilty of criminal intent. The leaders seek a distinction between unethical behavior and illegal behavior. One of the primary objectives of the foundation is to protect the rights of everyone to unlimited electronic communication.

There are several other organizations that believe in protecting the rights of computer users. See Figure 13.3.

## ▶ **M**inimizing **S**ecurity **P**roblems

Precautions and controls can be employed to protect hardware and software from illegitimate use. Several of the critical ones are described in this section.

### CONTROL ACCESS TO HARDWARE AND SOFTWARE

An organization should protect its hardware and software to ensure that unauthorized personnel cannot have physical access to the computer system or other resources. A centralized computer system as well as local PCs should be housed in locked rooms to protect hardware from theft and to prevent unauthorized people from accessing data or programs. An alarm should be installed. The facility should be monitored during

A survey by the Executive Information Network in 1992 showed that 55% of all computer data losses could be attributed to human errors or omissions. Dishonest and disgruntled employees accounted for another 25% of losses. External situations such as natural disaster caused the remaining 20%. Outside intrusion is rarely a major factor, although lines can be tapped. Backup media have their own problems. An 8-mm tape cartridge hidden in a shirt pocket and holding 5 GB of data—the equivalent of 180 file drawers—can be stolen from a computer site with relative ease. Virtually all of these losses could be eliminated or minimized with rigorous security and control procedures.

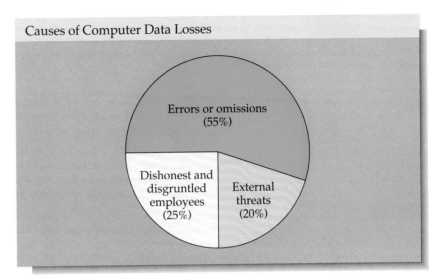

Causes of Computer Data Losses

and after working hours. Complete control, however, is difficult, especially when networks enable devices at remote locations to access a central computer's resources any time, day or night.

Specific physical and electronic access control techniques are useful for facilities with large computer systems as well as for PCs. These include keyboard locks, automatic logs, restricted access to systems, and limited after-hour use. Use of log-on codes and passwords that change periodically can also help to keep a system secure. Access control by voice-print and fingerprint techniques are becoming popular as the technology improves.

PCs and other small devices should be bolted to tables or otherwise secured to the facility if portability is not required. But when users want the flexibility to move devices or to physically remove them from the premises, it becomes very difficult to provide adequate control.

## MAKE BACKUP COPIES OF DATA AND PROGRAMS

Creating backup copies, or making extra copies, of programs or data safeguards against the risks from natural disasters, computer crime, or just plain human error. Data and software should be backed up each time they are updated or changed in any way. Incremental backups, which make copies of only the changes to files, can be performed at short intervals—hourly for large systems or daily for PCs. Full backups, which make copies of all files, can then be performed less frequently—for example, daily for large systems or weekly for PCs.

Because backups represent the safety net in case original data or programs are destroyed, they must be protected with the same care as the originals. Protection techniques include keeping them under lock and key in a fireproof container and storing them in a location separate from the originals. These procedures protect files from natural disasters, such as fire or flood, as well as computer crime and error.

## IMPLEMENT NETWORK CONTROLS

 Networks provide organizations with the ability to access both data and programs from remote locations. They also pose serious control problems because they leave computer files vulnerable to unauthorized access from off-site locations. For example, a network increases (1) the opportunities for employees to commit crimes or make errors, (2) the potential for hackers to wreak havoc and, (3) the capability of competitors to tap into the network and monitor transmissions for their own benefit. In addition to the controls mentioned previously, the common controls used for protecting data on networks are data encryption and callback systems.

**Data encryption** involves encoding data so that it cannot be understood unless it is first decoded. To encrypt data, a program uses an algorithm that either encodes or scrambles data before it is sent over the network. Another program at the receiving end then decodes the data. If an unauthorized person tapped into the database, the encrypted data would not be readable. Fax machines can use data encryption equipment as well to limit the threat of wiretapping for the purpose of intercepting faxes. Because data encryption is cumbersome and expensive, it is generally used only for very sensitive data or in cases where wiretapping is suspected. Access to both the encryption and the decoding programs must be tightly controlled.

A **callback system** ensures that a user accessing a computer by telephone is calling from an authorized telephone number. Each authorized user is given a password and asked to supply the phone number from which calls will be made. After validating the user's password, the callback system breaks the phone connection and then immediately calls back the telephone number in the file that corresponds to the password. This blocks entry to the system by someone who may have accessed a valid password but is not using a telephone at the authorized user's location. A callback system often involves added phone costs for the receiving party who must call back the sender and hence pay for the connect charges, but the extra security may be worth the cost.

## SEPARATE AND ROTATE FUNCTIONS

Another way to minimize the threat, however remote, of current employees misusing a system is to segment the work done so that each task requires the involvement of several different people. This is called separation of duties. It minimizes the risk of unauthorized and fraudulent use or modification of data and programs, because two or more perpetrators within the department would be required to commit a fraud. Separating tasks is not only good practice for minimizing the threat of crime, it also reduces the risk of errors, since one person can check the work of another.

In addition to separating duties, it is advisable to rotate jobs among individuals within a functional area from time to time. This arrangement is also likely to reduce errors as well as reduce the possibility of fraudulent collusion among employees. If, for example, a particular data entry operator who enters only payroll data and a programmer who works exclusively on payroll programs intend to conspire to commit a computer crime, they may find it difficult to perpetrate the crime if their jobs are periodically rotated. Similarly, if errors occur because both employees fail to perform a certain checking routine, other employees who perform the tasks are likely to detect this omission.

Audits can also result in early detection of crimes, mishaps, and unethical use of computers. The risk for computer errors and crime is increased not only when networks are used but when companies rely on outsourcing to satisfy their needs.

## USE MECHANISMS TO PROTECT AGAINST NATURAL DISASTERS

Security measures should also be taken to protect against natural disasters. Fire alarms are necessary as are surge protectors and uninterruptible power supplies in case of power outages. An uninterruptible power supply automatically supplies power in cases of brownouts as well as blackouts. They often have surge protection features as well.

## PROVIDE PROTECTION FROM VIRUSES

We have focused on viruses throughout this text, but particularly in this chapter, because of the serious threat they pose. Organizations can take the following 11 measures to minimize the risk of viruses infecting computers.

1. Use an antiviral program (e.g., Viruscan or Norton Antivirus) each time the computer is turned on or reset.
2. Discourage employees from using the same floppies at work and at home.
3. Discourage downloading of programs from electronic bulletin board systems that do not screen for viruses.
4. Always make backups.
5. Do not use bootlegged software.
6. Educate users about dangers.
7. Avoid using programs whose origin is unknown.
8. Control computer use: Do not allow people to run their own programs on the company's system.
9. Purchase only sealed packages of software.
10. Change passwords frequently.
11. Delete passwords of former employees.

Figure 13.4 summarizes some of the ways people could use computers improperly.

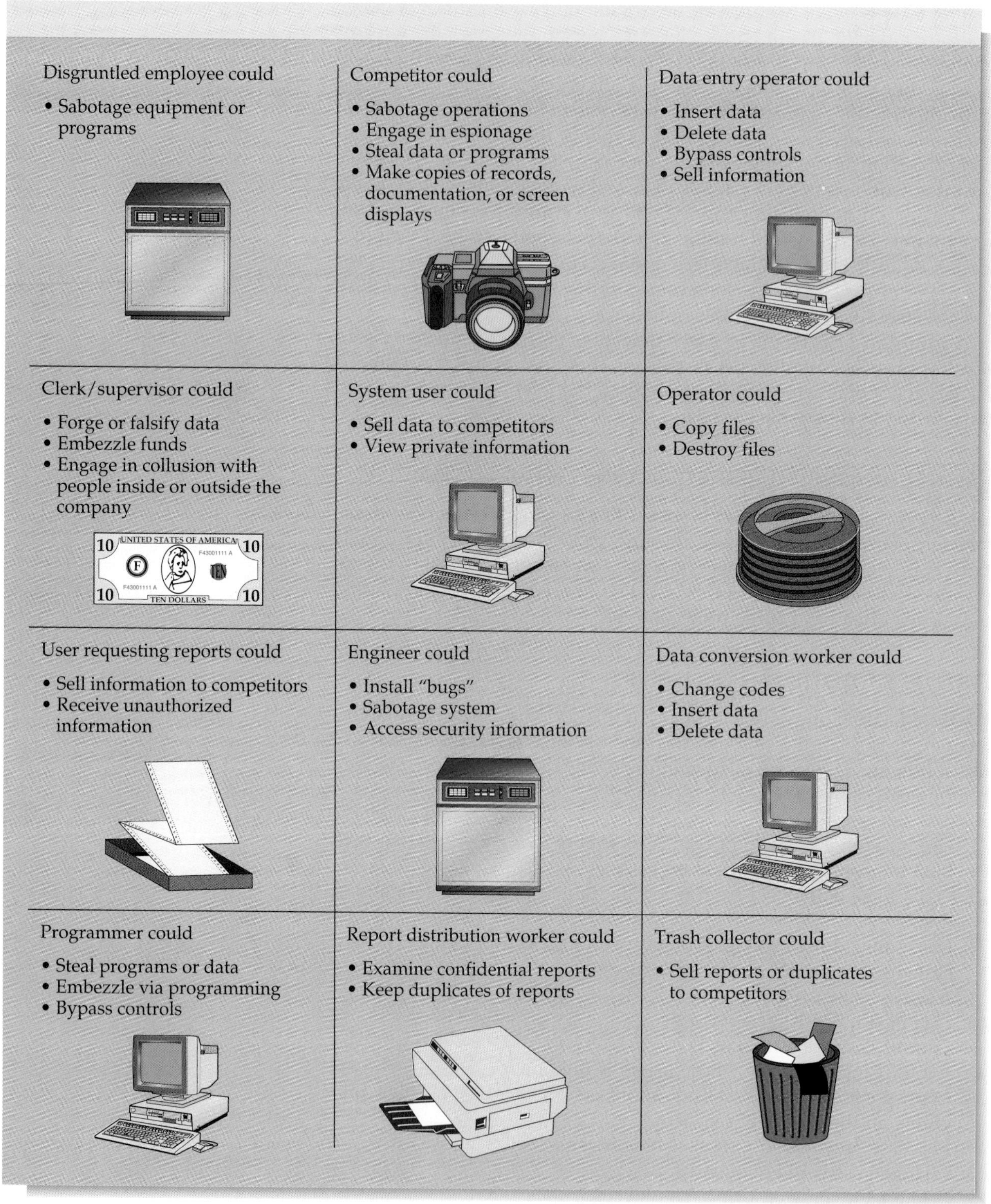
Disgruntled employee could
• Sabotage equipment or programs
Competitor could
• Sabotage operations
• Engage in espionage
• Steal data or programs
• Make copies of records, documentation, or screen displays
Data entry operator could
• Insert data
• Delete data
• Bypass controls
• Sell information
Clerk/supervisor could
• Forge or falsify data
• Embezzle funds
• Engage in collusion with people inside or outside the company
UNITED STATES OF AMERICA
TEN DOLLARS
System user could
• Sell data to competitors
• View private information
Operator could
• Copy files
• Destroy files
User requesting reports could
• Sell information to competitors
• Receive unauthorized information
Engineer could
• Install "bugs"
• Sabotage system
• Access security information
Data conversion worker could
• Change codes
• Insert data
• Delete data
Programmer could
• Steal programs or data
• Embezzle via programming
• Bypass controls
Report distribution worker could
• Examine confidential reports
• Keep duplicates of reports
Trash collector could
• Sell reports or duplicates to competitors

***Figure 13.4*** *Here are numerous ways in which people could use computers, data, or software improperly.*

## ▶ SELF-TEST

1. (T or F) Virus detection is typically performed using hardware controls.
2. (T or F) Rotating job functions within an organization minimizes the threat of computer crimes.
3. (T or F) Once a computer crime is detected, it is relatively easy to find the perpetrator.
4. (T or F) Both hardware and software controls are necessary to effectively minimize security risks.

### Solutions
1. F—Software is typically used.
2. T
3. F
4. T

# INFORMATION SYSTEMS AND PEOPLE | 13.3

## ▶ Managing the Work Environment

A computer's data and programs need to be protected for both legal and ethical reasons. It is also important to ensure that computers in the office are used in a socially responsible way. When computers are used appropriately, they have the potential for improving people's quality of life. We discuss here some elements that can have an impact on the quality of life.

How do information systems and computer networks affect the quality of life?

### ERGONOMICS

The emergence of computers in the workplace has created a number of new organizational issues in areas such as space planning, health, and safety. Consider what happened to a telephone company that installed an automated telephone system for its operators. Operator productivity suddenly decreased because:

- Light reflecting onto terminal screens from a large bank of windows bothered the operators. Although the windows were a much desired change for the operators, the bright, natural light was sometimes so intense that it caused eyestrain.
- The operators' workstations were designed for the average operator.

There was little, if any, flexibility for changing the position of the screen, keyboard, or desk to satisfy individual tastes and needs.

- Each operator was given a U-shaped desk with side panels for privacy. Many operators had been more comfortable seeing their colleagues while they worked and now felt cut off from their peers.

What can be done to help users cope with the physical, mental, and social problems caused by new office technologies? As noted in Chapter 5, ergonomics is the science of adapting machines and work environments to people. Ergonomically designed workplaces provide the best physical environment for people using computers and other technology, and have the potential for improving the quality of life of employees.

*Figure 13.5 This figure illustrates a screen filter that can be placed on a monitor to reduce glare.*

**Reducing Office Glare.**   Perhaps the most obvious problem in the work environment, and the one easiest to deal with, is office lighting. Improper lighting conditions create glare on video display terminals. There are two common ways to reduce glare: provide indirect lighting, which may almost totally eliminate the problem, and/or provide antireflection filters that reduce glare on the screen and also reduce the intensity of the screen image. The trend in many organizations is to eliminate all direct overhead lighting, such as fluorescent lights, and to substitute softer, indirect lighting in its place. See Figure 13.5.

**Reducing Sound Pollution.**   Well-planned offices eliminate distracting sounds yet make provisions for private conversations. Because noise created by keyboards, printers, and even the computer itself can be annoying and distracting, an effective noise control plan focuses on three areas: efficient sound-absorbing materials on furniture, walls, ceilings, and floors; sound-masking devices such as printer covers; and well-designed office layouts.

**Designing Ergonomically Sound Workstations.**   Workstations should be designed to allow users the greatest economy of movement. As shown in Figure 13.6, factors such as reach lengths, arm angles in keyboarding, and eye viewing angles all contribute to the comfort of employees performing necessary office tasks. See Figure 13.7 for how workstations are ergonomically designed. Poor workstation design will ultimately result in user fatigue, a high rate of error, and slow task performance as well as employee dissatisfaction.

**Reducing Hazards to Health.**   As we saw in Chapter 5, another hotly debated issue is whether monitors or video display terminals emit harmful radiation. Numerous studies have failed to detect radiation above acceptable levels, but not everyone is satisfied with these findings. Questions center around the long-term biological effects of low-level radiation from VDTs on users. Many people are concerned about whether prolonged exposure of pregnant women to VDTs can cause birth defects. Until conclusive evidence is available to resolve these issues, a corporate policy requiring periodic testing for malfunctioning video display ter-

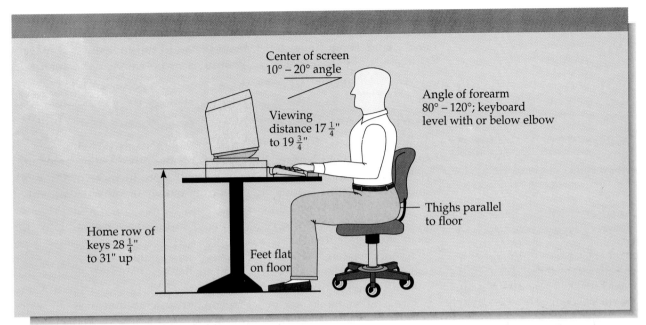

Center of screen
10° – 20° angle

Viewing distance $17\frac{1}{4}$" to $19\frac{3}{4}$"

Angle of forearm 80° – 120°; keyboard level with or below elbow

Thighs parallel to floor

Home row of keys $28\frac{1}{4}$" to 31" up

Feet flat on floor

*Figure 13.6 Ergonomically designed workstations are intended to make the user comfortable and to reduce health problems.*

*Figure 13.7 Attention should be paid to workstation design and setup for the comfort and health of employees.*

minals that emit radiation above safety limits might be appropriate.

The emission of radiation from monitors is just one health risk. Many people are concerned about the potential risk from wireless networks. This is likely to be addressed as well in the next few years.

Employee experiences with computer systems affect their attitude toward new technology. In a poorly managed computer environment, employees may believe that their computer system displaces workers, adversely affects their health, and limits their freedoms. In another environment, employees may believe that computers provide new opportunities, enhance employee control over tasks, and improve their decision-making ability. The perception of the effects of computers in a given business depends on the leadership and vision of the company's managers as well as on the attitude of computer professionals who plan and develop information systems.

## COMPUTER MONITORING

**CRITICAL THINKING**

Should employees have a role in the use of monitoring procedures? Some companies post individual performance data; is this likely to motivate people? Are high-level achievers likely to be ostracized by other employees? What impact do you think monitoring will have on overall productivity and the quality of the work performed?

Two objectives of managing the work environment are (1) to improve job satisfaction for employees and (2) to make the office setting ergonomically sound. Another goal is to monitor the productivity of the work force—a goal that is not very popular among employees and could adversely affect their quality of life.

Computer monitoring is widespread in businesses employing, for example, data entry clerks, reservation agents, insurance claim processors, and customer service agents. Typically, network software or the software for processing transactions includes monitoring utilities that compile usage statistics about each terminal or PC linked to a host. Many insurance companies are installing image systems that include "work flow software," which keeps track of how documents are handled by different levels of employees and where bottlenecks occur. A 1991 survey by the Communication Workers of America, which focused on 762 video display terminal users at telephone companies, indicates that such electronic monitoring of work flow dramatically increases the level of stress and stress-related pain, as shown in Figure 13.8.

Thus, while some monitoring devices are designed to test for ergonomically sound work environments, many others are actually designed to monitor computer workers themselves. This has prompted some unions to compare today's office environment to "sweatshops" where constant supervision and the need to meet minimum levels of productivity are the norm.

Critics of monitoring devices want legislation to limit electronic "sur-

*Figure 13.8 Evidence suggests that workers whose productivity is monitored have more physical problems on the job than those who are not monitored.*

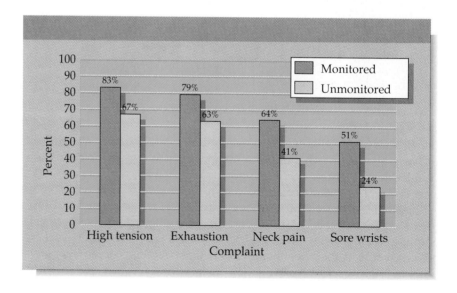

veillance" of employees. They also want laws to require employers to notify workers that they are being monitored. Employers claim that notifying workers would negate the results because normal patterns of work are likely to be altered when people know they are being watched. The U.S. House of Representatives is considering a bill, currently called The Privacy for Consumers and Workers Act, that would limit employers' rights to monitor production and require that workers be notified by a flashing light or tone when they are being monitored.

## ▶ Do Computers Result in Unemployment?

Almost all recent studies have demonstrated that the fear of mass unemployment resulting from automation is essentially unfounded. In total, more jobs have been generated by computers than have been eliminated by them. Nonetheless, in some areas computers have substantially reduced the work force—automated factories and typesetting companies for instance. In general, computers need an operating staff, and when they generate growth, this means an increased need for labor. Many publishing firms, for example, once feared that desktop publishing would result in fewer opportunities for publishers. But the evidence suggests otherwise. As many as 10,000 new publishing companies with desktop publishing capability emerged in the past decade. A large number of these new companies are involved in publishing magazines that target special interest groups in the computing field.

Computers have minimized tedious tasks that workers in all functional areas once performed. Now that the fear of being replaced by a computer has been allayed somewhat, and mundane, rote tasks have been offloaded to computers, one might think that the average worker has it easier today than a decade ago. But this is not always true. As we have seen, many companies now use computers to monitor their workers' productivity, which often increases the level of stress at work. Workers who sit and look at a computer screen all day have health problems that range from eyestrain to muscle strain to fears about the effects of radiation. Computer phobia adds to the stress as well: Many people continue to be afraid of computers and fear the depersonalization that they may bring. Computer professionals and computer users should be sensitive to such concerns, be informed about measures to allay them, and help future users understand and appreciate some of the benefits of computing.

## ▶ Certifying Computer Professionals as a Method of Improving Social Responsibility

What happens if a computer professional fails to satisfy the needs of the user? What happens if the information system developed is so poor that processing errors are rampant and huge delays occur? If the professionals responsible for a poorly designed information system work for the organization, then their jobs could be in jeopardy. If outside consultants were responsible, users may be able to bring legal action to recoup any losses resulting from the poor design, but it is difficult to prove liability in such instances. In fact, the reasons for poorly designed systems may not always be the fault of the designer. Users may have supplied incorrect information or too little information, or the needs of the organization may have changed. What is clear, however, is that because unsatisfactory information systems do exist, lawsuits abound and resolving them equitably continues to be problematic.

Ethical conduct goes beyond merely adhering to laws. For example, what should you do if you are a systems analyst or programmer responsible for a system or program that invades privacy? Or how responsible are you if you are part of a team that creates a software package with known bugs? There are, of course, no simple answers to questions such as these. Many people with high ethical standards have argued against holding computer professionals totally responsible for their work, because the way an information system is used may not be under the developer's control. Some people argue that, just as Alfred Nobel cannot be held accountable for the immoral use of his invention of dynamite, computer professionals should not be held accountable for programs that are used illegally or unethically. (How's that for an analogy?)

Most professionals have a code of ethics that broadly sets standards for professionals where such standards may not be covered by specific legislation. As the debate over the issues goes on, many leaders in the computing field believe that a code of ethics is needed to enable computer professionals to police themselves before the government finds it necessary to pass strict laws. Appendix B considers some organizations with certification programs aimed at establishing codes of ethics for computer professionals.

## ▶ **D**eveloping, **P**romoting, and **S**upporting **S**tandards

Throughout this text, we have discussed the lack of hardware and software standards in the computing field and how this lack has adversely affected computerization. The absence of transmission standards, for example, impedes the effectiveness of networks.

We saw in Chapter 12 that the ISDN (Integrated Services Digital Network) has as its goal the implementation of a universal standard for transmission of voice, data, and video information to people and organizations throughout the world. ISDN standards are being developed by a standards committee within the United Nations called the International Telegraphy and Telephony Consultative Committee. The standards being considered relate to physical interfaces, communications protocols, message formats, and services offered. Telephone companies, hardware and software suppliers, and service organizations that agree to adhere to these standards will develop systems that permit ISDN users ready access to a wide variety of network-based information services. Once a standard is widely accepted, then more appropriate procedures for controlling access can be implemented. It is often difficult, however, to convince users to adopt a standard, especially if it means they will need to change their procedures.

Many people advocate a National Information Act to develop new technology standards and to consolidate telecommunications control under a single agency. With the seven "Baby Bell" telephone companies formed as a result of the AT&T breakup, and the recent court decisions that give these Baby Bells the right to provide information services, national regulation may become a necessity for standardization to be achieved.

## ▶ The Impact of Computers on the Quality of Life

Despite widespread use of computers, the predictions that they would completely alter the way we live and work have not really materialized. There are, however, specific areas in which computers have had a dramatic impact on the quality of life.

### THE DISABLED

On the whole, the disabled have benefited greatly from computer technology. See Figure 13.9. Scanners convert printed text to verbal output for the visually impaired. Voice recognition equipment converts speech to printed or displayed output for the hearing impaired. People confined to their home can be productive by working on computers that have access to an office and all of its resources.

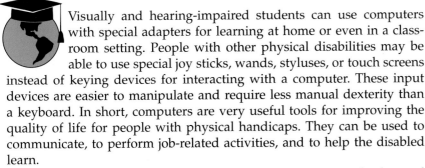

Visually and hearing-impaired students can use computers with special adapters for learning at home or even in a classroom setting. People with other physical disabilities may be able to use special joy sticks, wands, styluses, or touch screens instead of keying devices for interacting with a computer. These input devices are easier to manipulate and require less manual dexterity than a keyboard. In short, computers are very useful tools for improving the quality of life for people with physical handicaps. They can be used to communicate, to perform job-related activities, and to help the disabled learn.

Through artificial intelligence technology, computers can also be used to compensate for certain disabilities. Vision systems have sensors built into special glasses; computerized walking sticks help blind people "sense" the presence of large objects and even determine what the objects are. Computerized devices—some experimental and some in widespread use—also help the physically impaired become more mobile. Some of these devices are implanted in limbs and actually cause muscles to flex so that movement can occur. In other cases, wheelchairs, prosthe-

(a)

(b)

(c)

*Figure 13.9* Computers have benefited the handicapped. (a) *This is a large display for the visually impaired. (b) Here, a patient is linked by a chip in his skull to a computer. By looking at the screen, he can actually run the computer. (c) This is a computerized device to aid those who have difficulty working with their hands.*

ses, and other "smart" equipment can be programmed to help the disabled person be more ambulatory.

The federal government estimates that the lifetime cost of an unemployed disabled person to the country is more than 1 million dollars. Because of computerized devices, many disabled people will be able to lead more productive lives. The Americans with Disabilities Act, put in effect on July 26, 1992, requires organizations previously unconcerned about providing access and work for the disabled to cease discrimination. As a result of this act, companies are likely to become more attuned to how computer technologies can be used by the disabled both in the office and at home to enhance their contribution to the workplace and to improve their overall quality of life.

## PCS, TELECOMMUTING, AND LEISURE TIME

It was once believed that as a result of computers, a large segment of the work force would perform some of their normal duties at home on a regular basis rather than in the office, a concept known as telecommuting. Telecommuting would not only decrease the time and expense associated with commuting, but would decrease environmental and social concerns associated with energy use and mass transportation systems. It would also increase the quality of people's lives by enabling them to spend more time with their families and to have more personal leisure time as well.

But businesses have been slow to accept the virtues of telecommuting as an alternative to working in an office. They fear the loss of management control and the potential for misrepresenting the number of hours worked. Probably most importantly, they worry about the effects that decreased face-to-face interactions will have on the organization as a whole.

The result is that employees often take their computers home, but they do so in order to be productive in the evenings or on weekends, not during the work day. This type of "telecommuting" actually *reduces* a person's free time. As the computing field matures and as communications facilities enable users to be in constant touch with the office, telecommuting, in its truest sense, will likely become more prevalent and may then enhance the quality of people's lives in the years ahead. See Figure 13.10.

The ability of workers to connect their laptops to their office network from anywhere and at any time certainly improves flexibility and may increase productivity, but it does not always improve the quality of life. Just like the cellular phones that businesspeople take to restaurants, the movies, and even the beach, the laptop or palmtop can go with you anywhere. It, in effect, often extends your work day leaving *less time* for leisure activities. Many sociologists worry that such devices result in employees who are "on call" every hour of every day regardless of where they are.

**Figure 13.10** *Telecommuting enables employees to work at home yet have computer resources at their disposal and have access to their office as well.*

## PCS IN EDUCATION

Early predictions proclaimed that PCs would revolutionize the way people learn. Computer simulations would enable chemistry students to perform experiments, medical students to enhance their diagnostic skills, pilots to learn to control airplanes, and so on. But, in general, computer-based training still tends to be most widely used for simple tutorials and self-tests of the drill-and-practice variety except for some high-profile projects funded by large corporations. See Figure 13.11. One reason why computers have not had the predicted impact on education is the expense: many schools cannot afford the requisite hardware and software. Another reason is that instructors do not have the training necessary to teach others to use them.

**Figure 13.11** *Studies have shown that children using multimedia PCs learn more effectively because sound and video are included as well as interactive communication.*

As a result of the recent availability of multimedia tools for PCs, we are seeing a renewed attempt to use micros to teach a variety of subjects. People raised in the MTV generation are likely to respond favorably to educational software that has video and audio components. Educational software with multimedia components not only provides the ability to select lessons that present information dynamically in video and audio form, but also provides the ability to respond to that information interactively. Students can navigate through lessons at their own pace and in any sequence they choose. They can take self-tests at any point and then get additional information on topics that they do not understand fully.

Currently, multimedia teaching tools are popular for corporate training where cost is less of a constraint than it is in public education. As the cost of hardware and software decreases, however, and as multimedia standards are developed, such training is likely to be integrated into many educational environments.

---

**CRITICAL THINKING**

Do you think that a lesson on John Fitzgerald Kennedy that includes excerpts from some of his speeches or a lesson on Hamlet that includes monologues taped by Sir Laurence Olivier improves learning? Are students likely to remember better? Are they likely to be more informed about subjects if multimedia systems are used as teaching tools?

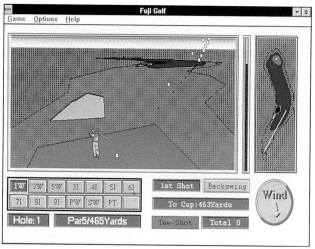

(a)

(b)

*Figure 13.12* *Computers are currently used for some leisure time and household activities. (a) Game-playing is a popular use. (b) Homemakers use computers to store recipes.*

## PCS FOR PROVIDING IN-HOME SERVICES

Shopping at home and banking at home were once thought to be natural areas for computer use. In fact, such services have been available for years, but relatively few people have taken advantage of them. One reason is that PCs are not all that popular with the average consumer. In general, most consumers view micros as nonessential items. When they buy them, it is usually because their children have a real interest or the family needs word processing capability. PCs are *not* considered necessities like a phone, TV, or even a VCR. Moreover, people without training view them as difficult to use, despite manufacturers' claims of user-friendliness.

But as more and more young people learn about computers in school

*Figure 13.13* *Today you can shop at home by viewing products on a screen, getting any additional information you need, and placing orders.*

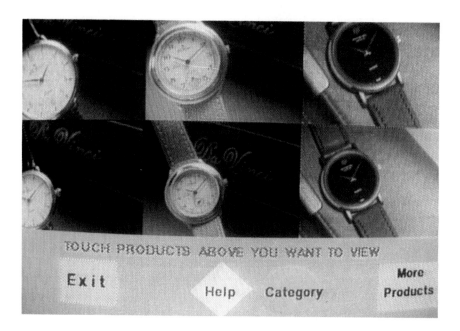

and become adults themselves, many more computers are likely to be used at home by consumers. See Figures 13.12 and 13.13. In the interim, the more familiar electronic products (phones and TVs) will become "smart," that is, equipped with computer capabilities. In this way, people who consider themselves computer illiterate will use computers without really knowing it. Purchasing goods and services via a smart phone, for example, is likely to be more widespread than using a conventional PC, because people are accustomed to placing orders over the telephone.

## THE OFFICE OF THE FUTURE

Some of us have observed firsthand the dramatic changes that have occurred in the office environment during the past years. For example, typewriters and ledgers have been replaced by personal computers with word processing and with spreadsheet software. Similarly, sophisticated voice-mail systems and telephone equipment permit office personnel greater latitude in communicating with their colleagues.

The office of the future is likely to be as different from today's office as the current office is from that of the past. Some of the changes predicted are

- The number of employees who work at home, in the field, and on the road will increase. Wireless LANs will permit personal computers to communicate with an organization's databases from virtually anywhere.
- Pen-based computing and voice systems will make office automation more "natural."
- Multimedia brought to the desktop with video and audio capabilities will enable employees to obtain information from databases in more meaningful ways.
- Customized workstations will allow employees to create their own work environment, one that suits their individual needs and style.

One of the original objectives of bringing computers to the office was to eliminate paper documents or at least to minimize their use. But that goal has not been realized. Indeed, many office workers believe that far more paper is generated now than before. When people have a great deal of information at their fingertips, they are apt to want to capture it on paper. After all, children are still growing up with paper. Will they, as most adults nowadays, still trust paper more than a flickering screen or a disk that cannot be read manually?

The pundits believe—or hope—that paper will be virtually nonexistent in the future. All mail will be received electronically as either text, verbal messages, or even video form. Any documents that need to be signed will be displayed on a screen and signed by means of a stylus and image processing software; that is, the document will be displayed on a screen, you will add your signature by writing to the screen, and the signed document will be safely stored on an optical storage device. See Figure 13.14.

At meetings, notepads will be replaced by pen-based computers that

*Figure 13.14 Computers in insurance, banking, and other application areas are being used with increasing frequency for image processing—scanning documents and images, storing them, and making them available when needed.*

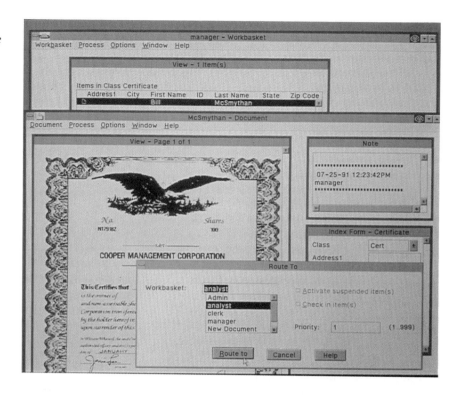

*Figure 13.15 Pen-based computers are now widely used for filling out forms and taking notes.*

will enable users to handwrite notes at the computer with the pen. Presentations will no longer be in the form of hard-copy reports; instead they will employ multimedia tools and will be available to all who need to view them via a computer. See Figure 13.15.

Computers themselves will not only be smaller but more natural. You will be able to talk to your computer in a normal voice and obtain either verbal or displayed responses—whichever you prefer. There will be fewer add-ons, because phones, modems, faxes, and so on, will be built in.

 Massive external databases will be at your disposal and you will have the ability to determine what you want to access on a regular basis. In fact, expert systems will be available that scan your personal computer database and suggest external resources that could prove useful to you. When you turn your computer on each morning, the news of the day that pertains to your area of expertise could be instantly available, along with any changes in the organizational structure of companies with which you do business. Recently published articles in areas in which you are currently working could also be displayed on the screen. Investment analyses of selected companies could be displayed, along with the number of shopping days until Christmas!

Even though some of these innovations may sound farfetched, the technology to achieve every one of them is currently available, albeit sometimes in primitive form. Consider mail systems, for instance. While electronic mail is still essentially a supplement to, rather than a replacement for, traditionally delivered mail, it is possible now for mail to be scanned and transmitted electronically rather than in envelopes. You might object to the potential invasion of privacy, but the capability is there.

The point is that a customized, paperless office could be achieved tomorrow *if* that became a major goal of organizations. At the moment, most of us still prefer the use of paper for some applications—banking, for instance. Because of personal preferences, the likelihood of becoming paperless in the near future is remote. The likelihood of becoming less paperbound is, however, much more feasible. Moreover, image processing systems are widely available to capture forms and other documents and store them on disks for easy access. This technology as well is likely to decrease the amount of paper generated in an office.

## *LOOKING AHEAD*

**THE WELL-CONNECTED OFFICE**

In the future, intelligent, bundled office machines will have integrated telephones, fax machines, photocopiers, color printers, and computers. These super machines will be linked to corporate databases as well as external databases, thereby providing access to enormous amounts of information.

## ▶ SELF-TEST

1. What do we call the science of adapting machines and work environments to people?
2. (T or F) Numerous studies have demonstrated conclusively that there are no long-term biological effects of low-level radiation from video display terminals.
3. (T or F) Overall, more jobs have been generated by computers than have been eliminated by them.
4. (T or F) Businesses have been slow to accept the virtues of telecommuting as an alternative to working in an office.
5. (T or F) In general, most consumers view micros as essential devices for the home.

Solutions
1. ergonomics
2. F—There has been no conclusive evidence to that effect.
3. T
4. T
5. F

## ▶ Chapter Summary

The proliferation of information systems and computer networks has raised many issues about privacy and security that involve legal as well as ethical questions. In addition, sociological questions concerning the effects of computers on the quality of life in this Information Age must be addressed.

### 13.1 PROTECTING THE PRIVACY OF USERS

As a result of the widespread development of information systems and computer networks, many legal issues have arisen that were neither anticipated nor addressed when various privacy laws were enacted. Con-

What personal, legal, and ethical issues are raised by the proliferation of information systems and computer networks?

sider, for example, privacy issues related to electronic mail. Currently, no federal law addresses the rights or obligations of e-mail users. State laws are vague in regard to liability if an individual's e-mail messages are intercepted. Because laws differ from state to state, an individual's rights can vary dramatically, depending on which state's laws apply if a lawsuit is brought.

The existence of large databases has raised other privacy concerns. Many organizations and government agencies maintain databases containing individual credit histories, income statements, criminal records, and so on. What rights does an individual have if, for example, hackers illegally gain access to financial databases and then sell the information to market research companies, telemarketing firms, or companies that buy mailing lists? Although laws have been enacted on the federal level to protect an individual's privacy, many of these laws are considered inadequate by privacy advocates.

## 13.2 MAKING INFORMATION SYSTEMS AND NETWORKS MORE SECURE

Why should security be an integral component of information systems and computer networks?

Businesses need security measures (1) to guard against computer crime, which can take the form of sabotage, espionage, and theft, and (2) to protect hardware, software, and data from natural disasters such as fire, flood, and earthquake.

Computer crime is difficult to detect and even more difficult to prevent. **Computer crimes** include (1) theft of computer time, (2) tampering with computer programs or data, (3) theft of data and assets, and (4) illegal copying of software. The prevalence of viruses mandates that organizations as well as individuals use **antiviral software** as a protection. To prevent **bootlegging of software,** or the making of unauthorized copies, software vendors sometimes sell copy-protected software. **Copy-protected software** means that the software cannot easily be copied to other disks, or can only be copied a limited number of times.

Organizations must take other precautions and institute controls to protect their hardware and software. Such measures include (1) controlling physical access to the computer system, (2) creating backup copies of data and software, (3) implementing network controls such as data encryption and callback systems, (4) separating and rotating functions among employees, and (5) using mechanisms for protection against natural disasters. **Data encryption** involves encoding data so that it cannot be understood unless it is first decoded. A **callback system** ensures that a user calling in by phone is calling from an authorized telephone number.

## 13.3 INFORMATION SYSTEMS AND PEOPLE: SOME CRITICAL ISSUES

How do information systems and computer networks affect the quality of life?

Ergonomics is the science of adapting machines and work environments to people. Ergonomically designed workplaces provide the best physical environment for people who use computers and other office technologies. Problems that are typically addressed include (1) reducing glare on video display terminals, (2) reducing sound pollution, (3) designing ergonomically sound workstations to reduce user fatigue and discomfort, and (4) reducing hazards to health.

Some organizations use monitoring devices and/or software to measure the productivity of employees. Critics of monitoring devices want legislation that will significantly limit electronic "surveillance" of employees.

The use of computers has raised some serious social issues. We must also consider, however, the areas where computers have already improved the quality of life for many people. When computers are used as tools by the disabled, for computer-based training, for providing in-home services, and for enhancing leisure time, they can indeed enhance one's quality of life.

## ▶ Chapter Self-test

1. (T or F) Most privacy advocates believe that existing federal laws adequately address privacy issues related to the proliferation of large databases.
2. (T or F) Computer crime is difficult to detect and even more difficult to prevent.
3. A _____ is a self-replicating computer code that is typically designed to destroy data and programs or cause other damage to a computer system.
4. Software vendors sometimes sell _____ software to prevent it from being copied to other disks or to limit the number of times that it can be copied.
5. (T or F) As a rule, prosecutors have had little difficulty in prosecuting computer criminals under existing criminal laws, even though these laws do not specifically address computer crime.
6. Creating _____, or making extra copies of programs or data, safeguards against the loss of programs or data.
7. (T or F) Almost all networks use some form of data encryption before data is transmitted.
8. (T or F) A callback system is used in some networks to verify that transmitted data was received without errors.
9. _____ is the science of designing workplaces to provide the best physical environment for people who use computers and other technology.
10. (T or F) Telecommuting has the potential for reducing energy consumption and improving the quality of life.
11. (T or F) Computer-based training is most widely used for simple tutorials and self-tests of the drill-and-practice variety although multimedia systems are likely to change that in the future.
12. (T or F) Purchasing goods and services via a smart phone is likely to be more widespread in the coming years than using a conventional PC for that purpose.

13. (T or F) The presence of computers in offices has led to the virtual elimination of paper documents.
14. (T or F) The lack of transmission standards has generally impeded the effectiveness of networks.

Solutions
1. F
2. T
3. virus
4. copy-protected
5. F
6. backups
7. F—It is generally used only for very sensitive data or in cases in which wiretapping is suspected.
8. F—It is used to ensure that a user calling in by phone is calling from an authorized telephone number.
9. Ergonomics
10. T
11. T
12. T
13. F
14. T

## ► Key Terms

Antiviral software, *p. 526*
Bootlegging of software, *p. 527*

Callback system, *p. 530*
Computer crime, *p. 525*

Copy-protected software, *p. 527*
Data encryption, *p. 530*

## ► Review Questions

1. Discuss major privacy issues that have resulted from the proliferation of large databases.
2. Why are detection and prosecution of computer crimes so difficult?
3. Discuss techniques that an organization can use to protect its hardware and software from computer crimes and natural disasters.
4. What measures can be taken to minimize the risk of viruses infecting a computer system?
5. What factors should be considered when designing a workplace that is to provide the best physical environment for those using computers?
6. Discuss how computers help the handicapped.
7. Discuss major changes that we can expect to find in the office of the future.
8. It is illegal to make copies of licensed software. What can colleges and universities do to convince students that bootlegging software is wrong? What can colleges and universities do to minimize the practice on campus? Some schools have been sued by software companies for permitting illegal copying. Is that fair?

## Solitude: A Status Symbol of the Future?

There are numerous benefits to having computers and databases make our world more interconnected, but with such benefits come risks to our personal privacy. Let us look first at computerized telephone systems and telephone companies that offer information services. Although such services often enhance the quality of our lives, they present problems as well.

An AT&T catalog, for example, has stirred some controversy because of the manner in which AT&T selected households to receive it: the company searched its telephone records to identify callers who frequently dial 800 phone numbers, based on the belief that these callers spend more money for consumer goods. Many people believe that practices such as this, which are widely used by telephone and information service organizations, invade an individual's privacy.

Automated telephone dialers can be programmed to call every phone number in a telephone exchange or to dial any other set of numbers. Most of us find telemarketing, which depends on these automated telephone dialers for promoting and selling products, to be not only a nuisance but an invasion of privacy. In fact, Congress is considering legislation that will ban telemarketing calls to people who expressly indicate that they do not want them.

The twenty-first century is likely to bring even more consumer-oriented technology into the home. Expect to be able to make purchases from electronic catalogs by means of broadband fiber-optic links to telephones, TVs, and computers. Imagine the type of databases that could then be created to keep track of your purchasing habits. Combine this problem with the ability of outsiders to intercept wireless telephone messages and faxes and we could have a privacy crisis.

Some organizations and people are not content to wait and see what will happen. The American

*Telemarketing operators make phone calls to potential customers who sometimes complain about invasion of privacy.*

Newspaper Publishing Association, among others, is lobbying to prevent phone companies from providing information and other services to consumers in an effort to help prevent abuses.

Often, the risks are more subtle. Recently a computer company offered to sell PCs to physicians at substantial discounts in exchange for patient data that the computer company planned to sell to drug and other health care organizations. Believe it or not, no federal laws protect the confidentiality of medical records, although some states require signed consent before records can be released. Consider, then, that simply consulting with your doctor might result in your medical history being shared with drug companies!

If privacy is eroded, solitude will likely become a rare commodity—a status symbol of sorts. Individuals intent on maintaining their privacy will rely solely or mainly on cash, pay extra fees for unlisted phone numbers, forgo discounts and frequent flyer bonuses, and perhaps visit a doctor under an alias.

### Analysis

1. Do you think that telephone companies should be restricted in the services they provide in order to protect individual privacy?

2. Drug companies claim they could develop more effective medications if they had access to patient data to determine the effects of current medicines. Is that a sufficient reason for permitting these companies access to patient data?

3. Overall, computers can definitely improve the quality of people's lives. Are we not, therefore, making too much of this privacy issue?

# DOS

What Is DOS?
File Naming in DOS
DOS Files
You Are Ready to Begin

**A.1** **LESSON 1—STARTING UP AND BASICS**
Starting Your System
Formatting Disks
Finding Out What Version of DOS You Are Using
Moving Between Disk Drives
Listing Disk Directories
Looking at the Contents of a File
Printing from Your Screen
Using Wildcard Characters
Turning Your Computer Off (Powering Down)

**A.2** **LESSON 2—FILE MANAGEMENT**
Copying Files
Renaming Files
Erasing and Deleting Files

**A.3** **LESSON 3—MANAGING SUBDIRECTORIES ON DISKS**
Creating New Subdirectories
Moving Between Subdirectories
Copying Files into a Subdirectory Structure
Removing Subdirectories

*Hardware needed:*

▶ IBM PC, IBM PS/2, or IBM-compatible microcomputer

*Software needed:*

▶ DOS 2.0 or later version
▶ two blank diskettes
▶ any disk with data or programs on it

*When you have completed this tutorial, you will be able to:*

▶ Turn on your computer and boot up your system
▶ Format floppy diskettes
▶ List disk directories
▶ Print the screen contents
▶ Use the ? and * wildcards
▶ Copy files and disks
▶ Create backup copies
▶ Rename files
▶ Delete files
▶ Create and manage subdirectories

## ▶ What Is **DOS**?

DOS is the software that allows you and your applications to interact with your microcomputer's central processing unit (CPU). PC-DOS is the disk operating system designed by Microsoft for the IBM PC and IBM PS/2 families. A virtually identical operating system, MS-DOS, is used on microcomputers designed to be compatible with either of these two IBM families. We will refer to both MS-DOS and PC-DOS as DOS.

You probably have DOS version (or release) 3.0 or later on your computer. A later release is represented by a higher number. The first number represents a major revision of DOS; for example, release 4.0 is a major update of release 3.0 and release 5.0 includes even more significant changes. The decimal number, on the other hand, refers to a slightly changed version, not a major revision. Thus, release 3.1 includes only minor changes of 3.0. Any release later than 2.0 will work for this tutorial, but the screens we show will be from release 3.3 or release 5.0. Releases 1.0 to 3.3 are quite similar in their command structure. If you are using release 4.0, 5.0, or higher, however, screens may look quite different because these releases allow you to choose commands from a menu called a shell. Figure A.1 shows examples of various DOS screen displays.

All users of IBM microcomputers and their compatibles need to learn some of the DOS commands, because DOS must be up and running before an application can be loaded. Thus, Lesson 1 of this tutorial begins with starting up your microcomputer. You also need DOS to do all the everyday control functions necessary in microcomputing: to prepare and manage your floppy diskettes; to copy, rename, and delete files; to find

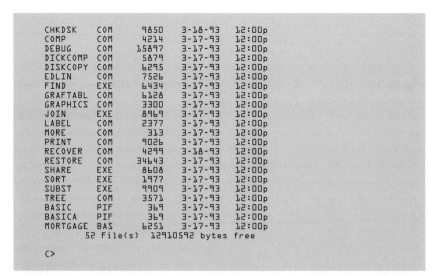

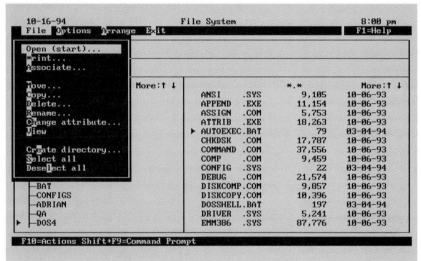

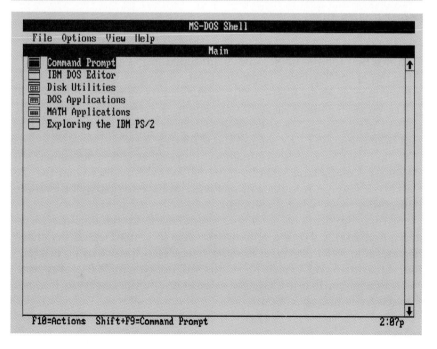

*Figure A.1* *Screens from various versions of DOS. The later releases have added menu choices that make it easier for new users to learn commands.* (a) *DOS version 3.3.* (b) *DOS version 4.0.* (c) *DOS version 5.0.*

(a)

(b)

(c)

out what files are on a disk and how much free space is remaining; to format and copy disks; and so on.

Before starting up your computer, however, you need to know some things about DOS files and file-naming rules.

## ▶ File Naming in DOS

A file can contain a program or data. Data files are named by the user, and there are a few rules, or **file-naming conventions,** that you must follow when you name your files. All file names, including program files, usually have two parts, separated by a period. The first part can have up to eight letters, digits, or symbols; the second part, which is optional, is called the **file-name extension** and can have up to three letters, digits, or symbols. Not all symbols are permitted in file names. The following symbols may be used in file names:

```
~ ! @ # $ ^ & ( ) - _ { } '
```

File names cannot include a space, so many people substitute an underline for a space. For example, here is what you might name a word processing file that contains the first report to your client, the ARP Corporation:

```
report_1.arp
```

Here are two examples of invalid file names:

```
report 1.arp
```

Spaces are not valid.

```
report_1.arpx
```

Extensions can only have three letters.

Notice that the file names above are typed in lowercase. You can use either upper- or lowercase letters for your file names. In this tutorial, we will use uppercase to highlight file names and commands, but we will use lowercase for the things you will type in. You might as well form the habit of using lowercase, because it is easier to type without having to hold down the [SHIFT] key or use the [CAPS LOCK] key.

Try to give files meaningful names—names that will mean something to you six months later when you are trying to remember what the file contains. If you can recognize it, you will not have to display or load the file in order to see what it contains.

For some applications, the file-name extension for the data file is created automatically. For example, worksheets in Lotus 1-2-3 always have the extension .WK1 (or .WKS in older releases). If the extension is something other than .WK1 or .WKS, Lotus will not recognize it as a spreadsheet. Remember that a file-name extension is not necessary if it is not required by your application.

## ► DOS Files

The COMMAND.COM program file on the DOS disk is necessary to start, or **boot up,** the system. If you try booting up on a disk that does not include this file (as well as two "hidden" files that we will talk about when you learn to format disks), you will see an error message on your screen, and your computer will not complete the booting process. For hard disk users, COMMAND.COM and the hidden files must be on the C drive when the computer is turned on; for diskette-only users, the files must be on the disk in the A drive. Once your microcomputer is turned on with these files in the A or C drive, the DOS functions in the COMMAND.COM file are loaded into main memory and are available to you no matter what disks are moved into the disk drives. We will go through the booting-up process in Lesson 1.

Other DOS files are not required for starting up. They execute specialized functions; if you want to use one of those commands, the appropriate DOS file must be present in one of your disk drives. Table A.1 summarizes the commands we will cover in this tutorial, as well as the names of the files that execute those commands.

Some DOS file-name extensions indicate the type of file they are.

.COM    Command file
.EXE    Executable program file
.BAT    Batch file—a series of program files to be executed in
        sequence

When you give DOS a command—FORMAT, for example—it looks for a file named FORMAT with one of the above extensions, and then it executes the instructions in that file.

**Table A.1** | BASIC DOS COMMANDS AND THEIR FILE NAMES

| Command | File Used | Function |
|---|---|---|
| DATE | COMMAND.COM | Allows current date to be set or changed |
| TIME | COMMAND.COM | Allows current time to be set or changed |
| FORMAT | FORMAT.COM | Initializes diskettes |
| VER | COMMAND.COM | Displays the DOS version number |
| DIR | COMMAND.COM | Displays the file in a disk's directory or subdirectory |
| TYPE | COMMAND.COM | Displays the contents of a file |
| COPY | COMMAND.COM | Copies files |
| DISKCOPY | DISKCOPY.COM | Formats a disk and copies all files from one disk to another |
| CHKDSK | CHKDSK.COM | Checks for the disk's available space and specifies whether there are faulty files on the disk |
| RENAME or REN | COMMAND.COM | Renames files |
| DEL or ERASE | COMMAND.COM | Deletes files |
| MKDIR or MD | COMMAND.COM | Creates new subdirectories |
| CHDIR or CD | COMMAND.COM | Changes the current directory |
| RMDIR or RD | COMMAND.COM | Removes empty subdirectories |

## TWO BOOTING FILES: AUTOEXEC.BAT AND CONFIG.SYS

Two optional files, AUTOEXEC.BAT and CONFIG.SYS, are often created by users so that their computers will boot up in special ways needed by their applications. These files must be located on the same disk as the COMMAND.COM file. When you turn on your computer, it will look for these two files and follow their instructions; but if they are not present, the computer will still boot up successfully.

The AUTOEXEC.BAT file allows users to load special functions or programs into storage as part of booting up. After executing COMMAND.COM, the computer will look for an AUTOEXEC.BAT file and execute it if it is there. You can create this file so that it changes the default disk drive, moves to a specific subdirectory, loads application programs, and so on.

The CONFIG.SYS file, which configures the system, allows users to customize their systems in a number of ways. For example, in DOS version 3.1 or later, you can specify a country and DOS will display the date, time, currency symbol, and so on, in that country's format. You can also specify how many buffers (i.e., storage areas) DOS should save. Some application packages require numerous buffer areas. Buffers are a part of RAM set aside by DOS to hold data that has been read, that is waiting to be written to disk, or that is on its way to the printer.

Experienced users can easily create AUTOEXEC.BAT and CONFIG.SYS files. These files can be created with a standard word processing package. For instructions, consult a book that includes advanced DOS functions or your DOS manual.

## DOS SYNTAX

DOS is very precise about the way commands must be entered. Although you may type them in lowercase or uppercase as you do with file names, you must use the proper wording and follow spacing rules exactly. When you see a blank on a line in the tutorial examples, you must leave a space in the specified position; if you omit the blank, the command may not work. The rules for proper wording of commands are called **syntax.** Throughout this tutorial, the commands you will use will be followed by notes about proper syntax. If you make a mistake in typing a command, DOS will let you know by displaying a message such as "Bad command or filename." If that happens, all you need to do is retype the command correctly.

## ► You Are Ready to Begin

This tutorial will take you through the basic DOS commands in three lessons, beginning with how to start up your microcomputer. The commands we will cover are all very useful, so you might consider doing the lessons twice to make sure you can remember them without looking anything up.

Most of the procedures in this tutorial begin with instructions for how to use a particular DOS command on a microcomputer with two floppy disk drives. If you are working on a micro that has a hard disk, the commands are the same, but the disk drive orientation is somewhat different. If you have a hard disk, you will load DOS from the C drive, where it has already been installed. If you have a diskette-only system, you will load DOS from a diskette that is placed in the A drive.

Throughout the tutorial, all entries you are to type are printed in **bold** type. And note that the Enter key is represented by the symbol ENTER. If you are using a computer on a network, a menu will appear when you turn on your computer and you will be told how to proceed or how to exit the menu to get to the DOS command line. To get to the DOS command line from the DOS 4 and DOS 5 shell, press SHIFT plus F9—the shift key and the F9 function key.

## LESSON 1 — STARTING UP AND BASICS

*After completing this lesson, you will be able to:*

▶ Turn your computer on and off, and boot up your system
▶ Set the date and time on your system
▶ Format a disk so that you can write on it
▶ Move between disk drives
▶ List disk directories
▶ Print what is on your screen
▶ Use wildcard characters to list files

We will begin with start-up procedures for a dual diskette system that has no hard drive, then give procedures for systems that have a hard disk with one or more external floppy disk drives.

### ▶ Starting Your System

If you have a dual diskette-only system, insert the DOS disk in drive A. (If you have a hard disk or are running on a network, skip this and the next paragraph.)

> Drive A is the upper or leftmost drive, depending on your system. Insert the DOS disk in drive A *before* you turn the switch on, because your micro will not start—or boot up—properly unless it finds the DOS disk when the power goes on. You will not hurt the micro if you forget to insert a disk, but you will have to start all over again.

Close the door on drive A if it has one; only 5¼-inch diskette drives have a door.

> The "door" refers to the lever or handle on your disk drive. The disk in a 5¼-inch diskette drive cannot be read by DOS unless the

door is closed. If you forget to close it and then try to address that drive, DOS will give you an error message such as: "Not ready error reading drive A. Abort, Retry, Fail?"

Close the door and press R for Retry, and DOS will continue with your instruction.

## If you have a hard disk system or are on a network, be sure drive A has no diskette in it.

Because DOS is typically installed on the hard disk or on a network, you do not need the DOS disk in the A drive. You should not have a disk in drive A when you boot up from a hard disk or network system.

You now have either a DOS disk in drive A for a dual-diskette system, or no disk in drive A for a system with a hard disk (Table A.2) or if you are on a network. Now:

## Switch on your computer.

Microcomputer switches are usually the rocker type: if it is pushed down on one side, it is ON; if it is pushed down on the other side, it is OFF. Switch locations vary. Look on the right or left side or on the back of the chassis. You may also have to turn on your screen, which is sometimes called the monitor. Some systems have separate switches for the monitor, printer, and other devices.

After you turn the switches on, you will hear the fan go on. A series of diagnostic tests on the hardware is then performed, and if there are no problems, a blinking cursor will appear after a few seconds in the upper left-hand corner of the screen.

### WHAT THE LIGHTS MEAN

As you work your way through this tutorial, you will see that after you execute each command, a light associated with each disk drive goes on and off, sometimes several times for one activity. This means that the disk drive is doing its work.

---

**WARNING**

Do not open a diskette drive door or insert or remove disks while the light for that drive is on.

---

Learn to watch the screen for the signal that the command has been completely executed. In DOS, the drive prompt that appears on the screen—A>, B>, C>, or other letter—indicates which drive is currently active.

## Table A.2 | STARTING YOUR SYSTEM

| | |
|---|---|
| Hard-disk systems | DOS is already on drive C. Drive A should be empty. |
| Dual-diskette systems | Place first DOS disk in drive A before starting up the system. |

## SETTING THE DATE AND TIME

Your micro may have a built-in battery-operated calendar-clock. If so, you may skip this section on setting the date and time, because the date and time on your micro are automatically kept current by the calendar-clock.

For systems without a battery-operated calendar-clock, the first words that appear on your screen ask you to supply the current date (Figure A.2). Respond with the current date. For example, if it is November 6, 1993, you would type 11-6-93. If you make a mistake in typing, simply back up using the [BACKSPACE] key and retype the date correctly. Press the Enter key when you are done.

Type today's date and press the [ENTER] key.

The screen will then display the current time and ask you to supply a new time (Figure A.3). Respond with a new time, if you wish. For

*Figure A.2* *When you turn your computer on, the first screen to appear is the DATE screen.*

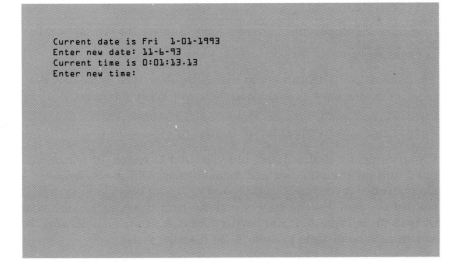

*Figure A.3* *After you type in the date, you are queried for the time.*

*Figure A.4 When you see the DOS copyright statement, your computer is fully booted up.*

```
Current date is Fri  1-01-1993
Enter new date: 11-6-93
Current time is 0:01:13.13
Enter new time: 10:30

The IBM Personal Computer DOS
Version 3.3  (C) Copyright International Business Machines Corp 1981, 1987
             (C) Copyright Microsoft Corp 1981, 1986

A>
```

example, if it is 10:30 a.m., you would type 10:30. (You must enter the time using the 24-hour clock.)

Type current time and press the ENTER key.

The computer then responds with a copyright DOS message (Figure A.4). On systems with dual diskettes and no hard drive, the prompt for drive A now appears just before the cursor. It looks like this:

```
A>
```

If DOS was loaded from a hard disk, the C prompt will be displayed as:

```
C>
```

You can use the DATE and TIME commands at any time to change or verify the date and time. For example, at the DOS command:

Type date

DOS will display the current setting. To leave the setting as it is:

Press ENTER

Alternatively, if you want to change the date, type in the new date. Follow the same procedure to change or verify the time.

## RESETTING THE SYSTEM—THE WARM BOOT

If your computer is already on, but you need to restart, or reboot, you could turn the computer off, and then on again. This is not, however, a recommended procedure. Instead, you can "warm boot" your system. If you have a dual-diskette system with no hard drive, make sure your DOS disk is in drive A. If you have a hard disk, or are on a network, be sure there is no diskette in drive A. To reset the system:

Press CTRL and, while holding it down, press ALT. Then, while holding them down, press DEL

> Your computer will go through the same screen sequence as if you had turned on the ON/OFF switch. Some IBM-compatible micros actually have a restart or reset button that can be pressed instead of the CTRL-ALT-DEL combination.

## ► Formatting Disks

Before disks can be saved for storing data or programs, they must be prepared electronically to receive data in a form that DOS can recognize. Preparing a disk in this way is called **formatting,** or **initializing,** a disk. Your first step will be to format any one of your blank disks so that you can use it to learn more about DOS commands.

---

**WARNING**

If your disk is not new, it may have files on it. Formatting wipes out **all** existing files on a disk. Be sure you want them deleted before you decide to format a used disk.

---

### FORMATTING DISKS IF YOU HAVE A DUAL-DISKETTE SYSTEM WITH NO HARD DRIVE

Your DOS disk should still be in drive A.

Insert a blank, unformatted disk in drive B.

> Next, you will type the FORMAT command. If you make a mistake in typing, either use the BACKSPACE key to correct it or, if you have already pressed ENTER, simply retype the command correctly. At the A> prompt:

Type format b:

Press ENTER

> The phrase "format b:" is DOS's abbreviated way of saying, "Format the disk in drive B." Be sure to include the colon after the letter B, and to press ENTER at the end. You must always press ENTER after typing a command.

> As soon as you press ENTER, a message similar to the one in Figure A.5 appears on your screen. Press any key when the blank disk is in the drive with the door closed. The disk drives both go to work, and you will hear whirring sounds, and the drive light will go on and off as the formatting proceeds. DOS will indicate that formatting is occurring by displaying:

> Formatting...

> When formatting is finished, a message similar to the one in Figure

***Figure A.5*** *When you enter the FOR-MAT command, DOS reminds you to insert a diskette.*

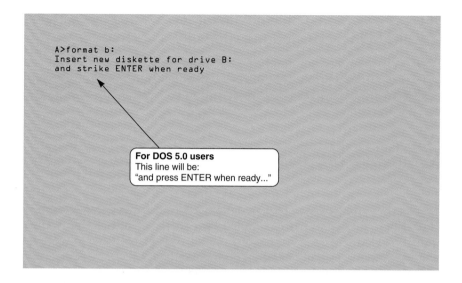

***Figure A.6*** *When formatting is complete, DOS tells you how many bytes are available on the disk, and asks whether you want to format another disk.*

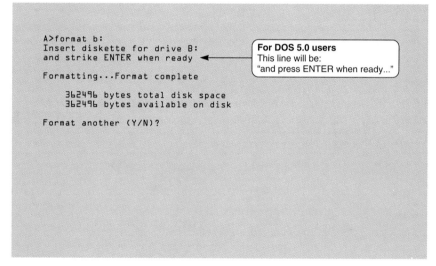

A.6 appears on your screen. Since you do not want to format another disk right now:

**Press N**

The cursor will return to the A> prompt.

Your newly formatted disk is ready to use.

### FORMATTING AND CREATING A BOOT DISK FOR DUAL-DISKETTE SYSTEMS WITH NO HARD DISK

You format blank disks in order to copy application programs onto them or to use them to store data files. If your disk is going to contain an application and you have a dual-diskette system with no hard disk, it is useful to be able to boot up using the application disk itself. Otherwise, you have to first start with the DOS disk in drive A, turn the computer on, take the DOS disk out, and put the software application disk in.

To be able to boot up directly with your new application disk, all you have to do is add /s to the FORMAT command; this not only formats the disk, but also puts the COMMAND.COM file and two hidden system files on the disk at the same time so that it can be used as a boot disk. You will now reformat the same blank disk, this time adding the command that puts the system files on it.

Type format b:/s

Press ENTER

Make sure that your spacing is correct—the only space follows the word "format." When formatting is complete, the message in Figure A.7 appears on the screen. It tells you how many total bytes of space are on the disk, how many bytes are used by the system files, and how many bytes are remaining for you to use.

Your formatted system disk is now ready for you to copy a software application onto it. Obtain a diskette label (it is packaged with the disk, or ask your lab instructor). With a soft, felt-tipped pen, label this disk with your name and the date. Then, when you are ready to boot up with the application disk, simply put it in drive A and turn on your computer.

## FORMATTING DISKS IF YOU HAVE A HARD DRIVE OR ARE ON A NETWORK

If the microcomputer you are working on has a hard disk or a file server, the DOS system and DOS files are probably on the hard disk or file server. In this tutorial, we assume that a hard disk is named drive C. If yours has another letter, just substitute that letter for C in this example. Make sure that you are in drive C if you are using a hard disk. If you

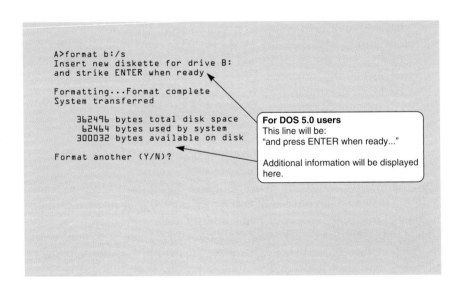

```
A>format b:/s
Insert new diskette for drive B:
and strike ENTER when ready

Formatting...Format complete
System transferred

     362496 bytes total disk space
      62464 bytes used by system
     300032 bytes available on disk

Format another (Y/N)?
```

For DOS 5.0 users
This line will be:
"and press ENTER when ready..."

Additional information will be displayed here.

*Figure A.7* When you use the /s parameter with the FORMAT command, DOS sets aside a section of disk space for the COMMAND.COM file and two hidden system files, which it copies onto the newly formatted disk.

are not, you can change the current drive to C as follows:

Type c:

Press [ENTER]

> Your cursor should now be at the C> prompt. If you are on a network your current drive might be F, or some other letter.

Insert a blank disk in drive A.

> Next you will type the FORMAT command. If you make a mistake in typing, either use the [BACKSPACE] key to correct it or, if you have already pressed [ENTER], simply retype the command correctly.

---

**WARNING**

Formatting from a hard disk has one ever-present danger: If you fail to add the name of another disk drive to the FORMAT command, the hard disk will format itself. Everything on the disk, including all files and all directories, will be wiped out. If you discover your mistake before formatting begins, you have one chance to recover—when the screen says "Strike Enter when ready" or "Press Enter when ready"). With DOS 3.0 and higher, you can press the [CTRL] key and, while it is depressed, press the [BREAK] key to cancel the FORMAT command. With earlier versions of DOS, pressing any key will start the formatting, including the [ESC] key, so your only option is to turn your computer off using the ON/OFF switch and reboot.

---

At the C> prompt:

Type format a:

Press [ENTER]

> The phrase "format a:" is the DOS abbreviation for, "Format the disk in drive A." Be sure to include the colon after the letter A and to press [ENTER] at the end. You must always press [ENTER] after typing a command.

> As soon as you press [ENTER], the message, "Insert new diskette for drive A" will be displayed on your screen. Press any key to begin formatting. The disk drives go to work; you will hear whirring sounds, and the C (or F) and A drive lights will go on and off as the formatting proceeds. When formatting is finished, a message similar to the one in Figure A.6 appears on your screen. Since you do not want to format another disk right now:

Press N

> The cursor will return to the C> or F> prompt.

The disk in drive A is ready to use. Obtain a diskette label (it is packaged with the disk, or ask your lab instructor for one). Using a soft, felt-tipped pen, label this disk with your name and the date.

Note that with hard-disk systems or networks, there is no need to put the system files on a diskette, because you will always be booting up from the hard disk in drive C or the file server, often called drive F.

## ▶ Finding Out What Version of DOS You Are Using

Now you can find out what version, or release, of DOS you are using. If you have a dual-diskette system, put your newly formatted disk that has the COMMAND.COM file on it in drive A. At the A> prompt (or the C> prompt if you have a hard disk system):

Type ver

Press [ENTER]

> Your screen will tell you what version you are using. If it is release 3.3, your screen will look like Figure A.8.

Note that release numbers have significance for formatting. If you are using a micro that was booted up with an earlier version, such as version 3.1, and you then attempt to use a disk that was formatted with a later version, such as 4.0 or 5.0 you will get an error message. Releases are upwardly compatible; that is, you can use a release 3.1 disk in a micro booted up on release 5.0 without any difficulty. The reverse, however, does not work.

## ▶ Moving Between Disk Drives

It is very easy to go back and forth between disk drives in DOS. There are many reasons for changing disk drives, and moving back and forth should become automatic for you. The following exercise will familiarize you with the process. If you have a dual-diskette system with no hard drive:

> Put a disk with data or programs—we call this a student disk—in

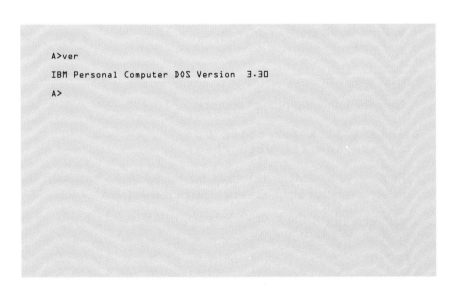

```
A>ver

IBM Personal Computer DOS Version  3.30

A>
```

*Figure A.8* Use the VER command to find out what version of DOS you are using.

drive A and your newly formatted blank disk in drive B.

Since you have just formatted a disk from drive A, you should see the A> prompt on your screen. At the A> prompt:

Type b:

Press ENTER

Now the prompt for the B drive appears, telling you that you are in drive B. To return to drive A:

Type a:

Press ENTER

The A> prompt reappears.

### MOVING BETWEEN DISK DRIVES IF YOU HAVE A HARD DRIVE OR ARE ON A NETWORK

If you have a hard drive or a file server with only one floppy drive, you can still perform operations between drive A and drive B as directed in this tutorial. The computer will use the same floppy drive as both the A drive and the B drive on an alternating basis, and will prompt you to insert and remove the diskettes. To see how the computer prompts you to alternate between drive A and drive B with just one floppy drive:

Place your student disk in drive A.

Make sure you close the drive door. Since you have just formatted a disk from drive C (or the network drive F), you should see the C> (or F>) prompt on your screen. At the C> or F> prompt:

Type a:

Press ENTER

Now the prompt for the A drive appears, telling you that you are in drive A. To move to drive B:

Type b:

Press ENTER

Now the following prompt appears:

```
Insert disk for drive B
Strike any key when ready
```

Remove your student disk from the floppy drive and insert the newly formatted blank diskette. Then strike any key.

The prompt for the B drive appears, telling you that you are in drive B. To return to drive A:

Type a:

Press ENTER

The following prompt appears:

```
Insert disk for drive B
Strike any key when ready
```

Remove your blank diskette from the floppy drive and insert your student disk. Then strike any key.

The prompt for the A drive appears, telling you that you are in drive A.

## ▶ Listing Disk Directories

Next you will take a look at the files on your student disk. This disk should be in drive A. (Note that the instruction to press ENTER after typing a command will no longer be included in the rest of this tutorial. This step should be automatic for you now.) At the A> prompt:

### Type dir

A list of files on the data disk will scroll by on the screen. This list of files is called the **disk directory.** It will look something like the directory in Figure A.9, although some of the file names will be different. Sometimes there are more files than your screen can hold. To ask for a single screen of files at a time:

### Type dir/p

This time the scrolling will stop as soon as the screen is filled. You can continue listing files by pressing any key.

### Press any key.

The screen will fill again. These displays will continue until the

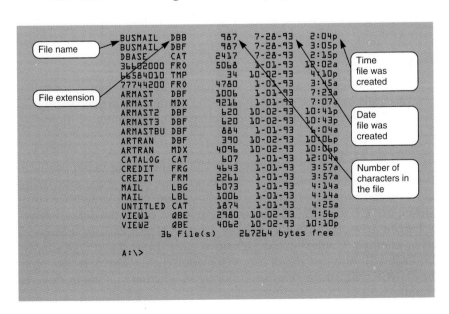

*Figure A.9 The DIR command lists file names and their extensions, the storage space used for each file, and the date and time each was created or last modified.*

**Figure A.10** *The /w parameter added to the DIR command gives you a wide-screen listing of files.*

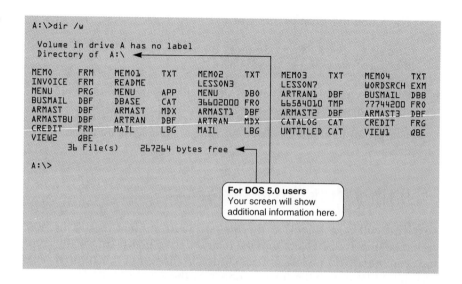

```
A:\>dir /w

 Volume in drive A has no label
 Directory of  A:\

MEMO       FRM   MEMO1      TXT   MEMO2      TXT   MEMO3      TXT   MEMO4      TXT
INVOICE    FRM   README           LESSON3          LESSON7          WORDSRCH   EXM
MENU       PRG   MENU       APP   MENU       DBO   ARTRAN1    DBF   BUSMAIL    DBB
BUSMAIL    DBF   DBASE      CAT   36602000   FRO   66584010   TMP   77744200   FRO
ARMAST     DBF   ARMAST     MDX   ARMAST1    DBF   ARMAST2    DBF   ARMAST3    DBF
ARMASTBU   DBF   ARTRAN     DBF   ARTRAN     MDX   CATALOG    CAT   CREDIT     FRG
CREDIT     FRM   MAIL       LBG   MAIL       LBG   UNTITLED   CAT   VIEW1      QBE
VIEW2      QBE
        36 File(s)     267264 bytes free

A:\>
```

**For DOS 5.0 users**
Your screen will show additional information here.

entire directory listing is complete. An alternative way to look at a file directory is to ask for a wide-screen version.

Type dir/w

You will see a wide-screen directory in the form shown in Figure A.10. This type of listing just includes file names and extensions, not storage used or date and time that each file was created.

Note that all DIR commands indicate the number of files on the disk as well as the number of bytes that are still available.

### ASKING FOR A DIRECTORY ON A DIFFERENT DISK DRIVE

You can also ask for a directory for a disk in another disk drive.

Put your DOS disk in drive A and your student disk in drive B. At the A> prompt:

Type dir b:

Even though you are in the A drive, the directory listing for drive B scrolls by on the screen. Notice the command's syntax: there is a space after the command DIR, followed by the letter of the drive and then a colon.

You can use all the DOS commands to direct something to happen in a drive other than the one you are in. The **current drive** is the one designated by the prompt—if you see the A> prompt, you know that your current drive is drive A. The current drive is also called the **default drive** or **logged drive,** because it is the only drive DOS will look for when you give a command, unless you designate another drive. If you type simply dir, DOS will only list the directory for your current drive. If you type dir b:, DOS will list the directory in drive B, whether you are in drive B or not.

# ► Looking at the Contents of a File

Sometimes you will want to look at text or document files that are designed to be read as is. The DOS command TYPE allows you to do this. One such file commonly found on application or program disks is called README. It contains pertinent information about the program or application. If your student disk has such a file and it is in drive B, move to drive B by typing **b:**. At the B> prompt,

Type *type readme*

> The contents of the file README will scroll by on the screen (Figure A.11).

> A README file is actually a data file created so that it can be read by the user. Most program files, however, are not written in English, because they have been translated into special programming code for use by an application. If you ask your computer to type one of the WordPerfect program files, for example, you will get surprising results. To illustrate, put your WordPerfect disk in drive A. Move to drive A by typing **a:**. At the A> prompt:

Type *type wp.mrs*

> What you will see on the screen is words mixed up with a lot of strange symbols, including Greek letters and other symbols that you will not find on the keyboard. Your computer may also beep alarmingly. Do not worry—you cannot hurt anything. To stop the TYPE command:

Press CTRL and then, while holding it down, press BREAK

> The file listing and beeping will stop and your cursor will return to the A> prompt.

The TYPE command is useful for displaying data files that contain text

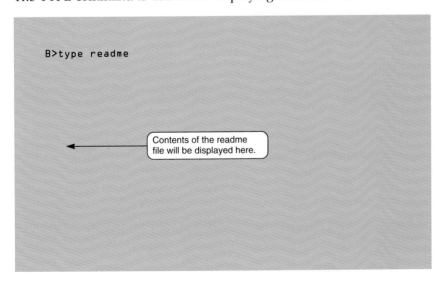

B>type readme

Contents of the readme file will be displayed here.

*Figure A.11 The TYPE command displays the contents of a file.*

material, or a document created by a word processing program, although word processed files may contain many nontext symbols.

If a readable file is longer than one page in length, you can type:

**more< readme**

which pauses after each page. After you read a page, press any key to continue.

## ▶ Printing from Your Screen

It is often useful to print a copy of what you see on your screen. For example, when you ask for a disk directory, you might want to print it out so that you have a record of the directory to tape to the disk's envelope. For this exercise, we will print a copy of the files on your disk. First, make sure your printer is on and that there is paper in the printer. Move to drive B. At the B> prompt:

Type dir

The names of all files will appear on your screen. If you have an IBM PC or XT or compatible:

Press SHIFT , while holding it down, press the key labeled "PrtSc" or "Print Screen."

Or, if you have an IBM PS/2, simply

Press "PrtSc" or "Print Screen."

The file names that are currently on the screen will be printed. You can also turn the print-screen function on and leave it on, so that it prints all your screens. Then, when you no longer want what is on the screen to print, you can turn the print-screen function off again. A key that turns a function on and off in this manner is called a **toggle** key. To make the "PrtSc" key act as a toggle, you combine it with the CTRL key.

Press CTRL , then, while holding it down, press "PrtSc" or "Print Screen."

The print-screen toggle is now on. Now take a look at how it works. At the B> prompt:

Type dir/w

As the directory listing appears on the screen, it also goes to the printer. Everything you type from this point on will go to the printer. This is called **echo printing** because it "echoes" what appears on the screen. To turn the toggle off:

Press CTRL , then, while holding it down, press "PrtSc" or "Print Screen."

In other words, simply repeat the same sequence you used to turn the toggle on.

SHIFT + "PrtSc" prints what is on the screen: CTRL + "PrtSc" prints whatever will be displayed on the screen from that point on.

# ▶ Using Wildcard Characters

Sometimes you want to look for specific files in your directory, but if there are a lot of files, it may be difficult to locate the ones you want. DOS gives you a method for narrowing your search; you can use the **wildcard characters,** the question mark (?) and the asterisk (*), to substitute for other characters in a filename. They are called wildcards because, as in poker, they can stand for any character in a file name. The question mark stands for any single character in that exact position, and the asterisk stands for any group of characters in that position.

### USING THE ? WILDCARD

You can practice using the ? wildcard by looking for some files on your student disk. Suppose some files are text files with the extension .TXT as in Figure A.12 while others are forms and have the extension .FRM. Suppose you want to find the memo files with the extension .TXT. Put your disk in drive A and move there by typing **a:**. First, ask for a directory listing. At the A> prompt:

Type **dir**

> You will see a list of files scrolling by on the screen. There may be too many to quickly find out whether a particular file is there. There may be only one or two of them on the disk, but you do not know which ones. At the A> prompt:

Type **dir memo?.txt**

> This command lists all file names that begin with *memo*, have one additional character in the file name, and have an extension of .TXT.

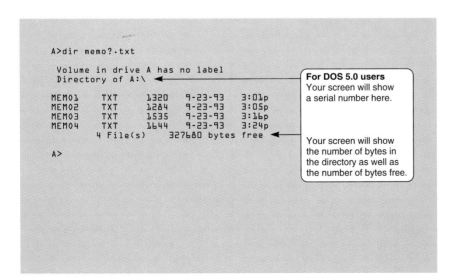

```
A>dir memo?.txt

    Volume in drive A has no label
    Directory of A:\  ◄──────────          ┌─────────────────────────┐
                                            │ For DOS 5.0 users       │
    MEMO1    TXT     1320    9-23-93  3:01p │ Your screen will show   │
    MEMO2    TXT     1284    9-23-93  3:05p │ a serial number here.   │
    MEMO3    TXT     1535    9-23-93  3:16p │                         │
    MEMO4    TXT     1644    9-23-93  3:24p │                         │
          4 File(s)    327680 bytes free ◄─┤ Your screen will show   │
                                            │ the number of bytes in  │
    A>                                      │ the directory as well as│
                                            │ the number of bytes free.│
                                            └─────────────────────────┘
```

*Figure A.12* *Using the ? wildcard with the DIR command lists all the files whose names match MEMO?.TXT, and have any character in the ? position.*

Our screen shows that there are four such files (Figure A.12). Notice that the ? character shows you only files that begin with *memo* and have only one other character in the fifth position of the file name. Check this out. At the A> prompt:

Type dir ?.wks

This time, no files show up, because there are no files with only one character before the extension.

If you want to list whole groups of related files, you need the other wildcard, the * character.

### USING THE * WILDCARD

Suppose you do not know exactly how the memo files were named, but you want to see all files on the disk related to memos. If you have a disk with memo files in drive A, at the A> prompt:

Type dir memo*.txt

If we use the same disk used for the display in Figure A.12, the same four files that were found before will be displayed again. But if the disk contained a file named MEMO12.TXT, for example, it would appear here and *not* in a DIR command that used a ?, which stands for only one character. Now you will look for all the forms files, those with the extension .FRM. At the A> prompt:

Type dir *.frm

All the files with the extension .FRM will scroll by on the screen, no matter how many characters precede the extension. As always, the directory also lists the total number of files and the amount of storage space left on the disk.

## ▶ Turning Your Computer Off (Powering Down)

When it is time to turn the computer off, remove your disks, then turn the power switch for the CPU, and the monitor, to the OFF position.

This completes Lesson 1. Do the following practice exercises before going on to Lesson 2.

## ▶ Practice

1. Turn your computer off and then boot up. Set the date and time (unless your computer has a built-in calendar-clock that does this automatically).
2. When your computer is fully booted, reboot it with a warm boot. Reset the date and time.

3. Move back and forth between disk drives several times. If you have two floppy disk drives, put a disk in each drive and move between drive A and drive B; each time, ask for a directory of the disk in the current drive. If you have a hard-disk drive, put a disk in drive A and move between drive C and drive A; each time, ask for a directory of the current drive.

4. From one drive, ask for a directory for the other drive. Move to the other drive and ask for a directory of the first drive.

5. If you have two floppy-disk drives, put your DOS disk in drive A, and at the A> prompt use the * wildcard to ask for a directory of all files that have the .COM extension. If you have a hard drive, do the same thing from the C> prompt.

# LESSON 2 — FILE MANAGEMENT

*After completing this lesson, you will be able to:*

▶ Copy files
▶ Copy an entire disk
▶ Create a backup copy
▶ Rename files
▶ Delete files

## ▶ Copying Files

Copy is the DOS command that you will probably use the most. Think about some of the reasons you will have for copying files.

- To make backup copies in case the original files are lost or damaged accidentally.
- To give someone else a copy of data or program files.
- To make a different version of the same file without losing the first version.
- To put related files together on the same disk.

The syntax, or wording, of the COPY command is typical of other DOS commands. The syntax calls for abbreviating the English equivalent by leaving out the prepositions "from" and "to." Instead of saying "Copy from drive A to drive B," the proper wording is:

```
copy a:filename b:filename
```

Notice that there is a space after the word *copy* and after the file name to be copied from. There is no space between the drive letters and the file names. Not all the elements of this example are needed for all uses of the COPY command. For example, if you are already in drive A, you do not need to specify the A drive. The above command sequence would then be:

**Table A.3** | SYNTAX FOR COPY COMMAND APPLICATIONS

| | | |
|---|---|---|
| To copy a file of same name in current drive to another disk | copy *(filename) (drive):* | copy memo1.txt b: |
| To copy a file of same name from one drive to another, where neither drive is current | copy *(drive):(file name) (drive):* | copy a:memo1.txt b: |
| To copy a file to another disk and rename it | copy *(drive):(file name) (drive):(new name)* | copy a:memo1.txt b:letter1.txt |
| To copy a file to the same disk and rename it | copy *(file name) (new name)* | copy memo1.txt letter1.txt |
| To copy a file from another disk to current drive | copy *(other drive):(file name)* | copy b:memo1.txt |
| To copy a file from another disk and rename it | copy *(other drive):(file name) (new name)* | copy b:memo1.txt letter1.txt |

```
copy filename b:filename
```

In this COPY command, a: is assumed for the file to be copied from.

If the file name will be the same in both copies, you do not need to repeat the file name. To copy the file named MEMO1.TXT from drive A to drive B and leave the name the same, the command is:

```
copy memo1.txt b:
```

See Table A.3 for a summary of the minimal syntax elements needed for each copying application.

Remember that DOS commands must be exact. If a file name has an extension, that extension must be included in the COPY command; without it, DOS will tell you "File not found."

You can use the wildcard characters * and ? with the COPY command. For example, if you want to copy all your files that have the extension .TXT, you simply use the syntax COPY *.TXT, and all .TXT files will be copied to the drive you designate.

### COPYING FROM ONE DISK TO ANOTHER

If you have not already done so, boot up your computer. Then insert your student disk in drive A and a formatted blank disk, which we will call your working disk, in drive B. Suppose you have a file called MEMO2.TXT on your student disk, which you will copy to your working disk. (If not, get a directory of files on your student disk and select one to be copied.) At the A> prompt:

Type **copy memo2.txt b:** (or **copy** *filename* **b:** where *filename* is the name of any file on your disk)

You will see the lights go on each disk drive as the computer does the work of copying from one drive to the other. Notice that you do not need to specify that the file is in drive A, because you are already in drive A. You also do not need to specify the name of the file after the b:, because it will have the same name. If you used the full statement, "copy a:memo2.txt b:memo2.txt," the result would be exactly the same.

Always look at the drive B directory after copying, to verify that the file was copied. At the A> prompt:

Type dir b:

The MEMO2.TXT file should now be listed in the directory for the new disk in drive B.

## COPYING TO ANOTHER DISK AND RENAMING THE FILE

It is often useful to change the name of a file when you copy it. For example, you might want to make a second version of a business form letter as a backup without losing the first version; or you might copy a spreadsheet so that you can use the format you designed for a different application, although you want to keep using the first one as well.

**WARNING**

If you use the COPY command to send a file to a disk that already has a file of that exact name, DOS simply copies the new file over the old one, thereby erasing it, often without giving you any warning. This can be disastrous if you needed the old version, so be careful when naming and copying files.

Now you will copy your MEMO2.TXT file again to your working disk in drive B, only this time you will rename it in the process. At the A> prompt:

Type copy memo2.txt b:letter2.txt

You could have renamed it anything, as long as you used no more than eight characters before the period, or three characters in the file-name extension after the period. Check the directory of the disk in drive B to see whether you now have both files. At the A> prompt:

Type dir b:

Both files are listed in the directory.

## COPYING FILES ONTO THE SAME DISK

You will sometimes want to make a second copy of a file on the same disk as the first one. DOS allows you to do this as long as you give the second file a new name. Unlike copying to another disk, where a file of the same name would be erased by the new copy, if you try to copy to a file of the same name on the same disk, DOS will give you the following message:

File cannot be copied onto itself

You can now make a second copy of your MEMO2.TXT file (or any file you selected) on your student disk. At the A> prompt:

Type copy memo2.txt letter2.txt

> After the copying is complete and the light on drive A is out, check the directory to see that the copying was done.

Type dir

> Both files are listed.

## COPYING FROM ANOTHER DRIVE

You can also copy a file from another drive to the current or default drive. You can either copy it with the same name or rename it in the process. We will now copy MEMO2.TXT from drive B to drive A and rename it REPORT2.TXT, since we already have a MEMO2.TXT file on our disk in drive A. At the A> prompt:

Type copy b:memo2.txt report2.txt

> Notice the syntax. Since you are already in drive A, you do not need to tell DOS to copy the file to drive A. Check the directory for drive A to make sure REPORT2.TXT was copied there. At the A> prompt:

Type dir

> The newly copied file REPORT2.TXT will be listed.

## COPYING AN ENTIRE DISK TO ANOTHER DISK

It is sometimes useful to copy all files from one disk to another disk. One important reason to copy an entire disk is to create a **backup copy** to use in case the original is lost or damaged. You will use your working disk to back up your student disk in the following exercise.

One way to copy all files from one disk to another is to use the * wild-card character. With your student disk still in drive A, and your working disk in drive B:

Type copy *.* b:

> All your files on your student disk are now copied onto your working disk.

A second way to copy all files is to use the DISKCOPY command. DISK-COPY does something more than copy files: it also formats the target disk before it copies the files.

---

**WARNING**

Before you use DISKCOPY, make sure that the disk to be copied to does not have files on it that you will need, because formatting will delete them.

---

For this exercise, use your other blank disk, which is still unformatted.

You will use DISKCOPY to format it and to create another backup copy of your student disk. The DISKCOPY command is not included in the COMMAND.COM file, so you must put the DOS disk in drive A (or be in drive C if you have a hard disk). From drive A (or C):

Type diskcopy a: b:

DOS then displays the message shown in Figure A.13.

Insert your student data disk in drive A and your blank unformatted disk in drive B. Press any key.

The two drives go to work, formatting the disk in drive B and then copying all the files from the disk in drive A to the disk in drive B. During copying, you will see the message, "formatting while copying . . .," displayed on your screen. When copying is complete, you will see the message,

```
Copy complete
Copy another (Y/N)?
```

Since you do not want to copy another disk:

Press N

Label this backup "student disk backup" and store it in a safe place so you can use it if something happens to your original student disk. You will continue to use your working disk in the following exercises.

The DISKCOPY command is particularly useful if you are planning to make more than one copy of the same disk or if you are copying entire disks onto unformatted disks. However, you should note that it is easier to use the * wildcard method if you are copying a disk with a great many files.

```
A>diskcopy a:  b:

Insert SOURCE diskette in drive A:

Press any key when ready . . .

Insert TARGET diskette in drive B:

Press any key when ready . . .
```

*Figure A.13* The DISKCOPY command can only be called up from the DOS disk. You are then instructed to remove the DOS disk from drive A and insert your source disk—the one you want to copy.

## ▶ Renaming Files

The DOS RENAME command allows you to change the name of a file. The syntax of the command is similar to the COPY command (Table A.4).

### RENAMING FILES ON THE SAME DISK

To practice renaming, we will give one of the .TXT files a new name. Assume your student disk has a MEMO3.TXT file. Put your student disk in drive A. At the A> prompt:

Type rename memo3.txt letter3.txt

> The light on the A drive comes on briefly, then you are returned to the A> prompt. The file has been renamed, so MEMO3.TXT will have disappeared and LETTER3.TXT now appears in the directory. Check the directory listing to see whether that happened. This is a good chance to use one of the wildcard characters to list all the files with the extension .TXT. At the A> prompt:

Type dir *.txt

> For our disk, there will be four files listed.

### RENAMING FILES ON ANOTHER DISK

You will sometimes want to rename a file in another drive without having to change drives. You are now in drive A. Put your working disk in drive B. Assume that it contains a MEMO2.TXT file. You will rename the MEMO2.TXT file on your working disk. At the A> prompt:

Type rename b:memo2.txt report2.txt

> Notice that you have to designate the B drive by putting the drive letter and a colon in front of the original file name. If you did not, DOS would look in your current drive (drive A) and might be unable to find a file by that name, or if it did find the file, it would rename a file in the wrong drive.

## ▶ Erasing and Deleting Files

You will often find that you want to remove a file from a disk, either because it is out of date, or you do not need it any more, or because you need the space on the disk. The two DOS commands ERASE and DEL (or DELETE) are identical. Many people use the DEL command just because it has fewer characters.

**Table A.4** | THE RENAME COMMAND

| | | |
|---|---|---|
| To rename a file on the same disk | rename *(file name) (file name)* | rename memo3.txt letter3.txt |
| To rename a file on another disk | rename *(drive):(file name) (file name)* | rename b:memo3.txt letter3.txt |

## DELETING FILES ON THE SAME DISK

We will now delete all the extra MEMO.TXT variations on our student disk. First, with the student disk in drive A, we use the DIR and wildcard * to take a look at what is there. At the A> prompt:

Type **dir *.txt**

> For our disk, six files will be listed: MEMO1.TXT, MEMO2.TXT, MEMO3.TXT, MEMO4.TXT, LETTER2.TXT, and REPORT2.TXT. The two files LETTER2.TXT and REPORT2.TXT are the copies of MEMO2.TXT that we made earlier. At the A> prompt:

Type **del letter2.txt**

> Try the ERASE command to delete the other file. At the A> prompt:

Type **erase report2.txt**

> Now check the directory to see whether the two files are really gone. At the A> prompt:

Type **dir *.txt**

> The only files left with the .TXT extension are the original MEMO files.

## DELETING FILES ON ANOTHER DISK

Deleting a file on another disk works just like renaming or copying— you just precede the file name with the drive name followed by a colon. To delete all the files with the extension .TXT on a working disk in drive B, use the wildcard * character.

Type **del b:*.txt**

> We can check the directory for drive B to verify that all .TXT files are gone. At the A> prompt:

Type **dir b:**

> There should be no .TXT files remaining on the working disk.

## DELETING ALL FILES FROM A DISK

We will now completely clear all the files on our working disk with a single command.

Type **del b:*.***

> DOS gives you a chance to make sure that you are really ready to part with all your files by asking for verification with the following question:

> `Are you sure (Y/N)?`

Press **Y**

We can check the directory for drive B to verify that all files are gone. At the A> prompt:

Type **dir b:**

The working disk should now be blank again.

---

**WARNING**

Be very cautious when you are deleting files or groups of files—you may be able to recover them with an UNERASE command if you are using DOS 5.0 or higher (or a special utility program), but other versions do not have this feature.

---

This completes Lesson 2. Do the following practice exercises before going on to the next lesson. When you are ready to turn the computer off, remove your disks, then turn the power switch for the CPU, or the CPU and the monitor, to the OFF position.

**PRACTICE**

1. Use the COPY command to copy and rename any file on your student disk. Make two copies on your student disk, but change the names of two files.
2. Use the ? wildcard to copy any files with a .COM extension to a blank, formatted disk.
3. Use the ? wildcard to delete any files with a .TXT extension from the disk in #2.
4. Move to the disk drive that holds your blank, formatted disk. Then copy any README files that are on your student disk to your blank disk.

# LESSON 3 — MANAGING SUBDIRECTORIES ON DISKS

As you get more sophisticated in your use of microcomputers, you will appreciate DOS's ability to organize files in sections and subsections, called **subdirectories,** on your disks. This is often useful on a floppy disk, but it is essential on a hard disk, which may hold the equivalent of hundreds of floppy disks and thousands of files.

Disks with numerous files work best when they are organized in tree-like directories (see Figure A.14). The main or **root directory** is the initial directory created by DOS. It is the directory that you find yourself in after turning your system on, and the one you return to if you need to use any of the DOS commands such as FORMAT or DISKCOPY. Any additional subdirectories created by the user are considered to be subordinate to the root directory.

As Figure A.14 shows, those subdirectories that branch off the root are called simply directories (<DIR>), but they really are subdirectories. Subdirectories make it much easier to find things on your hard disk.

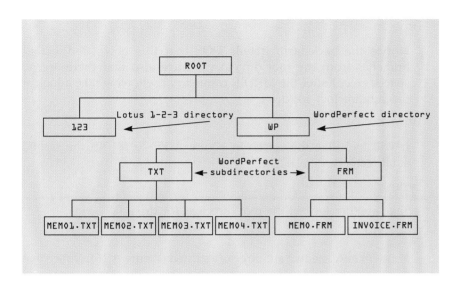

*Figure A.14 You are going to set up two subdirectories. This can be done on a diskette or on a hard disk.*

Think of a filing cabinet as an analogy: a drawer represents a directory and the files within it represent subdirectories. DOS provides a similar convenience in that it enables you to group files that will be used together into a single subdirectory. Remember that a "directory" can be a root directory or a subdirectory.

Typically, each software package is copied to its own subdirectory, and you may establish subdirectories within them for different applications of that package. For example, you might set up a subdirectory for WordPerfect with subordinate subdirectories for text files and forms files, as shown in Figure A.14.

In this part of the DOS tutorial, you will practice setting up or making subdirectories (MKDIR or simply MD), moving between or changing subdirectories (CHDIR or CD), and removing subdirectories (RMDIR or RD). Practice these procedures on a floppy disk, even if you are working on a computer with a hard disk. If you are working on a hard disk, use the root directory on the C drive to create subdirectories on a disk in your A drive. Be sure not to tamper with the hard disk's root directory structure unless you are directed to do so by your lab instructor.

## ▶ Creating New Subdirectories

You are going to set up your working floppy disk with subdirectories for two applications packages: Lotus 1-2-3 and WordPerfect. You can then put the Lotus or WordPerfect program disk in drive A, and work on your files in the corresponding directory in drive B.

Put your DOS disk in drive A and your working disk in drive B. First you will set up the Lotus 1-2-3 subdirectory. It is important to give the subdirectory a short, easily recognizable name, because you will have to type it each time you want to move to that subdirectory. In directory command syntax, the "branches" between directories or subdirectories are indicated by the **backslash** (\) character. At the A> prompt:

Type mkdir b:\123

Notice the backslash; it tells DOS that this new subdirectory branches from the root directory. Notice also that there are no spaces except after the MKDIR command itself. Now take a look at the subdirectory for drive B.

Type dir b:

It will look like the screen in Figure A.15. To set up the second subdirectory:

Type mkdir b:\wp

Take another look at the root directory for drive B.

Type dir b:

You will now see two subdirectories listed (Figure A.16). Notice that

***Figure A.15*** *Your 1-2-3 directory is listed with a <DIR> label.*

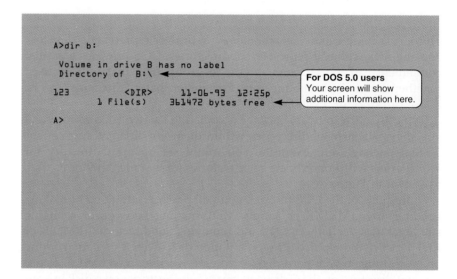

***Figure A.16*** *You now have two directories on your disk.*

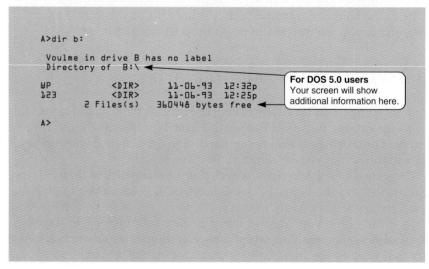

subdirectories are identified by <DIR> in the column used for file-name extensions.

Now you will set up two lower-level subdirectories in the subdirectory called SP. Some of the files on your student disk may have the extension .TXT (for text), while others may have the extension .FRM (for forms). Now, within the WP subdirectory itself, make a separate subdirectory for each kind of file. At the A> prompt:

Type mkdir b:\wp\txt

> You can also use the abbreviated form of the MKDIR command, which is MD. Use it to create a subordinate subdirectory.

Type md b:\wp\frm

> The MD form works just like the longer form.

Now you have TXT and FRM subdirectories within the WP subdirectory.

## ▶ Moving Between Subdirectories

When you decide to move to a different subdirectory, DOS requires a strict syntax that defines the **path** it will follow along the **tree hierarchy**. The command for changing directories is CHDIR, or its abbreviated form, CD. Practice moving between subdirectories. First, move to the B drive. Then, at the B> prompt:

Type chdir\wp\txt

> This moves you to the TXT subdirectory of the WP directory. Now, to make sure you are actually in the subdirectory of that name:

Type dir

> Your screen will look like Figure A.17. You can see that you are in

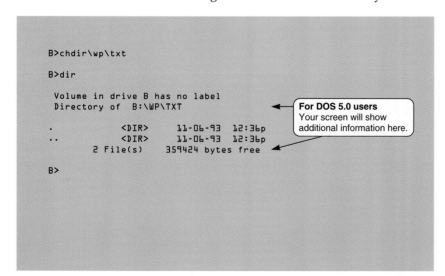

```
B>chdir\wp\txt

B>dir

     Volume in drive B has no label
     Directory of  B:\WP\TXT
                                                    ◀── For DOS 5.0 users
     .            <DIR>      11-06-93  12:36p            Your screen will show
     ..           <DIR>      11-06-93  12:36p            additional information here.
          2 File(s)     359424 bytes free  ◀

B>
```

*Figure A.17* An empty subdirectory looks like this when you ask for a file listing.

the \wp\txt subdirectory, and that there are no files in it. Now, move to the other WordPerfect subdirectory; this time, use the abbreviated CD command.

Type cd\wp\frm

Check the directory again to verify that you are now in the other WordPerfect subdirectory.

## ► Copying Files into a Subdirectory Structure

Remove the DOS disk from drive A and insert your student disk instead. You will copy files from the student disk into your new subdirectories on the disk in drive B. At the B> prompt:

Type cd\wp\txt

This sets the path that DOS will follow for copying. Then:

Type copy a:*.txt b:\wp\txt

This uses the wildcard * character to copy all files that have the extension .TXT from drive A to the subdirectory of the WP directory. Check your results.

Type dir

DOS will follow the current path that you set earlier on the B drive to give you a list of files in that subdirectory (Figure A.18).

Now you will copy any .FRM files into the FRM subdirectory. Reset the path for DOS. At the B> prompt:

Type cd\wp\frm

*Figure A.18* *After you copy the .TXT files into the \wp\txt subdirectory, the DIR listing might look like this.*

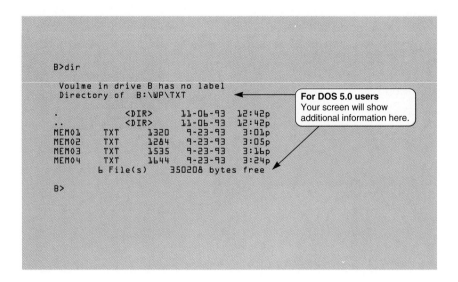

```
B>dir

    Voulme in drive B has no label
    Directory of   B:\WP\TXT

    .              <DIR>       11-06-93   12:42p
    ..             <DIR>       11-06-93   12:42p
    MEM01    TXT      1320      9-23-93    3:01p
    MEM02    TXT      1284      9-23-93    3:05p
    MEM03    TXT      1535      9-23-93    3:16p
    MEM04    TXT      1644      9-23-93    3:24p
          6 File(s)    350208 bytes free

    B>
```

For DOS 5.0 users
Your screen will show
additional information here.

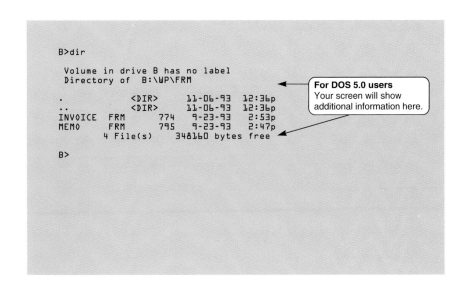

```
B>dir

  Volume in drive B has no label
  Directory of  B:\WP\FRM
  .            <DIR>       11-06-93  12:36p
  ..           <DIR>       11-06-93  12:36p
  INVOICE  FRM       774   9-23-93   2:53p
  MEMO     FRM       795   9-23-93   2:47p
          4 File(s)     348160 bytes free

B>
```

For DOS 5.0 users
Your screen will show
additional information here.

*Figure A.19* The DIR listing for the FRM subdirectory might look like this after files are copied into it.

The path is now changed to the other subdirectory. Now:

Type copy a:*.frm b:\wp\frm

Now check to see that the files were copied.

Type dir

Our screen will look like the one in Figure A.19.

## ▶ Removing Subdirectories

From time to time you will reorganize your disk and need to delete a subdirectory with the DOS command RMDIR (remove directory). There are two steps in deleting subdirectories. First, the subdirectory must be empty of files. Second, you must reposition yourself at the root directory before deleting the empty subdirectory, because DOS can only remove subdirectories *below* the current position. You can practice on the WordPerfect subdirectory called \WP\FRM. First, position yourself in the subdirectory of that name. At the B> prompt:

Type cd\wp\frm

Now you are in the subdirectory you are going to delete. Check the subdirectory, and notice that there are only two files in it, both with the extension .FRM. First, you must delete the files before you can remove the directory.

Type del *.frm

This deletes all files with a .FRM extension. There should be no files left in this directory. Check the subdirectory to make sure it is empty. You are now prepared to remove the subdirectory

**Figure A.20** *One subdirectory has been deleted from the wp subdirectory.*

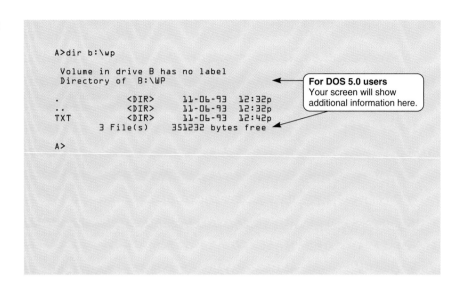

```
A>dir b:\wp

 Volume in drive B has no label
 Directory of  B:\WP

 .            <DIR>     11-06-93  12:32p
 ..           <DIR>     11-06-93  12:32p
 TXT          <DIR>     11-06-93  12:42p
        3 File(s)    351232 bytes free

A>
```

> **For DOS 5.0 users**
> Your screen will show additional information here.

\WP\FRM. Reposition yourself at the root directory. At the B prompt:

Type cd\

You are now in the root directory of the disk in drive B. Now return to drive A, and put your DOS disk back in the drive, because the RMDIR command can only be called from the DOS disk. At the A> prompt:

Type rmdir b:\wp\frm

You can also use an abbreviated form of this instruction: **rd b:\wp\frm**

Check to make sure the subdirectory is really gone from the \WP directory. At the A> prompt:

Type dir b:\wp

The screen now looks like the one in Figure A.20. There is only one subdirectory left.

This completes Lesson 3. When you are ready to turn the computer off, remove your disks, then turn the power switch for the CPU, and the monitor, to the OFF position.

## ▶ Practice

1. On your practice disk, copy files to the \wp\txt directory and then delete them. Then delete the \wp\txt subdirectory itself.
2. Move back to the root directory on your practice disk.
3. Create a new directory for dBASE IV data files. Call the directory \db4.

## ▶ Key Terms

| | | |
|---|---|---|
| Backslash (\), *p. 581* | File-name extension, *p. 554* | Subdirectory, *p. 580* |
| Backup, *p. 576* | File-naming conventions, *p. 554* | Syntax, *p. 556* |
| Boot up, *p. 555* | Format, *p. 561* | Toggle, *p. 570* |
| Current drive, *p. 568* | Initialize, *p. 561* | Tree hierarchy, *p. 583* |
| Default drive, *p. 568* | Logged drive, *p. 568* | Wildcard characters, *p. 571* |
| Disk directory, *p. 567* | Path, *p. 583* | |
| Echo printing, *p. 570* | Root directory, *p. 580* | |

## ▶ Review Questions

1. Why is it important to know whether a DOS command is included in the COMMAND.COM file or in a separate file?
2. Why is it sometimes desirable to have the COMMAND.COM file on a disk other than the DOS disk?
3. What happens if you copy a file to another disk when there is already a file with that name there?
4. What danger can you encounter in using wildcard characters to delete groups of files?
5. What is the function of the backslash (\)?
6. What is the relationship of subdirectories to directories?

# CAREER AND INFORMATION RESOURCES

## COMPUTING CAREERS

### ▶ Entry Level

Most college graduates who have majored in the computing field begin their careers as programmers or software developers. Some start out as liaisons to user groups and help them build information systems and customize programs or packages.

As a matter of policy, many organizations start off entry-level computer professionals as maintenance programmers, people who are responsible for maintaining existing software and modifying it when the need arises. The role of a maintenance programmer is to modify existing programs so that they are more up-to-date and efficient. Maintenance programming familiarizes novices with the types of programs typically coded at the organization and it also makes programmers better appreciate the value of well-documented, highly structured software. The hope is that the experience gained in maintenance programming will help employees be more effective application programmers, programmer analysts, or systems programmers. A common complaint of maintenance programmers, however, is that the work tends to be tedious, unless one has a keen interest in troubleshooting.

Application programmers write, debug, and document programs for specific business tasks and information systems. They generally have a long-range goal to become systems analysts or managers (programming, systems operations, or network managers).

In addition to maintenance and application programmers, many organizations employ programmer analysts and systems programmers. Programmer analysts help develop information systems like systems analysts do: they work with users to define and solve problems. They also follow through by doing the programming themselves or determining what software package to acquire and then customizing it.

Systems programmers develop operating system components designed to maximize the overall processing efficiency of the computer system. They may also develop utilities or interfaces to help users interact with computers.

## REQUIREMENTS FOR ENTRY-LEVEL PROGRAMMING POSITIONS

Entry-level programming jobs usually require a college degree, some knowledge of, and experience in, programming, and the right set of personal qualities.

**College Degree.**  Depending on the company, its requirements, and the salary offered, the degree needed might be one of the following:

- A four-year degree—bachelor of science (BS) or bachelor of arts (BA) in computer science or bachelor of business administration (BBA) in information processing.
- Associate's degree (AAS or AS) in computer science or business data processing.
- Masters in business administration (MBA) with an emphasis on management information systems, or a computer-related master's degree.

In general, people with more education can expect higher-paying and more responsible programming positions. Most organizations view a student's grade point average, particularly in computing courses, as a major factor in evaluating job applicants. An MBA or master's degree in computer science generally paves the way for a position higher than entry-level programmer.

**Programming Knowledge and Experience.**  This is the Catch-22 for many graduates. Some organizations require entry-level programmers to have some business or programming experience, but they can't get experience without a job, and they can't get a job without experience. If most organizations in a particular location require previous work experience in computing, it becomes difficult to break into the field.

The situation is, however, rarely insurmountable. Many students can earn extra money and gain experience by working (1) in their college's computing center, (2) in local firms as interns, or (3) for their instructors who have consulting jobs.

**Personal Attributes.**  The personal characteristics that employers seek vary widely, but a logical mind and a demonstrated interest in problem solving are usually standard requirements. Because many organizations believe that communication barriers between users and computer professionals account for a large number of failures, they are intent on hiring individuals who are sensitive, good listeners, and able to communicate both orally and in writing. Courses in business writing and public speaking could be useful for providing these communication skills, and in fact, many schools require them for computer majors.

Companies generally rely on an interview to determine whether a prospective candidate has the personal attributes needed. Sometimes a battery of aptitude and achievement tests is administered as well.

Jobs are available in a wide variety of organizations, both large and small. In larger organizations, there is apt to be a standard training procedure and a more specific job definition for each position. In smaller organizations, there probably will be more flexibility but less technical supervision. Before accepting a position, think about the environment in which you will be working and try to decide if it really suits your personality, skills, and interests.

IN A

**TYPICAL REQUIREMENTS FOR ENTRY-LEVEL PROGRAMMERS**
- College degree
- Programming knowledge and experience
- Personal attributes: logical mind, interest in problem solving, good communication skills

## THE EMPLOYMENT OUTLOOK

The need for computer professionals has always been great: the demand typically exceeds the supply in almost all areas of the United States and on virtually all levels. The expectation is that this trend will continue through the 1990s. In fact, the estimates are that 60% of new jobs in the United States in the 1990s will be computer related.

The federal Bureau of Labor Statistics announced that the number of computer professionals employed in 1990 was twice as great as it was in 1980. During the same period, overall employment growth increased only 20%.

The reasons for the increased need for computer professionals are as follows:

- The use of computers has been expanding greatly in many organizations.
- More and more small businesses purchase computers but do not have the expertise to use them; they need to hire or contract with computer professionals.
- With increasing frequency, user departments are hiring computer professionals to computerize decentralized operations and to serve as a liaison with a centralized computer department. (In the past, the need

for computer professionals was limited almost entirely to computer departments.)

The need for qualified professionals is sometimes so great that in good economic times, companies offer new employees not only high salaries but perks such as (1) microcomputers or laptops for personal use, (2) flexible hours and the use of terminals for communicating with the office from home, (3) a greater than usual allowance for vacation time, and (4) stock options.

## ▶ Career Paths for Experienced Computer Professionals

After working as a programmer or software developer, or in some other entry-level position, for a year or two, some people are ready to advance. The path for advancement in the computing field is not really standardized; that is, there are various positions to which you can be promoted after you have had some programming experience (Figure B.1). Some people bypass the entry-level stage altogether by completing a computer-related master's degree or master's in business administration. The following career paths are open to an experienced programmer or a computer professional with an advanced degree. Keep in mind that experience is the key to advancement in computing.

### THE LATERAL MOVE

Many programmers seek greener pastures at other organizations after they have gained experience. Most programmers with experience find that they are in demand and can obtain higher-paying jobs in prime locations with good benefits. Many choose a career path in which they change jobs every few years to earn higher salaries and to broaden their knowledge of computer systems and business application areas.

### THE TECHNICAL PATH

Programmers—particularly those with a computer science orientation—sometimes seek opportunities to expand their technical skills. After gaining some experience, they become interested in positions in the more advanced areas of software engineering, compiler design, operating system design, computer graphics, data communications and networking, systems programming, and so on. These jobs tend to be filled by highly skilled, experienced programming professionals.

### THE MANAGEMENT PATH

Many programmers view the computer primarily as a tool to facilitate management decision making. This tends to be particularly true of people with business-related BBA or MBA degrees or those with extensive

## LOOKING AHEAD

**JOBS, JOBS, JOBS**

1. Six out of 10 new jobs in the United States will be computer related.
2. Demand for programmers is likely to increase at an average annual rate of 20%.
3. Computer professionals will begin their training at an earlier age and will, as a consequence, thus enter the job market with substantial expertise.
4. By the end of the century, job satisfaction will become increasingly important to computer professionals as a major criterion for accepting a position.
5. Managers and executives will need to take a more active role in determining how they can best retain computer professionals.

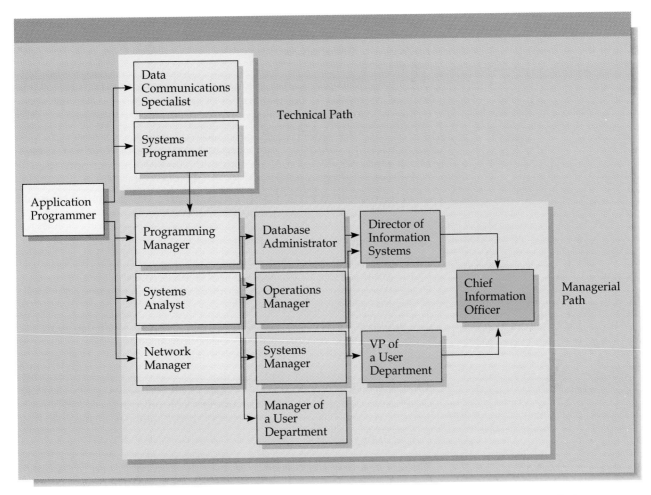

business experience. For these professionals, promotion to management is a primary goal. Numerous management positions are available for skilled computer professionals with good communication skills.

*Figure B.1 Career paths for programmers include both technical and managerial jobs.*

**Programming Manager.**  The first step in management for many computer professionals is to supervise other programmers as a programming manager.

**Systems Analyst and Systems Manager.**  In many organizations, a systems analyst supervises the work of programmers and works closely with top management to determine the organization's overall information processing needs. Even though technical responsibilities are part of the job, the position of systems analyst is considered a management-level job. In general, the more business experience systems analysts have, the more attuned they will be to the needs of specific departments and to the company as a whole. This is the most common second-level job for an experienced programmer.

After serving as a systems analyst, the computer professional could advance to systems manager. A systems manager oversees the activities of all systems analysts in an organization. A person with systems experience and good management and communication skills is likely to be promoted to a systems manager.

**Operations Manager.**   After some experience, a computer professional may be promoted to the position of operations manager. An operations manager supervises all computer and data entry operations. The job includes general operating responsibilities in which the manager directly supervises the data entry operators and computer operators. The operations manager has overall responsibility for the efficient and effective use of the computer equipment; he or she also makes recommendations for new acquisitions. The security and integrity of the computer system are the operations manager's responsibility as well.

**Database Administrator.**   A database administrator is responsible for organizing, designing, and maintaining the database and all other data used by the organization. Control of the use, security, and integrity of the database is the responsibility of this professional. Programmers who report to a database administrator may be responsible for creating, modifying, and updating databases. Typically, a programmer or analyst with several years of database experience and good communication skills may be promoted to the position of database administrator.

**Network Manager.**   A network manager is the individual responsible for organizing, designing, and maintaining a computer network. He or she controls the use, security, and integrity of the network. Data communications specialists typically report to the network manager.

**Manager of a User Department.**   As user departments in an organization become more computerized, the need for computer expertise within the departments themselves increases. A primary source of failure in computerizing information systems is poor communication between users and computer professionals. A computer professional within the user area may help to bridge this communication gap. As a result, increasing numbers of organizations are hiring programmers and analysts to serve as technical liaisons with user departments. On occasion, such people may eventually become managers of the user departments.

**Director of Information Systems.**   The director of information systems is usually the highest-level position within the computing group. It is often a vice presidential position, but this varies widely depending on the organization. The director of information systems, sometimes called vice president of MIS, has overall responsibility for all computer operations and for the entire staff of programmers, analysts, and other computer professionals and managers. The director of information systems usually has considerable experience at all levels of computing and demonstrated management and technical skills.

**Chief Information Officer (CIO).**   In some corporations, the combined function of acquisition, use, and control of hardware and software throughout the organization requires its own management, separate from and on a higher level than that of the information processing department. CIOs are responsible for coordinating the corporate computing systems and monitoring the acquisition of hardware and software by the company's different areas. Their goal is to ensure that the diverse computing resources of the company are integrated into an efficient and secure system. A CIO is responsible for planning for the future hardware and software needs of a company, controlling the use of current hardware and software, training users, and educating the staff in how computers can be used most effectively. Currently, half of the Fortune 500 companies have a CIO. It is likely that this trend toward an information resource executive who has responsibilities different from the director of information systems will continue.

## CREATING A BUSINESS OR CONSULTING

Many experienced programmers are eager to form their own consulting organizations. Some begin by doing freelance programming and systems work, troubleshooting for clients, or developing packages that they then sell or lease to customers. The advantage of establishing your own company or consulting practice is that you are working for yourself. In addition, you have the potential to earn an excellent income. The disadvantages are the obvious ones of greater risk and instability.

# ► Average Salaries of Computer Professionals

Salaries vary widely among organizations and depend generally on the following factors.

- Type of organization.
- Specific responsibilities.
- Geographic location.
- Number of years of experience.

Sometimes a company offers special benefits in place of high salaries. As noted, benefits used to attract employees include grants of micros, travel opportunities, long vacation periods, and so on. Figure B.2 illustrates average salaries for computing professionals.

# ► Getting a Job

## WHERE TO LOOK

Most schools have placement offices for matching the needs of local businesses with their graduates. This is a good place to begin the search for a position, because most organizations that have contacted the placement

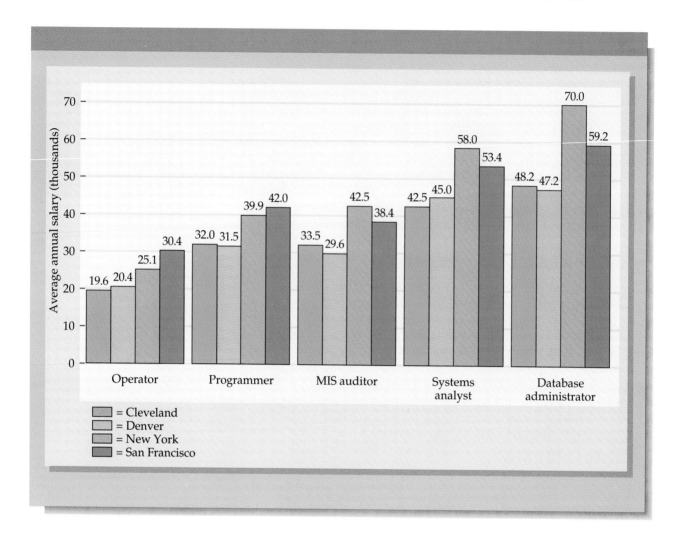

*Figure B.2 Sample average salaries for computer professionals. Source: Source EDP.*

office are familiar with the degree requirements and course offerings at the school. Moreover, scheduled on-campus interviews can make your search easier.

A wide variety of books are published listing companies that hire entry-level people directly from school. Your placement office or library should have some of these publications. Many graduates obtain job offers by simply mailing resumes to the organizations listed in the publications.

Although newspaper ads focus on positions for experienced personnel, sometimes there are ads for entry-level people as well.

Another option is to register with a placement agency. There are both benefits and disadvantages associated with that. Successful placement usually depends on the quality of the agency. Reputation is one way of determining the quality of an agency. Ask others who have used the agency about their experiences or ask the agency for the names of some of their clients and contact them. In most instances, the hiring company pays the agency's fee, so there is usually no financial obligation on the part of the applicant. The agency should be able to (1) pinpoint your strengths and weaknesses, (2) make recommendations for improving your image, (3) set up interviews in which the potential employer is looking for someone with your qualifications, and (4) provide you with background information on the potential employer.

## THE RESUME

The resume is the document that formally describes your credentials to a company. There is no standard way to prepare a resume, but guidelines do exist. The resume should be typed (use a word processing package!) and segmented into specific sections such as the following.

- Identifying information: Centered at the top of the resume should be your name, address, and telephone number.
- Career objectives: Indicate the type of position you are currently seeking. You may also include your long-range career objectives.
- Personal background: Include items that will describe you to a potential employer. The following are typically included, but they can be omitted if you so desire: birth date, citizenship, marital status, number of children (and ages), health, and special interests or talents.
- Educational background: Include all education after high school, degrees, graduation dates, major, grade point average, awards, honors, and relevant extracurricular activities. In addition, it is advisable to include a list of computer courses you have taken, programming languages you have learned, and computers with which you have had experience.
- Relevant work experience: Work experience should be listed chronologically, beginning with your most current position. Indicate dates, job titles, and responsibilities. Emphasize hands-on experiences, where appropriate. Include major projects you have completed as a student.
- Other work experience: Include, chronologically, noncomputer-related jobs you have held; indicate dates, job titles, and responsibilities.
- Certification and membership: If you hold a **Certificate of Data Processing (CDP)** or you are a **Certified Computer Professional (CCP),** this should be clearly indicated. Membership in professional organizations should also be included because that demonstrates a commitment to computing. We will discuss issues relevant to certification and membership later in this appendix.
- References (supply on request): It is useful to include a list of people who can attest to your expertise in the computing field. These may include professors, employers, and supervisors.

Keep in mind that before potential employers make a job offer, they typically check references. This means either requesting letters of recommendation or actually telephoning one or more references and asking pertinent questions. Thus, you should ask permission before including an individual as a reference.

As a general rule, do not include any information pertaining to salary requirements. This is best left to the interview.

Since there is no universally accepted standard format for resumes, you may choose to make some alterations to highlight significant facts about yourself. See Figure B.3 for a sample resume.

If you are mailing your resume to potential employers, include a cover letter indicating that your resume is enclosed, explaining how you heard about the job opening, and stating the position for which you are applying. Your cover letter may also include the best time to reach you by telephone. See Figure B.4 for a sample cover letter.

## THE INTERVIEW

If a company believes there is a possible match between your qualifications and its needs, you will be contacted for an interview. The interview is of great significance in determining whether an applicant will fit in well in the organization and determining whether the position available is of serious interest to the applicant.

Thus, an interview has a dual purpose. It is not simply a technique that potential employers use to make their decision. It is a technique that *you* should use to determine if the available job is one that you are likely to find challenging and interesting.

**Preparing for the Interview.**   Learn as much as you can about the company, its products, its financial position, its potential for growth, and so forth, before the interview. The information can be learned from a variety of sources, for example, the company's annual report.

Dress appropriately. When in doubt, a conservative suit is appropriate. Makeup should be minimal. Being punctual for the interview is, of course, essential.

**Communicating with the Interviewer.**   Answer all questions honestly and succinctly. Be prepared for the following types of questions.

- "What are your career objectives and goals?"
  Be specific. Include both your immediate and long-range career objectives and goals.
- "Why are you changing jobs?" (if you are currently employed)
  Indicate the reasons relevant to your career objectives. To indicate that money is the primary reason for changing jobs would probably not make an appropriate impression. Do not dwell on personality conflicts that may exist at your present job.
- "Tell me about yourself."
  Don't be tempted to ramble. Focus on your career self.
- "What do you know about the company?"
  The more you know, the more impressed the interviewer will be.
- "Do you have any other offers?"
  Indicate that you are looking, but it is probably wise to be vague about your options.
- "Would you be willing to relocate?"

Nancy Stern
4 Main Street
Anywhere, USA 48732

| PERSONAL | Social Security No. | Birthdate | Married | | Citizen | | Number of Dependents | Maximum Percent Travel Desired | Health |
|---|---|---|---|---|---|---|---|---|---|
| | | | Yes | No | Yes | No | | | |
| | 355-24-2121 | 12/29/51 | X | | | X | 3 (ages 4, 8, 10) | 10 | Excellent |

POSITION DESIRED
  Systems Analyst

TECHNICAL BACKGROUND
  Programmer analyst for 3 years with large banking firm

PROGRAMMING LANGUAGES
  COBOL on IBM 4341

REFERENCES

| | Name | Company | Position | Telephone |
|---|---|---|---|---|
| 1. | John Marley | University of Louisville | Professor | (502) 893-3304 |
| 2. | Don Wood | Touche Ross, Inc. | Partner | (312) 589-6200 |
| 3. | John Sterling | U. S. Senator (Ohio) | | (513) 812-5069 |

EDUCATION

| | Educational Institution | Field of Study | Degree | No. of Years | Year Degree Received | G.P.A. |
|---|---|---|---|---|---|---|
| 1. | University of Illinois | Computer Science | BS | 4 | 1982 | 3.4 |
| 2. | Northwestern University | Finance | MBA | 2 | 1984 | 3.2 |

EXTRACURRICULAR ACTIVITIES
  Computer Club, Yearbook Committee

LICENSES,
CERTIFICATION,
MEMBERSHIPS     1. CPA Illinois     2. Phi Beta Kappa     3. Member, ACM

OTHER
INTERESTS   1. Republican Party State Chairman   2. Chamber of Commerce   3. Oriental languages
            4. Karate tournament

LOCATION PREFERENCE     Northeast

*Figure B.3* Sample resume.

Home Address
Date

Address of
organization

To Whom It May Concern:

    Enclosed you will find a copy of my resume which I am submitting in response to your advertisement which appeared in _____ on _____. Please note that I am applying for the position of _____.

    I can be reached at the above address or by phone at_____ during business hours and _____ in the evening.

    References and other material will be supplied to you on request.

    I look forward to hearing from you.

Sincerely yours,

**Figure B.4** *Sample cover letter for a resume.*

Answer this question honestly. Otherwise you might be wasting your time as well as the interviewer's time.

In general, remember that the primary purpose of the interview, from the company's perspective, is to determine the personal attributes of the applicant. The following are typical attributes sought by interviewers: intelligence, motivation, honesty, respect for others, enthusiasm, and potential for remaining with the company. The checklist that follows provides additional guidelines that should prove helpful in preparing for the interview.

1. Speak clearly and crisply. Avoid the use of slang.
2. Bring your resume and use it where appropriate to point to items pertinent to the discussion.
3. Pay attention to the interviewer—listening is as important as talking.
4. Ask about whether you will need to travel.
5. Avoid criticizing your current boss, company, salary, and so on.
6. Avoid exaggerations or bragging.
7. Ask about whether you will need to work extra hours often or on a regular basis.
8. If you really want the job, indicate your interest.
9. Be aware of your strengths and weaknesses. If you had poor grades or did not do well in a previous position, be prepared to discuss the reasons.
10. Be prepared to discuss your career objectives.

**Using the Interview to Help You Decide About the Job.** The interviewer may be a company executive, computer manager or supervisor, or personnel officer. If the interviewer is a personnel officer, he or she will generally not be able to assess your professional skills; on the other hand, he or she will need to determine whether your personal attributes fit the "company image." If the interviewer is a computer manager, he or she will generally be more interested in your professional expertise. If the interviewer is a company executive, he or she will probably be more interested in how effective you are apt to be in improving the overall decision-making process at the company.

It is perfectly acceptable, indeed encouraged, that you ask questions about these aspects of the job.

- The company: Even if you learned something about the company before the interview, ask for an insider's view.
- Specific job responsibilities: Do not assume that a title says it all. Frequently, for example, the title "systems analyst" really means a job involving programming. Be sure you understand exactly what functions you will be performing and what your specific responsibilities will be. Determine what sort of training you will receive, how closely you will be supervised, and what decision-making responsibilities you might have.
- Potential for promotion: Express an interest in advancement. You

might ask, for example, if one excels in one's job, how long a period must one typically wait for a promotion?

- Fringe benefits: In addition to the standard medical, pension, and life insurance benefits, determine whether the company will pay your tuition for an advanced degree, whether you can take information processing seminars, whether you will receive bonuses, and so on.
- Salary: There is no *specific* rule about salary negotiations. Most companies do, however, have a standard salary for entry-level positions. Hence, when applying for your first job, it is probably best to wait until the interviewer discusses money. For higher-level positions, it is probably best to indicate your salary requirements during an interview because this might be a negotiable item. Although you may regard salary as a critical factor, try to view it as only one aspect, albeit a major one, of an overall package. To accept a position solely on the basis of the highest offer may be a mistake. Job satisfaction and promotion potential are viewed by many professionals as more important than salary.

## ▶ SELF-TEST

1. Why do many companies hire entry-level programmers as maintenance programmers initially?
2. (T or F) A programmer with several years of experience could be promoted to systems analyst.
3. An application programmer who wants to learn more about computer architecture might seek a position as a _____.
4. (T or F) In an interview, always let the interviewer ask all the questions.
5. (T or F) Salary is always the major factor in determining what job is best.

Solutions
1. Maintenance programmers learn about company practices and experience firsthand and about the value of well-documented structured programs.
2. T
3. systems programmer
4. F—If you ask questions, you will get a better idea if the job is one you will like.
5. F

## KEEPING UP WITH THE PROFESSION

Successful computer professionals, no matter what area of the profession they are in, must be informed about the latest technological and industry developments so they can provide the best possible solutions for business problems. Professionals keep abreast by joining computer societies, reading the major journals, and attending conferences. We look at each of these here in more detail.

# ▶ Major Computing Societies

Many computer professionals belong to societies that provide their members with journals and general information about the field. These societies also sponsor key activities in the computing field. We will briefly consider three of the most common societies, all of which offer student memberships. Both students and active professionals find computer societies an excellent vehicle for learning about advances in the field and for communicating with other professionals.

## ASSOCIATION FOR COMPUTING MACHINERY

Founded in 1947, the **Association for Computing Machinery (ACM,** 11 West 42 St., New York, NY 10036) is the oldest and largest computing society. It has more than 75,000 members, publishes over a dozen major periodicals, and has numerous special interest groups in various computing subjects. Figure B.5 is an ACM application for membership that you can copy and fill out.

## DATA PROCESSING MANAGEMENT ASSOCIATION

With over 35,000 members in the United States, Canada, and abroad, the **Data Processing Management Association (DPMA,** 505 Busse Highway, Park Ridge, IL 60068) is the largest professional association for computer management. The purpose of the DPMA is to focus on education and research activities designed for self-improvement of its members.

## THE COMPUTER SOCIETY OF THE INSTITUTE OF ELECTRICAL AND ELECTRONICS ENGINEERS

The **Institute of Electrical and Electronics Engineers (IEEE)** has many societies in addition to the Computer Society (P.O. Box 639, Silver Spring, MD 20901). The aim of the Computer Society is to advance the theory and practice of computer and information processing technology.

# ▶ Journals

One important way to keep abreast of developments in the field is to read professional journals. Because the computer field is so diverse, there are literally hundreds of computer journals. In addition, major business publications like *Forbes, Fortune, Business Week,* and *The Wall Street Journal* always include articles, even feature stories, on computing. Even more general publications like *Time, U.S. News and World Report,* and *The New York Times* run major stories on computing.

If you are a member of one of the three major computer societies, journals and reports will be sent to you.

The list on the top of page 606 comprises what we consider the five major journals in computing.

# MEMBERSHIP  APPLICATION

*ADVANCING HUMAN CAPABILITIES* **acm** *THROUGH INFORMATION TECHNOLOGY*

**Mail to:**

**ACM, P.O. Box 12114**
**Church Street Station**
**New York, NY 10257**

You may use this ACM Membership Application to: 1) Join ACM and take advantage of the special Publication and SIG rates for ACM members; 2) Join the Special Interest Group(s) of your choice at the SIG Member (non-ACM member) rates on the reverse side; individuals joining SIGs using these rates are not entitled to ACM membership privileges.

*Please print*

_____
First, Middle Initial, Last Name

_____
Address

_____
Address

_____
City / State /Zip or City / Country / Postal Code

( )_____ For Office Use Only_____
Day Telephone Number

## ACM Membership

ACM Membership includes a subscription to the monthly *Communications of the ACM.* Check the membership class desired.

☐ **$77.00 Voting Member Applicants**
You must subscribe to the Purposes of ACM; have attained professional stature as demonstrated by intellectual competence and ethical conduct in the arts and sciences of information processing; and must satisfy at least one of the requirements at the right.

1. Bachelor's Degree. Institution:_____

2. Equivalent level of education. Institution:_____

3. Four full-time years of experience (attach a brief statement).

I attest the above is correct_____
*Signature*

☐ **$77.00 Associate Member Applicants**
You must subscribe to the purposes of ACM. Associate Members may convert to Voting Member status at any time by writing ACM Headquarters for a "Self-Certification" form.

☐ **$23.00 Student Member Applicants**
You must be registered in an accredited educational institution and a Faculty Member must certify your full-time status.

Institution:_____

Faculty Member's Signature_____

Expected Graduation Date:_____/_____
MM YY

## ACM Member Services Dept.

Phone: (212) 626-0500
Fax: (212) 944-1318
E-mail:
ACMHELP@ACMVM.BITNET

☐ **$72.00 Joint Membership—IEEE-CS**
Members of the IEEE-CS receive a $5 dues discount.
(not Affiliates with "N9" member #'s).

Society:_____

Member #:_____

☐ **$62.00 Joint Membership—International Computing Societies**
ACS (Australia), ADIG (Guatemala), AFCET (France), AICA (Italy), API (Portugal), ATI (Spain), BCS (United Kingdom), BIRA/IBRA (Belgium), CIPS (Canada), CSIS (Czechoslovakia), CSZ (Zimbabwe), DD (Denmark), GI (Germany), HKCS (Hong Kong), ICS (Ireland), IPA (Israel), IPSJ (Japan), NGI (Netherlands), NZCS (New Zealand), SCCC (Chile), SCS (Shanghai), SCS (Singapore).

☐ **Spouse Membership:** For more information, please write to ACM Membership Services Department, 1515 Broadway, New York, NY 10036

## SIG Membership

Non-ACM Members Only

☐ **SIG Membership only. (Non-ACM Members only.)**
Membership in special interest group(s) of your choice includes a newsletter subscription. SIG non-ACM members are not eligible for ACM SIG member rates or ACM membership privileges. *See "SIG Member (non-ACM) Rates" on reverse.*

## Mailing List

Optional

ACM occasionally makes its membership list available to companies and societies for computer-related mailings. If you wish to restrict the use of your name for these purposes, please check one of the following:

☐ ACM announcements only.

☐ ACM and sister society announcements only.

**For Office Use:**
**Recruit/Promotion Code**

## Purposes of ACM

*Signature Required*

**Note:** Membership dues include $32.00 ($23.00 for students) toward a subscription to *Communications of the ACM.*

To advance the sciences and arts of information processing; to promote the free interchange of information about the sciences and arts of information processing both among specialists and among the public; and to develop and maintain the integrity and competence of individuals engaged in the practice of information processing.

I hereby affirm that I subscribe to the purposes of ACM and understand that my membership is not transferable.

_____
*Signature*                      *Date*

Effective 7/92

### (OVER)

**Figure B.5** *Membership application for the Association for Computing Machinery (ACM).*

## Publications

**Air Options:** Available to overseas members. Circle desired rate(s) and add to publication subscription and/or SIG membership rate(s).

**Partial Air Services** - Air freight to Amsterdam and Dutch surface mail. Available only to Europe, India, Africa, and Mideast.

**Full Air Service** - Air service from U.S. Available to all overseas locations including Hawaii.

*Circle appropriate rate(s) and indicate subtotal. Membership includes a subscription to ACM's flagship publication Communications of the ACM. If air service is desired for member copy of CACM, circle appropriate Air Option.*

*Add Appropriate Overseas Air Option(s) to Voting/Associate or Student Rate(s)*

| | Code # | Voting/ Associate | Student | Partial | Full Air | Total |
|---|---|---|---|---|---|---|
| **Communications of the ACM** (monthly) addt'l subscriptions only | 101 | $26.00 | $21.00 | + $30.00 | $60.00 | = $_____ |
| Membership includes a subscription to *CACM* | | | | | | |
| **Journal of the ACM** (quarterly) | 102 | 23.00 | 18.00 | + 20.00 | 25.00 | = $_____ |
| **Computing Surveys** (quarterly) | 103 | 16.00 | 11.00 | + 15.00 | 30.00 | = $_____ |
| **Computing Reviews** (monthly) | 104 | 35.00 | 30.00 | + 20.00 | 30.00 | = $_____ |
| **Collected Algorithms,** Vols I, II, III, IV, V & 1 yr's quarterly updating supplements | 105 | 220.00 | 195.00 | + 10.00 | 20.00 | = $_____ |
| **ACM Guide to Computing Literature** (annual) You will receive the current published edition. | 160 | 98.00 | 93.00 | + 30.00 | 40.00 | = $_____ |
| **ACM No-Nonsense Guide to Computing Careers** | 120 | 20.00 | 16.00 | + 6.00 | 8.00 | = $_____ |
| Transactions on: (all quarterlies) | | | | | | |
| **Mathematical Software** /TOMS | 108 | 27.00 | 22.00 | + 10.00 | 20.00 | = $_____ |
| **Database Systems** /TODS | 109 | 26.00 | 21.00 | + 10.00 | 20.00 | = $_____ |
| **Programming Languages and Systems** /TOPLAS | 110 | 25.00 | 20.00 | + 10.00 | 20.00 | = $_____ |
| **Graphics** /TOG | 112 | 31.00 | 26.00 | + 10.00 | 20.00 | = $_____ |
| **Information Systems** /TOIS | 113 | 27.00 | 22.00 | + 10.00 | 20.00 | = $_____ |
| **Computer Systems** /TOCS | 114 | 27.00 | 22.00 | + 10.00 | 20.00 | = $_____ |
| **Software Engineering & Methodology** /TOSEM | 115 | 23.00 | 18.00 | + 10.00 | 20.00 | = $_____ |
| **Modeling & Computer Simulation** /TOMACS | 116 | 31.00 | 26.00 | + 10.00 | 20.00 | = $_____ |
| **Letters on Programming Languages and Systems** / LOPLAS | 117 | 26.00 | 21.00 | + 10.00 | 20.00 | = $_____ |
| **IEEE/ACM Networking** /TON (bi-monthly) | 118 | 22.00 | 17.00 | none | * | = $_____ |

*Contact Member Services for rates.

**PUBLICATION SUBTOTAL $_____**

## Special Interest Groups (SIGs)

**Note:** SIG members who are not ACM members do not receive a subscription to *Communications of the ACM*.

**Definitions:**
**Air Options:** Available to overseas members. Circle desired rate(s) and add to publication subscription and/or SIG membership rate(s).

**Partial Air Service** - Air freight to Amsterdam and Dutch surface mail. Available only to Europe, India, Africa, and Mideast.

**Full Air Service** - Air service from U.S. Available to all overseas locations including Hawaii.

*Circle appropriate rate(s) and indicate subtotal. SIG Membership includes a Newsletter subscription.*

*Add Appropriate Overseas Air Option(s) to Voting/ Associate, Student or SIG Member Rate(s)*

| | Code # | ACM Members Voting/ Associate | Student | SIG Mbrs Non-ACM Mbr. Rates | Partial | Full Air | Total |
|---|---|---|---|---|---|---|---|
| **SIGACT** (Algorithms and Computation Theory) | 001 | $15.00 | $7.50 | $40.00 | + $ 8.00 | $29.00 | = $ _____ |
| **SIGADA** (Ada) | 037 | 20.00 | 10.00 | 42.00 | + 22.00 | 70.00 | = $ _____ |
| **SIGAPL** (APL) | 032 | 20.00 | 15.00 | 50.00 | + 9.00 | 31.00 | = $ _____ |
| **SIGAPP** (Applied Computing) | 042 | 15.00 | 7.50 | 39.00 | + 3.00 | 8.00 | = $ _____ |
| **SIGARCH** (Computer Architecture) | 002 | 28.00 | 14.00 | 54.00 | + 22.00 | 65.00 | = $ _____ |
| **SIGART** (Artificial Intelligence) | 003 | 15.00 | 8.00 | 41.00 | + 11.00 | 26.00 | = $ _____ |
| **SIGBIO** (Biomedical Computing) | 005 | 20.00 | 7.00 | 30.00 | + 6.00 | 16.00 | = $ _____ |
| **SIGBIT** (Business Information Technology) | 004 | 18.00 | 12.00 | 38.00 | + 6.00 | 11.00 | = $ _____ |
| **SIGCAPH** (Computers and the Physically Handicapped-Print Edition) | 006 | 15.00 | 6.00 | 42.00 | + 6.00 | 9.00 | = $ _____ |
| **SIGCAS** (Computers and Society) | 007 | 18.00 | 9.00 | 51.00 | + 7.00 | 10.00 | = $ _____ |
| **SIGCHI** (Computer and Human Interaction) | 026 | 30.00 | 10.00 | 52.00 | + 16.00 | 50.00 | = $ _____ |
| **SIGCOMM** (Data Communication) | 008 | 22.00 | 15.00 | 50.00 | + 10.00 | 40.00 | = $ _____ |
| **SIGCPR** (Computer Personnel Research) | 010 | 18.00 | 7.00 | 20.00 | + 7.00 | 20.00 | = $ _____ |
| **SIGCSE** (Computer Science Education) | 011 | 16.50 | 7.50 | 43.00 | + 12.00 | 44.00 | = $ _____ |
| **SIGCUE** (Computer Uses in Education) | 012 | 19.00 | 10.00 | 55.00 | + 10.00 | 20.00 | = $ _____ |
| **SIGDA** (Design Automation) | 013 | 15.00 | 15.00 | 27.00 | + 7.00 | 15.00 | = $ _____ |
| **SIGDOC** (Documentation) | 033 | 18.00 | 10.00 | 44.00 | + 7.00 | 11.00 | = $ _____ |
| **SIGFORTH** (Forth) | 039 | 20.00 | 11.00 | 46.00 | + 5.00 | 13.00 | = $ _____ |
| **SIGGRAPH** (Computer Graphics) | 015 | 26.00 | 16.00 | 59.00 | + 20.00 | 55.00 | = $ _____ |
| **SIGIR** (Information Retrieval) | 016 | 20.00 | 10.00 | 65.00 | + 6.00 | 37.00 | = $ _____ |
| **SIGLINK** (Hypertext/Hypermedia) | 043 | 22.00 | 12.00 | 56.00 | + 5.00 | 12.00 | = $ _____ |
| **SIGMETRICS** (Measurement & Evaluation) | 019 | 20.00 | 10.00 | 46.00 | + 9.00 | 33.00 | = $ _____ |
| **SIGMICRO** (Microprogramming) | 020 | 21.00 | 8.00 | 38.00 | + 5.00 | 20.00 | = $ _____ |
| **SIGMOD** (Management of Data) | 014 | 20.00 | 12.00 | 23.00 | + 16.00 | 55.00 | = $ _____ |
| **SIGNUM** (Numerical Mathematics) | 021 | 16.00 | 7.50 | 23.00 | + 8.00 | 16.00 | = $ _____ |
| **SIGOIS** (Office Information Systems) | 027 | 18.00 | 10.00 | 40.00 | + 10.00 | 35.00 | = $ _____ |
| **SIGOPS** (Operating Systems) | 022 | 15.00 | 8.00 | 41.00 | + 14.00 | 44.00 | = $ _____ |
| **SIGPLAN** (Programming Languages) | 023 | 25.00 | 10.00 | 52.00 | + 50.00 | 181.00 | = $ _____ |
| **FORTRAN FORUM** (Fortran) Newsletter Only | 038 | 10.00 | 6.00 | 20.00 | + 7.00 | 16.00 | = $ _____ |
| **LISP POINTERS** (LISP) Newsletter Only | 040 | 12.00 | 7.00 | 25.00 | + 6.00 | 16.00 | = $ _____ |
| **OOPS MESSENGER** (Object-Oriented Programming Systems) Newsletter Only | 041 | 10.00 | 6.00 | 20.00 | + 7.00 | 24.00 | = $ _____ |
| **SIGSAC** (Security, Audit & Control) | 036 | 18.00 | 9.00 | 44.00 | + 7.00 | 15.00 | = $ _____ |
| **SIGSAM** (Symbolic & Algebraic Manipulation) | 024 | 17.00 | 6.00 | 25.00 | + 8.00 | 12.00 | = $ _____ |
| **SIGSIM** (Simulation) | 025 | 15.00 | 5.00 | 41.00 | + 9.00 | 17.00 | = $ _____ |
| **SIGSMALL/PC** (Small & Personal Computing Systems & Applications) | 031 | 17.00 | 10.00 | 38.00 | + 8.00 | 17.00 | = $ _____ |
| **SIGSOFT** (Software Engineering) | 034 | 23.00 | 10.00 | 46.00 | + 17.00 | 60.00 | = $ _____ |
| **SIGUCCS** (University & College Computing Services) | 028 | 15.00 | 5.00 | 40.00 | + Free | Free | = $ _____ |

**SIG SUBTOTAL $ _____**

## Payment Information

**Mail this application with your payment to:**
ACM
P.O. Box 12114
Church Street Station
New York, NY 10257

ACM accepts payment by personal check, money order, or credit card. For international residents, payment must be in U.S. dollars drawn on a U.S. bank. Please make checks payable to ACM, Inc.

I wish to pay by: ☐ Check (make payable to ACM, Inc.)  ☐ Credit Card
☐ American Express  ☐ MasterCard  ☐ VISA

Card #: ☐☐☐☐☐☐☐☐☐☐☐☐☐☐☐☐  Card Exp. Date:_____/_____

Signature:_____

| | |
|---|---|
| **ACM Member Dues** (from reverse side) | $ |
| **Publication Subtoal** | $ |
| **SIG Subtotal** | $ |
| **GRAND TOTAL** | $ |

*Computerworld* (more mainframe in orientation)
P.O. Box 9171
375 Cochituate Rd.
Framingham, MA 01701-9171
508-874-0700

*Datamation* (more mainframe in orientation)
8601 Georgia Avenue
Silver Spring, MD 20910
301-650-2000

*InfoWorld* (good mix of mainframes and PCs)
1060 Marsh Rd.
Menlo Park, CA 94025
415-328-4602

*PC Magazine* (PC oriented)
P.O. Box 54093
Boulder, CO 80322-4093
800-289-0429

*PC World* (PC oriented)
P.O. Box 55029
Boulder, CO 80322-5029
800-234-3498

These journals provide current articles on recent advances in computing, editorials, and advertisements from mail-order companies that often have the least expensive prices.

A list of the more popular general computing journals in the field and journals that regularly include articles in computing follows:

*ACM Computing Surveys*
*ACM Transactions on Computer Systems*
*ACM Transactions on Graphics*
*ACM Transactions on Information Systems*
*ACM Transactions on Programming Languages & Systems*
Association for Computing Machinery
11 W. 42nd St.
New York, NY 10036
800-638-6423

*AI Expert*
Miller Freeman Publications
500 Howard St.
San Francisco, CA 94105
415-397-1881

*AT&T Technical Journal*
AT&T Bell Laboratories
101 John F. Kennedy Pkwy.
Short Hills, NJ 07078
201-564-2000

*Business Week*
McGraw-Hill
1221 Avenue of the Americas
New York, NY 10021
212-512-2000

*Byte*
McGraw-Hill
1221 Avenue of the Americas
New York, NY 10021
212-512-2000

*Communications of the ACM*
Association for Computing Machinery
11 W. 42nd St.
New York, NY 10036
800-638-6423

*Computer (IEEE)*
Institute of Electrical and Electronics Engineers
345 E. 47th St.
New York, NY 10017
212-705-7900

*Computer Security Journal*
Computer Security Institute
43 Boston Post Road
Northboro, MA 01532
508-393-2600

*Computer Systems News*
CSN
CMP Publications
600 Community Dr.
Manhasset, NY 11030
516-562-5000

*Computerworld*
CW Communications
P.O. Box 9171
375 Cochituate Rd.
Framingham, MA 01701-9171
508-879-0700

*Data Communications*
McGraw-Hill
1221 Avenue of the Americas
New York, NY 10020
212-512-2000

*Datamation*
Cahners-Ziff Publishing Associates
8601 Georgia Avenue
Silver Spring, MD 20910
301-650-2000

*Dr. Dobb's Journal*
M&T Publishing
501 Galveston Dr.
Redwood City, CA 94063
415-366-3600

*EDGE* (on and about AT&T)
EDGE: Work-Group Computing Report
Edge Publishing
P.O. Box 471
Hackettstown, NJ 07840
201-852-7217

*EDN*
Cahners Publishing Co.
44 Cook St.
Denver, CO 80206
303-388-4511

*Educational Technology*
Educational Technology Publications
720 Palisade Ave.
Englewood Cliff, NJ 07632
201-871-4007

*Forbes*
Forbes
60 Fifth Ave.
New York, NY 10011
212-620-2200

*Fortune Magazine*
The Time Inc. Magazine Co.
Time & Life Bldg.
1271 Ave. of the Americas
New York, NY 10020
212-522-1212

*Government Computer News*
Cahners-Ziff Publishing Associates
8601 Georgia Avenue
Silver Spring, MD 20910
301-650-2000

*IBM Systems Journal*
International Business Machines Corp.
Armonk, NY 10504
914-765-1900

*IEEE Network*
*IEEE Transactions on Computers*
*IEEE Transactions on Robotics and Automation*
*IEEE Transactions on Software Engineering*
Institute of Electrical and Electronics Engineers
345 E. 47th St.
New York, NY 10017
212-705-7900

*Information Week*
CMP Publications
600 Community Dr.
Manhasset, NY 11030
516-562-5000

*InfoWorld*
Popular Computing
1060 Marsh Rd.
Menlo Park, CA 94025
415-328-4602

*InTech*
ISA Services
67 Alexander Dr.
Research Triangle Park, NC 27709
919-549-8411

*Journal of Object-Oriented Programming*
SIGS Publications
310 Madison Ave.
New York, NY 10017
212-972-7055

*Journal of Systems Management*
Association for Systems Management
24587 Bagley Rd.
Cleveland, OH 44138

*Journal of the ACM*
Association for Computing Machinery
11 W. 42nd St.
New York, NY 10036
800-638-6423

*Los Angeles Times*
Times Mirror Corp.
Times Mirror Sq.
Los Angeles, CA 90053
213-237-5000

*Lotus Magazine*
Lotus Publishing Corp.
55 Cambridge Pkwy.
Cambridge, MA 02142
617-225-6808

*MacUser*
Ziff-Davis Publishing Co.
1 Park Ave.
New York, NY 10016
212-503-3500

*MacWEEK*
Coastal Associates Publishers
301 Howard Street
San Francisco, CA 94105
415-882-7370

*Macworld*
PC World Communications
501 Second St.
San Francisco, CA 94107
800-525-0643

*MIS Quarterly*
University of Minnesota MIS Research Center
271 19th Ave. S.
Minneapolis, MN 55455
612-625-5000

*Modern Office Technology*
Penton Publishing
1100 Superior Ave.
Cleveland, OH 44114
216-696-7000

*PC Magazine*
P.O. Box 54093
Boulder, CO 80322-4093
800-289-0429

*PC World*
P.O. Box 55029
Boulder, CO 80322-5029
800-234-3498

*Systems Integration*
Cahners-Ziff Publishing Associates
8601 Georgia Avenue Suite 300
Silver Spring, MD 20910
301-650-2000

*T H E Journal*
*(Technological Horizons in Education Journal)*
Information Synergy
P.O. Box 17239
Irvine, CA 92713
714-261-0366

*UNIX World*
Tech Valley Publishing
444 Castro St.
Mountain View, CA 94041
415-940-1500

*The Wall Street Journal*
Dow Jones & Co.
22 Cortland St.
New York, NY 10007
212-416-2000

## ▶ Conferences

Computing conferences offer technical state-of-the-art sessions along with exhibits at which the newest technologies are displayed. Special-interest, or niche, conferences focus on hot topics widely publicized in the major computing journals. Conferences on topics such as multimedia, artificial intelligence, and object-oriented programming are scheduled frequently.

General, micro-oriented "PC Expos" come to major U.S. cities annually. These conferences display the latest hardware and software and have sessions on the newest technologies.

Every year there are two Comdex conferences, which are gatherings that attract more than 100,000 computer people who come to see the most recent advances in computing. They are usually held in Las Vegas in the fall and Atlanta or Chicago in the spring. For more academically-oriented professionals, fall and spring joint IEEE-ACM conferences focus more on scholarly activities and have fewer exhibits.

## ▶ Electronic Bulletin Boards and Subscriber Services

As we have noted in this text, there are numerous electronic bulletin boards and subscriber services available. Many provide information about recent advances in computing and enable you to download public domain software and shareware as needed. The cost of some services is just the cost of a phone call (sometimes a long distance call). Other services charge by the minute and by the resource being used, or they charge a flat rate. The following are major sources of information.

CompuServe: 800-848-8199
Prodigy: 800-424-8580
Dow Jones Information Services: 609-520-4000

Most professionals seek ways to keep abreast of their field, but people differ in how they best learn about advances. In the beginning experiment with different resources, keep your options open, and then select sources best suited to your needs and method of learning.

## ▶ Companies

The following list describes major companies that manufacture or develop computing products and have annual sales that are among the highest in the industry. (From *Computer Select*, June 1992.)

Company:   ABB Industrial Systems, Inc. (Automation Division)
Address:   16250 W. Glendale Dr.
           New Berlin, WI 53151
           414-785-3200

Company:    Apollo Computer, Inc. (division of Hewlett-Packard Co.)
Address:    300 Apollo Dr.
            Chelmsford, MA 01824
            508-256-6600
            FAX: 508-256-9374
            Tech support: 800-227-6556

Company:    Apple Computer, Inc.
Address:    20525 Mariani Ave.
            Cupertino, CA 95014
            408-996-1010

Company:    AT&T Computer Systems
Address:    1776 On The Green
            Morristown, NJ 07960
            800-247-1212; 908-898-8000
            FAX: 908-644-9768
            Tech support: Use main no.

Company:    Bank of America
Address:    555 California St.
            San Francisco, CA 94104
            415-953-0484

Company:    Boeing Computer Services
Address:    PO Box 24346
            Seattle, WA 98124-0346
            206-865-5000

Company:    Bull HN Information Systems, Inc.
Address:    2 Wall St., Technology Park, M/S 111N
            Billerica, MA 01821-4199
            508-294-6000
            FAX: 508-294-4508
            Tech support: Use main no.

Company:    CADAM, Inc. (subsidiary of IBM)
Address:    1935 N. Buena Vista St.
            Burbank, CA 91504
            800-255-5710; 818-841-9470
            FAX: 818-840-8428
            Tech support: 800-423-2351; 818-840-8587

Company:    COMPAQ Computer Corp.
Address:    PO Box 692000
            Houston, TX 77269-2000
            800-231-0900; 713-370-0670
            FAX: 713-374-1402
            Tech support: 800-345-1518

Company: Control Data Corp. (Business Management Services Division)
Address: 8100 34th Ave., S
Minneapolis, MN 55425
800-PAYROLL; 612-853-4303
FAX: 612-853-6662

Company: The DATA Group Corp. (a NYNEX Co.)
Address: 77 S. Bedford St., Burlington Business Center II
Burlington, MA 01803
617-272-4100, ext. 580
FAX: 617-229-6189

Company: Digital Equipment Corp.
Address: 146 Main St.
Maynard, MA 01754-2571
508-493-5111
FAX: 508-493-8780
Tech support: 800-332-8000

Company: Du Pont Electronics (Electro-Optic Products Group)
Address: 3300 Gateway Center Blvd.
Morrisville, NC 27560
800-888-5261; 919-481-5100
FAX: 919-481-0753

Company: Eastman Kodak Co. (Copy Products Division)
Address: 343 State St.
Rochester, NY 14650
800-242-2424; 716-724-4000
FAX: 716-724-0663
Tech support: Use main no.

Company: EDICON Systems (division of Eastman Technology, Inc.)
Address: 95 Allens Creek Rd.
Rochester, NY 14618
716-271-2950
FAX: 716-244-0192

Company: Ektron Applied Imaging, Inc. (subsidiary of Eastman Kodak Co.)
Address: 23 Crosby Dr.
Bedford, MA 01730
800-242-2424; 617-275-0475
FAX: 617-271-1997

Company: Electronic Data Systems Corp. (EDS) (subsidiary of General Motors Corp.)
Address: 7171 Forest Lane, Room A347
Dallas, TX 75203
214-661-6000

Company:    Fluor Daniel, Inc. (Maintenance Management Systems
            Division)
Address:    301 N. Main St., PO Box 19019
            Greenville, SC 29602-9019
            803-298-2752
            FAX: 803-298-2336
            Tech support: 803-298-2337

Company:    GE Information Services (division of General Electric Co.)
Address:    401 N. Washington St.
            Rockville, MD 20850
            800-433-3683; 301-340-4000
            FAX: 301-340-4488
            Tech support: 800-638-8730

Company:    Hewlett-Packard Co.
Address:    3000 Hanover St.
            Palo Alto, CA 94304
            800-752-0900; 415-857-1501
            Tech support: Use tollfree no.

Company:    Honeywell, Inc. (Industrial Automation and Control Divi-
            sion)
Address:    16404 N. Black Canyon Hwy.
            Phoenix, AZ 85023
            602-869-2311
            FAX: 602-863-5692

Company:    IBM (International Business Machines Corp.)
Address:    Old Orchard Rd.
            Armonk, NY 10504
            800-426-2468; 914-765-1900
            Tech support: Use tollfree no.

Company:    Intel Corp.
Address:    3065 Bowers Ave.
            Santa Clara, CA 95051
            408-765-8080
            FAX: 408-765-1821

Company:    MCI Communications Corp.
Address:    1133 19th St., NW
            Washington, DC 20036
            800-333-1000; 800-333-4000 (DC); 202-872-1600
            FAX: 800-950-4329

Company:    Memorex Telex Corp.
Address:    6422 East 41st St.
            Tulsa, OK 74135
            800-950-3465; 918-627-1111
            FAX: 918-624-4581
            Tech support: Use main no.

Company:   Metrum Information Storage
Address:   PO Box 5227
Denver, CO 80217-5227
800-231-8202; 303-773-4700
FAX: 303-773-4762

Company:   Motorola, Inc. (Digital Signal Processor Operation)
Address:   6501 William Cannon Dr., W
Austin, TX 78735
800-521-6274; 512-891-2030
FAX: 512-891-2947
Tech support: 512-891-3230

Company:   NCR Corp.
Address:   1700 S. Patterson Blvd.
Dayton, OH 45479
800-225-5627; 513-445-5000
FAX: 513-445-2008
Tech support: 800-CALL-NCR

Company:   Northern Telecom, Inc.
Address:   200 Athens Way
Nashville, TN 37228
615-734-4000

Company:   Northern Telecom, Inc. (Meridian Business Systems Group)
Address:   2100 Lakeside Blvd.
Richardson, TX 75081
800-328-8800; 214-437-8000
FAX: 214-437-8912

Company:   Olivetti Office USA
Address:   PO Box 6945, 765 U.S. Hwy. 202, S
Bridgewater, NJ 08807-0945
800-527-2960; 908-526-8200
FAX: 908-526-8405
Tech support: 908-704-6501

Company:   Panasonic Communications & Systems Co. (Office Automation Group)
Address:   2 Panasonic Way
Secaucus, NJ 07094
201-348-7000
Tech support: 800-222-0584

Company:   Racal-Vadic (subsidiary of Racal Electronics PLC)
Address:   1708 McCarthy Blvd.
Milpitas, CA 95035
800-482-3427; 408-432-8008
FAX: 408-434-0188
Tech support: 408-922-3350

Company:   Schlumberger (CAD/CAM Division)
Address:    4251 Plymouth Rd., PO Box 986
            Ann Arbor, MI 48106
            313-995-6000
            FAX: 313-995-6171

Company:   Seagate Technology
Address:    920 Disc Dr.
            Scotts Valley, CA 95066-4544
            800-468-3472; 408-438-6550
            FAX: 408-438-4127
            Tech support: Use tollfree no.

Company:   Siemens Nixdorf Printing Systems
Address:    5500 Broken Sound Blvd.
            Boca Raton, FL 33487
            407-997-3100
            Tech support: Use main no.

Company:   SONY Corporation of America (Component Peripheral
            Products Co.)
Address:    655 River Oaks Pkwy.
            San Jose, CA 95134
            408-432-0190
            FAX: 408-943-0740
            Tech support: Use main no.

Company:   Sprint International (division of US Sprint Communica-
            tions Corp.)
Address:    12490 Sunrise Valley Dr.
            Reston, VA 22096
            800-736-1130; 703-689-6000
            FAX: 703-689-5176

Company:   Sun Microsystems, Inc.
Address:    2550 Garcia Ave.
            Mountain View, CA 94043
            800-821-4643; 800-821-4642 (CA); 415-960-1300
            FAX: 415-969-9131
            Tech support: 800-USA-4SUN

Company:   Tandy Corp.
Address:    1800 One Tandy Center
            Ft. Worth, TX 76102
            817-390-3011
            FAX: 817-390-2774
            Tech support: 817-390-3861

Company:   Tektronix, Inc. (Redmond Division)
Address:   PO Box 1197
           Redmond, OR 97756
           800-833-9200; 503-923-0333
           FAX: 503-923-4434
           Tech support: Use main no.

Company:   Texas Instruments, Inc.
Address:   PO Box 655012, M/S 57
           Dallas, TX 75265
           800-527-3500; 214-995-2011
           FAX: 214-995-4360
           Tech support: 512-250-7407

Company:   3M (Information Systems Group)
Address:   3M Center, Bldg. 225-3S-05
           St. Paul, MN 55144-1000
           612-733-9222
           FAX: 612-736-3094
           Tech support: Use main no.

Company:   UNISYS Corp.
Address:   PO Box 500
           Blue Bell, PA 19424-0001
           215-542-4011
           Tech support: 800-448-1424

Company:   U S West Communications
Address:   1999 Broadway, Ste. 1140
           Denver, CO 80202
           800-888-4948; 303-896-9258
           FAX: 303-896-1320

Company:   Ventura Software Inc. (subsidiary of Xerox Corp.)
Address:   15175 Innovation Dr.
           San Diego, CA 92128
           800-822-8221; 619-673-0172
           Tech support: 800-848-5222

Company:   Wang Laboratories, Inc.
Address:   One Industrial Way, M/S 014-A1B
           Lowell, MA 01851
           800-835-9264; 508-459-5000
           Tech support: 800-247-9264

Company:   Xerox Corp. (U.S. Marketing Group)
Address:   PO Box 24
           Rochester, NY 14692
           800-832-6979

### ▶ SELF-TEST

1. Name three computer societies.
2. Why do people join professional societies?
3. Name three professional computer journals.

Solutions
1. ACM, DPMA, Computer Society of IEEE
2. To obtain information about the field and to share experiences with other professionals
3. *PC Magazine, InfoWorld, PC World, Datamation, ComputerWorld,* and so forth

## ▶ Key Terms

Association for Computing Machinery (ACM), *p. 603*
Certificate of data processing (CDP), *p. 597*
Certified computer professional (CCP), *p. 597*
Data Processing Management Association (DPMA), *p. 603*
Institute of Electrical and Electronics Engineers (IEEE), *p. 603*

# AN OVERVIEW OF
# THE HISTORY OF COMPUTING

**500 BC** The abacus was the first known mechanical counting machine.

**1673** Gottfried von Leibniz developed an automatic calculator that could multiply and divide.

| 500 BC | 1642 | 1673 | 1804 |

**1642** Blaise Pascal invented the Pascaline, considered to be the first automatic calculating machine. It could only add and subtract, and was considered a commercial failure.

**1804** Joseph-Marie Jacquard invented a punched-card loom attachment that revolutionized the French silk-weaving industry by automating the process of entering input data. The principles used in Jacquard's loom were later applied to many computing devices.

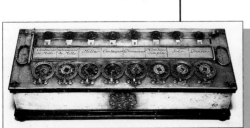

**1822** Charles Babbage began work on his Differential Engine, abandoned it, and then conceived the idea of an Analytical Engine, which, in principle, contained concepts now found in modern computers.

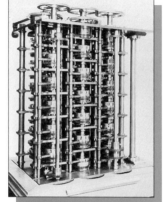

**1884** Herman Hollerith, a statistician with the U.S. Census Bureau, introduced his electromechanical punched-card system to compile the 1890 census. Hollerith's company grew and merged with other companies, and eventually became the International Business Machines Company (IBM).

| 1822 | 1833 | 1884 | 1939 |

**1833** Augusta Ada, Countess of Lovelace and daughter of the poet Lord Byron, worked closely with Babbage to show that it was possible to program the Analytical Engine with a single set of cards that specified a series of instructions.

**1939** John Atanasoff and Clifford Berry designed a prototype for their ABC (Atanasoff Berry Computer), which was intended to be a special-purpose electronic digital computer.

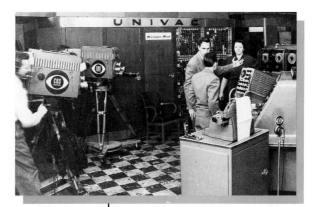

**1951** The UNIVAC, the first commercially available stored-program, electronic digital computer, was developed by John Mauchly and J. Presper Eckert.

**1943** John Mauchly and J. Presper Eckert began work on the ENIAC, the first operational general-purpose electronic digital computer. It was completed in 1946.

**1957** Fortran, the first high-level programming language for scientists and engineers, was introduced by IBM.

| **1943** | **1946** | **1951** | **1957** | **1964** |
|---|---|---|---|---|

```
INPUT "ENTER THE EMPLOYEE'S NAME"; NAME$
INPUT "ENTER THE HOURS WORKED"; HOURS
INPUT "ENTER THE PAY RATE"; PAYRATE
REM
REM CALCULATE GROSS PAY
LET GROSSPAY = HOURS * PAYRATE
REM
REM PRINT RESULTS
PRINT "EMPLOYEE NAME:      "; NAME$
PRINT "HOURS WORKED:       "; HOURS
PRINT "PAY RATE:           "; PAYRATE
PRINT "GROSS PAY           "; GROSSPAY
END
```

**1964** BASIC programming was introduced at Dartmouth College by Thomas Kurtz and John Kemeny.

**1964** Control Data Corporation introduced the first supercomputer, the CDC 6600.

**1946** The concept for a stored program computer was introduced by John von Neumann and his associates.

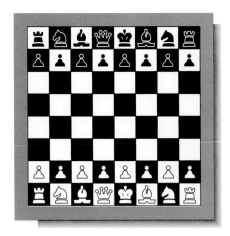

**1967** MacHack, a program written at MIT, was the first to play chess so successfully it could enter tournaments and win at the novice level.

**1971** The first expert system, DENDRAL, was completed. It was used as an "expert" chemist to determine the structure of molecular compounds.

**1965**   **1967**   **1968**   **1971**

**1965** The first commercially available minicomputer, the PDP-8, was introduced by the Digital Equipment Corporation.

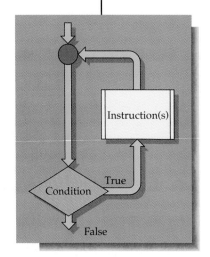

**1968** Edsger Dijsktra introduced the concept of structured programming, which became a standard for third-generation languages.

**1971** Intel introduced its first microprocessor chip, developed by Ted Hoff.

**1977** The Apple II computer was introduced. It was developed by Stephen Wozniak (left) and Stephen Jobs (right).

**1980** The now defunct Ashton-Tate, developer of dBase, the most popular database management system for PCs, was founded.

**1975** Bill Gates and Paul Allen establish the Microsoft Corporation. Gates (pictured here) is currently chairman of the board of Microsoft.

| 1974 | 1975 | 1977 | 1979 | 1980 |
|------|------|------|------|------|

**1974** Intel announced its microprocessor, later used in the original IBM computers and their compatibles.

**1979** VisiCalc introduced the first commercial spreadsheet program designed for inexperienced users of PCs. Its success helped to drive the PC market to greater heights.

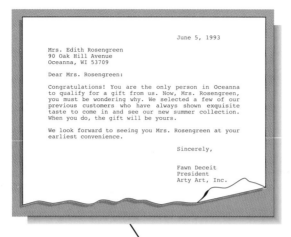

June 5, 1993

Mrs. Edith Rosengreen
90 Oak Hill Avenue
Oceanna, WI 53709

Dear Mrs. Rosengreen:

Congratulations! You are the only person in Oceanna
to qualify for a gift from us. Now, Mrs. Rosengreen,
you must be wondering why. We selected a few of our
previous customers who have always shown exquisite
taste to come in and see our new summer collection.
When you do, the gift will be yours.

We look forward to seeing you Mrs. Rosengreen at your
earliest convenience.

Sincerely,

Fawn Deceit
President
Arty Art, Inc.

**1982** WordPerfect announced its word processing package, which became the biggest selling package of its kind.

**1982** Compaq Inc. was founded. Their original luggables proved that PCs did not have to be desktop — or IBM!

**1980** WordStar shipped its first word processing package. Productivity tools made it to the top in 1980.

## 1980    1981    1982

**1980** The installed base of micro-computers reached 700,000 — one year before the IBM PC was introduced.

**1981** The IBM PC was introduced and quickly made it to the top of the microcomputer market and, with it, Microsoft's DOS operating system.

**1982** Hayes brought the 300 bps smart modem to the PC market, and it became an instant success.

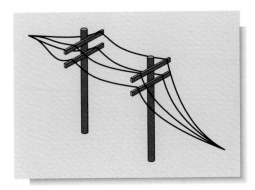

**1982** The breakup of AT&T created a new market for corporate networks by making it feasible for companies to create their own wide area communication networks.

**1984** IBM AT was introduced. Operating at 8 MHz, this 80286 16-bit computer ushered in the next generation of micros. In that same year, Apple unveiled the Macintosh (pictured below).

**1982**     **1983**     **1984**

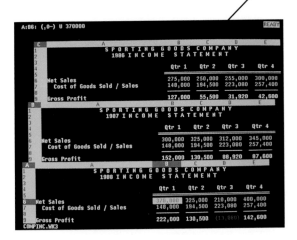

**1983** Lotus Development Corporation was founded. Their spreadsheet software, which cost $340,000 to develop, became the best-selling program for the PC.

**1983** IBM PC Jr. was introduced for the home market. It became that company's Edsel and died in 1985.

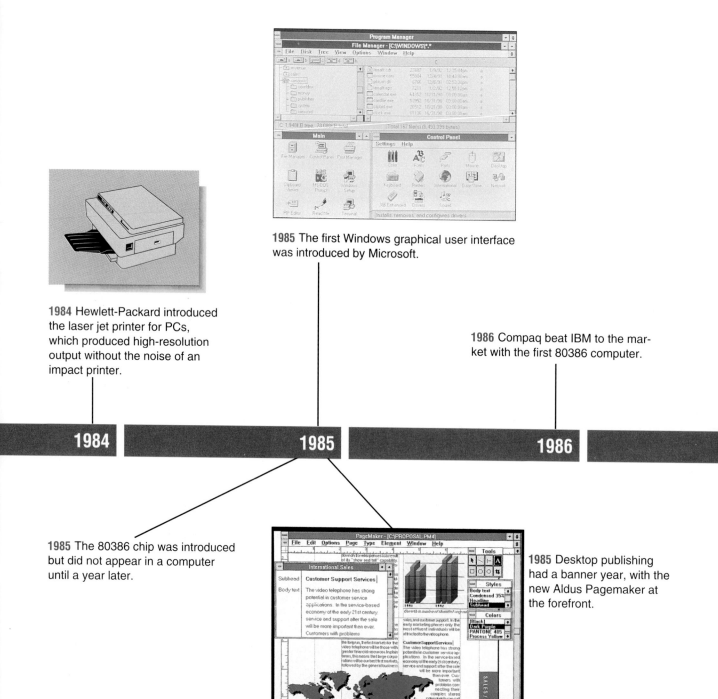

**1985** The first Windows graphical user interface was introduced by Microsoft.

**1984** Hewlett-Packard introduced the laser jet printer for PCs, which produced high-resolution output without the noise of an impact printer.

**1986** Compaq beat IBM to the market with the first 80386 computer.

**1984**

**1985**

**1986**

**1985** The 80386 chip was introduced but did not appear in a computer until a year later.

**1985** Desktop publishing had a banner year, with the new Aldus Pagemaker at the forefront.

**1987** IBM and Microsoft announced the OS/2 operating system.

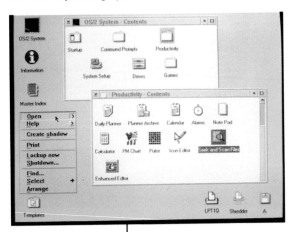

**1988** A new category of smaller notebook PCs, led by NEC's 4.4 pound UltraLite, appeared.

**1987**

**1988**

**1987** IBM replaced the original PCs with the PS/2 Line.

**1988** The first million-transistor microprocessor was introduced by Intel for the RISC (reduced instruction set computer) device. It became the technology standard for workstations.

**1990** 80486 computers became the models to beat.

**1990** The 10-year partnership between IBM and Microsoft began to fall apart as Microsoft promoted Windows for DOS and IBM promoted its OS/2 operating system.

**1992** The 80586 computer was announced; CD-ROMs became a popular storage medium; object-oriented programming grew dramatically; and multimedia standards were set.

**1989**      **1990**      **1991**      **1992**

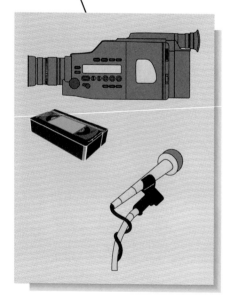

**1991** IBM and Apple agreed to share technology and develop software and hardware platforms together.

**1989** Multimedia was highly touted but it took years to catch on, because software and hardware products initially were very expensive, and development costs were high.

# GLOSSARY

**Absolute addressing** Copying a cell address in a spreadsheet formula so that it remains constant in every new location in which the formula appears; contrast with relative addressing.

**Access time** The time needed to locate data on a secondary storage device; typically measured in thousandths of a second.

**Acoustic coupler** Type of modem that has two cups into which a telephone handset is placed to transmit and receive computer data.

**Ada** Third-generation programming language that uses the structured concepts first used in Pascal; an extremely powerful and sophisticated language specifically designed for real-time and embedded systems.

**Address register** Temporary storage in the control unit of the CPU that holds the main memory address of (1) data to be processed or (2) the next instruction to be executed.

**Analog signal** Signal in the form of electronic waves that is often transmitted over telephone lines.

**Antiviral software** Programs designed to detect and disable viruses.

**Application** A specific use of a computer such as for payroll or inventory.

**Application generator** Software that generates application programs from descriptions of the problem and the processing required.

**Application package** Type of prewritten software designed for business or personal use that can be purchased off-the-shelf.

**Application programmer** Computer professional who writes, debugs, and documents programs for specific business tasks.

**Application software** Any program designed to satisfy a user need.

**Architecture** The technology used in a computer for processing data.

**Arithmetic/logic unit (ALU)** Part of the CPU that performs arithmetic and comparison operations.

**Artificial intelligence** Simulated human decision making by means of a computer.

**ASCII** Acronym for *American Standard Code for Information Interchange*; the computer code widely used by micros and for data communications, where each byte consists of 7 or 8 bits.

**Assembler** Program for translating an assembly program into machine language.

**Assembly language** Second generation programming language that uses symbolic instruction codes and symbolic names for storage areas; it is a programming language that is most machinelike and least user-friendly.

**Association for Computing Machinery (ACM)** A society for computer science professionals.

**Asynchronous transmission** Type of transmission in which one character at a time is transmitted over communications channels.

**Audio response unit** Output device that provides verbal responses which simulate the human voice; the output actually consists of prerecorded messages or phrases.

**Audit trail** Printout that lists all changes made to a file; produced for checking or control purposes.

**Authoring software** A set of programs used for multimedia presentations and computer-based training.

**Automated design tool** A technique for analyzing and developing systems.

**Automatic teller machine (ATM)** Interactive input/output device in which data entered at the point of transaction can either automatically and immediately update banking records in an online operation or store the transaction and update banking records later in batch mode.

**Auxiliary storage** Same as secondary storage.

**Backup** A copy of secondary storage files that is maintained in case something happens to the original.

**Band printer** Type of line printer that uses a flexible, stainless-steel print band that is photoengraved with print characters.

**Bandwidth** Transmission capacity of a computer or communications channel, measured in bits per second.

**Bar code reader** Device that reads or scans either the Universal Product Code on merchandise or other types of bar codes and transmits the data as input to a computer.

**Baseband** Communication technique in which data is transmitted over only one communications channel at medium speed.

**BASIC** Acronym for *Beginner's All-purpose Symbolic Instruction Code*; an easy-to-learn third-generation programming language.

**Batch processing** Type of processing in which input is read at fixed intervals as a file and operated on all at once; contrast with interactive processing in which input is operated on as soon as it is transacted.

**Baud rate** Speed at which data is transmitted over communications lines; it is commonly expressed in bits per second (bps).

**Benchmark test** Performance test that compares the capabilities of various computer devices.

**Binary numbering system** Numbering system in which there are only two possible digits: 0 and 1. Digital computers use binary codes to represent letters, digits, or special symbols.

**Bit** Short for binary digit—a single on- or off-state signal; characters are represented in a computer by 7- or 8-bit codes.

**Bit-mapped graphics** Graphic images created by painting and other programs in which the images consist of patterns of dots. Contrast with vector graphics.

**Bits per inch (bpi)** A measure of the density of data recorded on a magnetic disk or tape.

**Bits per second (bps)** Speed at which information is transmitted over communications lines.

**Block** Section of a data file that can be moved, copied, or placed anywhere in the same file or in a different one.

**Blocking** Process whereby records are placed as a unit or block on a disk or tape to make more effective use of the physical space on that disk or tape.

**Boilerplating** Word processing feature in which a section or block of a standard text can be used in many documents.

**Bootlegging of software** Making an unauthorized version of a program.

**Break-even analysis** Cost study that indicates when a new system design will start to be cost-effective.

**Bridge** Interface for connecting similar networks.

**Broadband** Communication technique in which data, voice, and video transmission can be transmitted at high speed along numerous channels.

**Bubble memory** *See* magnetic bubble memory.

**Budgetary constraints** Limits imposed on the time and money allocated to a business system.

**Buffer** Temporary print area where a queue of files to be printed is placed so that they can be printed while other processing is being performed.

**Bulletin board system** Service that enables people with PCs and modems to communicate with one another.

**Bundled software** Programs supplied along with the hardware by the manufacturer or vendor as part of a package.

**Bus** Special electronic path that carries data between the control unit, arithmetic/logic unit, and main memory.

**Bus configuration** Type of network topology in which each node can access not only the host computer but every other node as well.

**Business system** Integration of tasks and procedures in each functional business area.

**Byte** One storage position in main or secondary storage used to store a letter, digit, or symbol.

**C** Third-generation programming language that incorporates the advantages of both assembly language and high-level languages; the UNIX operating system was written in C.

**Cache memory** Type of memory that can double the speed of a computer; it stores and retrieves the most frequently used data in readily accessible form.

**Callback system** Security method to ensure that a user on a phone line is calling from an authorized telephone number.

**CASE structure** Logical control structure in a program typically used for selecting a course of action from a menu.

**CASE tool** Acronym for Computer *Assisted Software Engineering*; a systems analysis and design productivity tool for building information systems.

**Case-insensitive program** A program in which you can type commands or instructions using either uppercase or lowercase letters and get the same results.

**Cathode ray tube (CRT)** The most common type of screen or monitor used to display instructions and computer responses; can be either monochrome or color.

**CD-ROM (compact disk read-only memory)** Type of storage medium that uses the same technology as audio CDs. CD-ROMs cannot be written to—they can only be read. The disks are suitable for storing large amounts of fixed data (over 600 MB) for frequent reference.

**Cell** Intersection of a row and column in a spreadsheet program.

**Central processing unit (CPU)** Part of the computer system that controls all computer operations.

**Centralized processing** A single computer facility that serves all or most of the computing needs of an organization.

**Chain printer** Type of line printer that uses characters linked together on a chain as its print mechanism. The chain spins horizontally around a set of hammers and when the desired character is in front of the selected print position, the corresponding hammer strikes the paper into the ribbon.

**Character** A unit of data consisting of a single letter, digit, or special symbol.

**Chip** Integrated circuit that can hold millions of electronic components.

**CICS** An abbreviation for IBM's Customer Information Control System; a general-purpose communications interface designed to enable transactions entered at remote locations to be processed concurrently by a mainframe or host.

**Client-server** One method of using a LAN in which a file server does as much processing as possible before downloading to nodes.

**Clip art** Database of graphic displays that can be added to documents.

**Clock speed** Rate at which a computer can process data, as determined by the CPU's clock; in micros, it is measured in megahertz (MHz).

**Clone** A PC so similar to an IBM micro that it will run most of the software developed for IBM computers.

**Coaxial cable** A cable used for hardwired communications channels because it can carry large amounts of data.

**COBOL** Acronym for *CO*mmon *B*usiness *O*riented *L*anguage; a third-generation business-oriented programming language that is machine independent, relatively easy to maintain, and English-like.

**Command** Instruction given to an operating system or application package.

**Common carrier** A company that furnishes communication services to the general public.

**Communications channel** Linkage between nodes and/or hosts in a network.

**Compiler** Program for translating a source program into an object program. Compiling is a separate step that is completed before a program is run on the computer.

**Compression** Technique for storing files so that they require less storage space on disk.

**Computer-aided design (CAD)** Highly sophisticated drawing technique whereby engineers and architects use software to create complex drawings.

**Computer-aided manufacturing (CAM)** Technique whereby engineers use software to design the manufacturing components in a factory or production facility.

**Computer crime** Use of a computer to steal, embezzle, or defraud.

**Computer literate** Being aware of computers, how they operate, and how they are used for personal and business purposes.

**Computer output microfilm (COM) unit** A device that can be linked to a CPU to create output on microfilm or microfiche at very high speeds.

**Computer system** Group of devices that reads data, processes it, and produces information.

**Configure** To specially equip a computer system so that it includes components or devices designed to meet specific needs.

**Connectivity** Concept that enables different computer systems along with other technologies to interact with one another.

**Context-sensitive help** A level of on-screen help in which the displays pertain specifically to what is currently being done in an application.

**Continuous-form paper** Printed paper with small holes on either side that allow it to be fed through the printer without interruption.

**Control listing** Printout listing all changes made to a file; produced for checking purposes.

**Controls** Actions taken to minimize errors; they include techniques for verifying that data entered is correct.

**Control unit** Component of the computer's CPU that monitors the operations performed by the entire system.

**Coprocessor** Special chip that can be added to, or built into, microcomputers to speed up certain kinds of operations; for example, a math coprocessor speeds up the processing of mathematical operations for applications such as statistical analysis.

**Copy protection** Preparing software in such a way that the programs cannot be copied to other disks or can only be copied a limited number of times; copy protection is designed to prevent bootlegging.

**Cost-benefit analysis** Study that compares the cost of an existing system to the cost of a proposed system.

**CPU** *See* central processing unit.

**Cursor** Small blinking underline or rectangle that indicates where your input will actually appear on the screen.

**Cursor control keys** Keys on a terminal or microcomputer keyboard with arrows pointing in four directions; the arrows are used for positioning the cursor on the screen.

**Custom program** A set of instructions designed to meet the specific needs of users; it is written by a programmer within an organization or by an outside consultant.

**Cutting and pasting** Technique for moving, copying, or deleting blocks of text; first you define a block of text so that it can be "pasted" to another place.

**Daisywheel printer** Type of impact printer that prints fully formed characters from a flat disk that has petal-like projections containing individual characters.

**Data** Raw facts to be processed by a computer.

**Data definition language (DDL)** Set of technical specifications for a database's fields and the relationships among data in the database.

**Data dictionary** Descriptions of fields, records, and files in a database and the relationships among them.

**Data encryption** Encoding data so that it cannot be understood unless it is first decoded; used to protect data from unauthorized access.

**Data file** Collection of records in a specific application area.

**Data flow diagram** Tool used by analysts to depict an existing information system or one that is being developed; emphasis is placed on where data originates and where it goes during and after processing.

**Data integrity** The need to keep databases from being corrupted by input or programming errors or by deliberate attempts to tamper with the data.

**Data manipulation language (DML)** Computer language that is typically a proprietary part of a database management package and that allows users to create custom-designed applications. Query languages are types of data manipulation languages.

**Data Processing Management Association (DPMA)** A society for business computer professionals.

**Database** Collection of related files that are stored electronically and can be linked, joined, or cross-referenced.

**Database administrator** Individual responsible for organizing, designing, and maintaining the database and all other data used by the organization.

**Database file** Collection of data in a specific application area; database files can be linked or joined for reporting purposes or for providing responses to inquiries.

**Database management system (DBMS)** Software used to create, edit, and update database files and to inquire about the status of records in those files.

**Debit card** A form of bank card that handles transactions in the same way as your personal checking account. The instant you make a purchase with your debit card, the money is extracted from your bank account and placed in the bank account of the seller.

**Debugging** Finding and correcting all logic and coding errors, or "bugs," in a program.

**Decentralized system** Computer facility in which each business department within a company has its own computer system intended to accomplish its goals more directly.

**Decision support system (DSS)** Flexible management information system that allows managers to access corporate and other databases and to create their own reports and applications, even their own specialized databases. Such systems are used by managers to help them make decisions.

**Default** Standard setting or assumption made by a software package; default settings can be changed by users if the need arises.

**Density** Number of characters that can be represented in an inch of disk or tape.

**Desk-checking** Process in which a programmer manually traces through a program visually checking for syntax errors.

**Desktop computer** The most widely used type of PC in business; typically, it is a single-user device.

**Desktop organizer** Program that allows microcomputer users to keep track of information such as names, addresses, telephone numbers, notes, to-do lists, and appointment schedules. Typically included as part of a personal information manager.

**Desktop publishing** Software tools offering advanced capabilities that allow users to do page design for publications such as newsletters, magazines, and books.

**Device driver** A piece of software that expands an operating system's ability to work with peripherals.

**Digital audio tape (DAT)** Type of tape that can store a large amount of data very compactly.

**Digital computer** Electronic computer that processes data in discrete form as on-off electronic pulses.

**Digital signal** Signal in the form of an on-off electronic pulse.

**Digital video interaction (DVI)** Technique for compressing video images so that they can be stored more compactly for computer processing.

**Digitizer tablet** Input device for converting illustrations into digital form.

**Direct-connect modem** Type of modem built into a computer or directly attached to it by cable.

**Direct conversion** Method of converting from an old information system to a new one in which the company simply stops using the old system and immediately begins using the new system (no overlap).

**Direct file** Method of database organization in which a key field itself is used to calculate each record's address, thereby eliminating the need to look for the record in an index.

**Disk** Type of secondary storage in which data is recorded as magnetized bits and is randomly accessible at high speeds.

**Disk cartridge** Storage medium that combines the advantages of both diskettes and hard disks; cartridges are portable like diskettes yet store as much data as some hard drives.

**Disk drive** Device that gives the CPU access to programs and data stored on disks; widely used for secondary storage.

**Disk organizer** Application package that enables users to manage data and program files on their disks.

**Disk pack** Older type of disk used for some midrange and mainframe computers; consists of removable sets of hard disks.

**Diskette** *See* floppy disk.

**Distributed system** Integrated computer facility that allows individual users within a business to process data locally and to communicate with a central computer in the company; combines the advantages of centralized and decentralized environments while minimizing their disadvantages.

**Document** Letter, report, or other text produced with a word processing package.

**Documentation package** A set of manuals that details the procedures and techniques used in a new information system as well as the technical specifications of the hardware and software.

**DOS** The operating system for IBM micros and their compatibles. *See* PC-DOS and MS-DOS.

**Dot-matrix printer** Impact printer that creates characters using a rectangular grid of pins which press against a carbon ribbon to print on paper.

**Download** To copy files maintained by the host to remote or local nodes, which are typically microcomputers.

**Downsizing** Strategic plan in which applications are moved from large computers to smaller ones.

**Drum printer** Type of line printer that uses a cylindrical steel drum embossed with print characters to generate output.

**E-mail** *See* electronic mail.

**EBCDIC** Acronym for *Extended Binary Coded Decimal Interchange Code* (pronounced *eb-c-dick*). The standard 8-bit computer code for most IBM and IBM-compatible mainframes.

**EEPROM** Acronym for *electronically erasable programmable read-only memory.* A ROM chip that allows program information to be changed by software without removing the chips from the computer.

**Electroluminescent (EL) display** Type of flat-screen technology used in display screens that do not depend on cathode ray tubes; often used in laptop computers.

**Electronic mail (e-mail)** Productivity tool that enables users to electronically send, store, and retrieve messages that would otherwise be delivered verbally or by mail.

**Electronic spreadsheet** Software productivity tool that uses a row-and-column format for storing data and performing calculations; any data that can be displayed in row-and-column format, like ledger sheets used by accountants, can be prepared with this tool.

**Embedded system** Computers built into other systems, such as those in a video cassette recorder or on an airplane.

**Encryption** *See* data encryption.

**EPROM** Acronym for *erasable programmable read-only memory.* A ROM chip that must be removed from the computer if reprogramming is desired; a special process is required to erase old programs from EPROM chips.

**Equipment constraints** Limits on the type of computer hardware and other devices that can be used by a business system.

**Ergonomics** Science of adapting machines and work environments to people.

**Ethernet** A local area network used for connecting computer devices, typically within the same building. Ethernet operates over twisted pair and coaxial cable at speeds up to 10 million bits per second.

**Even parity** Method of verifying the accurate transmittal of data by checking to ensure that an even number of bits in a byte are always in the on state at any given time. Some computers use even parity and others use odd parity.

**Exception report** Report that calls attention to unusual situations in which certain predefined conditions occur.

**Execution cycle** CPU processing time during which instructions are executed and results produced.

**Executive information system (EIS)** Specialized form of decision-support system that requires no expertise on the part of the user and is often designed around the information needs of a single executive.

**Expansion slot** Receptacle on the main circuit board in which add-on units can be inserted.

**Expert system** Software that simulates the knowledge and analytical ability of an expert in a specific field; helps users make decisions.

**Facsimile (fax) machine** Machine that scans documents and transmits them to either computers or other fax machines.

**Fax board** Board that captures documents or screen displays stored by the computer and transmits them via a modem either to another computer with a modem or to a fax machine.

**Feasibility study** Study undertaken to determine if a new systems design is possible given current constraints.

**Feedback** Process of periodically evaluating a system to determine how well it meets user needs.

**Fiber optic cable** Communications channel using light impulses that travel through clear flexible tubing half the size of a human hair to transmit data at very high speeds with few or no errors.

**Field** Unit of information contained in a record (e.g., Social Security number or name).

**Fifth-generation language (5GL)** Nonprocedural programming language for querying databases or developing expert systems; typically uses artificial intelligence techniques.

**File** Collection of related records.

**File allocation table (FAT)** Table on a disk that keeps track of the disk address of each file; permits fast access of files on a disk.

**File conversion** Process of creating computerized files as part of implementing a new system.

**File extension** One to three characters added to a filename that helps to identify it; for example, Lotus 1-2-3 files are automatically given a WK1 file extension so that they are easily identified as worksheet files.

**File management system** Set of programs for storing simple data, such as a personal address book in which one file need not be linked in any way to data in another file. Also called a file manager.

**Filename** Name given to a file; it is typically from one to eight characters long.

**File server** Special host computer that makes programs and data available to nodes on a network.

**Financial planning language (FPL)** Fourth-generation programming language that uses sophisticated mathematical, statistical, and forecasting methods for analyzing data.

**Firmware** Read-only memory chips that contain permanent, nonvolatile instructions.

**First-generation language** Another name for machine language; it was the earliest type of programming language developed.

**Fixed disk** Another term for a hard disk.

**Fixed-head disk drive** Storage device that contains one or more hard disks and stationary access arms with separate read/write mechanisms for each of the tracks on the disks.

**Flash card** Credit-card-sized memory card that fits into a slot of some portable computers; used in place of disks in very small computers.

**Flat-screen technology** Technology such as liquid crystal display, electroluminescent display or gas plasma that is used in a display screen instead of a cathode ray tube; often used in laptop computers.

**Floppy disk** Portable disk on which data is stored; most commonly found in 5¼-inch and 3½-inch diameters; same as a diskette.

**Flowchart** Pictorial representation of the logic flow in a program or a system; illustrates major elements and how they are logically integrated.

**FORTRAN** Acronym for *FOR*mula *TRAN*slator; a third-generation programming language best suited for scientific and engineering applications.

**Fourth-generation language (4GL)** An easy-to-write, non-procedural programming language that simply states the needed output using English-like terms without specifying each step required to obtain that output.

**Friction feed mechanism** Print mechanism that moves paper through a printer by pressure between the paper and the carriage.

**Front-end processor** Microcomputer or minicomputer that helps offload the activities performed by a host computer so that it can run more efficiently.

**Full-duplex line** Communications channel that permits data to move in both directions at the same time (e.g., a telephone line).

**Function key** Any one of the keys numbered F1 through F10 or F1 through F12 on a microcomputer; each key typically performs a specific operation depending on the software package being used.

**Gantt chart** Chart depicting time lines that graphically show how long projects are scheduled to take and at what points parts of the project development can overlap; used for project planning and project control.

**Gas-plasma display** Form of flat screen technology for laptop computers that sandwiches a neon/argon gas mixture with grids of vertical and horizontal wires.

**Gateway** Software that connects small local area networks to mainframes or wide area networks.

**Gigabyte (GB)** One billion storage positions in main memory or auxiliary storage.

**Graphics software** Programs with tools for drawing, charting, and presenting graphics and illustrations.

**Hacker** Computer user who illegally or unethically accesses a computer system.

**Half-duplex line** Communications channel that permits data to move in two directions, but not at the same time, like a CB radio.

**Hard card** Series of circuit boards that can be added to a microcomputer by plugging them into the computer's internal expansion slots; functions like a hard disk.

**Hard copy** Output that is printed on paper.

**Hard disk** Rigid disk mounted permanently in a disk drive for storing data; can typically store hundreds of millions of bytes or more.

**Hard disk drive** Storage device that can typically store hundreds of millions of characters or more.

**Hardware** Set of devices that perform information-processing functions.

**Head crash** Loss of all data on a hard disk when a read/write head collides with a disk recording surface.

**Hierarchical database** Database organized like an upside-down tree with the root, or main segment, at the top in a one-to-many, or parent-child, relationship. Each data item or group of data items shown in the tree diagram is called a segment.

**Hierarchy chart** Program planning tool that graphically illustrates how programs are segmented into subprograms, or modules, and how the modules relate to one another.

**High-definition television (HDTV)** High-quality TV and sound system that can be used for converting TVs into interactive computers by bringing many services and information resources into the home.

**High-level language** A symbolic programming language that is similar to English, such as COBOL or BASIC; third-generation languages are high-level languages.

**Horizontal package** Software that meets a specific business need for organizations of all sizes.

**Host computer** Central processor in a network.

**Hypermedia** Software that links together not only text but graphics, sound, animation, and video using special navigation techniques.

**Hypertext** Software that allows a user to navigate through a database where information is linked together and accessible as desired, regardless of its location.

**Icon** Graphic symbol displayed on a video screen representing files or commands that a user can select.

**Illustration package** Painting or drawing software.

**Image processing system** System whereby software and hardware input actual images of documents, store them, and retrieve them when needed.

**Impact printer** Printer that uses some form of strike-on method, as a typewriter uses, to press a carbon or fabric ribbon against paper.

**Importing data** Copying files or portions of files into other files that may have been created using different programs.

**Incompatibility** Situation in which hardware or software produced for one computer system cannot be used with another system.

**Index** File that contains two lists: the disk address of each record in the main file and the corresponding key field for that record.

**Indexed file** File that uses a method of organization in which data is created along with an index which keeps track of the physical location on disk of each record; the most common method of file organization when records need to be accessed randomly.

**Inference engine** In an expert system, the software that examines facts and rules to draw conclusions.

**Information** Data that is processed or operated on by a computer.

**Information processing** Set of procedures for operating on data and producing meaningful information.

**Information system** System that uses computers to improve the efficiency of existing business operations.

**Inheritance** A feature of object-oriented programming where objects within a class share the same attributes.

**Ink-jet printer** Type of nonimpact printer in which tiny dots are shot onto paper to form characters; well suited for graphics applications.

**Input** Incoming data read by computers.

**Input device** Component of a computer system that accepts data from the user (e.g., a keyboard or mouse).

**Insert mode** Mode available with software packages so that when you are editing text you can add characters rather than replace them.

**Institute for the Certification of Computer Professionals (ICCP)** Organization that certifies computer professionals.

**Instruction cycle** CPU processing time during which the control unit fetches an instruction from primary storage and prepares it for processing.

**Instruction register** Temporary storage location within the CPU for processing data.

**Integrated circuit** A chip that can hold millions of electronic components.

**Integrated package** Software that combines the features of the four productivity tools (word processing, spreadsheet, database management system, e-mail) into a single package so that users need to learn only one common interface and so that they can easily move from one application to another.

**Integrated Services Digital Network (ISDN)** An international standard for the transmission of both voice and data over communications lines.

**Interactive processing** Immediate processing of data as soon as it is transacted.

**Interblock gap** Space separating blocks of records on a disk or tape.

**Interpreter** Translator program that converts instructions written in a high-level language into machine language one statement at a time as the program is being run on the computer.

**Iteration** One of the four logic structures in programming in which a program executes a series of steps repeatedly. Also called a looping structure.

**Joystick** Device used to position a cursor (similar to a mouse); minimizes the need for keyboarding.

**Jukebox** Device that can make available a number of optical disks.

**Justification** Ability of a word processing package to align both left and right margins.

**Kernel** Part of the operating system that manages the computer's resources including the CPU, primary storage, and peripheral devices; also called the supervisor.

**Keyboard** Common input device for entering data and instructions; similar to a typewriter.

**Key field** A main field that uniquely identifies each record and that is used to create an index for fast, random-access retrieval of records.

**Kilobyte (K)** Approximately 1,000 storage positions (actually 1,024 bytes) in main memory or auxiliary storage.

**Knowledge base** Part of an expert system that translates the knowledge from human experts into rules and strategies.

**Knowledge engineer** Computer professional who creates a knowledge base in an expert system.

**Laptop computer** Portable computer weighing 11 pounds or less.

**Laser printer** Nonimpact printer that produces high-quality output.

**Legal constraints** Limits on the design of an information system due to legal requirements, such as compliance with the rules for Social Security payroll deductions.

**Letter-quality printer** Printer capable of high-quality output. Each letter is composed of solid lines, just like typewriter output. Contrast with dot-matrix printer.

**Light pen** Special device that uses a light-sensing mechanism to transmit signals to a computer; typically used for selecting items from a menu.

**Line printer** Type of impact printer that prints an entire line at a time. These include band printers, chain printers, drum printers, and dot-matrix printers.

**Linkage editor** Utility program that links an object program to a computer so that it is ready to run.

**Liquid crystal display (LCD)** Type of flat screen in which a current runs through liquid crystals sandwiched between two sheets of polarized material.

**Local area network (LAN)** System of connecting devices that are in relatively close proximity to one another.

**Logic error** Mistake in a program that occurs because instructions are not sequenced properly or because the wrong instructions are used.

**Longitudinal parity** Method of verifying the accurate transmission of data in which a check byte is added to the end of each record; each bit of the check byte is used to preserve the appropriate parity of each bit position in each byte of the record.

**Looping** One of the four logic structures in programming in which a program executes a series of steps repeatedly. Also called an iteration structure.

**Machine cycle** The time during which the processing of a single instruction occurs.

**Machine language** Computer's own internal language; all programs must be in machine language to be executed.

**Macintosh operating system** A user-friendly operating system that uses windows and icons for selecting commands and processing data in a multitasking environment.

**Macro** Collection of instructions that can be executed as one unit to facilitate the processing of data.

**Magnetic bubble memory** Type of memory frequently used in addition to, or in place of, integrated circuits because it is nonvolatile; information is stored in a magnetic film as a pattern of oppositely directed magnetic fields.

**Magnetic ink character reader (MICR)** Device used by banks to read or scan the magnetic ink digits and symbols printed at the bottom of checks.

**Magneto-optical (MO) disk** Erasable compact disk that makes use of combined optical and magnetic technologies; can store hundreds of megabytes of data.

**Mail merge** A word processor feature that allows letters and a name and address file to be linked so that the letters are personalized.

**Mainframe** First computer used in business; widely used as a host or central computer in mid-sized and large companies.

**Main memory** Another term for primary storage; used for storing programs and data.

**Maintenance programmer** Computer professional who modifies existing programs to ensure that they are current and working efficiently.

**Management information system (MIS)** Information system designed to integrate the information needs of the entire organization, beginning at the top, with the company-wide goals set by high-level managers.

**Master file** Main collection of records relating to a specific application area.

**Megabyte (MB)** Approximately 1 million storage positions in main memory or auxiliary storage.

**Megahertz** A measurement of a computer's speed equal to a million ticks of a computer's clock; in general, the more megahertz per second, the faster the computer.

**Memory board** Extra memory that fits on a main circuit board; used to enhance a computer's primary storage.

**Memory management** A component of systems software that allocates and controls the effective use of a computer's memory.

**Menu** List of choices displayed on the screen from which required operations can be selected.

**Microcomputer** Smallest and least expensive type of computer system; used mainly by one individual at a time.

**Microjustification** Feature of word processing packages that produces automatic adjustment of spacing between characters on a line so that the text has flush right and left margins.

**Microprocessor** The CPU of a PC along with main memory and other components; typically contained on a single board.

**Microsecond** One millionth of a second.

**Midrange computer** Same as a minicomputer.

**Millions of instructions per second (MIPS)** Measurement of a computer processor's speed.

**Minicomputer** Computer system that is midway between a mainframe and a micro in terms of size, cost, and processing power.

**MIPS** *See* millions of instructions per second.

**Modem** Device that enables data to be transmitted over telephone lines by converting digital signals to analog signals and vice versa.

**Modula-2** Structured, high-level programming language developed as an alternative to Pascal.

**Module** Subprogram contained within a main program that performs a fixed set of operations.

**Monitor** TV-like screen that displays user instructions and the computer's responses. Also called video display terminal (VDT) or cathode ray tube (CRT).

**Monochrome monitor** Display screen with only one color, typically green or amber against a black background.

**Motherboard** Main circuit board of a computer that contains the microprocessor, battery-operated clock, and other components.

**Mouse** Handheld device with one or more buttons on the top that is slid around the desktop to electronically move the cursor on the computer screen, thereby eliminating the need to type commands.

**MPC (Multimedia PC)** A minimum specification for multimedia PCs developed by Microsoft. MPC computers must be an 80286 or higher, have 2 MB+ of RAM, a VGA monitor, a CD-ROM drive, and Windows 3.1.

**MS-DOS** The operating system for IBM-compatible micros.

**Multifunction drive** Drive that can read or write either WORM-CDs or erasable optical disks.

**Multimedia** Use of text, video, graphics, animation, and sound to communicate, make presentations, educate, store database files, and so on.

**Multiple virtual storage (MVS)** The high-end operating system for IBM's batch-oriented mainframes.

**Multiplexer** Device that collects messages from numerous nodes at one physical location and transmits them collectively at high speeds over a single communications channel.

**Multiprocessing** Linking of two or more CPUs so that different instructions or different programs can be executed simultaneously.

**Multiprogramming** Ability to store and process more than one program in a computer concurrently.

**Multitasking** A variation of multiprogramming implemented on many high-end microcomputers that allows the user to access several programs at the same time.

**Multiuser system** Computer system shared by many users.

**Nanosecond** One billionth of a second.

**National Research and Education Network (NREN)** Proposed super network based on Internet that will link educational institutions, scientists, and businesspeople to supercomputers across the nation.

**Natural language interface** Method of interacting with an expert system or database that allows users to conduct dialogs with the computer that seem as natural as talking to another human being.

**Near-letter-quality (NLQ) printer** Dot-matrix printer that produces relatively high-quality output but not quite as good as that produced with fully formed characters.

**Needs analysis** Description of an organization's needs.

**Network** System that permits the sharing of resources such as computing power, software, and input/output units by different computers.

**Network database** Similar to a hierarchical database except that more than one parent per child is permitted and a child with no parent is also permitted.

**Network operating system** Set of control programs that works in conjunction with the normal computer operating system to facilitate basic network management functions such as transmitting files, communicating with other systems, and performing diagnostics.

**Network topology** The specific type of configuration used in a network.

**Node** Terminal or computer at a remote location that is linked to a host computer in a network.

**Nonimpact printer** Printer that produces images by methods other than the strike-on method; thermal, ink-jet, and laser printers are nonimpact devices.

**Nonprocedural language** Another name for a fourth-generation programming language; languages are called nonprocedural because they only specify the output required, not the procedure by which the output is to be obtained.

**Nonvolatile memory** Type of memory typically composed of magnetic bubbles so that data stored in it can be retained for some time even after the power is shut off.

**Notebook computer** Portable computers weighing 7 pounds or less.

**Numeric keypad** Section of a keyboard containing numbers; used to make numeric data entry easier.

**Object-oriented database** Database that can link not only text but graphics, photos, video, and sound; objects consisting of data and functions are used to make information available.

**Object-oriented programming** Type of programming in which both the data and the set of operations that can act on that data are treated as one unit; object-oriented programs are designed to facilitate the use of reusable code.

**Object program** Program that has been translated into machine language.

**Odd parity** Method of verifying the accurate transmission of data in which an odd number of bits must always be in the on state at any given time. A computer is said to be an even-parity or odd-parity computer.

**Offline** Data entry in which data is entered on computers or terminals that are not connected to the main CPU. Used for collecting data for future batch processing.

**Offload** To reduce one computer's tasks by having those tasks handled by a second computer.

**Online** Data entry in which input entered is immediately used by the computer for updating files or answering inquiries.

**Open Systems Interconnection (OSI) model** A set of communications protocols defined by the International Standards Organization.

**Operating system** A set of control programs that moves data in and out of storage and monitors the running of application programs; a main component of systems software.

**Optical character reader (OCR)** Input device that scans data, eliminating the need for a keying operation. *See* bar code reader, optical mark reader, and optical scanner.

**Optical disk** Direct access storage medium that can store 600 MB or more. CD-ROMs and WORM disks are types of optical disks.

**Optical mark reader** Device that detects the presence of pencil marks on predetermined grids. Used to read test answer sheets and market research forms. Also called a mark-sense reader.

**Optical scanner** Device that scans text and graphics from typed or handwritten entries, eliminating the need for keying in the data.

**OS/2** An operating system for the IBM PS/2 family of computers.

**Output** Outgoing information produced by a computer.

**Output device** Part of the computer system that produces processed data or information. Monitors and printers are output devices.

**Outsourcing** Use of outside services to satisfy some or all of an organization's information processing needs.

**Packaged program** Program designed for a wide range of users and sold or leased by computer vendors, consultants, or software houses.

**Page printer** Nonimpact printer that uses a laser, thermal, or ink-jet technology to print a page at a time.

**Palmtop computer** Handheld portable computer weighing approximately a pound.

**Parallel conversion** Method of converting to a new design in which the old and new systems are used concurrently and output is compared at various stages to make sure the new system is running correctly.

**Parallel processing** Use of multiple CPUs to process data.

**Parallel transmission** Method of transmitting data in which each bit of a character is sent over a separate channel.

**Parity bit** A single bit attached to each byte to verify that data is being transmitted correctly.

**Partition** Section or portion of primary storage or disk space set aside for some purpose such as running an application program.

**Pascal** Third-generation programming language that is relatively easy to learn and is highly structured.

**PC-DOS** The operating system specifically for IBM micros.

**Pen-based system** A computer, usually a notebook or picocomputer (palmtop), that can accept input using a stylus or pen; commonly used for filling out forms or taking notes.

**Peripheral** Input or output device.

**Personal computer (PC)** Same as a microcomputer.

**Personal information manager** A software package that combines the features of project management software and desktop organizers for a manager's personal use.

**PERT chart** Chart that provides a method for keeping track of the progress of a project. PERT is an acronym for *program evaluation and review technique.*

**Phased conversion** Method of converting to a new design in which a gradual or stepwise implementation of the new system is used.

**Picocomputer** Palmtop or smaller general-purpose computer.

**Picosecond** One trillionth of a second; used to measure computing speed.

**Pilot conversion** Implementation of an entire system in only one part of the company until all problems are solved.

**Pixel** A tiny point of light or picture element on a screen or monitor.

**PL/1** High-level programming language designed to meet the needs of both business and science; it combines the advantages of FORTRAN and COBOL.

**Plotter** Printer that produces high-quality line drawings in color by moving either pens or electrostatic charges with different colors of ink over paper.

**Point-of-sale (POS) terminal** Input device used in retail establishments to enter data at the point where a transaction is made.

**Polling** Method of controlling transmissions in a LAN ring configuration so that two computers are prevented from sending a message at the same time.

**Port** Sockets for plugging peripherals into a computer.

**Portability** Ability to run the same program on two or more types of computers.

**Portable microcomputer** Compact and lightweight computer that is easy to transport.

**Presentation graphics software** Set of packaged programs

for producing graphic representations of data for business presentations.

**Primary storage** The main memory of a computer where data and programs are stored for processing.

**Printer** The most common output device for PCs; used to obtain printed or hard-copy reports.

**Problem definition** A report that presents the results of an analysis of the basic problem areas in an existing system.

**Procedural language** Another name for a third-generation programming language; the term *procedural* means that the programmer must develop the logic necessary to carry out each procedure.

**Processing** Manipulation of data by computer that results in quick and efficient information.

**Processor** The CPU of a computer along with main memory and other components; typically stored on integrated circuit boards.

**Productivity tool** Application package designed to help users perform day-to-day business tasks and to assist them in decision making; a spreadsheet package, a DBMS, a word processing package, and an e-mail package are considered productivity tools.

**Program** Set of instructions that inputs data, processes it, and produces output information.

**Program file** Software typically stored on a secondary storage device such as a disk.

**Programmer** Computer professional who writes, debugs, and documents programs.

**Programmer analyst** Computer professional who serves as both programmer and systems analyst and is responsible for integrating new software into an information system.

**Program testing** Execution of a program with different sets of data to find and eliminate errors.

**Project management software** A set of programs that allows users to set up schedules and allocate personnel and resources for projects.

**PROM** Acronym for *programmable read-only memory*; a ROM chip that can be programmed to perform user-defined tasks.

**Prompt** Message or blinking cursor that appears on a screen and requires action by the user.

**Protocol** Standard set of rules that regulates the way data is transmitted between two computers.

**Prototyping** Technique used by systems analysts whereby users experiment with parts of a proposed system in order to minimize the need for changes when the entire system is implemented.

**Pseudocode** Program planning tool that uses key words to depict the logical control structures to be used in a program.

**Public domain software** Noncopyrighted programs that developers make available free of charge.

**Pull-down menu** A submenu that is superimposed over a main menu, from which the user can select more specific entries.

**Query language** Type of fourth-generation programming language that allows a user to retrieve information from databases.

**QuickTime** An operating system extension developed by Apple to enable users to incorporate sound, animation, and video into their multimedia applications.

**Random-access memory (RAM)** The part of primary storage that stores programs and data during processing.

**Read-only memory (ROM)** Memory chip that permanently stores instructions and data.

**Read/write head** Mechanism used to read data from or write information to a disk (or tape).

**Real-time processing** Type of processing in which the interaction between user and computer is very fast; that is, there is no perceived delay between sending an inquiry and receiving a response.

**Record** Unit of information pertaining to one item in a file; a collection of related fields.

**Register** Special storage area in the arithmetic/logic or control unit of a CPU that is used to process data.

**Relational database** Type of database that presents files in table format to the users, that is, with the records as rows and the fields as columns; relational databases enable files to be linked together and are known for their flexibility.

**Relative addressing** Copying a cell address in a spreadsheet formula so that it adjusts for the columns and rows being copied to; contrast with absolute addressing.

**Remote data entry** Method of processing in which terminals or PCs are used for entering data at the place where transactions occur.

**Remote job entry** Method of processing in which users enter and run programs from terminals or PCs linked to a host computer.

**Report generator** Component of a database management system that produces customized reports using data stored in a database.

**Request for proposal (RFP)** A document prepared by a systems analyst to obtain specific technical information and cost bids from computer vendors.

**Resolution** Crispness of the characters or images on a monitor or screen.

**Reusable code** A goal of structured programming in which a module or combination of modules can be used in more than one program.

**Reverse video** Display screen feature for highlighting data in which background and foreground colors are reversed.

**RGB monitor** Color monitor in which the pixels each have

a dot of red, green, and blue that can create many hues and colors.

**Ring network** Network configuration that connects computers in a circle of point-to-point connections with no central host computer.

**RISC technology** RISC is an acronym for *reduced instruction set computer*. RISC technology makes it possible for CPUs to have fewer and simpler instructions programmed into ROM but still have the capability for performing complex tasks by combining simple instructions; a reduced instruction set greatly reduces processing time.

**ROM** *See* read-only memory.

**Root directory** Main directory on a disk drive.

**Scanner (optical scanner)** Device that converts images, pictures, and text into machine-readable data.

**Scrolling** Text that flows rapidly past on the screen.

**Search and replace** A word processing feature that searches for a specified word or phrase and replaces it with another, either automatically or after pausing for the user to verify the change.

**Secondary storage** A set of devices that stores data and programs in electronic form so that they can be accessed by computer. Also called auxiliary storage. Examples of auxiliary storage are floppy disks and hard disks.

**Second-generation language** Another name for assembly language, which is one step removed from machine language.

**Sector** A wedge-shaped segment of a track on a disk.

**Sequence structure** One of the four logic structures in programs whereby statements are executed in the order in which they appear.

**Sequential file** File that is stored in some sequence or order and that can only be accessed sequentially.

**Serial printer** Impact printer that prints one character at a time.

**Serial transmission** Method of transmission in which each bit is transmitted one at a time in sequence over a single channel.

**Shareware** Software typically distributed through bulletin boards free of charge on a trial basis; if you use it, you are asked to pay for it and you receive additional documentation.

**Shell** The user interface to an operating system; COMMAND.COM is the program that provides the command-driven user interface to DOS.

**Simplex line** Communications channel that permits data to flow in one direction only, such as from CPU to printer.

**Site license** The right to have multiple users at a site access or copy a single software product; the manufacturer agrees to sell or lease the rights to a fixed number of copies of the software for a set price.

**Smart card** Storage medium the size of a credit card that contains a microprocessor capable of recording and storing information.

**Smart phone** A telephone with built-in computing power for sending messages, making bank transactions, placing orders, and performing other computerized tasks.

**Soft copy** Output that is produced on a screen.

**Soft-sectored diskette** Diskette with a small hole near the center hub that tells the disk drive where the tracks begin. These diskettes do not have sectors already defined when you buy them and must, therefore, be formatted.

**Software** Total set of programs that enables a computer system to process data. Consists of both operating system and application programs.

**Software development cycle** Steps involved in creating a program. These include developing the program specifications and designing a solution; coding the program and translating it into machine language; debugging, testing, installing, maintaining, and documenting the program.

**Software engineering** The formal techniques for designing and developing software.

**Sound board** Circuit board that can generate a variety of sounds and audio responses.

**Source data automation (SDA)** Process of computerizing the procedures that convert source documents to machine-readable form.

**Source document** Document such as a purchase order, vendor invoice, or payroll change report that contains data to be used as input to a computer.

**Source program** Program written by a programmer in symbolic language; it must be translated into machine language before it can be executed.

**Spooling** Process of transmitting output that is to be printed to a disk first, in a high-speed operation, so that the CPU can do other processing while the output is printed from disk.

**Spreadsheet package** A program that can represent data in column-and-row format and can manipulate and present that data in a number of ways.

**SQL** Abbreviation for *Structured Query Language*; a nonproprietary data manipulation language that has become a standard for many database applications.

**Star network** A network configuration in which one or more small computers, or nodes, are connected to a host computer that coordinates the transmission of data from node to node.

**Statistical package** Type of software that performs data analysis such as determining standard deviations and variances.

**Status line** A display line, usually at the top or bottom of the screen, that an application package uses for providing key information about the current settings for that application.

**Storage capacity** Amount of data a storage device or memory unit can hold; most often measured in megabytes or gigabytes.

**Storage device** Part of the system that permanently stores programs and data so that they can be used again later.

**Stored-program device** A computer that requires a set of instructions to be entered and stored before data can be processed.

**Structure chart** *See* hierarchy chart.

**Structured analysis** Top-down method of systems analysis for describing a system.

**Structured programming** Standardized approach for creating a program using logical control constructs that make the program easier to write, read, debug, maintain, and modify.

**Structured walkthrough** A concept in which a group of programmers manually step through the logic of a program to help dubug it and to evaluate its structure.

**Subdirectory** Directory accessible from the root directory on disk; each subdirectory contains related files.

**Subprogram** Set of instructions that fit together as a unit; same as module or routine.

**Subscriber service** Service that allows a user with a computer, modem, and telephone to access a wide variety of databases and other resources.

**Summary report** Report that contains totals rather than detailed data; typically used by either the operating staff or by managers for decision making.

**Supercomputer** The fastest, largest, and costliest of all computer systems; used mainly for scientific and industrial research, by the government, and for networking.

**Supervisor** *See* kernel.

**Swapping** Process using virtual memory that permits a very large program to be executed by a computer with limited storage capacity; parts of the program are loaded into memory at different times, overlaying parts that have already been executed.

**Symbolic language** Programming language that uses instructions such as ADD or + instead of complex operation codes and allows the programmer to assign symbolic names to storage locations.

**Synchronous transmission** Method of transmission that enables blocks of characters called packets to be sent in timed sequences.

**Syntax error** Error that occurs when the programmer violates the grammatical rules of the programming language.

**System interrupt** Temporary suspension of some programs so that others can use the resources and devices of the computer.

**Systems analyst** Computer professional who studies the information needs of various groups in an organization and works with user groups to design, develop, and implement a new system.

**Systems development** Designing and implementing of information systems.

**Systems development life cycle** The five basic stages through which a business system passes: investigation and analysis; design and development; implementation; operation and maintenance; and replacement.

**Systems flowchart** Diagram that shows the relationships among inputs, processing, and outputs in a system.

**Systems programmer** Computer professional who develops operating systems, compilers, and other programs designed to maximize the processing efficiency of the computer system.

**Systems software** Set of programs, including the operating system, that supervises and controls the overall operations of a computer system.

**Telecommunications** A communications technology in which data is transmitted over telephone, microwave, or satellite lines.

**Telecommuting** Technique whereby employees with PCs in their homes can do word processing, access corporate data, and send messages to colleagues without having to be physically present in the office.

**Template** A shell of an application such as a spreadsheet which includes all the necessary design elements so that the user need only enter data.

**Terabyte** A trillion storage positions in main memory or auxiliary storage.

**Terminal** Any input/output device or PC that is not at the same site as the CPU; it usually has a keyboard and monitor.

**Test data** Data that closely resembles expected input data; used to test a program's logic.

**Text editor** A software package that enables you to make changes to a file; often used as a synonym for a word processing package.

**Thermal printer** Type of nonimpact printer that creates whole characters on specially treated paper that responds to patterns of heat produced by the printer.

**Third-generation language (3GL)** A high-level, symbolic programming language that uses English-like commands to instruct the computer. Also called a procedural language.

**Time-sharing** Technique whereby a large computer can be used or shared by many organizations or individuals.

**Time-slicing** Method of computer processing where a small "slice" of computer time is allotted to each user.

**Token ring network** A topology that allows one node at a time to transmit or receive data from the file server; it has become a de facto standard in the industry.

**Top-down design** Type of system design that is organized around the goals and informational needs of top managers.

**Touch screen** Screen that enables the user to select entries and choose commands by simply making contact with the screen to point to, or highlight, the desired item.

**Track** Invisible concentric circles on a disk that are segmented into wedge-shaped units called sectors.

**Trackball** Pointing device like a mouse; the user rotates a ball to position or move the cursor.

**Tractor feed mechanism** Printer mechanism that uses sprockets to feed continuous-form paper; the holes on the sides of the paper are inserted into the sprockets.

**Traditional systems approach** An approach to designing information systems that assumes that if each business system within an organization functions efficiently, then the organization as a whole will run smoothly.

**Transaction file** File of changes to be made to the master file.

**Transaction processing** Form of interactive processing that enables a user to input data and complete a transaction on the spot.

**Transaction report** Report that contains detailed information of business transactions; usually used by the operating staff.

**Transfer rate** Speed at which data is transferred from disk to main memory; it is typically measured in megabytes per second.

**Transmission protocol** Procedure that is part of communications software; used to set the speed at which data can travel accurately across communications channels.

**TSR program** Abbreviation for *terminate* and *stay* resident; some programs are loaded into main memory and remain there available for use while other software is being run.

**Twisted-pair cable** The typical telephone wires used in homes and also used for computer connections; the cable consists of two individual copper wires that are twisted to make them stronger.

**Typeover mode** A feature of application packages in which text that is currently on the screen will be replaced by the new text entered. Contrast with insert mode.

**Ultimedia** A multimedia system developed by IBM.

**Universal Product Code (UPC)** Bar code found on most consumer goods that indicates the manufacturer of a product as well as the product itself.

**UNIX operating system** An operating system written in the C programming language that can be used on many different sizes and types of computers.

**Update** Procedure for keeping a file of records current; includes operations to add new records, delete obsolete records, and make changes to existing records.

**Upload** To send data and programs to a central computer from a mini or micro.

**Upwardly compatible** Term used to indicate a family of computers for which software run on lower models in the family can also be run on higher models.

**User** Someone who uses a computer.

**User-friendly** Term describing hardware and software that is easy to use.

**User interface** Part of the systems software that permits interaction between the hardware and the user.

**Utilities** Component of a database management system that allows the user to maintain the database by editing data, deleting records, creating new files, and so on; can also be programs that perform standard procedures such as sorting files, merging files, and so on.

**Value-added service** Extra services offered by telephone companies.

**Vector graphics** Type of graphic image created by a drawing program in which images are produced by using combinations of lines, arcs, circles, squares, and other shapes or objects rather than dots. Contrast with bit-mapped graphics.

**Vertical package** Program designed to meet the highly specialized needs of a specific industry or business.

**Video display terminal (VDT)** A TV-like screen that displays instructions and the computer's responses. Also called cathode ray tube (CRT) or monitor.

**Videoconferencing** Using video transmissions, computers, and telephones to enable people to communicate with each other over long distances without the need to travel to central locations.

**Virtual machine** Processing concept whereby the real machine simulates a number of virtual machines, each capable of interfacing with its own operating system, so that it functions as though there were a number of separate systems.

**Virtual memory** Type of memory that allows the computer system to operate as if it had more primary storage than it actually does by segmenting the application program and storing parts of it in auxiliary storage. Also called virtual storage.

**Virtual storage** *See* virtual memory.

**Virus** Software added to operating systems or application programs that can destroy the product and damage files in a computer.

**Voice recognition equipment** Devices that can interpret spoken messages; they minimize the need for keying data and result in user-friendly interactions.

**Voice response unit** Output in the form of verbal responses.

**Volatile memory** Type of memory composed of microprocessor chips in which programs and data are lost when the computer is turned off or loses power.

**Wand reader** Handheld optical reader for scanning typewritten fonts, optical character fonts, and bar codes.

**What-if analysis** Using a spreadsheet or other software package to make hypothetical changes to data in order to determine the impact of those changes.

**Wide area network (WAN)** Similar to local area networks but used where nodes are far from the central computer and each other; uses microwave relays and satellites to enable people at nodes to communicate with a host or with each other over long distances around the world.

**Windows** Software package that serves as a graphical user interface for DOS; facilitates multitasking and maximizes the efficient use of the computer.

**Wireless transmission** Method for connecting computers to other computers or input/output devices; usually uses light beams or radio waves for transmission.

**Word** A group of consecutive bytes in storage; refers to a unit of data that can be processed at one time.

**Word processing package** Productivity tool used to enter, edit, and print documents.

**Word wrap** A feature of word processing packages that brings words down to the next line if there is no room on the current line, so that margins are aligned properly.

**Worksheet** Another term for an electronic spreadsheet.

**Workstation** High-powered supermicro; commonly used for generating graphics or as a file server in a small network.

**WORM (write once, read many) disk** Optical disk that can be written on one time only; typically used for storing reference or archived data.

**Write-protect notch** An indentation in a diskette that can prevent data from being changed on that diskette; cover the notch and you will not be able to write to the diskette.

**WYSIWYG** Acronym for *what you see is what you get*; word processing, desktop publishing, spreadsheet, and many other packages are capable of displaying text exactly as it would appear printed.

# PHOTO CREDITS

## Part One

*Page 0:* Ben Simmons/The Stock Market. *Page 1 (top):* Baker/Picture Group, *(center left):* IBM Watson Research Lab, *(center right):* Courtesy Compaq, *(bottom):* James D. Wilson/Woodfin Camp & Associates. *Page 2 (top):* Rich Friedman/Black Star, *(bottom left):* Dennis Budd Gray/Picture Group, *(center right):* Courtesy Grid. *Page 3 (top):* Courtesy Tandy Corporation, *(middle):* Sun Disk, *(bottom):* Courtesy IBM. *Page 4 (top):* Courtesy Compaq, *(middle):* Poquet Computer Corp., *(bottom):* Thomas Hoepker/Magnum Photos, Inc.

## Chapter 1

*Figure 1.2a:* Courtesy IBM. *Figure 1.2b:* Courtesy NCR. *Page 9 (left):* Jon Feingersh/The Stock Market, *(right):* James Sugar/Black Star. *Figure 1.3:* Courtesy Tandy Corporation. *Figure 1.4a:* Courtesy IBM. *Figure 1.4b:* Courtesy Apple Computers. *Figure 1.4c:* Courtesy Microsoft. *Figure 1.5a:* David Joel/Tony Stone World Wide. *Figure 1.5b:* Loren Santow/Tony Stone World Wide. *Figure 1.6:* Howard Grey/Tony Stone World Wide. *Figure 1.7a:* Courtesy Aetna. *Figure 1.7b:* Tony Stone World Wide. *Figure 1.8:* Roger Ressmeyer/Starlight. *Figure 1.9:* Steve Weber/Tony Stone World Wide. *Page 18 (top left):* Roger Ressmeyer/Starlight, *(top right):* Jim Argo/Picture Group, *(bottom):* Peter Menzel. *Figure 1.10a:* Dan McCoy/Rainbow. *Figure 1.10b:* Cameramann/The Image Works. *Figure 1.10c:* Hughes Medical Division/Peter Arnold, Inc. *Figure 1.11a:* Richard Pasley/Stock, Boston. *Figure 1.11b:* Courtesy IBM. *Page 24:* Robert Frerck/Tony Stone World Wide. *Page 25:* Roger Ressmeyer/Starlight. *Page 26:* Ed Kashi/Phototake. *Page 27:* Catherine Noren/Stock, Boston. *Page 32 (left and right):* Courtesy IBM.

## Chapter 2

*Figure 2.1:* Hartmann/Magnum Photos, Inc. *Figure 2.2:* Courtesy Apple Computers. *Figure 2.3:* Courtesy General Parametrics Corp. *Figure 2.4:* David Ximeno Tejada/Tony Stone World Wide. *Page 39 (top left):* Courtesy Compaq, *(top right):* Courtesy DEC, *(bottom left):* Courtesy IBM, *(bottom right):* David Parker/Science Photo Library/Photo Researchers. *Page 41:* Courtesy Moore School Computer Museum, University of Pennsylvania. *Figure 2.5:* Courtesy IBM. *Page 44 (top left):* Sun Microsystems, *(top center):* Courtesy IBM, *(far right):* Joe Sohm/The Image Works, *(bottom left):* Courtesy Compaq, *(bottom right):* Courtesy Hewlett Packard. *Page 45:* Hank Morgan/Science Source/Photo Researchers. *Page 46:* Courtesy Apple Computers. *Figure 2.6:* Courtesy Compaq. *Page 47 (bottom right):* Courtesy GRID, *(top):* Sun Disk. *Figure 2.7:* Courtesy Apple Computers. *Figure 2.8:* Courtesy IBM. *Pages 50, 51, and 53:* Courtesy IBM. *Figure 2.9b:* Courtesy Aetna. *Page 67:* Courtesy GEM Plus. *Page 68:* Richard Kalvar/Magnum Photos, Inc.

## Chapter 3

*Figure 3.1:* Courtesy Tandy Corporation. *Figure 3.3:* Courtesy Microsoft. *Figure 3.4:* Courtesy FoxPro. *Figure 3.5:* Courtesy Microsoft. *Figure 3.10:* Courtesy Data Perfect. *Figures 3.11 and 3.13:* Courtesy Microsoft. *Figure 3.22:* Courtesy Microsoft. *Figure 3.23:* Courtesy Wordstar Institute. *Figures 3.27 and 3.28:* Courtesy Borland International, Inc. *Figure 3.34c:* Courtesy dBase. *Page 117:* Courtesy Borland International, Inc. *Figure 3.43:* Courtesy Data Perfect.

## Part Two

*Page 124:* Dan McCoy/Rainbow. *Page 125 (top):* Courtesy GRID, *(middle):* Richard Pasley/Stock, Boston, *(bottom):* Kermani/Gamma Liaison. *Page 126 (top):* Dan McCoy/Rainbow, *(bottom):* Courtesy GEM Plus. *Page 127 (top left):* Gontier/Jerrican/Science Source/Photo Researchers, *(bottom):* Hank Morgan/Science Source/Photo Researchers, *(top right):* Diego Goldberg/Sygma. *Page 128 (top right):* Ken Sakamura/Tron Project, *(top left):* Hank Morgan/Science Source/Photo Researchers, *(middle):* James Wilson/Woodfin Camp & Associates, *(bottom):* Eric Preau/Sygma.

## Chapter 4

*Figure 4.1:* Roger du Buisson/The Stock Market. *Page 133:* Courtesy Intel. *Figure 4.2:* Courtesy Intel. *Figure 4.3:* Courtesy Motorola. *Figure 4.4:* Paul Silverman/Fundamental Photographs. *Page 151 (top):* Gill Kenny/The Image Bank, *(bottom):* Peter Silva/Picture Group. *Figure 4.14:* Richard Pasley/Stock, Boston. *Figure 4.15:* Courtesy IBM. *Figure 4.16:* AT&T. *Figure 4.18a:* Lalima Druskis/Stock, Boston. *Page 168:* Courtesy IBM.

## Chapter 5

*Page 173 (left):* The Computer Museum, *(right):* Courtesy IBM. *Figure 5.4:* Jim Pickerell/Tony Stone World Wide. *Figure 5.5a:* Courtesy Viewdata Corp. *Figure 5.5b:* Courtesy Tandy Corporation. *Figure 5.6:* Eric Futran/Liaison International. *Figure 5.7:* Courtesy Microsoft. *Figure 5.8:* Courtesy Lotus. *Figure 5.9a:* Courtesy Microsoft. *Figure 5.9b:* Courtesy Micro Touch Systems. *Figure 5.10:* Courtesy Unisys. *Figure 5.11:* Charles Gupton/Tony Stone World Wide. *Figure 5.12:* Alan Levenson/Tony Stone World Wide. *Figure 5.13:* David Frazier/Photo Researchers. *Figure 5.14:* Courtesy Handheld Products. *Figure 5.15:* Courtesy Blockbuster. *Figure 5.16a:* Bob Daemmrich/Stock, Boston. *Figure 5.16b:* Courtesy Associated Business Products. *Figure 5.18a:* Richard Pasley/Stock, Boston. *Figure 5.18b:* Courtesy Chinon. *Figure 5.19:* Hank Morgan/Science Source/Photo Researchers. *Figure 5.20:* Courtesy IBM. *Figure 5.21:* Spencer Grant/Stock, Boston. *Figure 5.22:* Courtesy GRID. *Page 190 (top):* Tom Tracy/The Stock Shop. *Figure 5.23:* Courtesy Poquet Computer Corp. *Figures 5.24b and 5.25:* Courtesy IBM. *Figure 5.26:* Courtesy Toshiba. *Figure 5.27a:* Hank Morgan/Science Source/Photo Researchers. *Figure 5.27b:* David Weintraub/Photo Researchers. *Figure 5.28:* Courtesy Intergraph. *Figure 5.29:* Roger Ressmeyer/Starlight Photo Agency. *Figure 5.30:* Chip Henderson/Tony Stone World Wide. *Figures 5.32 and 5.33:* Courtesy IBM. *Figure 5.34:* Courtesy Intergraph. *Figure 5.35:* Courtesy Tandy Corporation. *Figure 5.37:* Joel Gordon. *Figure 5.39a:* Courtesy Mitsubishi. *Figure 5.39b and c:* Courtesy IBM. *Figure 5.40a:* Courtesy Hewlett Packard. *Figure 5.40b:* Dick Luria/Photo Researchers. *Figure 5.41:* Robert Isear/Science Source/Photo Researchers. *Figure 5.42:* Courtesy Creative Labs. *Figure 5.43:* Courtesy IBM. *Figure 5.44:* Bob Daemmrich/The Image Works.

## Chapter 6

*Figure 6.1a:* Ken Ross/Liaison International. *Figure 6.1b:* Will & Deni McIntyre/Photo Researchers. *Figure 6.5:* Dan McCoy/Rainbow. *Figure 6.6:* Courtesy Maxtor Corp. *Figure 6.7:* Courtesy Quantum Corp. *Figure 6.8:* Courtesy Iomega Corp. *Figure 6.10:* Bryce Flynn/Picture Group. *Figure 6.11a:* Herb Snitzer/Stock, Boston. *Figure 6.11b:* Richard Pasley/Stock, Boston. *Figure 6.12:* Courtesy Micronet Technology. *Figure 6.16:* Gabe Palmer/The Stock Market. *Figure 6.17:* Richard Kalvar/Magnum Photos, Inc. *Page 237:* Courtesy Poquet Computer Corp. *Figure 6.18:* Courtesy Toshiba. *Page 242 (top):* Courtesy Shakespeare on Disk. *Figure 6.21:* Courtesy Corel Draw Software. *Figure 6.22:* Courtesy Microsoft. *Figure 6.23:* Courtesy Toshiba. *Page 253:* Courtesy Delome Mapping.

## Part Three

*Page 254:* Rich Friedman/Black Star. *Page 255 (top):* Courtesy Corel Draw Software, *(center top):* A. Tannenbaum/Sygma, *(center bottom):* Courtesy Pixar, *(bottom):* Courtesy Exxon Co. USA. *Page 256 (top):* Courtesy Autodesk Inc., *(center and bottom):* Courtesy IBM. *Page 257 (top left and right):* Courtesy IBM. *Page 257 (center):* Courtesy Authorware, *(bottom):* Alan Levenson/Tony Stone World Wide. *Page 258 (top right):* Litelzmann/Matrix International, Inc., *(top left):* Hank Morgan/Science Source/Photo Researchers, *(bottom):* Courtesy NEC Corp.

## Chapter 7

*Figure 7.1:* Courtesy Microsoft. *Figure 7.2:* Courtesy Symantec. *Figure 7.3:* Courtesy IBM. *Figure 7.5:* Courtesy IBM. *Figure 7.6:* Courtesy Central Point Software, Inc. *Figure 7.7:* Courtesy Aldus. *Figure 7.8:* Courtesy Ventura Publishing. *Figure 7.9:* Courtesy General Parametrics Corp. *Figure 7.10:* Courtesy Draw Perfect. *Figure 7.11:* Courtesy Lotus. *Figure 7.12:* Courtesy Micrografx. *Figure 7.13:* Courtesy Z-Soft. *Figure 7.14:* Courtesy Adobe Systems, Inc. *Figure 7.15:* Courtesy Micrografx. *Figure 7.16:* Courtesy Autodesk Inc. *Figure 7.17:* Courtesy SAS/Graph Software. *Page 277 (top):* Courtesy Autodesk Inc. *Page 277 (bottom):* Courtesy Microsoft. *Figure 7.18a:* Courtesy Authorware and American Airlines. *Figure 7.18b:* Courtesy Authorware. *Figure 7.19:* Courtesy Chip. *Figure 7.20a:* Courtesy Peachtree Software. *Figure 7.21:* Courtesy Medicus Systems. *Page 287:* Courtesy Hewlett Packard. *Page 290 (top and bottom):* Courtesy Central Point Software. *Page 295:* Courtesy Z-Soft.

## Chapter 8

*Page 308:* Charles Thatcher/Tony Stone World Wide. *Page 309 (top right):* Courtesy Digital Equipment Corp., *(bottom right):* Naval Surface Weapons Center. *Figure 8.7:* Courtesy TRW, Inc. *Figure 8.8:* Courtesy Lotus. *Page 329 (top left):* NYPL, *(top center):* The Science Museum, *(top right):* Culver Pictures, Inc., *(bottom):* Courtesy IBM.

## Chapter 9

*Pages 349 and 358:* Courtesy IBM. *Figure 9.11:* John Greenleigh, Courtesy Apple Computers. *Figures 9.12 and 9.13:* Courtesy Microsoft. *Figure 9.14:* Courtesy Lotus. *Figure 9.15:* Courtesy IBM. *Figure 9.16:* John Greenleigh/Courtesy Apple Computers. *Figure 9.17:* Courtesy Microsoft. *Page 364:* Courtesy DCA. *Page 376:* Blair Seitz/Photo Researchers.

## Chapter 10

*Figure 10.1:* Louis Psihoyos/Matrix International, Inc. *Figure 10.2:* Courtesy IBM. *Figure 10.4:* Tim Brown/Tony Stone World Wide. *Page 385 (bottom):* Courtesy IBM. *Figure 10.6:* Courtesy IBM. *Figure 10.14:* Michael Grecco/The Picture Group. *Page 413:* Peter Kaplan/The Stock Shop.

## Part Four

*Page 422:* Adam Hart-Davis/Science Photo Library/Photo Researchers. *Page 423 (top left):* Dale Boyer/Photo Researchers, *(top right):* Courtesy Tandy Corporation, *(bottom):* Courtesy Compaq. *Page 424 (top):* Jon Feingersh/The Stock Market, *(center):* Peter Morgan/Picture Group, *(bottom):* Malcolm Kirk/Peter Arnold, Inc. *Page 425 (top):* Courtesy CNN Studios, *(bottom):* Peter Arnold, Inc. *Page 426 (top):* Labat/Explorer/Photo Researchers, *(bottom):* Hank Morgan/Science Source/Photo Researchers.

## Chapter 11

*Page 439:* Courtesy Hewlett Packard. *Page 442:* Courtesy Borland International, Inc. *Figure 11.12:* Courtesy NASA. *Page 450:* Courtesy IBM. *Page 453:* Courtesy SAS/Graph Software. *Page 456 (left):* Paul Fusco/Magnum Photos, Inc., *(right):* Herman Kokojan/Black Star. *Page 457 (top):* Courtesy IBM. *Figure 11.20:* Courtesy Pilot Software. *Page 458:* Courtesy NCR. *Page 459 (top):* Courtesy Draw Perfect, *(bottom):* Courtesy OnTrack. *Figure 11.22:* Courtesy Shell Oil Company. *Page 462:* Courtesy Wang Laboratory.

## Chapter 12

*Figure 12.1:* Richard Kalvar/Magnum Photos, Inc. *Figure 12.2:* Michael Grecco/The Stock Shop. *Figure 12.4:* John Walsh/Science Photo Library/Photo Researchers. *Figure 12.7a:* Courtesy Hayes Smartcom. *Figure 12.7b:* Courtesy Hayes Smartcom. *Figure 12.7c:* Courtesy U.S. Robotics. *Figure 12.8:* Courtesy Tandy Corporation. *Figure 12.10a:* Tim Davis/Photo

Researchers. *Figure 12.11a:* Mikki Rain/Science Photo Library/Photo Researchers. *Figure 12.13:* Courtesy IBM. *Figure 12.14:* Loren Santow/ Tony Stone World Wide. *Page 490:* Courtesy Dow Jones Info Services. *Figure 12.16a:* Courtesy Compuserve, Inc. *Figure 12.16b:* Courtesy Prodigy Service Co. *Figure 12.17:* Courtesy Viewdata Corp. *Figure 12.19:* Chris Sorenson/The Stock Market. *Page 493:* Derek Benvin/The Image Bank. *Figure 12.24:* Courtesy Wandel & Gotterman Technologies, Inc. *Page 502:* Courtesy CFS Labs. *Figure 12.25a:* Mark Antman/The Image Works. *Figure 12.25b:* Courtesy Hams Corp. *Figure 12.26:* Courtesy Digiboard. *Figure 12.27a:* Michael McDermott/Black Star. *Figure 12.27b:* David York/The Stock Shop. *Figure 12.28:* AT&T. *Page 511:* Hank Morgan/Photo Researchers. *Figure 12.29:* Courtesy Hewlett Packard. *Page 513:* Simon Fraser/ Science Photo Library/Photo Researchers. *Page 518:* Courtesy Computerland.

## Chapter 13

*Figure 13.1:* G. Hall/Woodfin Camp & Associates. *Figure 13.2a:* Everett Collection, Inc. *Figure 13.2b:* United Artists Corp. *Figure 13.3:* Danford Connolly/Picture Group. *Figure 13.5:* Sheila Terry/Science Photo Library/Photo Researchers. *Figure 13.7:* Courtesy Herman Miller. *Figure 13.9a:* Hank Morgan/Rainbow. *Figure 13.9b:* Peter Menzel. *Figure 13.9c:* Susan Steinkamp/SABA. *Figure 13.10:* Courtesy IBM. *Figure 13.11:* Courtesy Tandy Corporation. *Figure 13.12a(1):* Courtesy Microsoft. *Figure 13.12b:* Courtesy Apple Computers. *Figure 13.13:* Ray Ellis/Photo Researchers. *Figure 13.14:* Courtesy IBM. *Figure 13.15:* Courtesy GRID. *Page 549:* Courtesy Hewlett Packard.

## Appendix C

*Page 617 (center and bottom left):* Courtesy IBM, *(top right):* Courtesy Monroe Systems for Business, *(bottom right):* Courtesy New York Public Library. *Page 618 (top left):* Courtesy New York Public Library, *(center and bottom left):* The Science Museum, *(top and bottom right):* The Computer Museum. *Page 619 (center left):* Courtesy Moore School Computer Museum, University of Pennsylvania, *(bottom left):* Institute for Advanced Study, Princeton, NJ. *Page 619 (top):* Sperry Univac, Division of Sperry Corporation. *Page 620 (bottom left):* Courtesy Digital Equipment Corp., *(bottom right):* Courtesy Intel. *Page 621 (center left):* Courtesy Microsoft, *(top and bottom right):* Courtesy Apple Computers. *Page 622 (bottom right):* Courtesy IBM, *(top right):* Courtesy Compaq. *Page 623 (bottom left):* Courtesy Lotus Development Corp., *(bottom right):* Courtesy IBM, *(top right):* Courtesy Apple Computers. *Page 624 (top):* Courtesy Microsoft, *(bottom):* Aldus. *Page 625 (bottom and top left):* Courtesy IBM, *(top right):* Courtesy Compaq, *(bottom right):* Courtesy Intel Corporation. *Page 626 (top left):* Courtesy Compaq. *Page 626 (top right):* Courtesy Tandy Corporation.